A DREAM OF EUROPE

A DREAM OF EUROPE

Jacob Ehrbahn

Dewi Lewis Publishing

FOREWORD

More than a million refugees and migrants headed for Europe in 2015. This caused the EU's asylum system to collapse and individual member states to focus on keeping as many refugees and migrants as possible outside their national borders. But razor wire fences, tear gas, border controls, tightened asylum procedures and the lack of humanitarian assistance could not put a stop to everyone who was trying to escape war, poverty and oppression.

On nineteen trips from 2015 to 2020 I photographed people who have fled to Europe with a dream of a better life.

I have watched as people drowned in the Mediterranean Sea. I have watched families break out in tears or shouts of joy when they reached the stony beaches of Lesbos in flimsy rubber dinghies. I have seen overcrowded reception centres and makeshift 'jungle' camps on the Greek islands of Samos and Lesbos, where people live with their children under inhumane conditions. I have seen people pray to their gods in abandoned industrial buildings. I have seen young men and boys hide in lorries or under the seats on trains to cross the borders within Europe. I have watched families with children crawl under the razor wire fence on the border between Hungary and Serbia. I have seen human traffickers charge high prices for almost nothing. I have met Danish and Swedish speaking young men who have lived in Scandinavia for three years and been refused asylum there, now living on the streets of Paris with broken dreams. I have watched people being beaten by border police. I have watched families flee the Moria camp with their few possessions while the flames consumed the last remains of makeshift houses. I have witnessed a lot, but by no means everything. Refugees and migrants are in a state of free fall. While they find themselves in terrible situations and living in hellish places, they struggle day after day to keep the faith that there is a better life at the end of their journey.

Since 2015 most European countries have imposed more asylum restrictions and the EU has entered into financial agreements with Turkey, Libya and other African nations in order to minimize the stream of refugees and migrants. This is a significant reason as to why not as many refugees and migrants arrive in Europe as before. The ones who do make it are still faced with chaos and extreme danger on their journeys, perhaps more now than ever. They have to navigate a landscape peopled with brutal border police, greedy human traffickers and racists. They do not meet many people who wish them well.

If you ask them what they dream of, most of them would like to go to a country where they have family or friends. Other simply wish to find any peaceful country that would grant them asylum so they can live legally in the safety of Europe. I have spoken with many people who have given up their hope of a good life for themselves, but who are willing to go through fire and water for their children to have one.

In the camps on the Greek islands, large numbers of refugees and migrants wait for months or years before they can continue on their journey or are deported. I have visited the Moria camp on Lesbos many times, from when it became an official reception centre in 2015 until it burnt down in September 2020. It is like stepping into a nightmare. The conditions are extremely primitive. The sense of insecurity is just as real as the uncertainty about the future. Even hopes and dreams have harsh conditions here. I find it hard to comprehend that places like this exist in Europe. The locals on the islands find it hard to believe too. They feel let down by their own government as well as the EU. It is as if no one is willing to acknowledge and take on the responsibility for the state of affairs in these camps.

Yet in the midst of the misery, I have witnessed how humans are able to adapt to the most inhumane conditions and create an everyday life with a structure of sorts. It is always life-affirming to watch a mother with her baby, or children forget time and place for a while as they laugh and play, or young men inside a dilapidated industrial building doing all they can to prepare the best possible meal out of very few ingredients. For me, these are glimpses of hope. And then there is the patchwork of good-hearted people who meet the refugees and migrants without judgement and offer them care and positive attention. In addition to Doctors Without Borders (MSF), I have come across numerous small NGOs, churches, local residents and volunteers who come from all around the world to help where they can and with whatever means they have. I cannot imagine what the situation would have been without these dedicated people.

This book offers insight into a parallel European reality, a reality in which thousands of refugees and migrants live. It is my hope that my pictures will serve to remind us that behind the numbers and statistics, and at the other end of policy decisions, there are real people. It is my hope that this book can serve as a counterpart to the cynicism and stigmatization with which these people are increasingly faced. I have often found it hard to believe what I have witnessed, that scenes like these can play out on European soil, and it is hard for me to connect these scenes with the idea of a humanistic Europe. In addition to being a document for posterity, it is my hope that this book can challenge the perceptions we have of ourselves as Europeans.

Jacob Ehrbahn
February 2021

In 2015 more than a million refugees and migrants head for Europe. According to the International Organization for Migration (IOM) more than 800,000 of them arrived in small boats to the Greek islands, and about half of them make land on Lesbos. By far the majority are fleeing war and repression in Syria, Afghanistan and Iraq.

The journey from Turkey across the Aegean Sea to one of the northern beaches on Lesbos usually takes around two hours if everything goes well. The human traffickers typically take $1,000 USD for a place on the overfilled rubber dinghies.

In the early summer of 2015 there is basically no one to assist the refugees and migrants except for individual locals who keep an eye on the stretch of coast and try to be ready with water, sandwiches and good advice when the dinghies come in. Depending on their place of arrival and the route, new arrivals are told that they have to walk 45-65 kilometres through hilly terrain in the baking heat of summer to get to the reception centre in Mytilini, the largest town on Lesbos. They are not allowed to take taxis, buses or stay in hotels. They are in the country illegally and the locals can be punished for helping them.

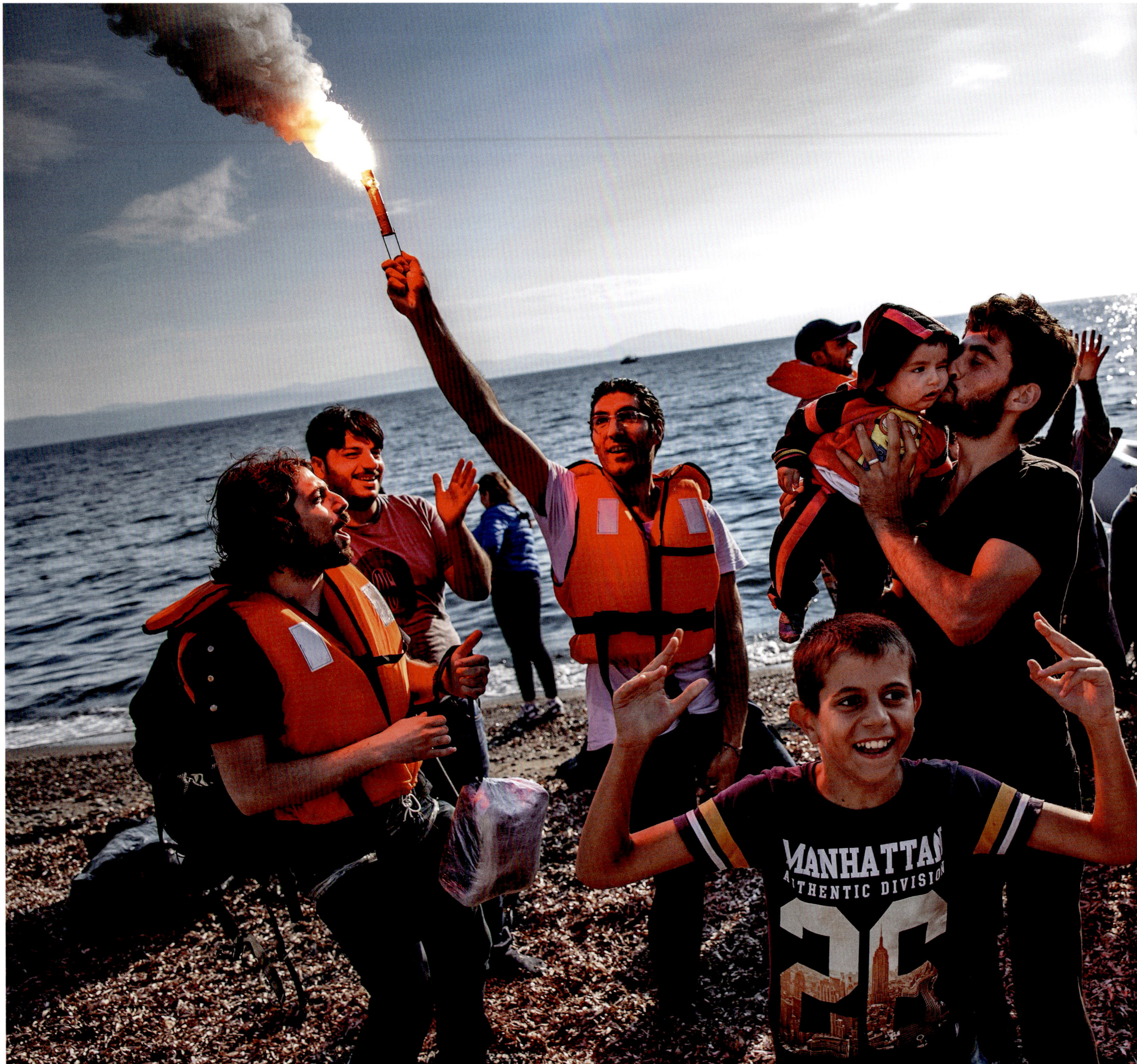

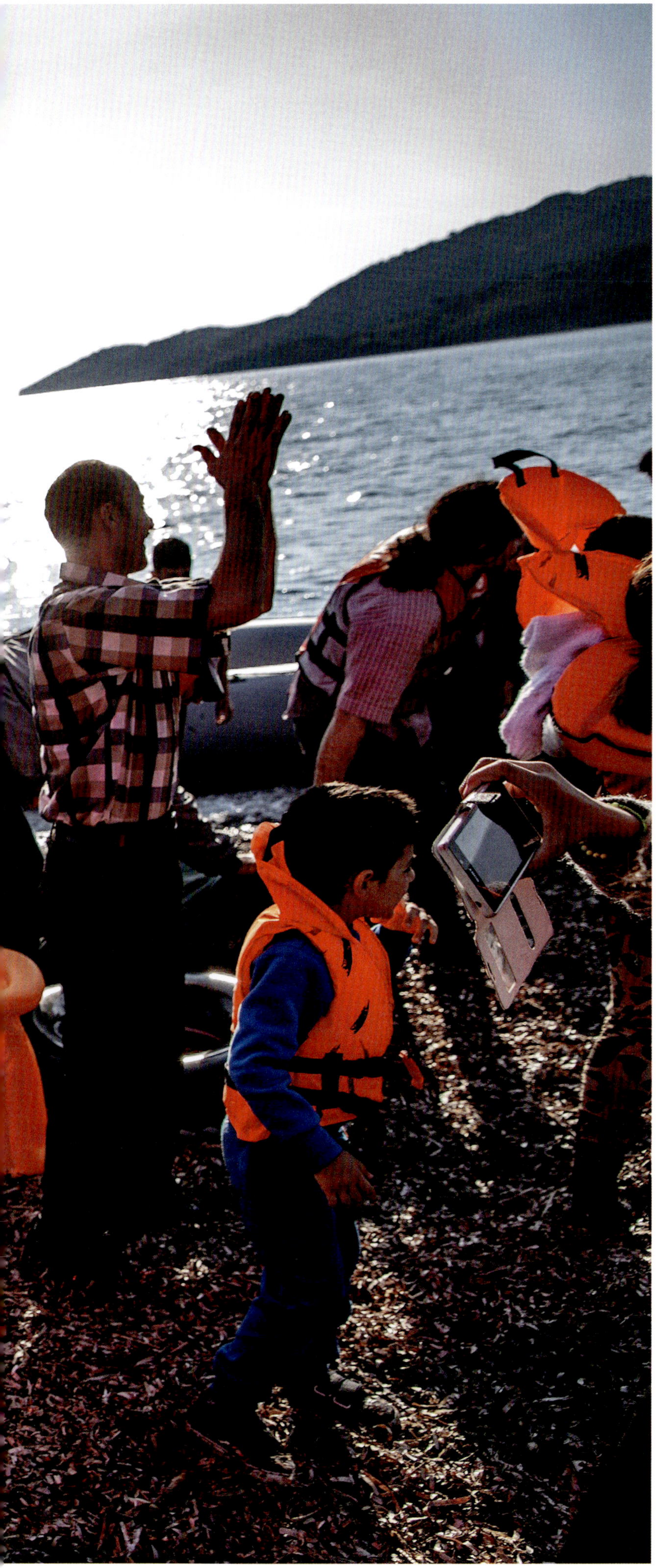

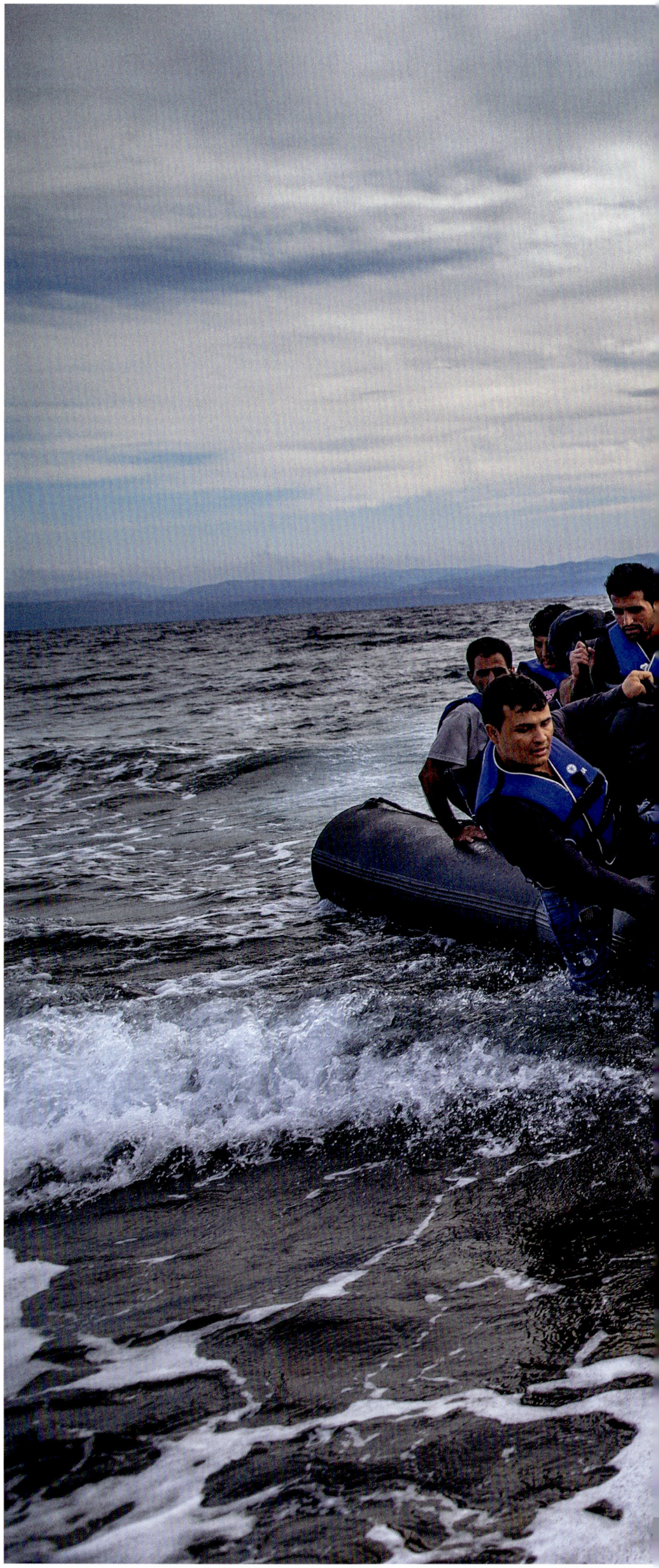

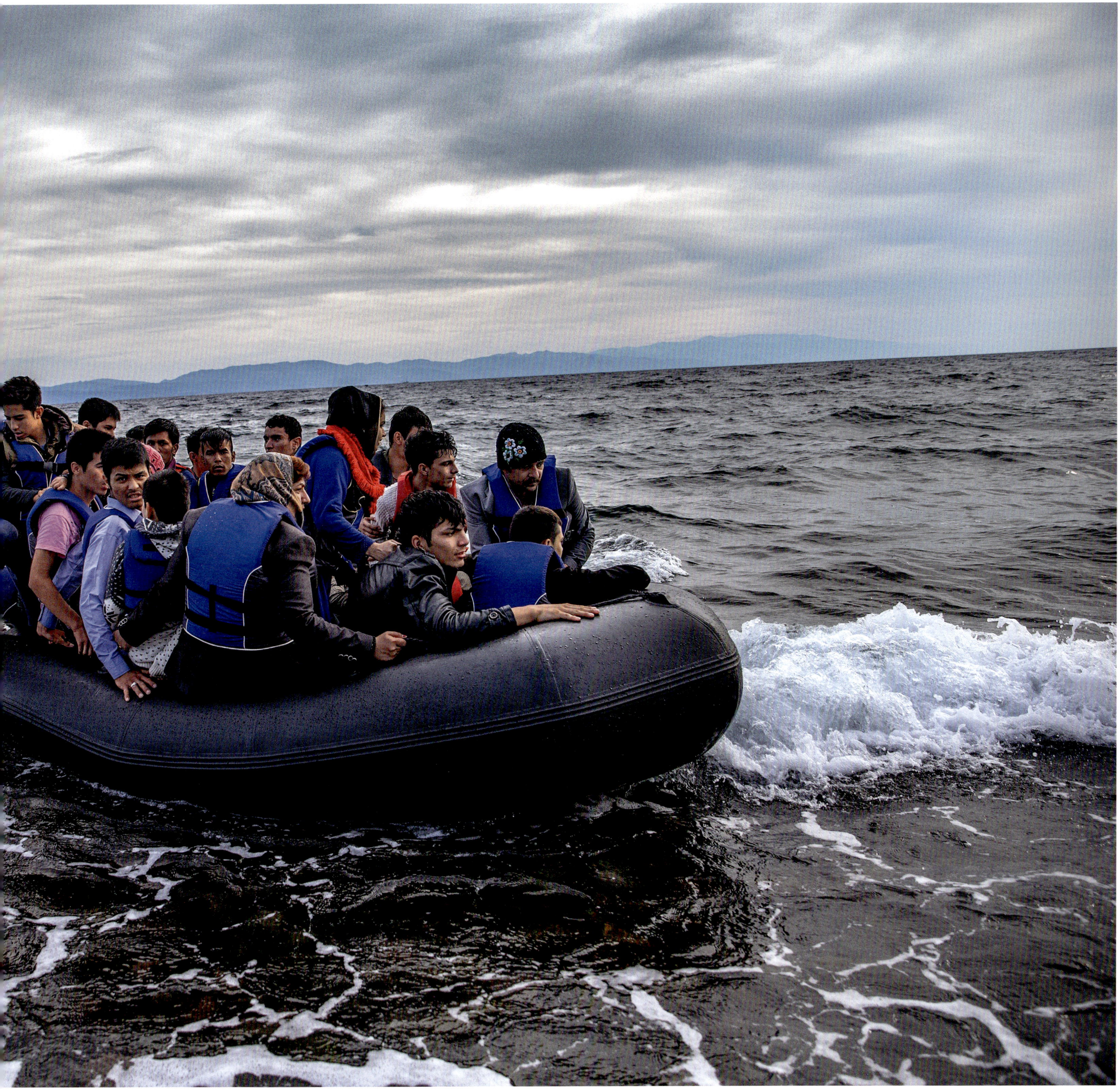

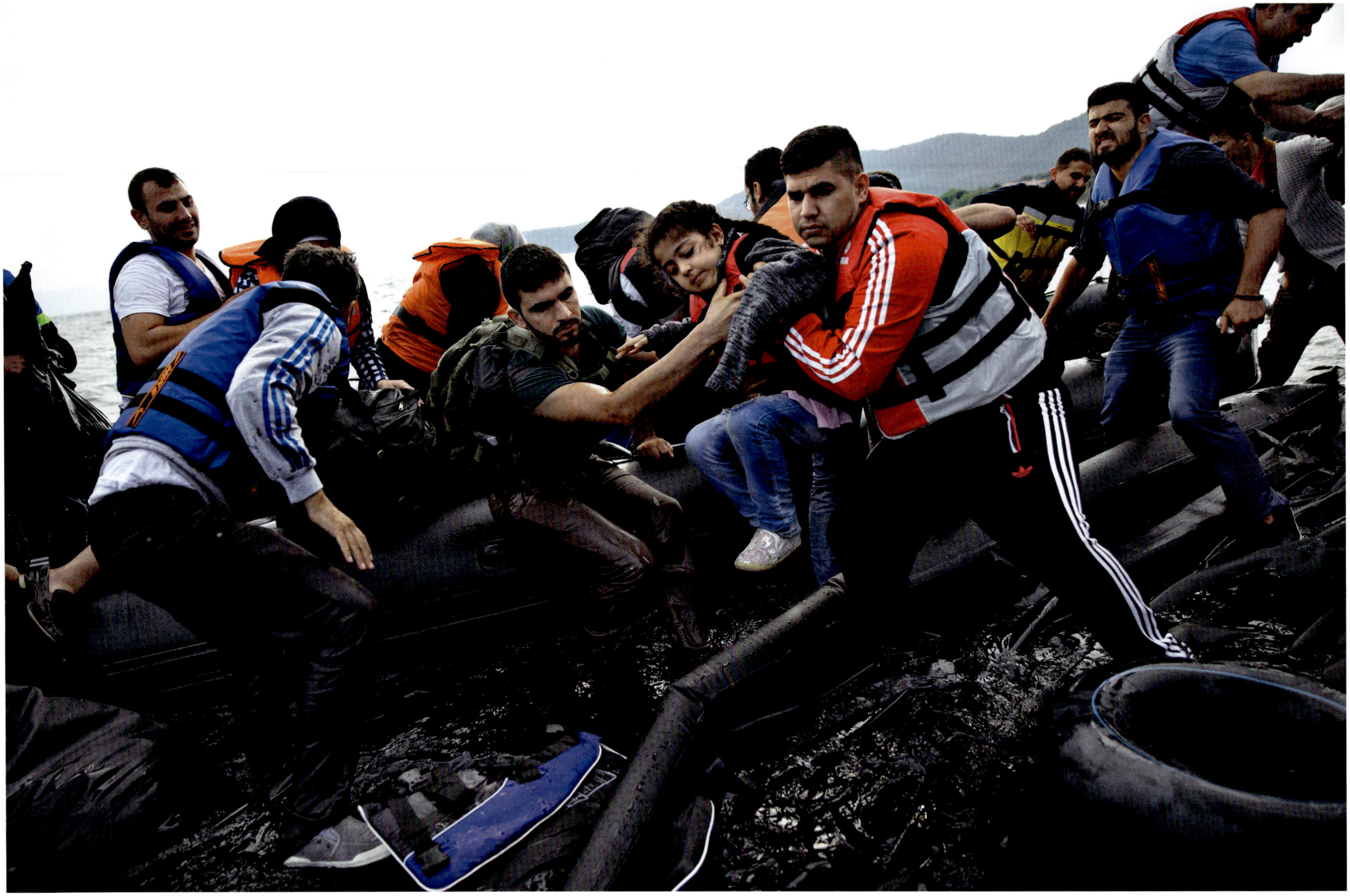

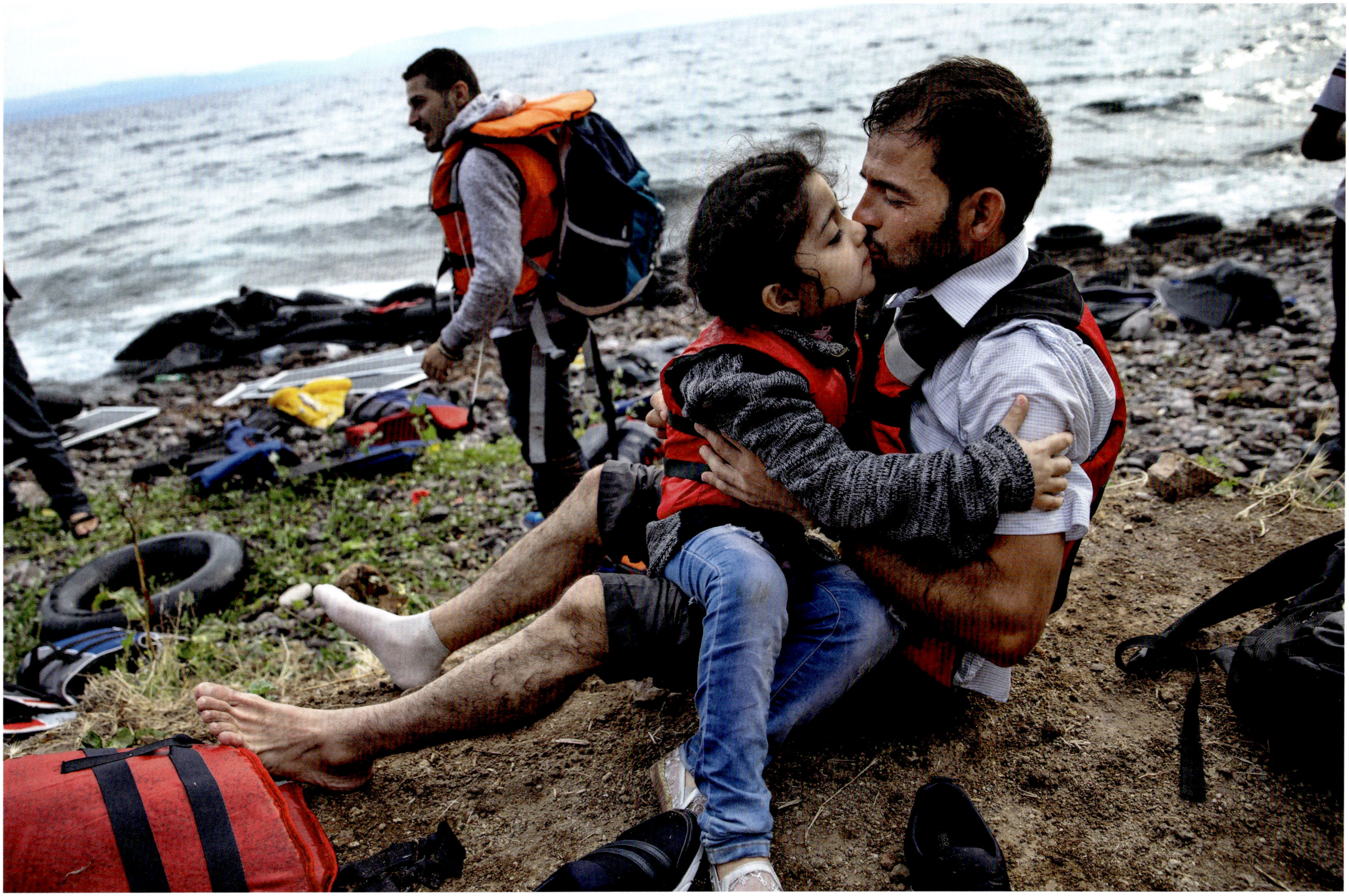

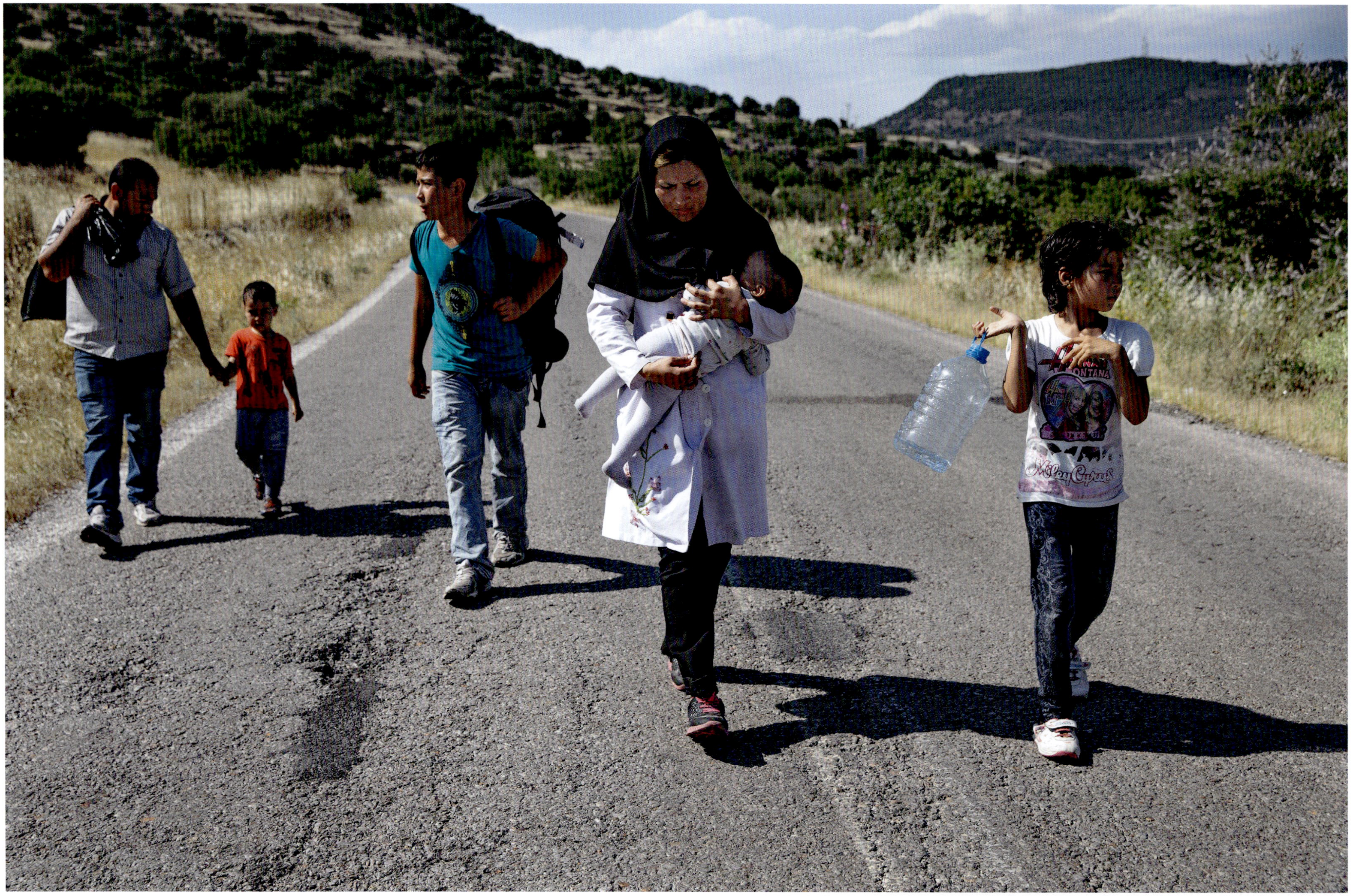
Miley Cyrus

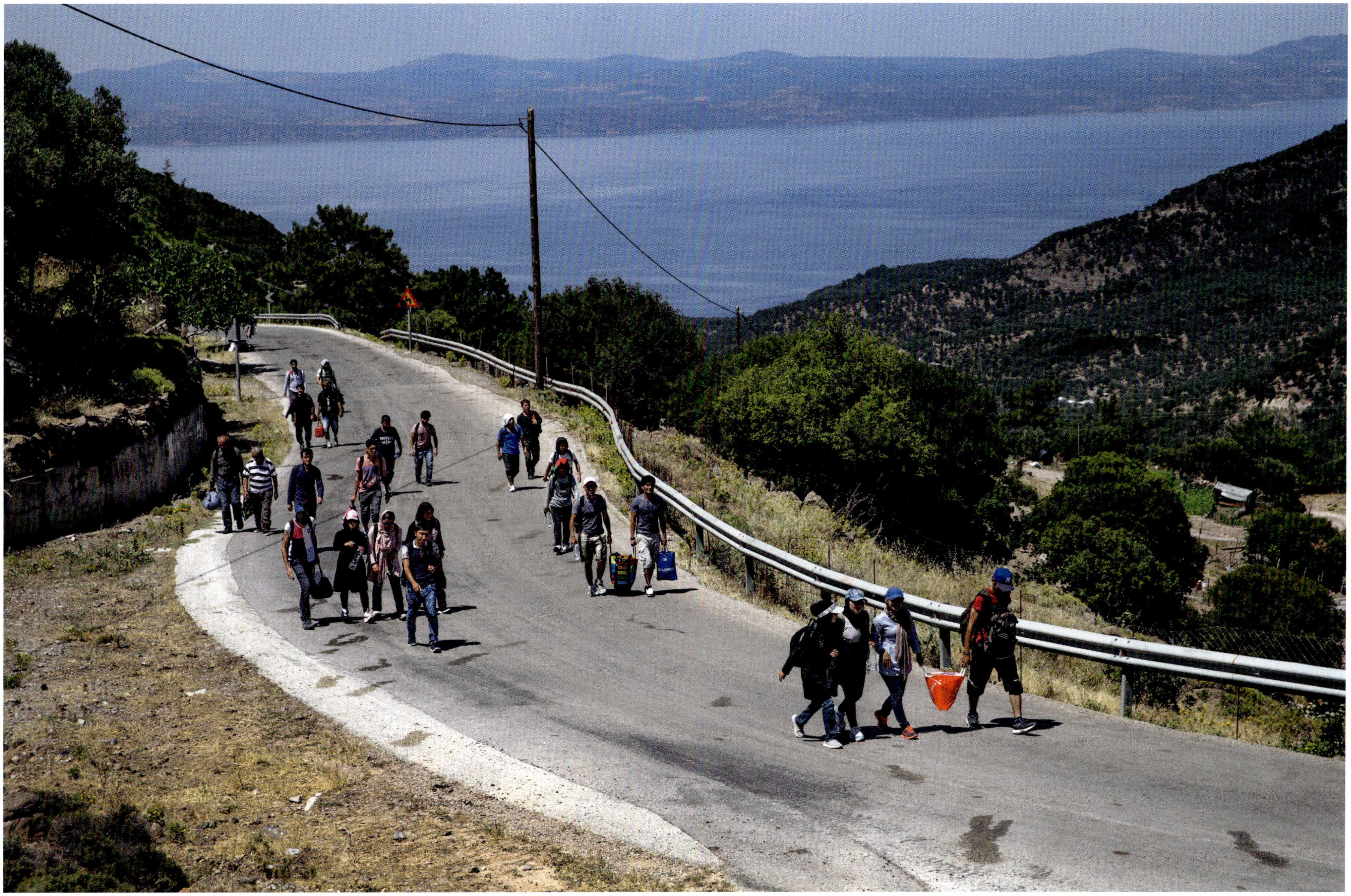

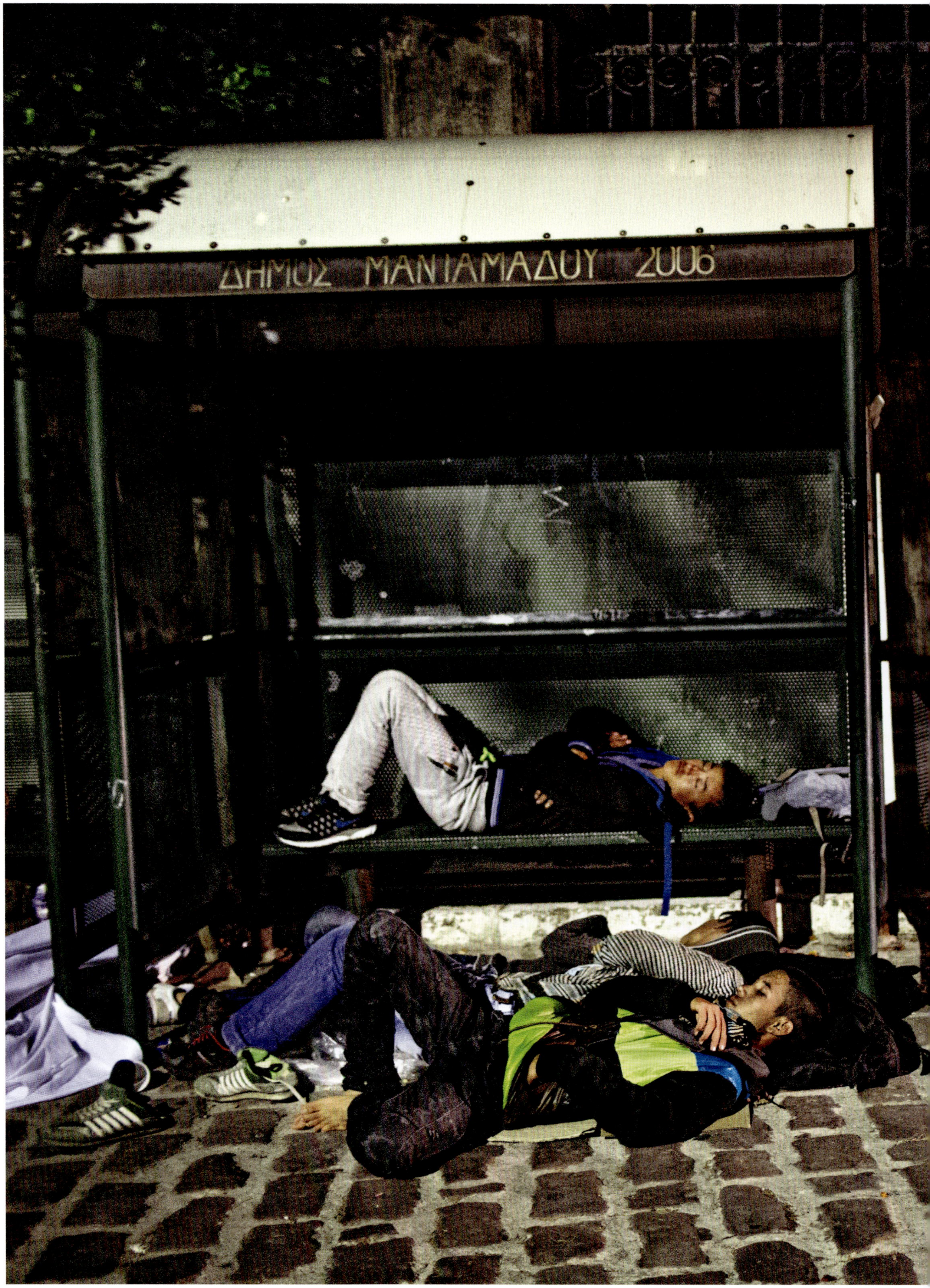
ΔΗΜΟΣ ΜΑΝΤΑΜΑΔΟΥ 2006

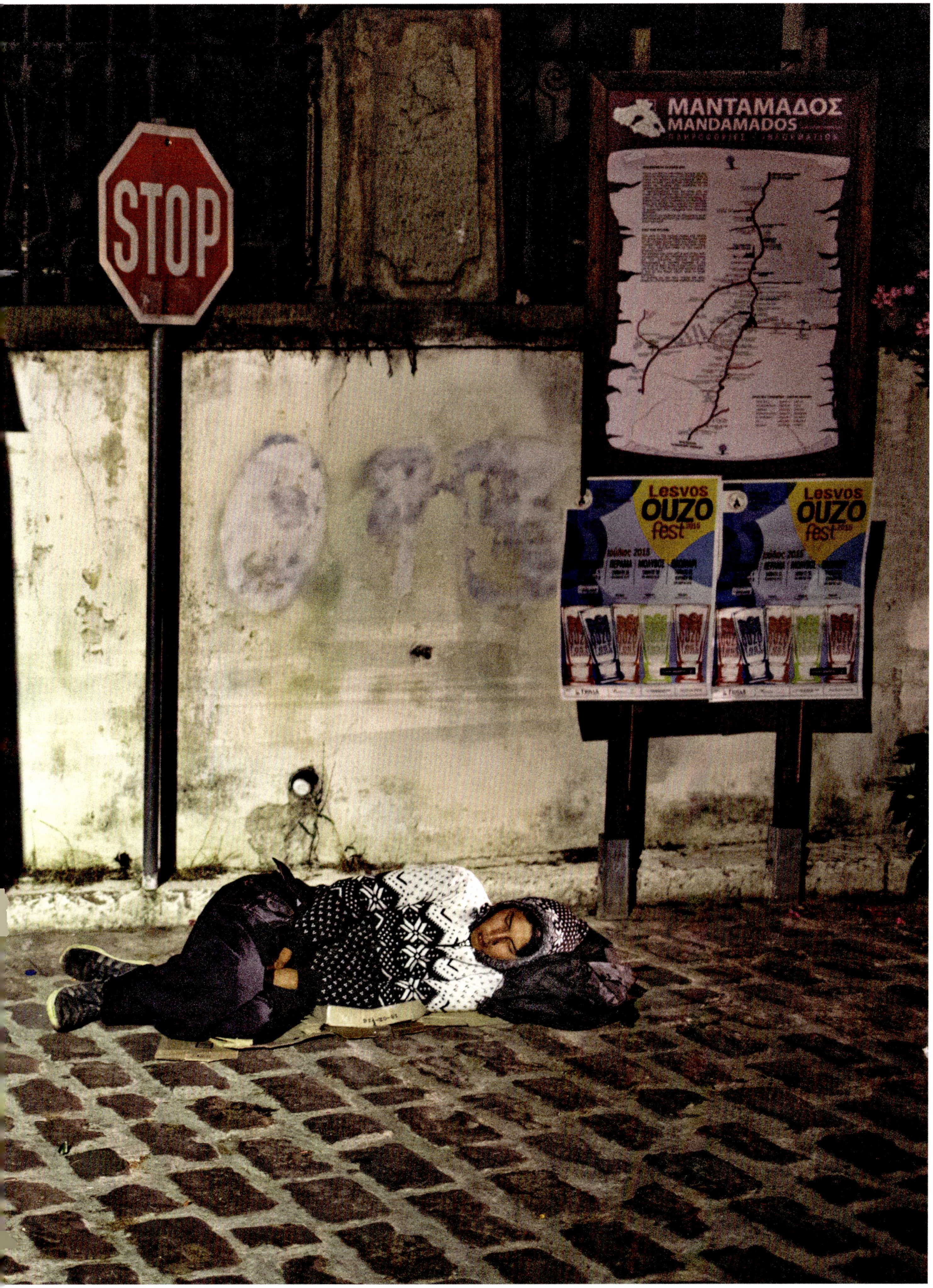
STOP
ΜΑΝΤΑΜΑΔΟΣ
MANDAMADOS
Lesvos
OUZO
fest
Lesvos
OUZO
fest

To slow the stream of refugees and migrants taking the Balkan route through Hungary, Prime Minister Viktor Orbán begins to build a controversial fence along the border between Hungary and Serbia.

While the fence is under construction, it is still possible to enter Hungary by following the railway track from Serbia near the Röszke-Horgoš border crossing point. But as soon as they cross the border, the refugees and migrants are met by the police. Many choose to force entry through the fence in order to elude the police, and avoid having to be registered and fingerprinted. According to the Dublin regulation, refugees must seek asylum in the first EU country in which they arrive. In principle this means that if they attempt to travel further they may be sent back here. Since the Greek asylum system has broken down in practical terms, many fear that they would be forced to seek asylum in Hungary if they are registered here and very few want their journey to end in Hungary.

On 14 September 2015, police and soldiers closed the border completely. As of 15 September, the Hungarian police have orders to take those attempting to cross the border illegally into custody. Everyone who manages to enter Hungary before the fence is completed and who does not want to seek asylum there is transported to the station in Röszke, where, early the following morning, they are placed on a special train that takes them to Austria.

In the days that follow, newly arrived refugees and migrants amass on the Serbian side of the newly completed fence at the border crossing near Horgoš. They are confused and frustrated that they cannot get any further. It ends with an intense confrontation with the Hungarian police. Later, everyone who was stranded in the area near the border is driven to Croatia by bus. The many refugees and migrants who are heading north through Europe can no longer travel through Hungary.

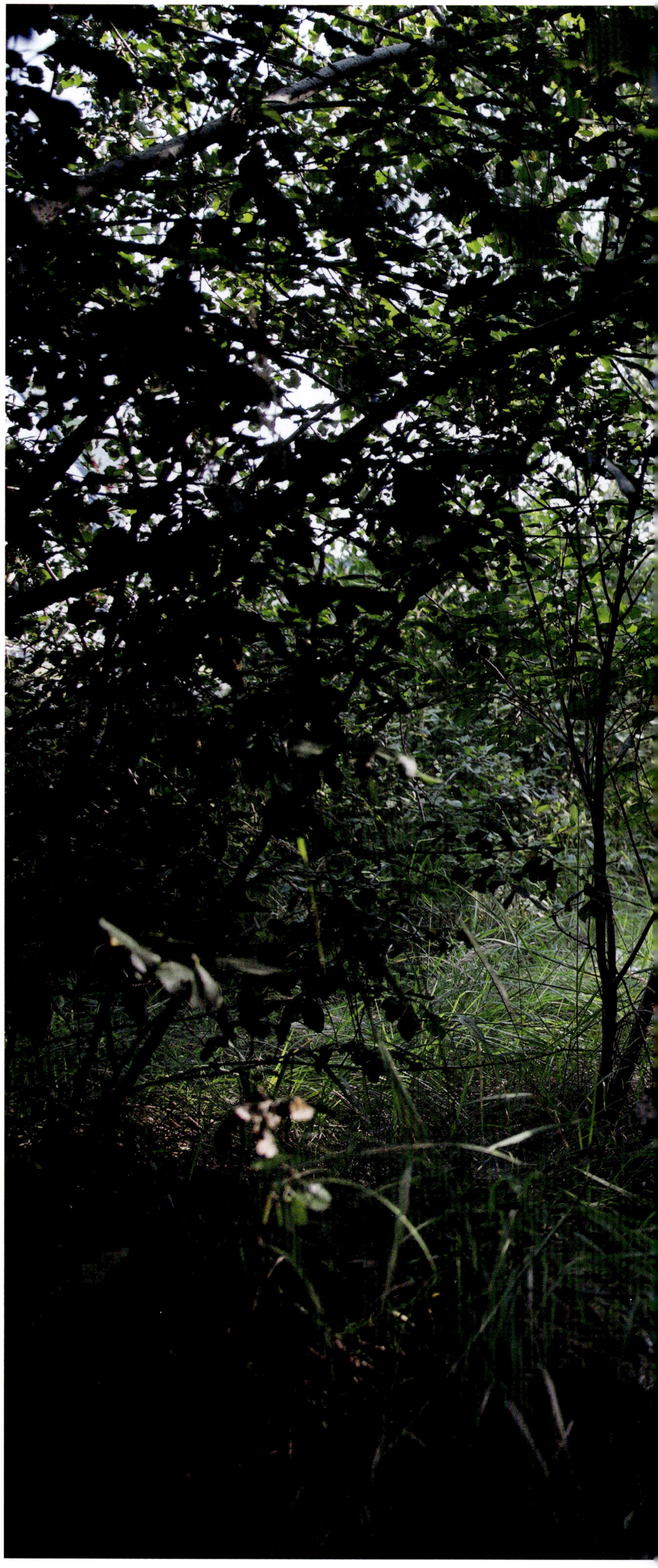

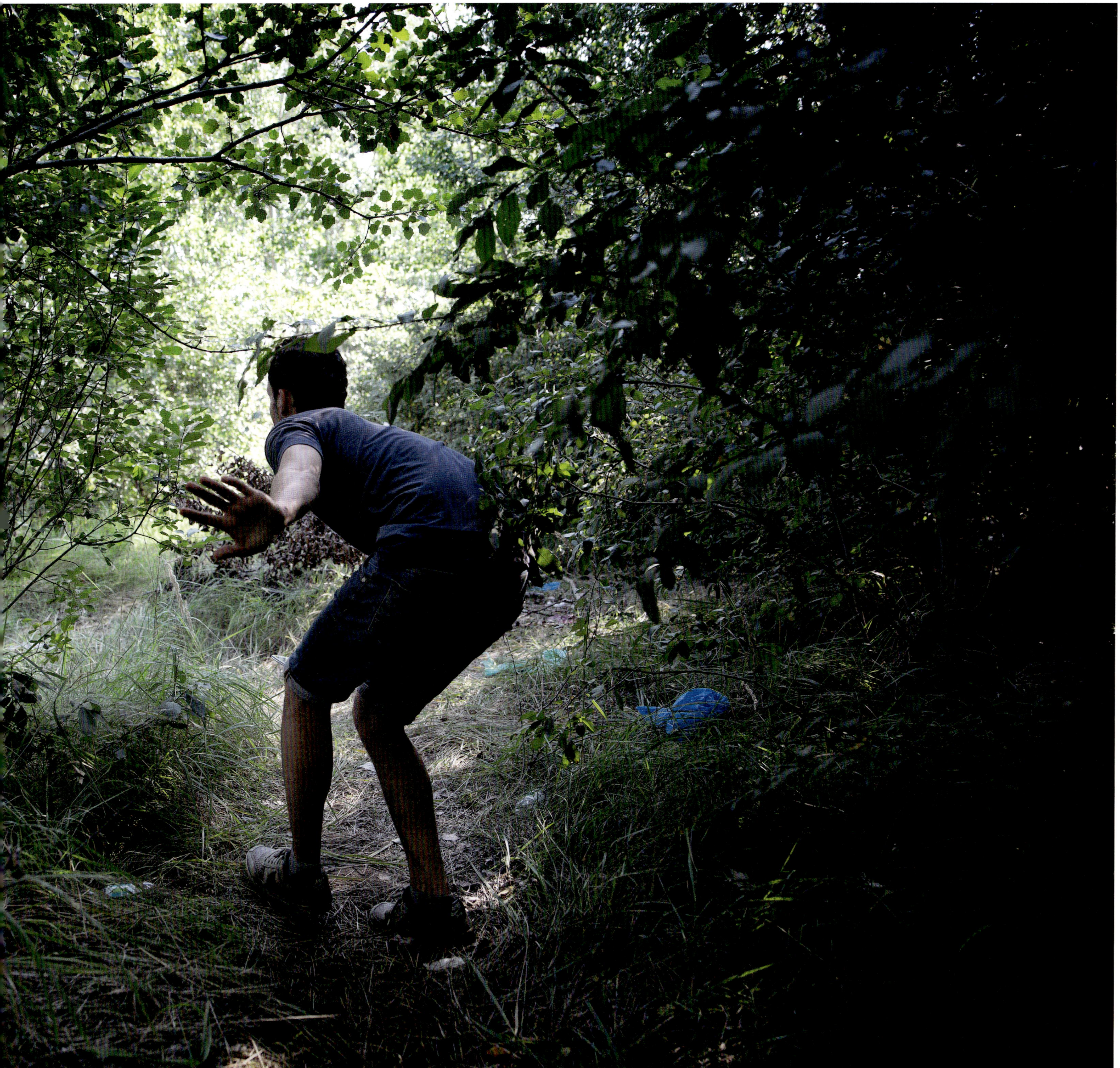

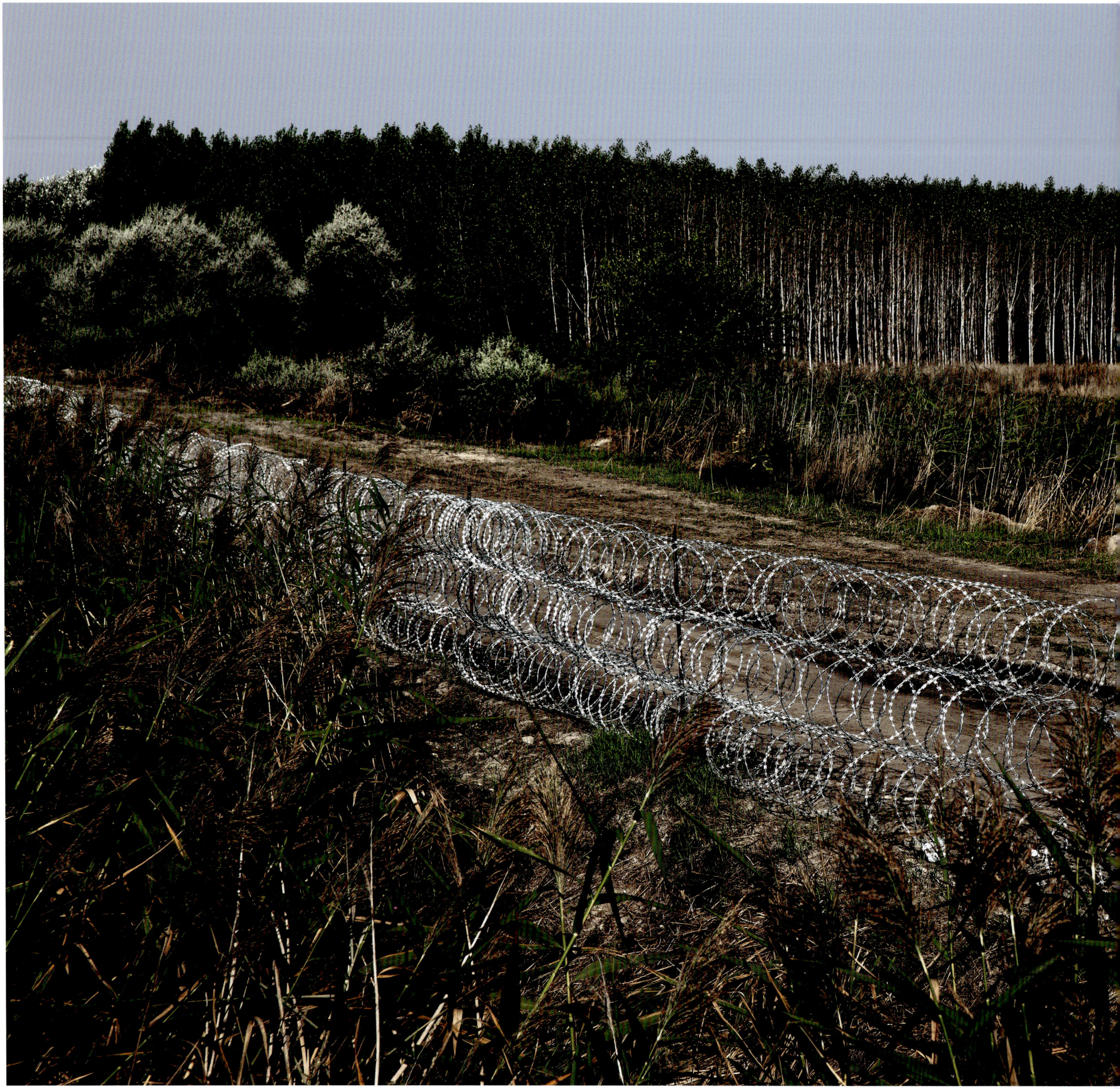

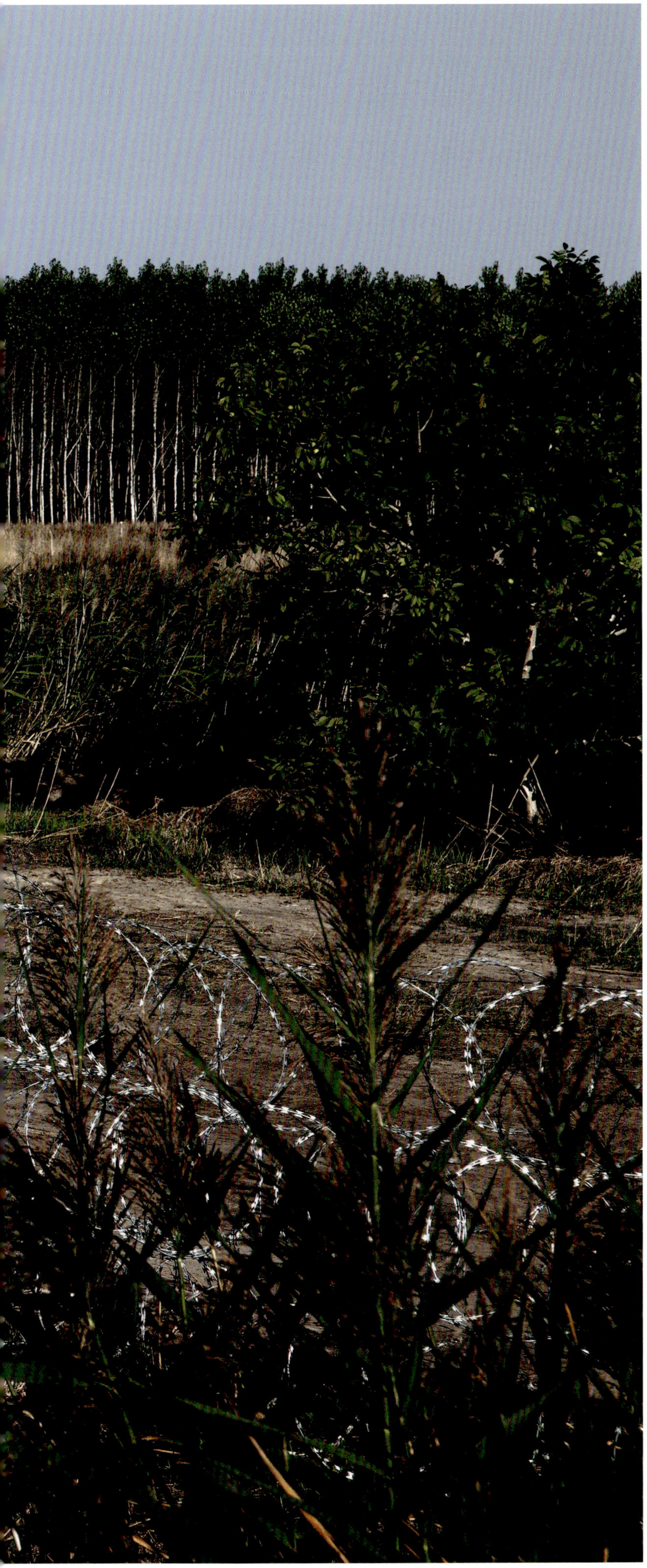

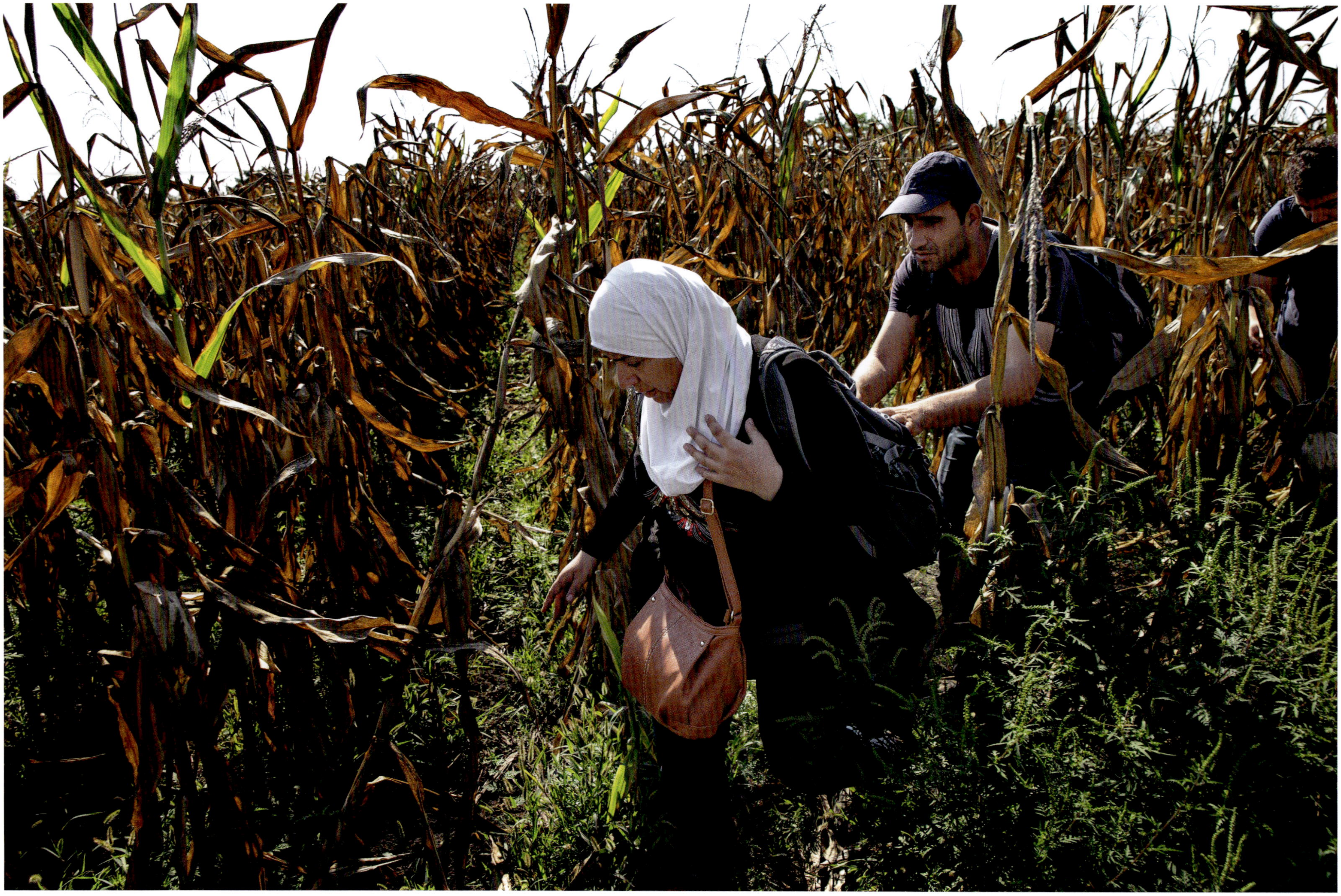

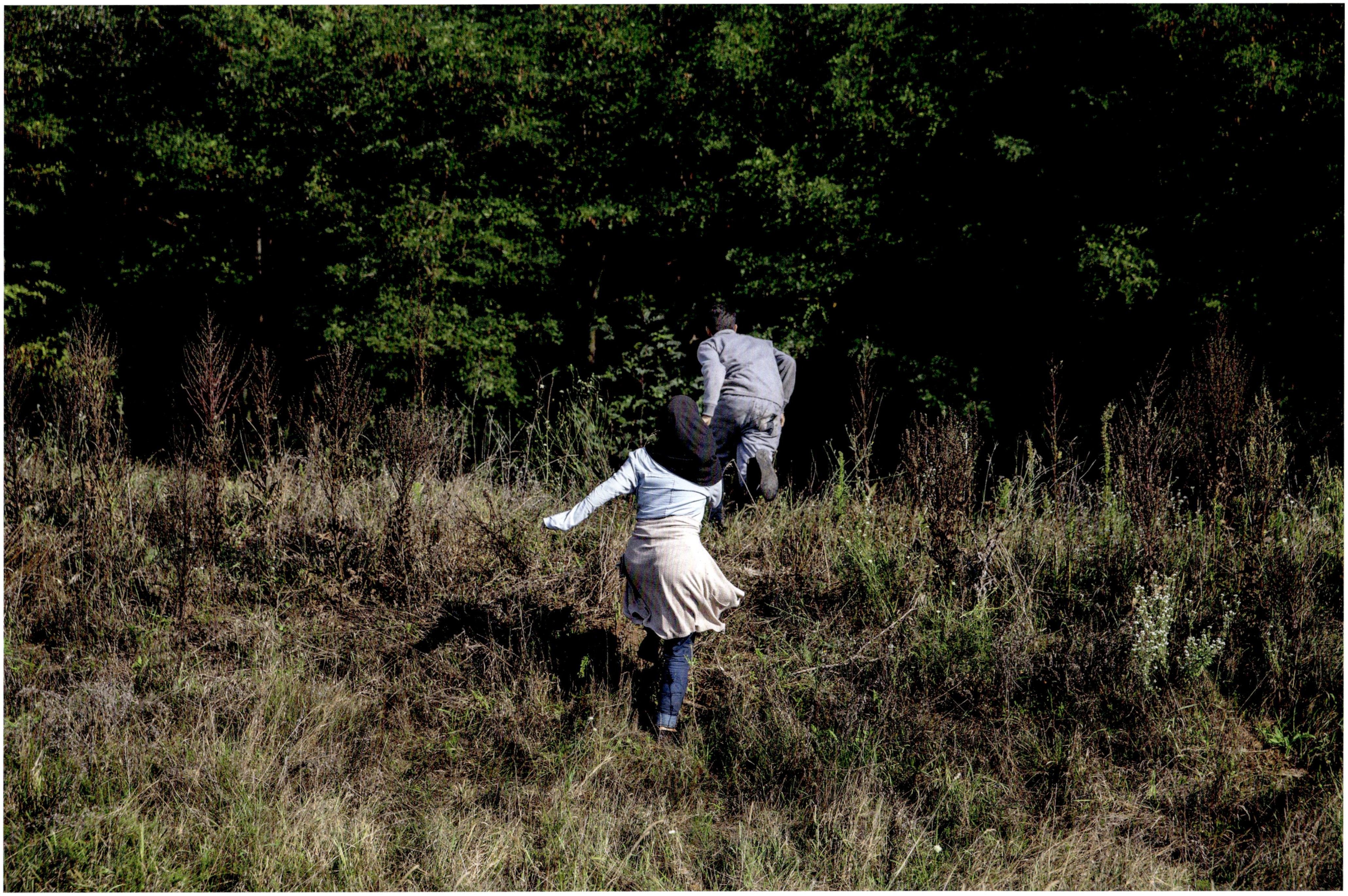

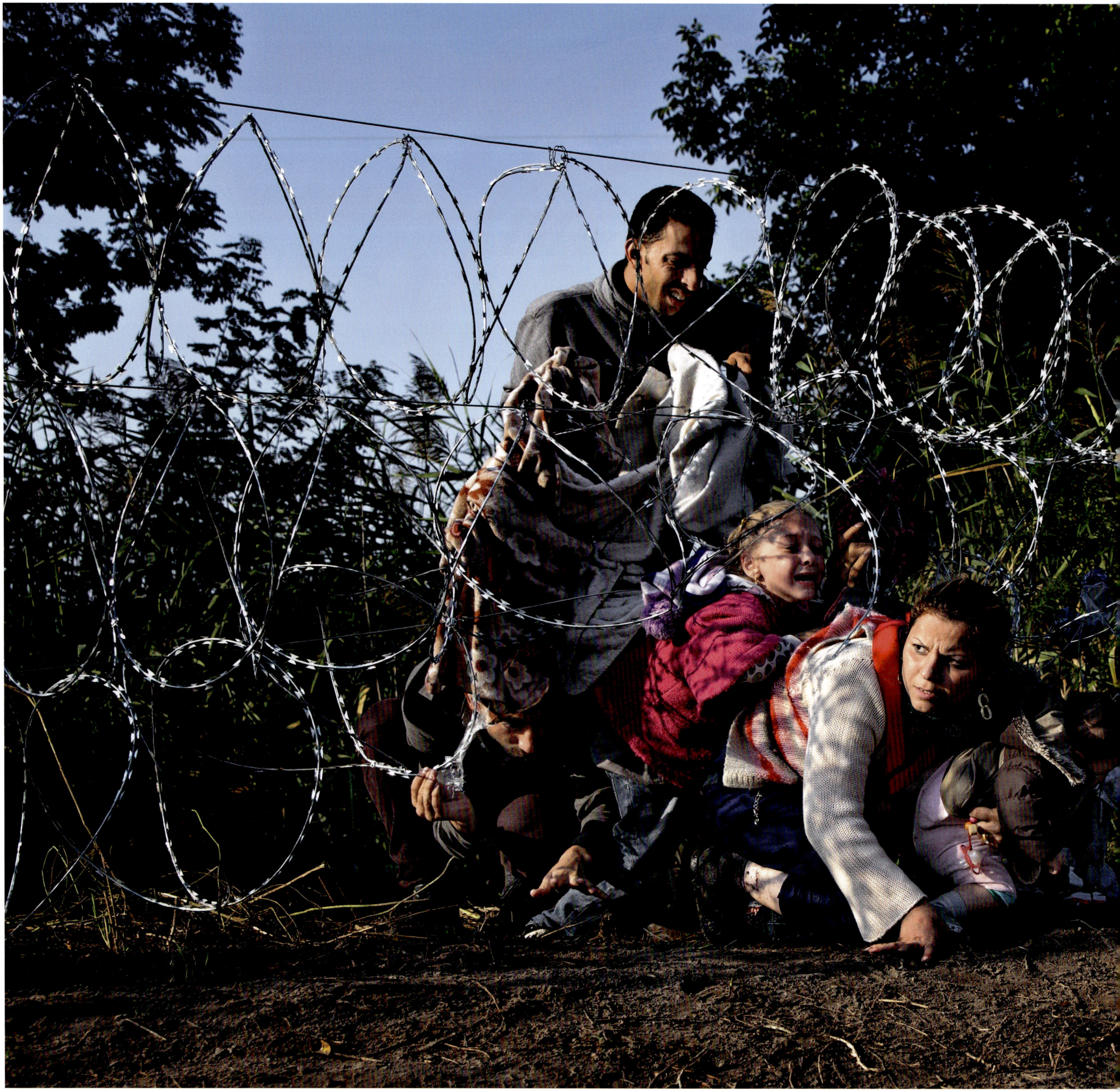

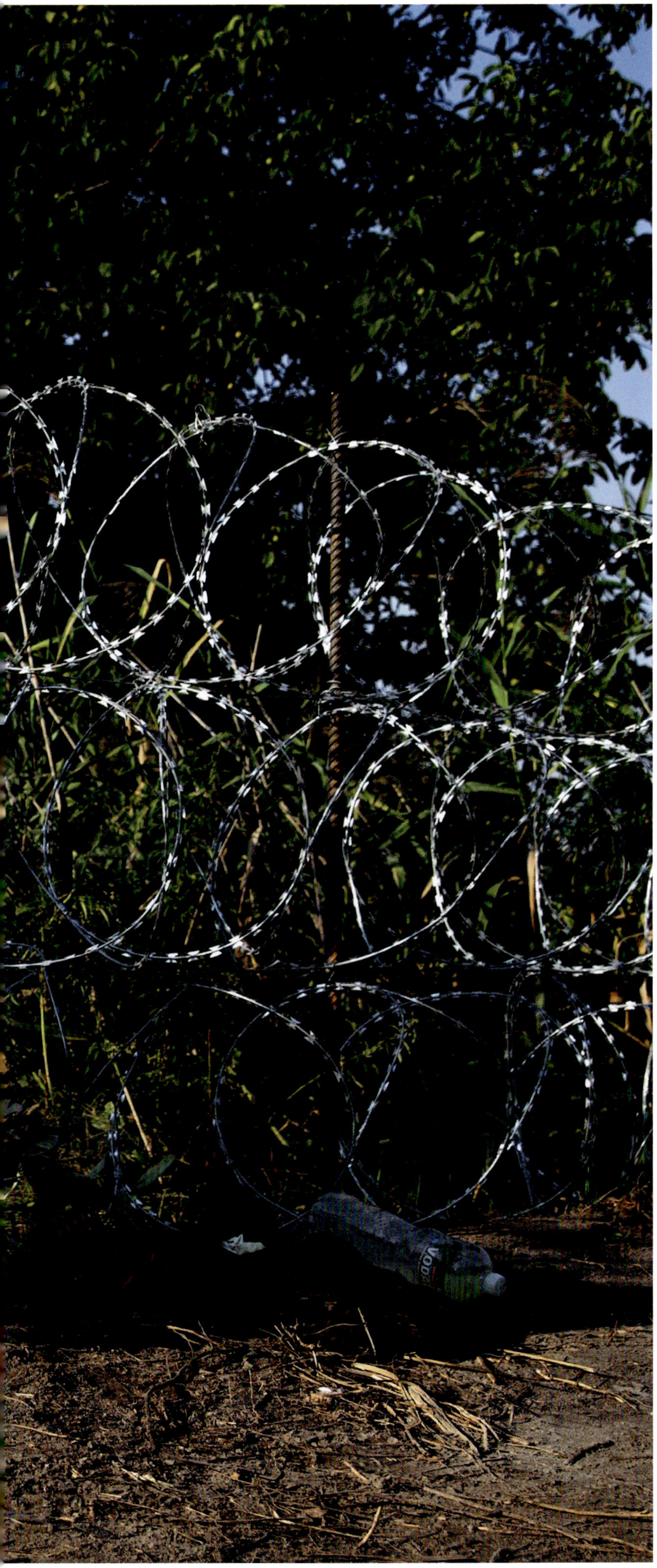

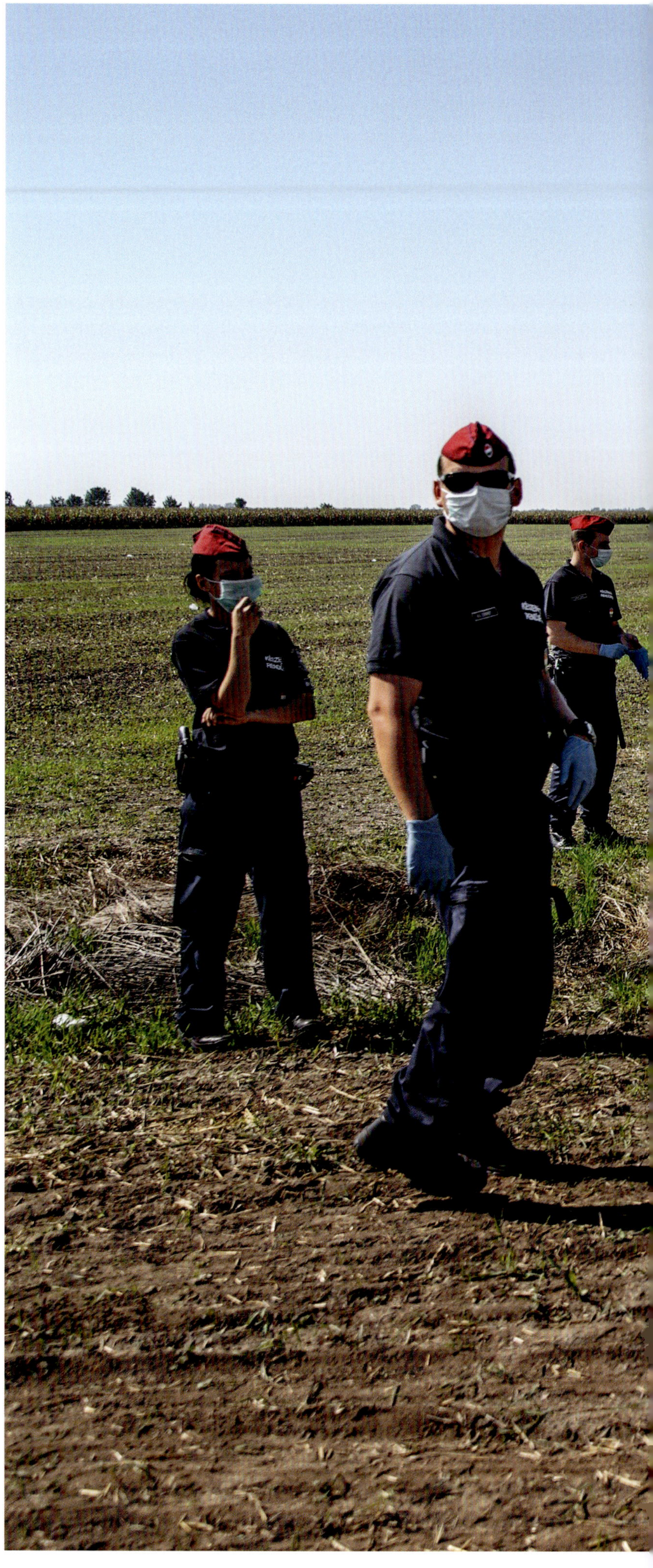

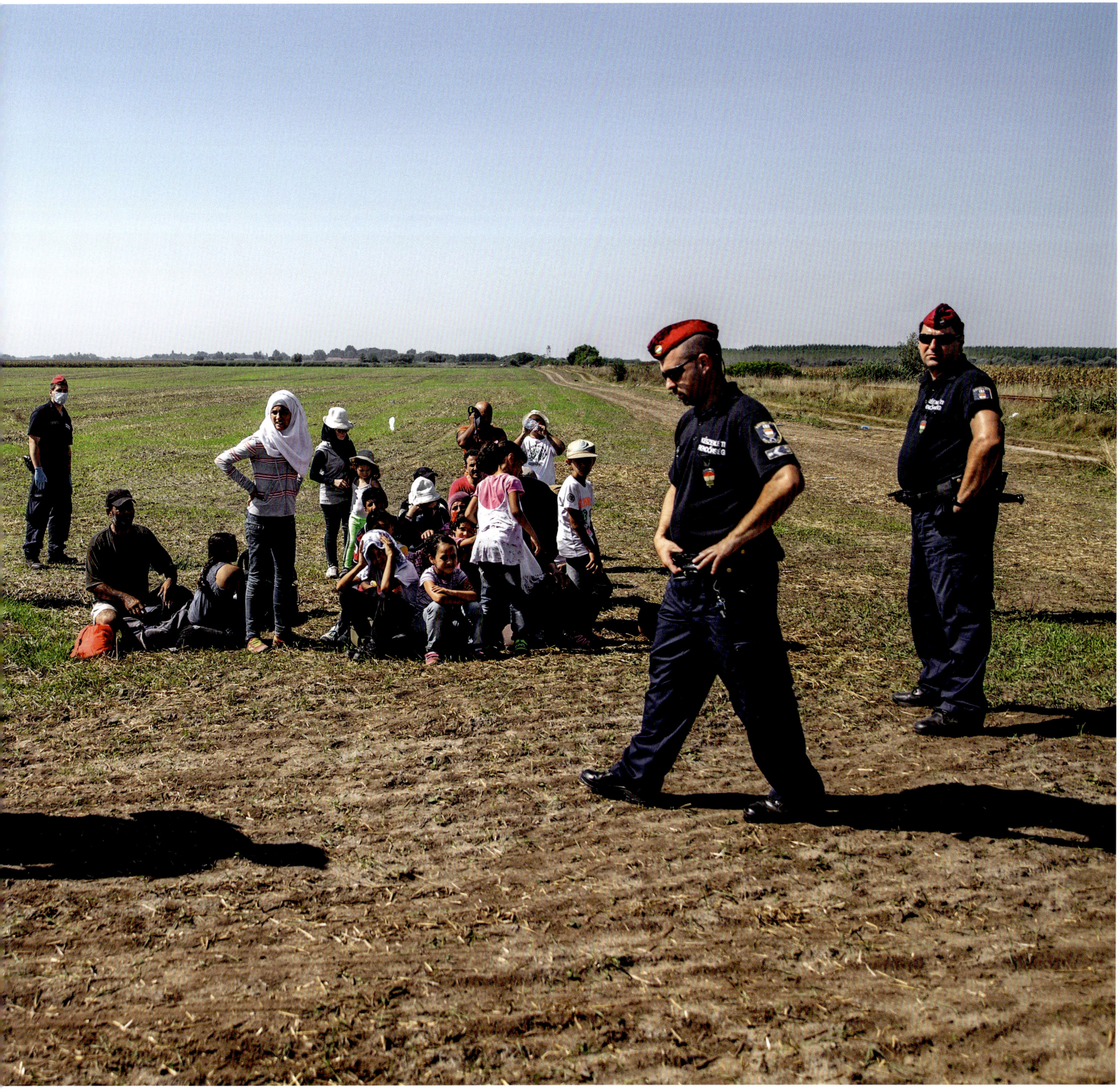

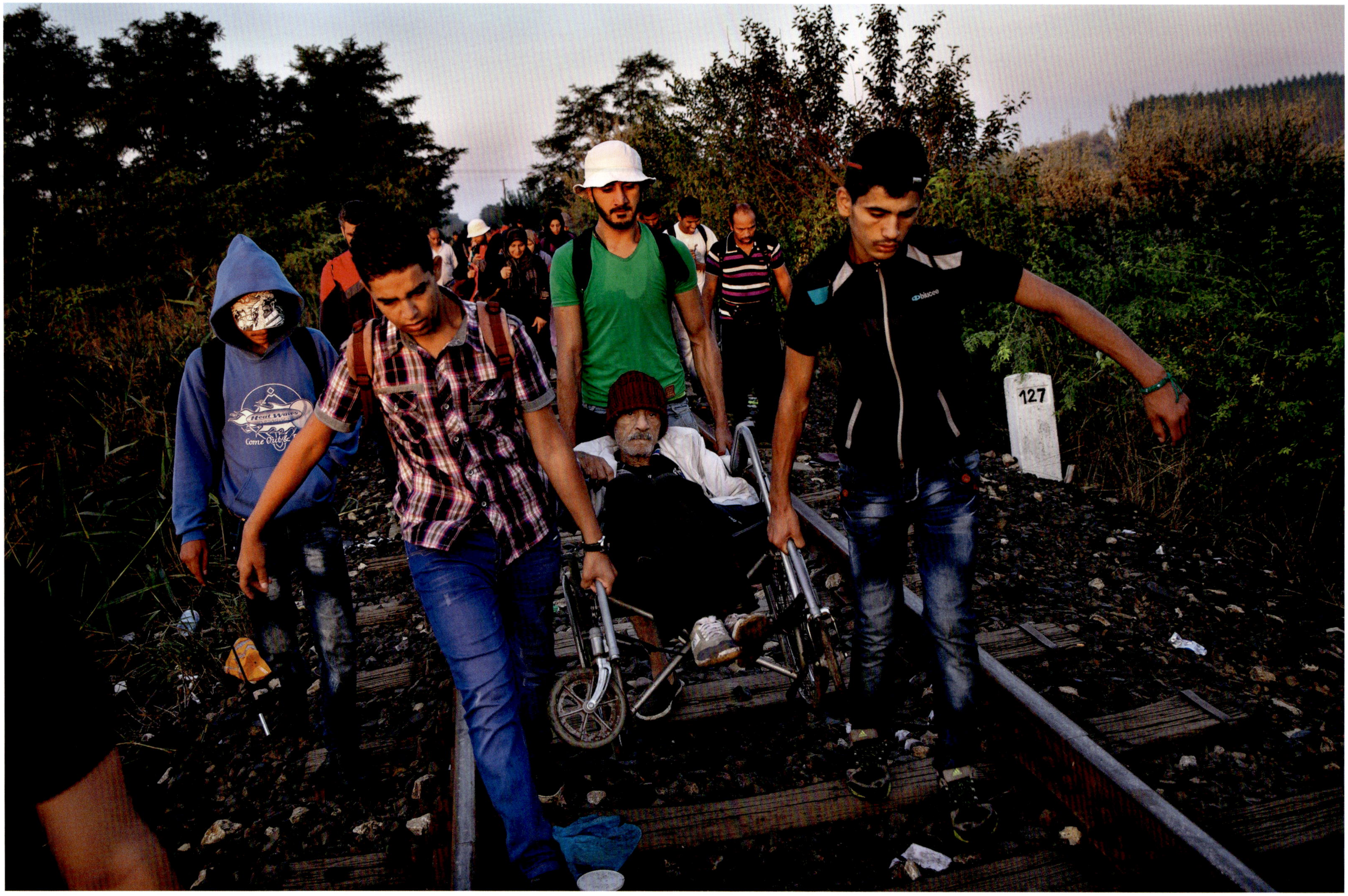
127

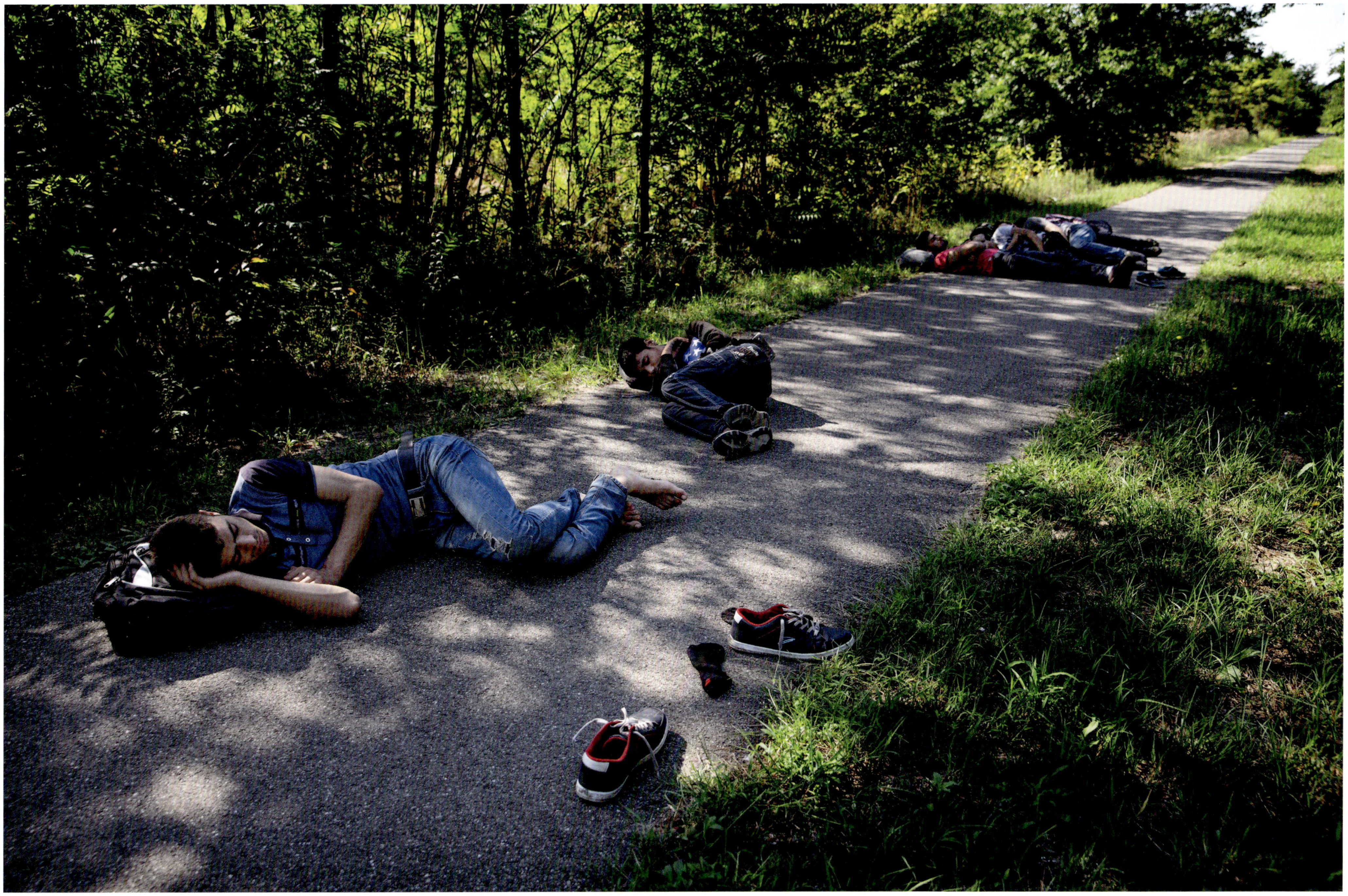

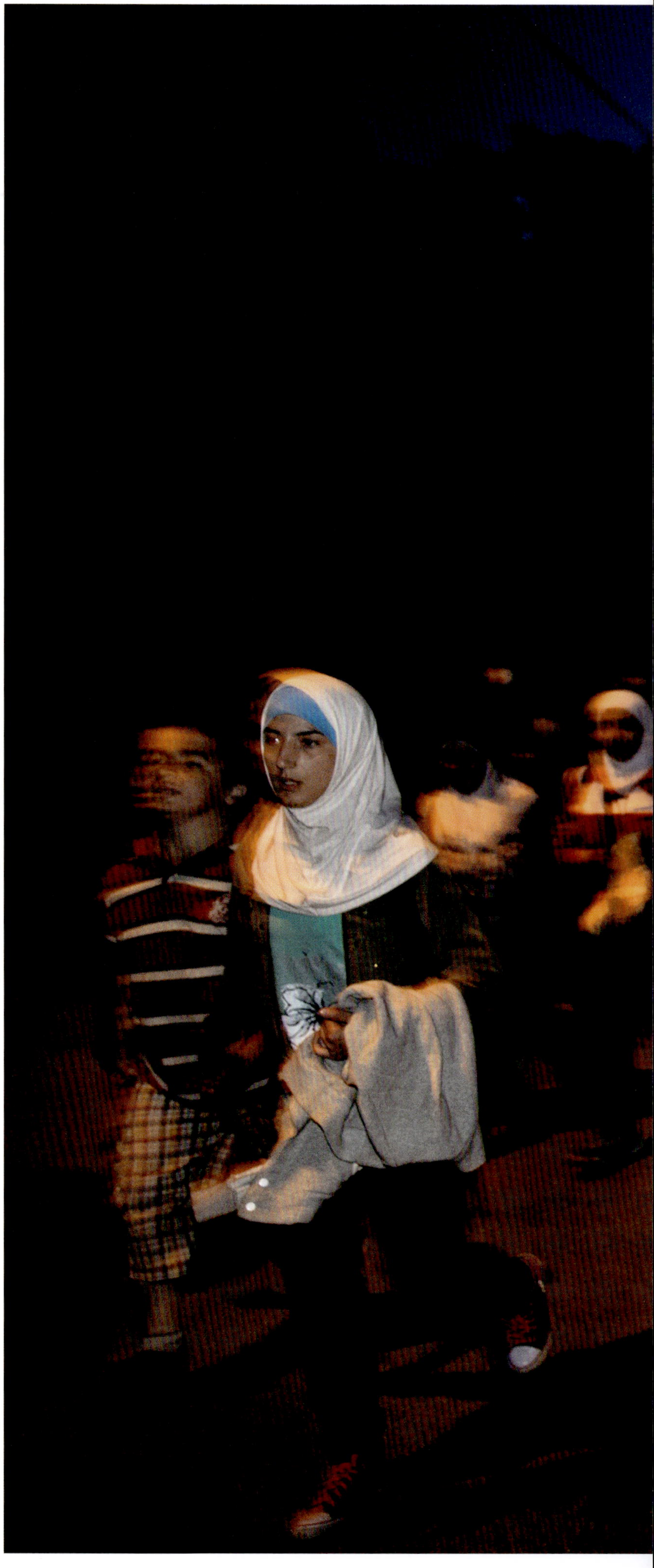

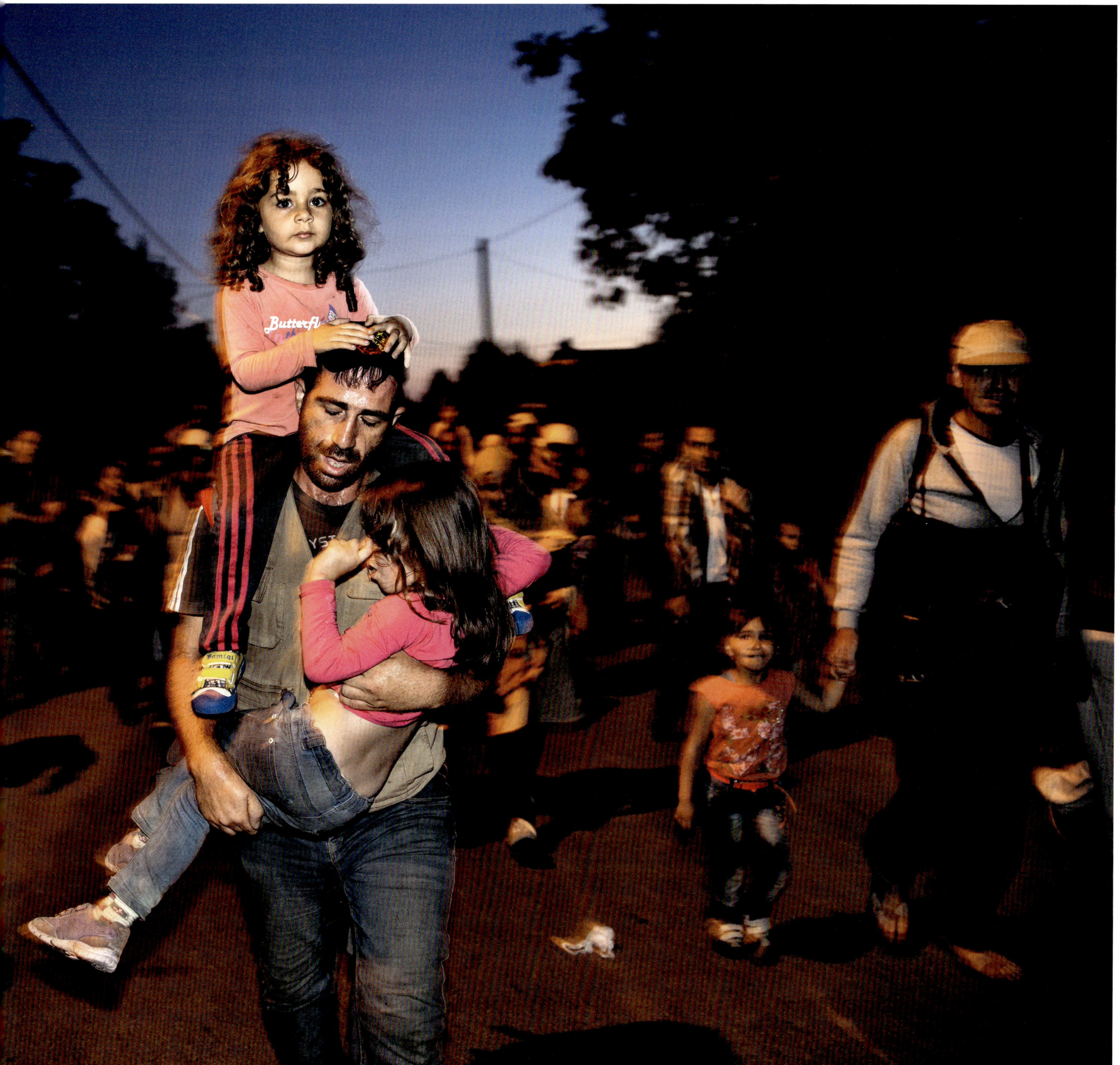

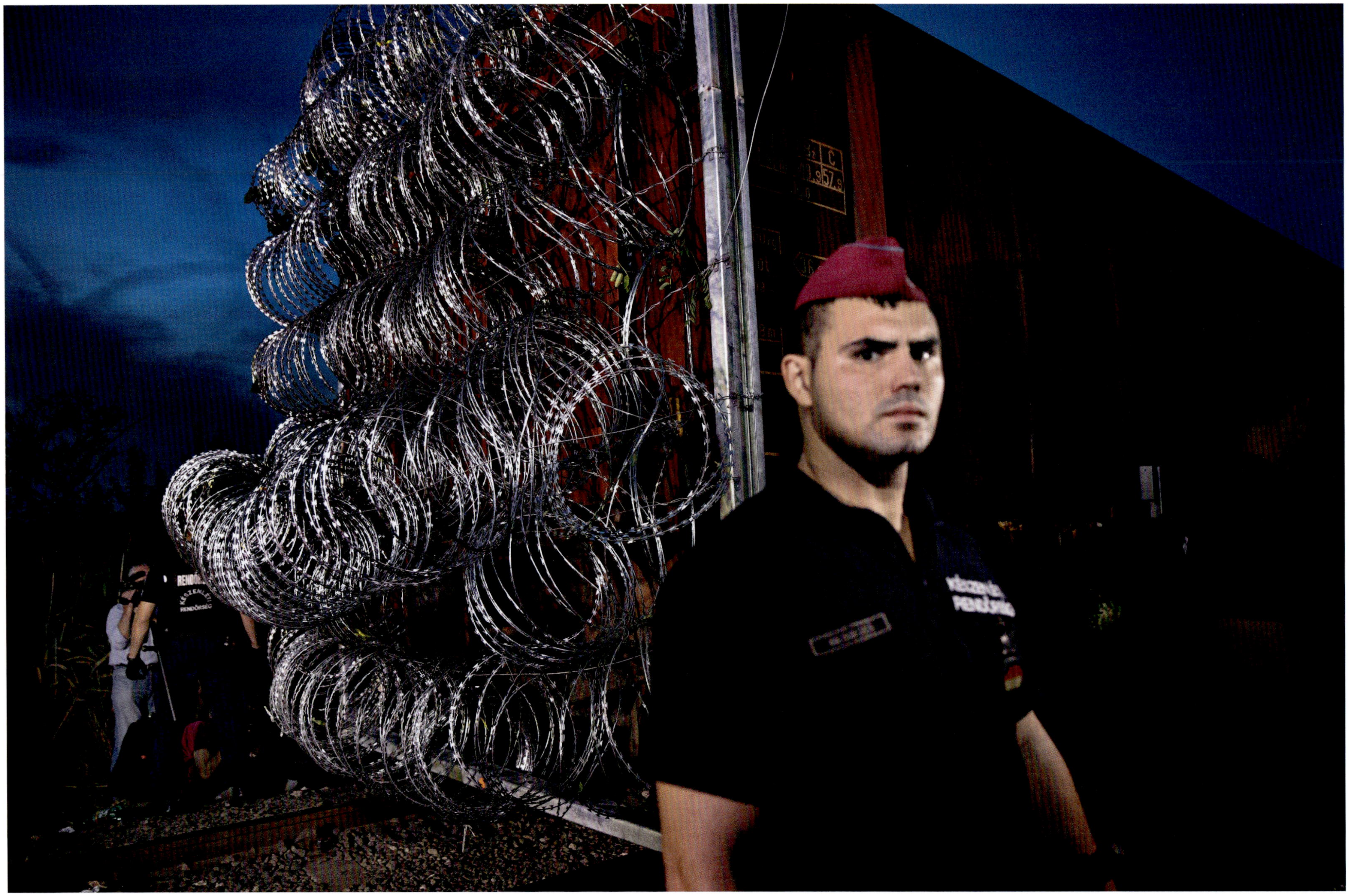

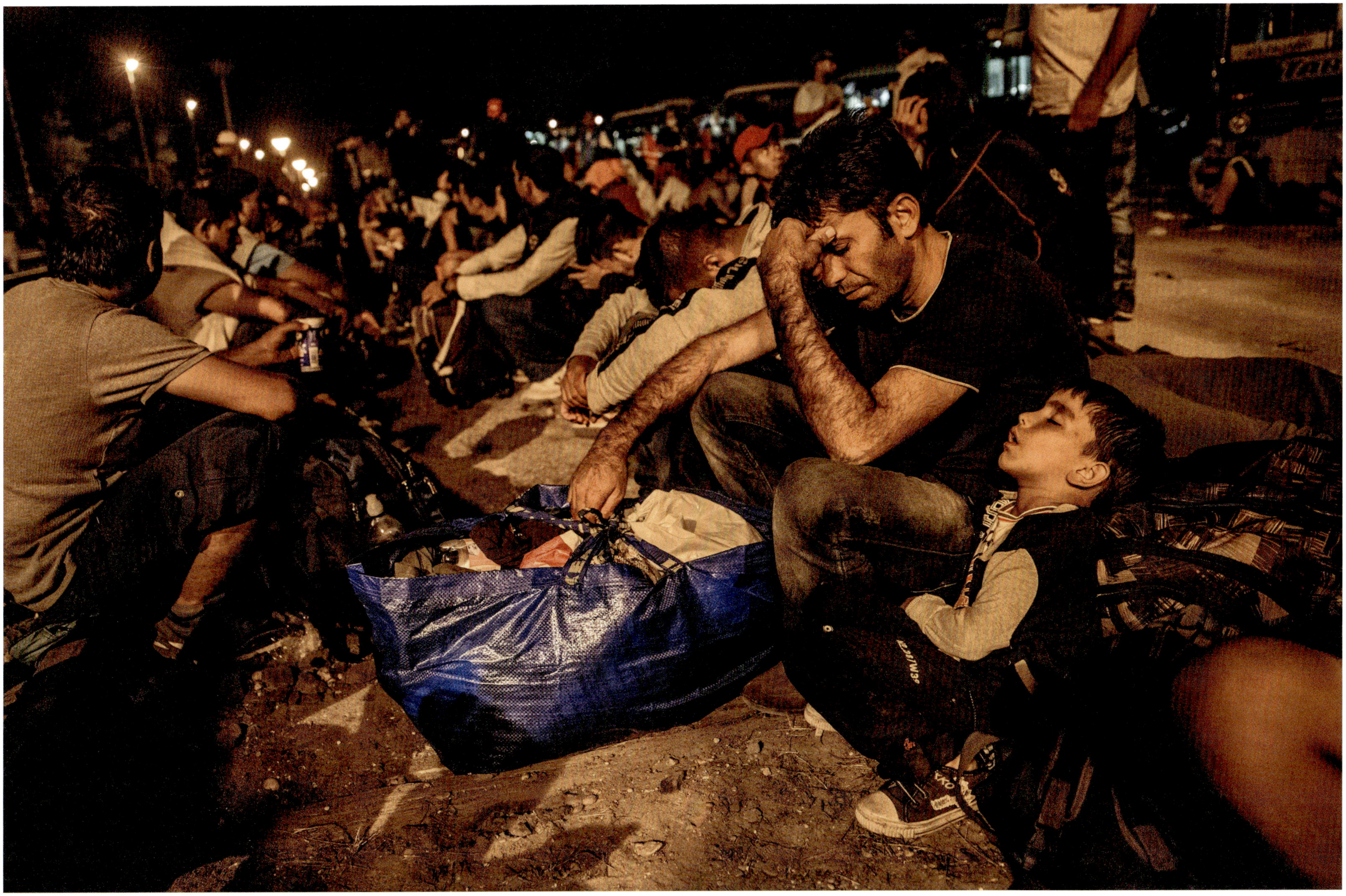

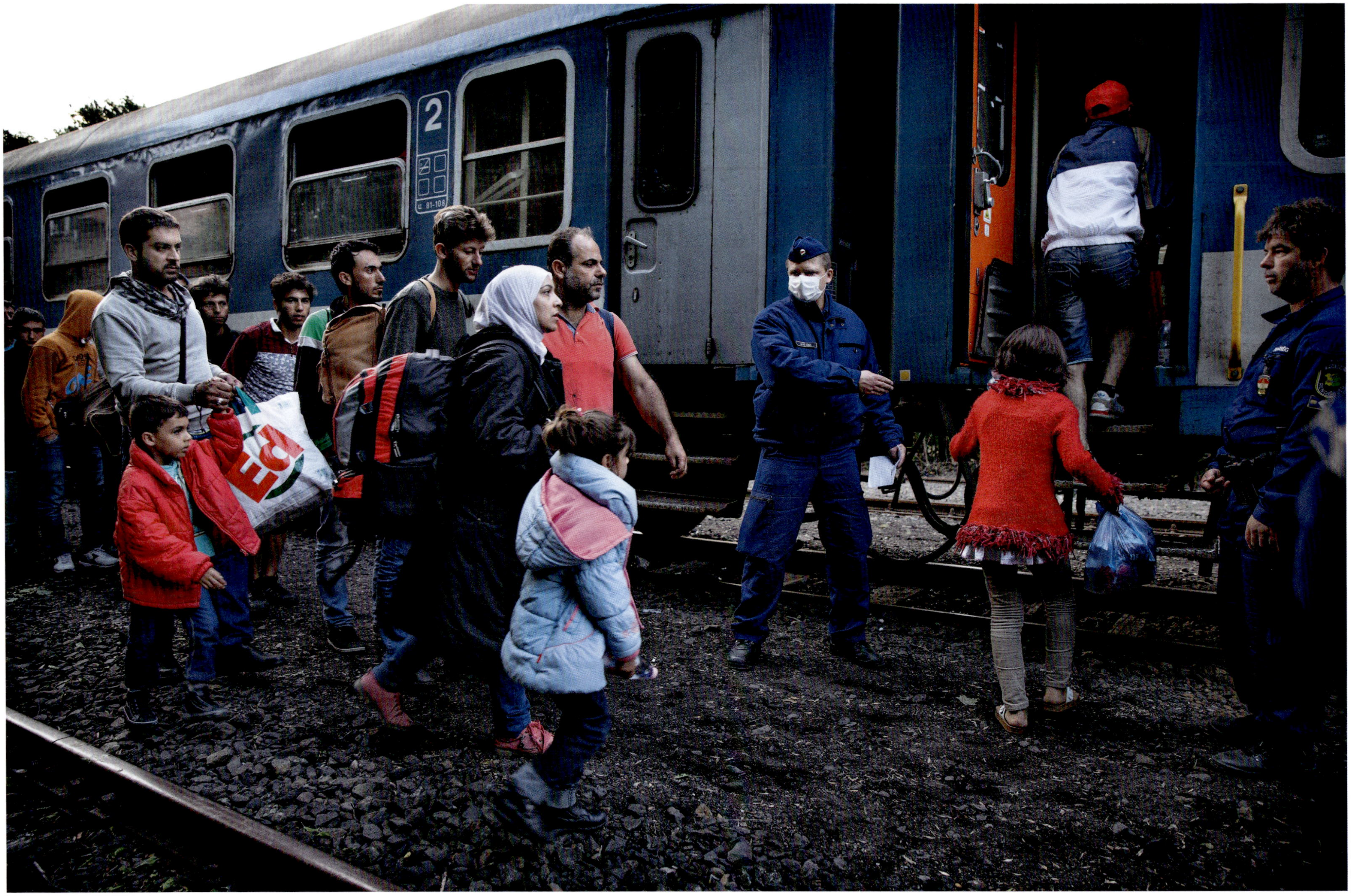
2

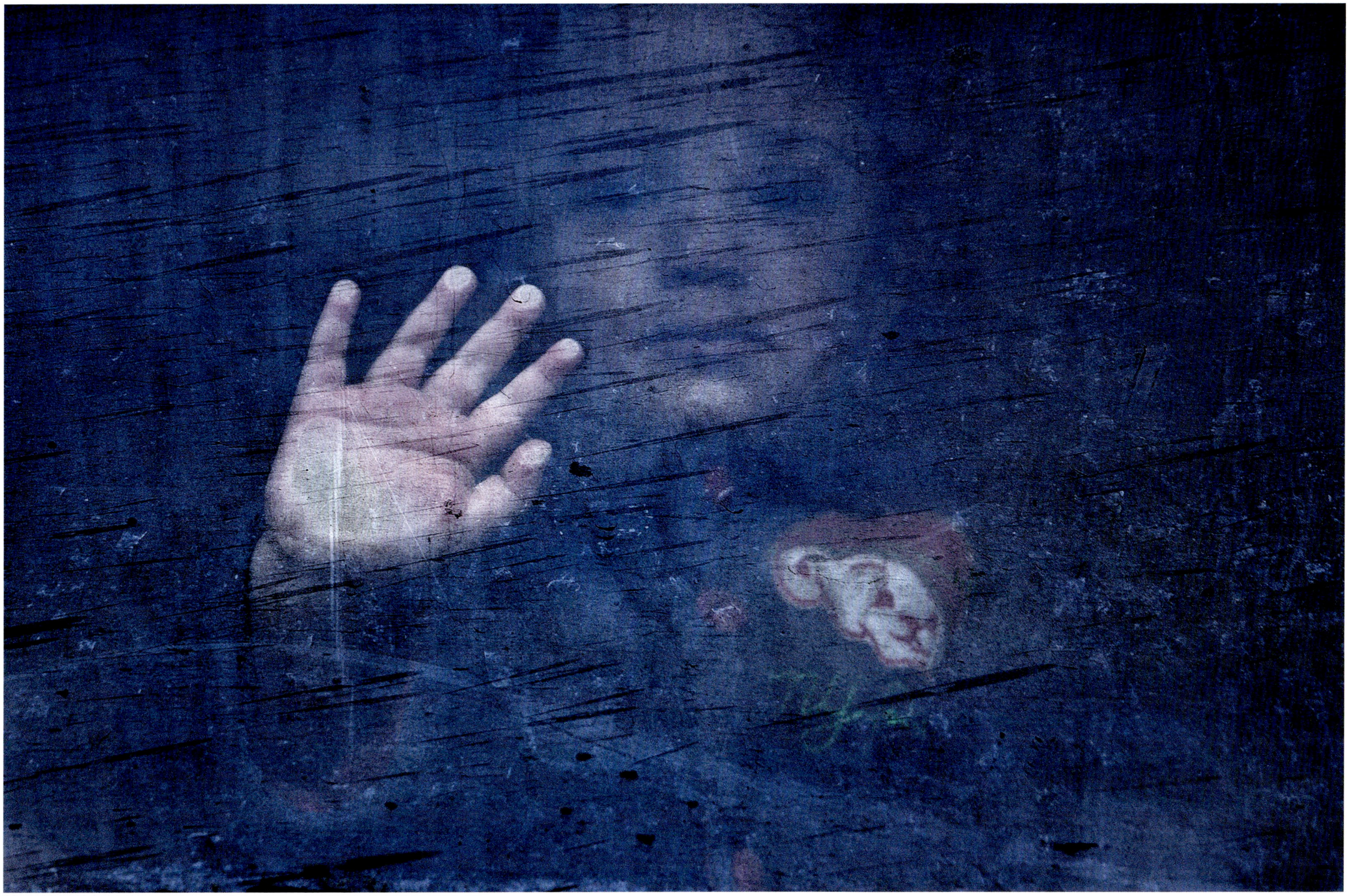

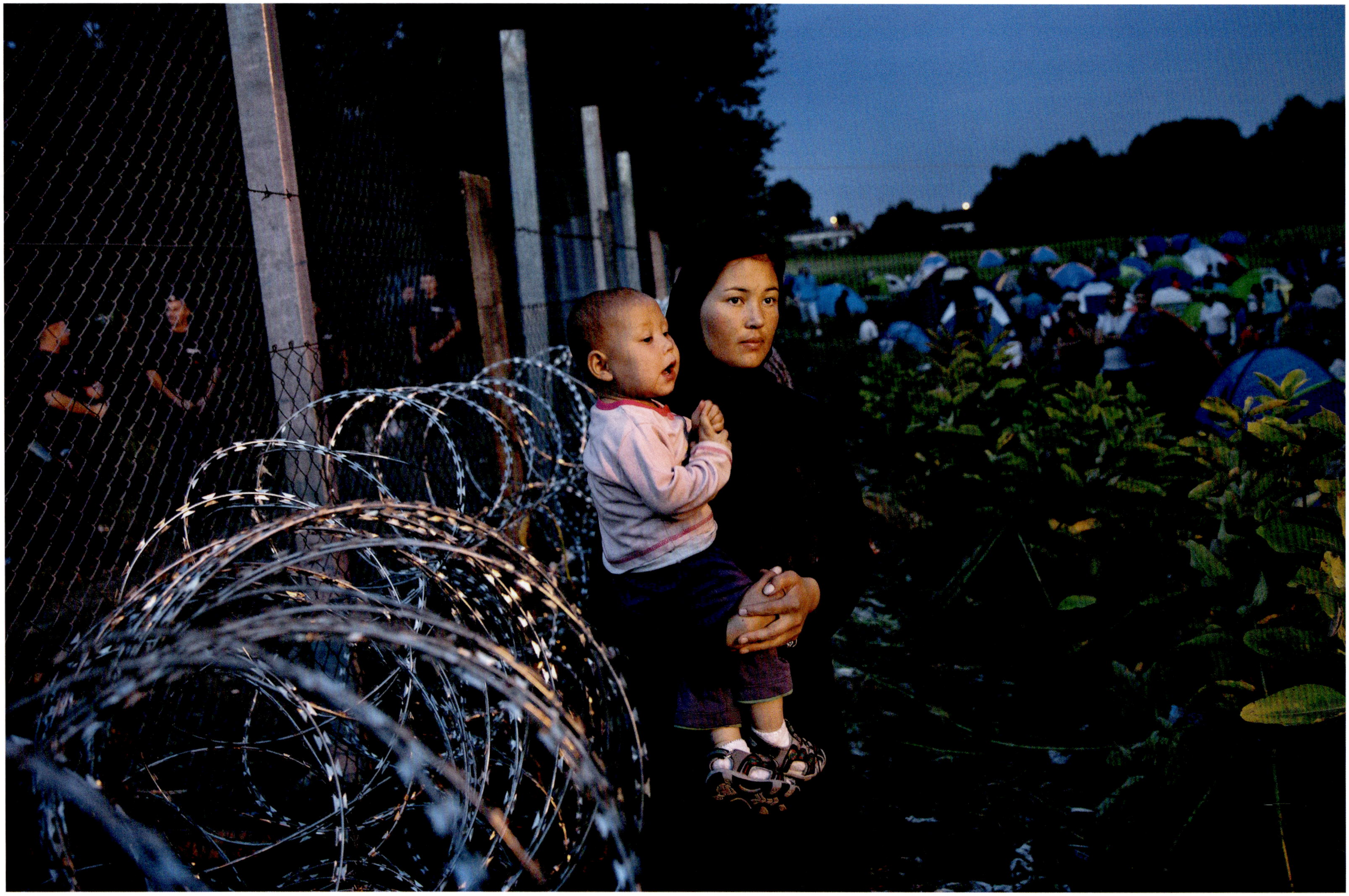

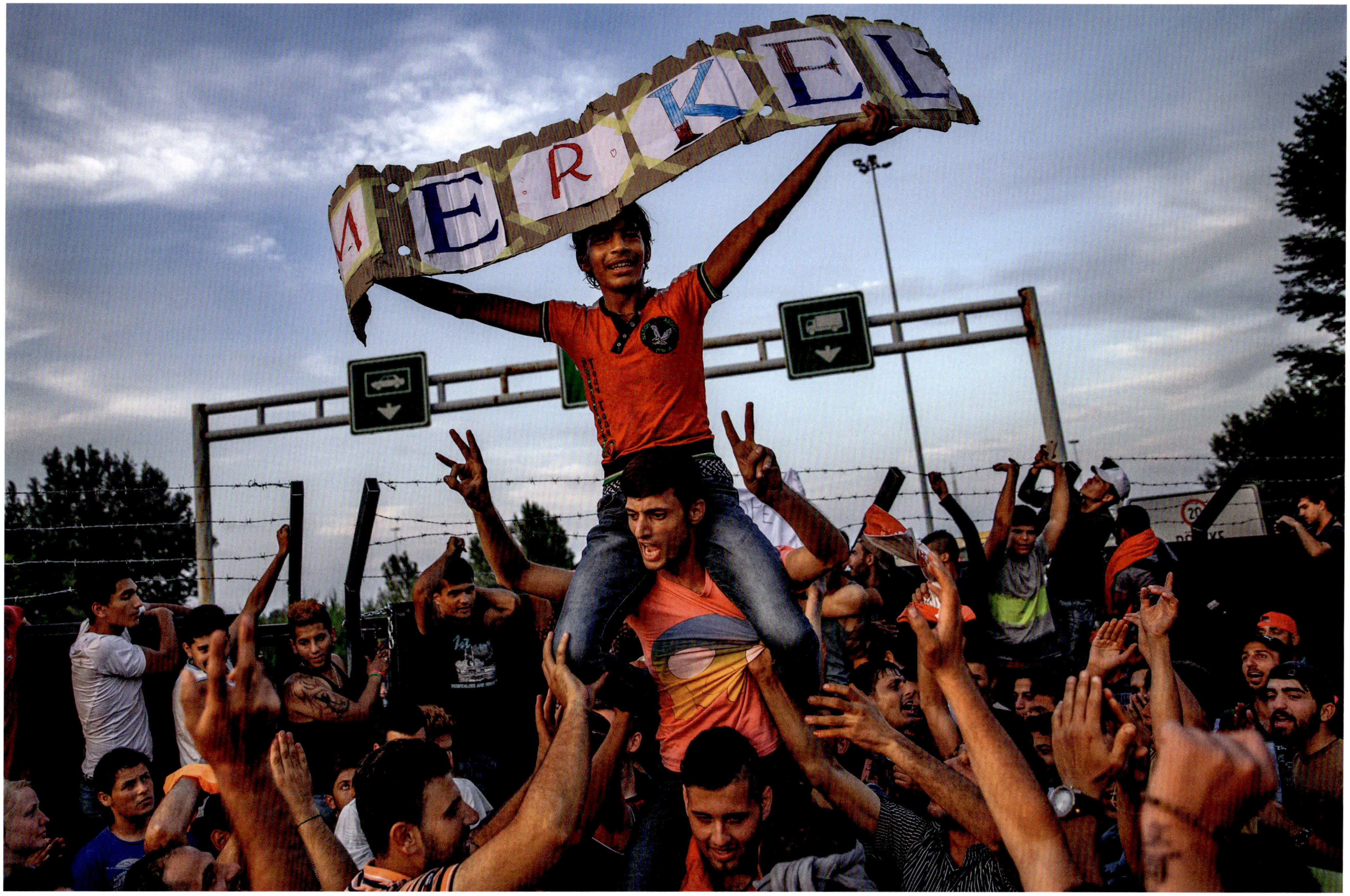
MERKEL

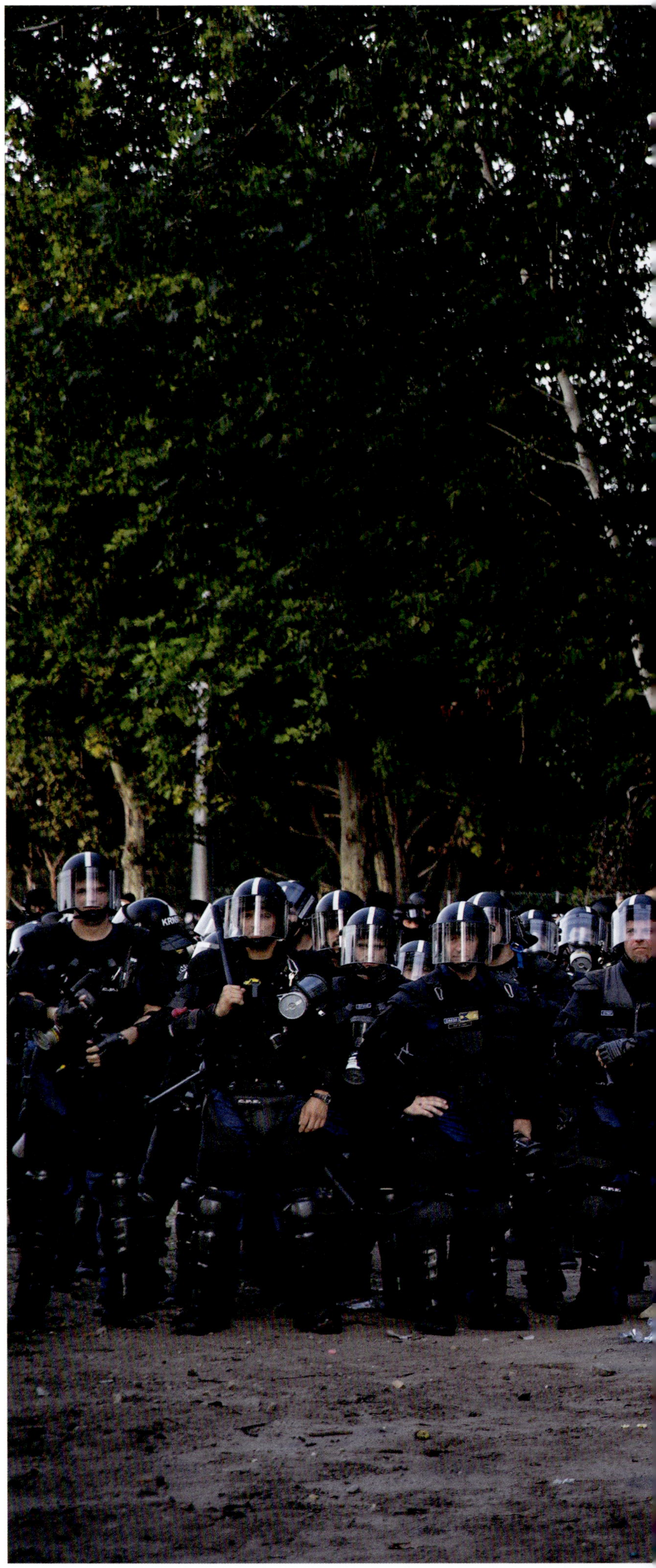

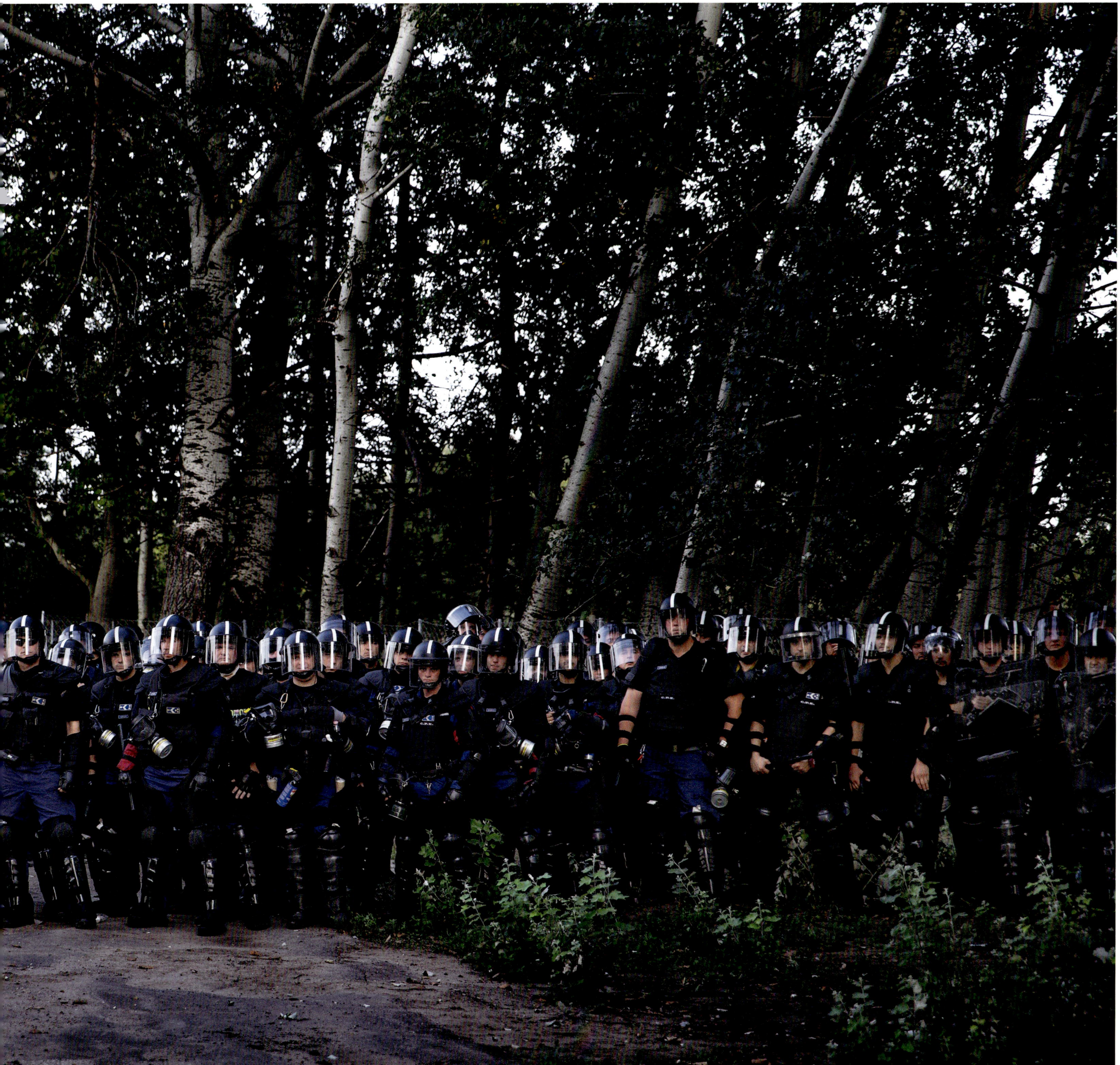

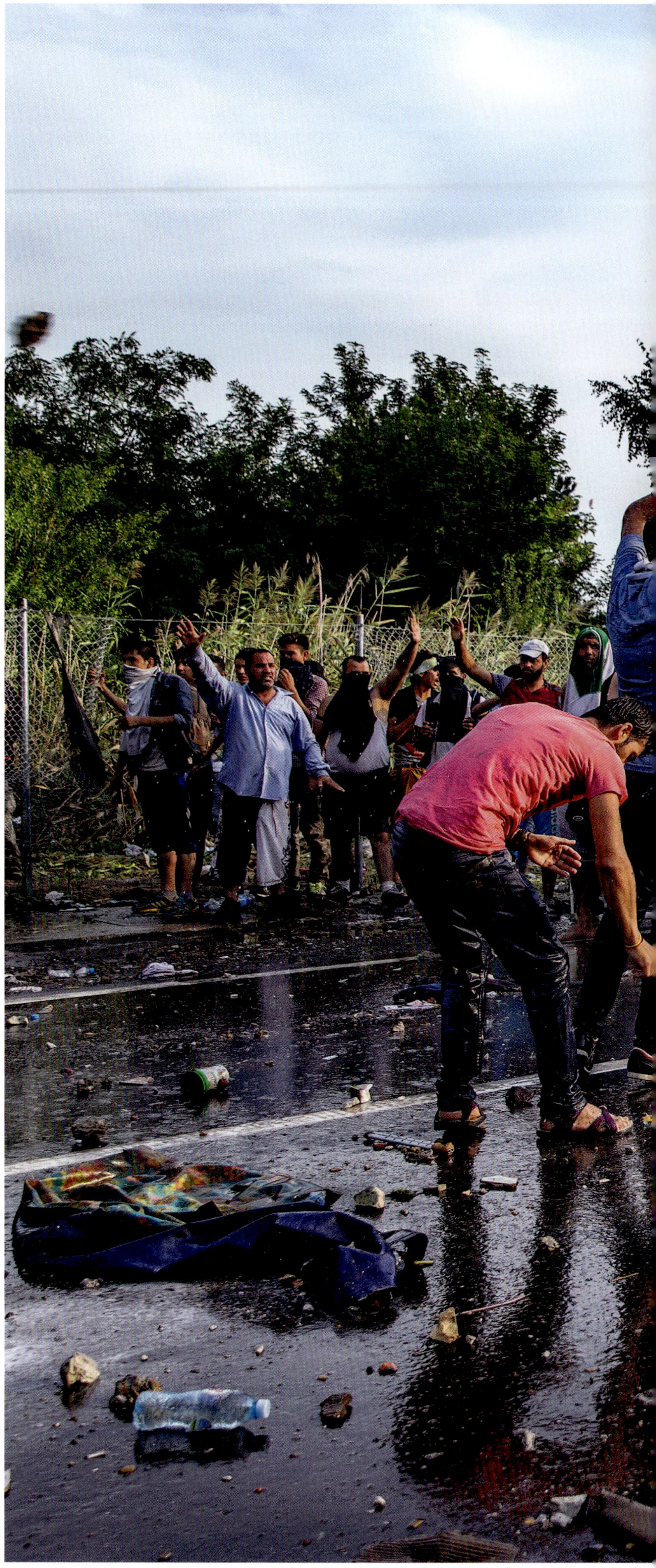

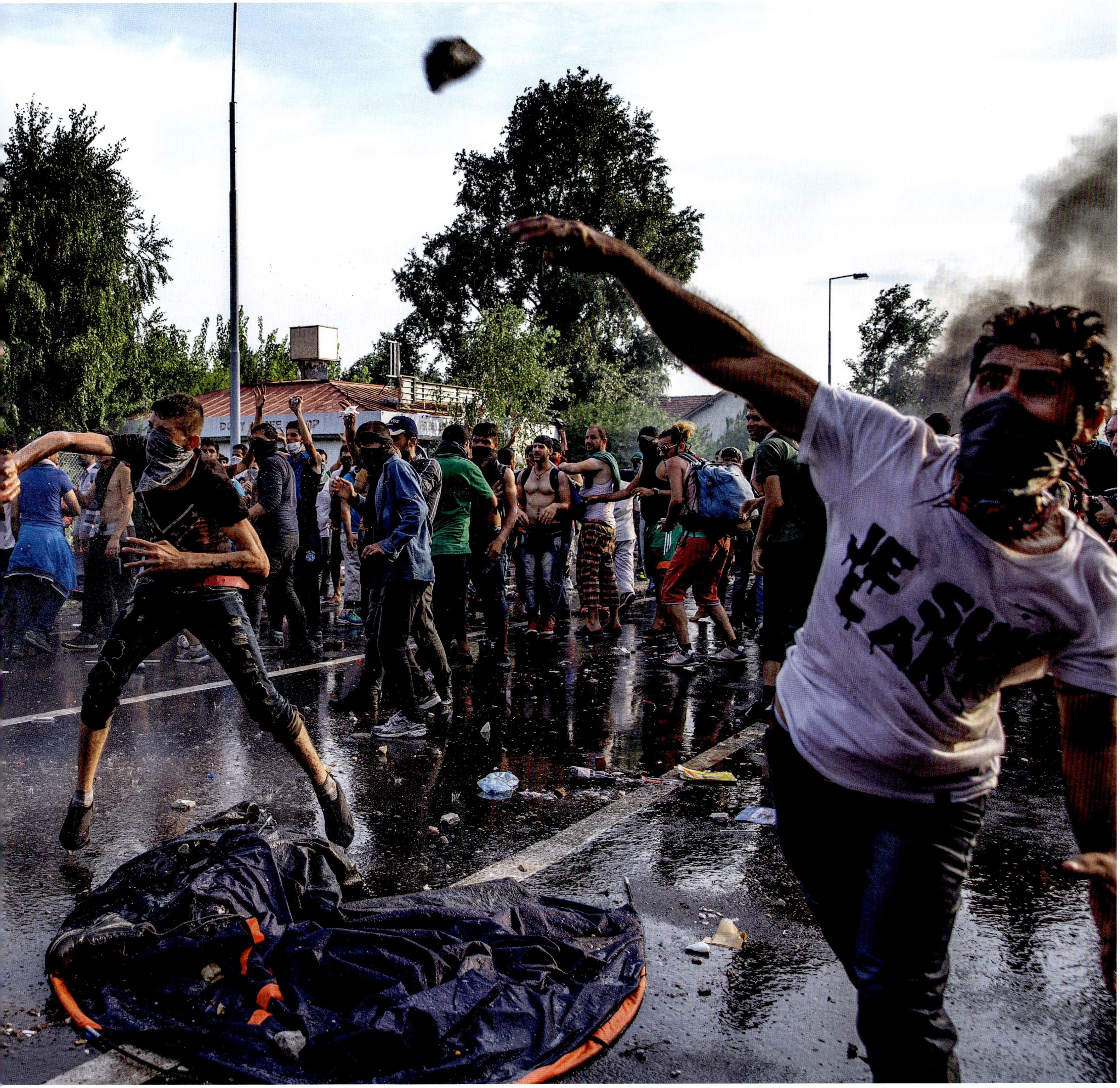

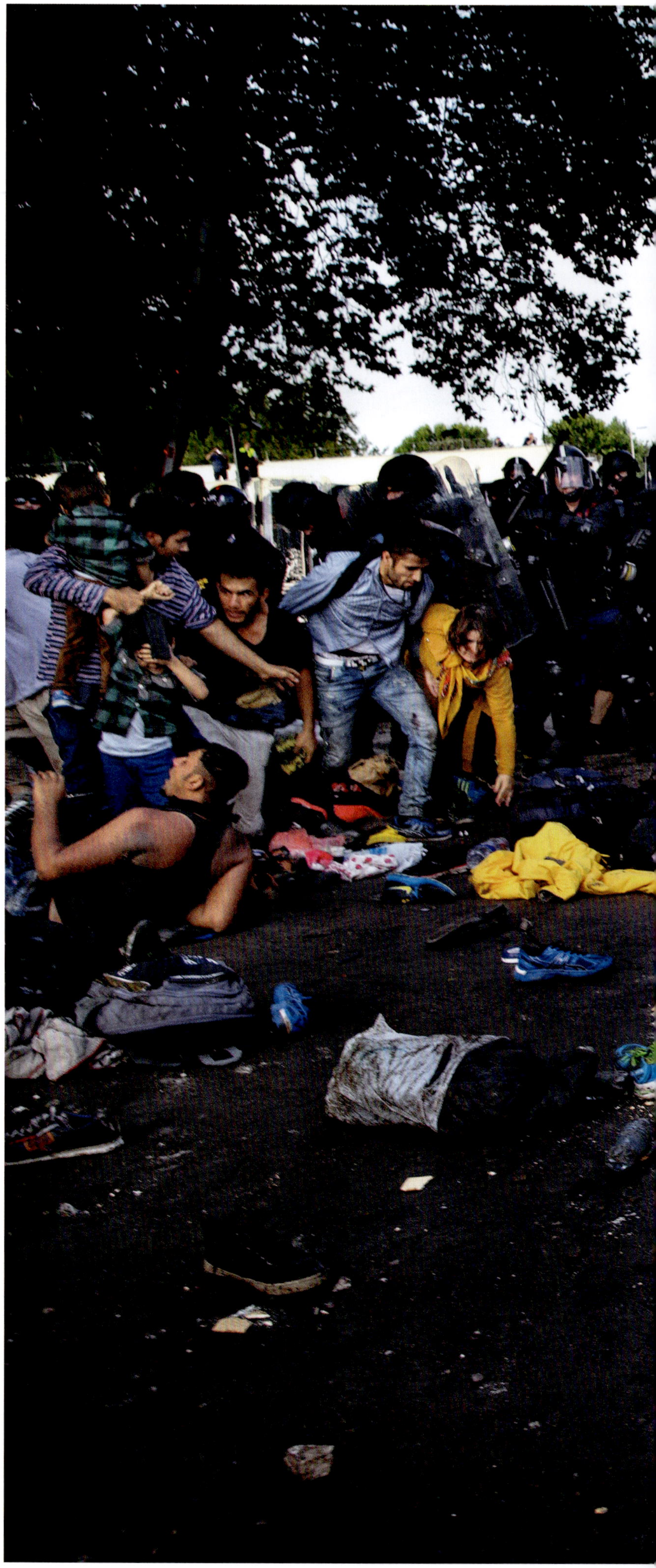

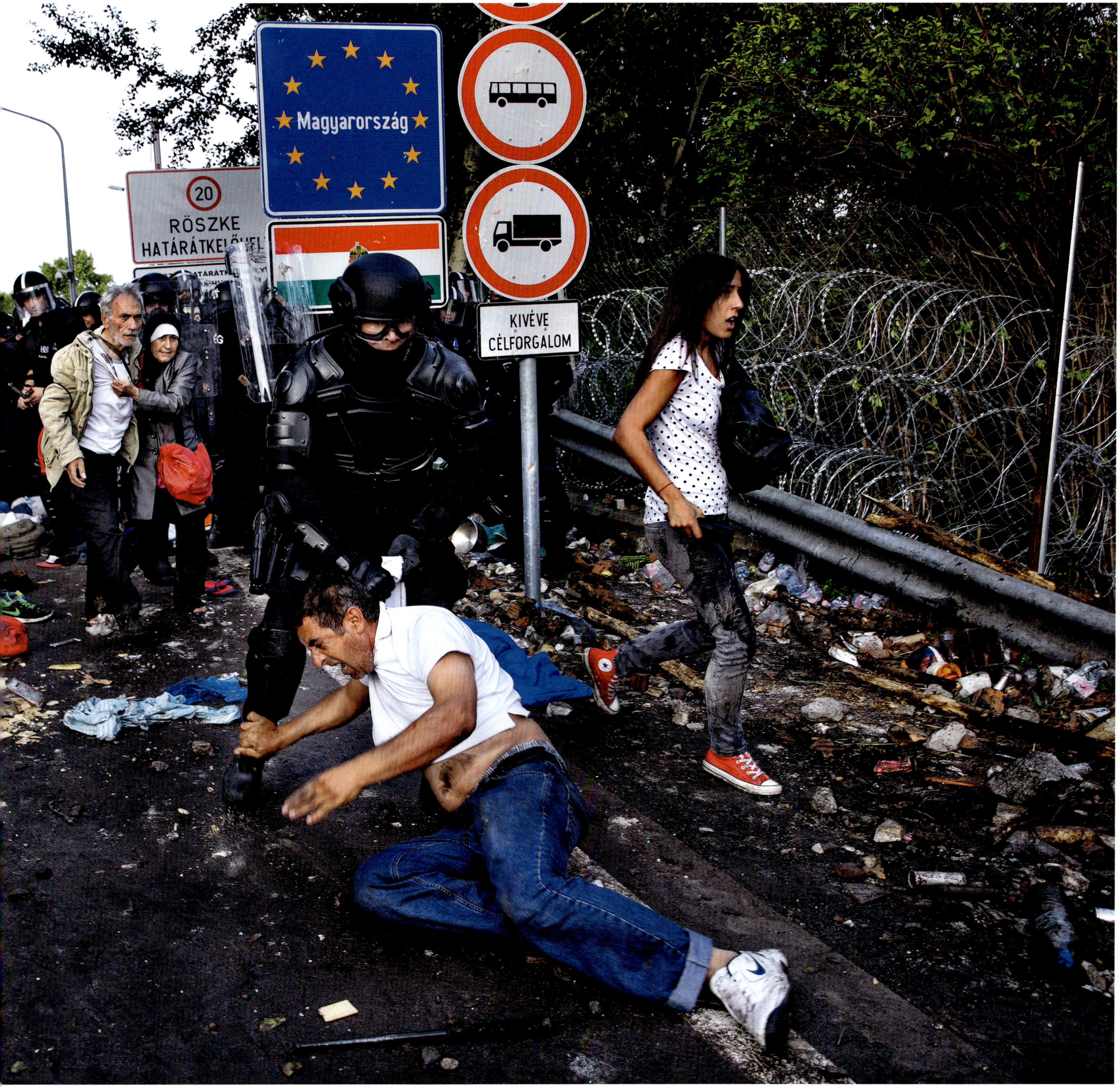

Magyarország
20
RÖSZKE
KIVÉVE
CÉLFORGALOM

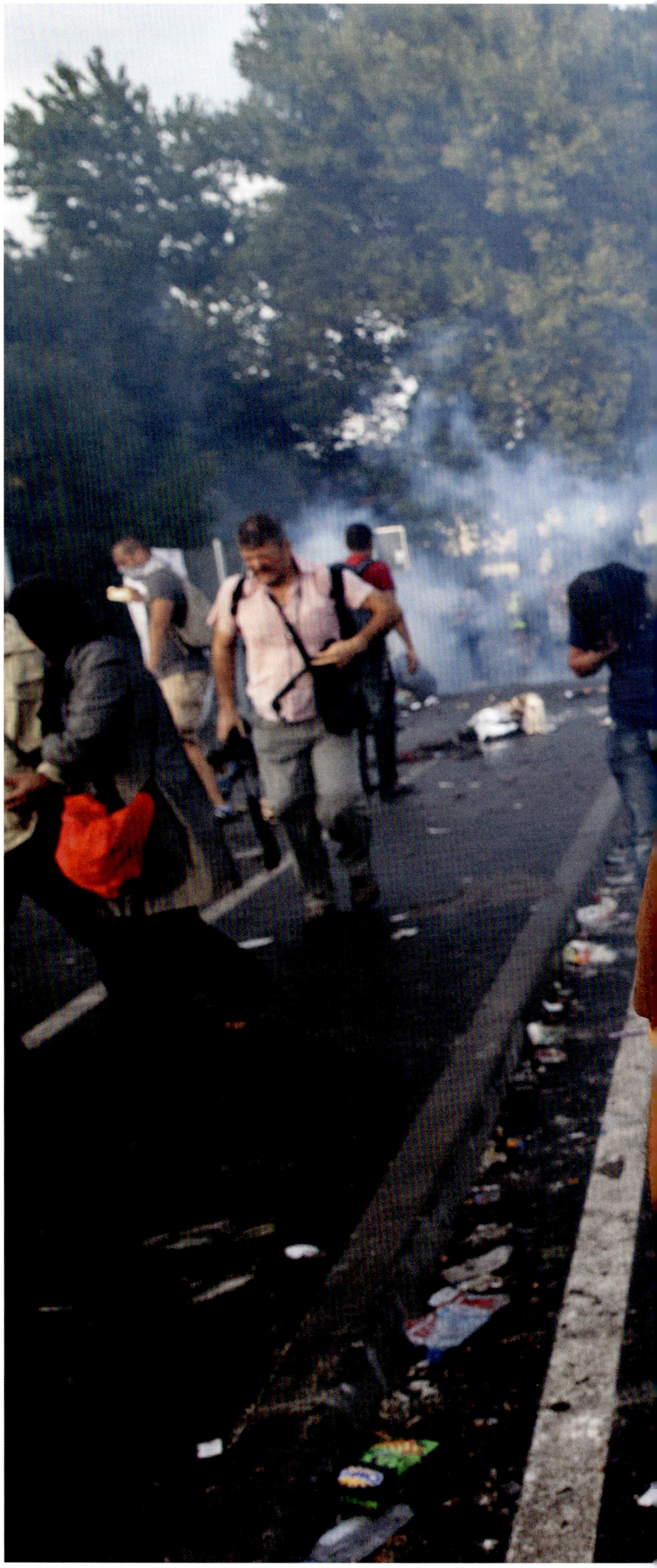

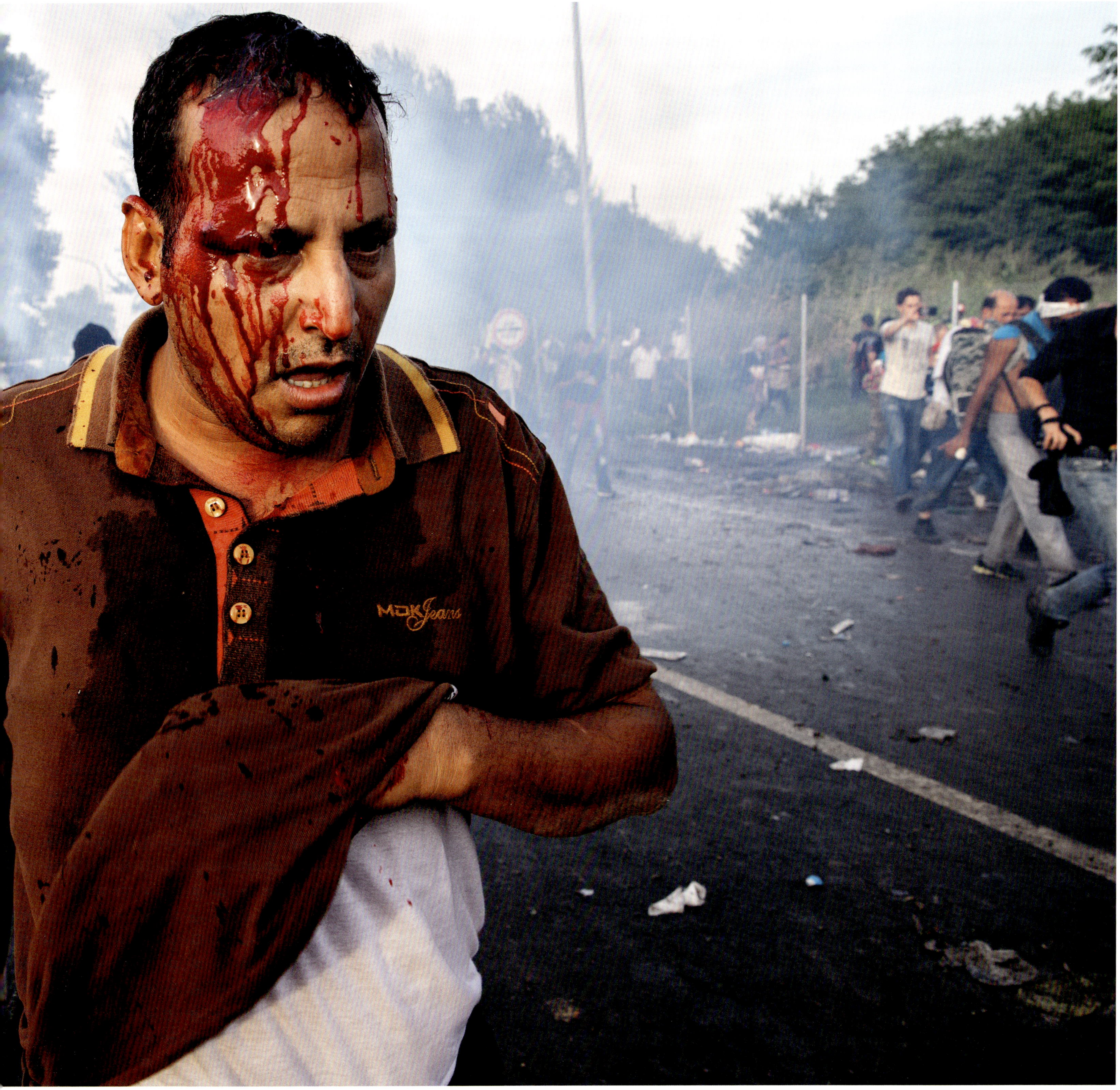
MDK Jeans

Despite the rough weather, in the autumn of 2015 large numbers of dinghies filled with refugees land on the Greek islands. According to the International Organization for Migration (IOM), between the 17th and 21st of October alone, 27,276 people arrived in Lesbos. Most boats land on a 15 kilometre stretch on the northern coast of Lesbos between Molivos and Skala Sikaminias. Small NGOs and volunteers from around the world arrive on the island to help in whatever way they can, but there is a lack of coordination and the situation is chaotic.

Everyone has to be registered and have their fingerprints taken at the reception centre in Moria, which was designated as the first European migration 'hotspot' in October 2015. Refugees and migrants must be quickly registered and screened so that a potential asylum application process can begin. The hotspot strategy is a central tool in the new European effort to relieve the recipient countries and redistribute the refugees throughout all of Europe, however, it turns out to be almost impossible for the EU member countries to agree on a redistribution policy.

The reception centre in Moria cannot keep up with the demand. There is not enough room for more people inside the centre, which has capacity for around 2,800 people. Outside, people lie in queues waiting for days. It can easily take a week or longer before they get documents that state that they can stay in Greece legally on a temporary basis, and which permit them to take a ferry to Athens. Syrians are given papers that put them in a better position compared to people of other nationalities.

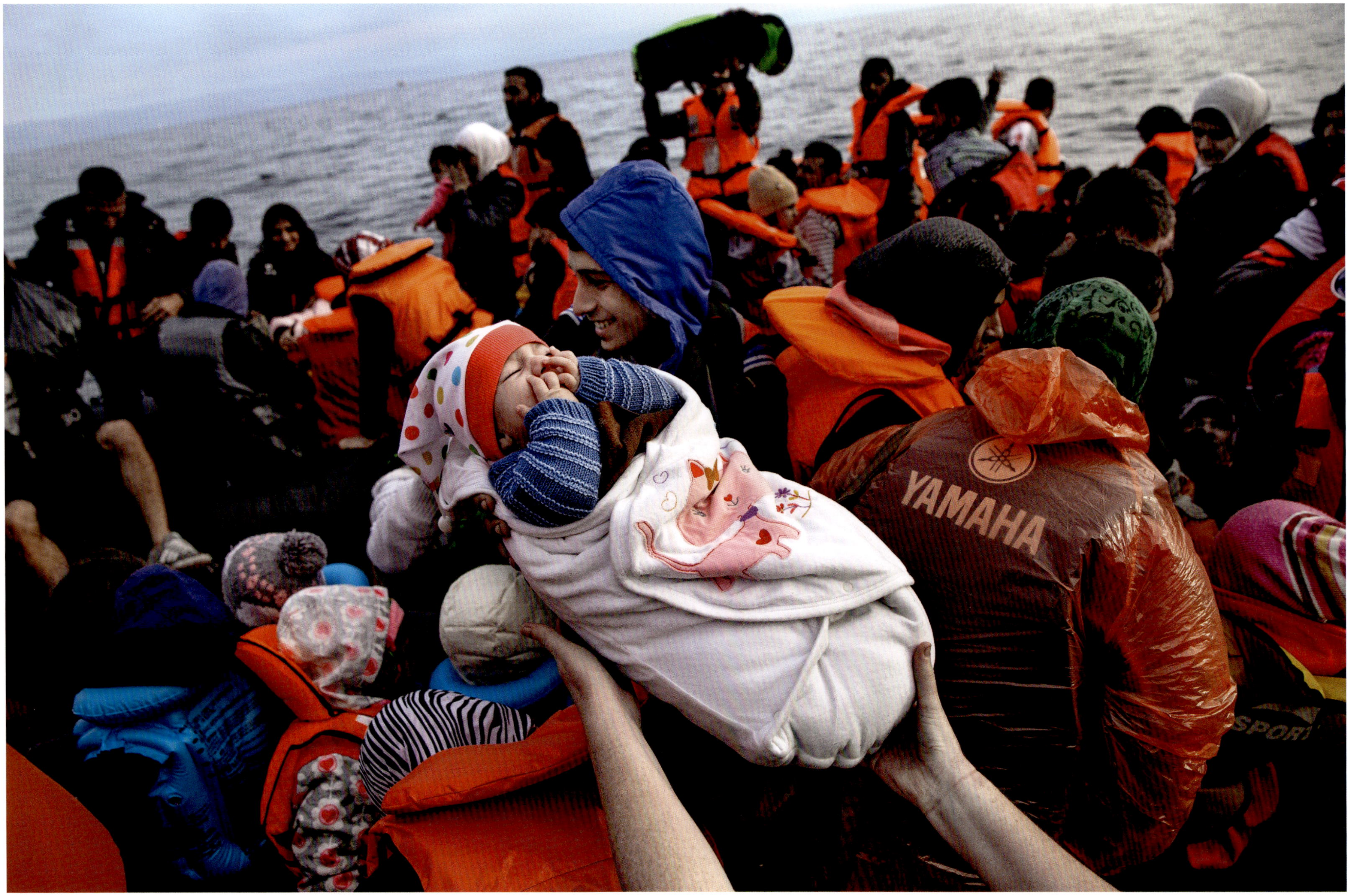
YAMAHA
SPORT

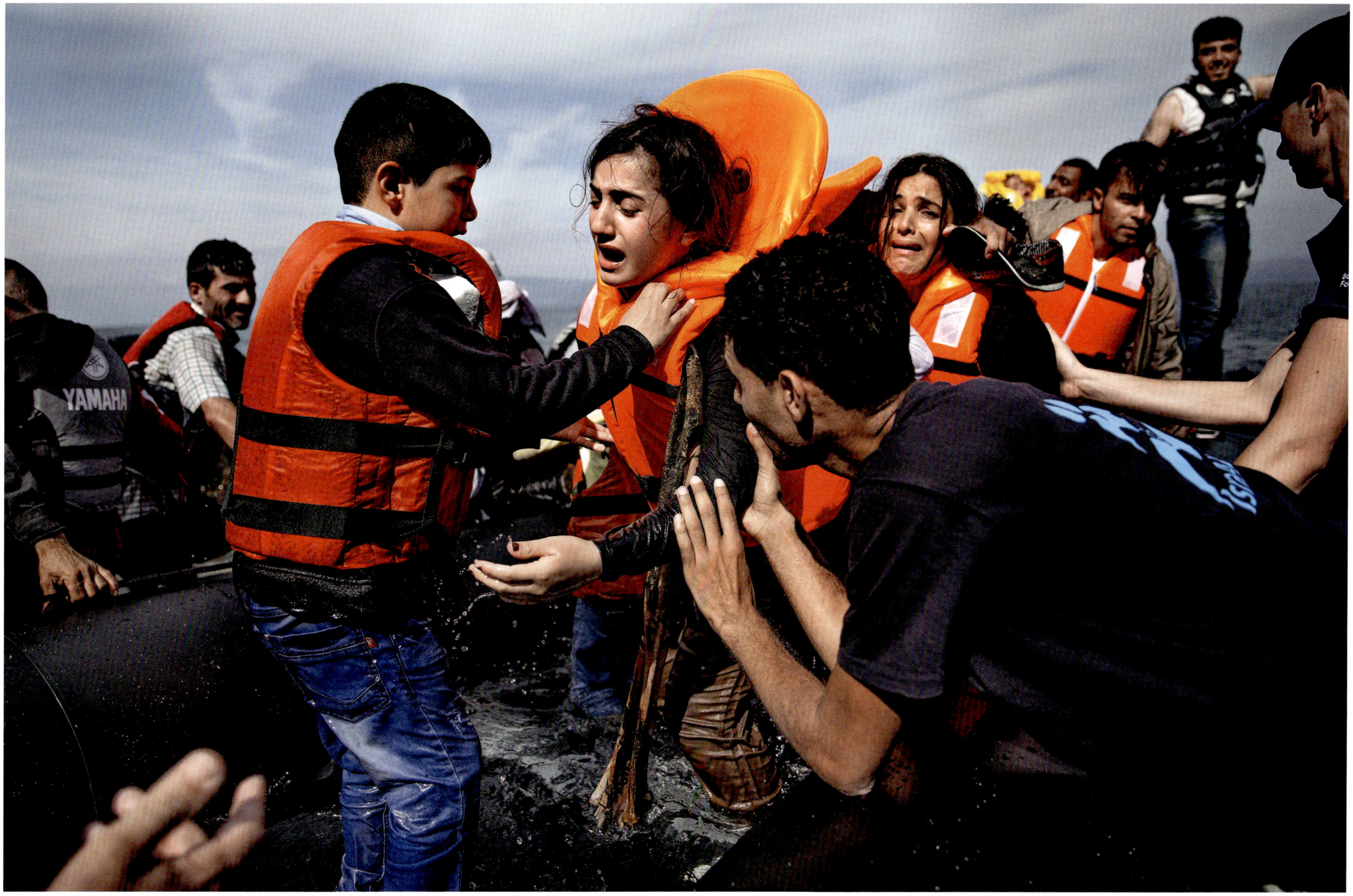
YAMAHA

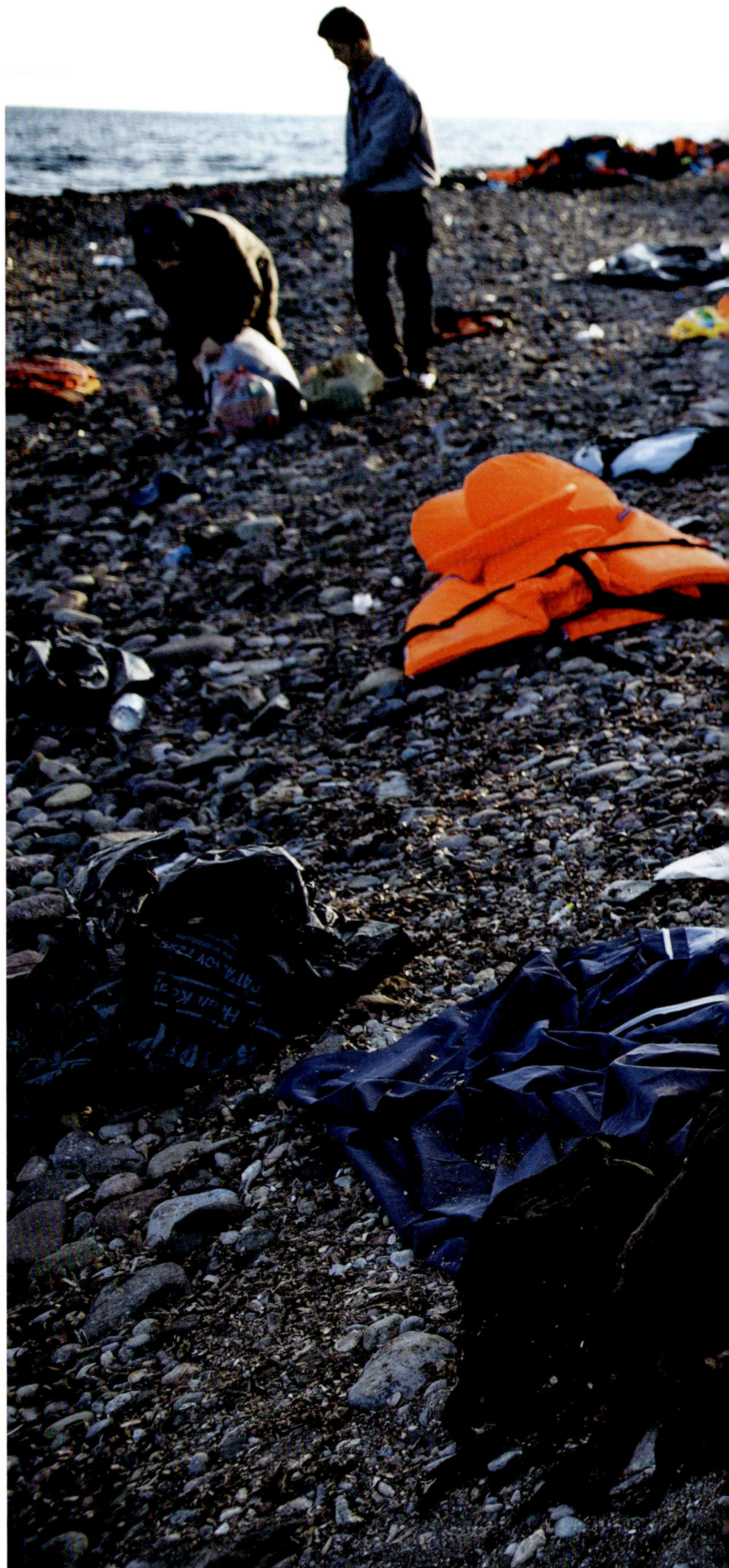

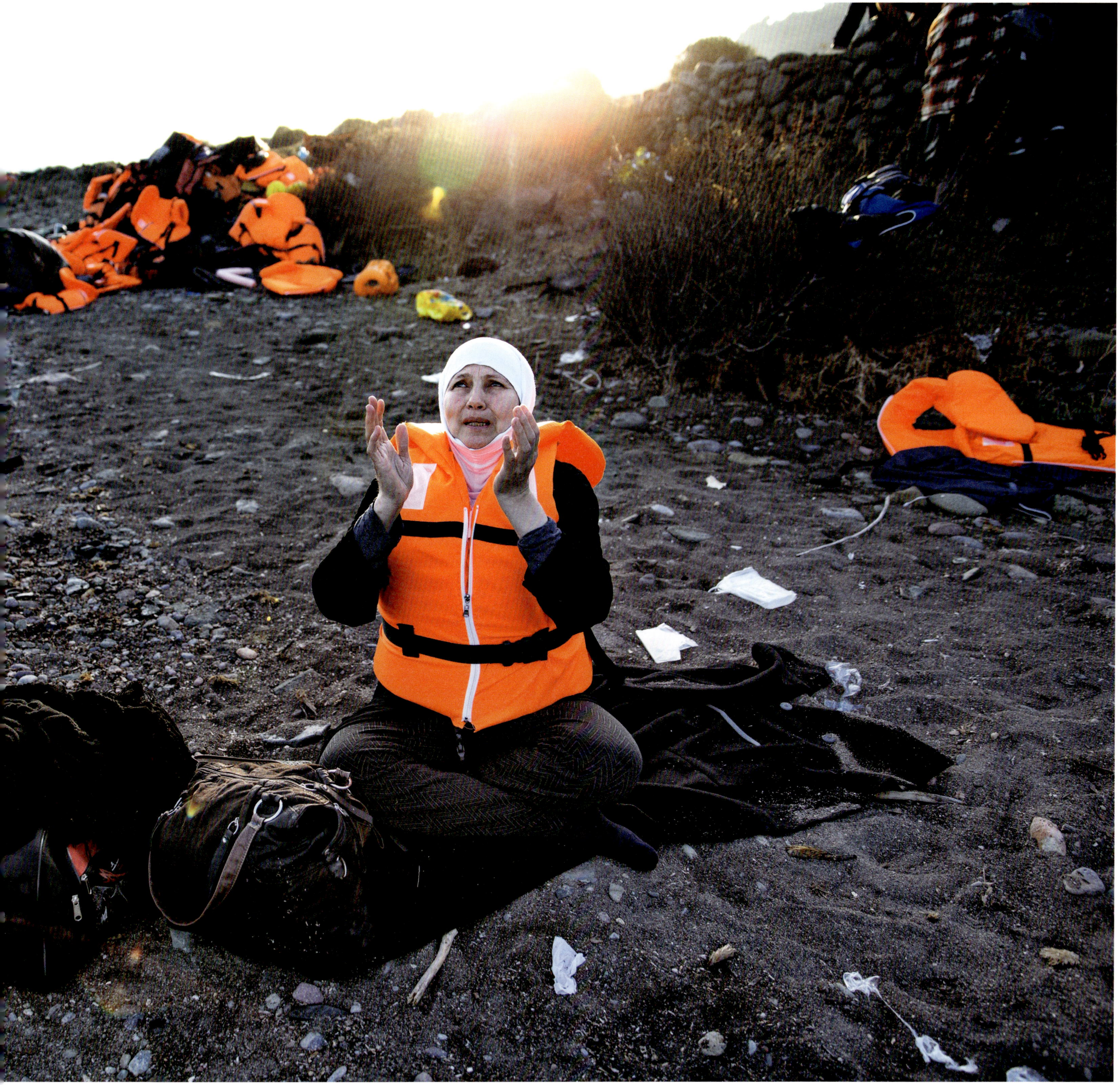

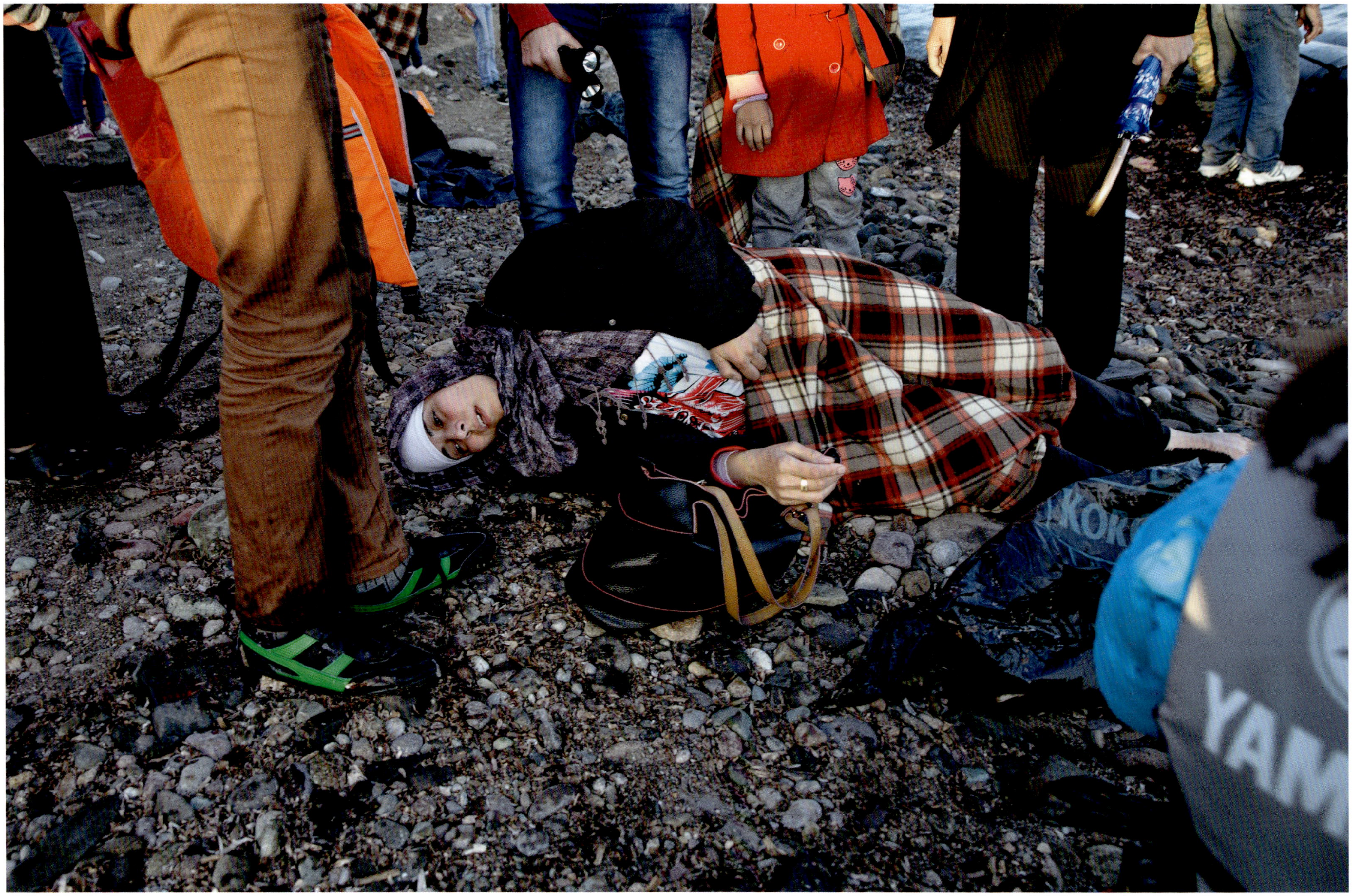

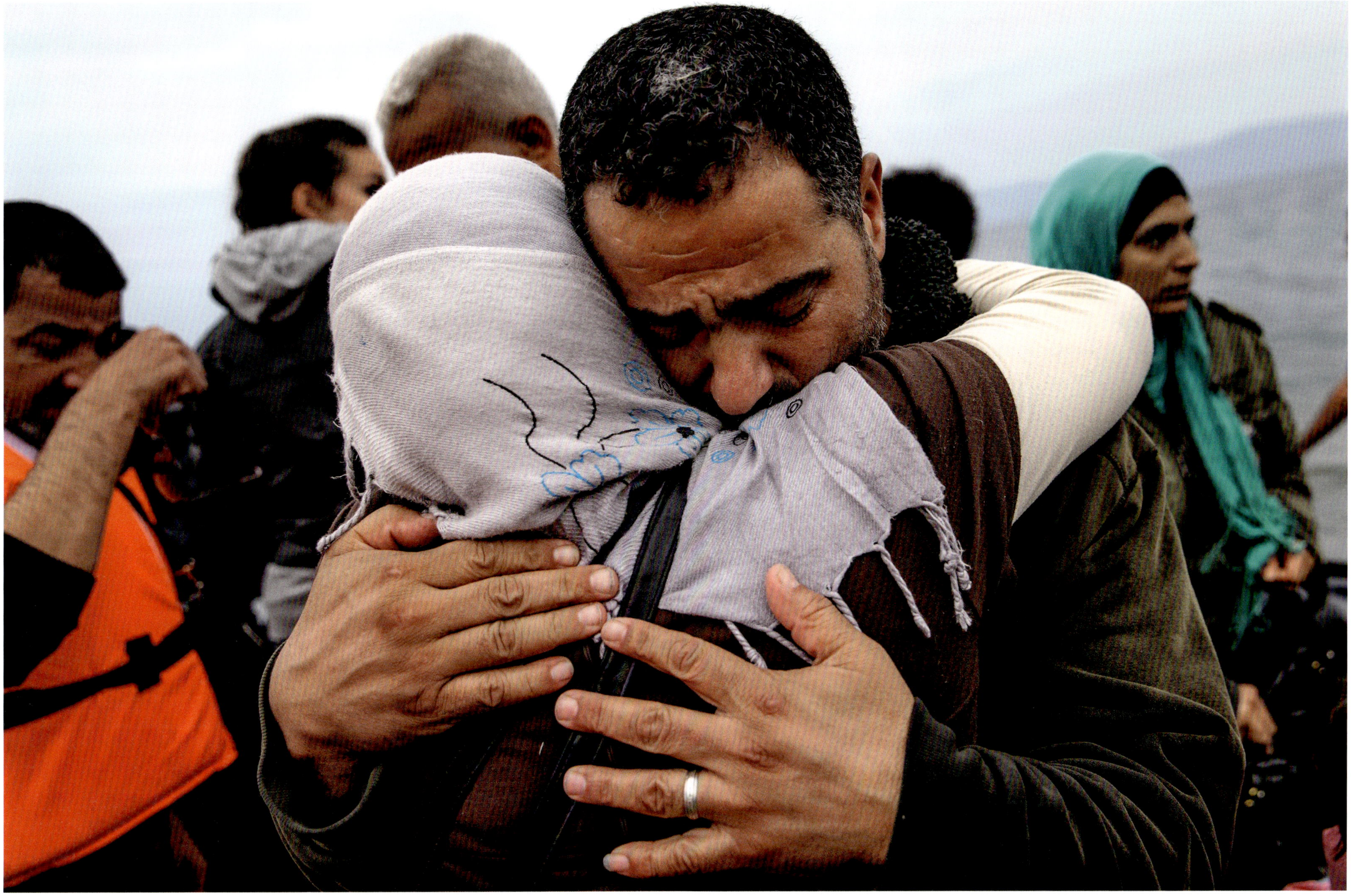

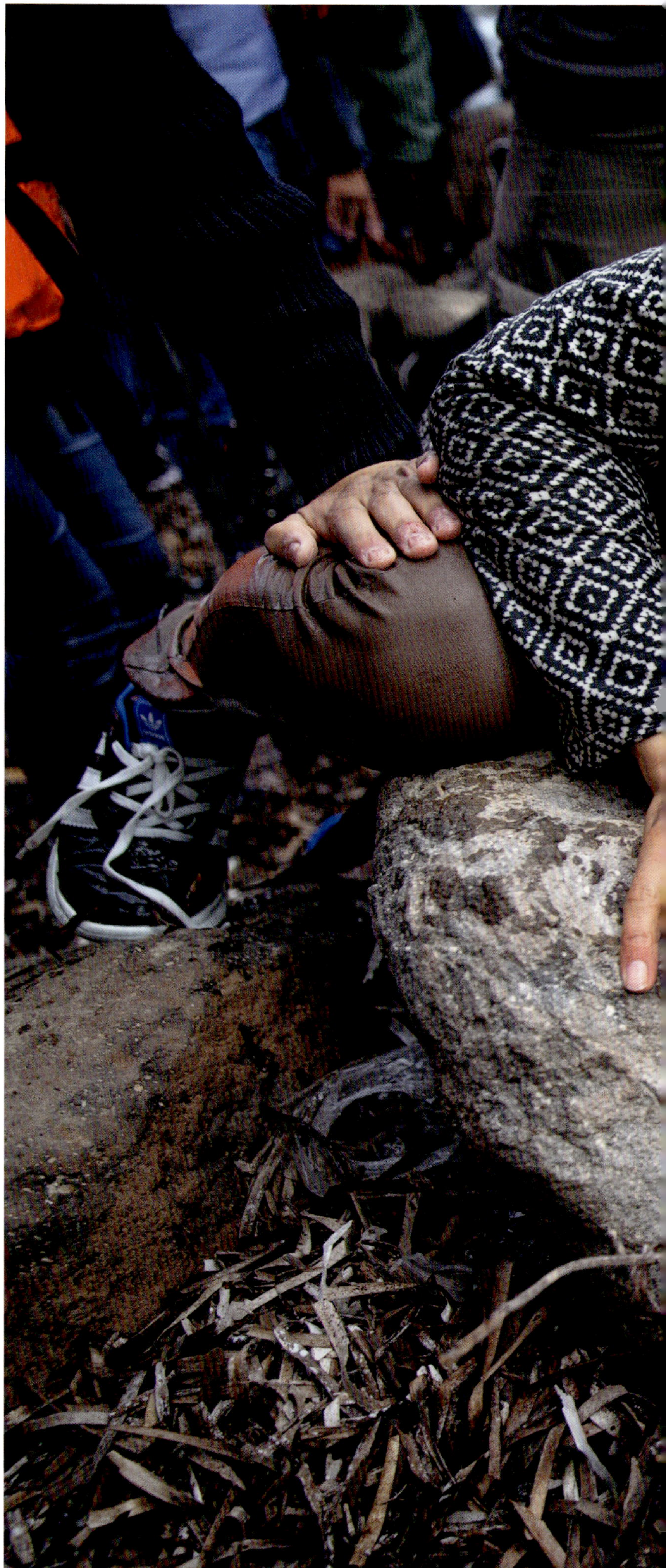

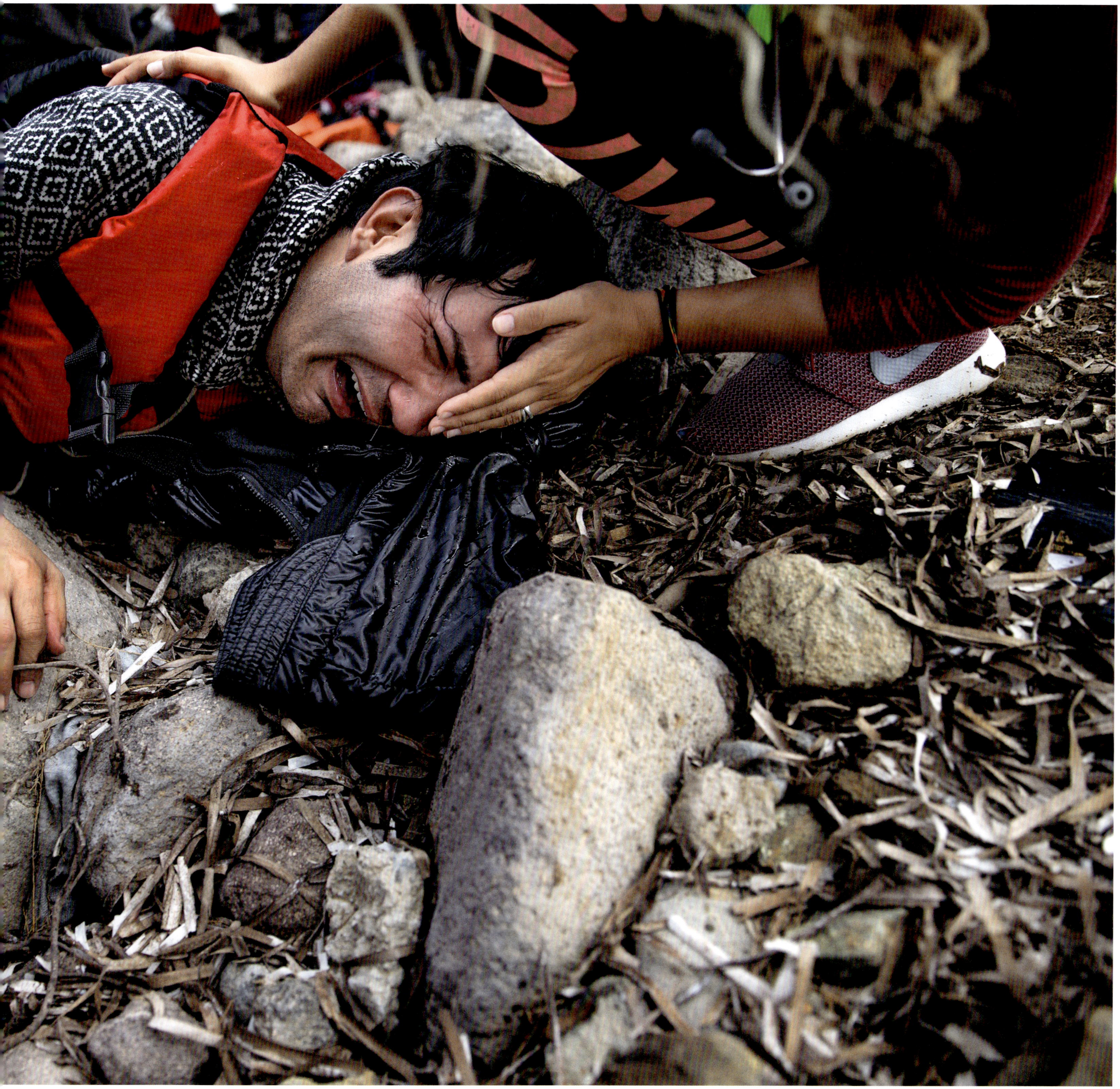

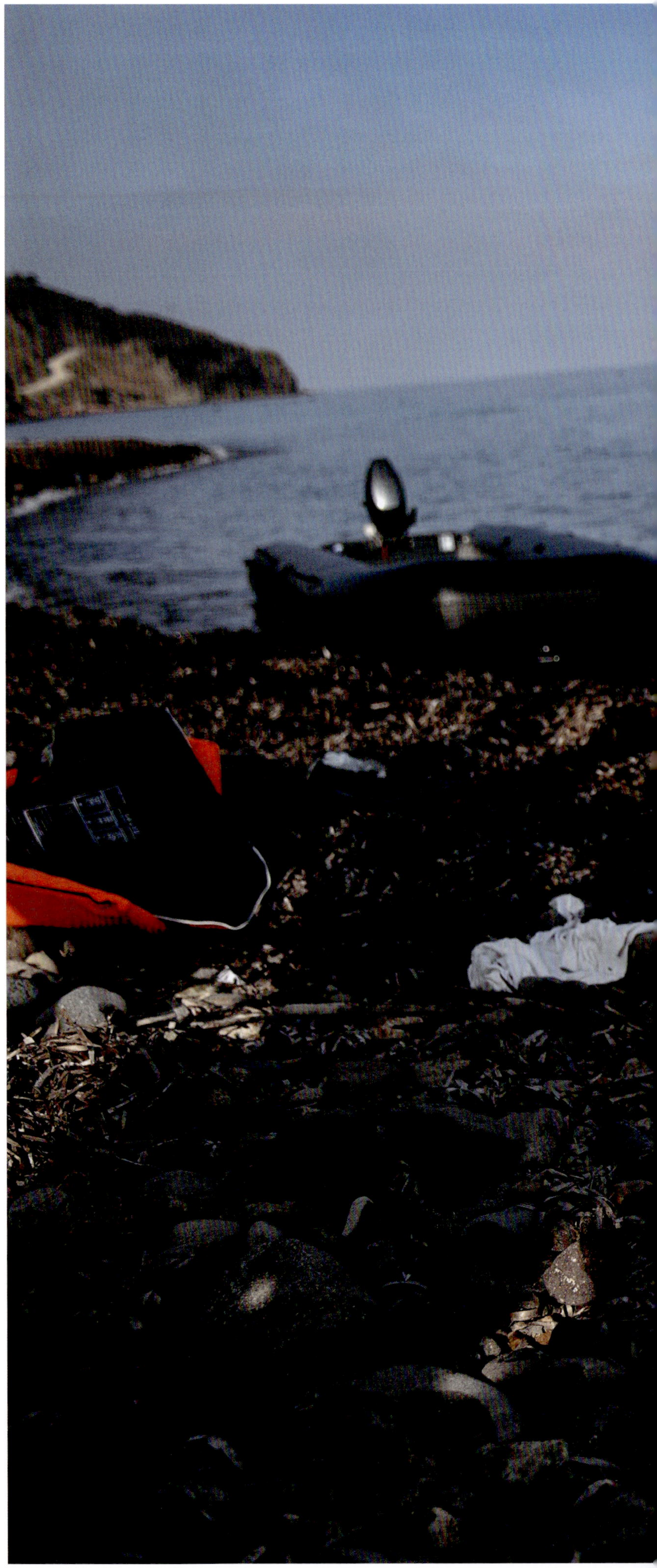

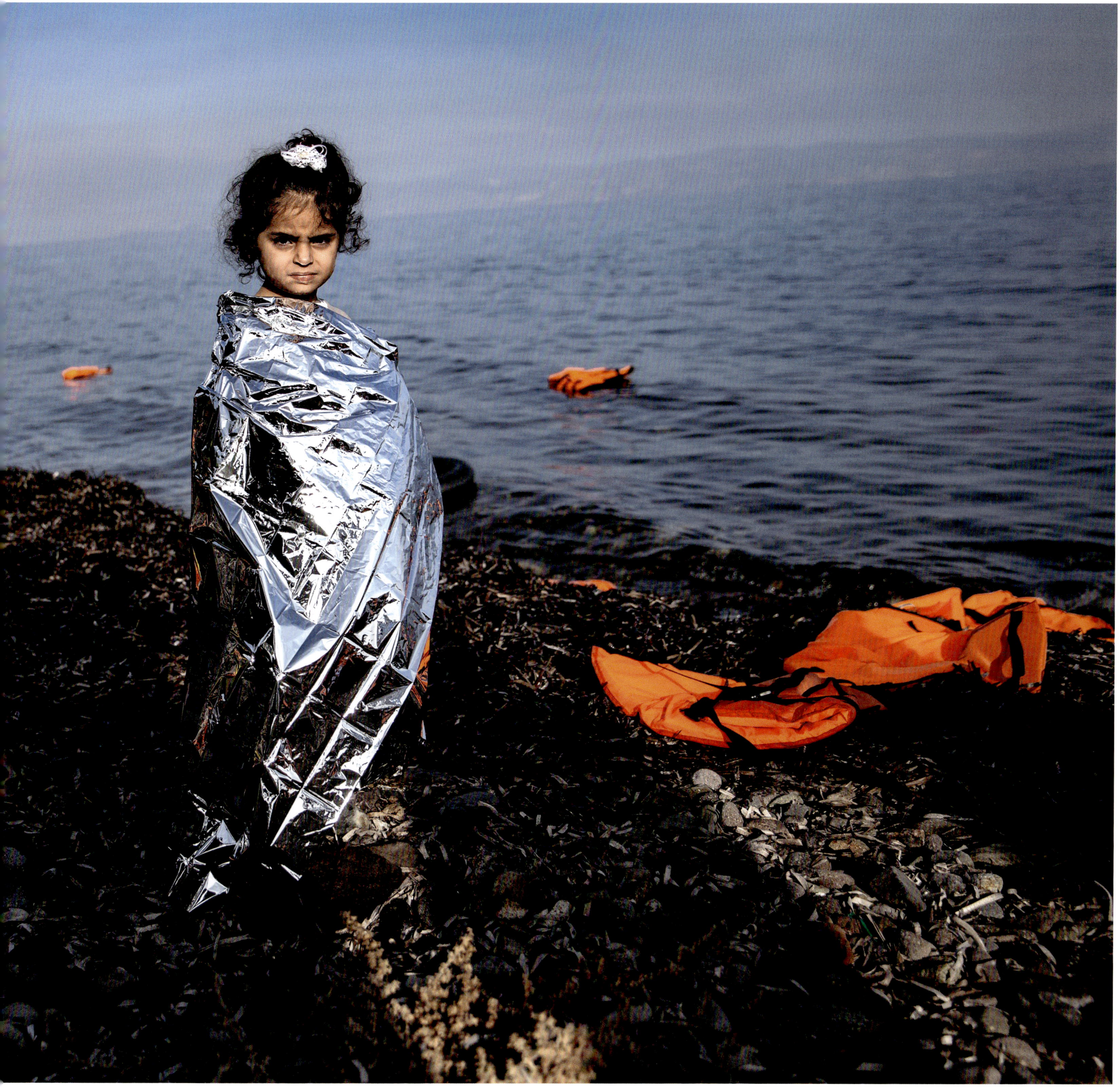

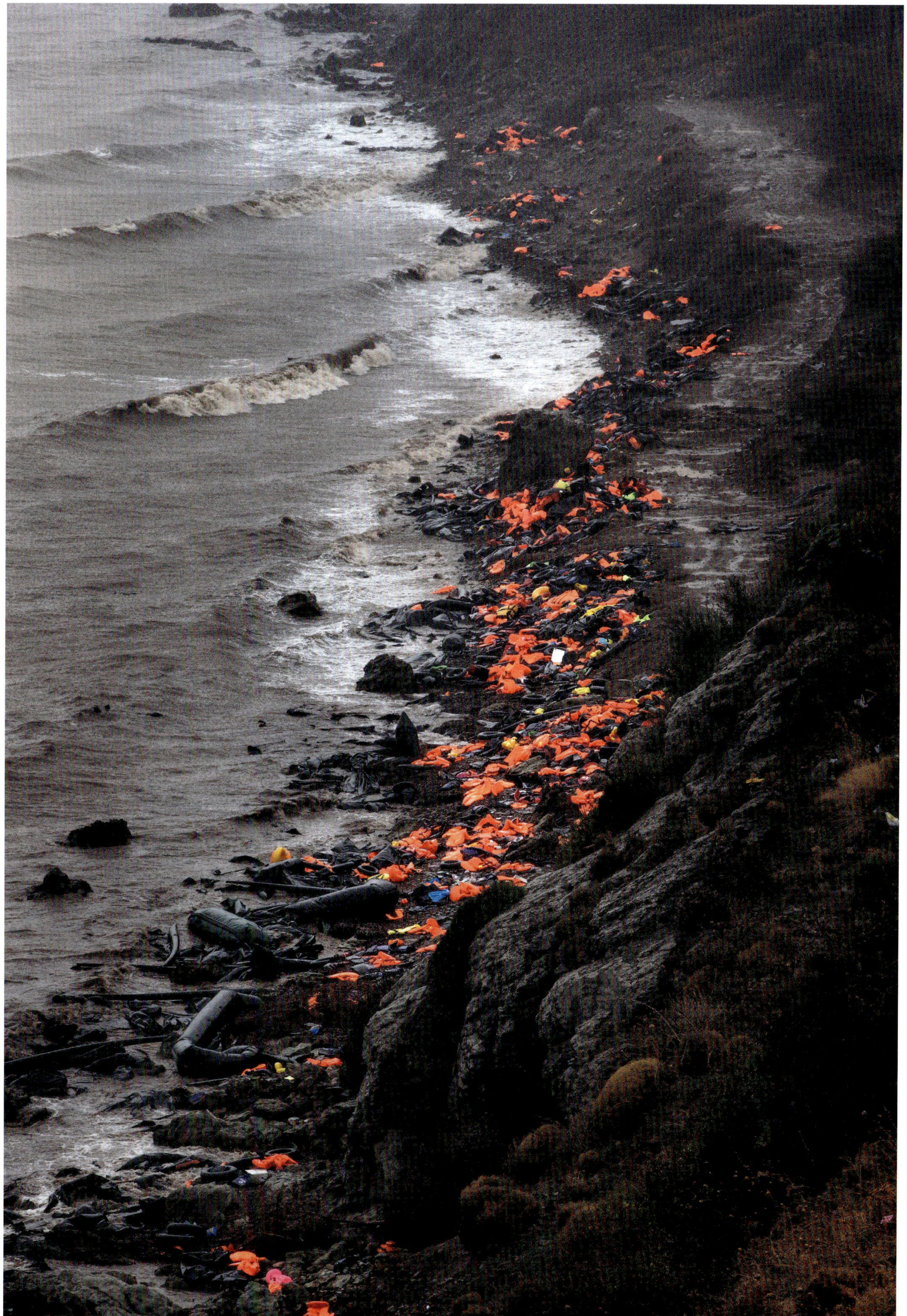

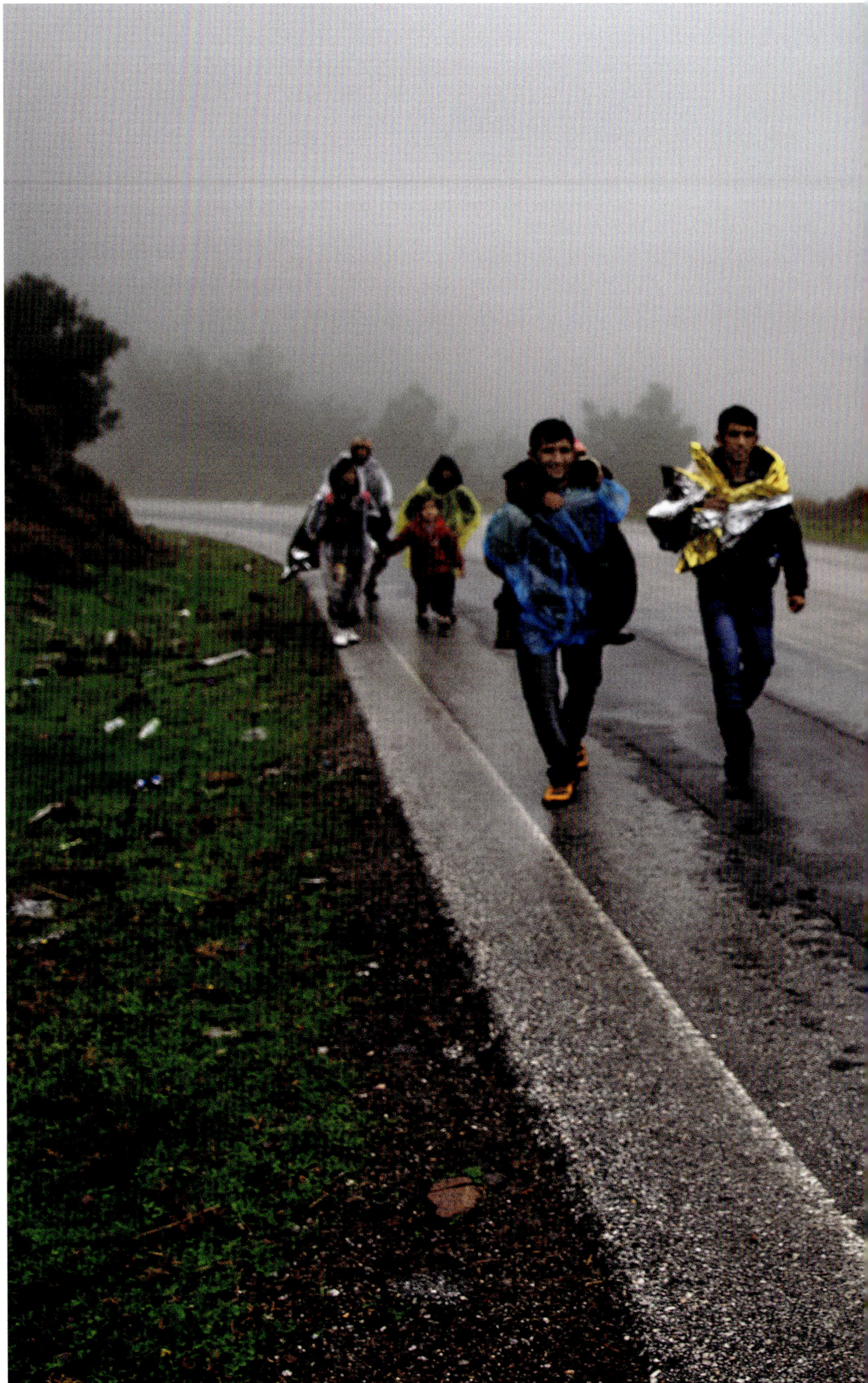

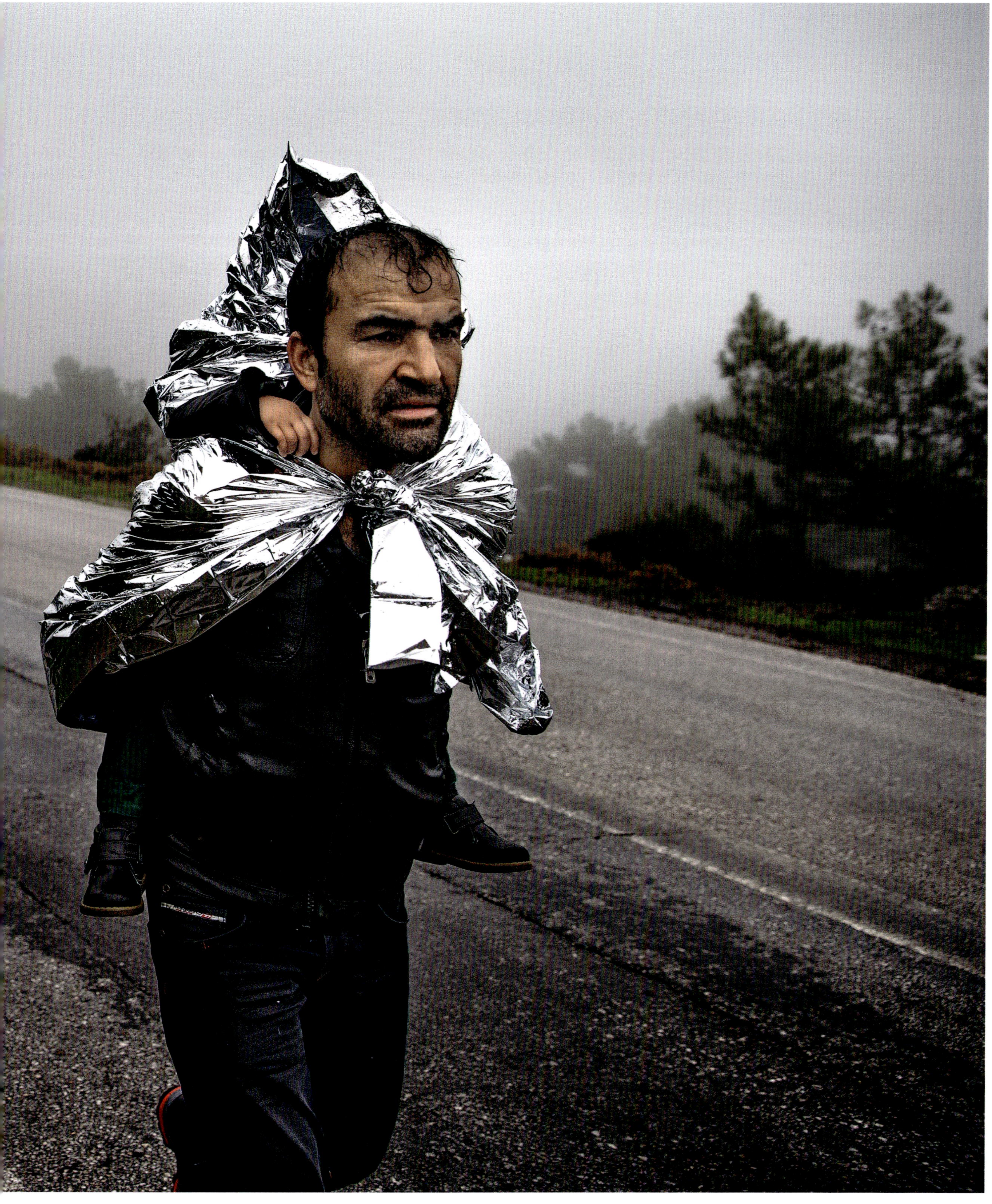

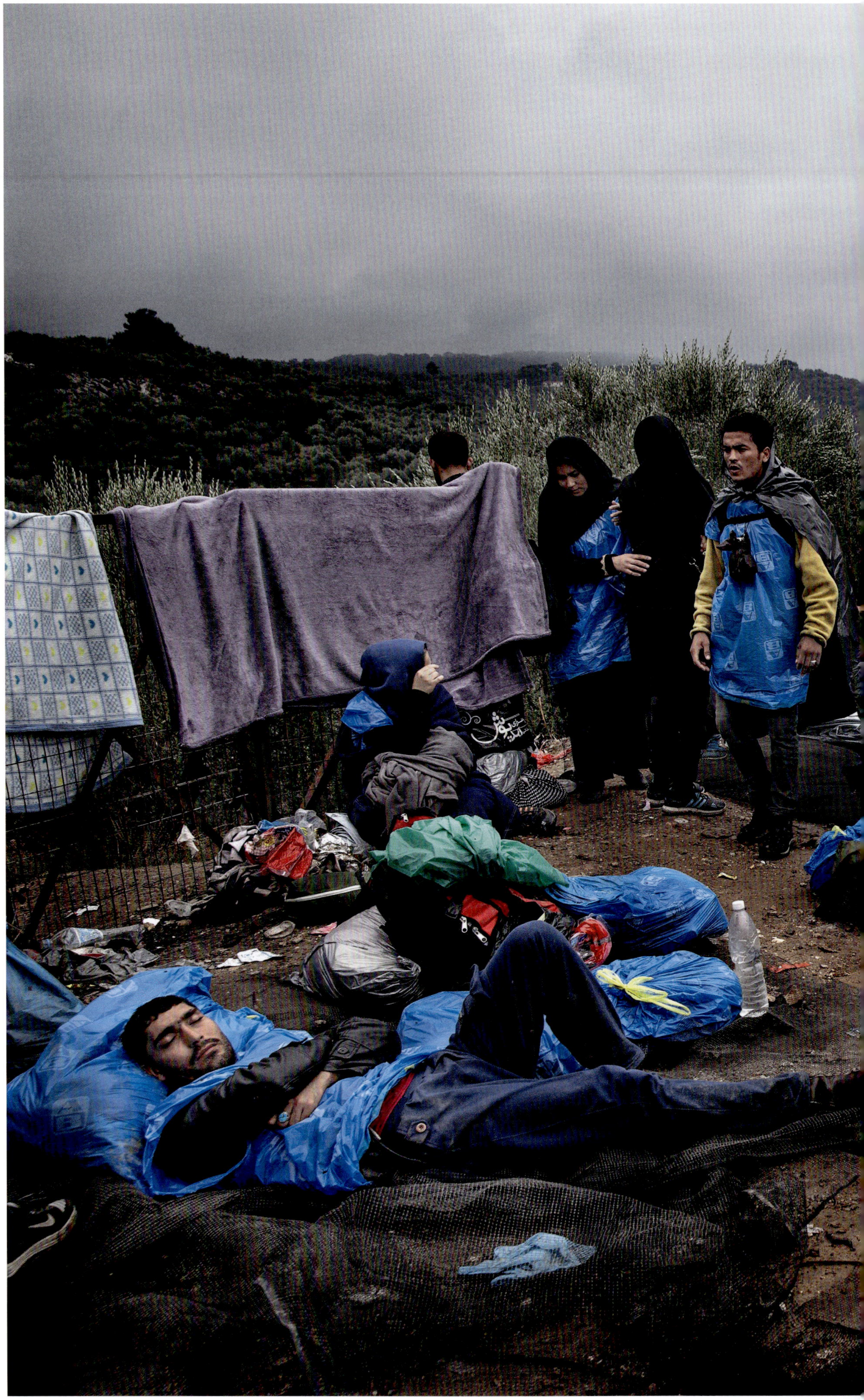

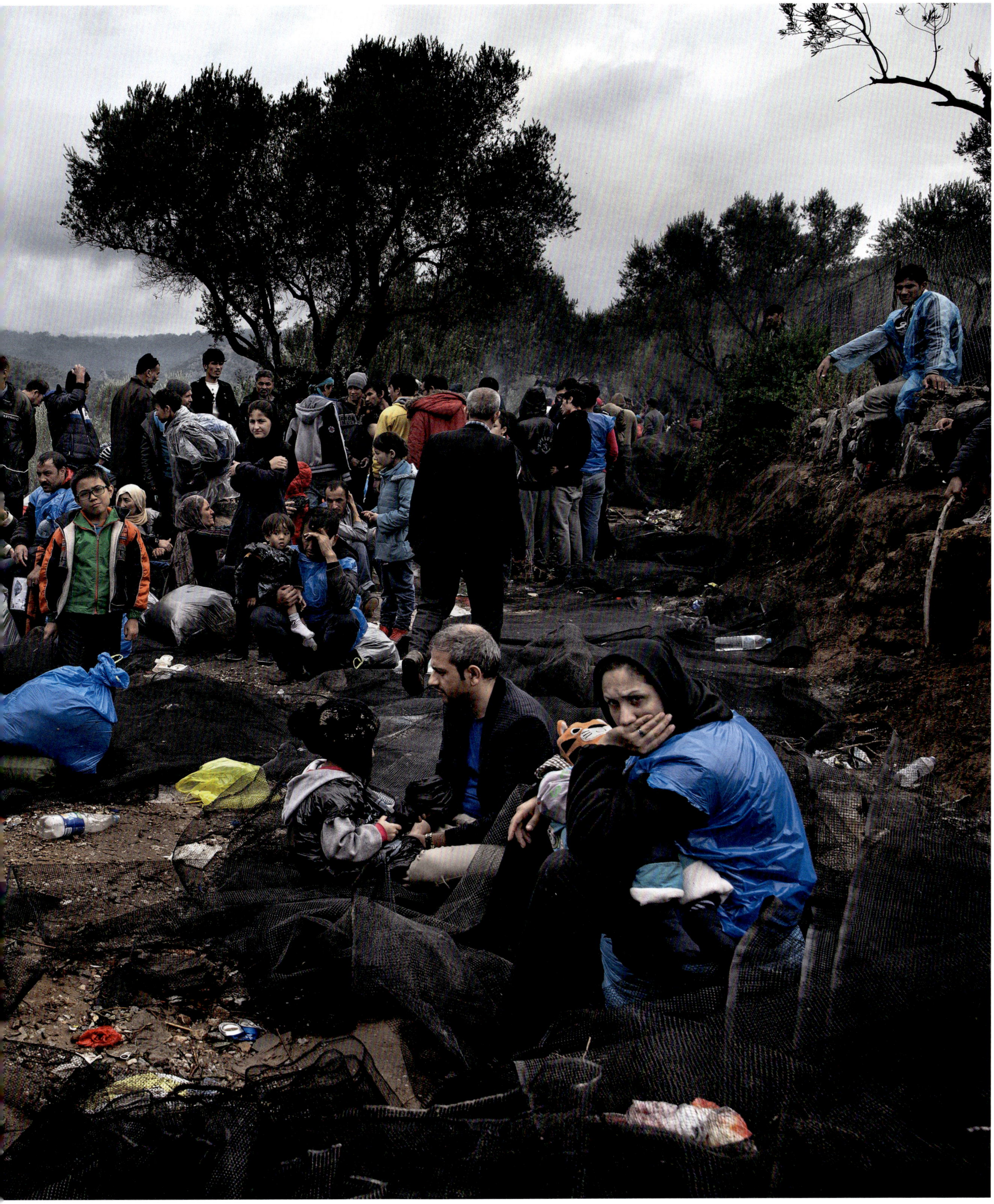

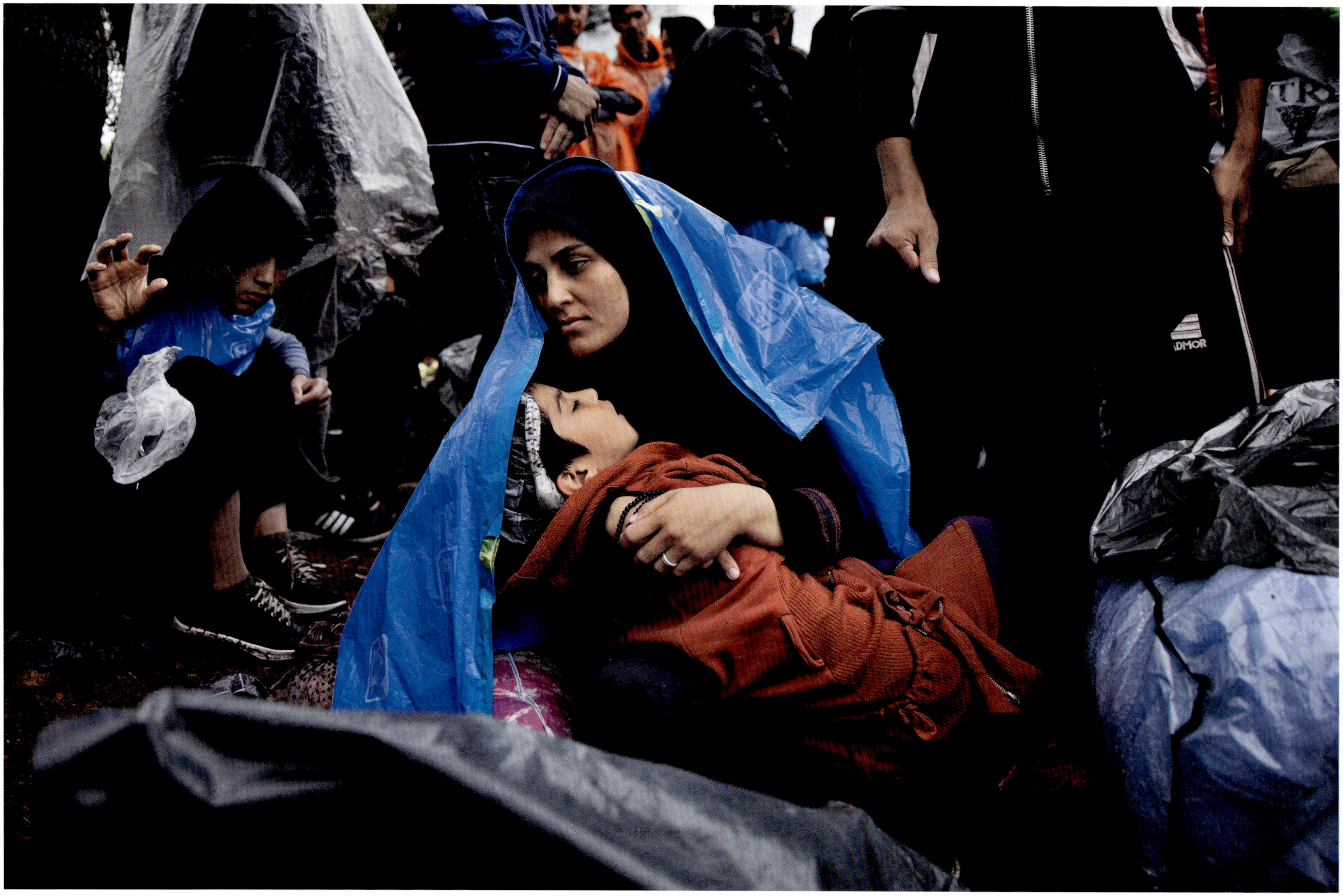

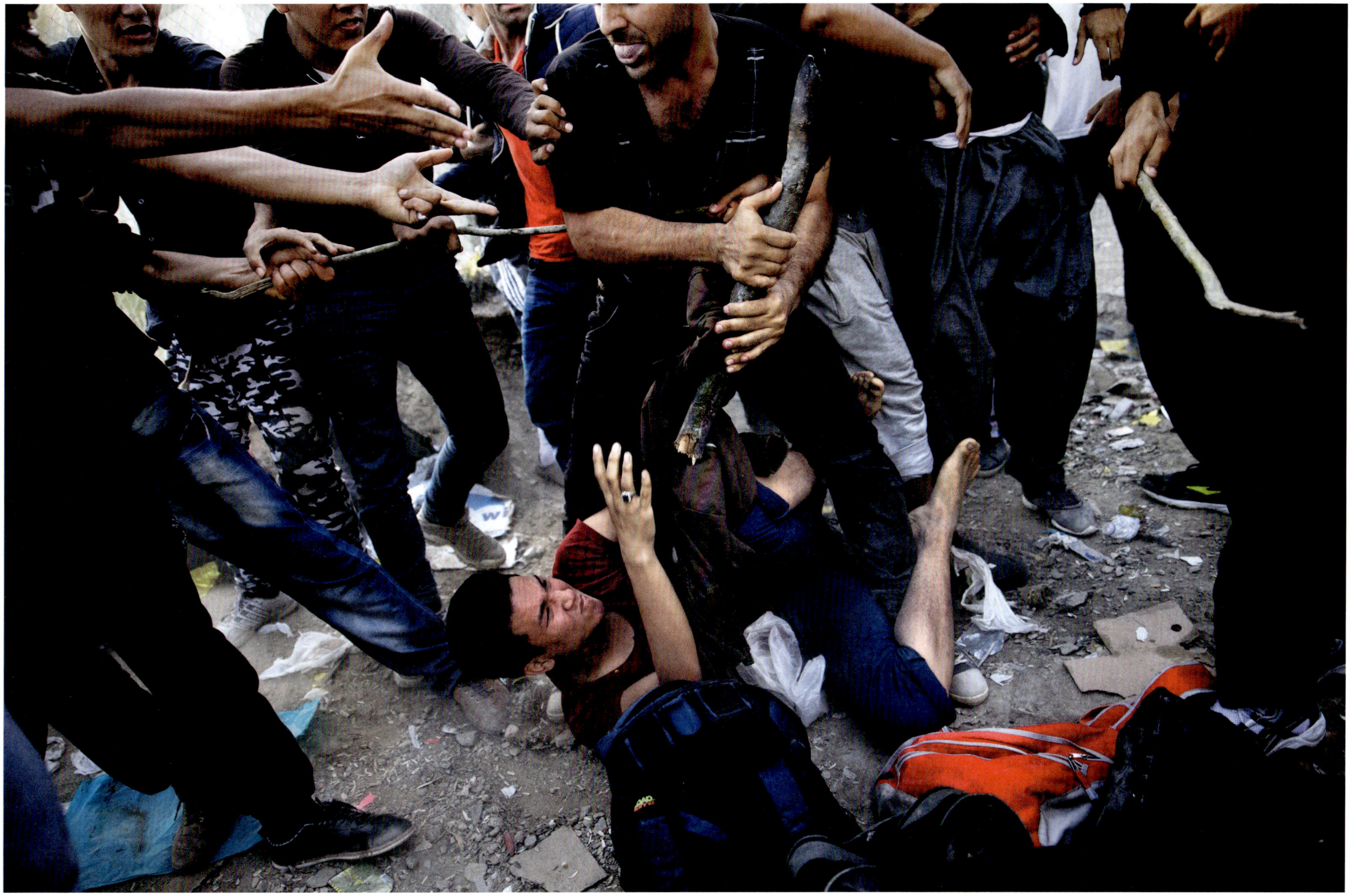

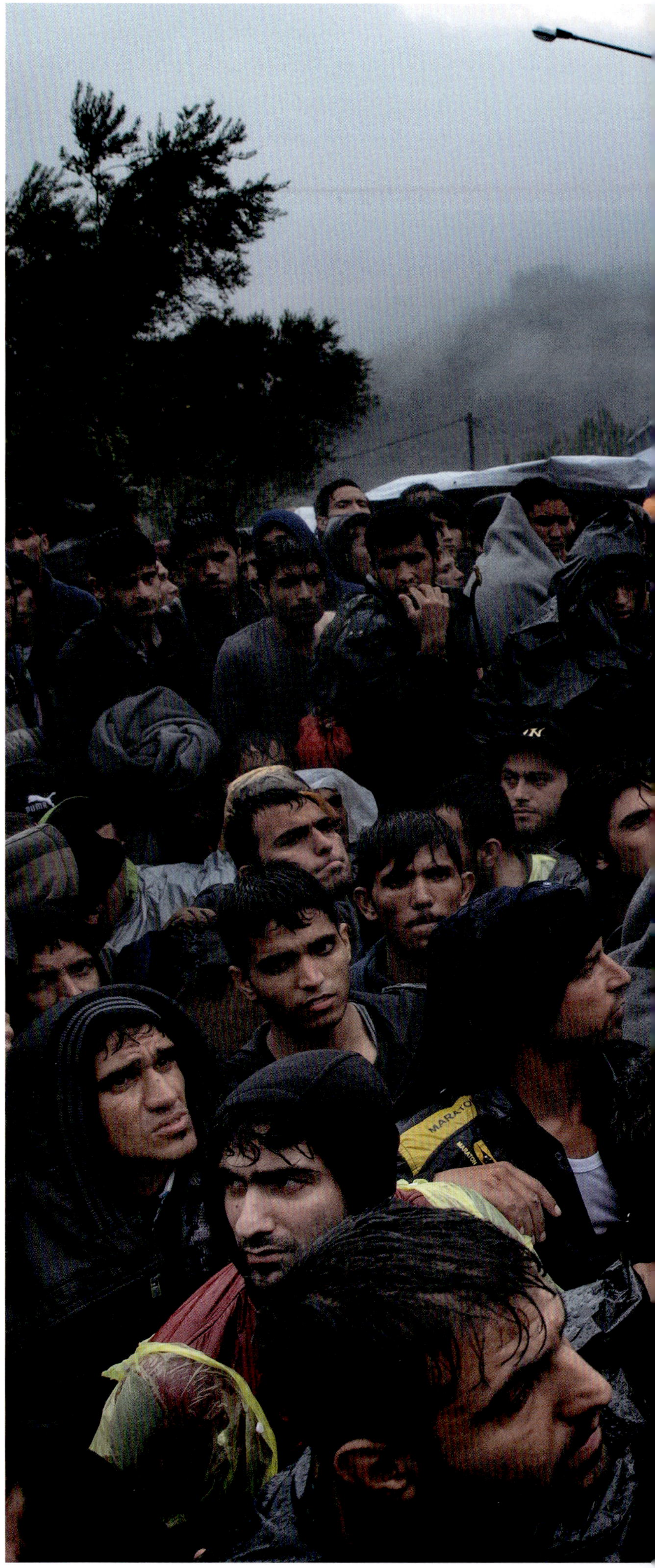

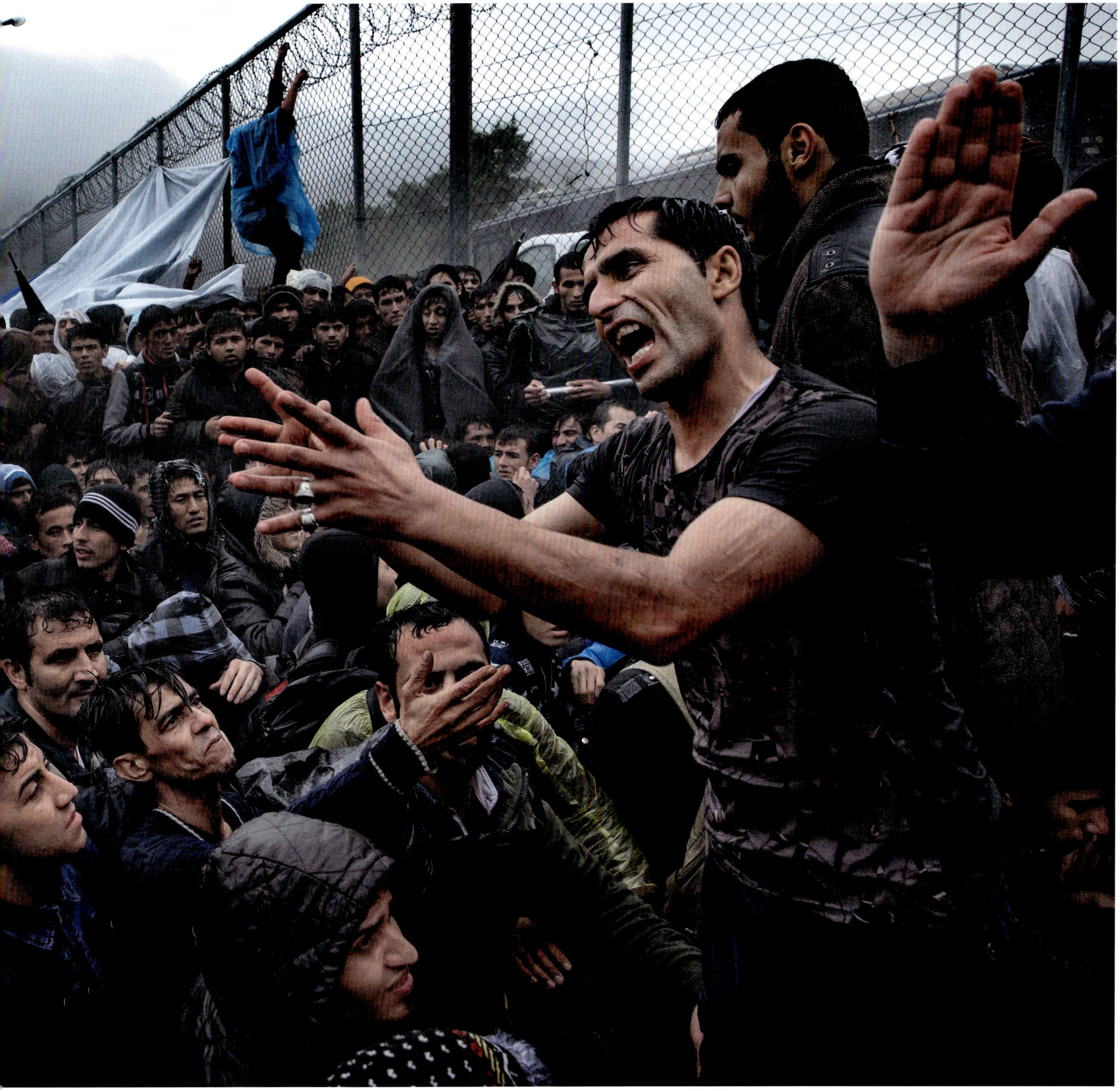

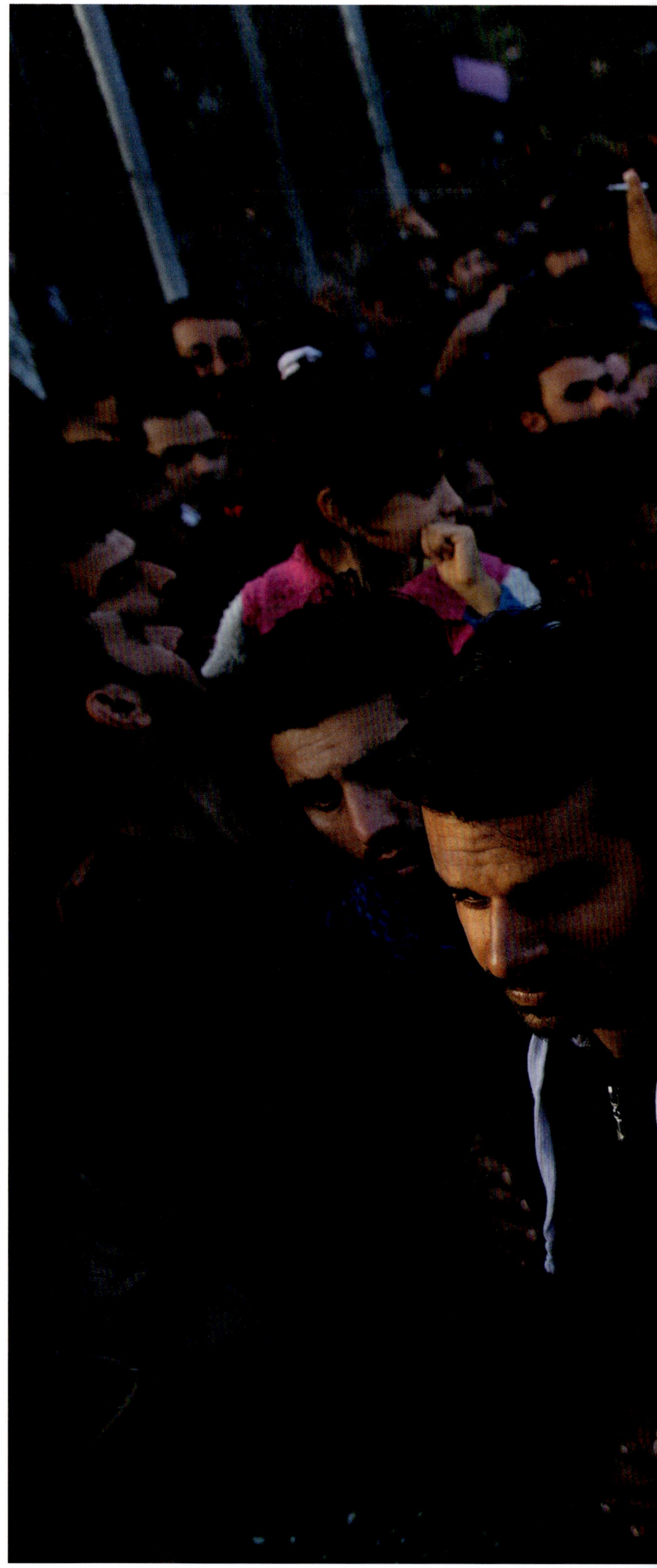

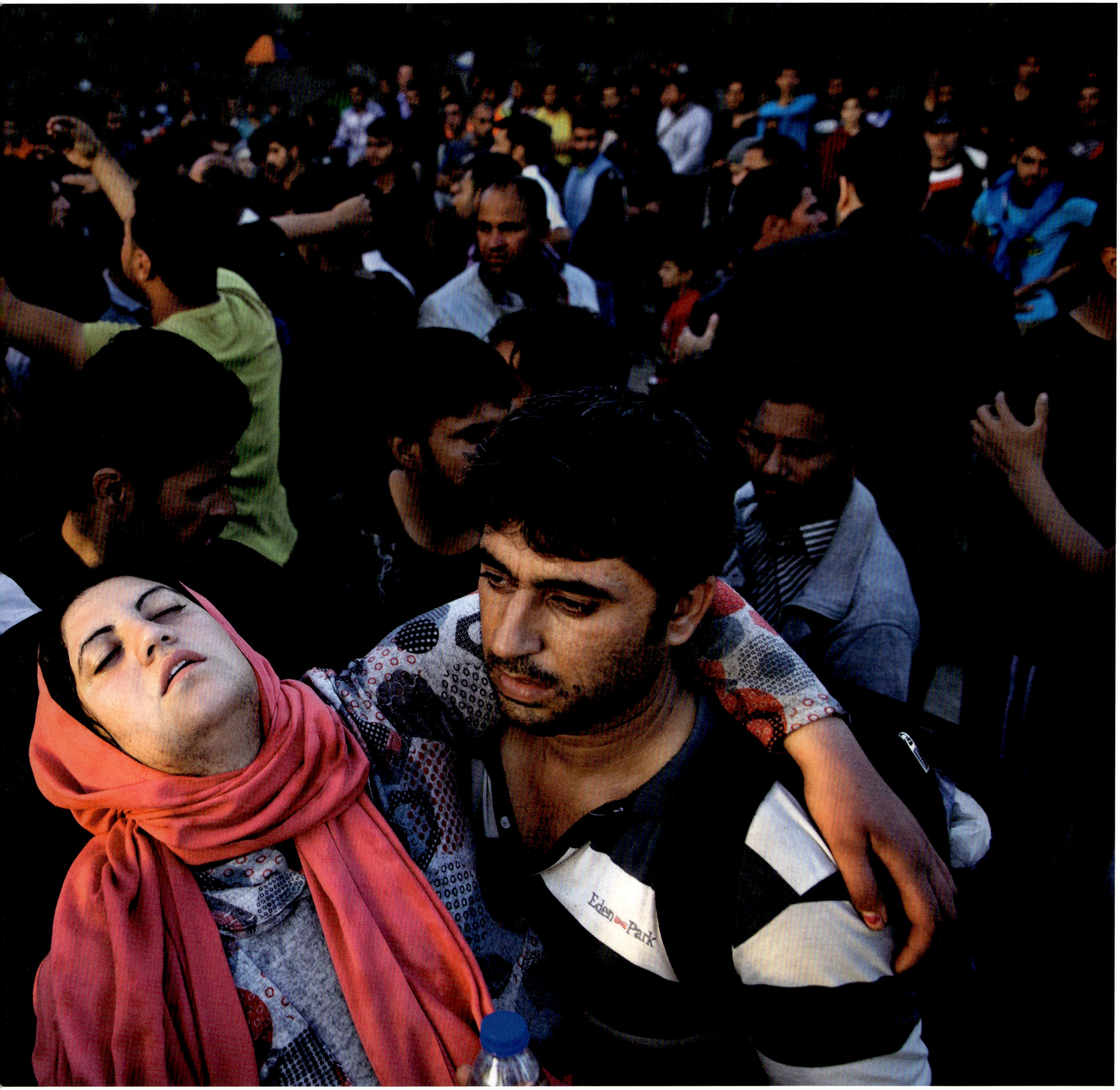
Eden Park

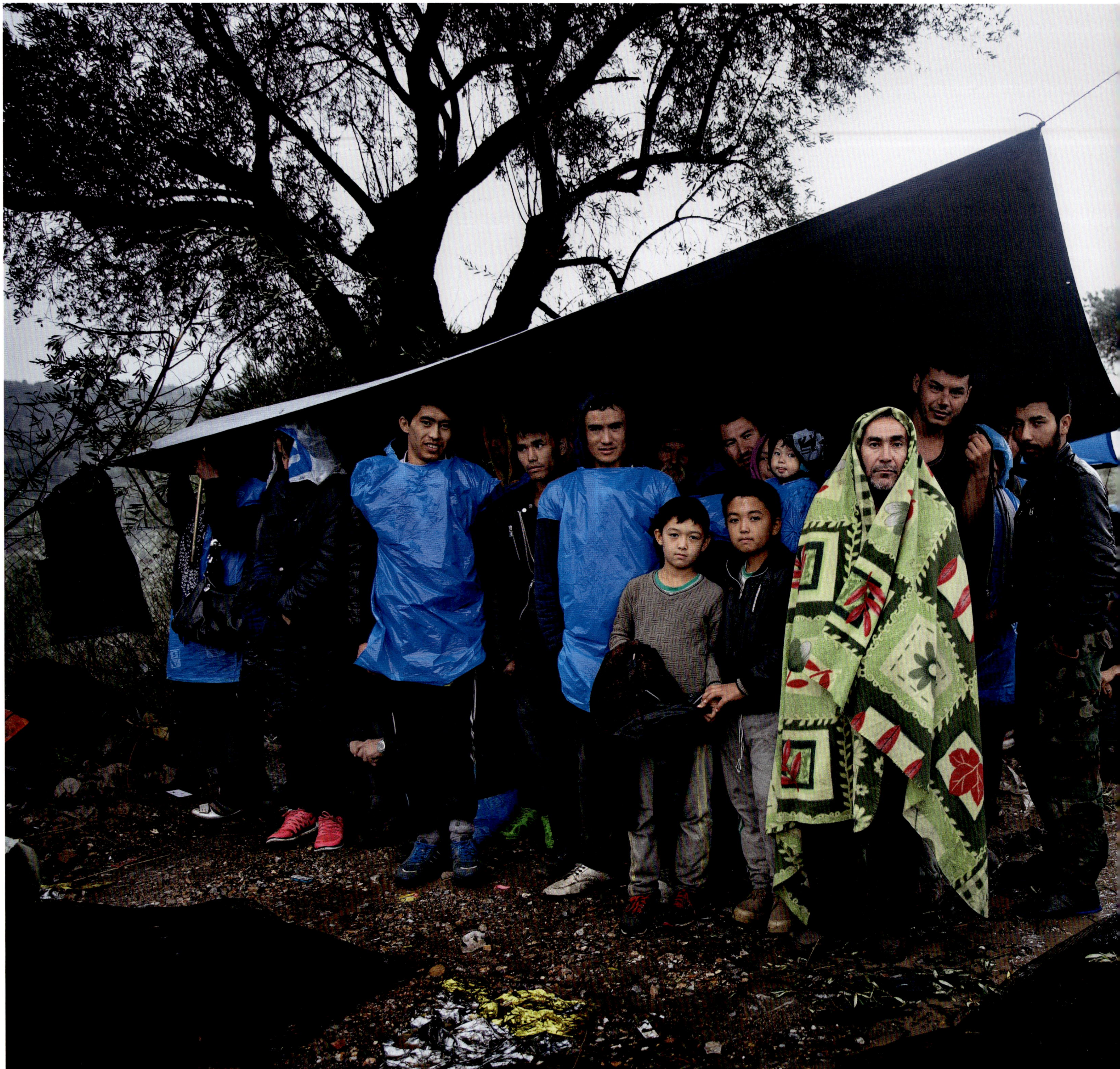

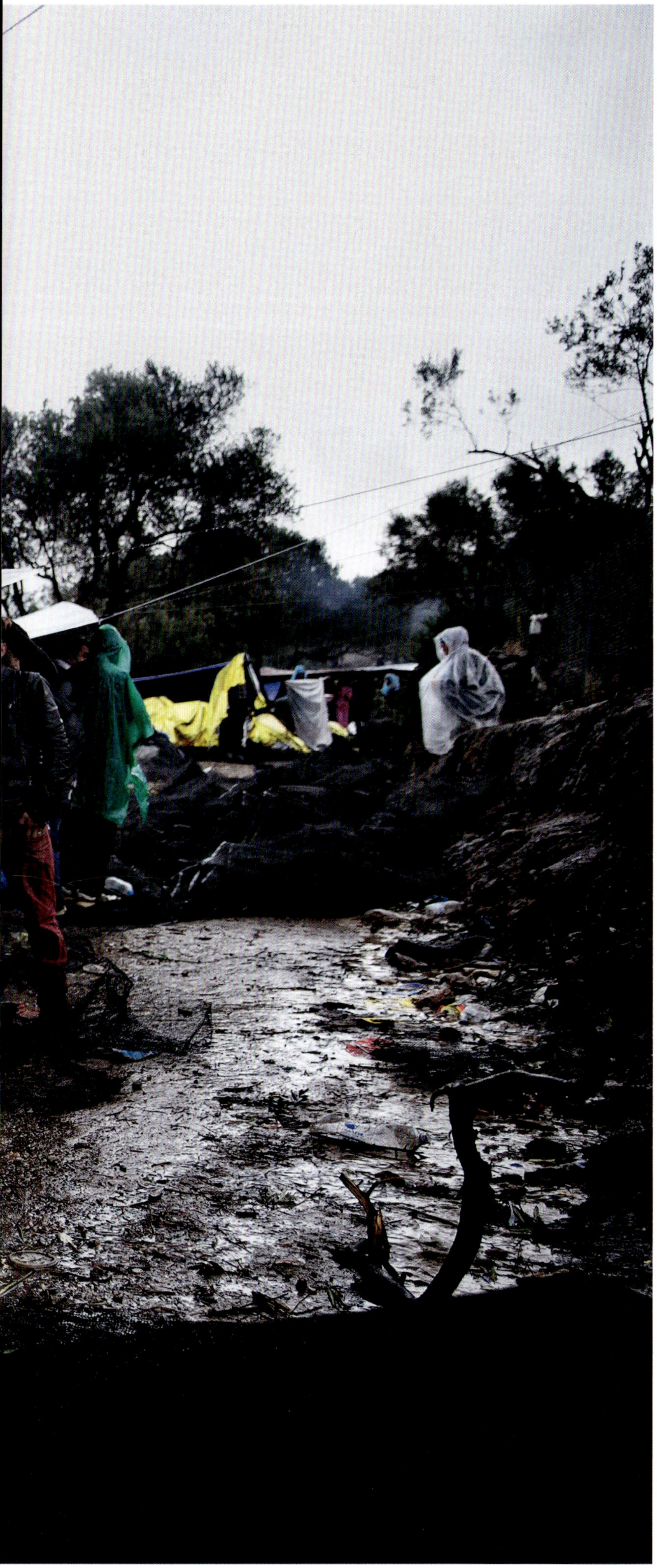

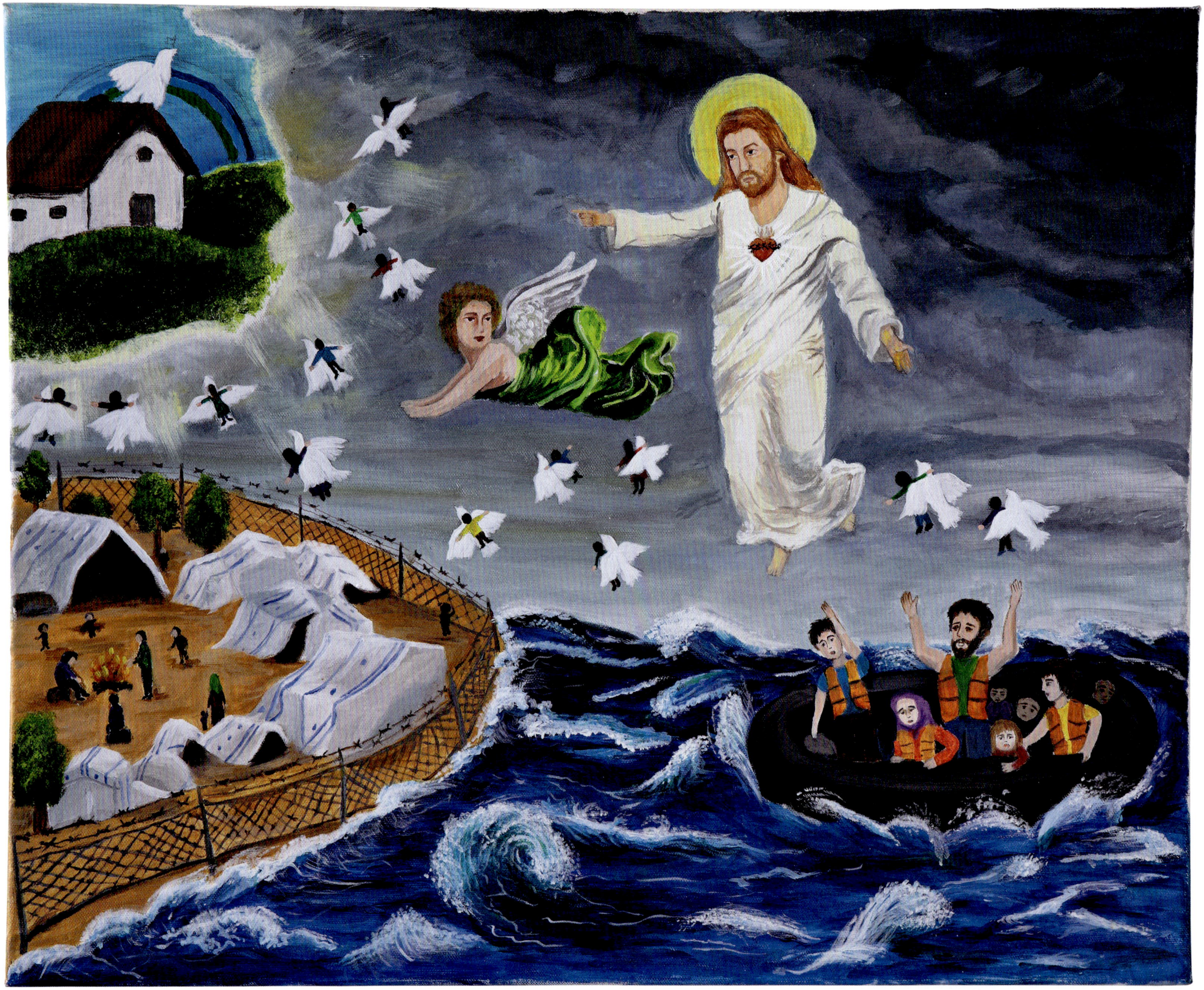

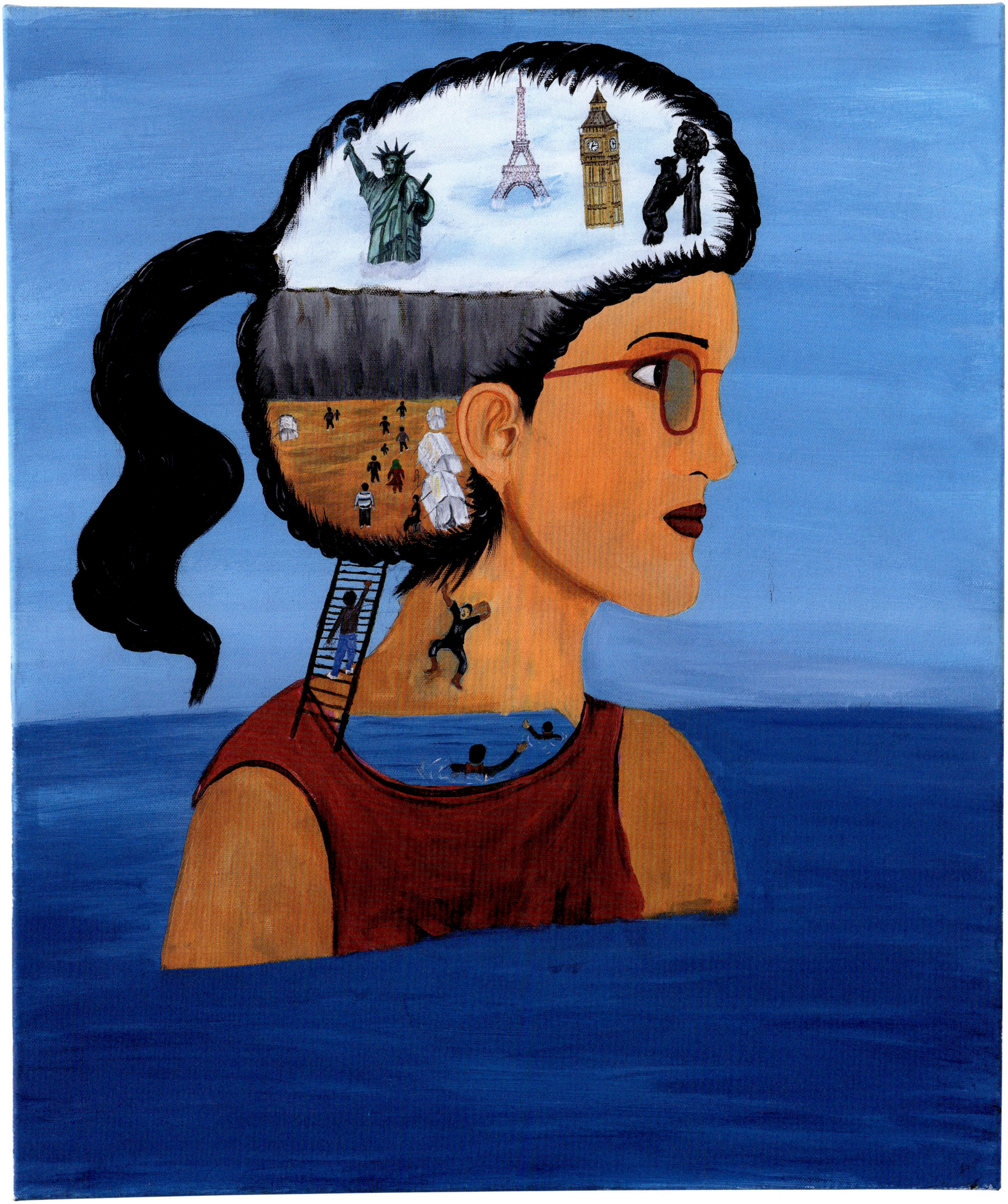

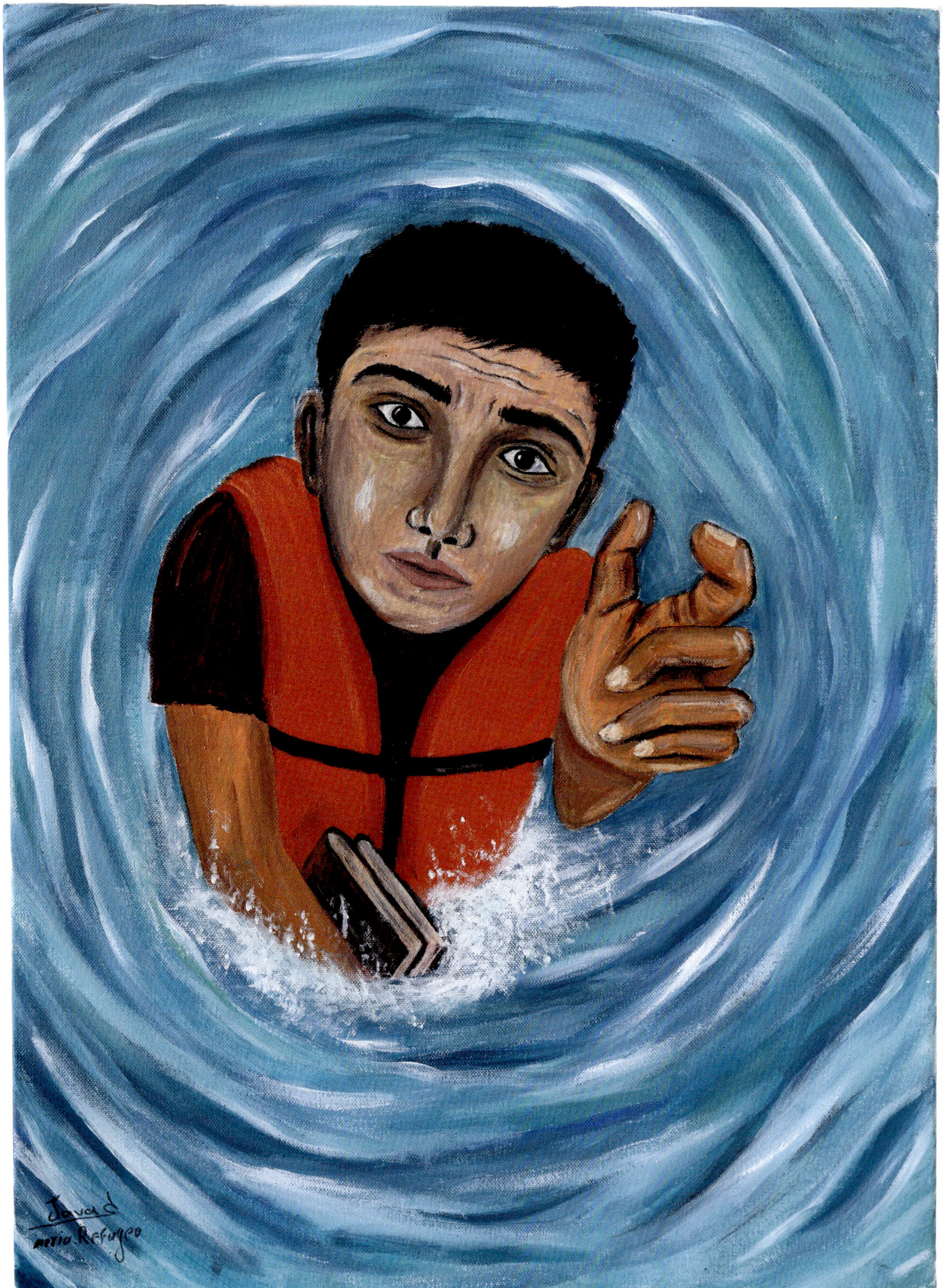
Javad

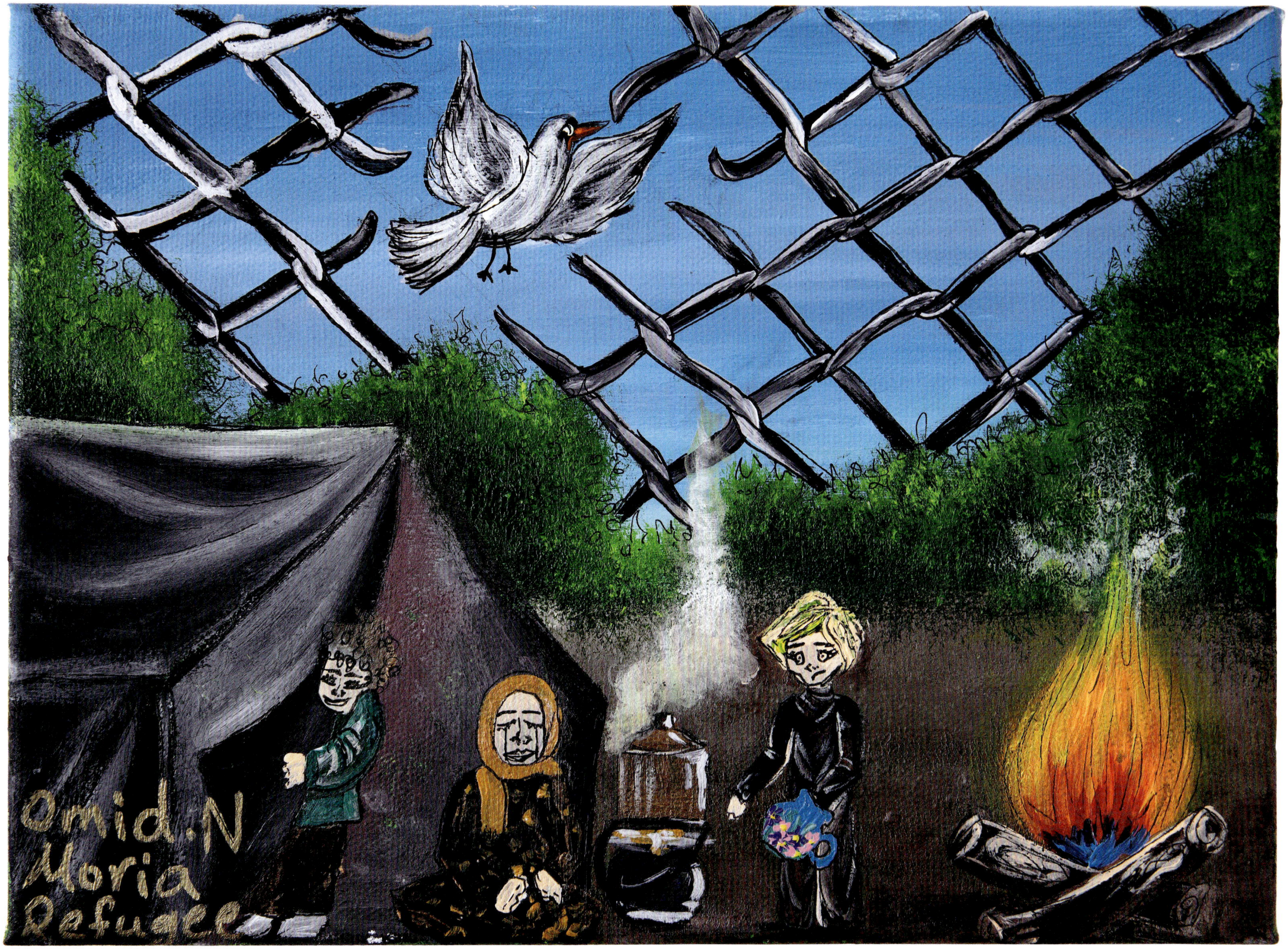
Omid.N
Moria
Refugee

Many of the refugees and migrants who arrive in Europe in 2015 are trying to reach Sweden, one of the few EU countries that has demonstrated great openness in accepting refugees.

When the asylum seekers arrive in Sweden, in most cases they get their fingerprints taken in Malmö and then the Swedish migration agency allocates them to governmental and privately run asylum centres around the country. It is not unusual to have to wait several years to receive a final answer as to whether one can remain in Sweden, and applicants often have to move many times during this period. It is easy to lose heart.

Granbacken is an old hotel that has functioned as a privately operated asylum centre since 2015. It is in the small village of Vrigstad, which has 1,500 residents.

In the summer of 2018, the Swedish migration agency decided to close all privately operated asylum centres due to the significant fall in the number of asylum seekers. This means that the forty-six asylum seekers still living at Granbacken will soon be moved to governmental centres or accommodated privately if they can make arrangements and these are approved by the authorities. Despite the uncertainty of their situation, most of the residents have been happy to stay at the old hotel and feel safe in the village community, so they are sorry that the place is closing.

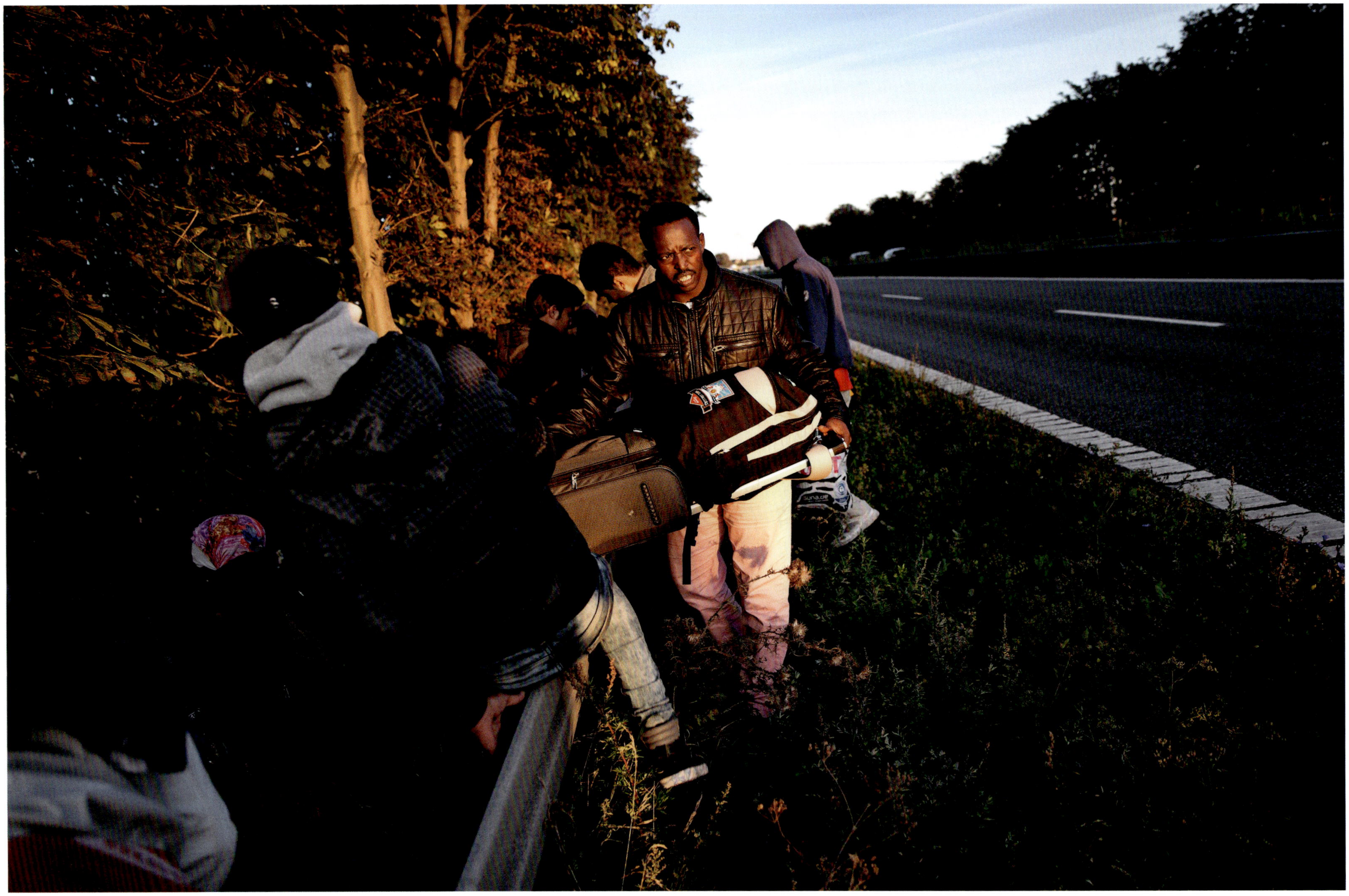

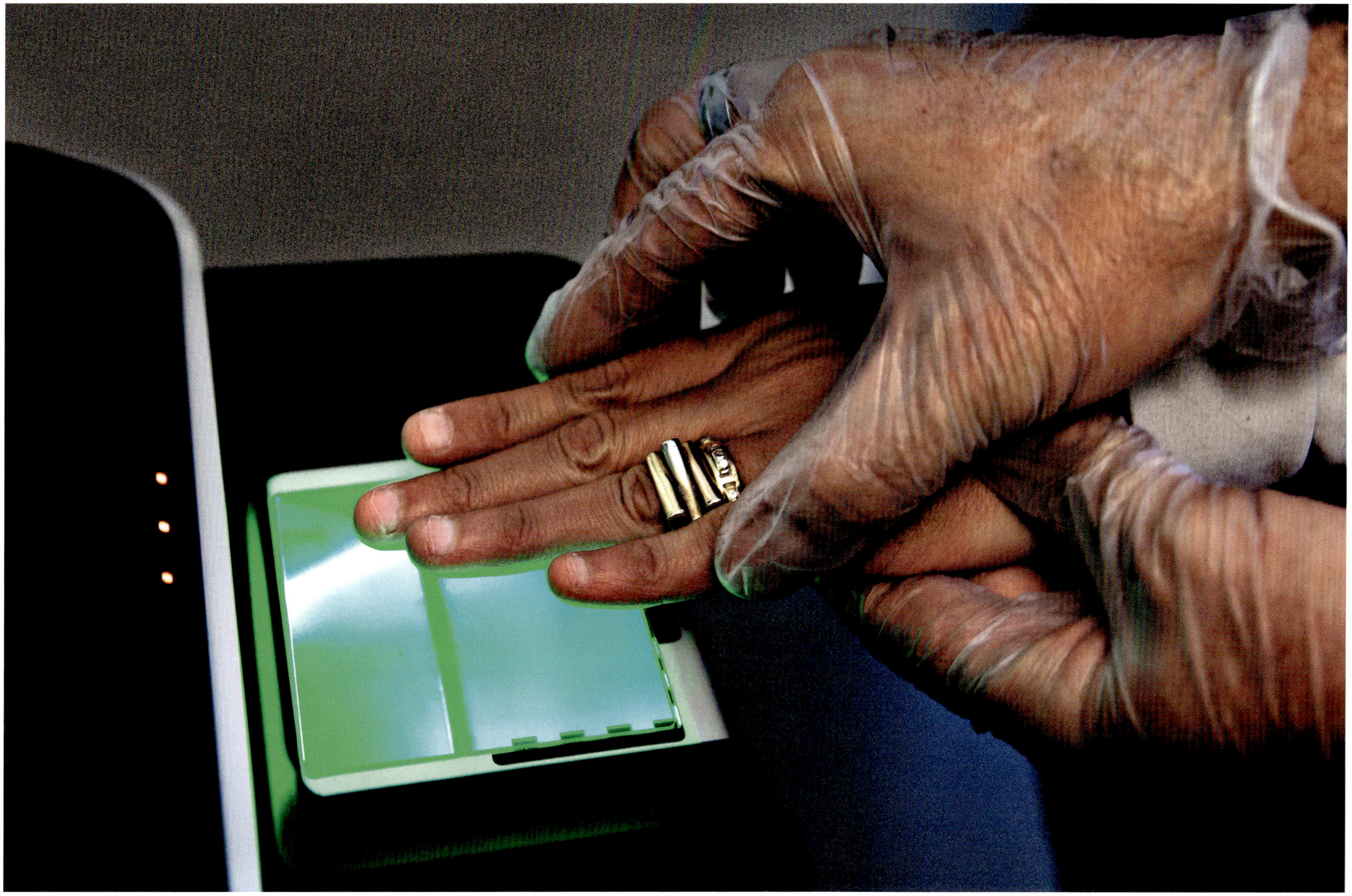

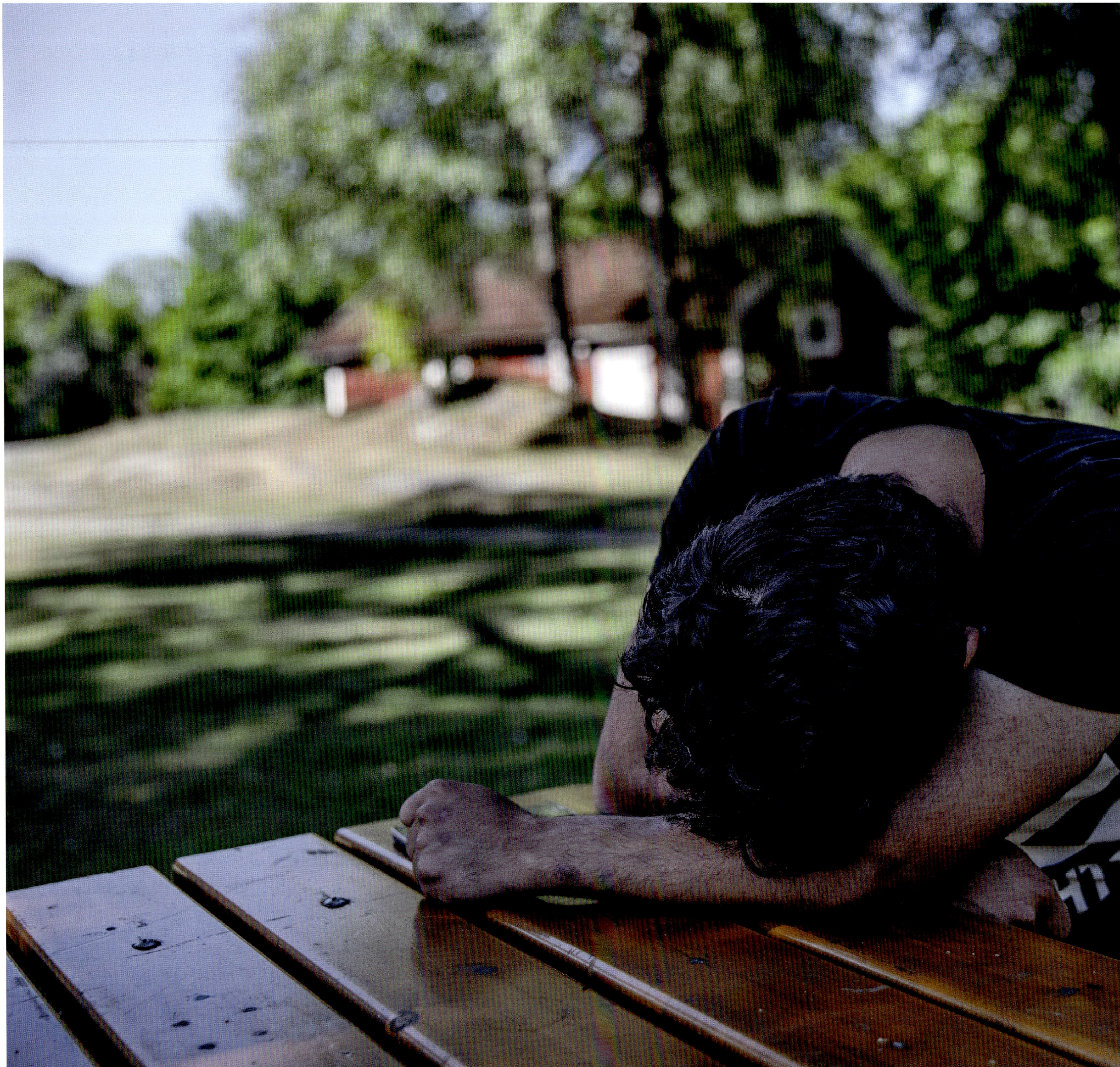

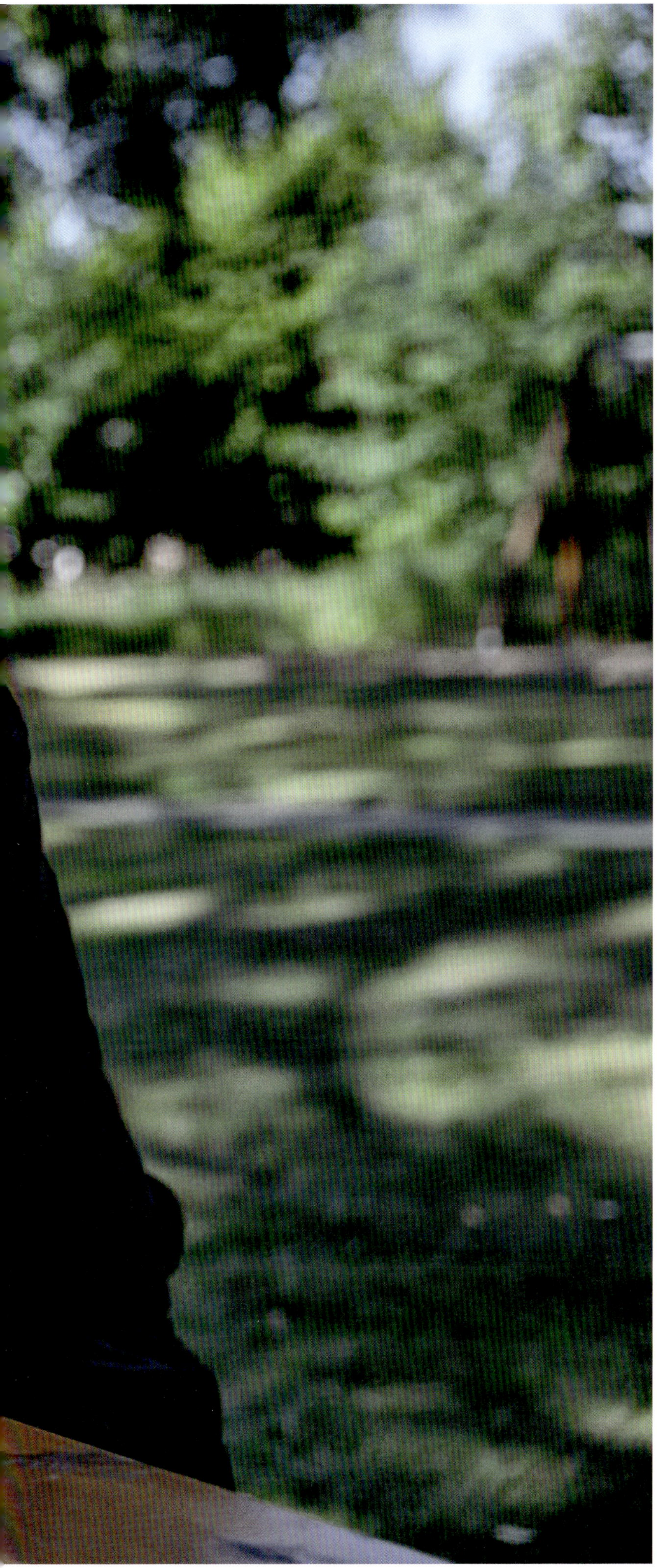

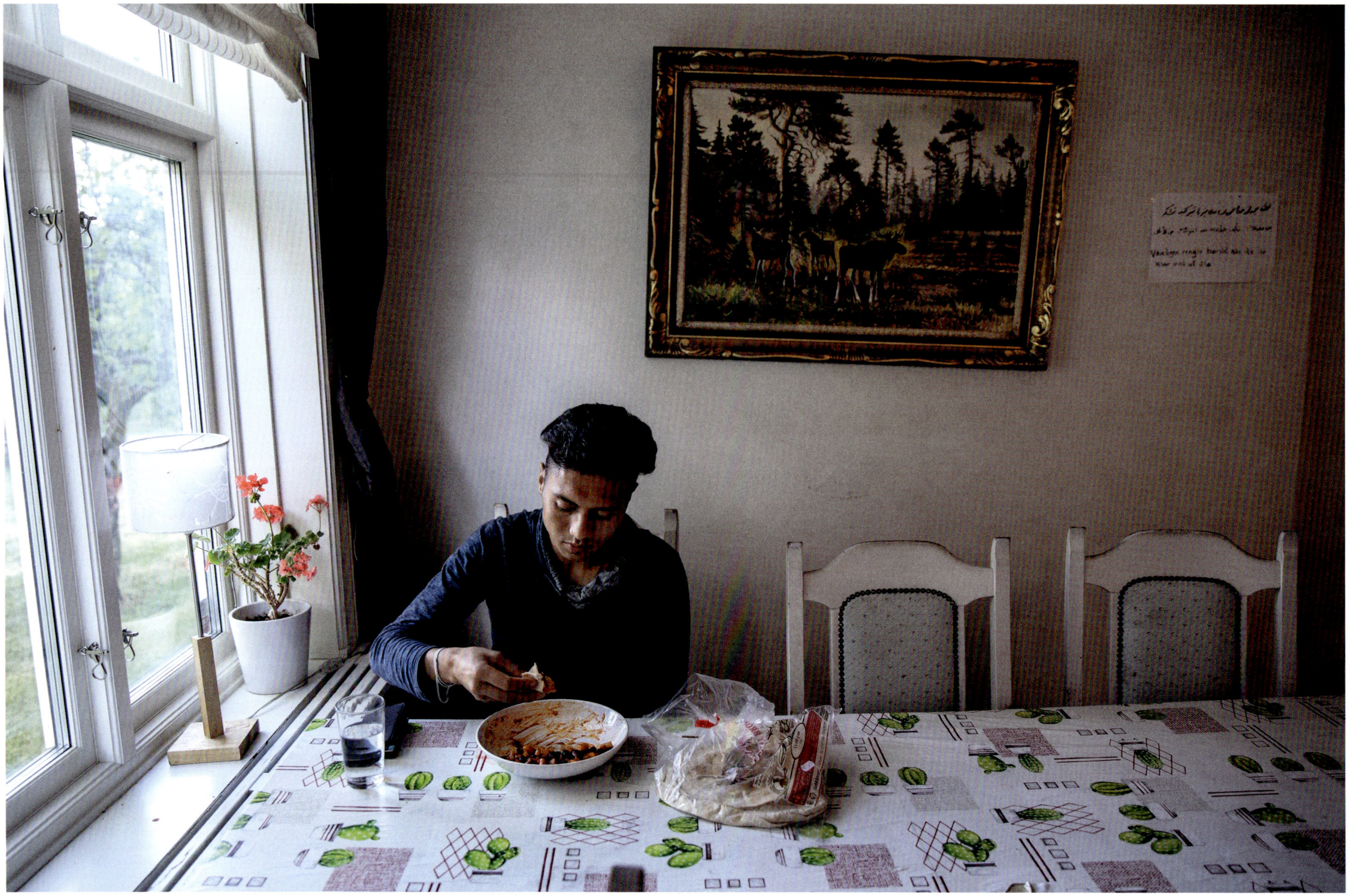

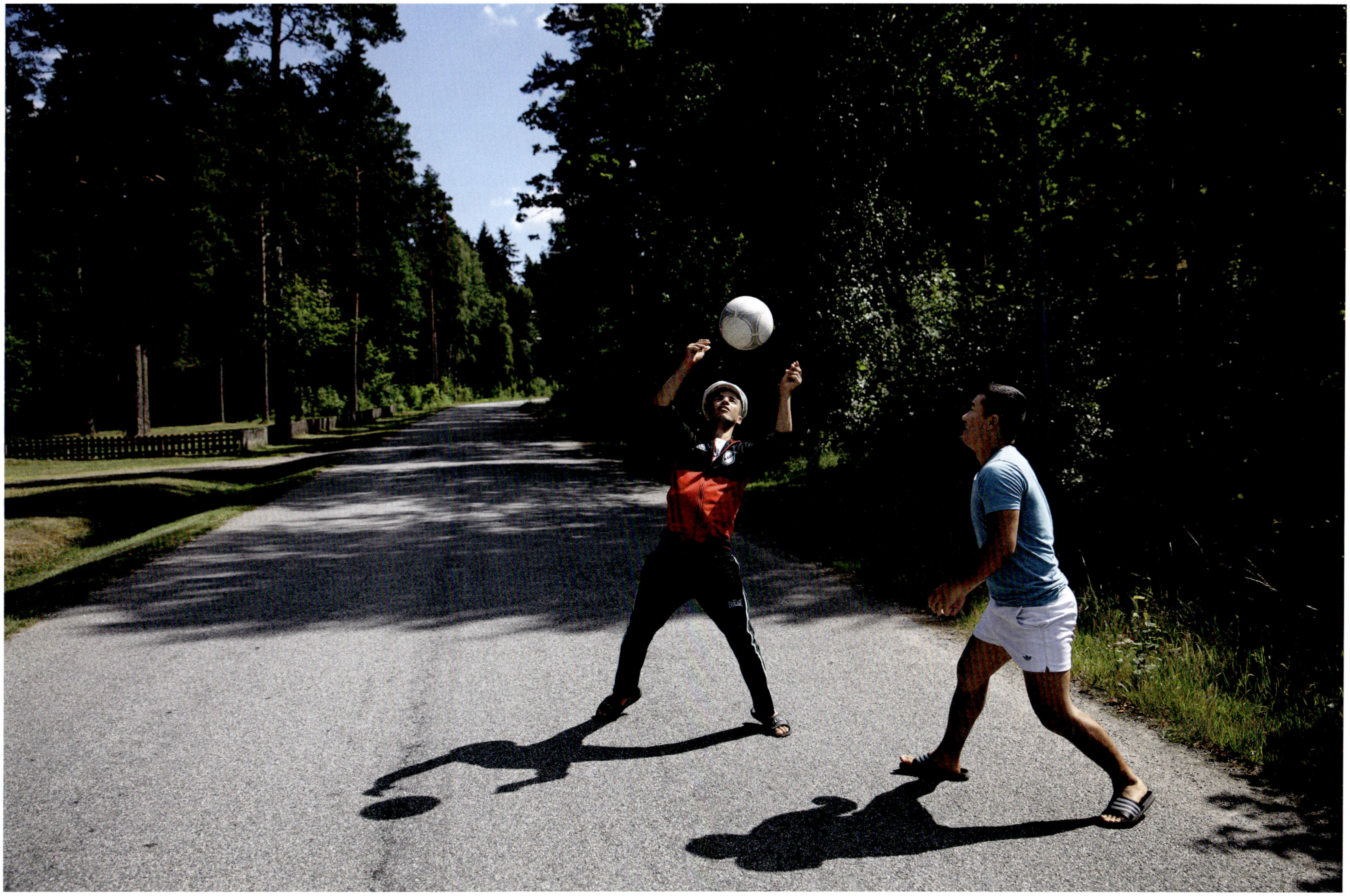

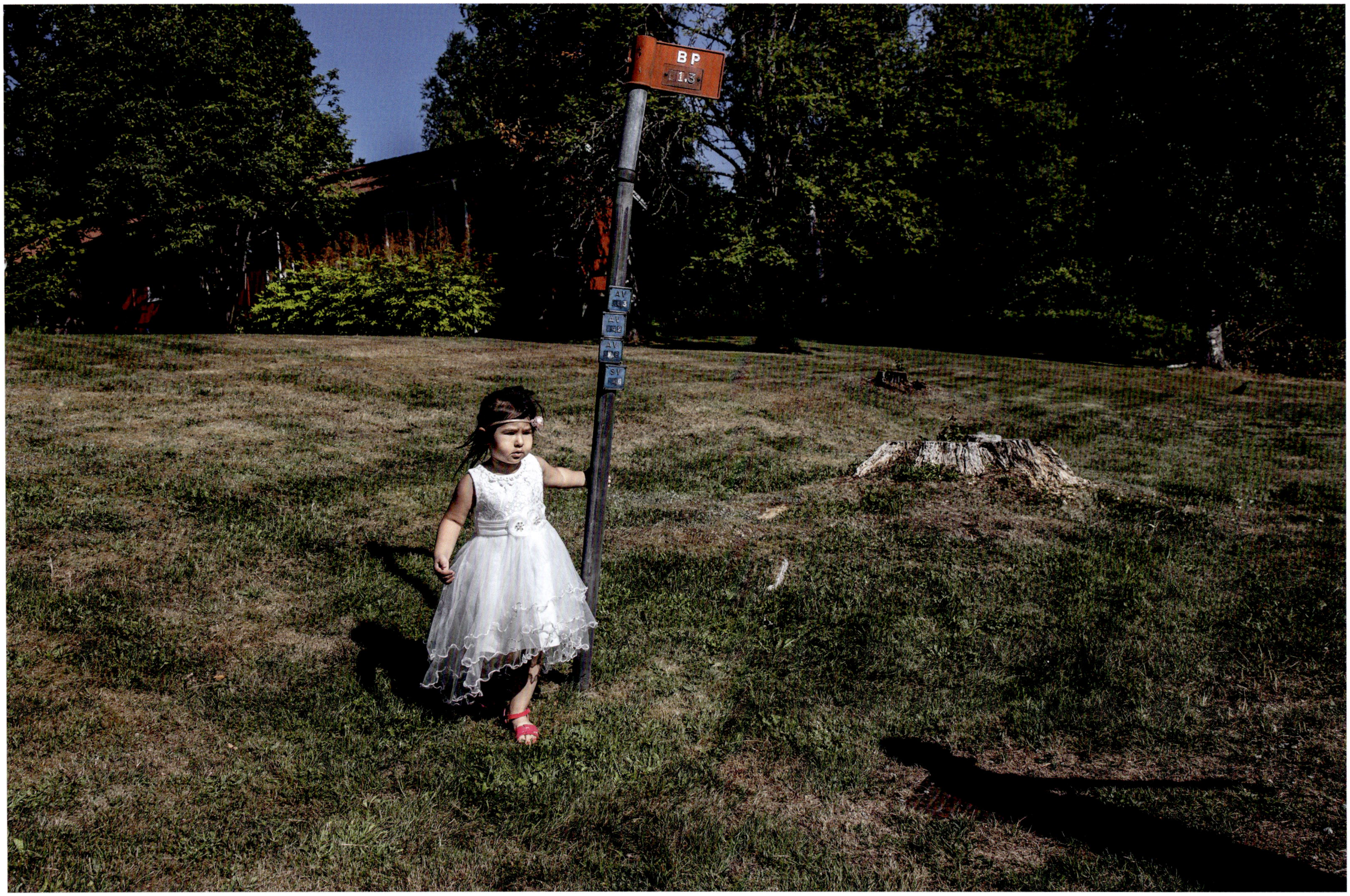
BP
1.3
AV
AV
AV
SV

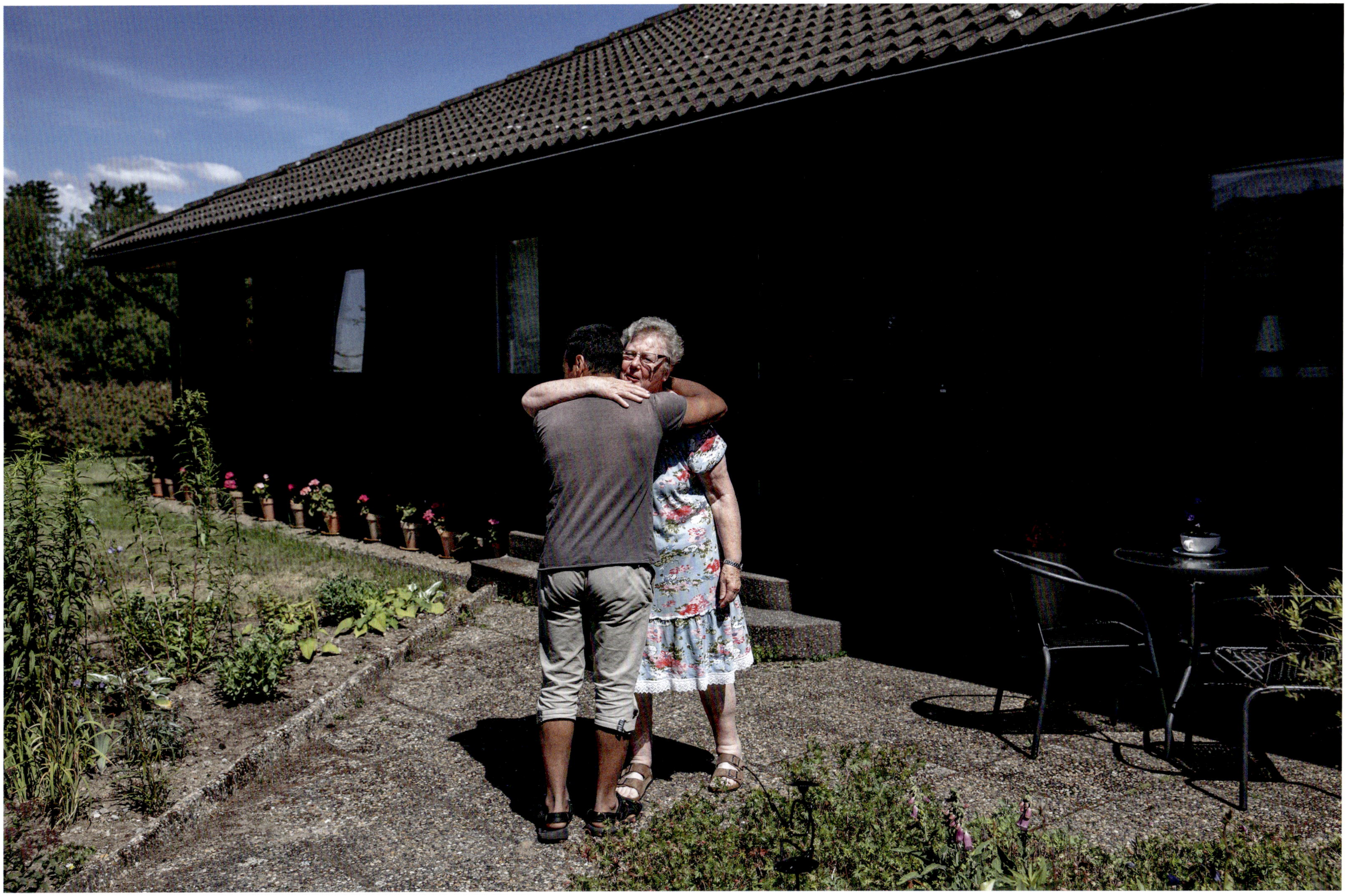

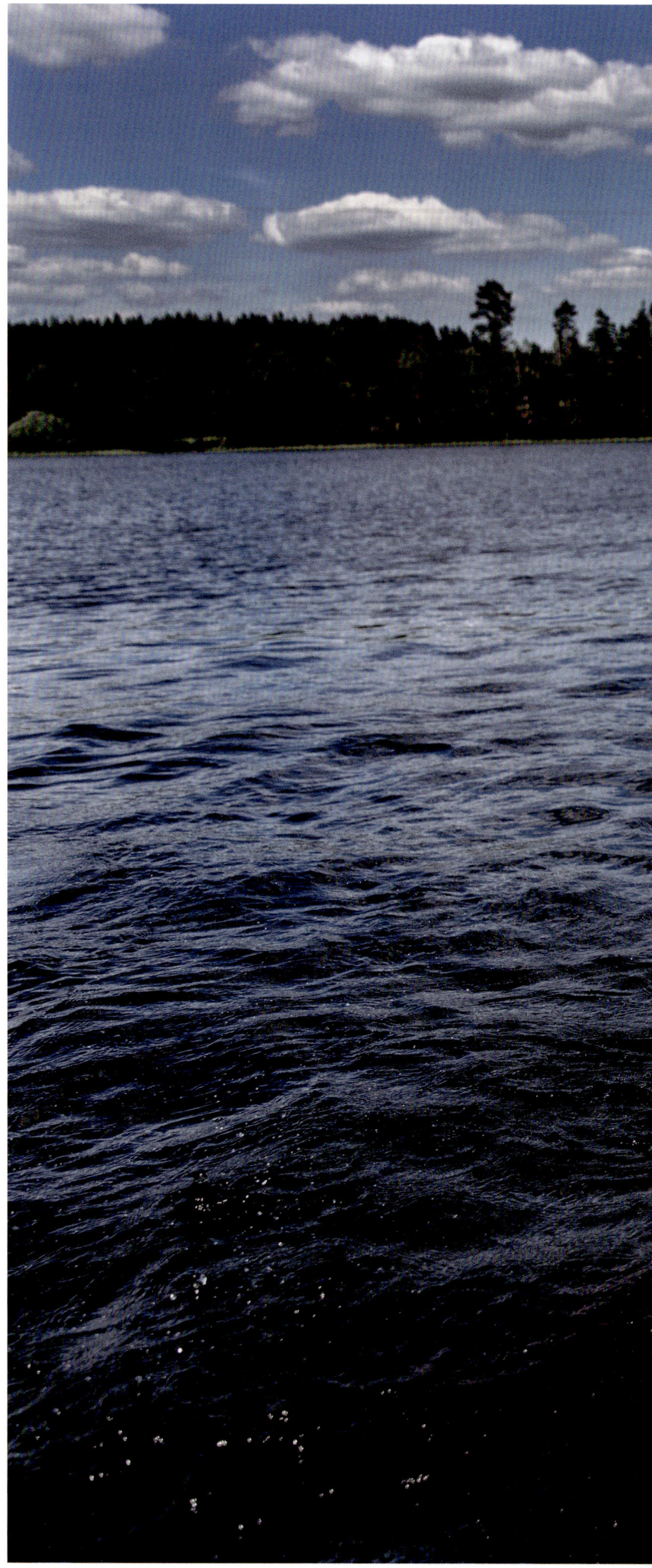

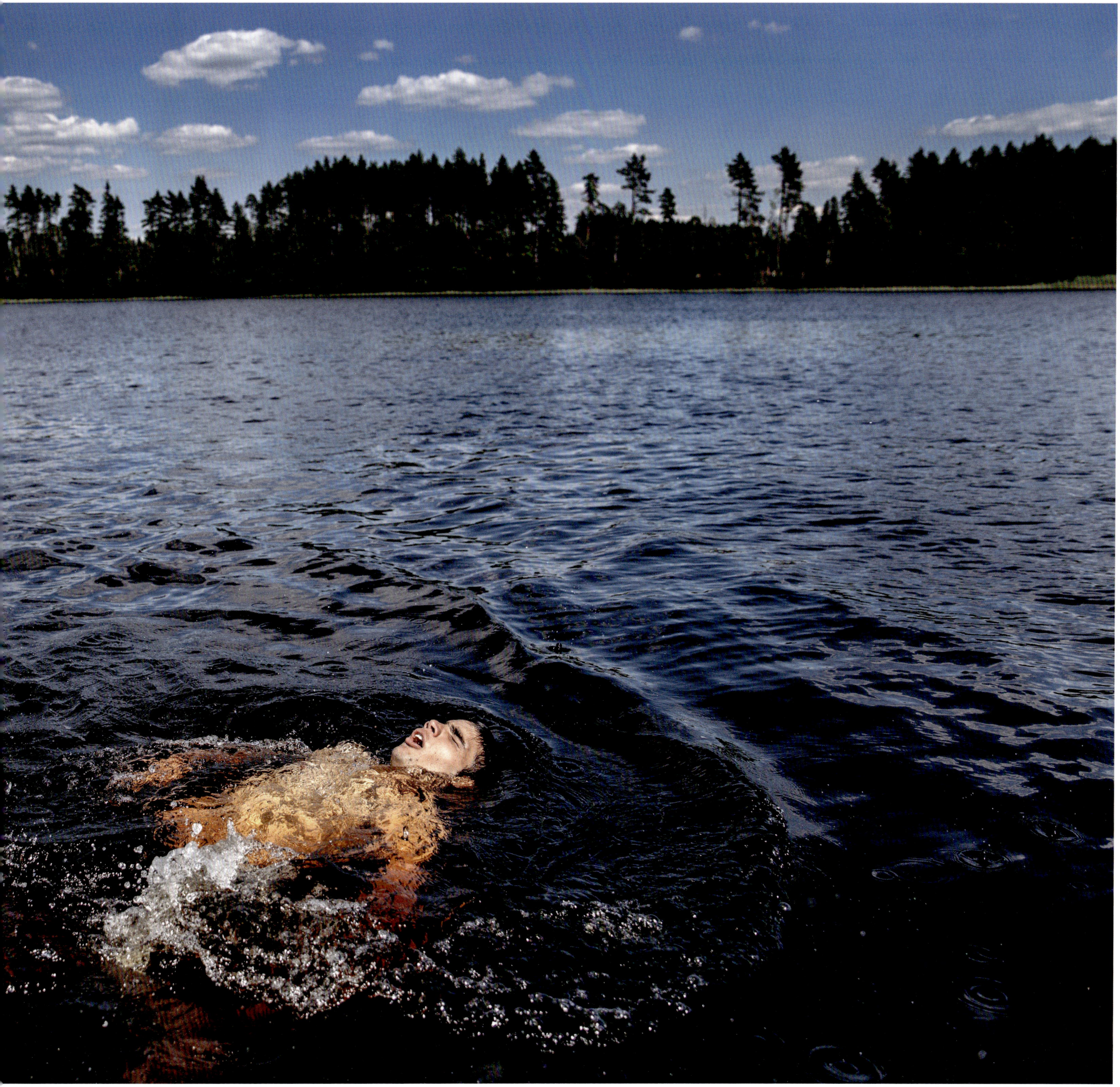

While president Emmanuel Macron tightens the French immigration and refugee policy, the number of refugees and migrants living on the streets of Paris increases. In the early spring of 2018, at least a couple of thousand people live along the canals, under bridges and on the city's warm air vents.

For many of them, Paris is a stop on the journey to the northern European countries. But for others, the city is more like an end station. After having been refused asylum in Scandinavia, Germany and other European countries, they go to Paris in the hope that French authorities will evaluate their personal safety in their home countries differently. Afghans in particular look to France as the last chance for an officially sanctioned life in Europe.

A number of the refugees and migrants living on the streets in the 'City of Lights' are heading for the port city of Calais, in northern France, risking their lives to go on to England, most of them as stowaways on lorries. Some have already been to Calais several times and have tried in vain to proceed to England. Now they are gathering the courage and strength to make another attempt.

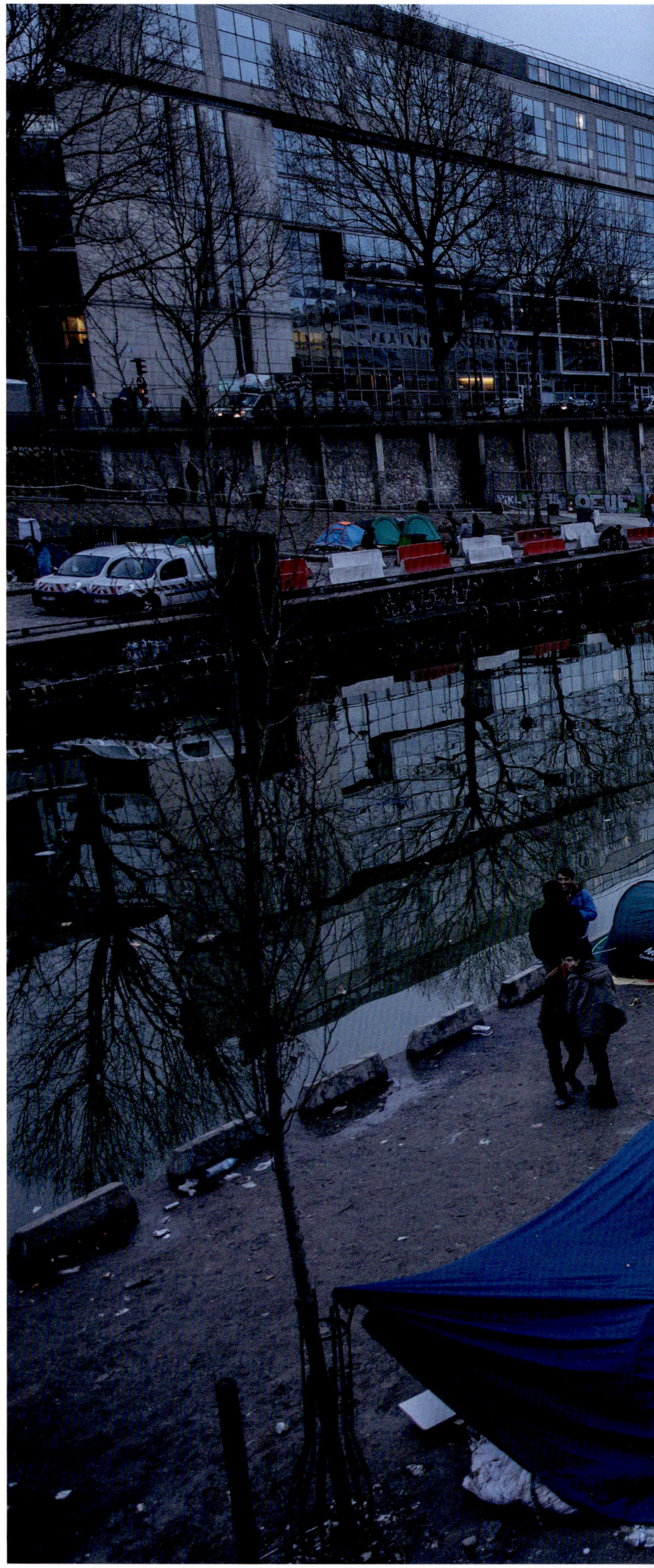

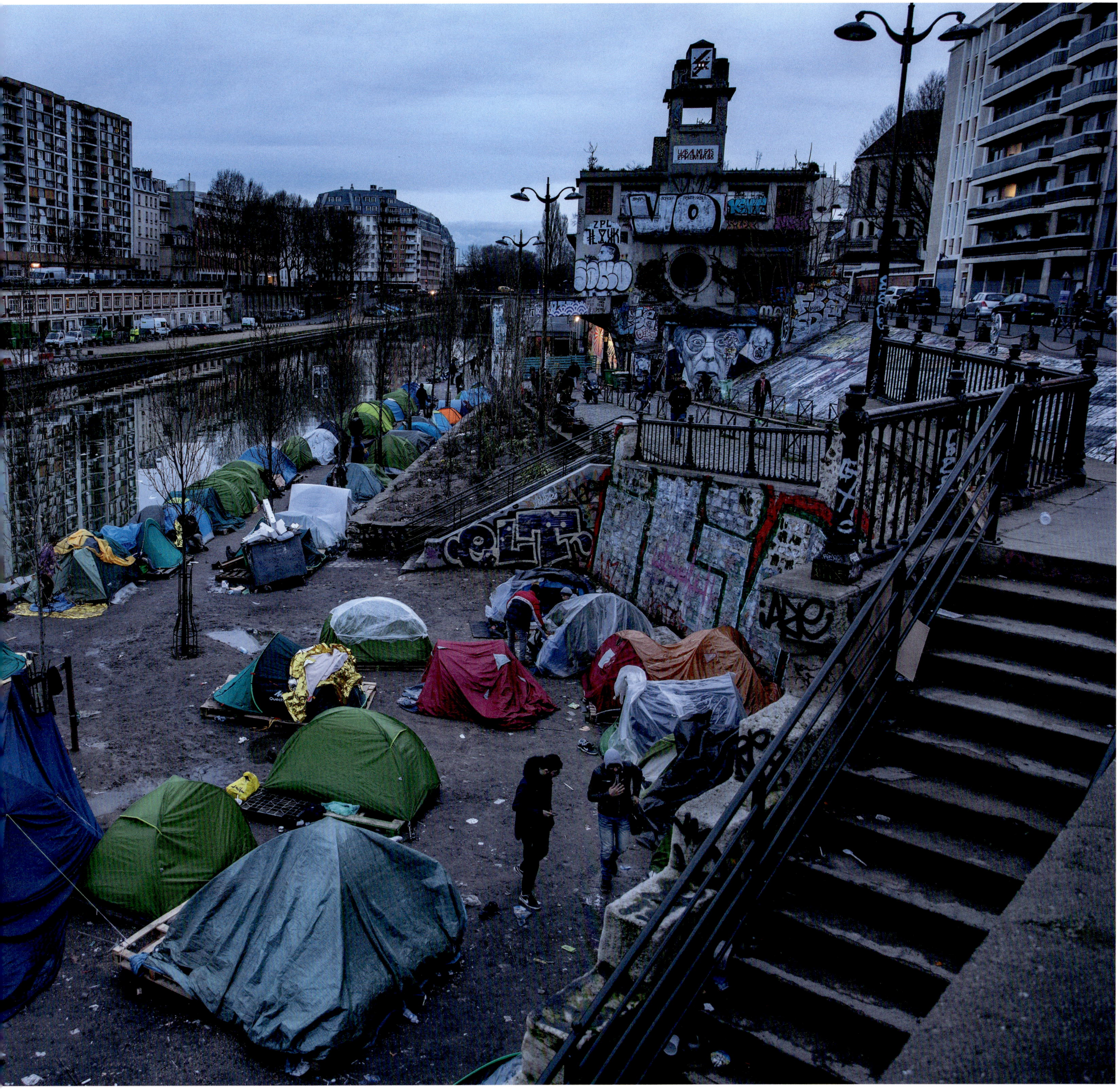

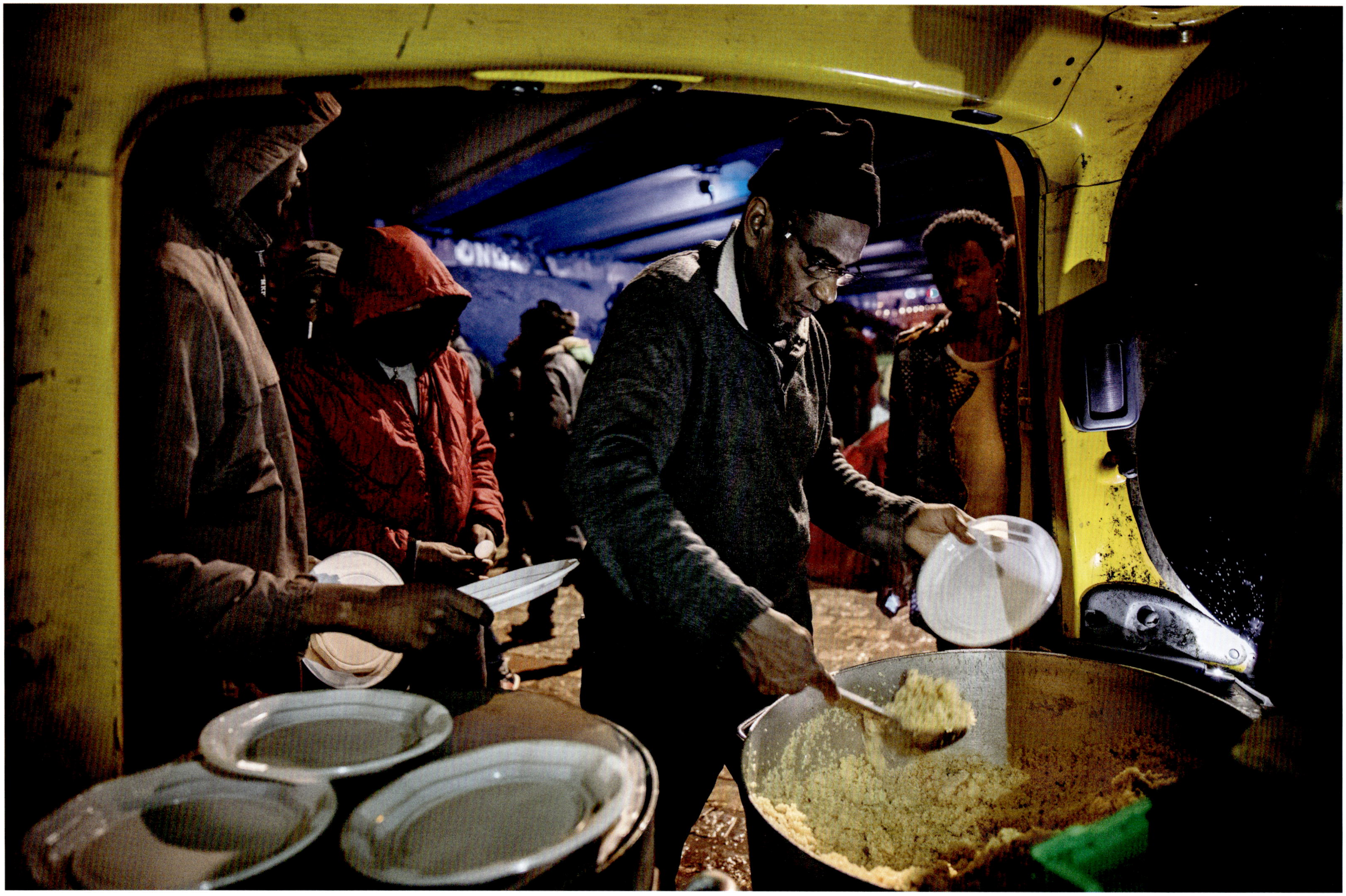

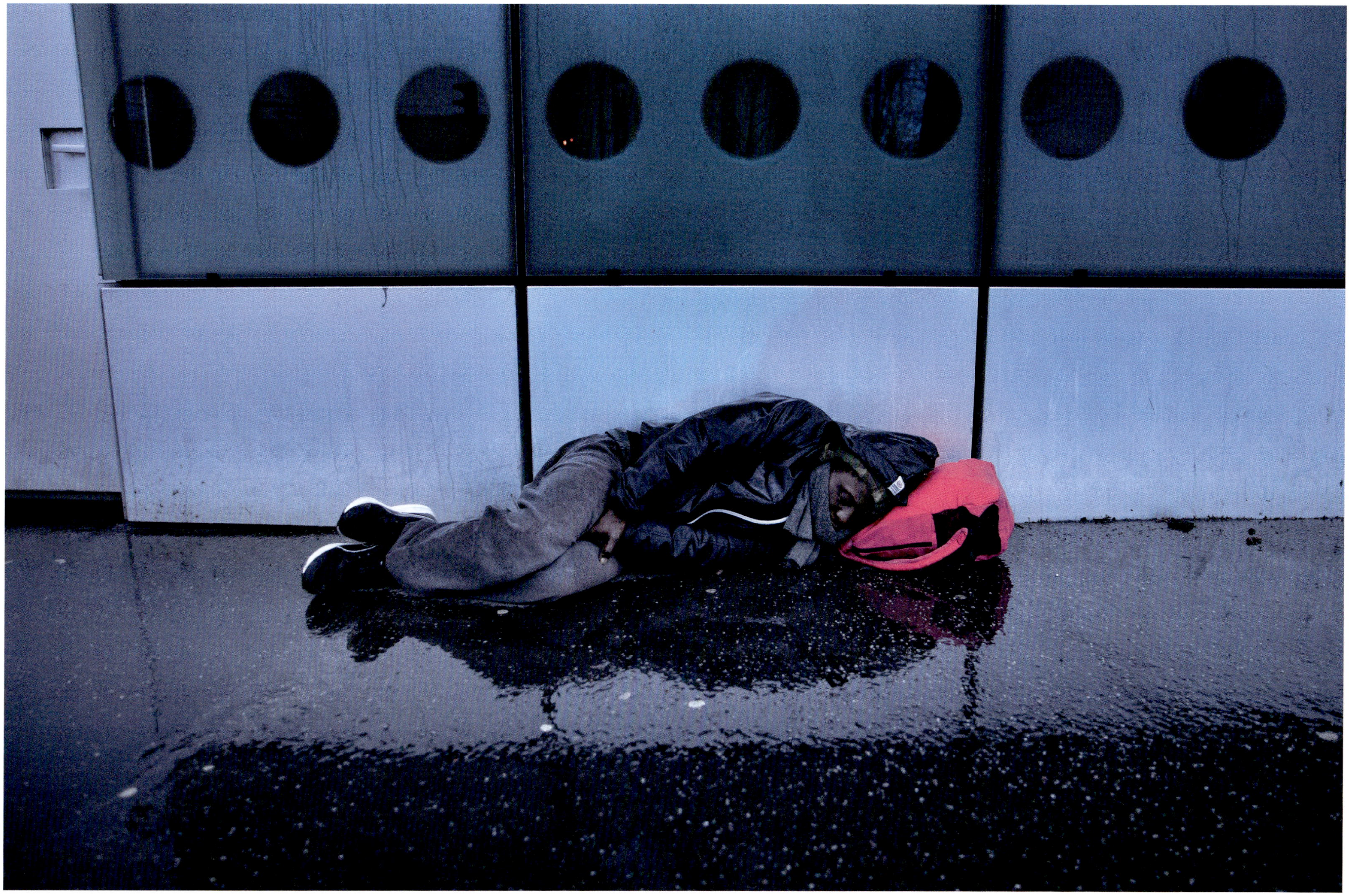

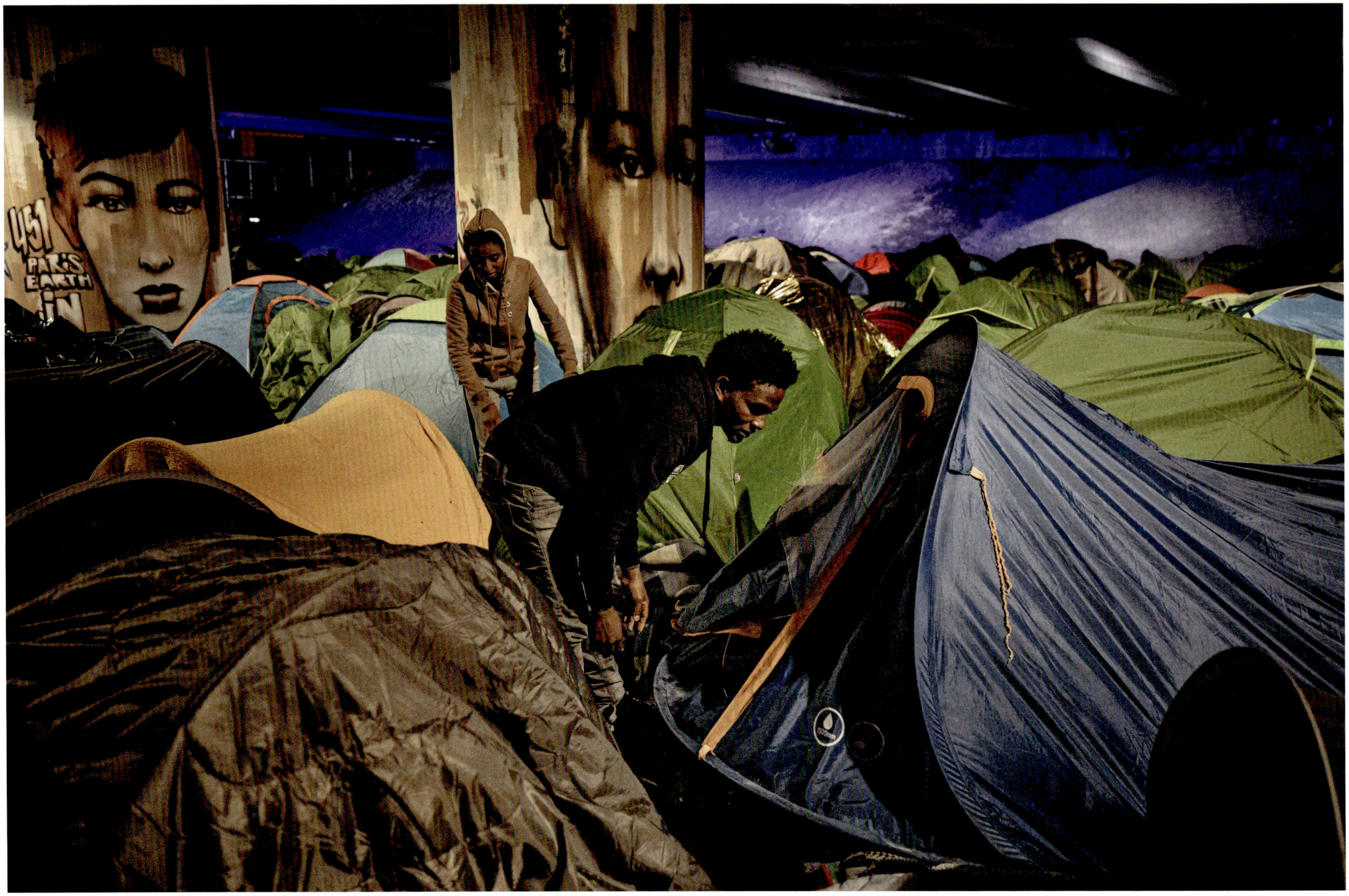
451
PARIS
EARTH
iN

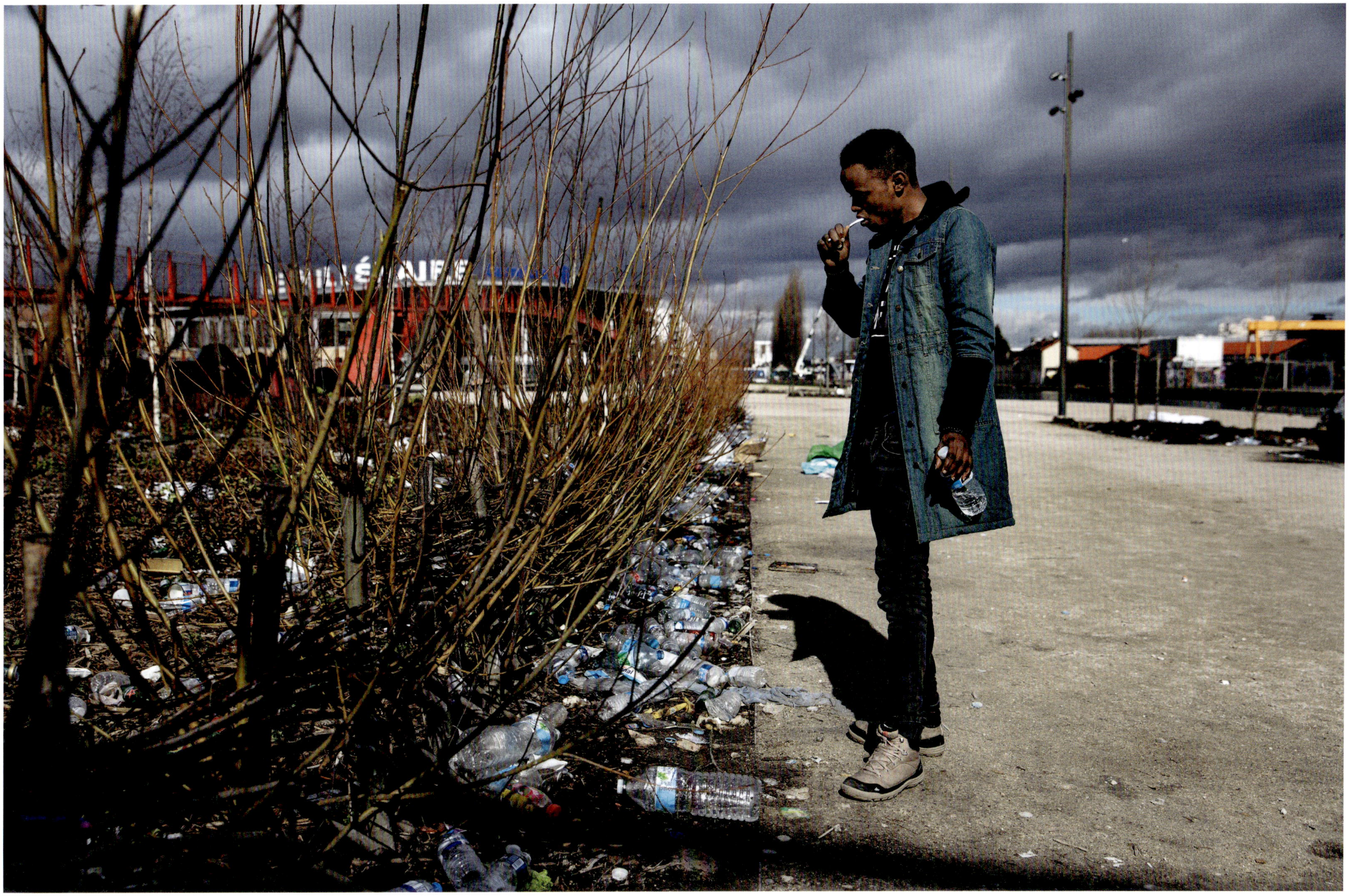

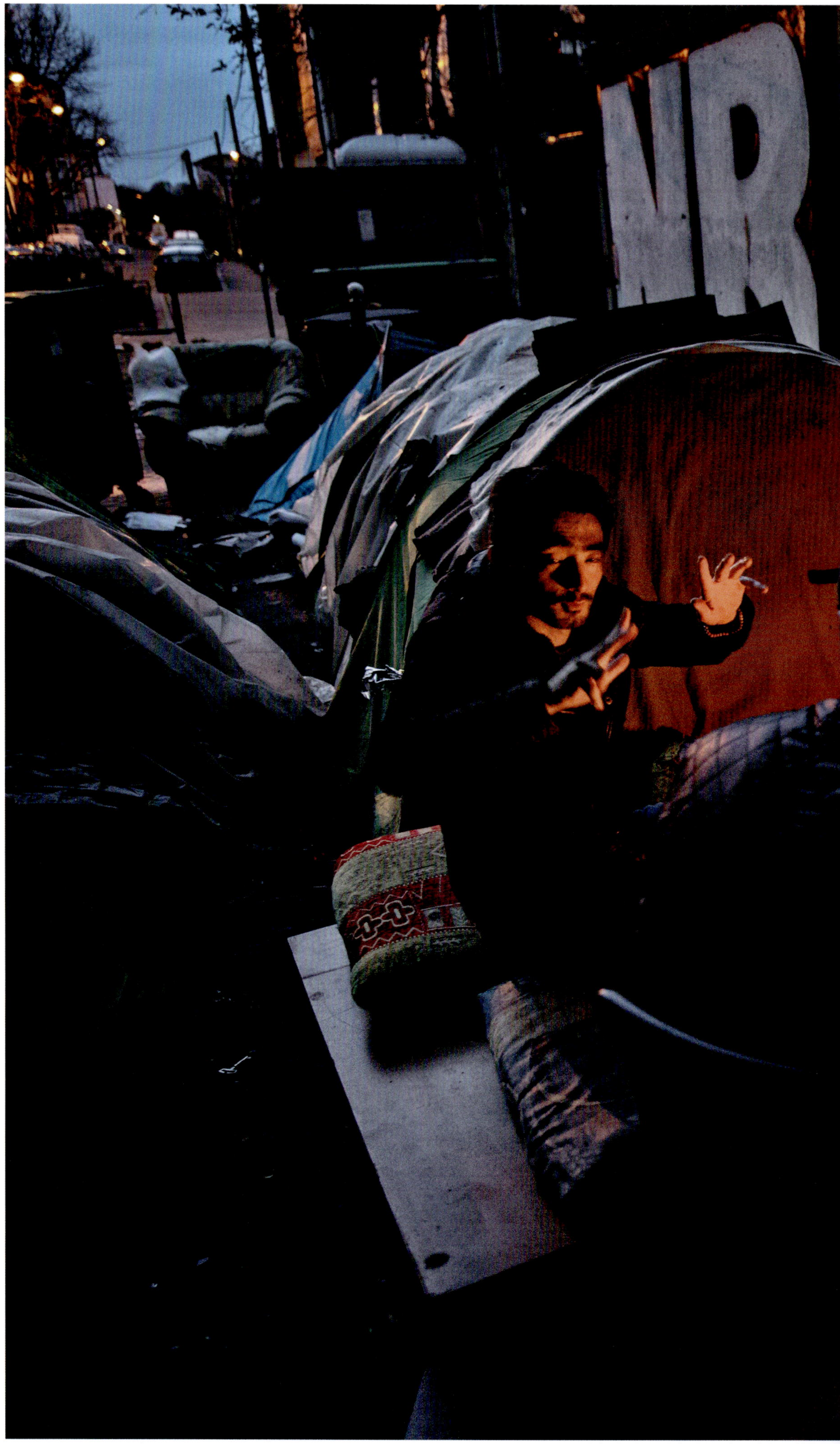

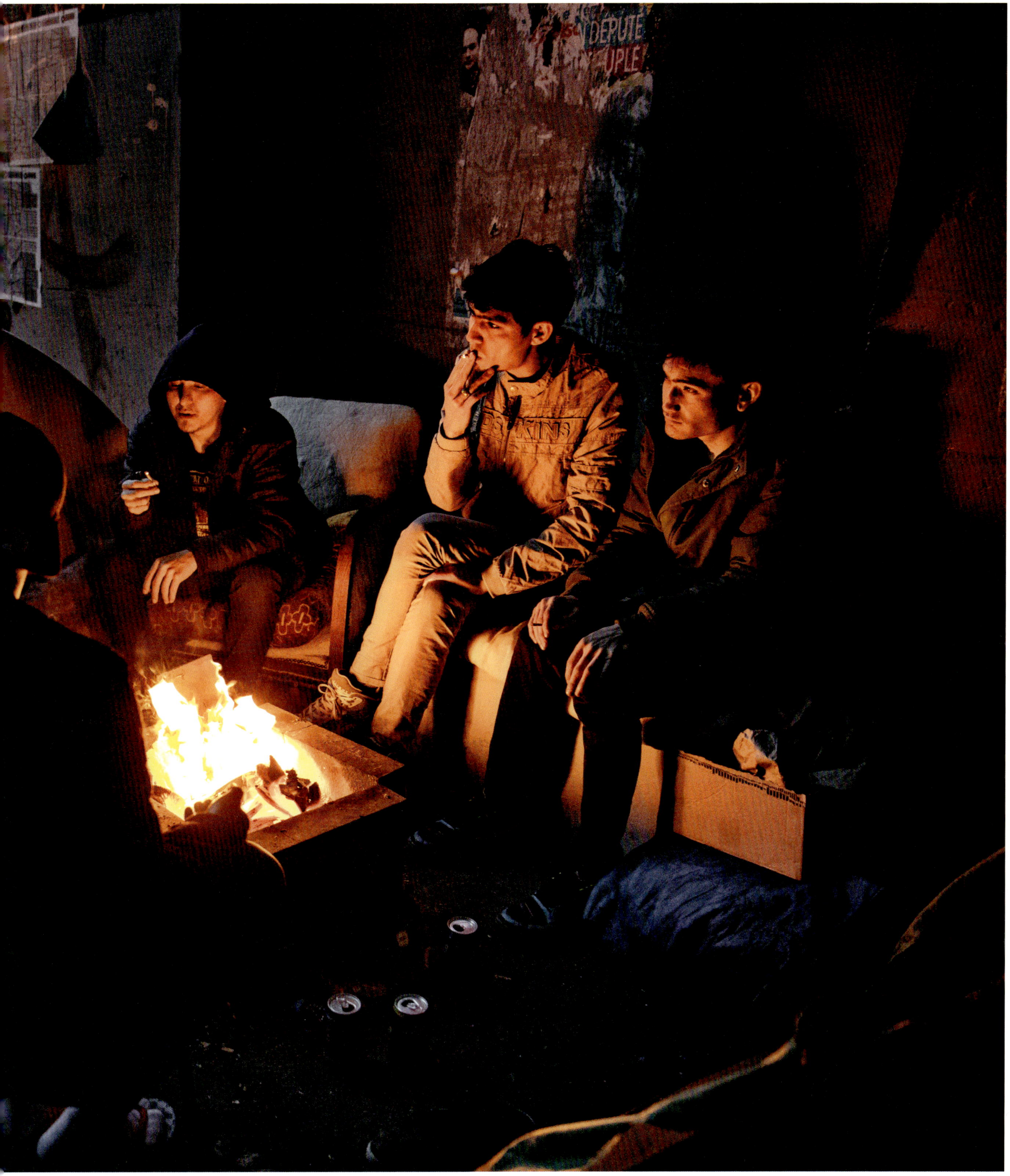
DEPUTE

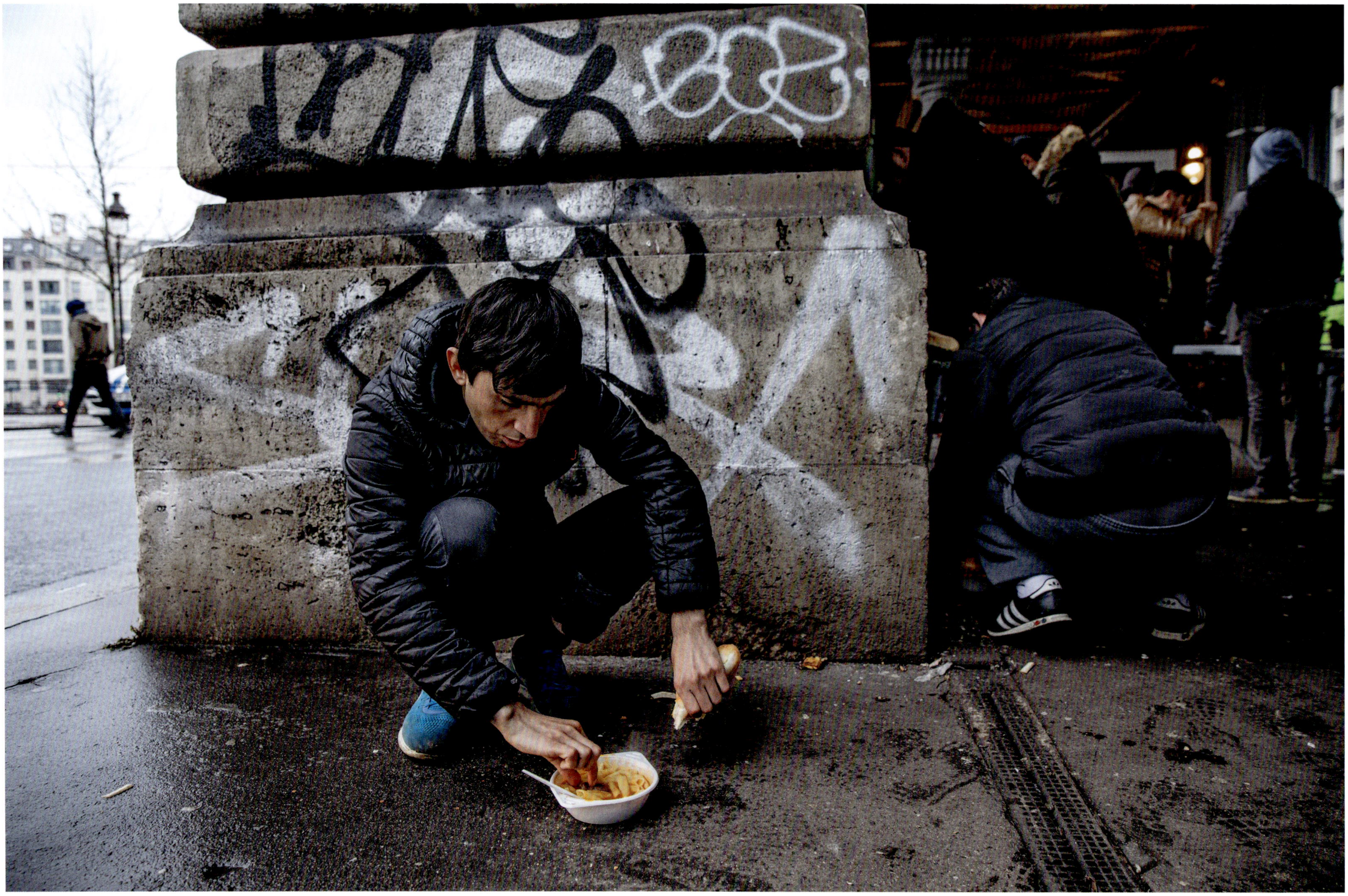

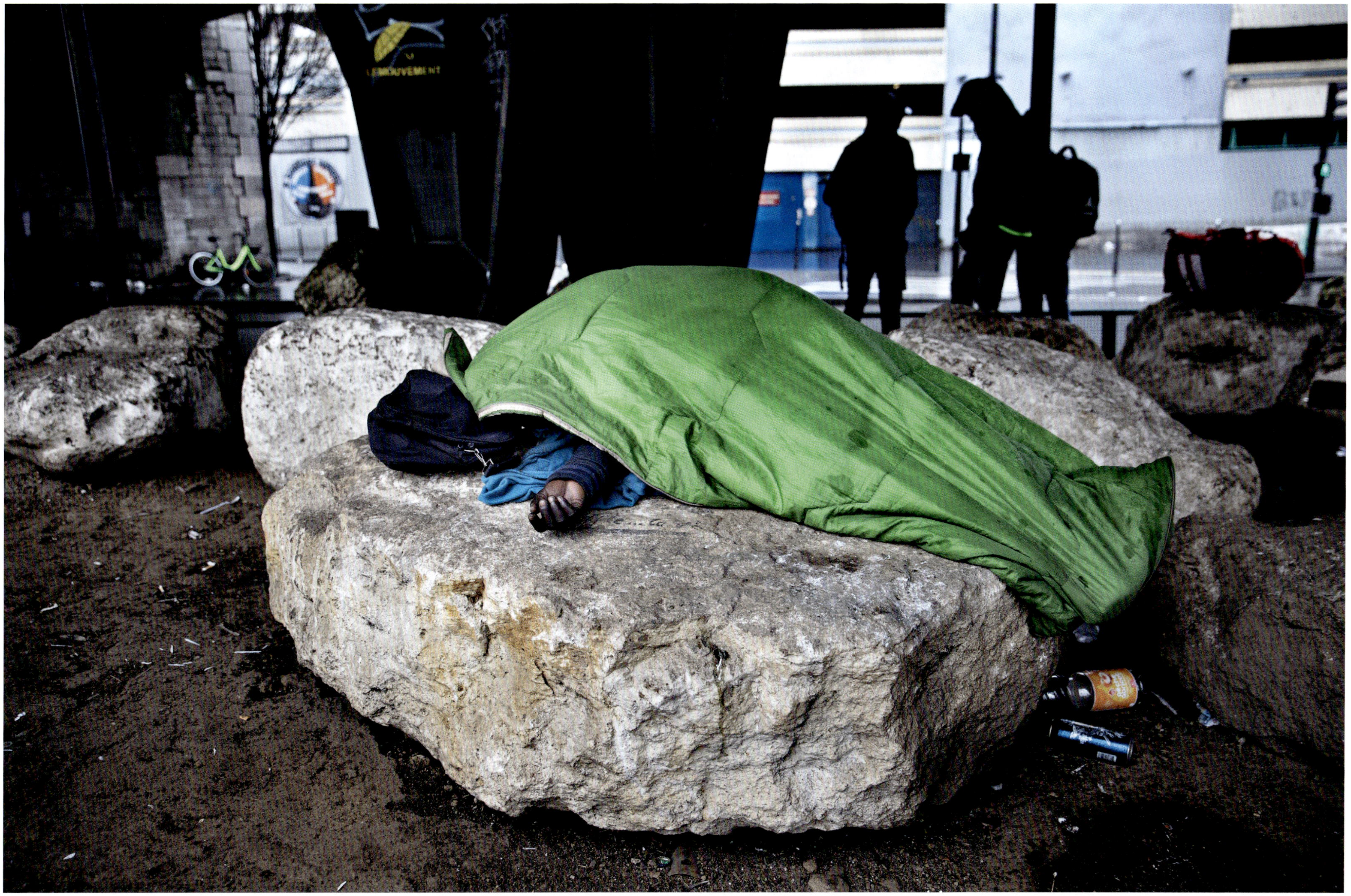

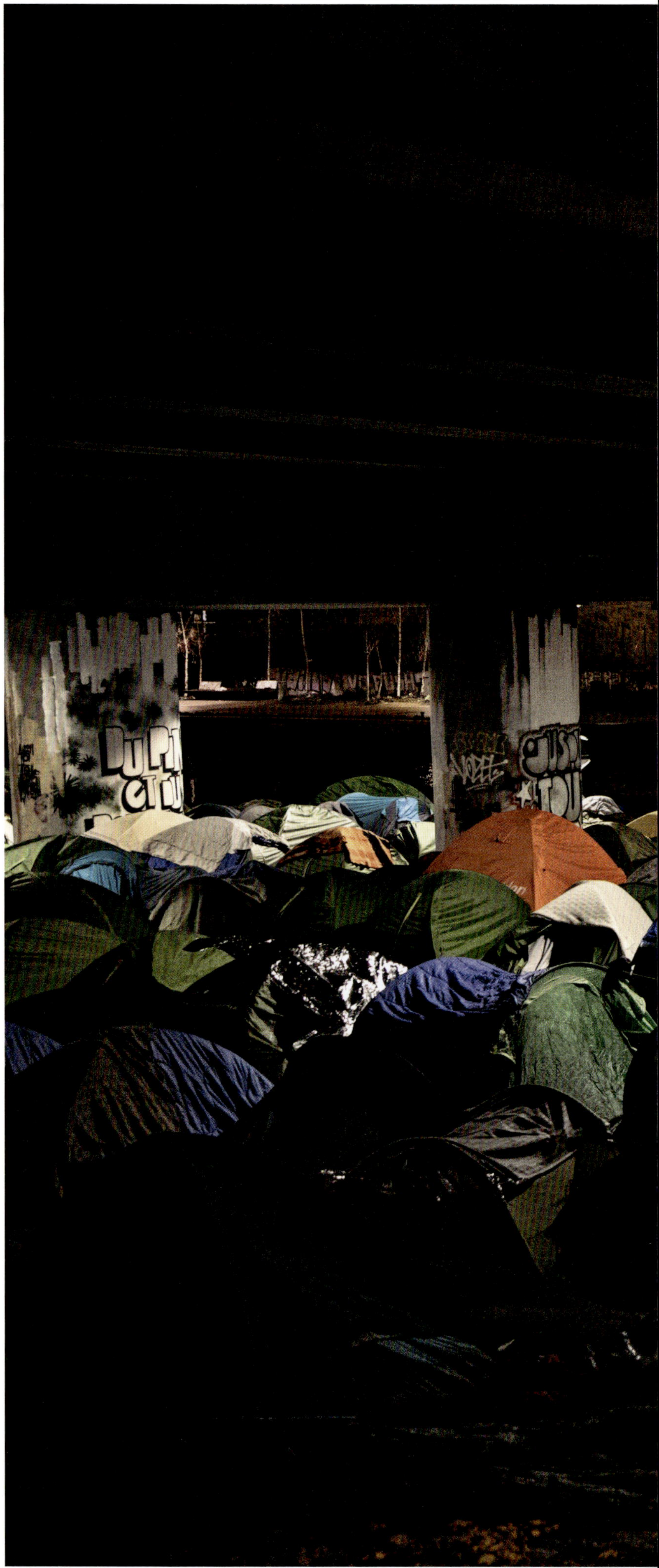

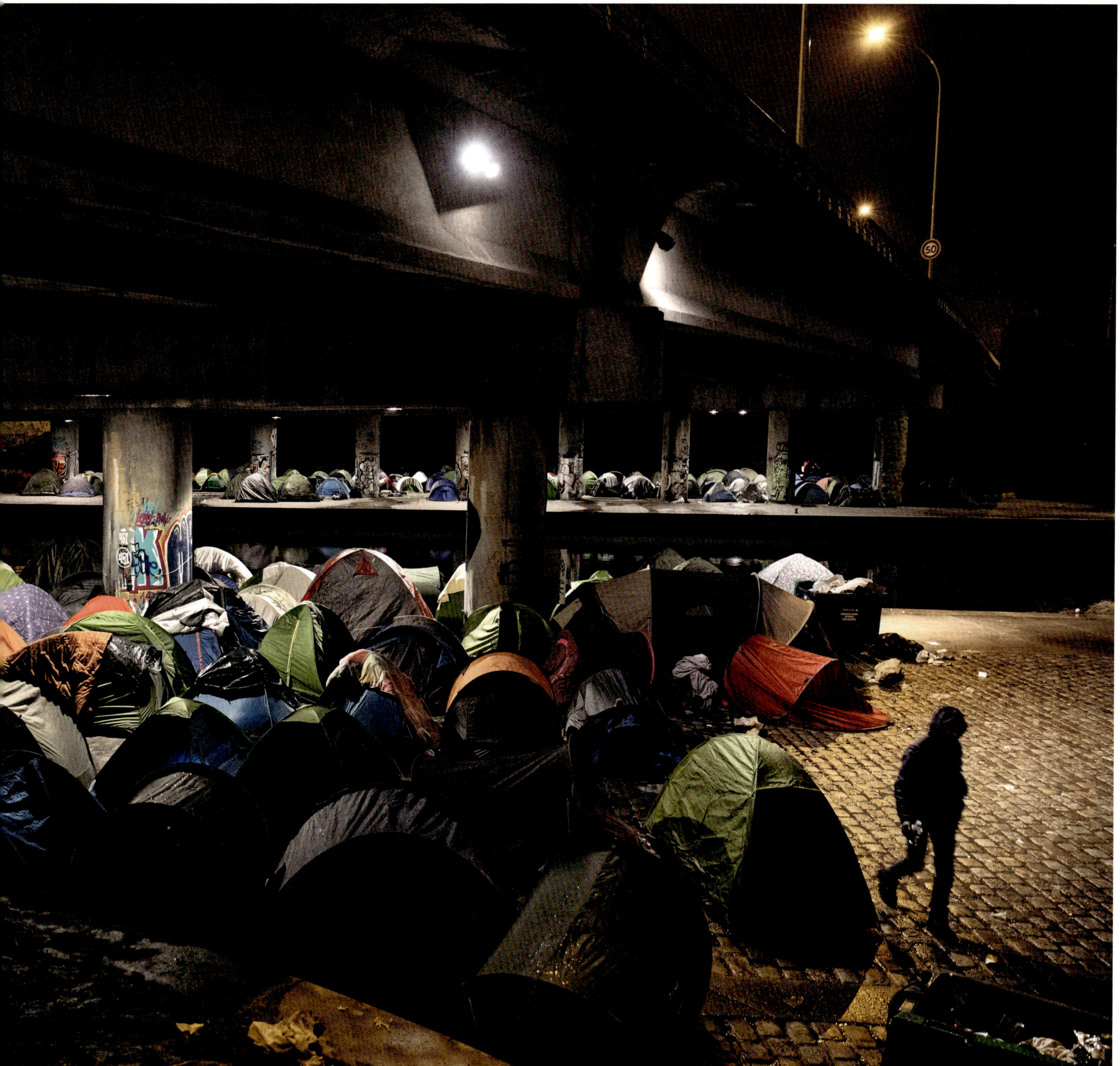
50

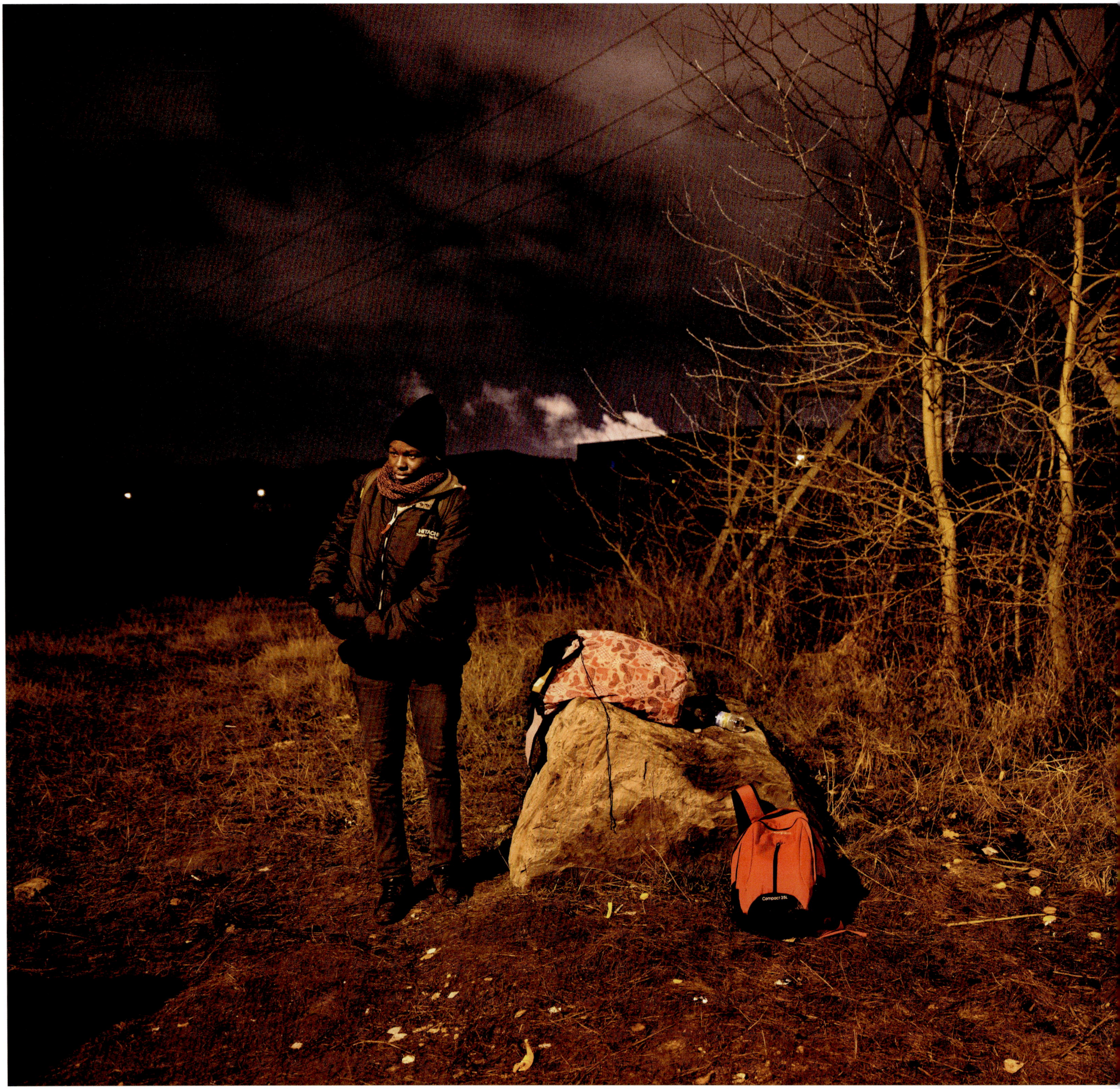

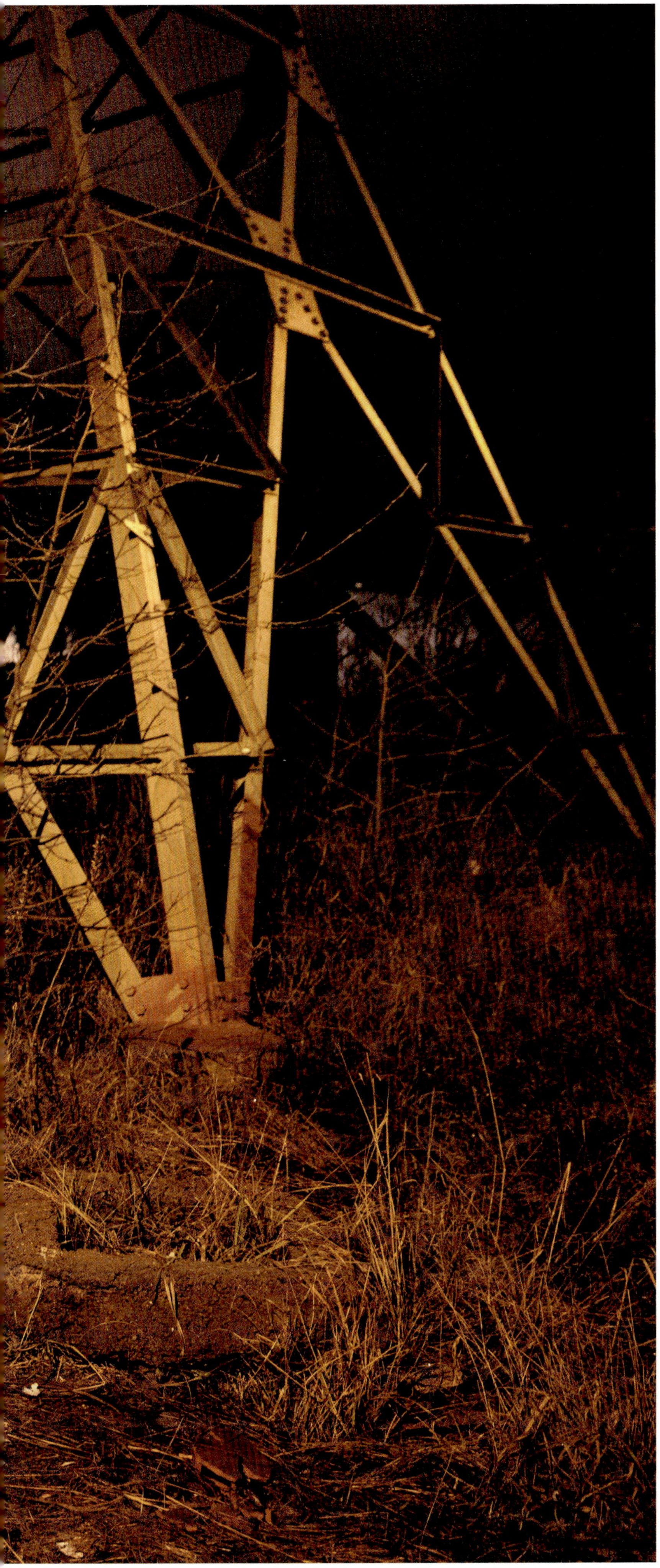

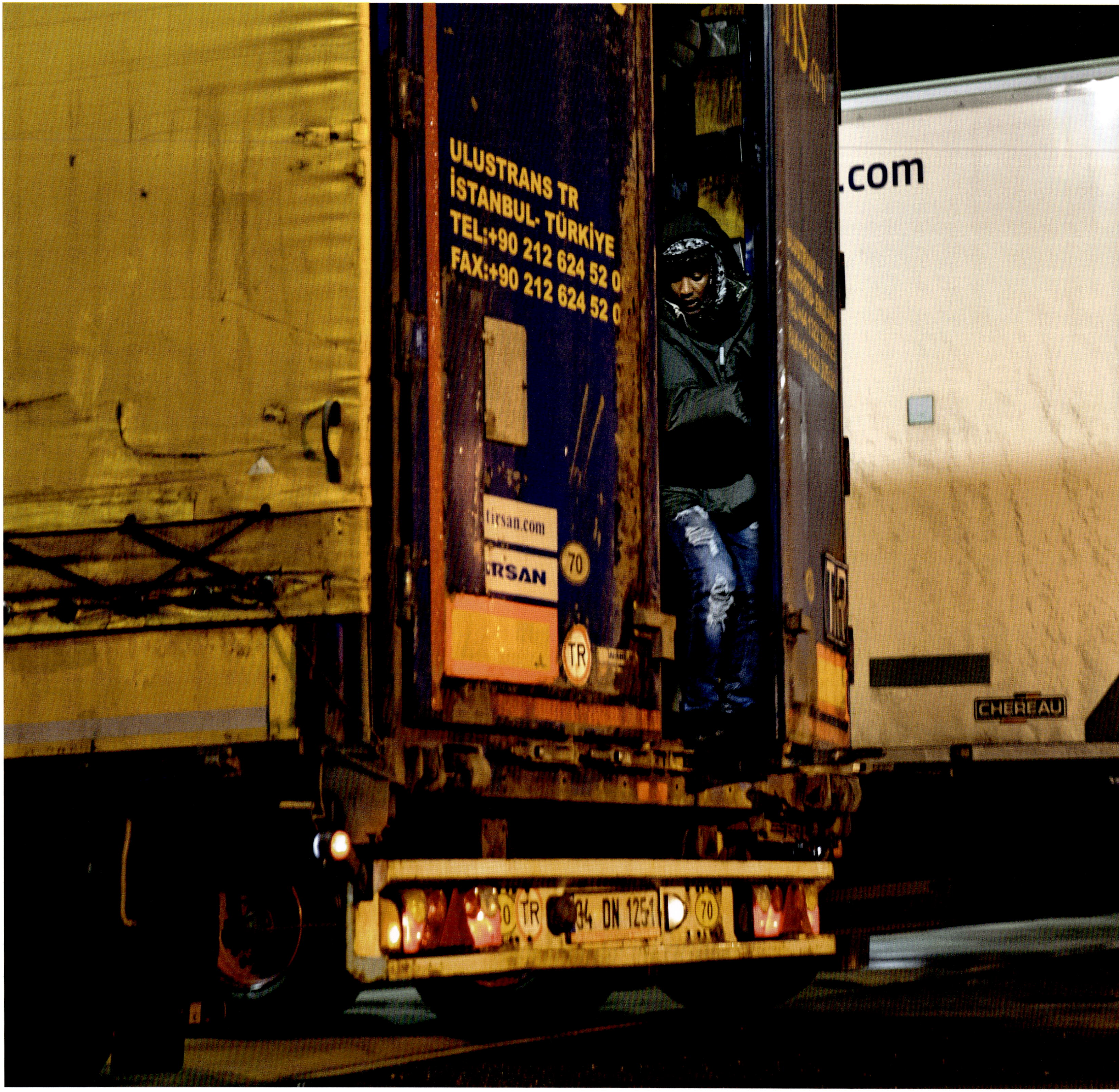
ULUSTRANS TR
İSTANBUL- TÜRKİYE
TEL:+90 212 624 52 0
FAX:+90 212 624 52 0
tirsan.com
RSAN
.com
CHEREAU

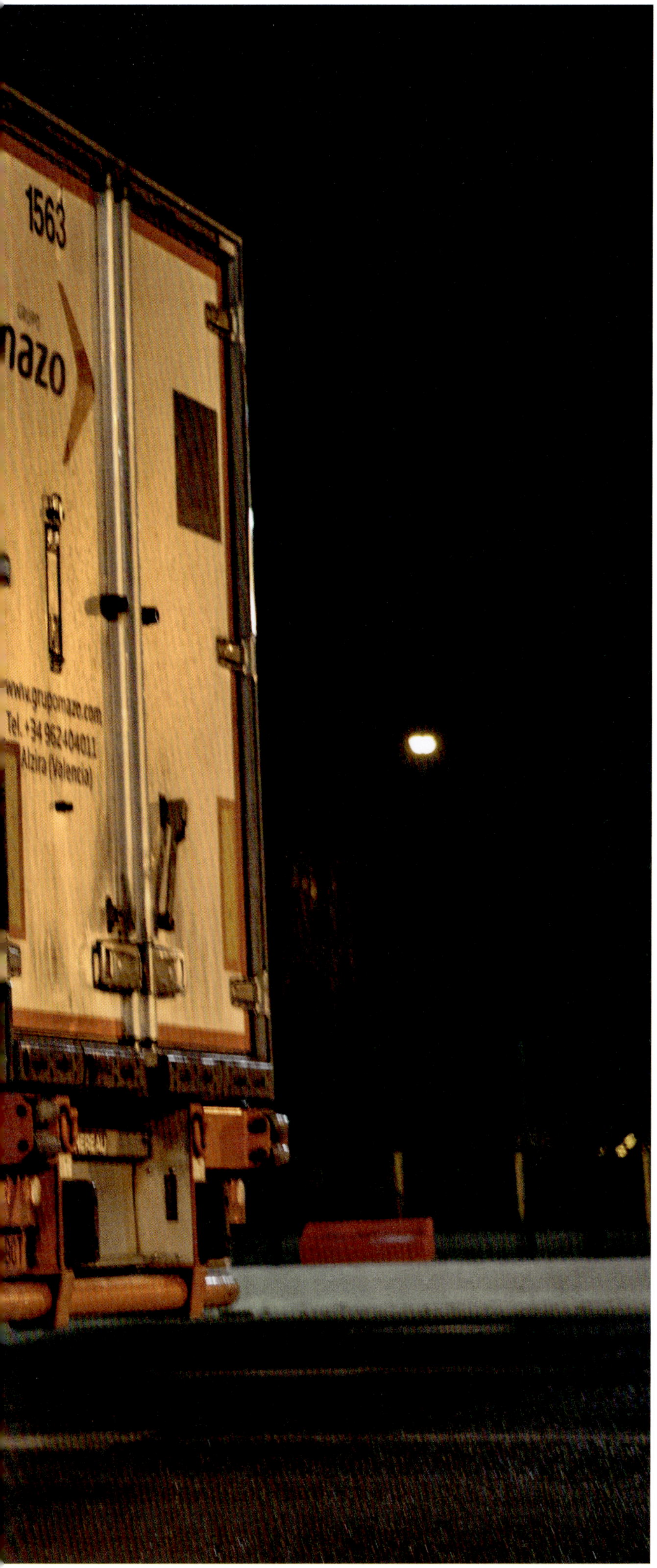
1563
www.grupomazo.com
Tel. +34 962404011
Alzira (Valencia)

Sea-Watch is a German NGO that has been coming to the rescue of African boat refugees in the Mediterranean since 2015. They operate in international waters which begin 12 nautical miles (22 kilometres) off the coast of Libya.

On 2 June 2017 a crew of seventeen volunteers embark on the sixth mission of the year on the ship Sea-Watch 2, a converted research vessel. Each mission lasts for two weeks and this one ends up involving fifteen rescue operations. Despite the fact that the EU, Libya and other African countries try to collaborate in slowing down the stream of refugees and migrants to Europe, the human traffickers still send them on overcrowded dinghies in terrible condition from the north African coasts. The people on board are highly unlikely to reach the shores of Italy, a journey that takes six or seven days, on dinghies with small outboard motors, so their survival depends on whether anyone finds them and picks them up.

Sea-Watch 2 does not bring the refugees and migrants they pick up to a safe harbour, but hands them over to other much larger NGO ships or to the Italian coast guard, which usually sails them to either Lampedusa or Sicily.

According to the International Organization for Migration (IOM), more than 3,100 people have died or were reported missing in the Mediterranean Sea in 2017.

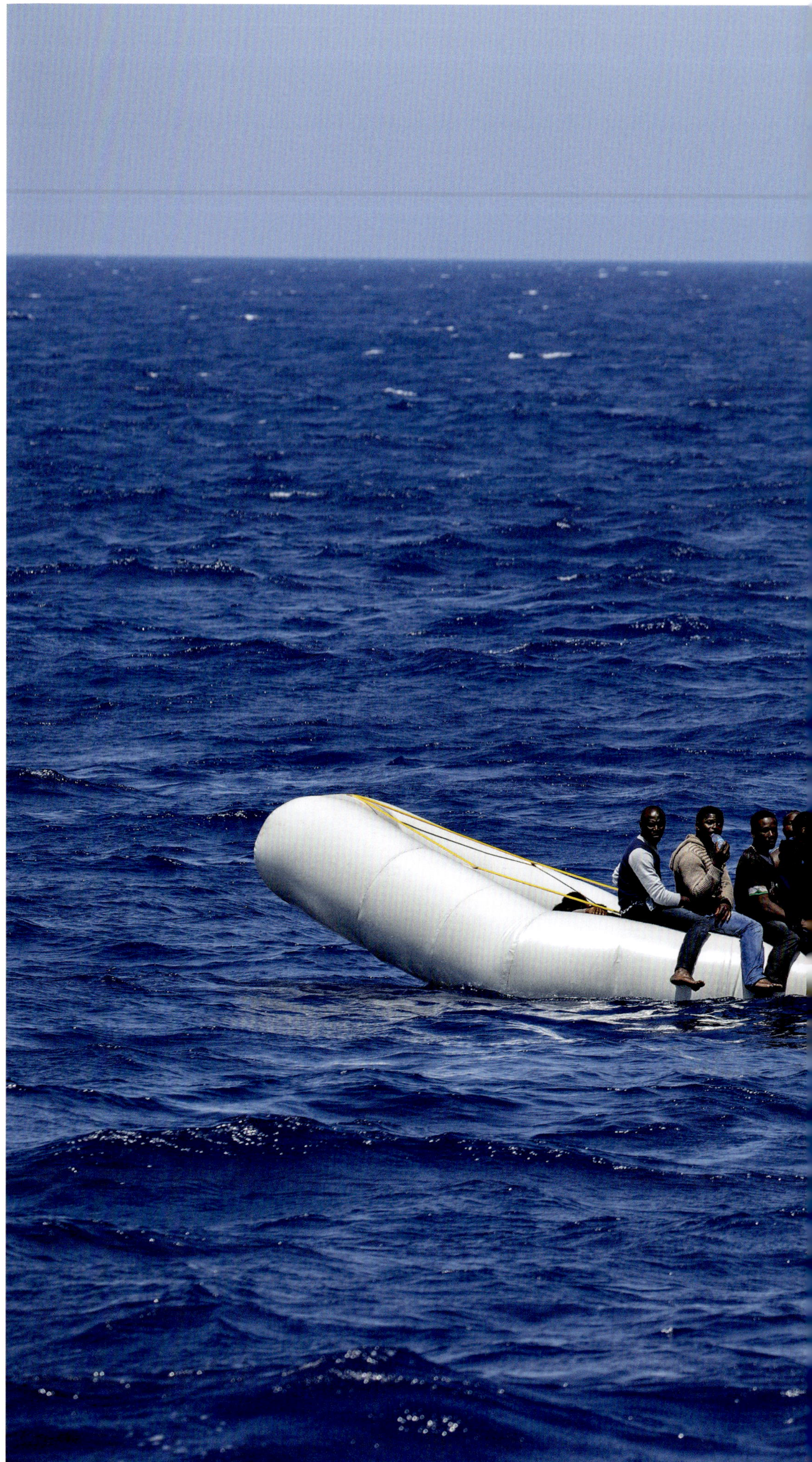

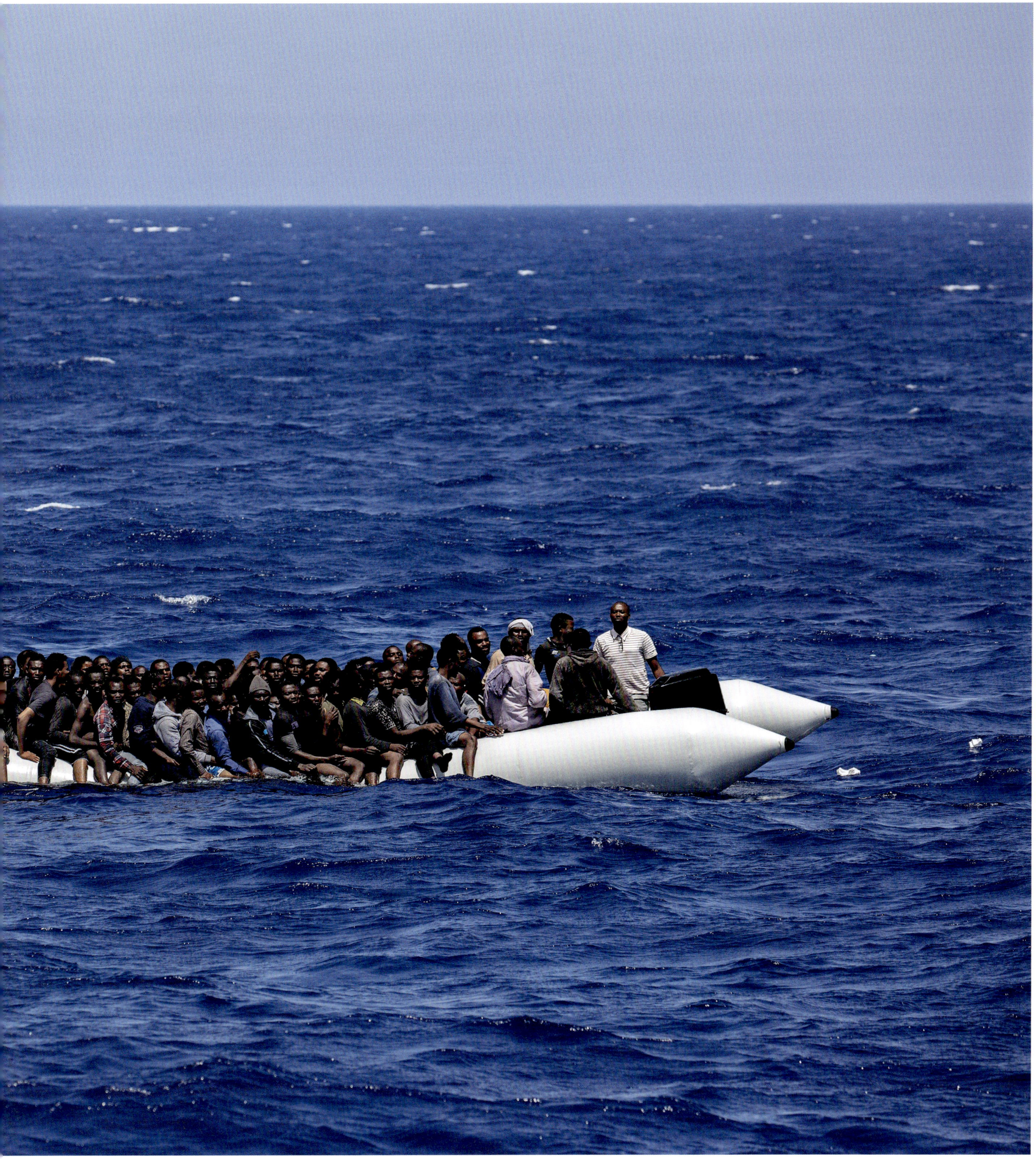

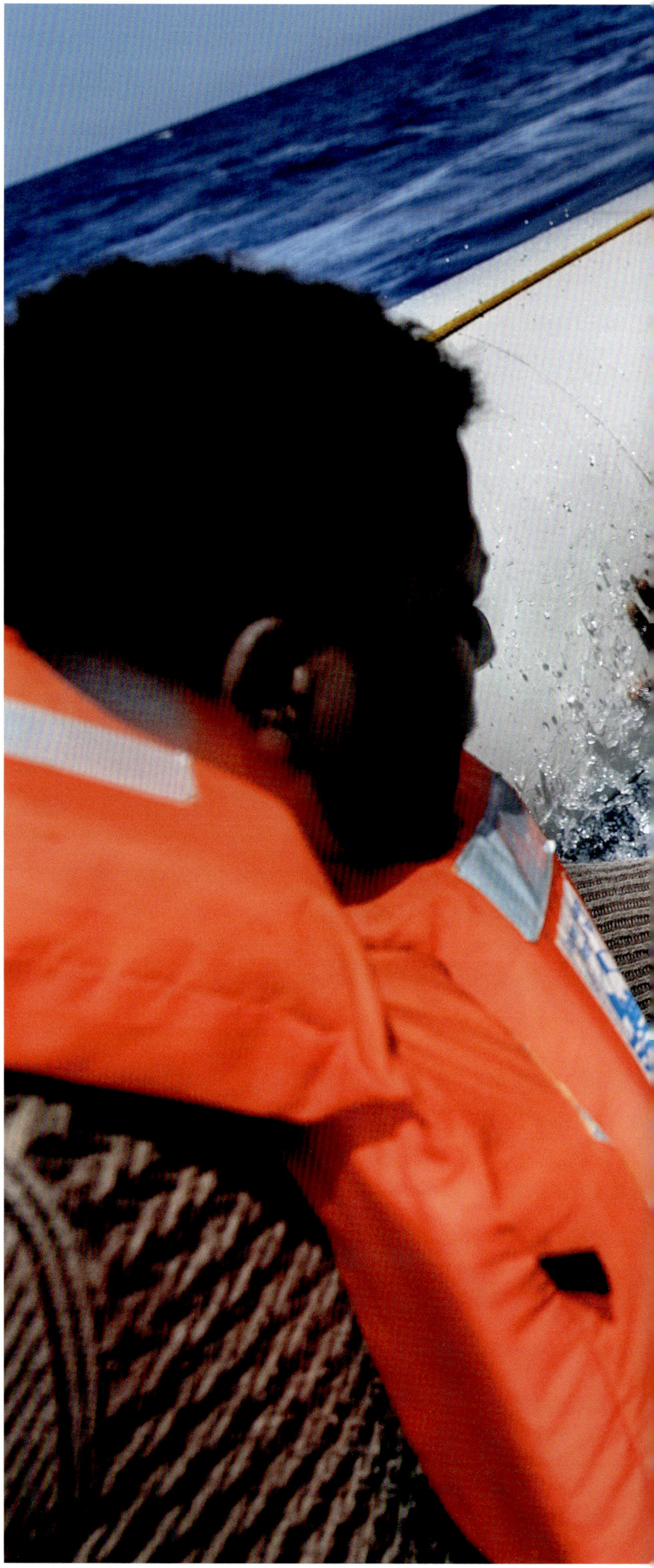

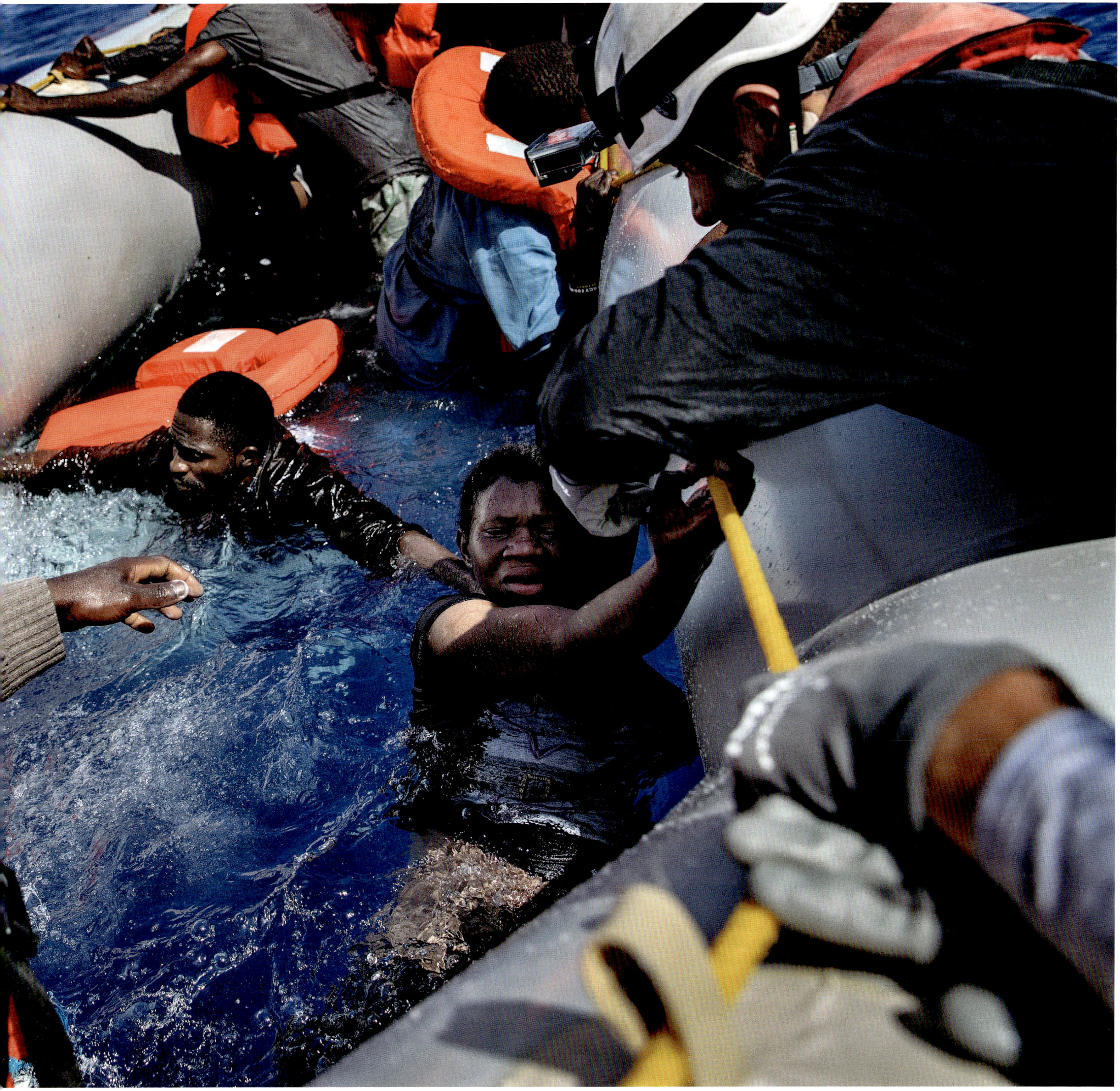

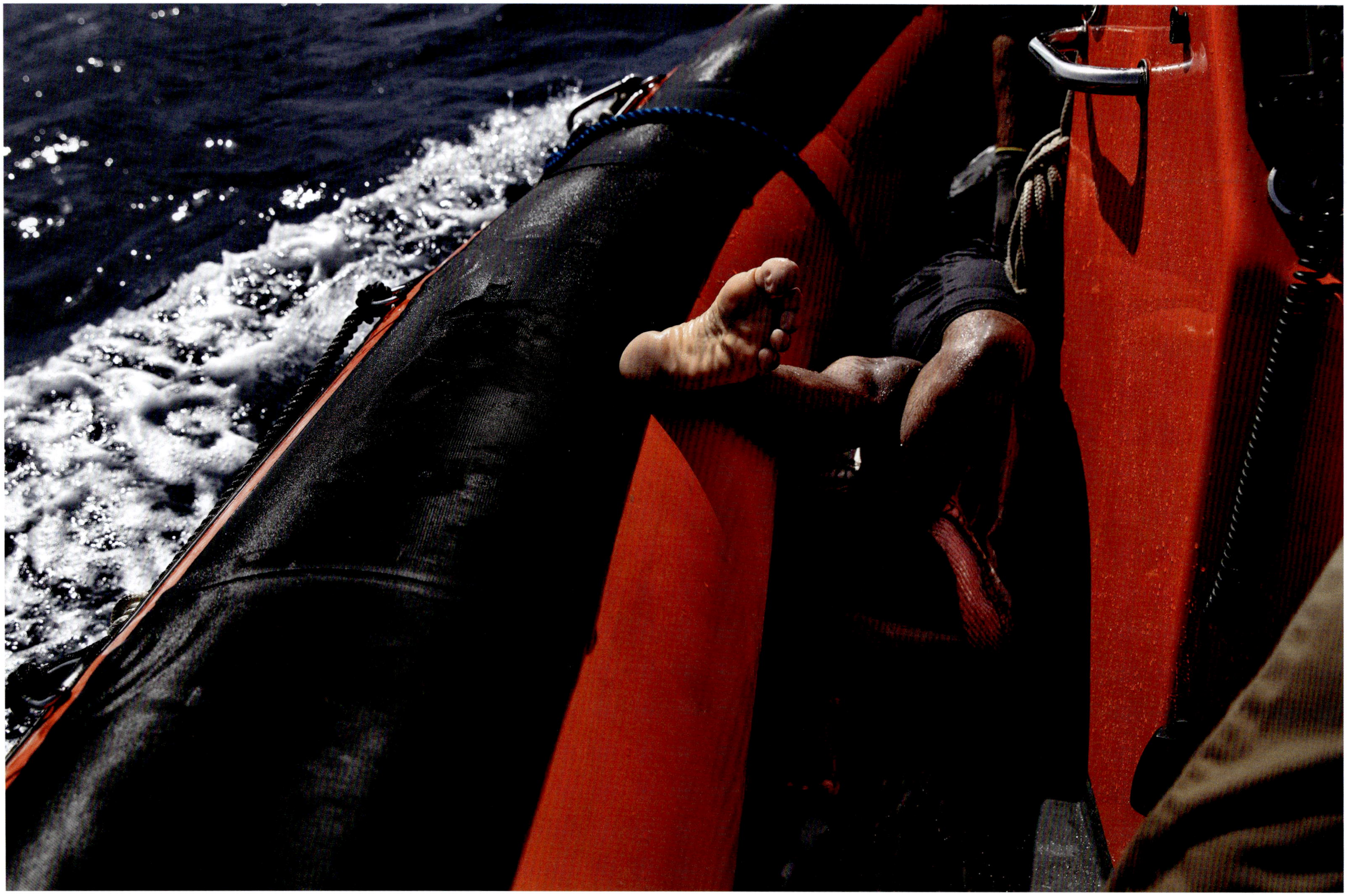

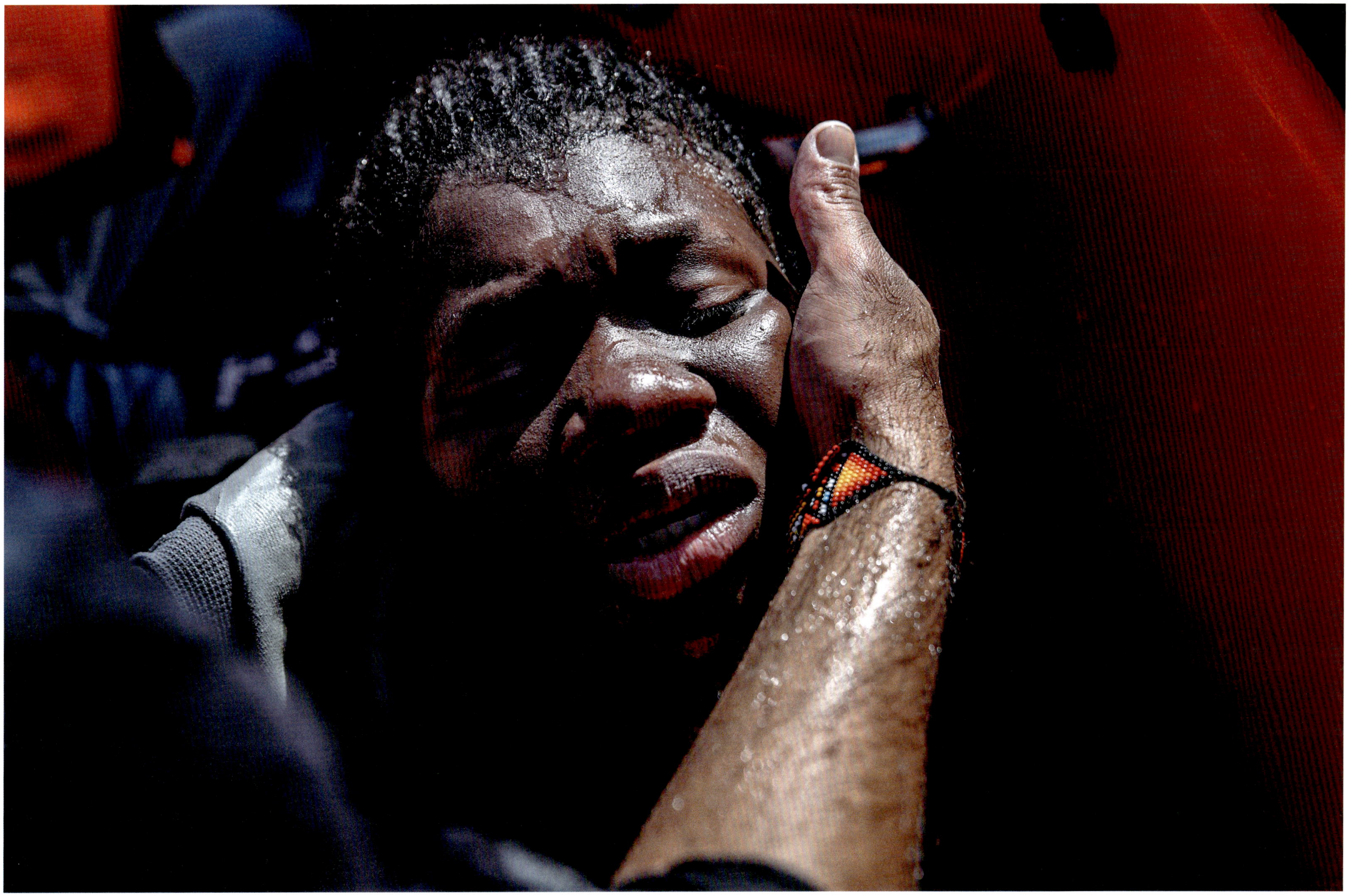

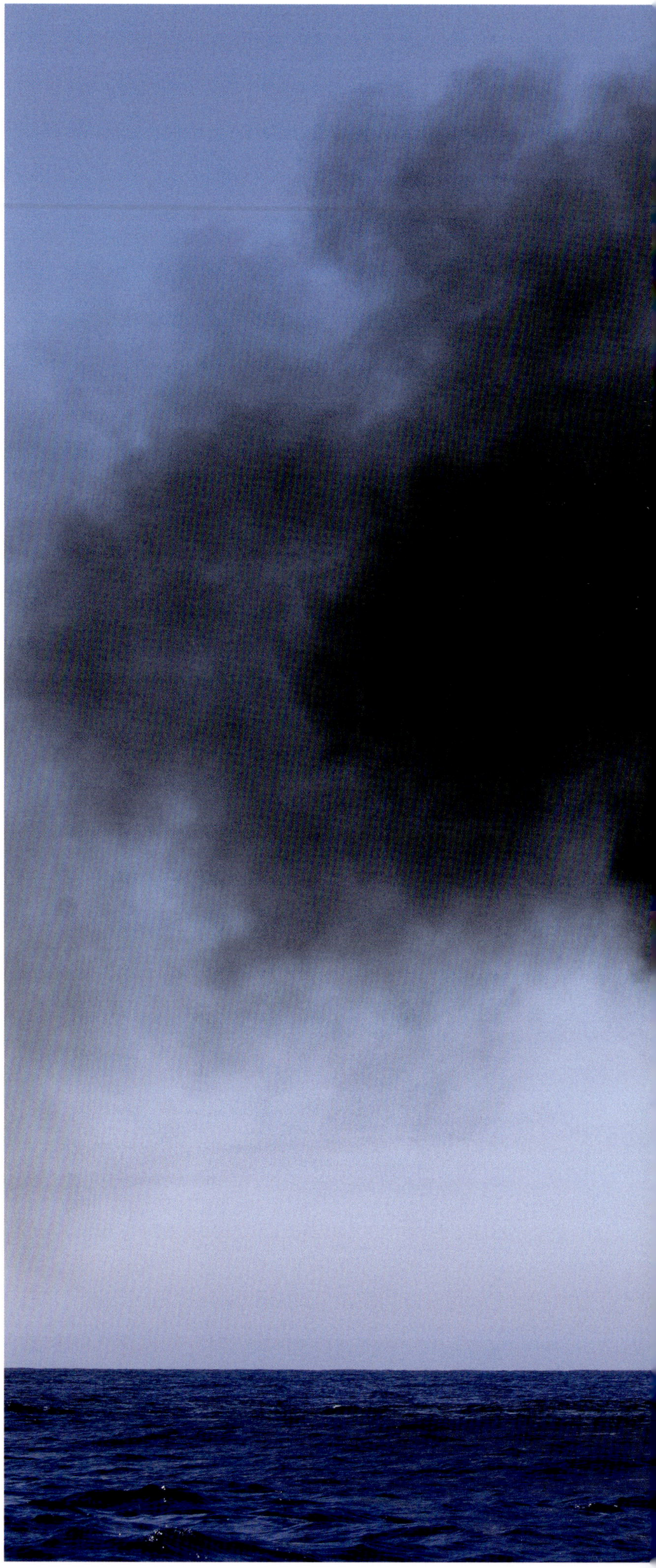

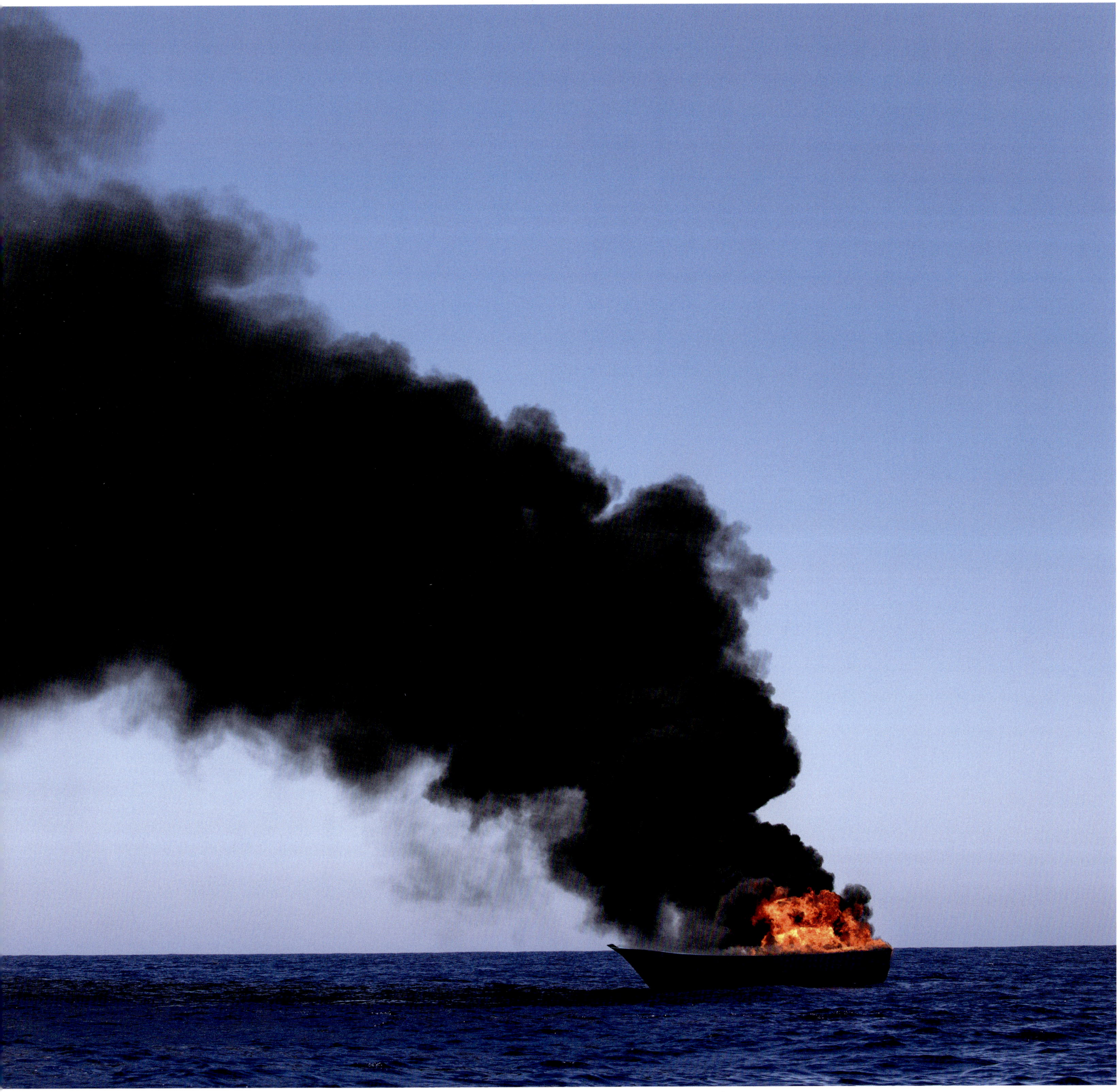

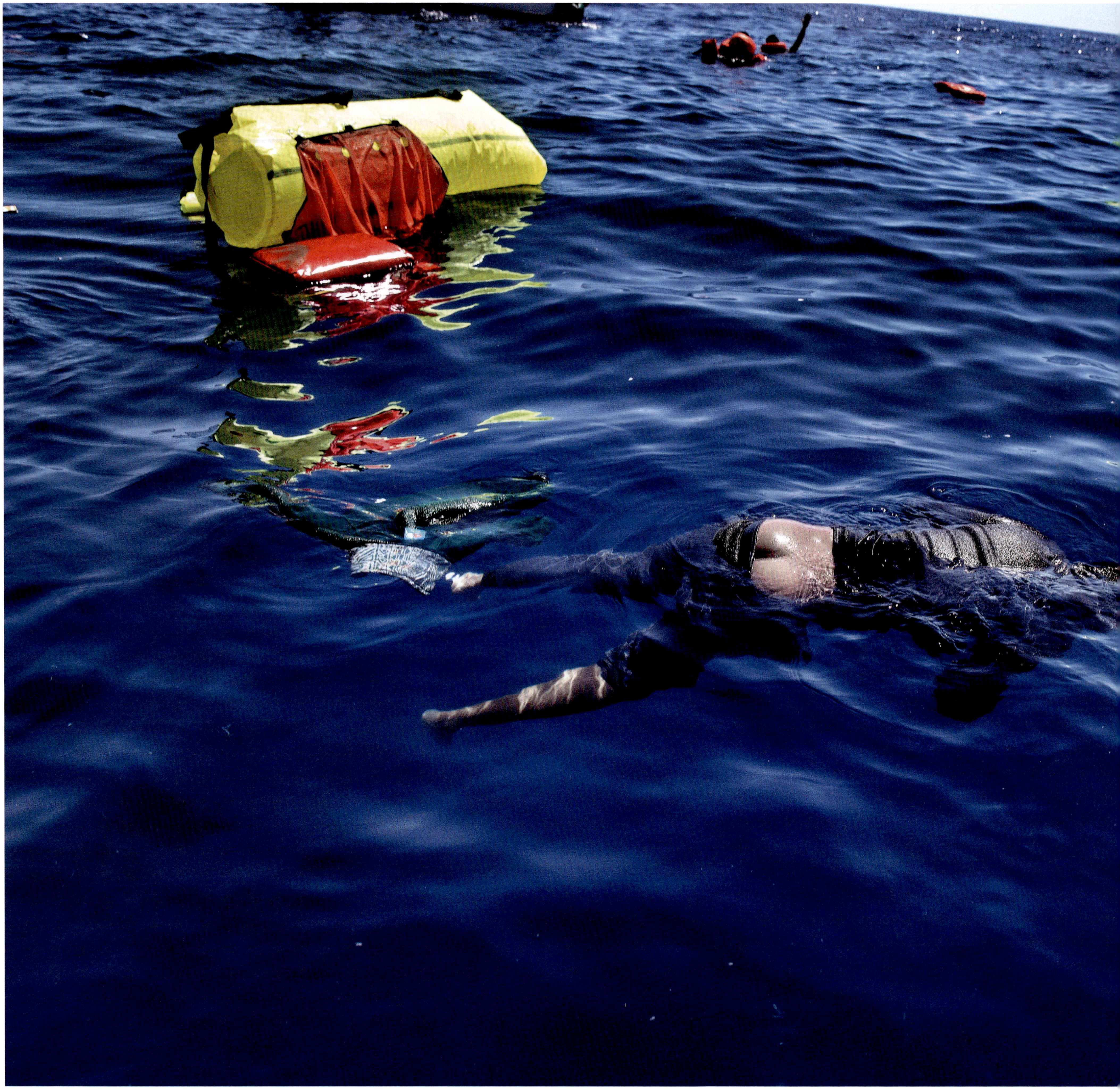

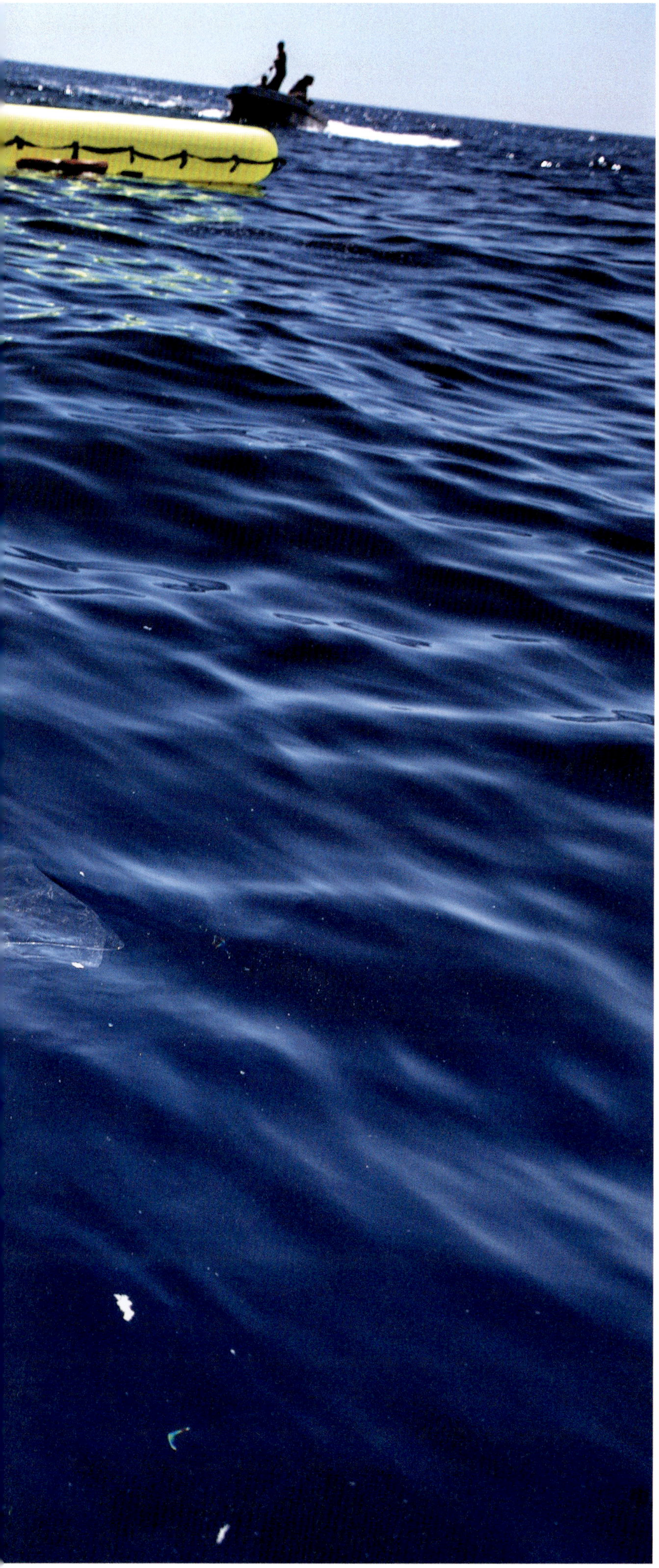

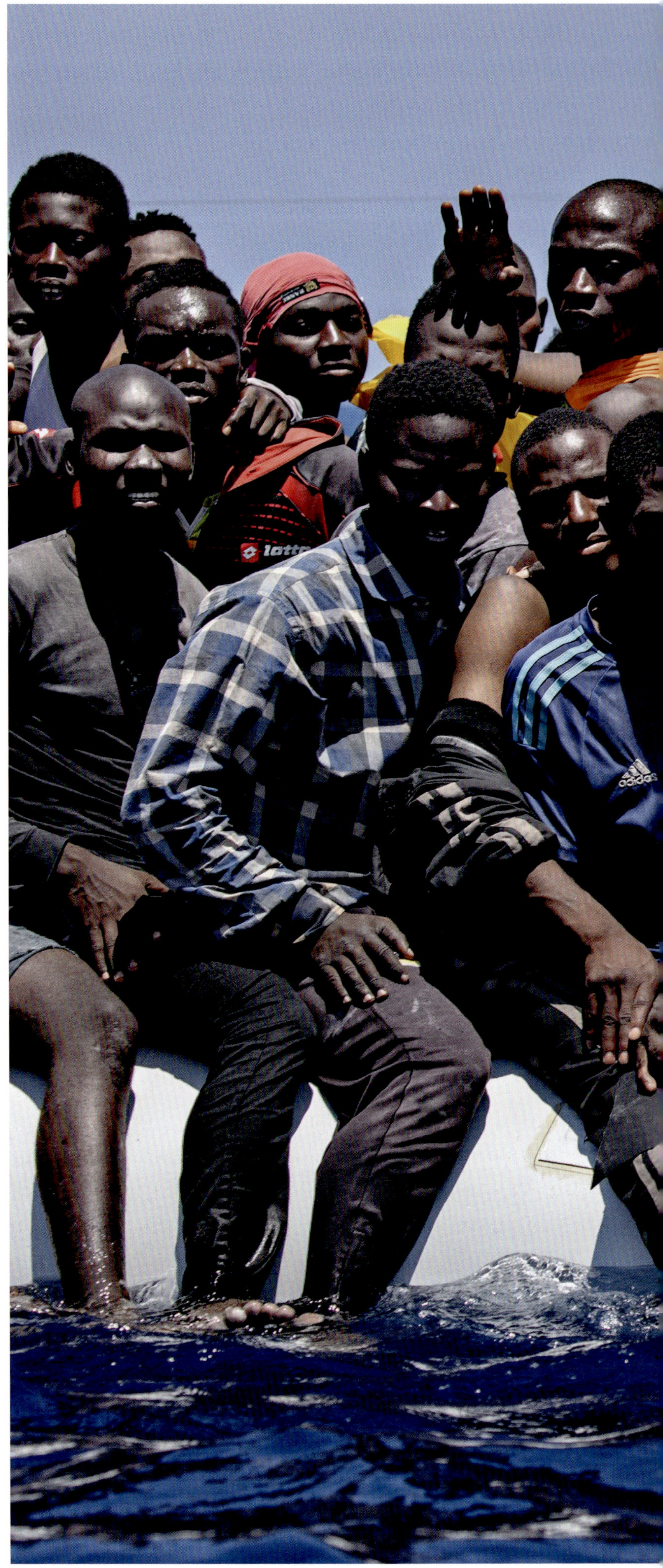

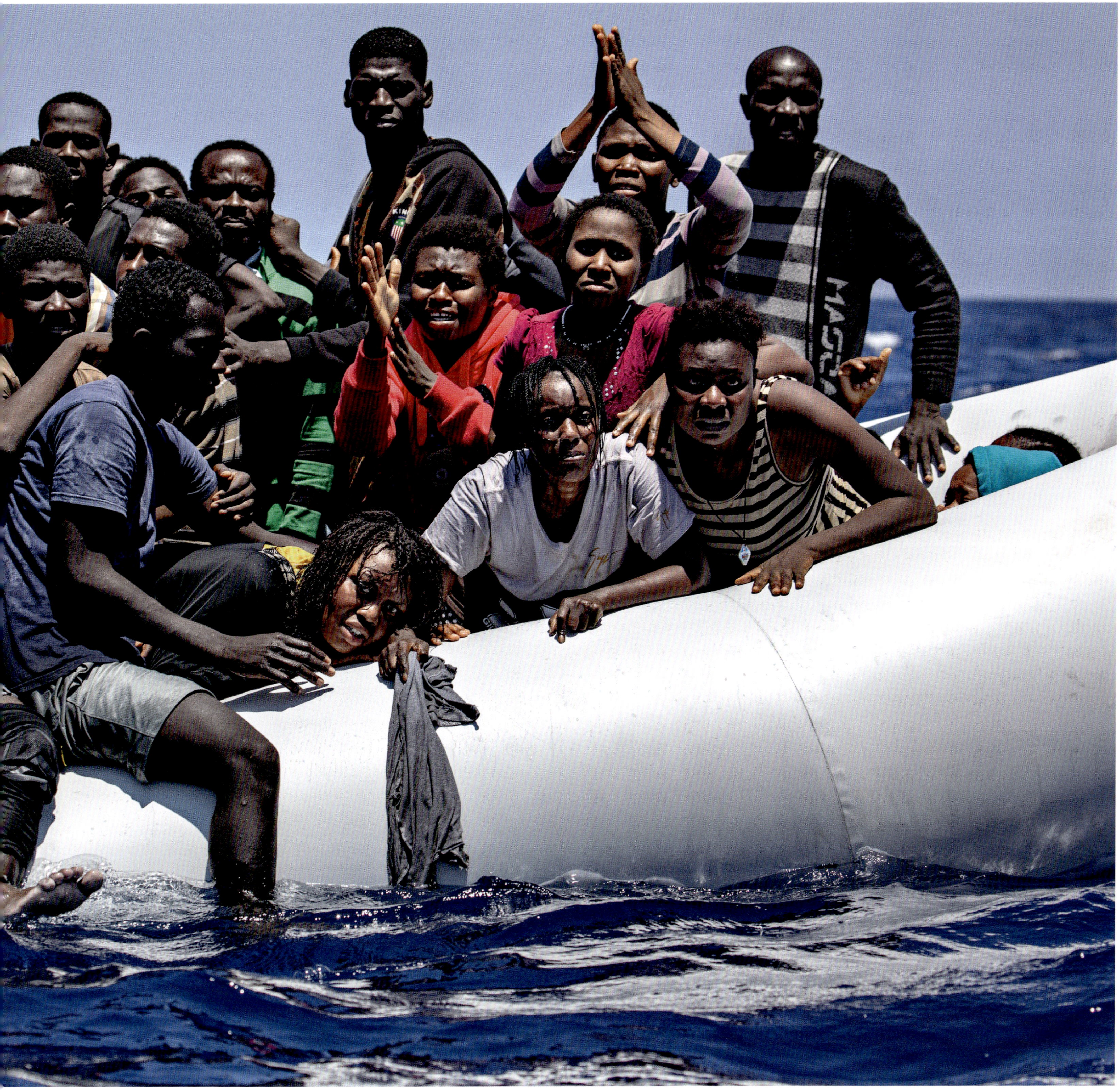

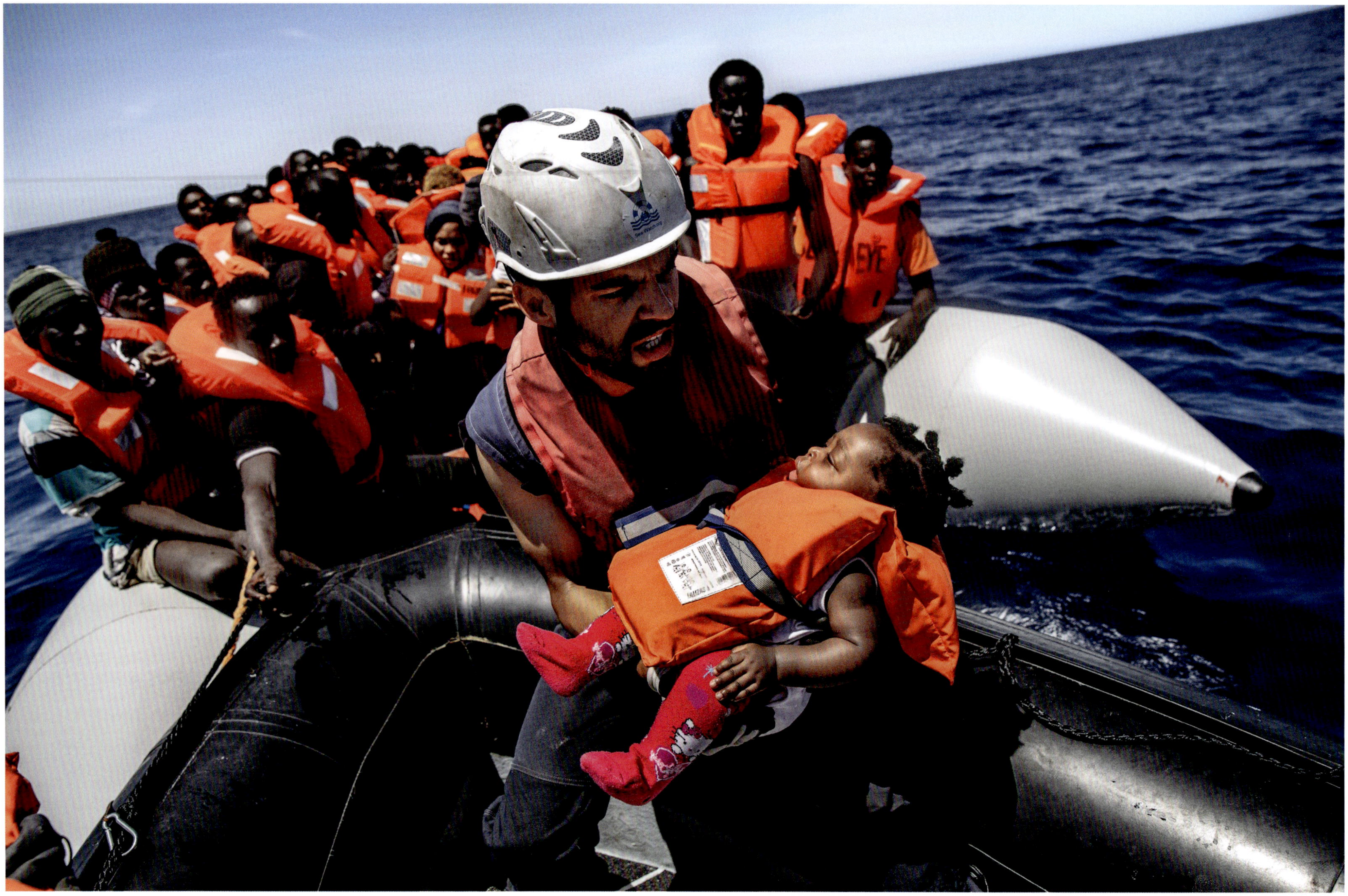

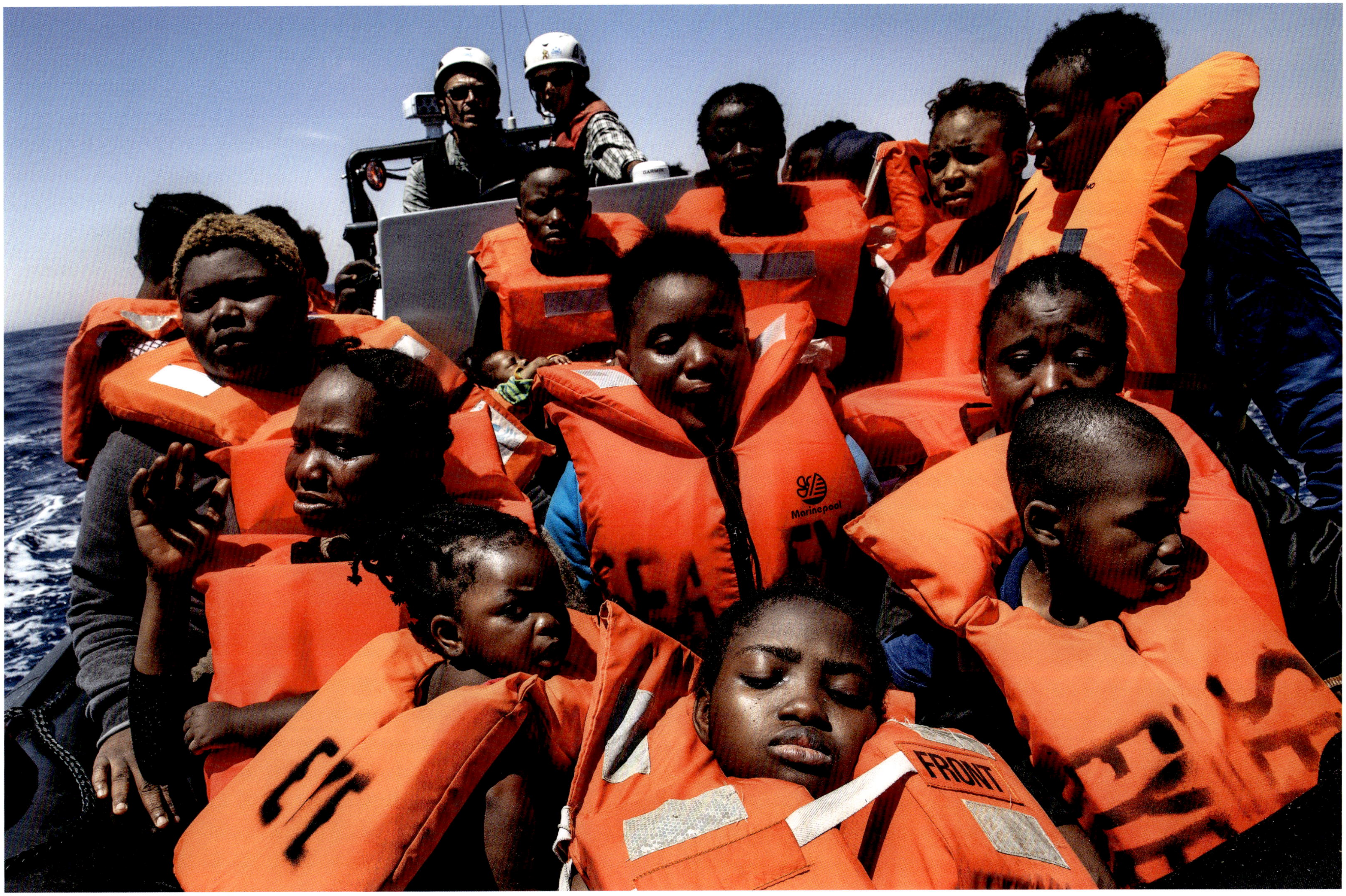
Marinepool
FRONT

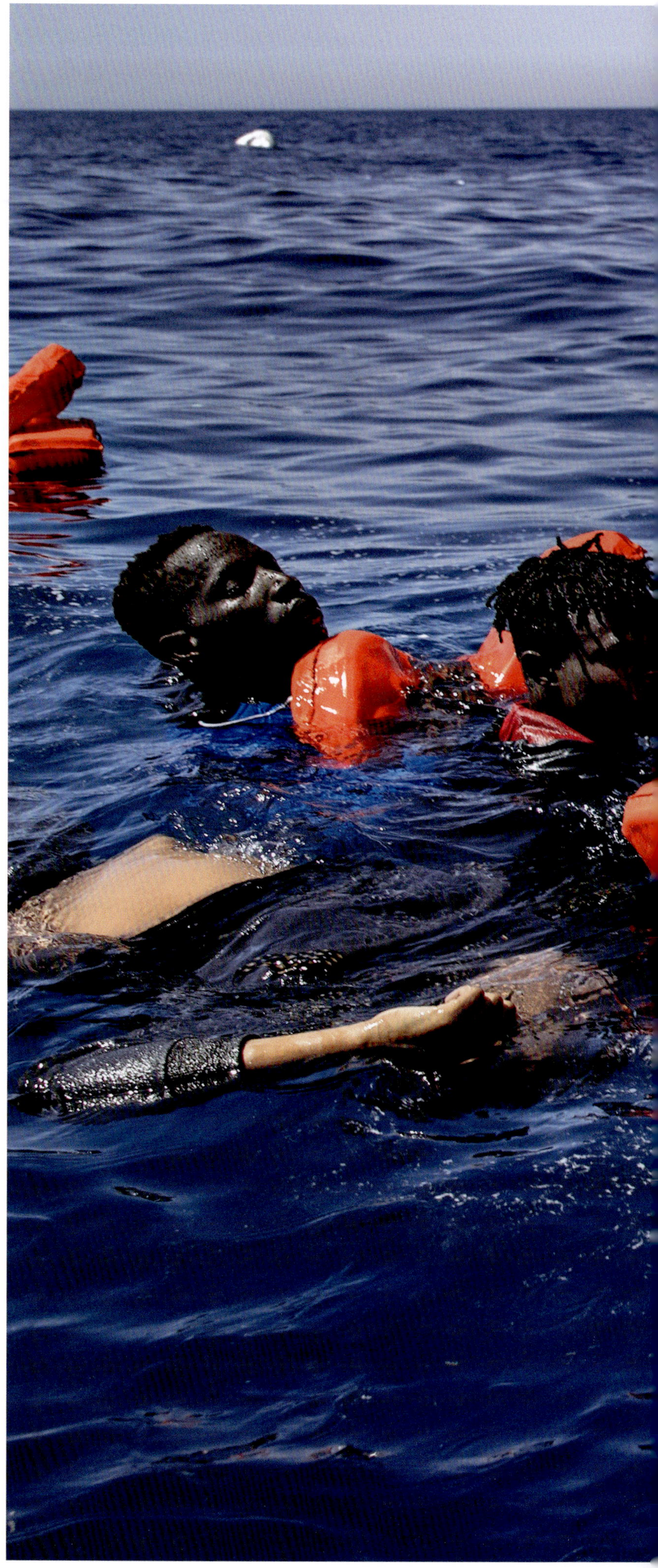

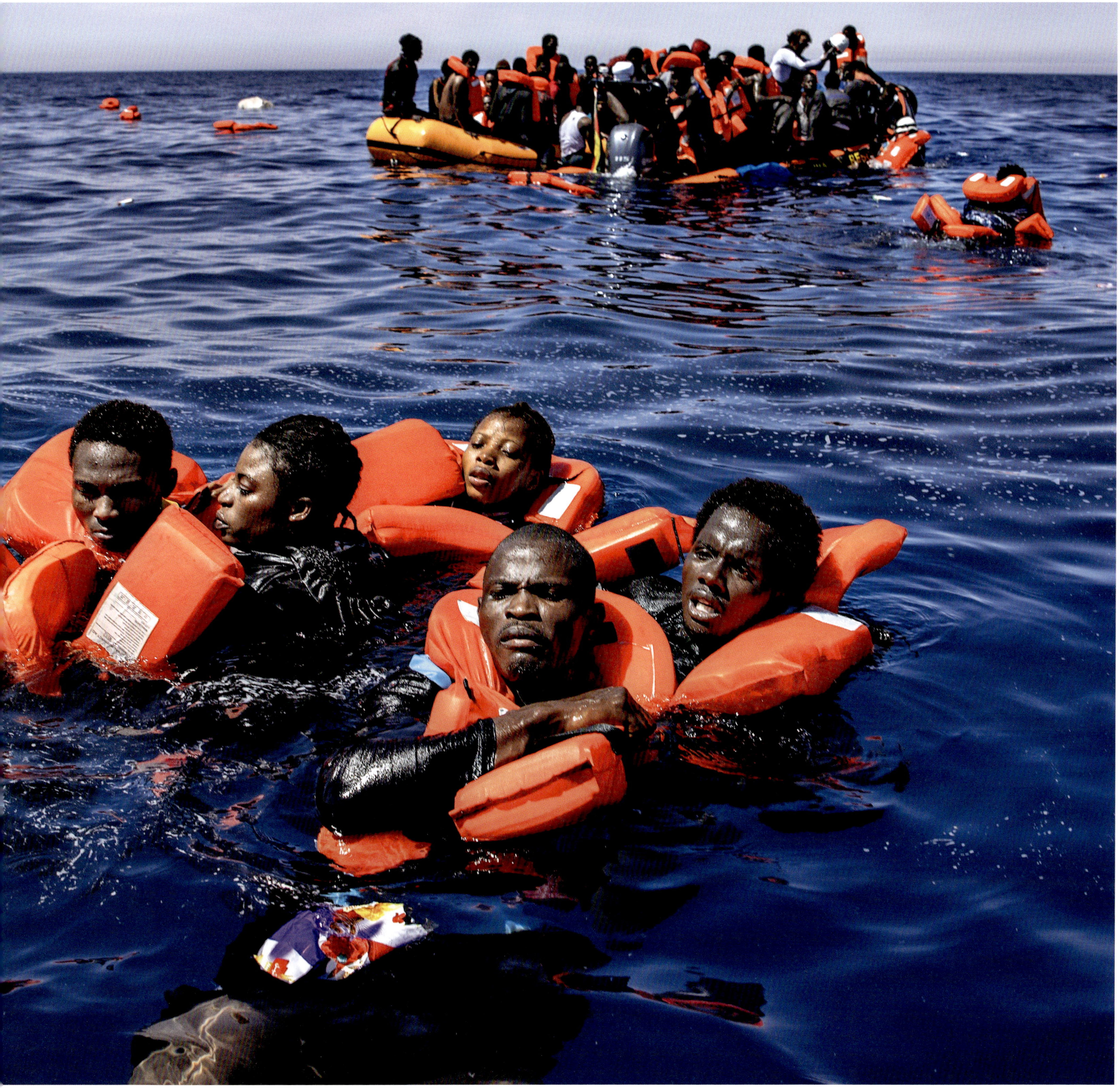

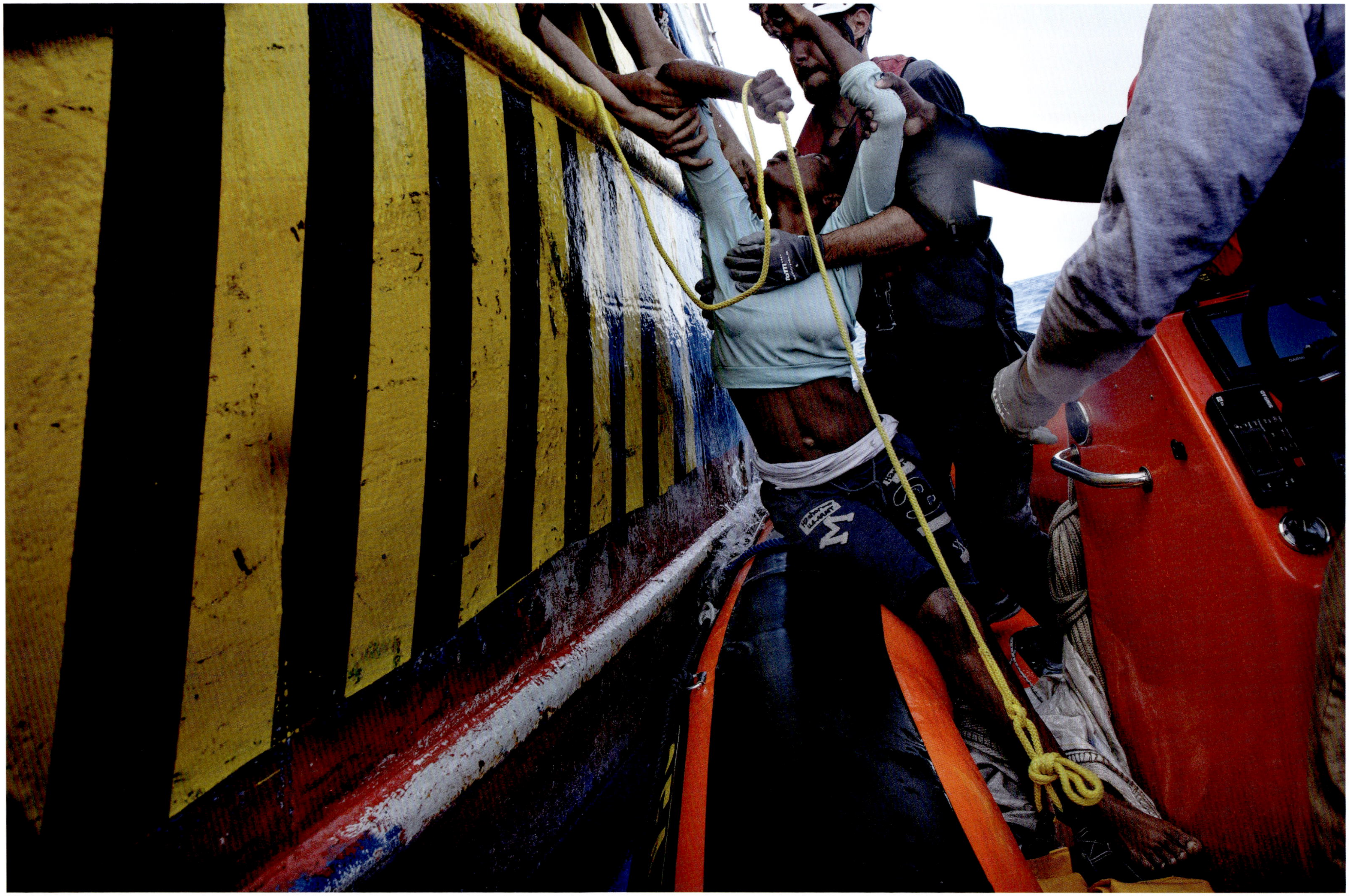

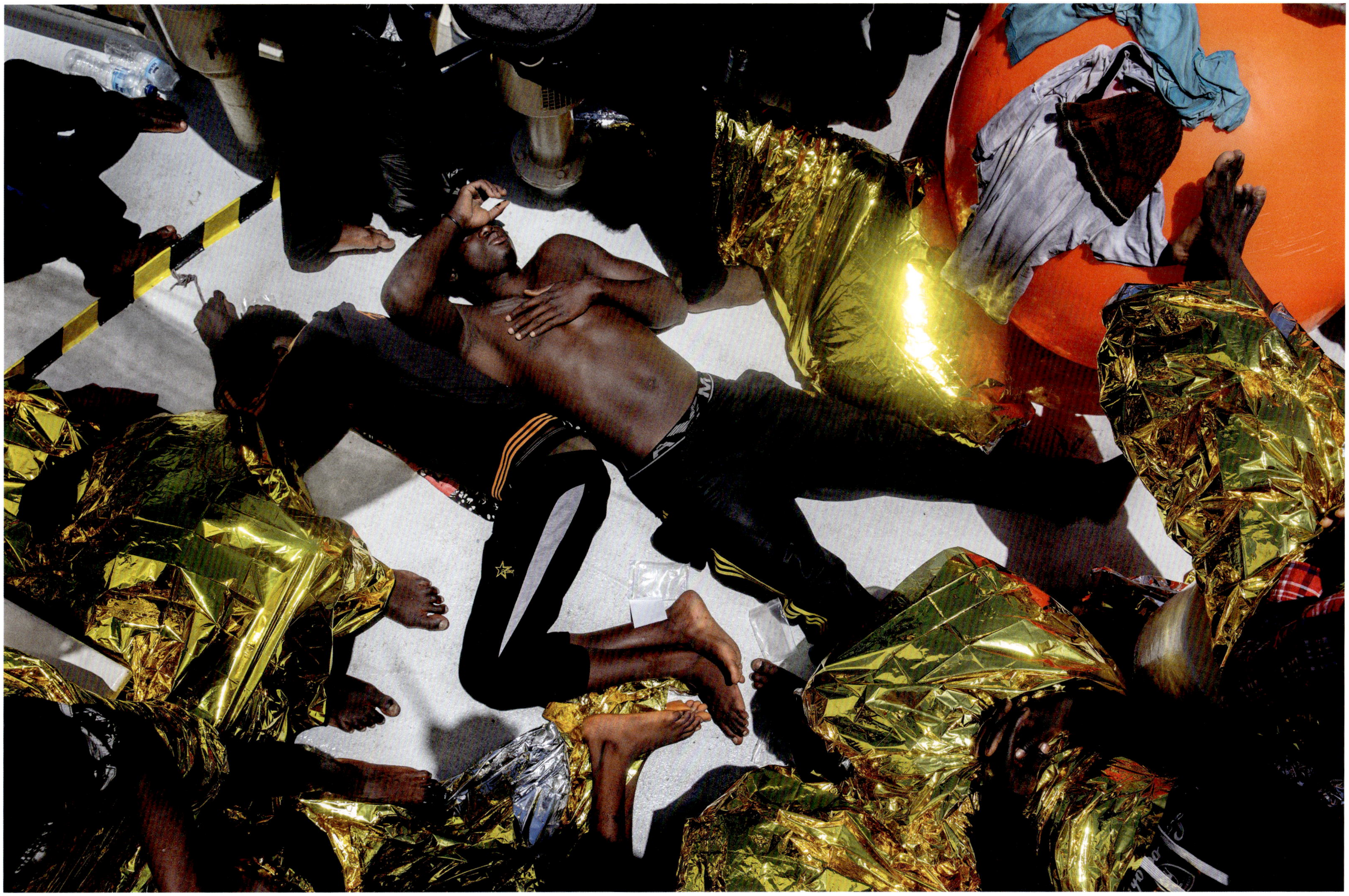

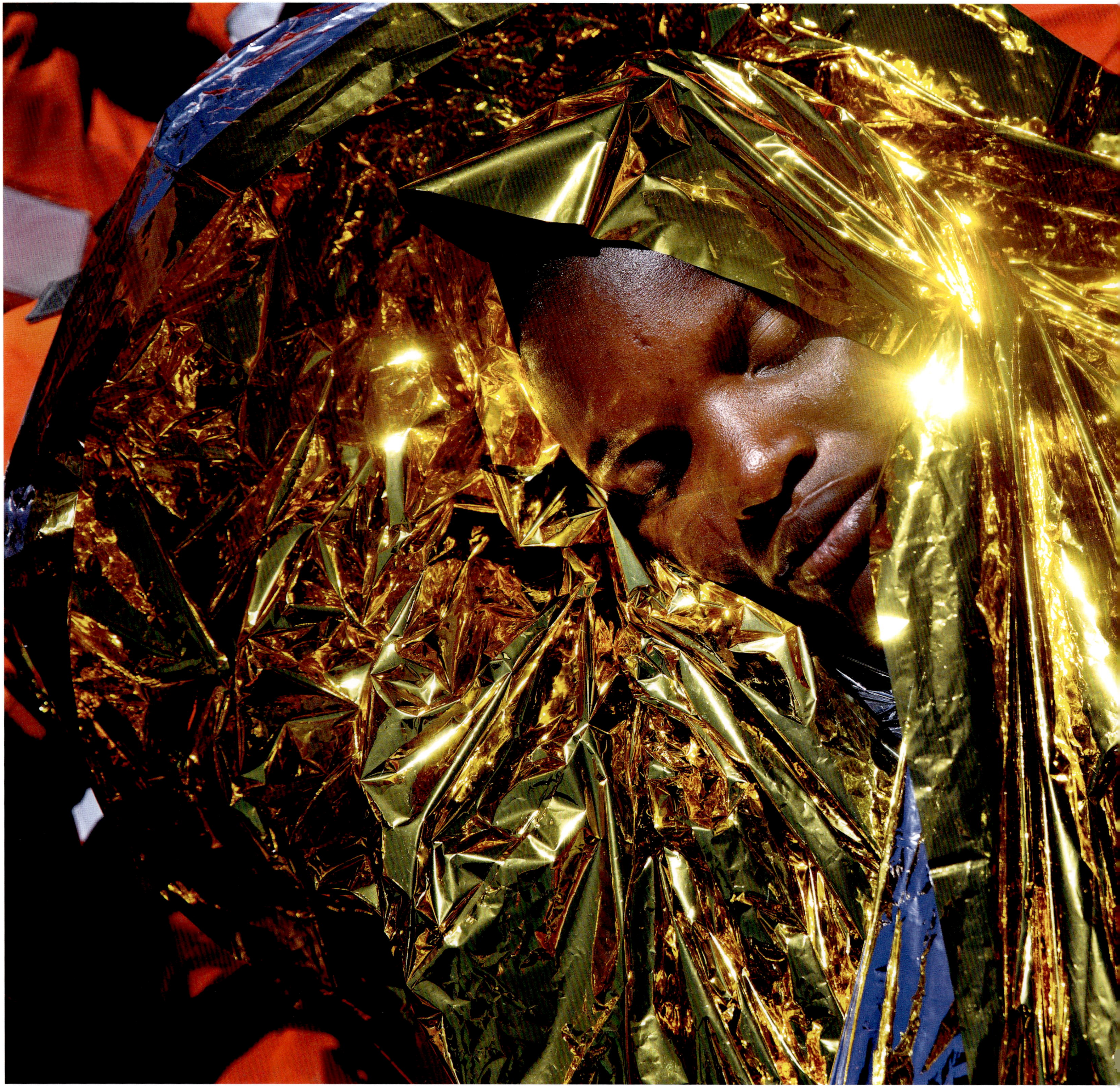

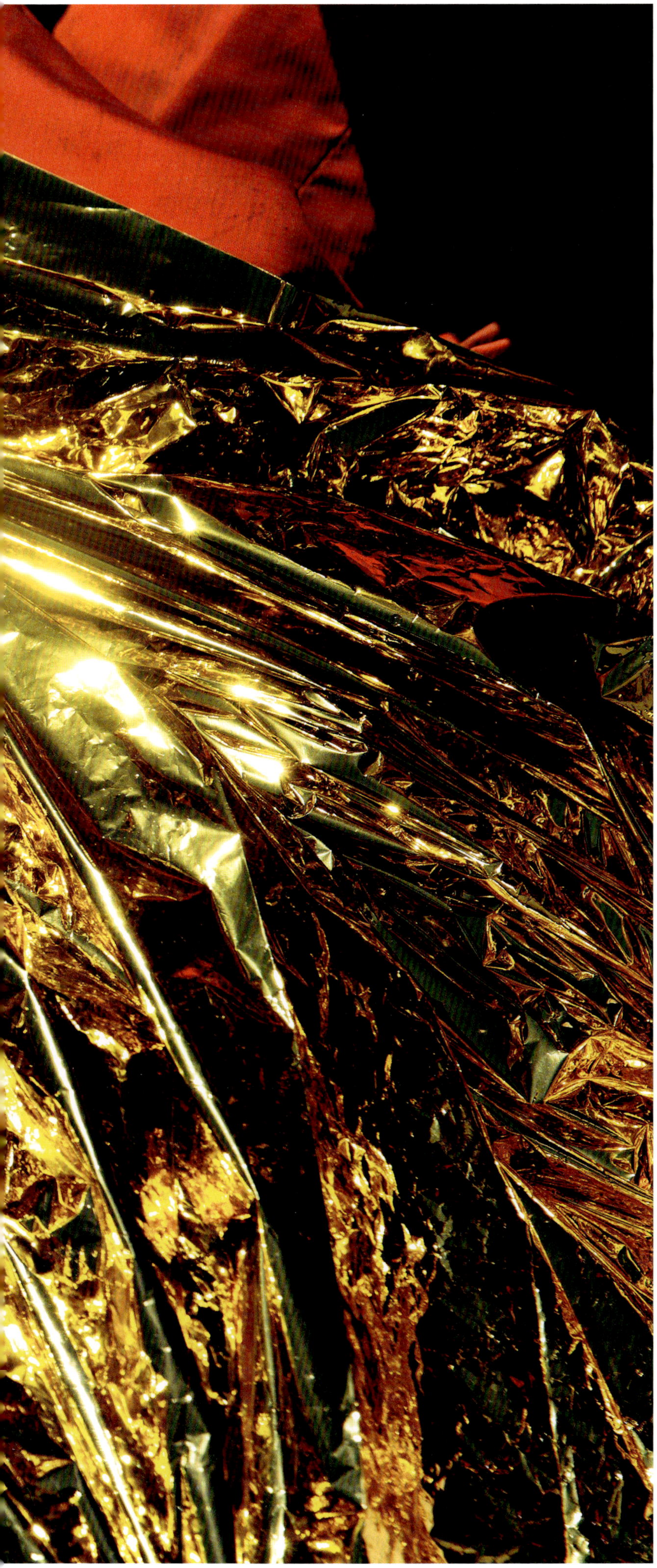

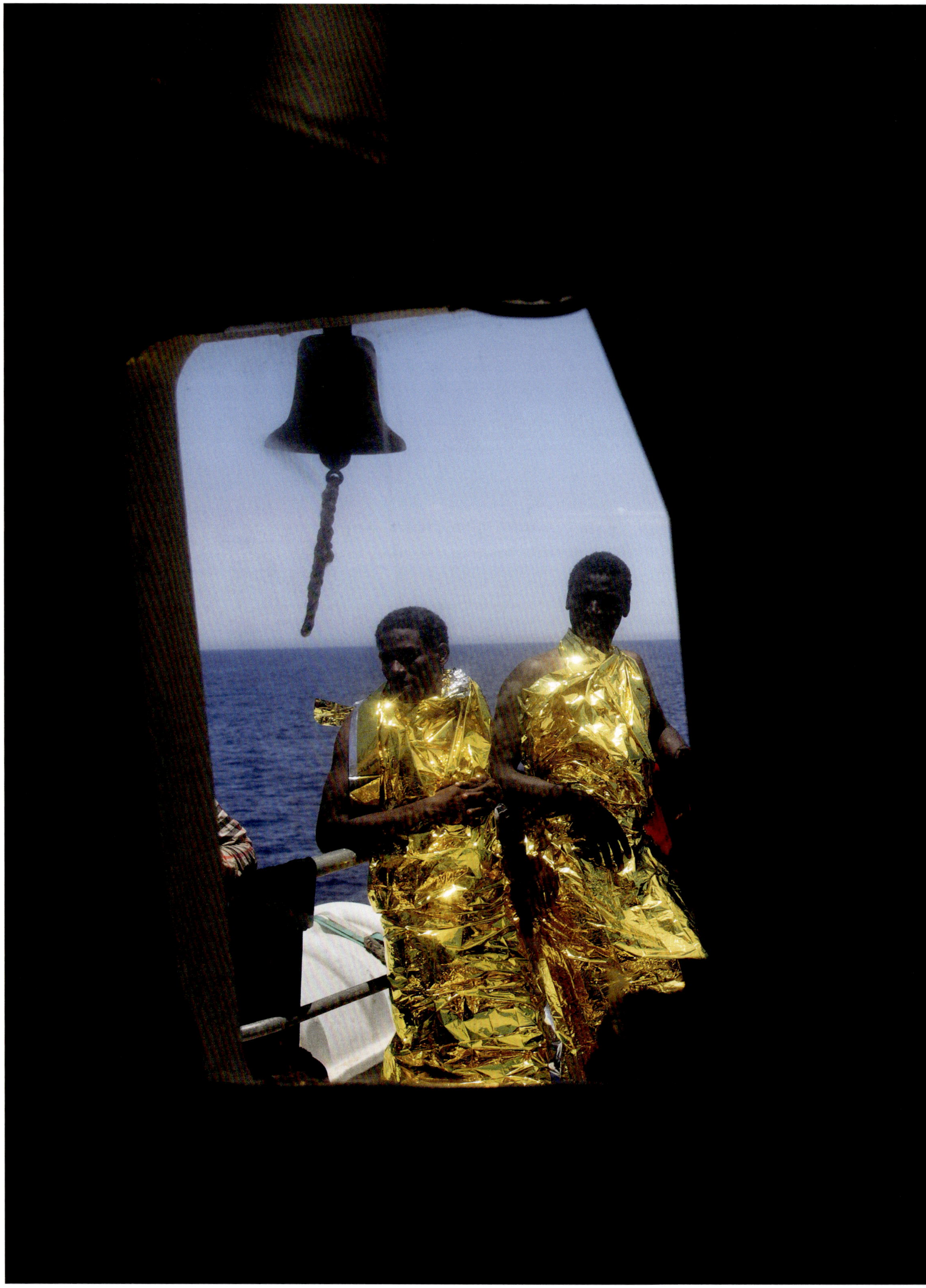

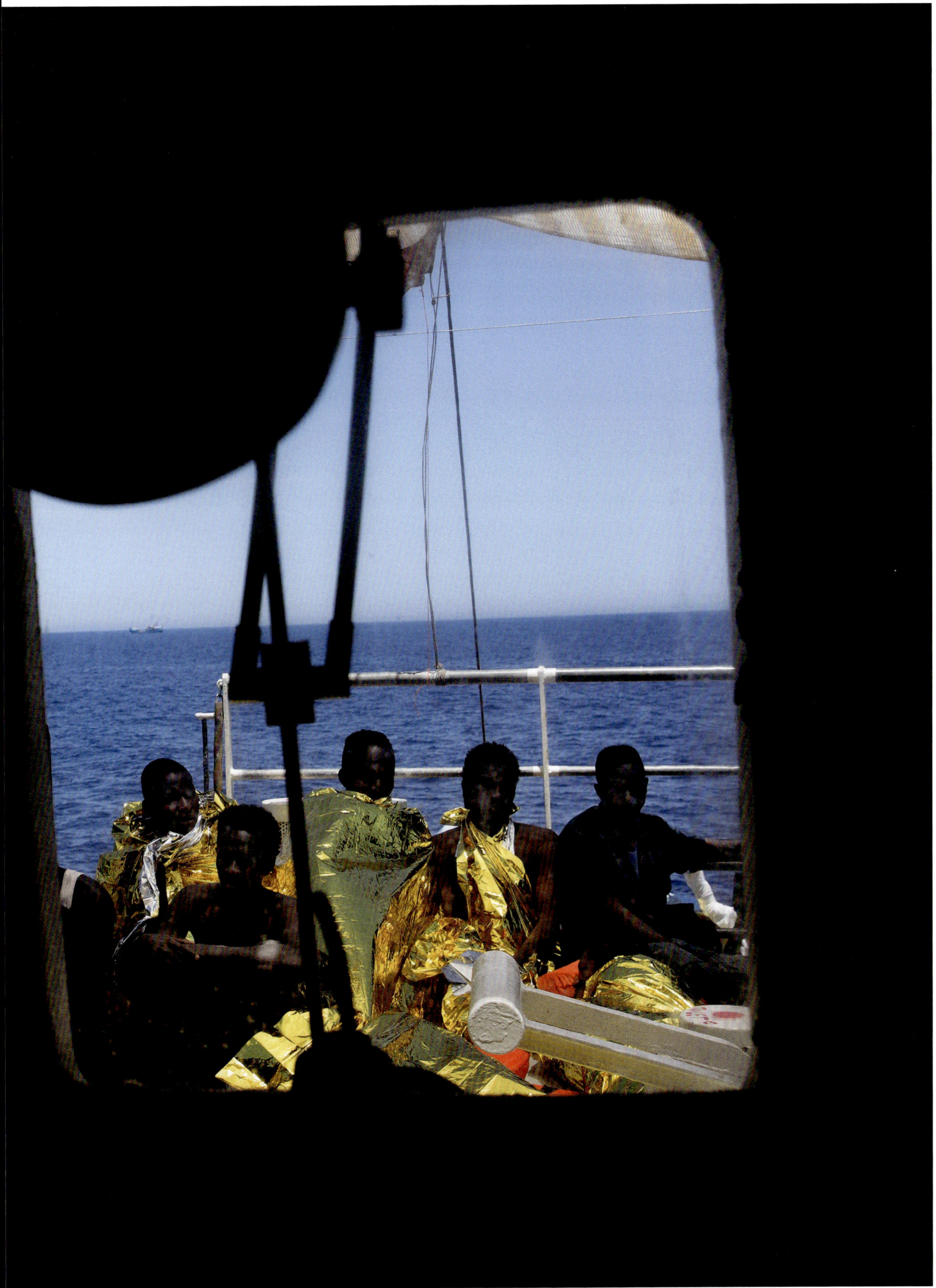

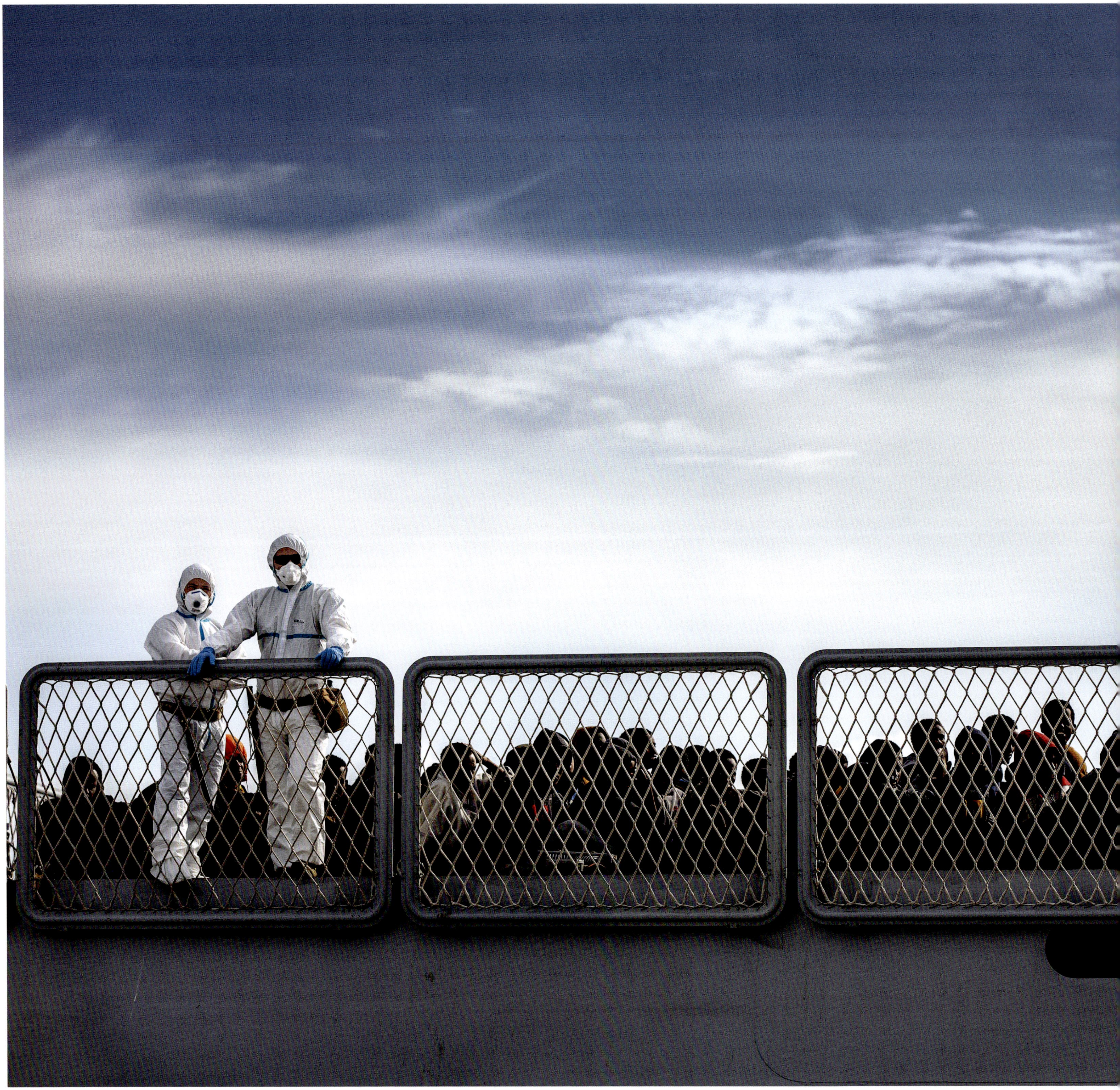

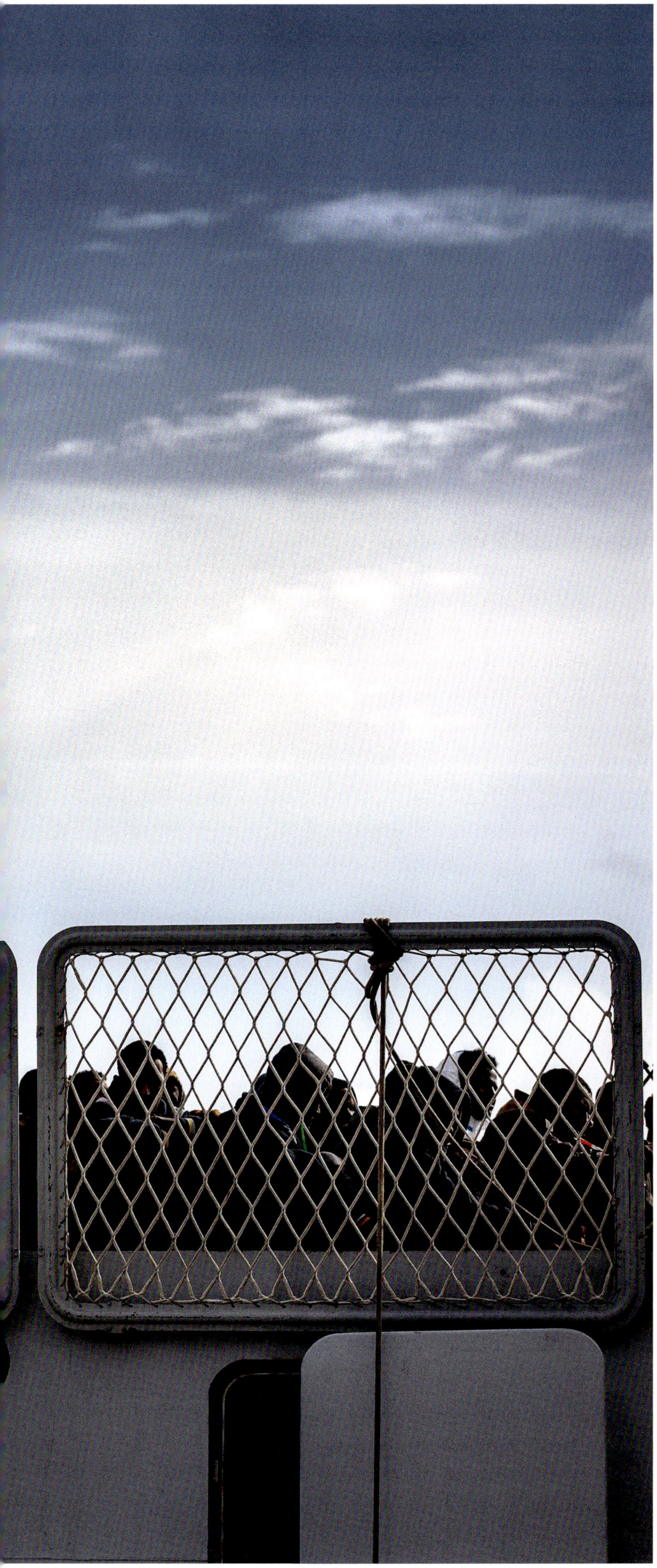

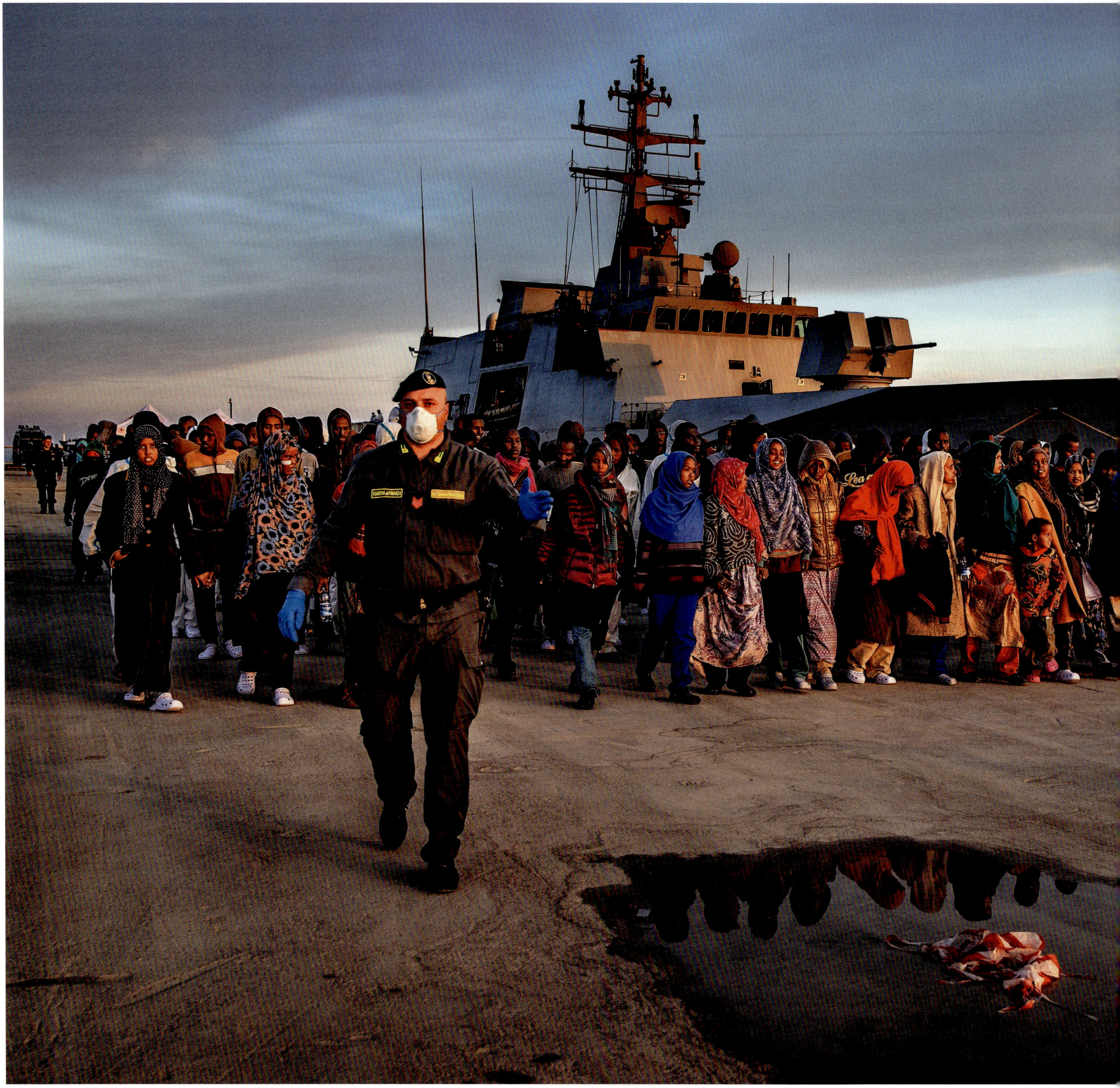

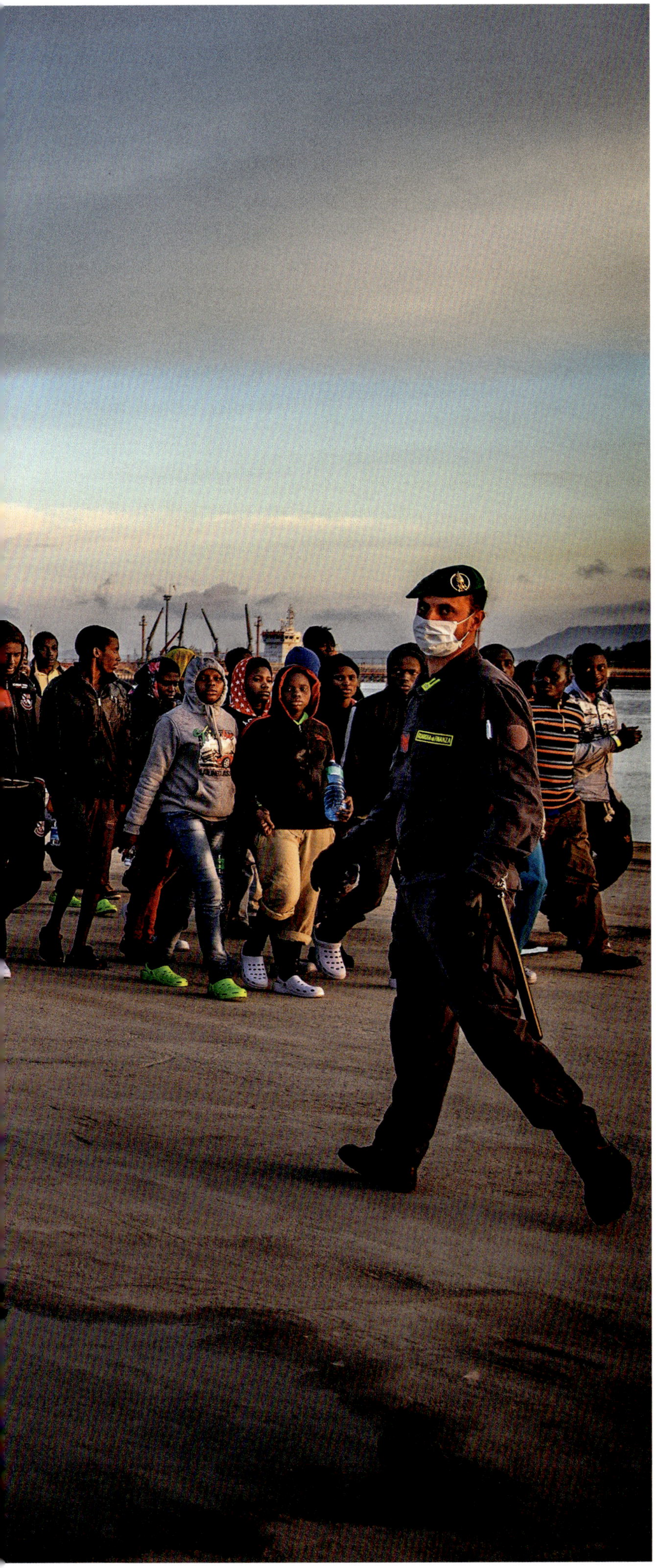

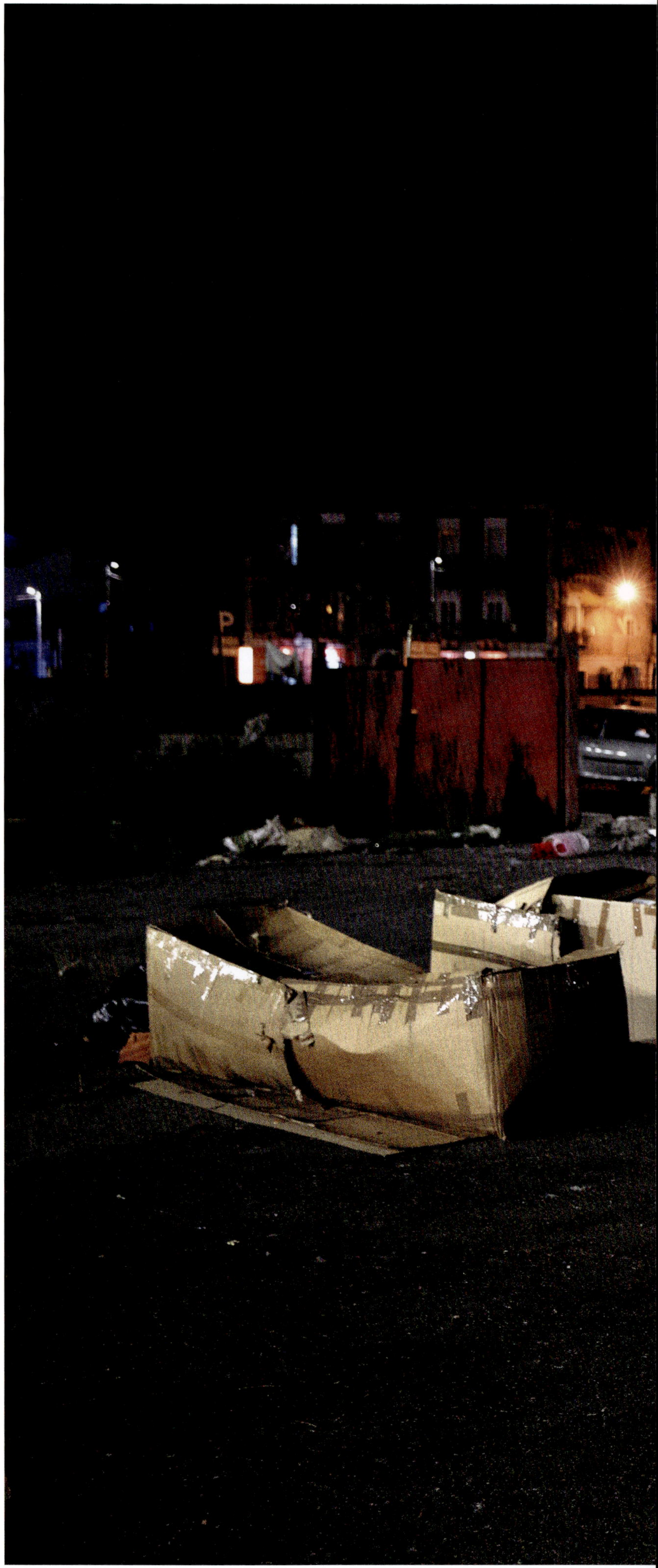

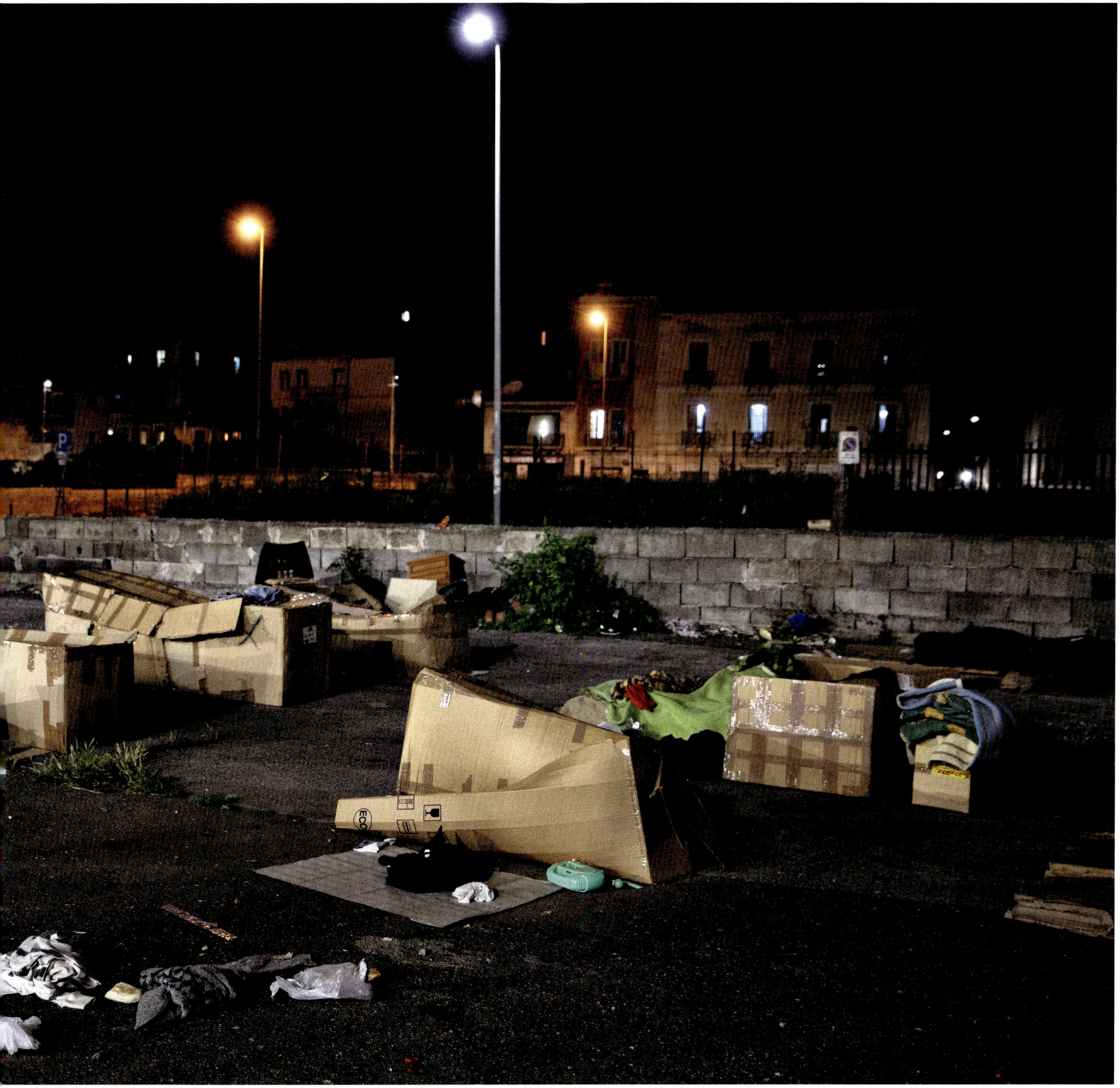

Although the EU entered into agreements with Turkey in 2015 and 2016 to stop the stream of people coming to Greece, in 2018 refugees and migrants are still crossing the Aegean Sea from Turkey to the Greek islands.

On Lesbos people gather in camps near the main city on the island, Mytilini. The largest is the Moria camp, a former military camp converted into a reception centre in 2015 and with space for around 2,800 asylum seekers. In January 2018 there were between 5,000 and 6,000 people. There is no access to hot water and the electricity supply is unstable. Asylum seekers stay in overpopulated accommodation containers or in tents. The toilets are overflowing with faeces. Sometimes there is not enough food for everyone. Fist fights, knife stabbings and suicide attempts are a part of everyday life at the camp.

Due to the cramped and poor conditions, a lot of people move to the other side of the barbed-wire fence. Here, most of them live in improvised tents in an olive orchard. This part of the camp is called the Olive Grove Camp and is later known as 'the Jungle'.

Some of the asylum seekers have been stuck at the Moria camp for two years.

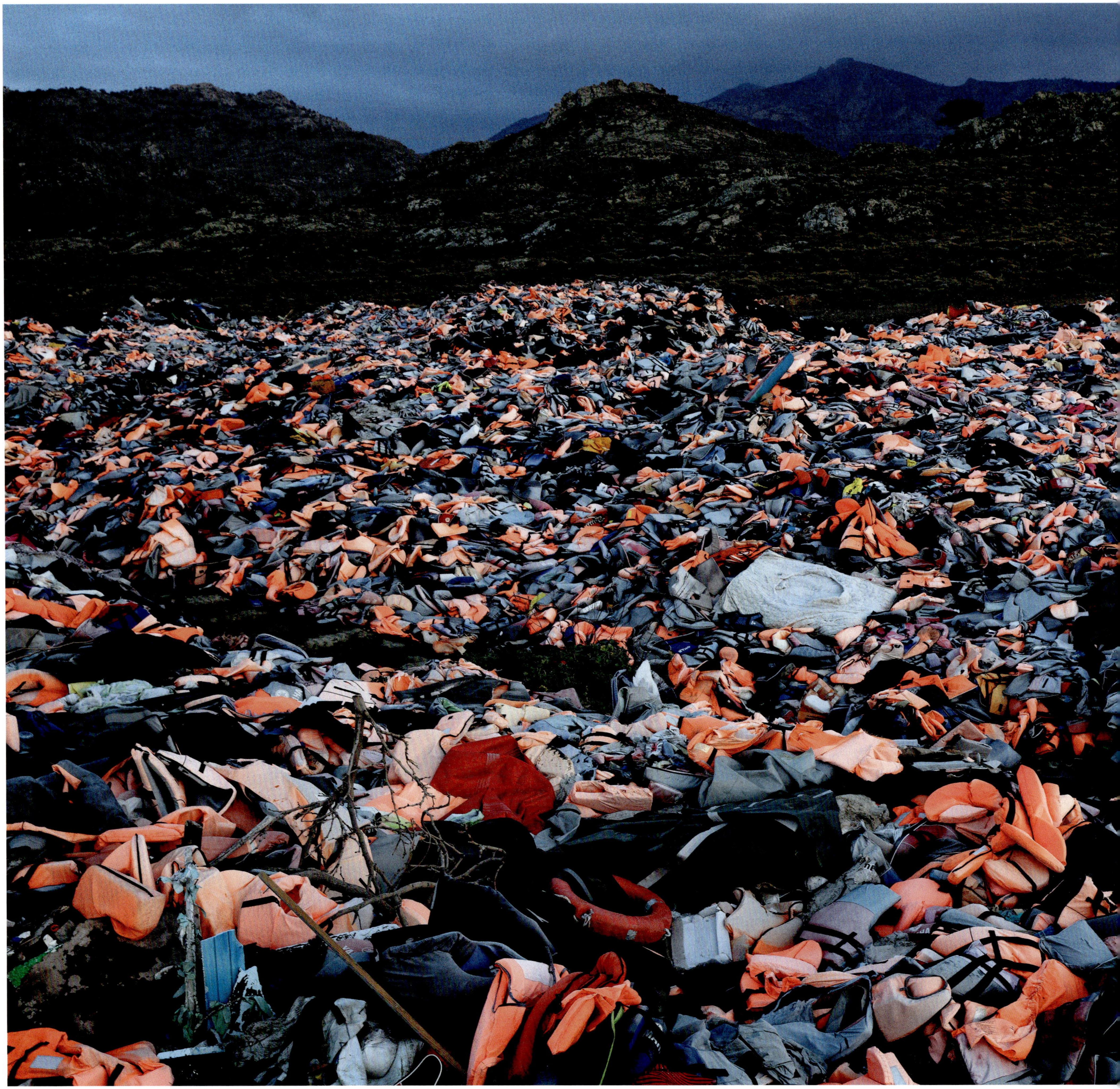

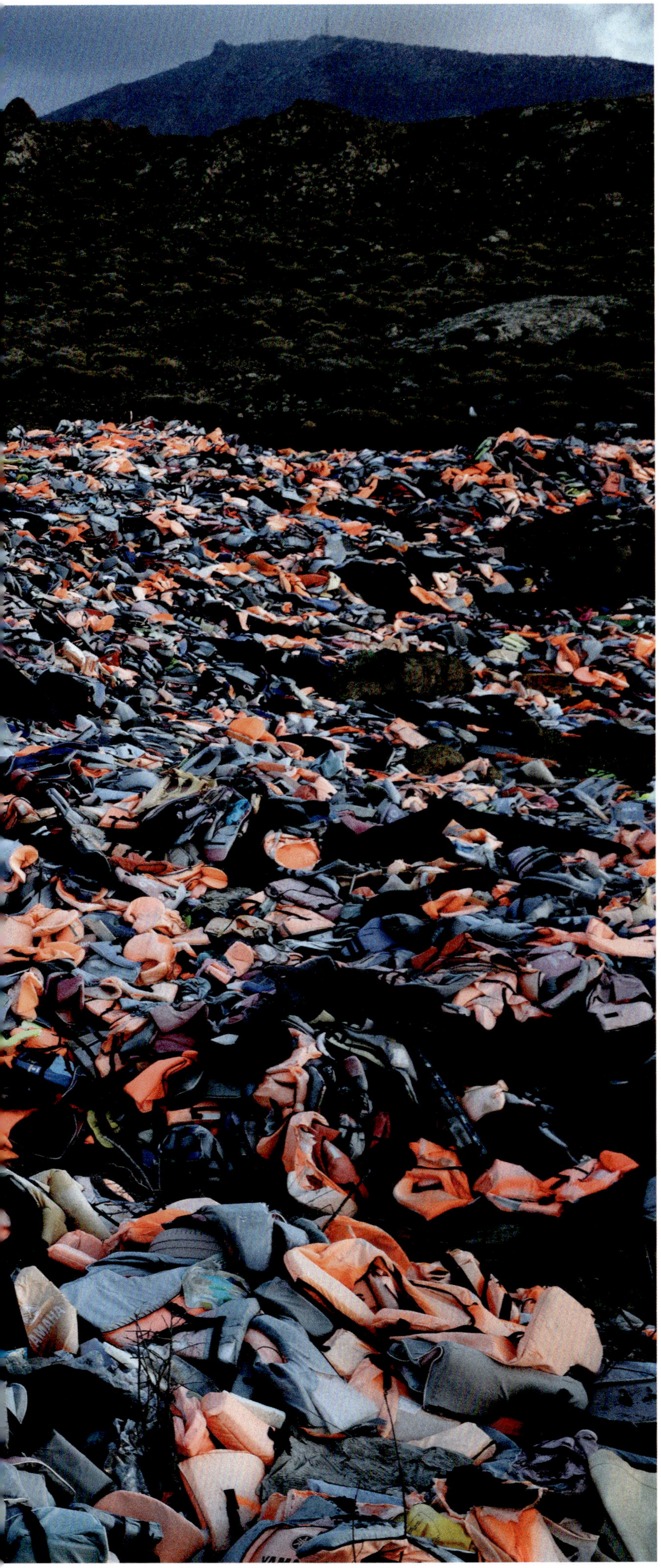

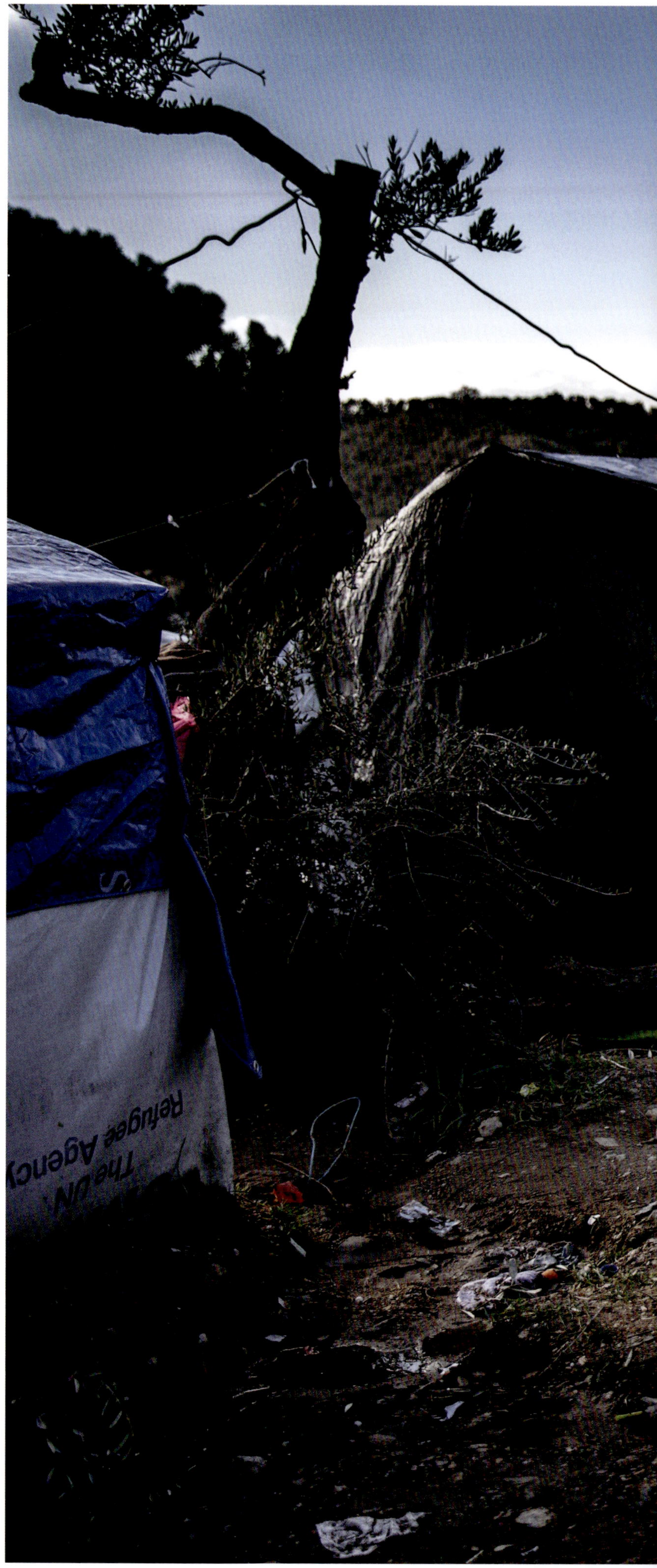

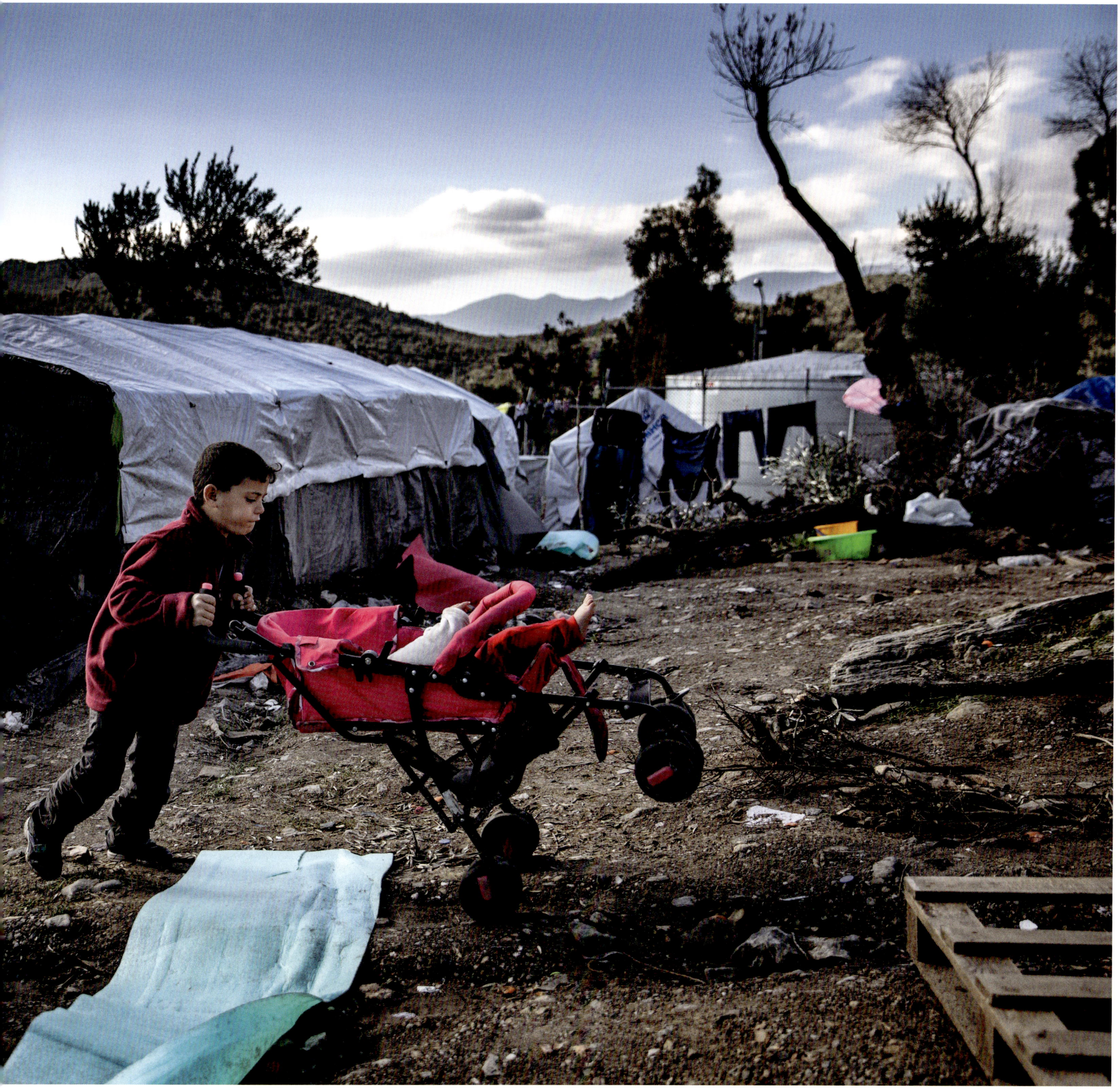

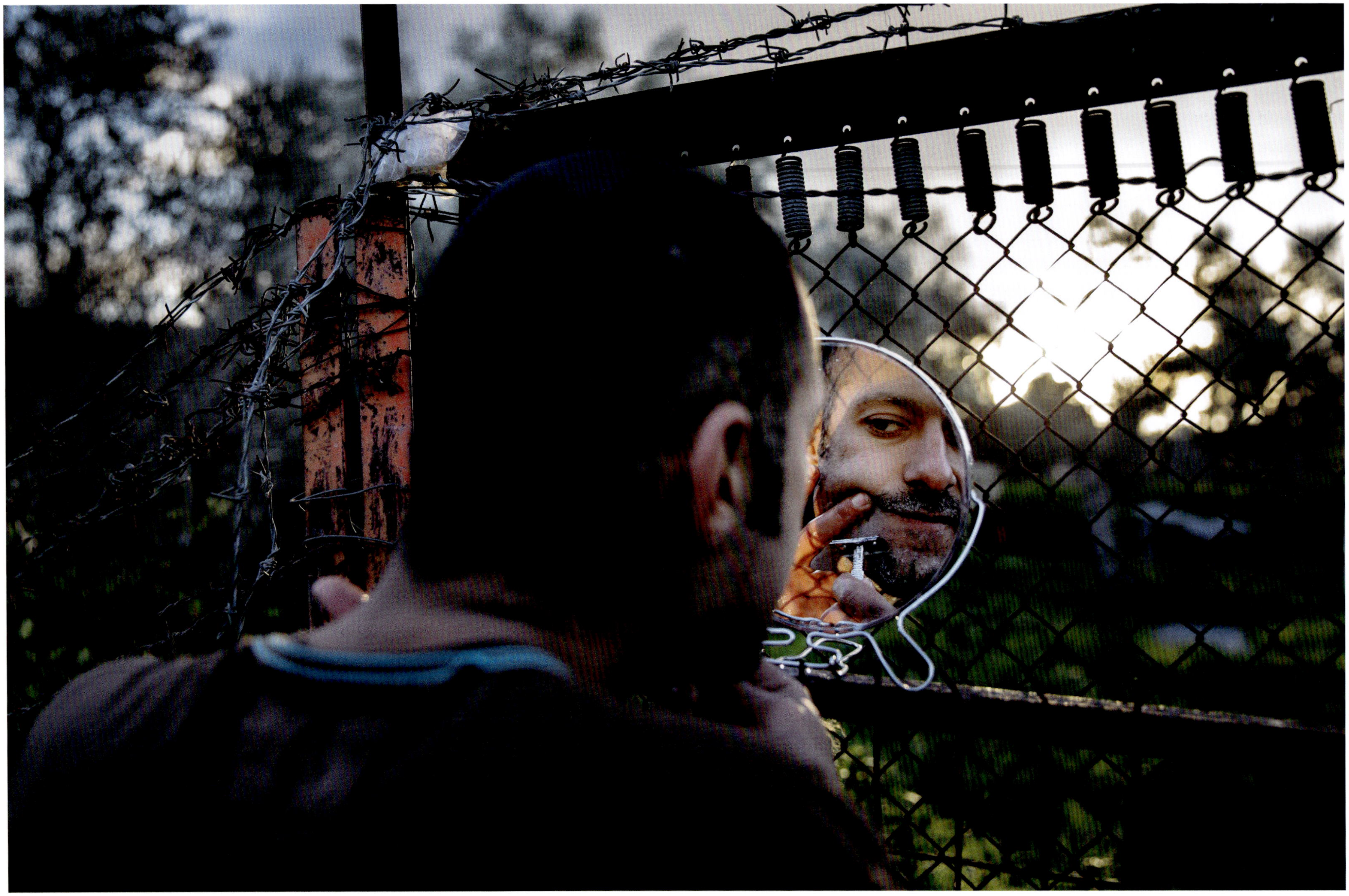

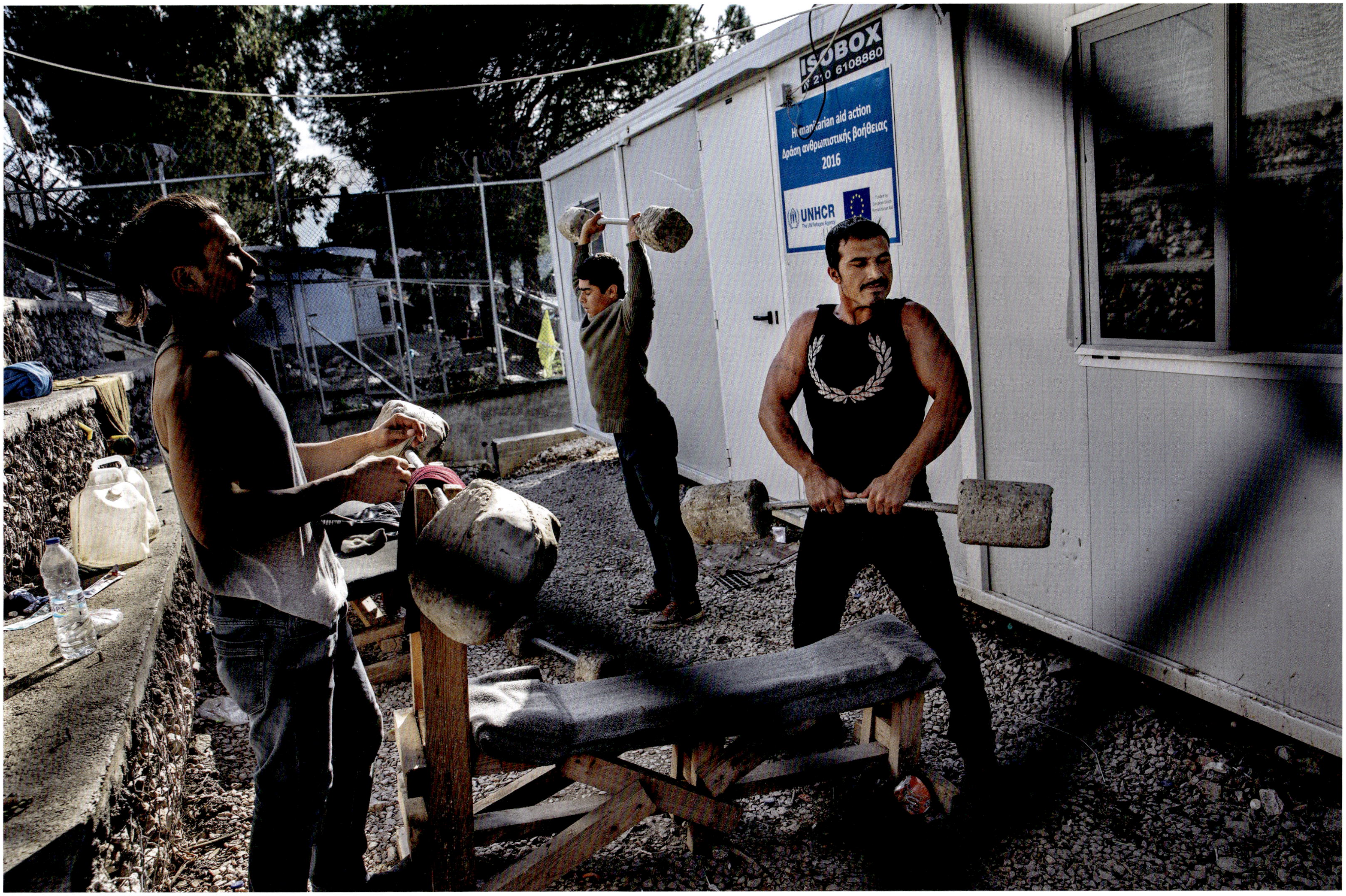
ISOBOX
210 6108880
Δράση ανθρωπιστικής βοήθειας
2016
UNHCR

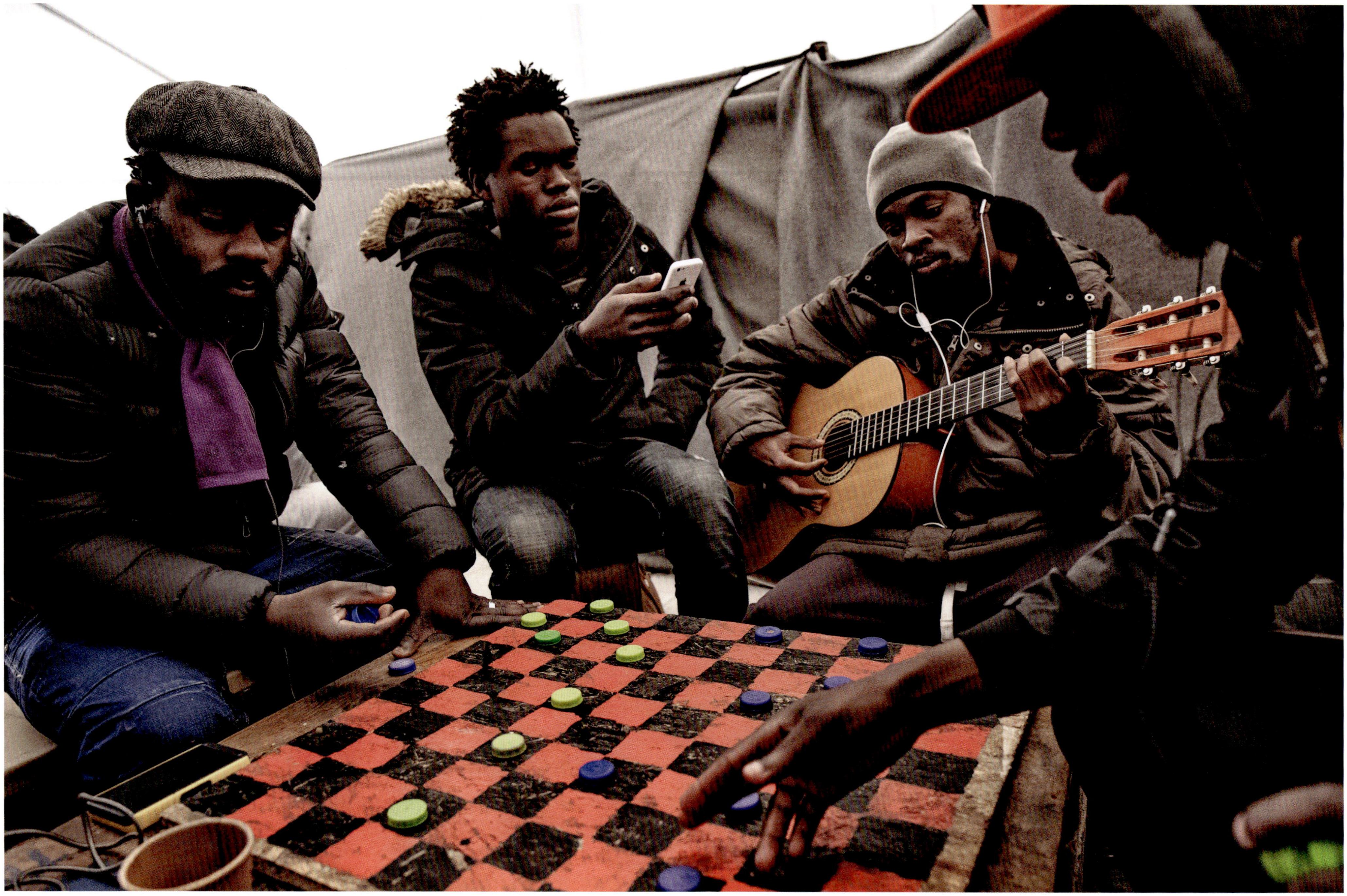

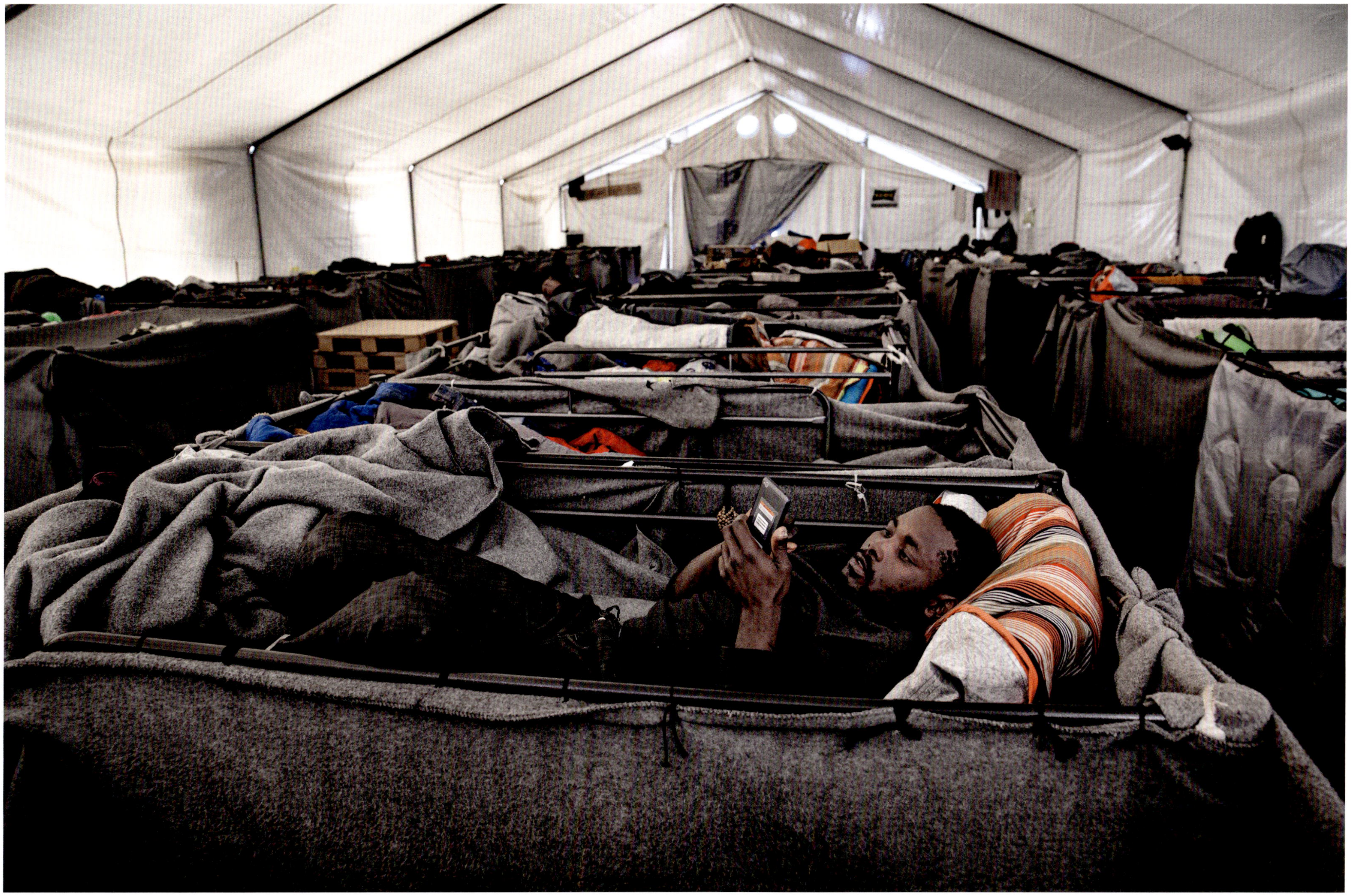

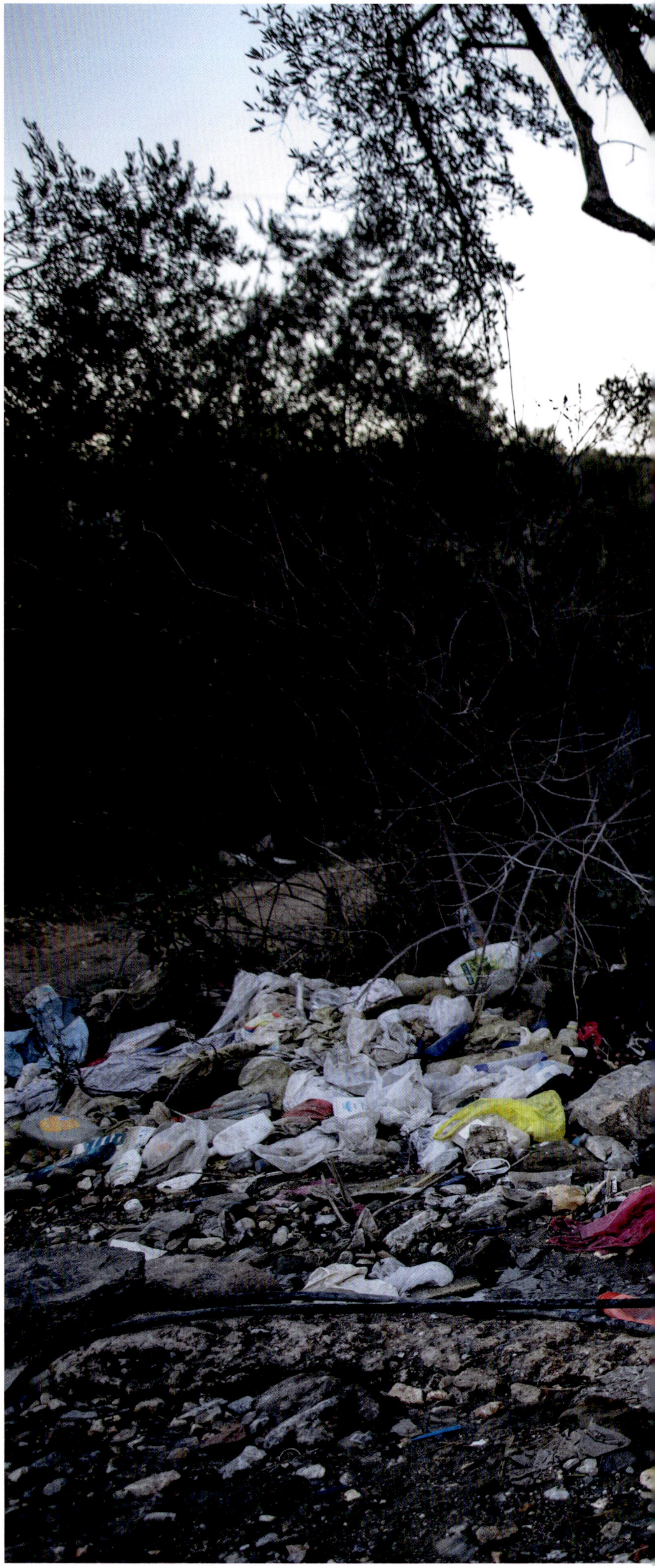

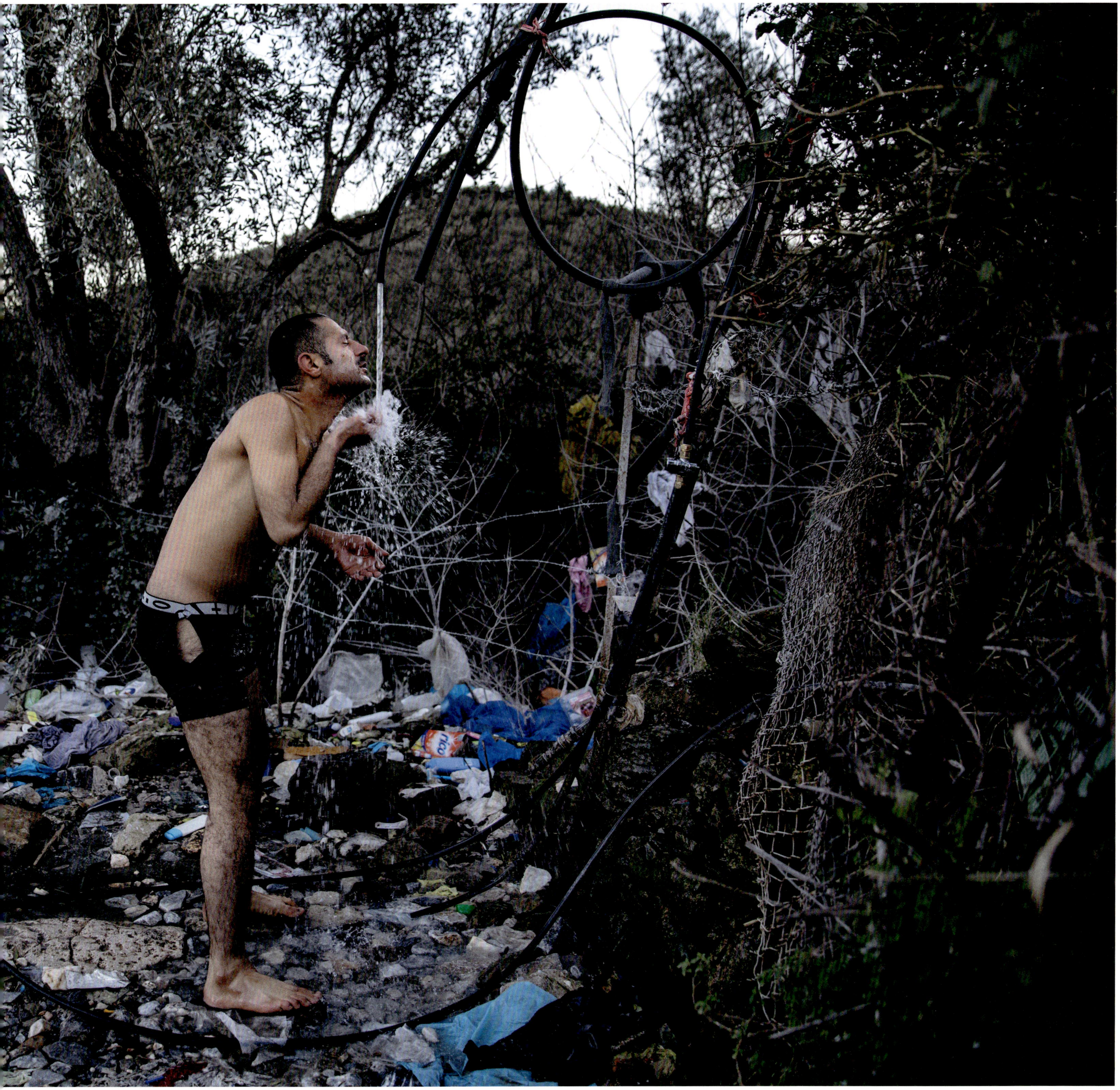

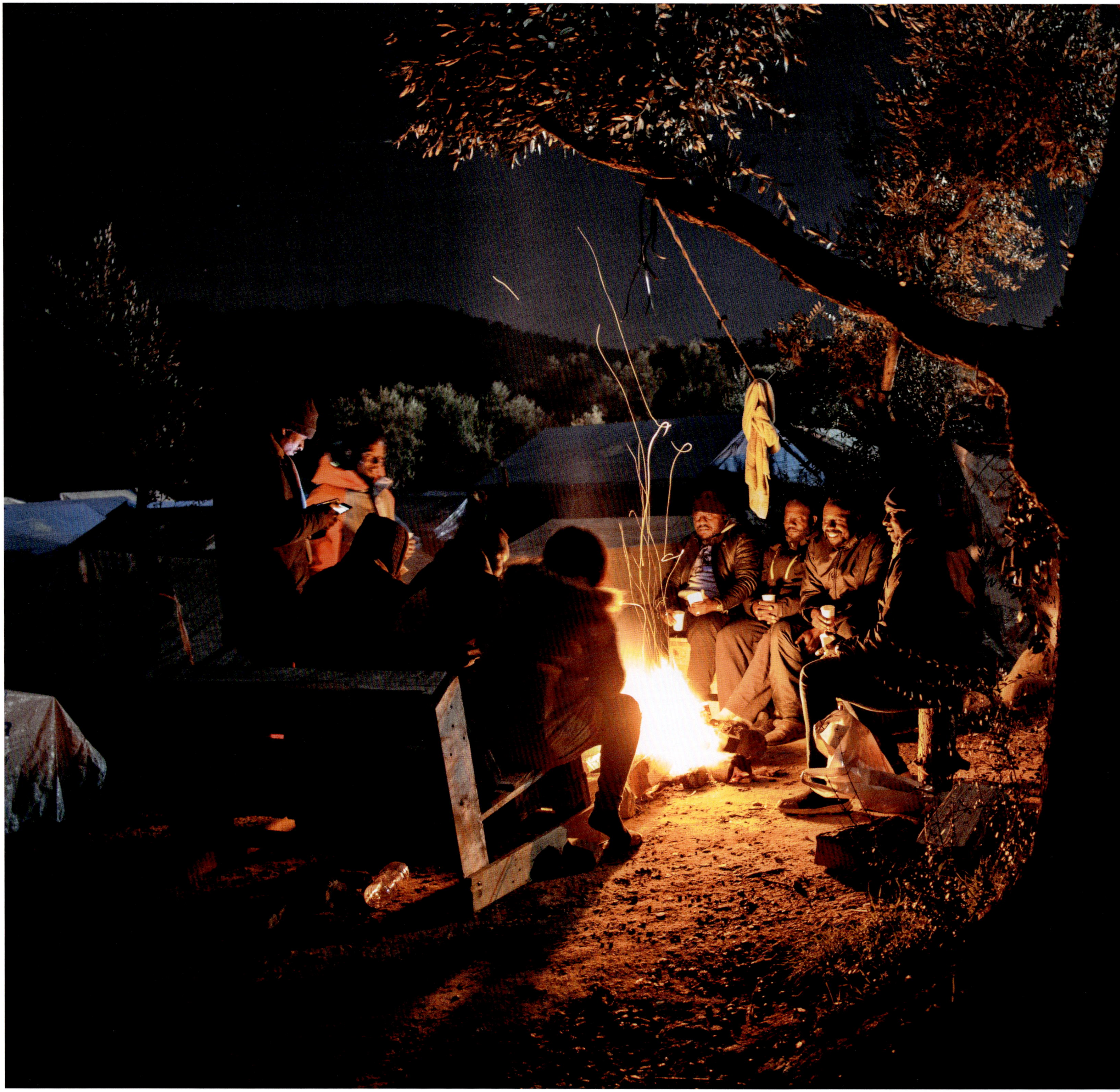

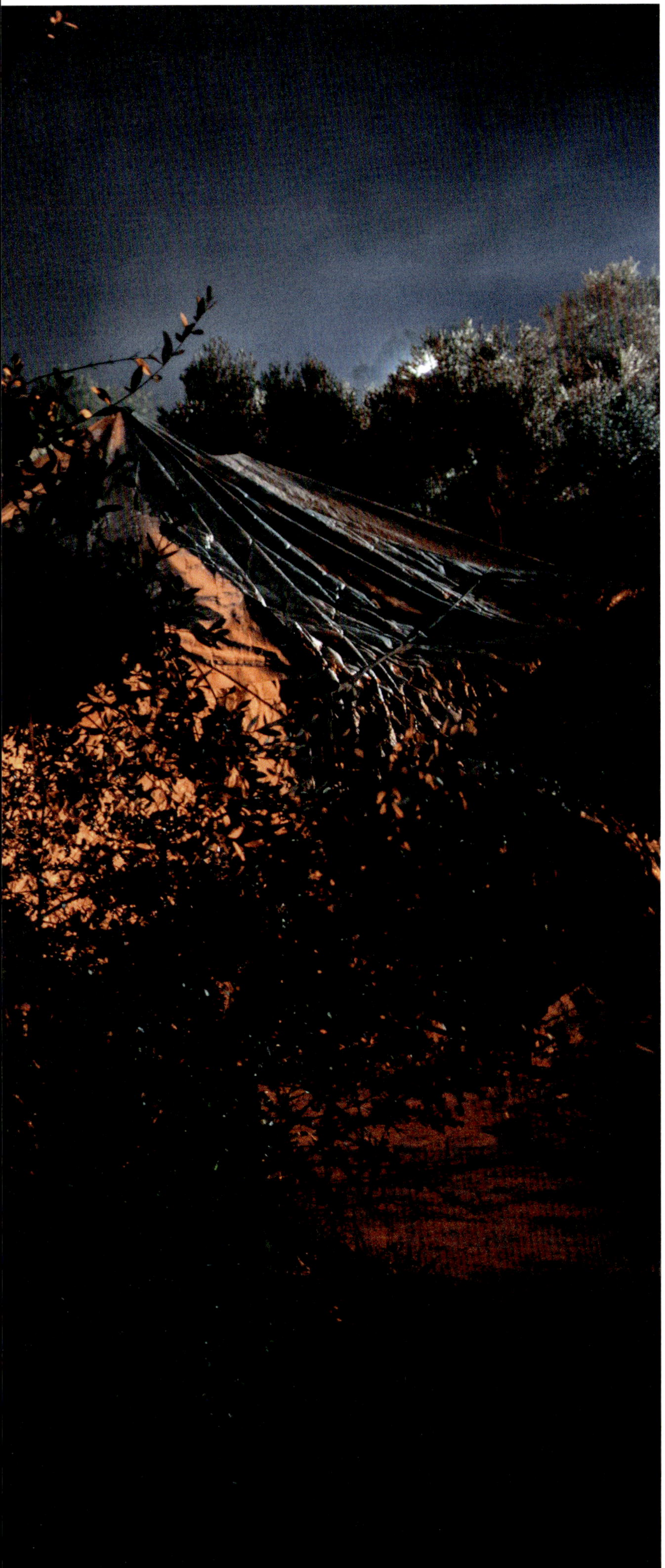

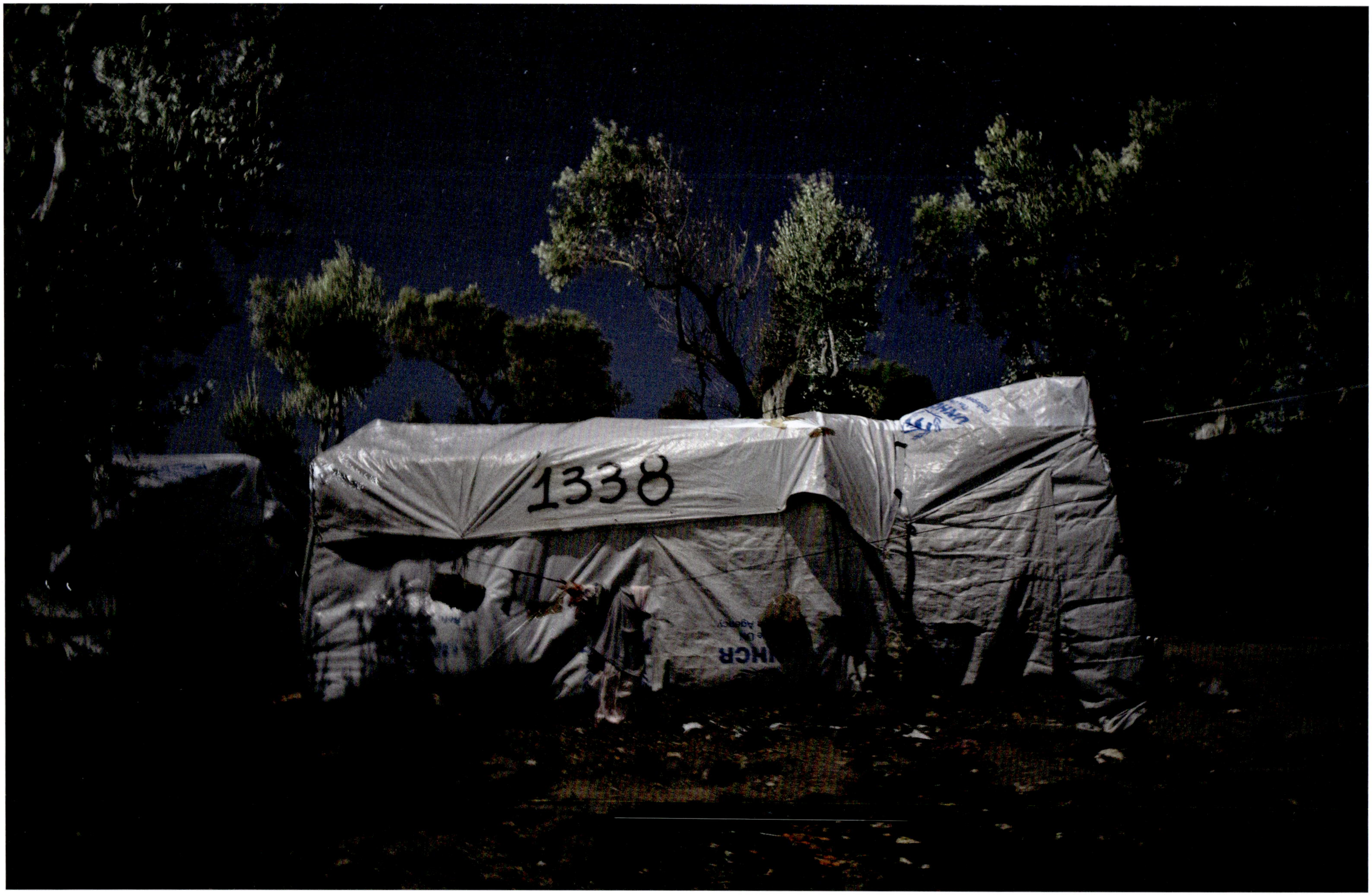
1338

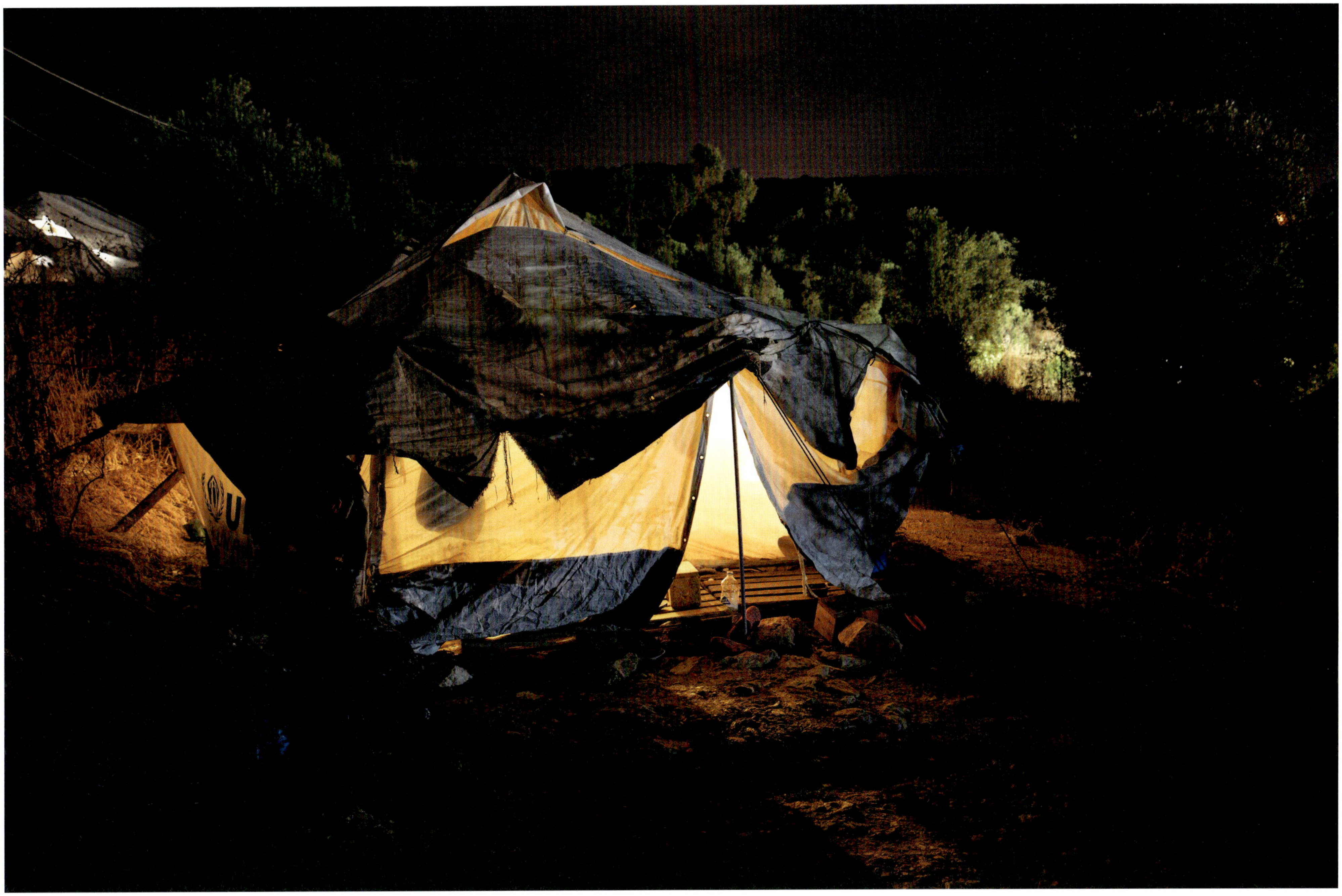

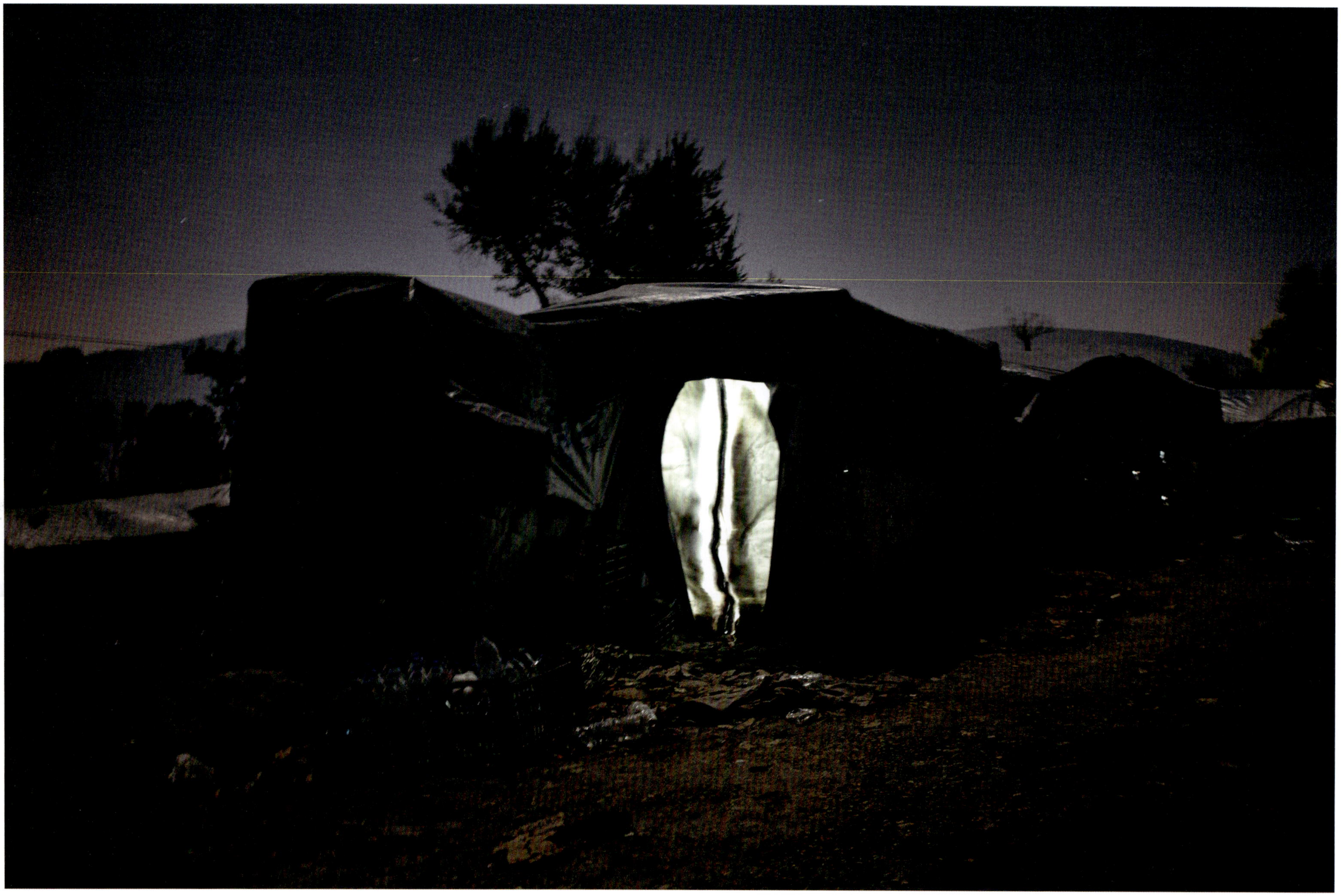

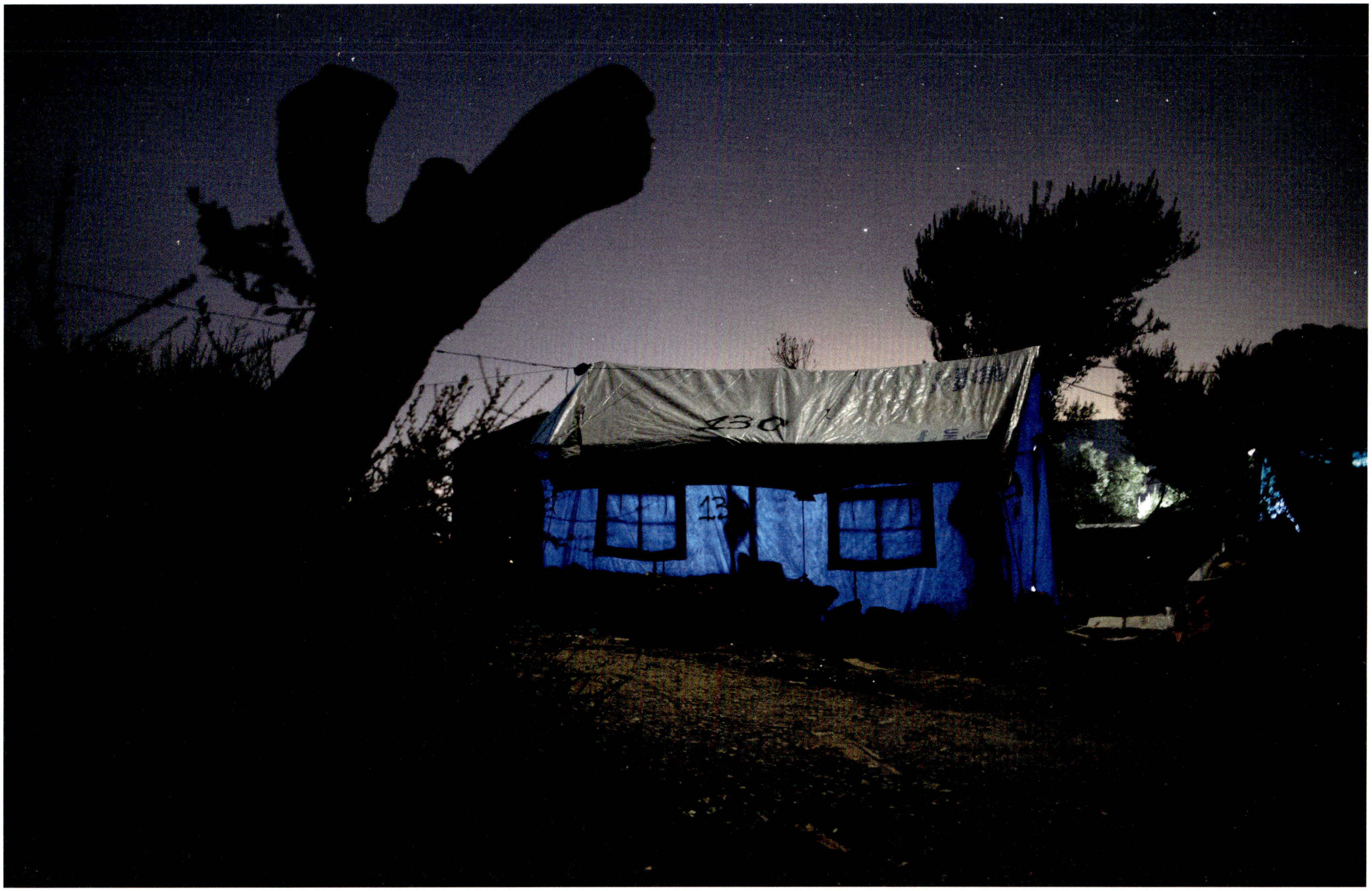
130

Large numbers of refugees and migrants pass through Italy, especially Africans. Most of them try to move on to other European countries, especially due to the tough Italian refugee policy.

France is often the next stop towards a better life in Europe. For large numbers of people, the journey passes through the Italian coastal city of Ventimiglia, 11 kilometres from the French border. Most people attempt to cross the border by train though others try to walk through motorway tunnels, along railway tracks or along narrow mountain paths in order to evade the border police. Some of them make it across at the first attempt while others have to try several times before they succeed. Anyone captured by the French border police, is typically detained for 12 to 24 hours.

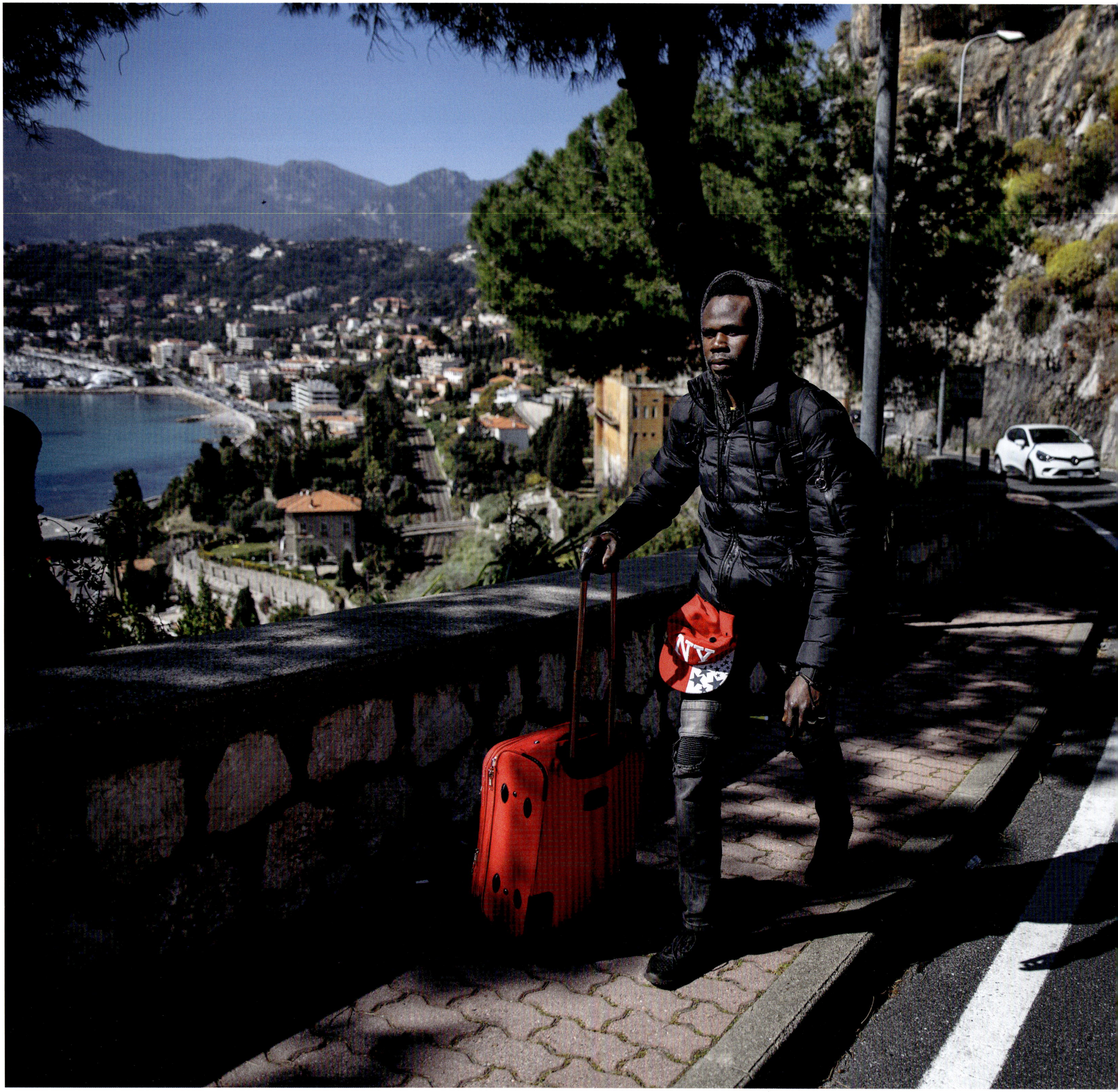
NY

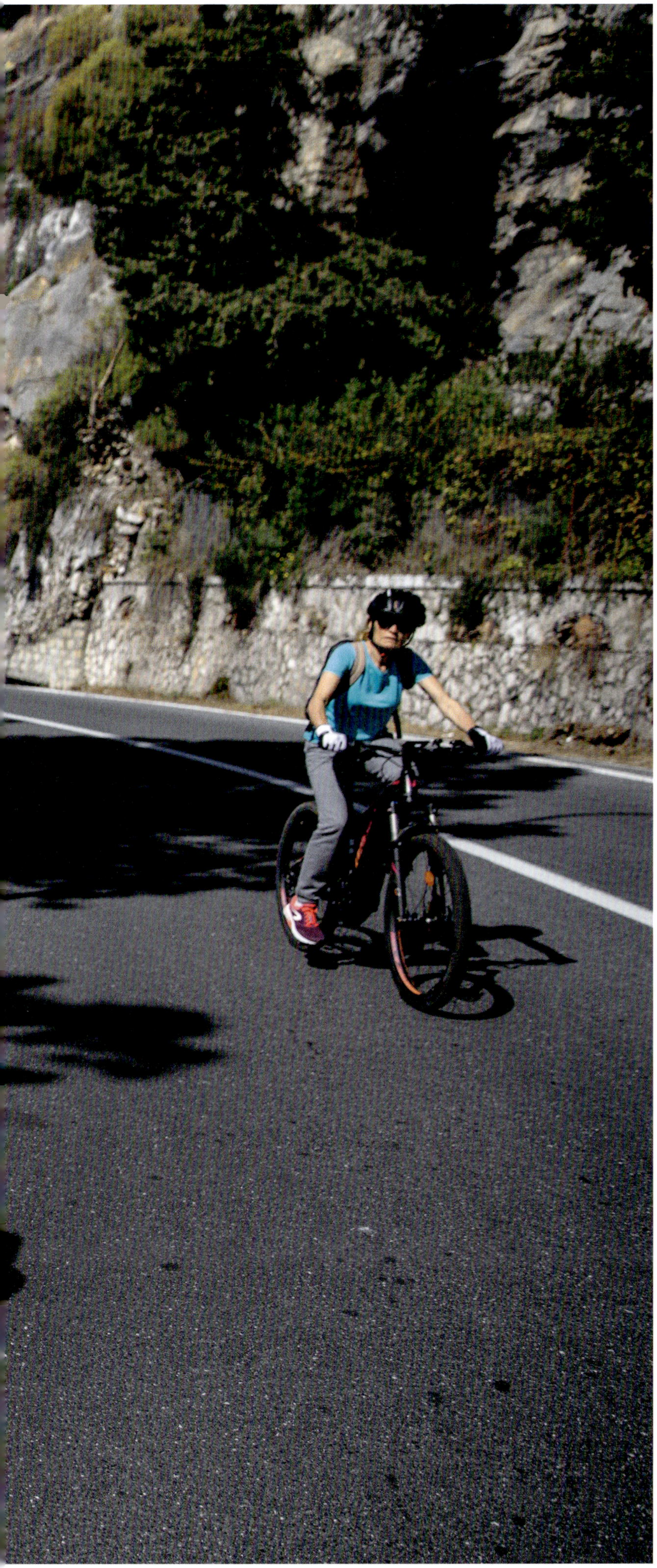

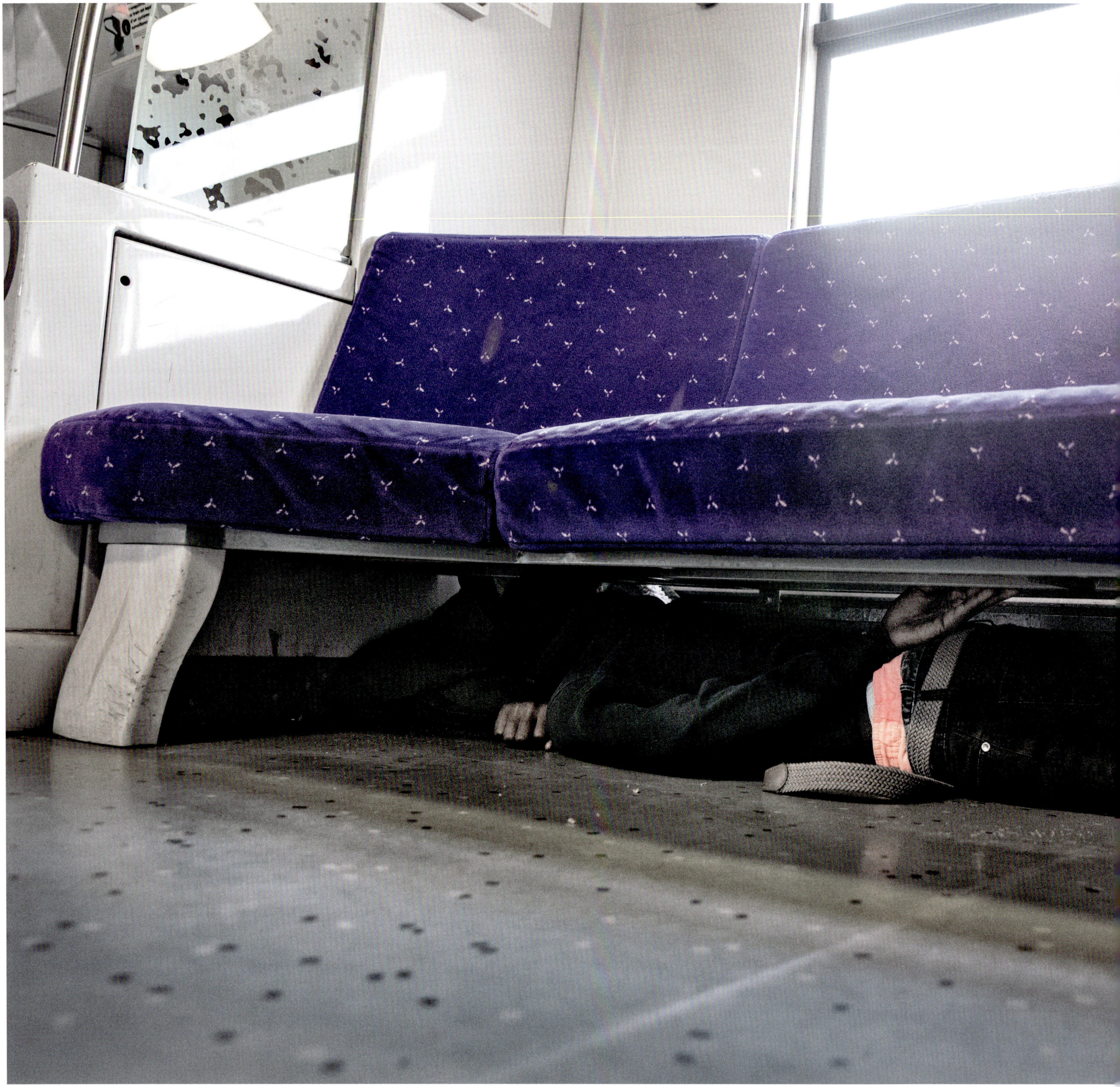

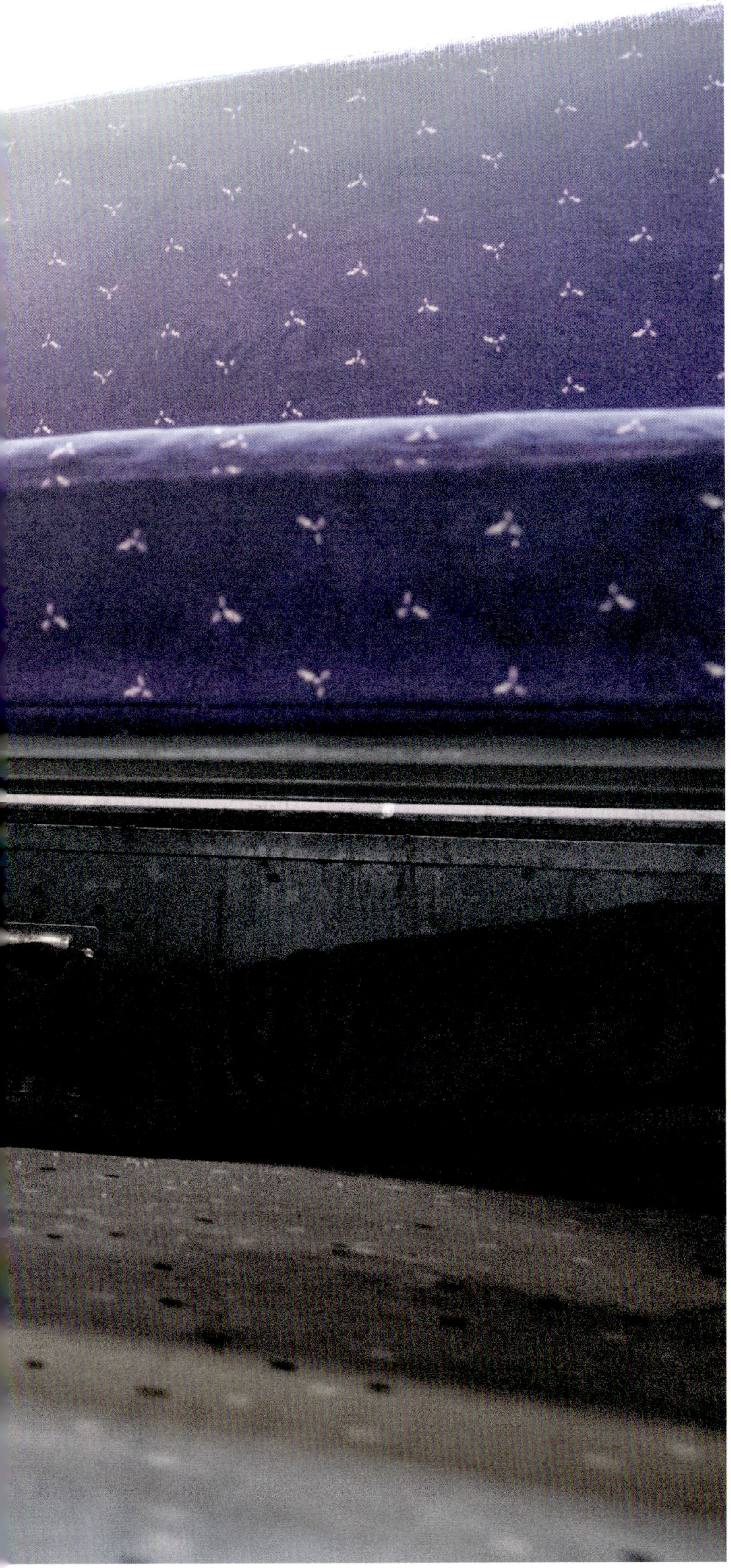

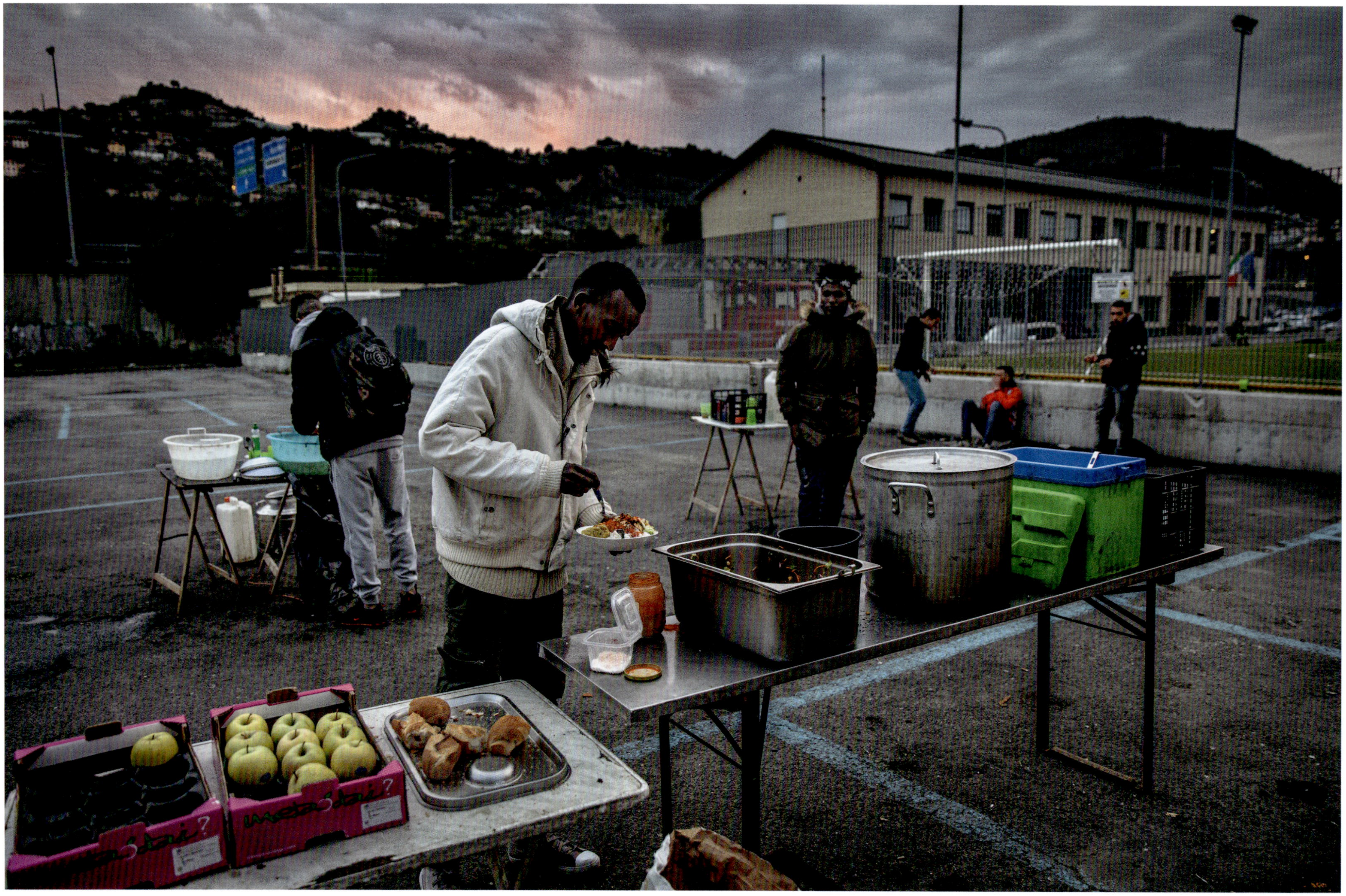

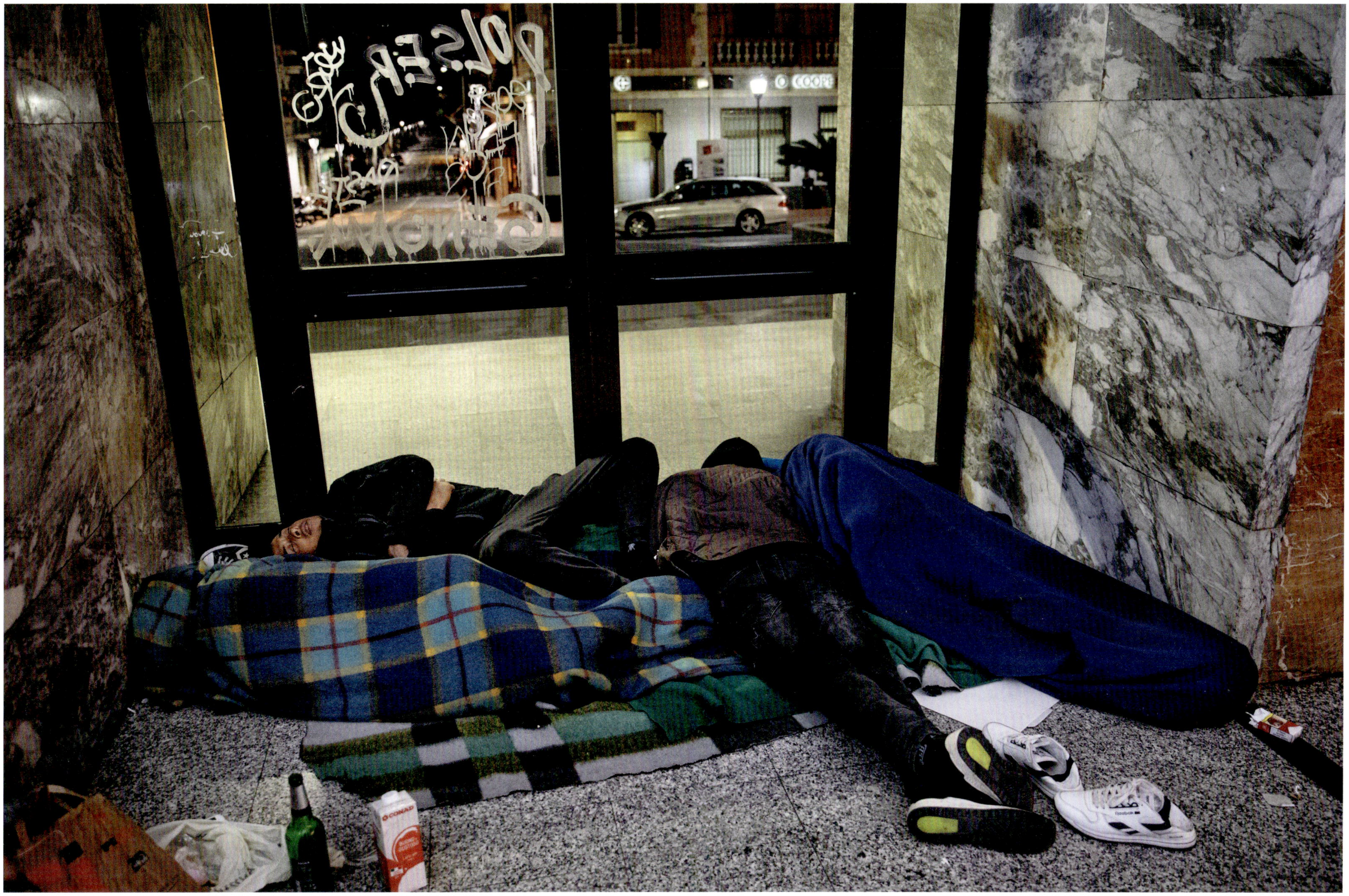

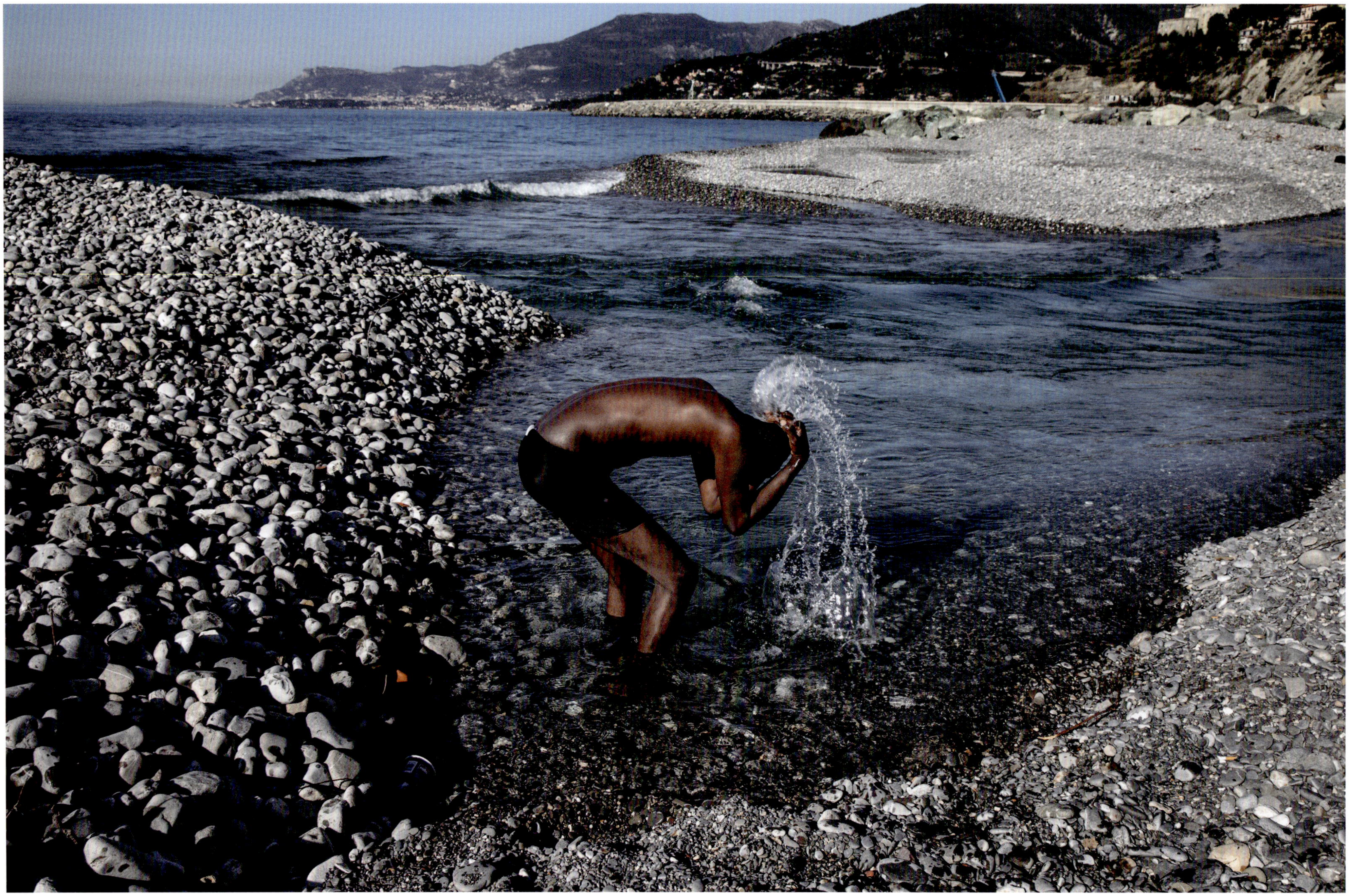

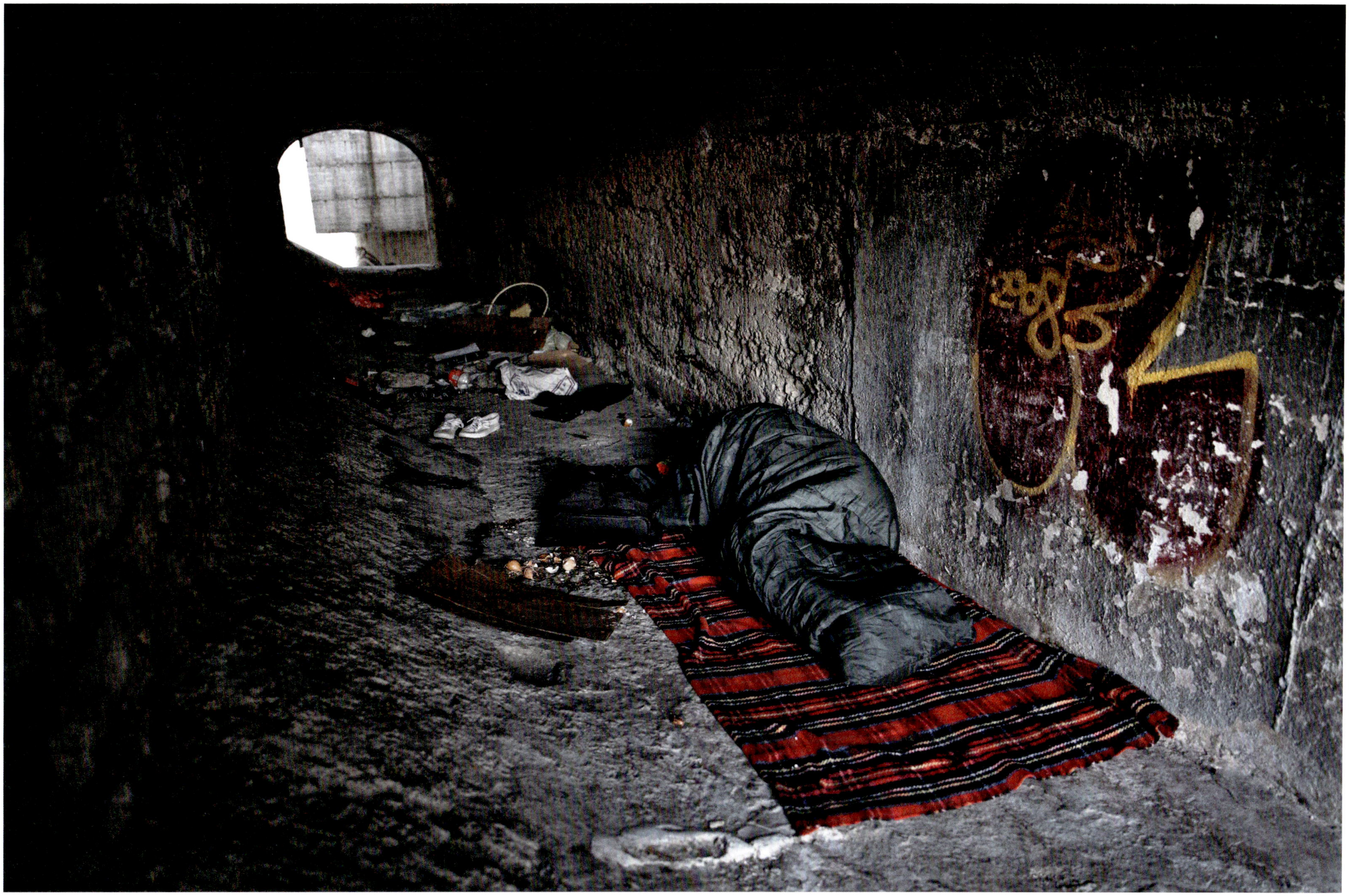

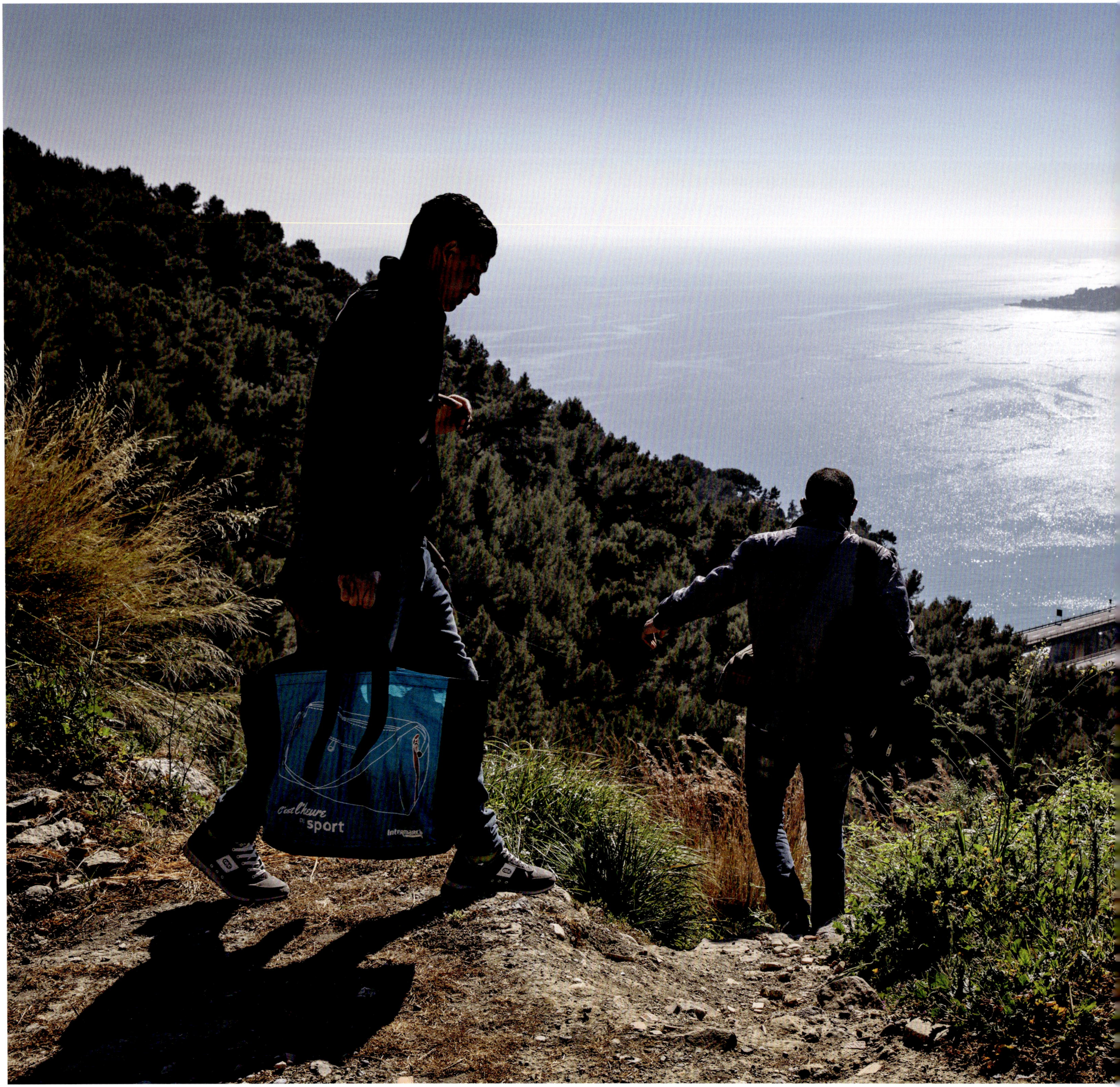
C'est l'heure
sport

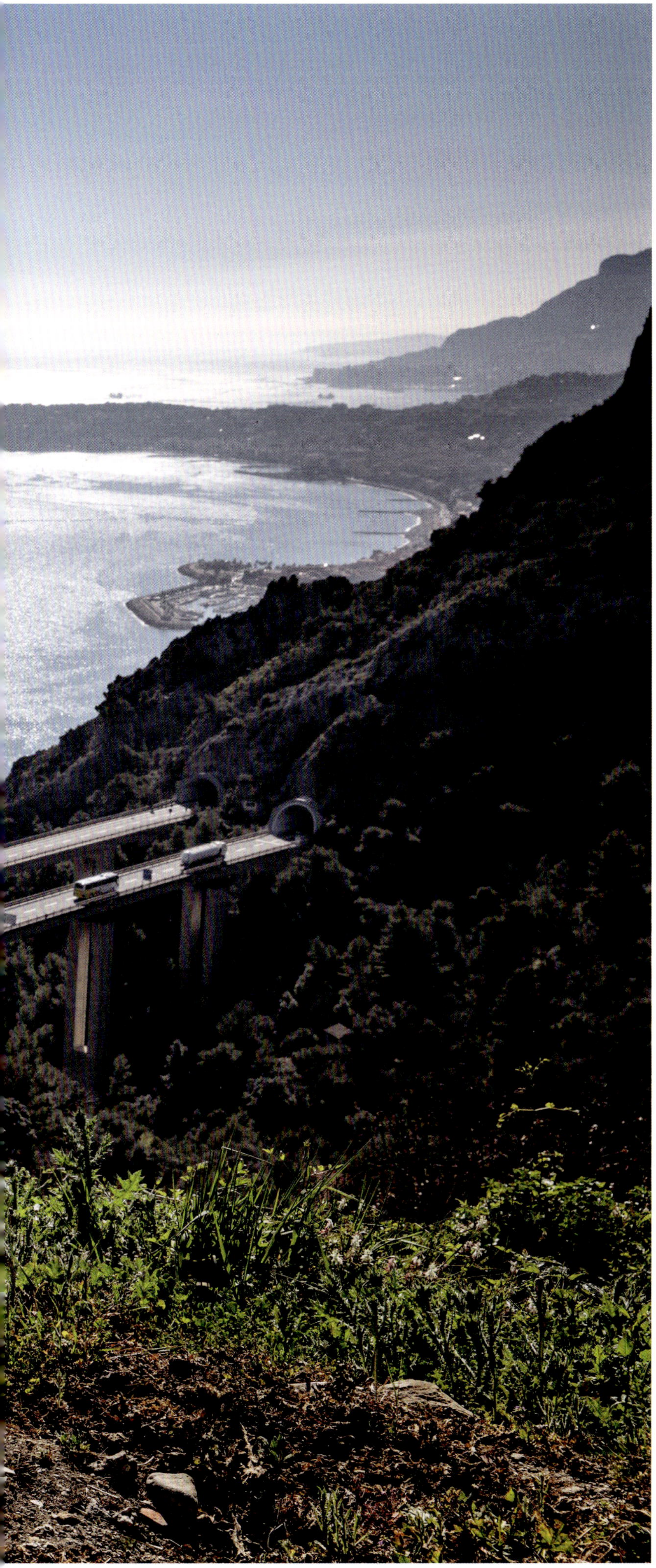

After Hungary closes its border with a fence in 2015, refugees and migrants trying to reach northern and western Europe via the Balkan route have to find new ways. Many travel to the northwestern corner of Bosnia-Herzegovina to cross the border to Croatia, an EU member state. After this, most people continue their journey through Slovenia to Italy, and many go even further.

In December 2018, winter sets in. The snow and cold make it even more dangerous for refugees and migrants to continue on their journeys, so many wait for better weather. With the consent of the Bosnian authorities, the Organization for Migration (IOM) sets up camps in old factory buildings in the cities of Bihać and Velika Kladuša in Bosnia-Herzegovina. In December 2018 the camps house at least 2,800 refugees and migrants, the majority of whom are young men.

After several years with many refugees and migrants in the area, some of the locals are tired of it. At the end of September 2020, in the run-up to a local election, the authorities close the IOM-run Bira camp in Bihać. Some of the men are moved 25 kilometers away to Lipa, a temporary camp of overfilled tents where it is hard to keep warm. Families can seek shelter in the two smaller IOM-run camps Sedra and Borići. The IOM estimates that in December 2020 there are 4,000 refugees and migrants in the area. When there is no room for them in the camps, many people settle down in abandoned houses and rundown factory buildings in and around the towns of Bihać and Velika Kladuša. The large majority of them are single men and boys from Afghanistan, Pakistan and Bangladesh, but there are also a number of families staying in the area who will try to cross the border before the winter really sets in.

Most of them have crossed the border to Croatia many times and have been sent back to Bosnia-Herzegovina. Many tell of Croatian border guards subjecting them to systematic violence and indignities, smashing their cell phones and taking their money, documents and things of value. Some say that the border police take their shoes so they have to walk back to the refugee camps in bare feet. Forcing people back without giving them the chance to seek asylum is called 'pushback'. According to all international laws and conventions, this is illegal.

The migrants and refugees refer to it simply as 'the game'. It is fatiguing, both physically and mentally, to gather the strength and the money again and again to stay in the game. Most of them will move on at any price.

In addition to watching out for the guards at the Croatian border, refugees and migrants moving through Croatian forests also risk stepping on land mines dating back to the wars in former Yugoslavia in the 1990s.

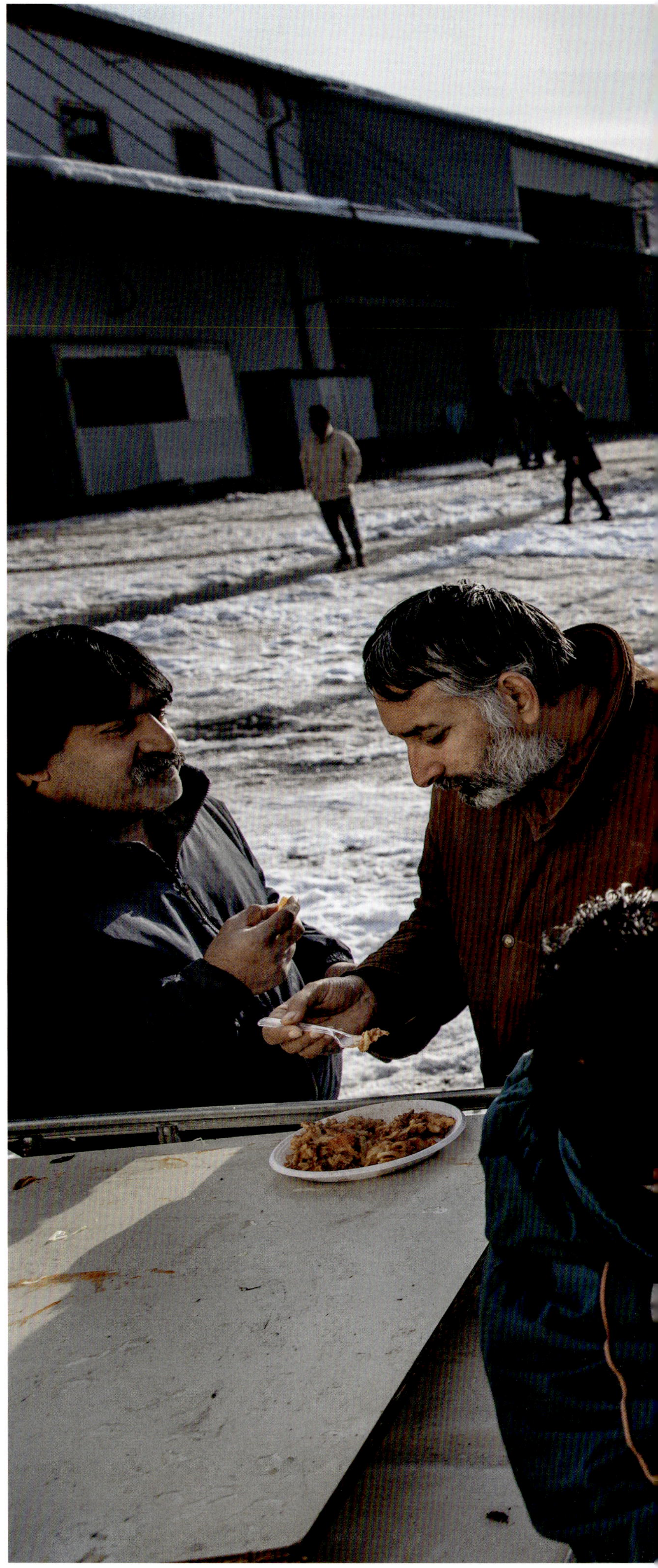

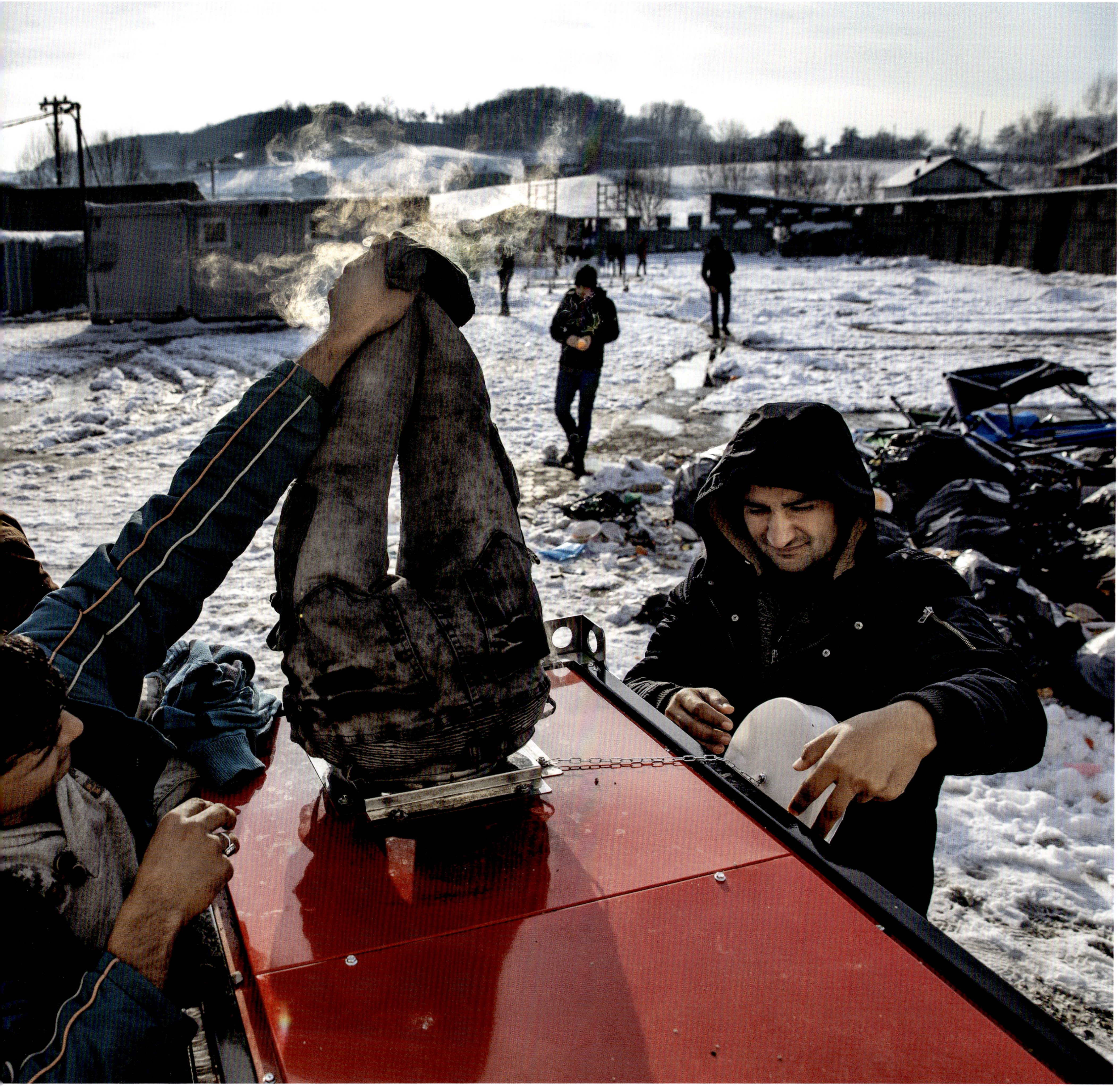

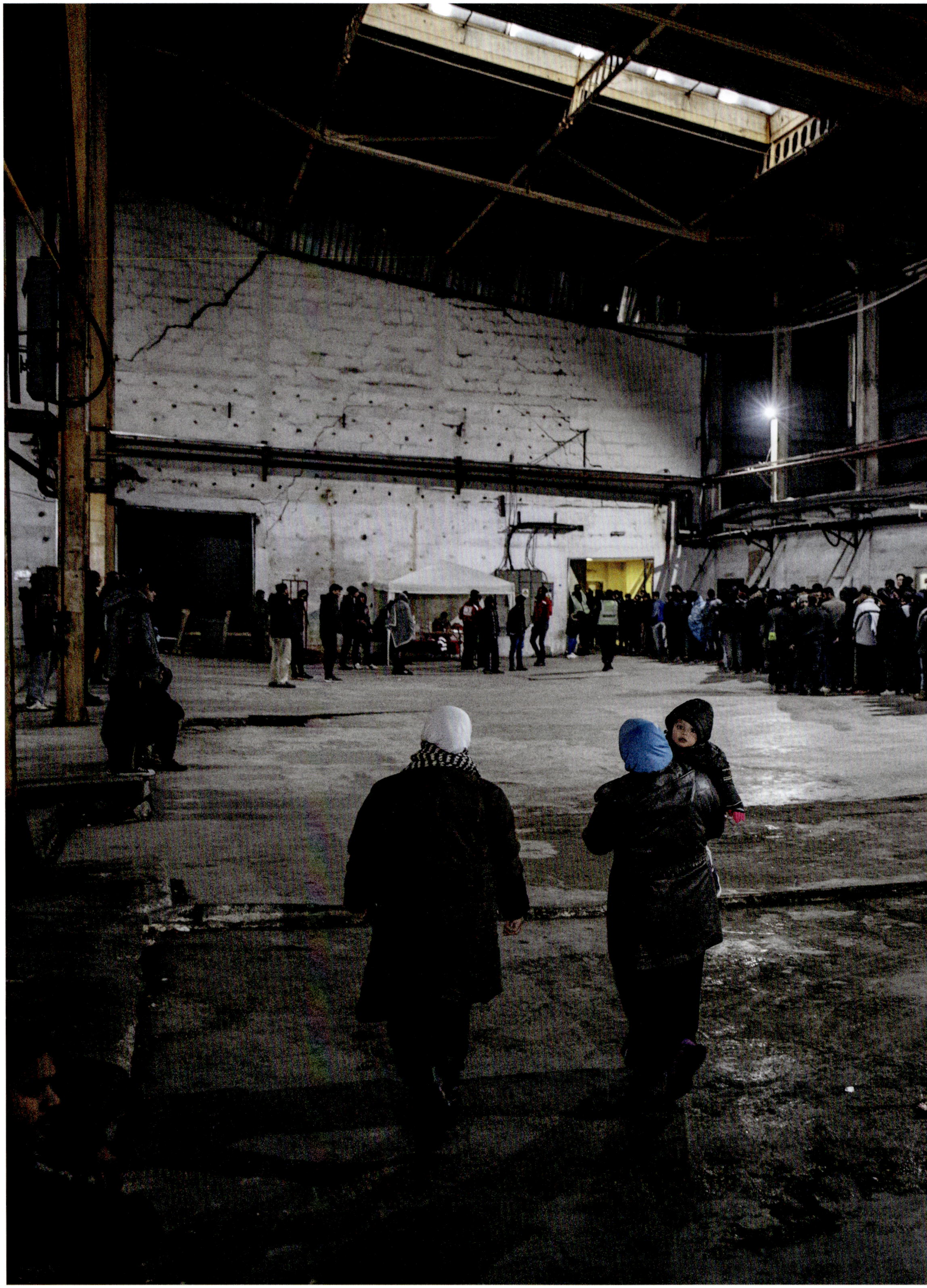

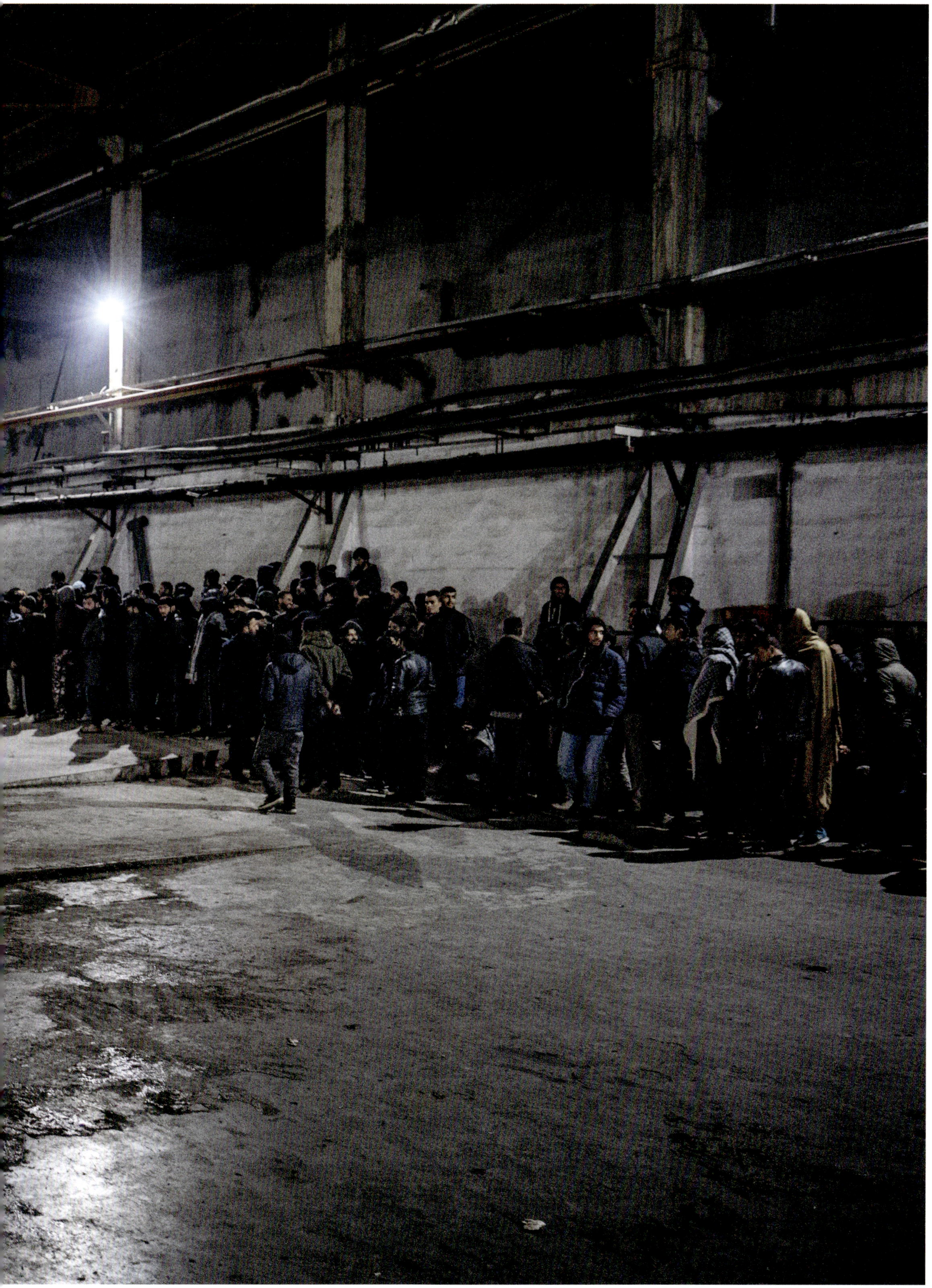

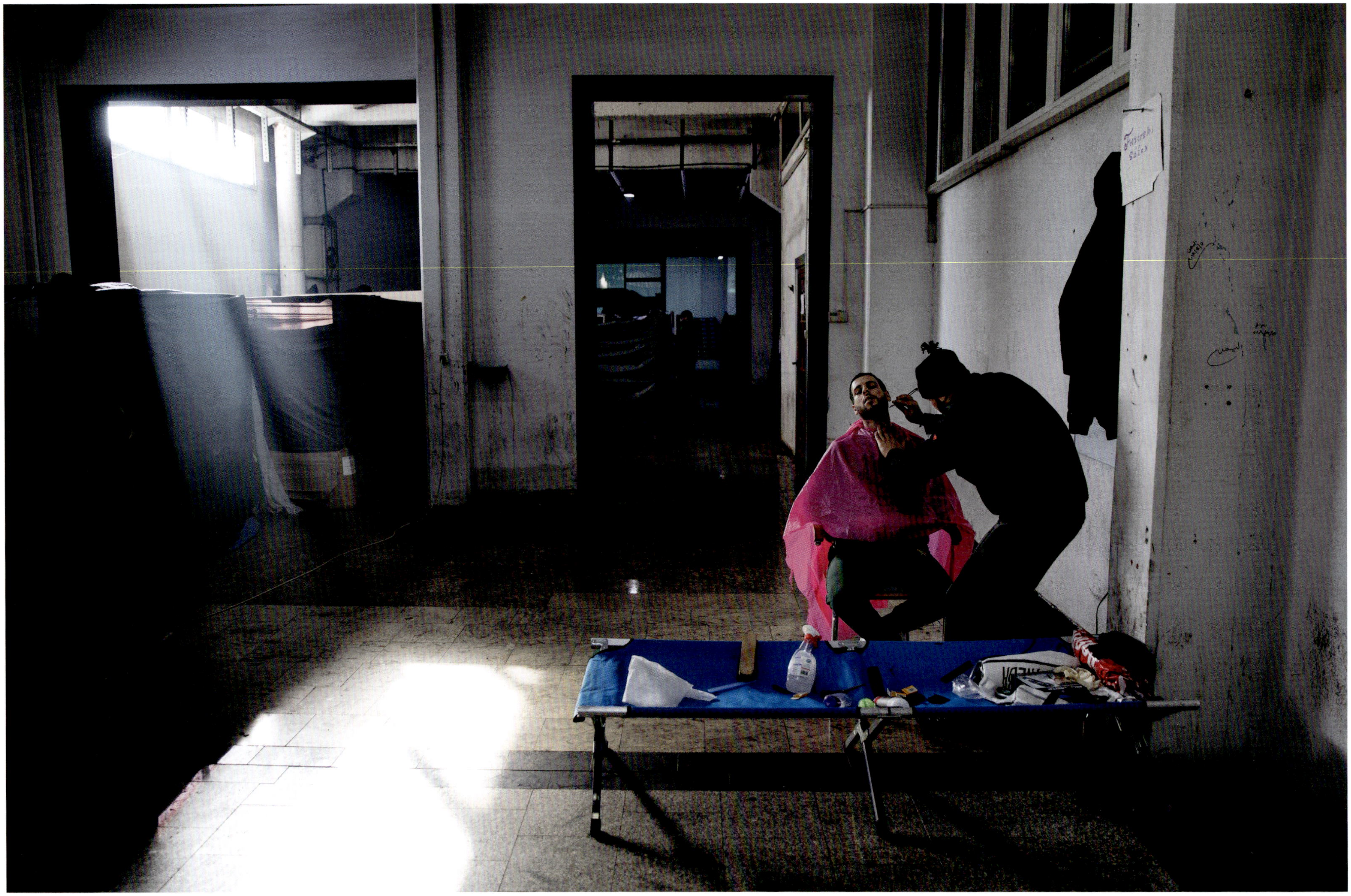

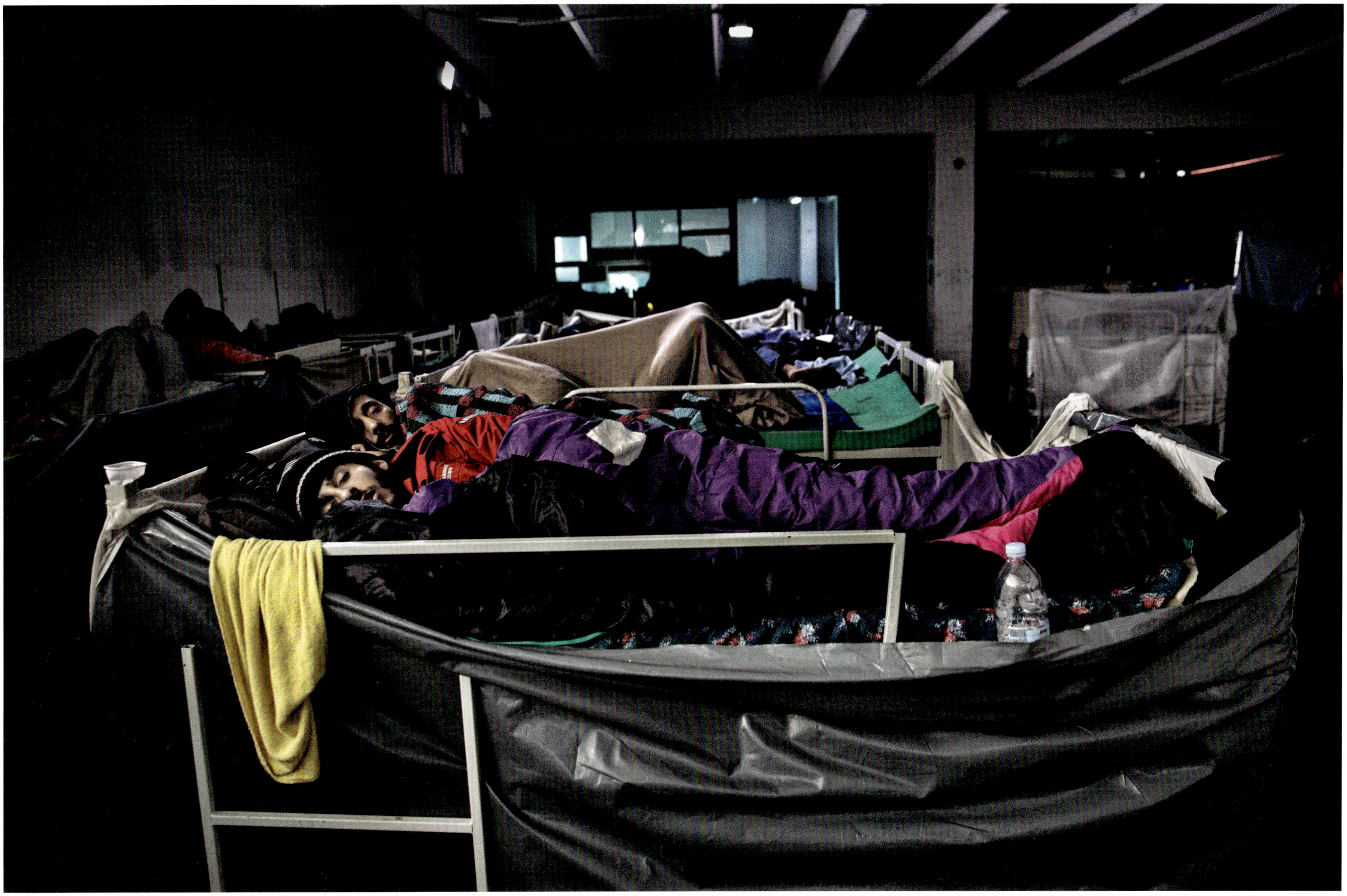

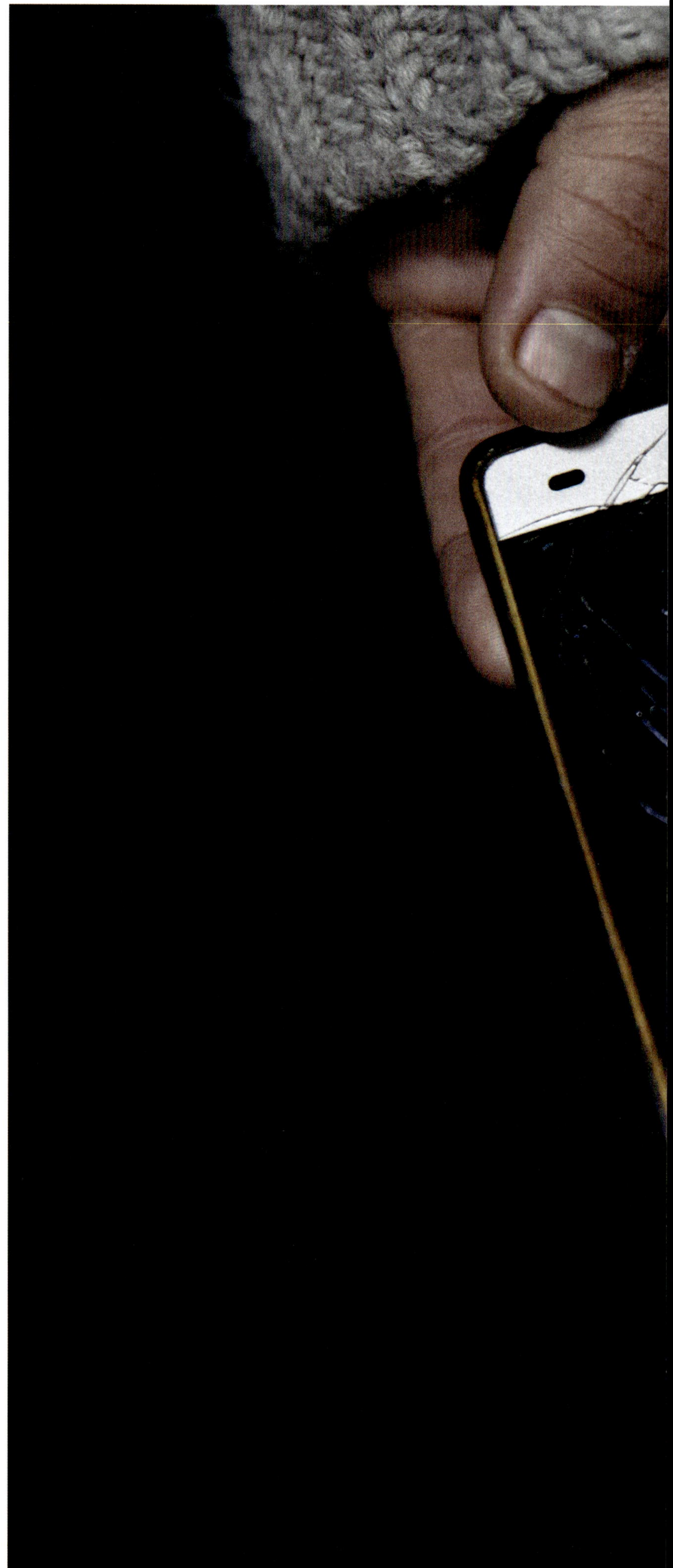

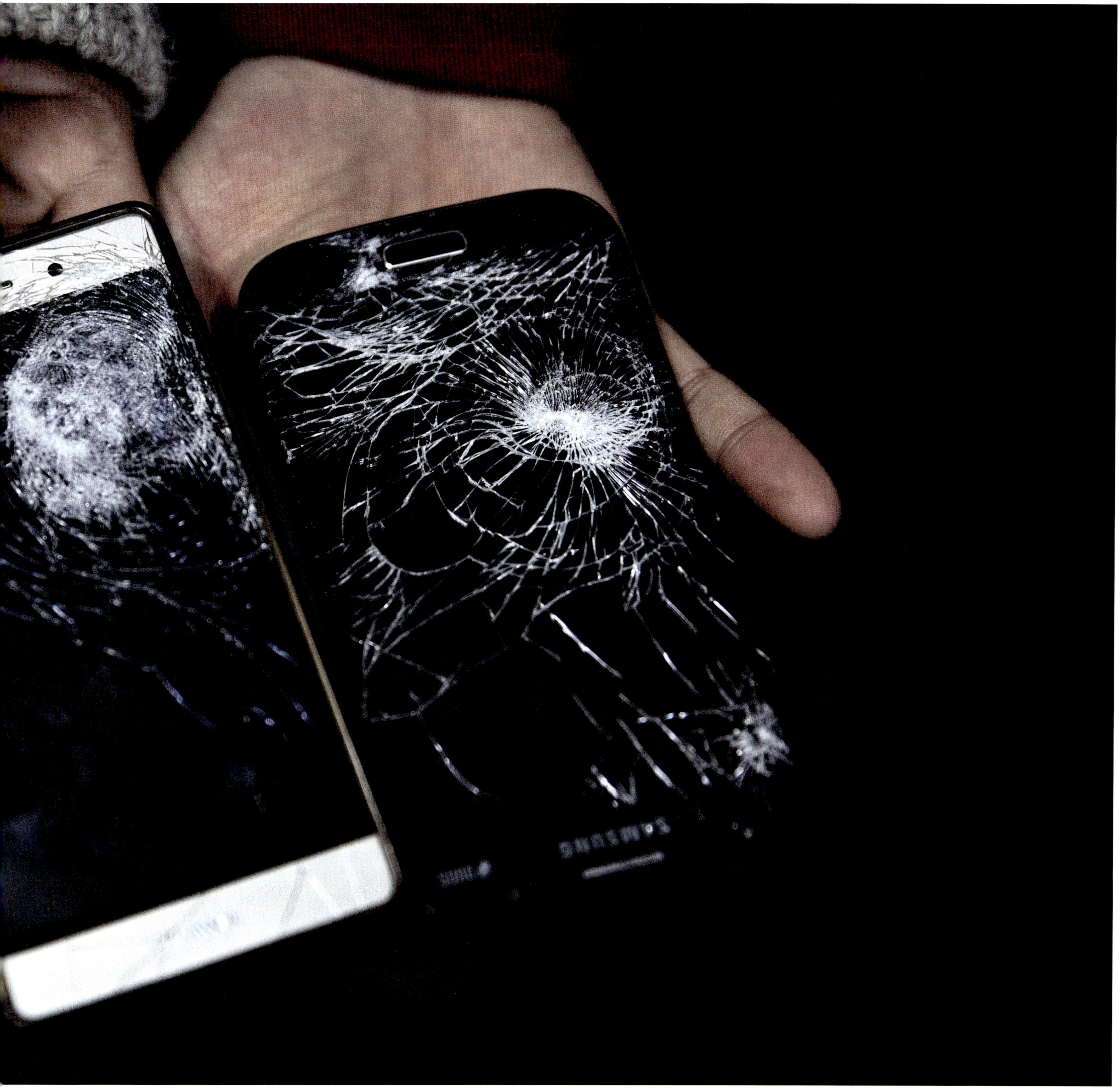

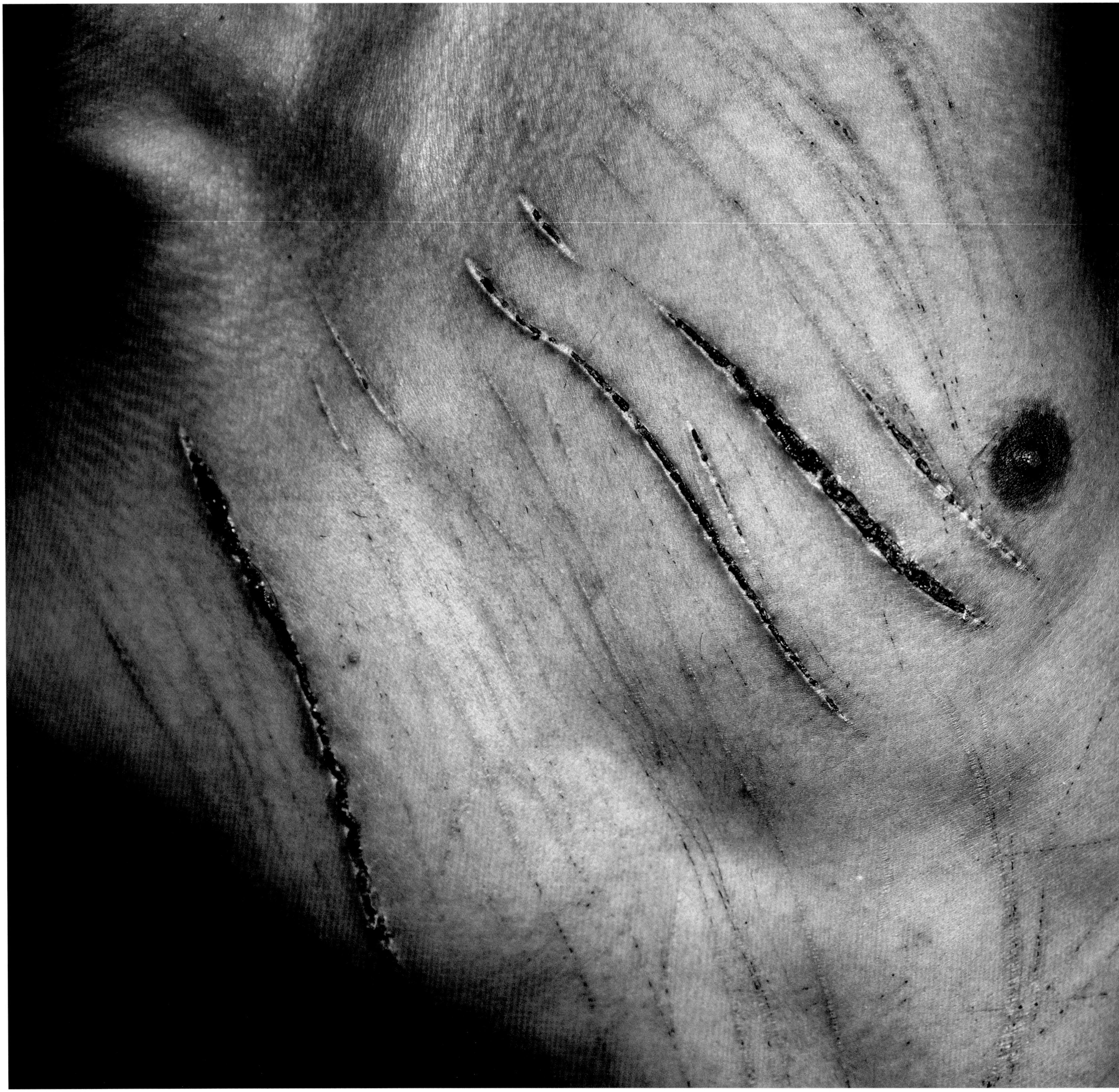

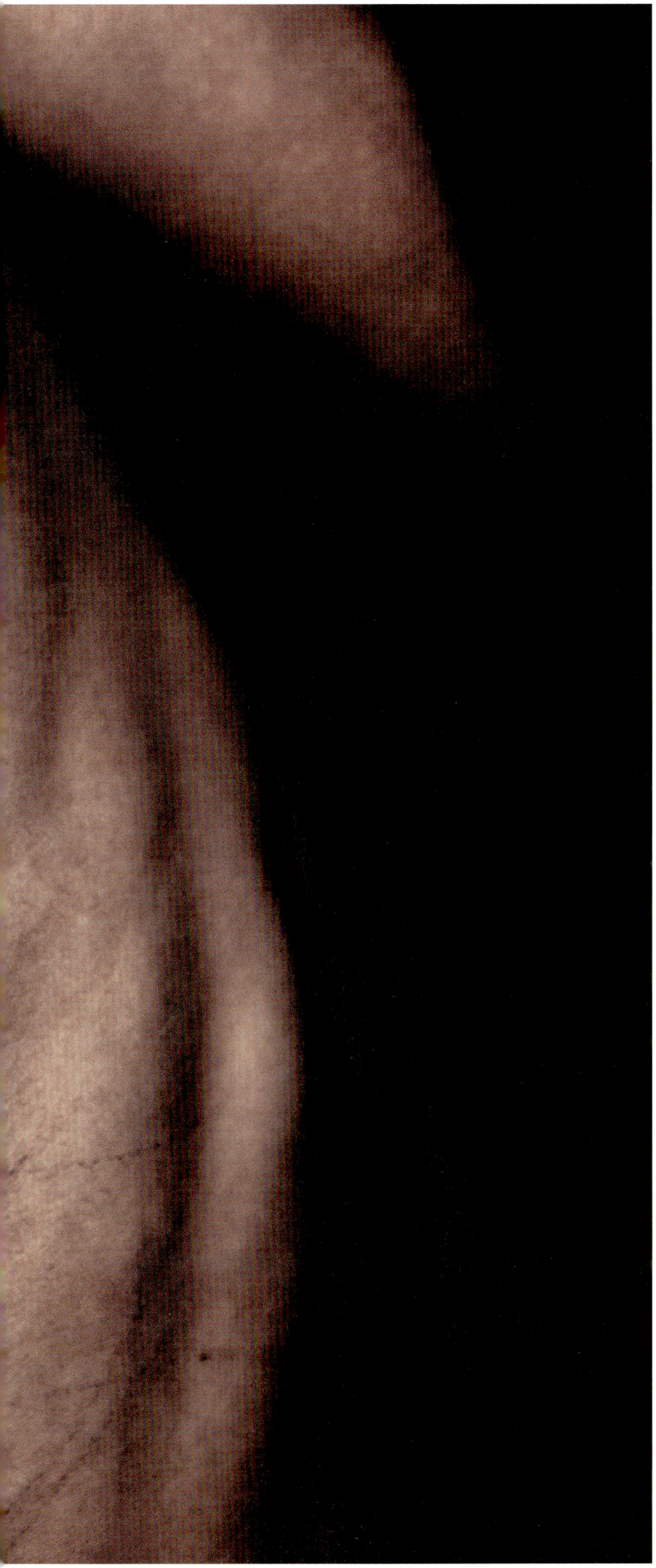

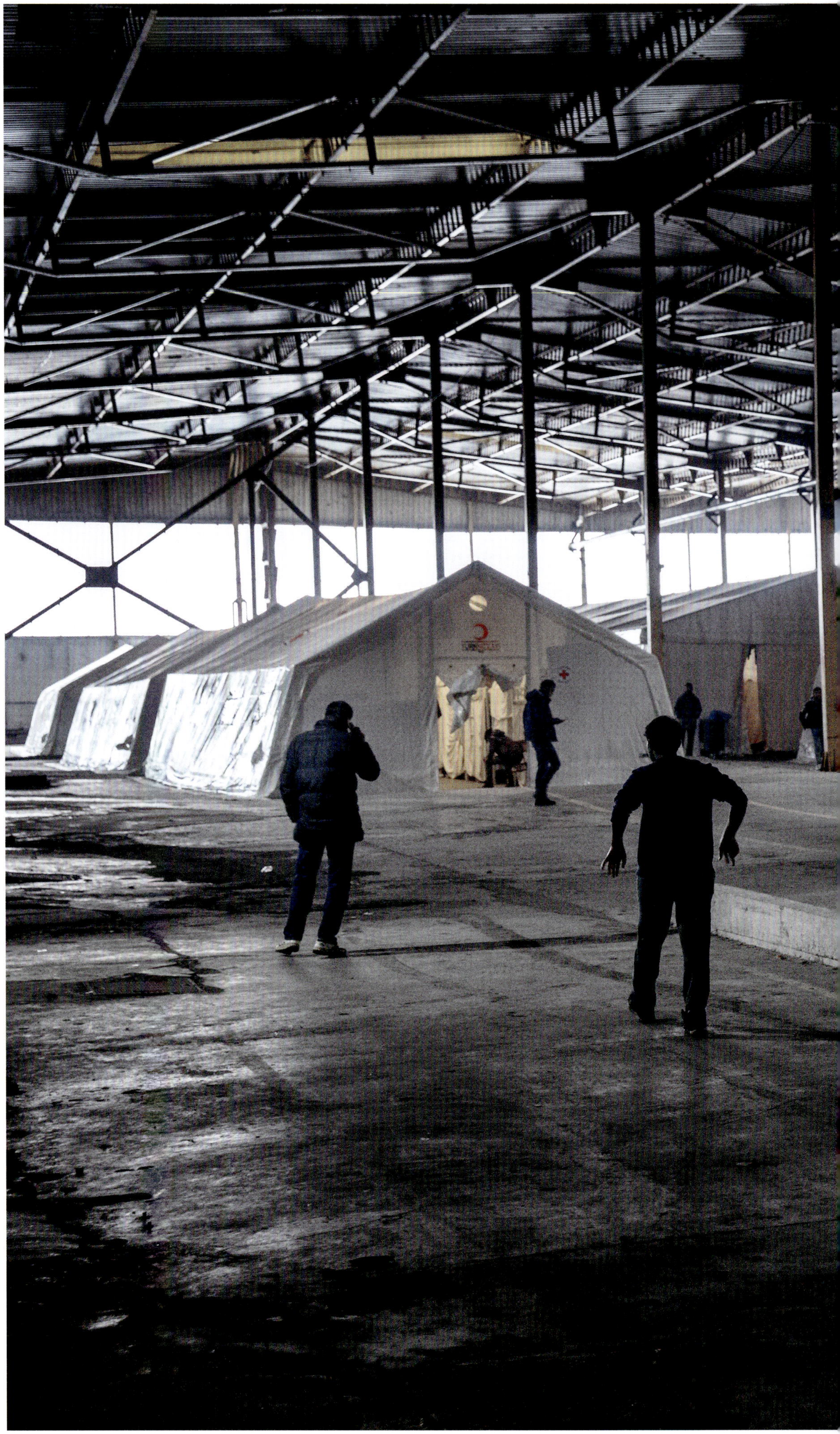

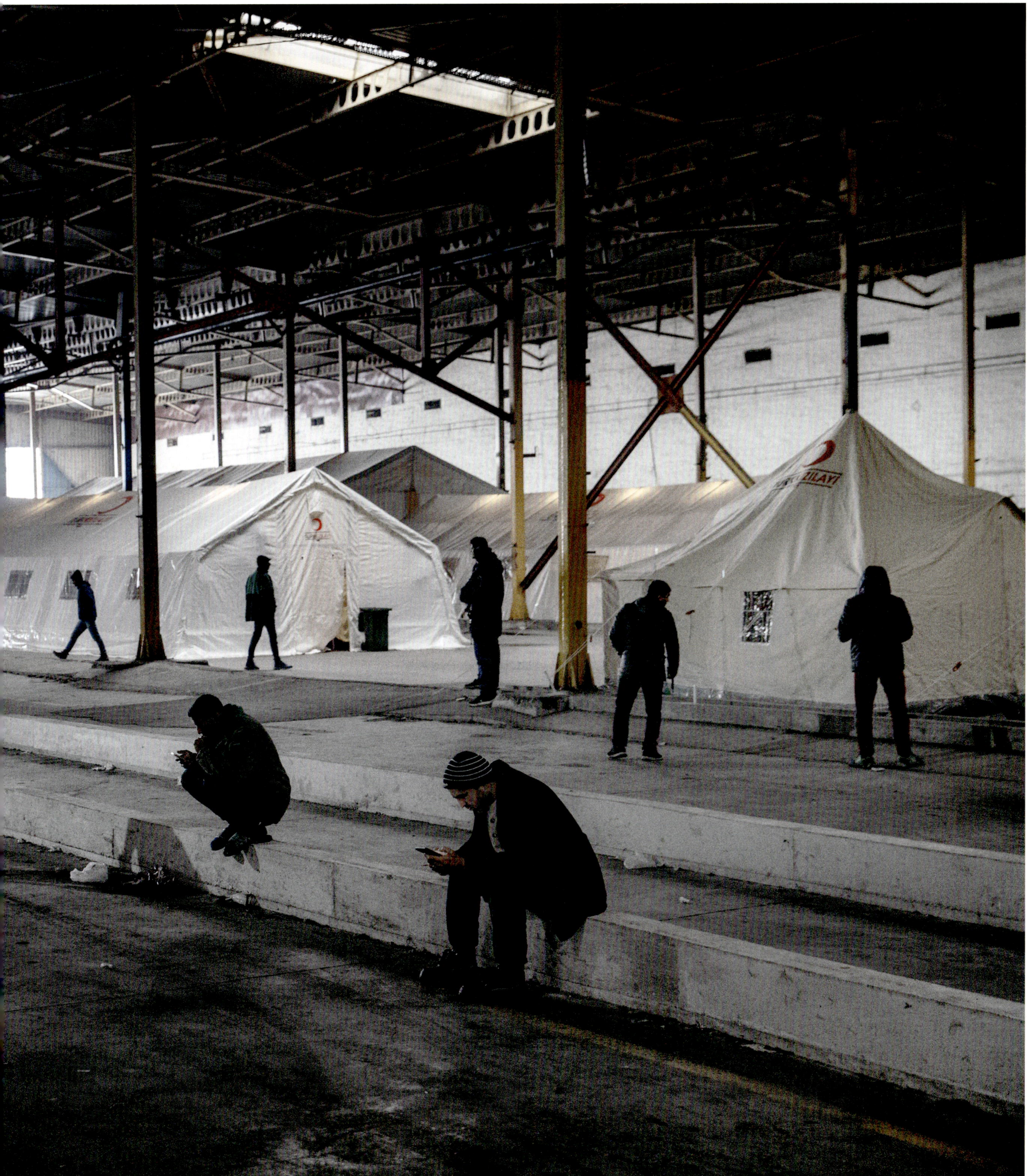

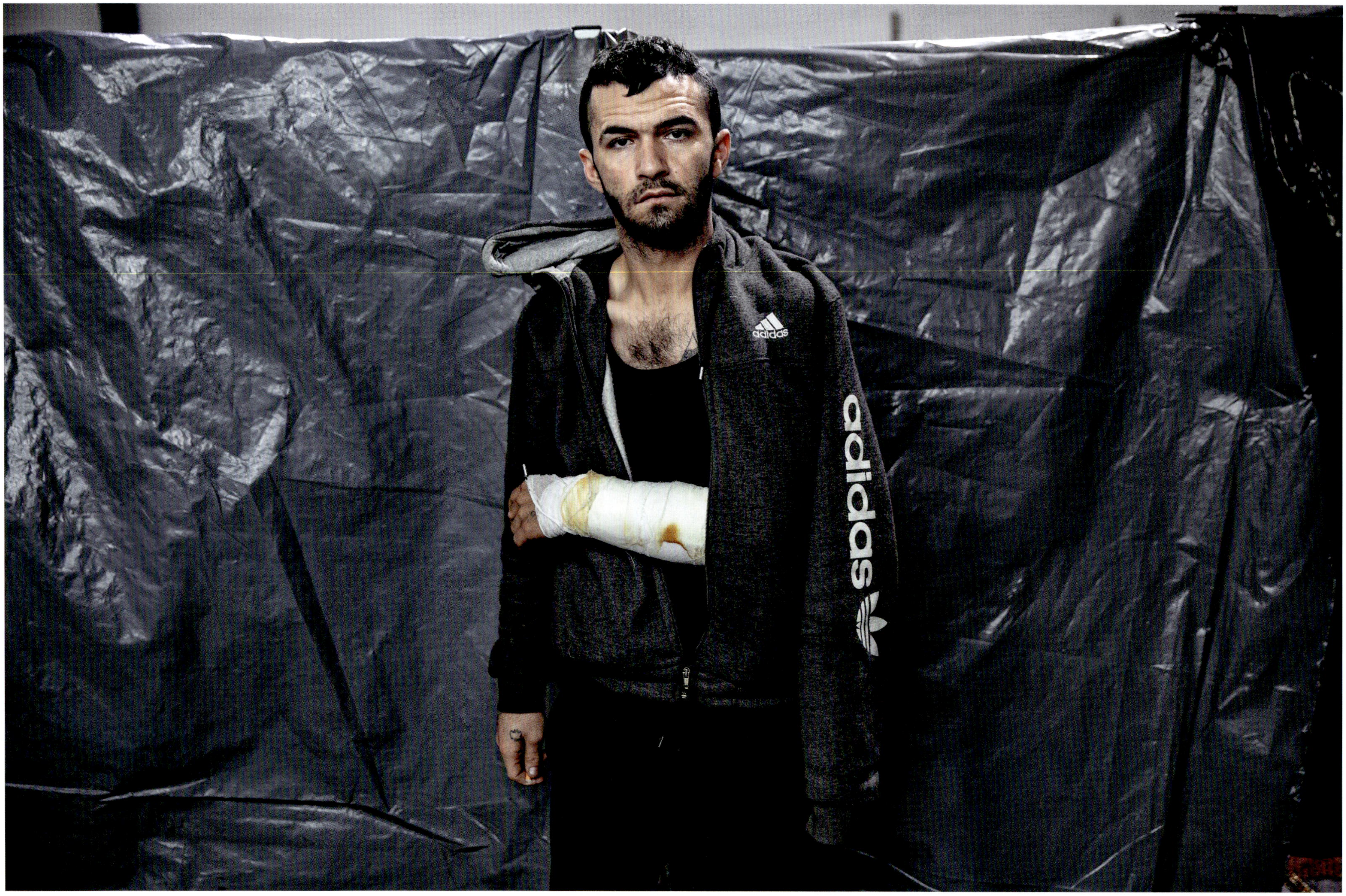
adidas
adidas

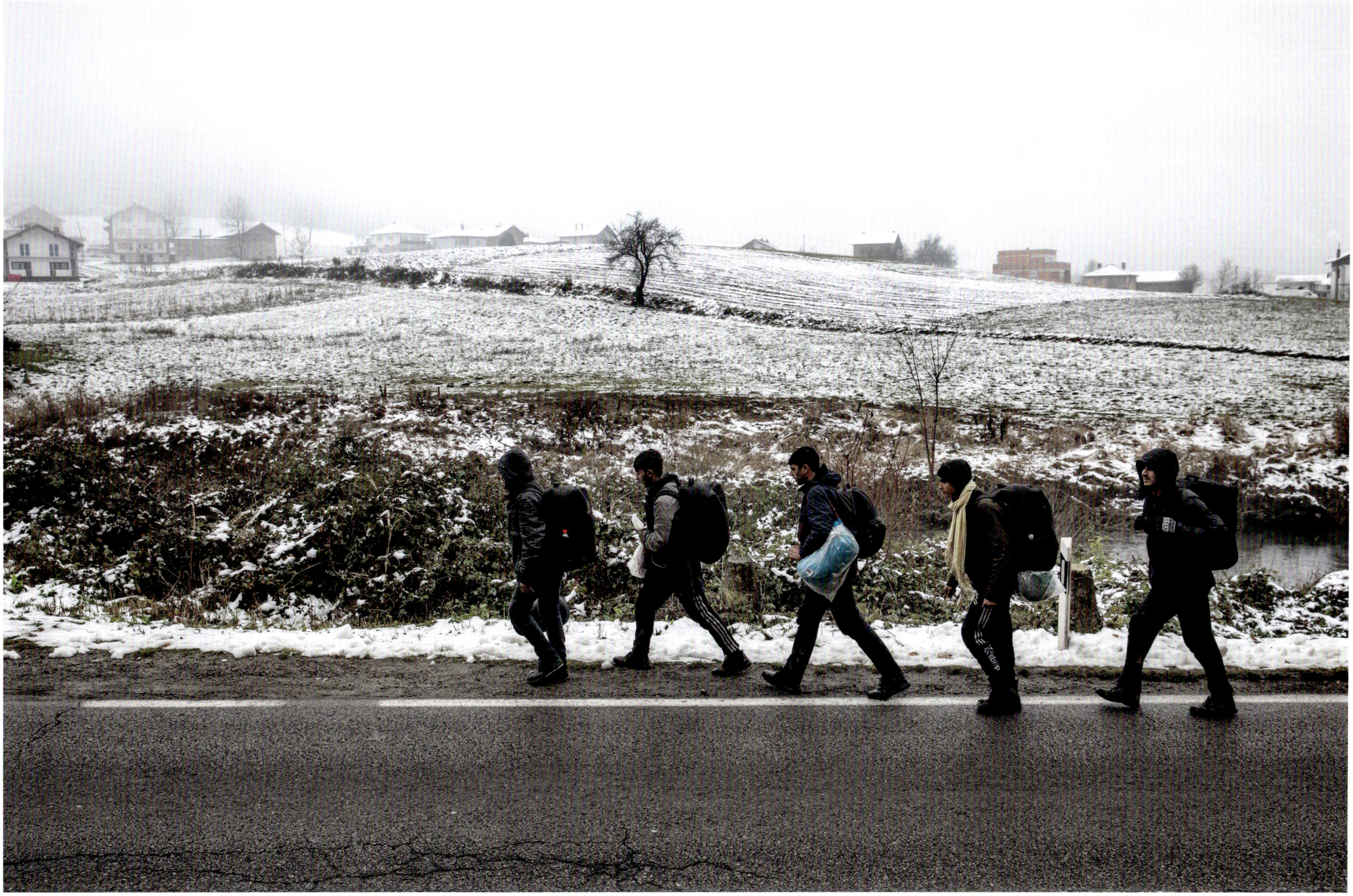

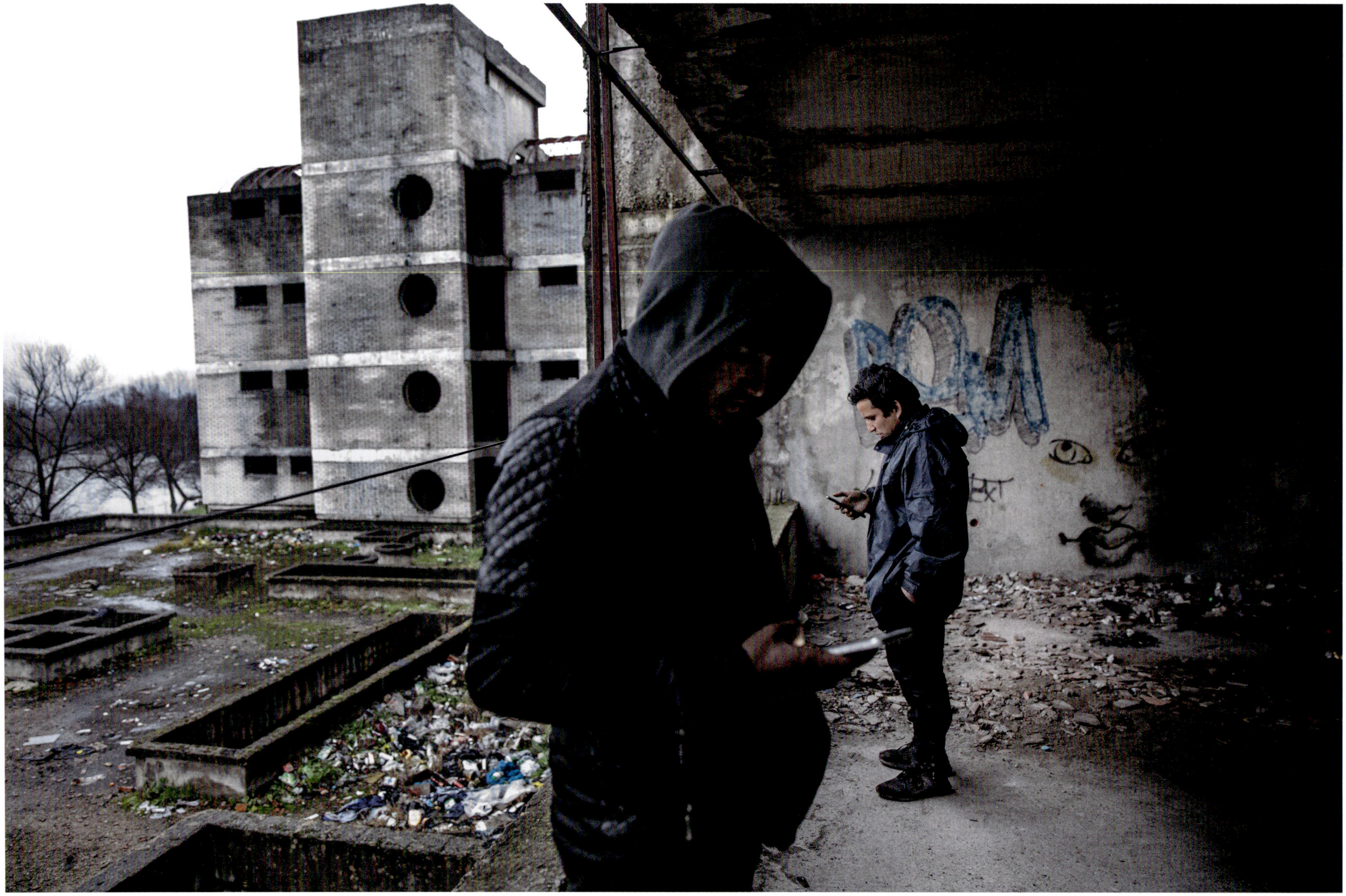

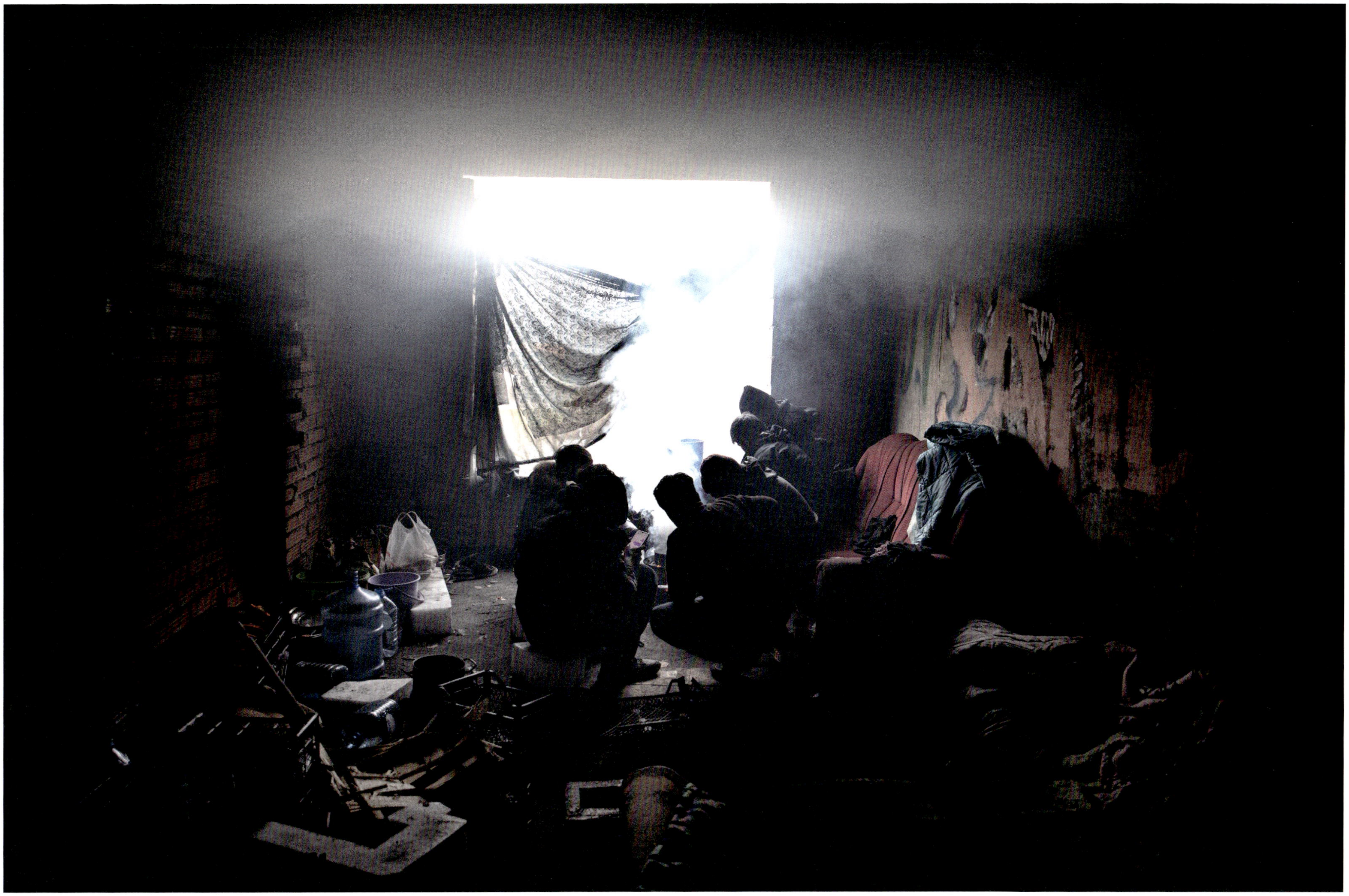

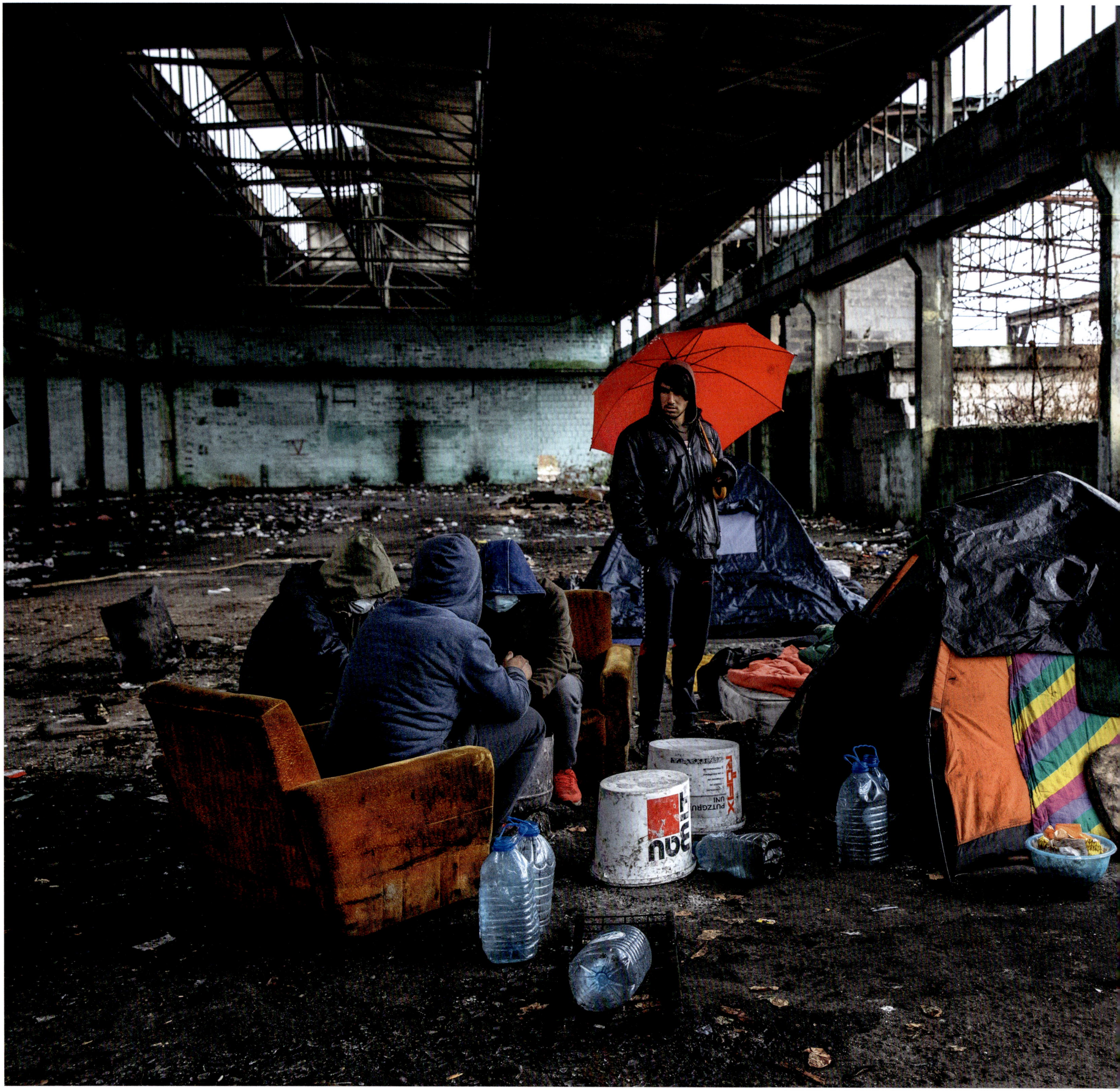
RÖFIX
UNI

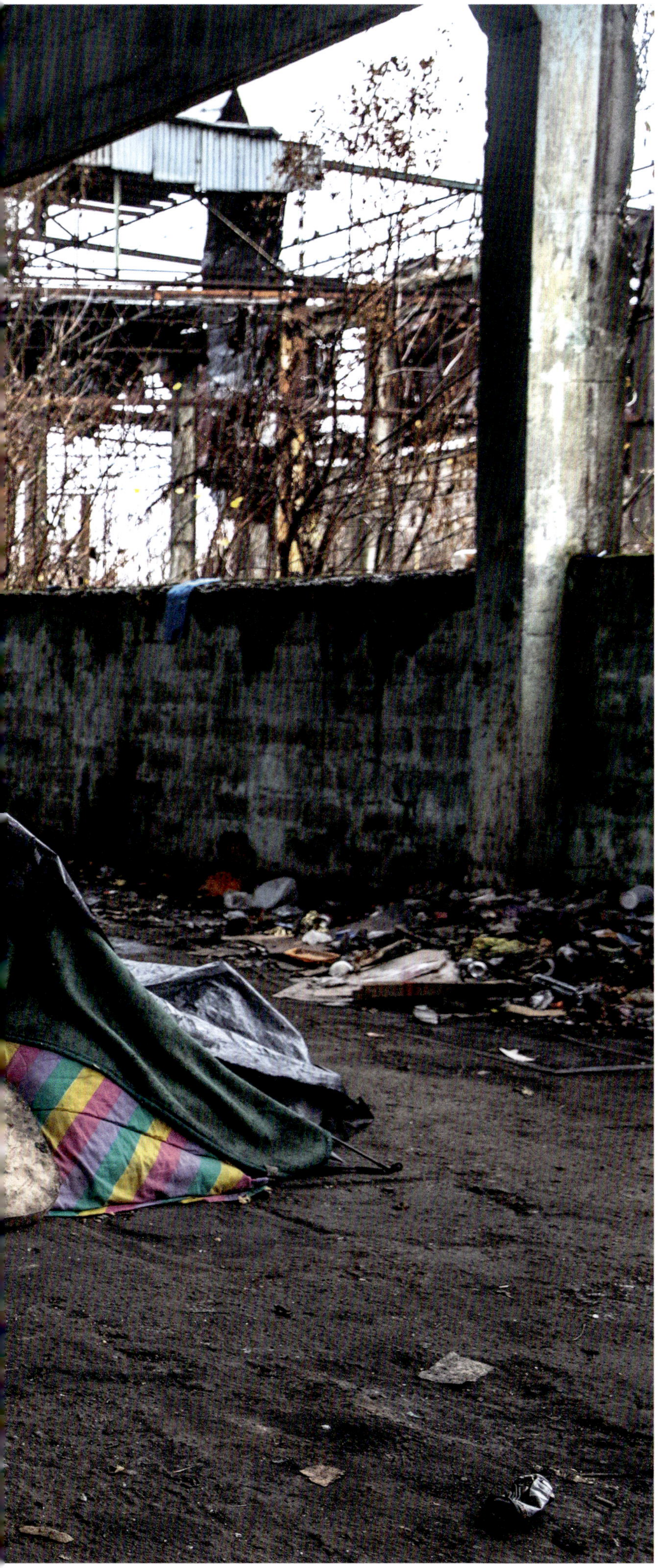

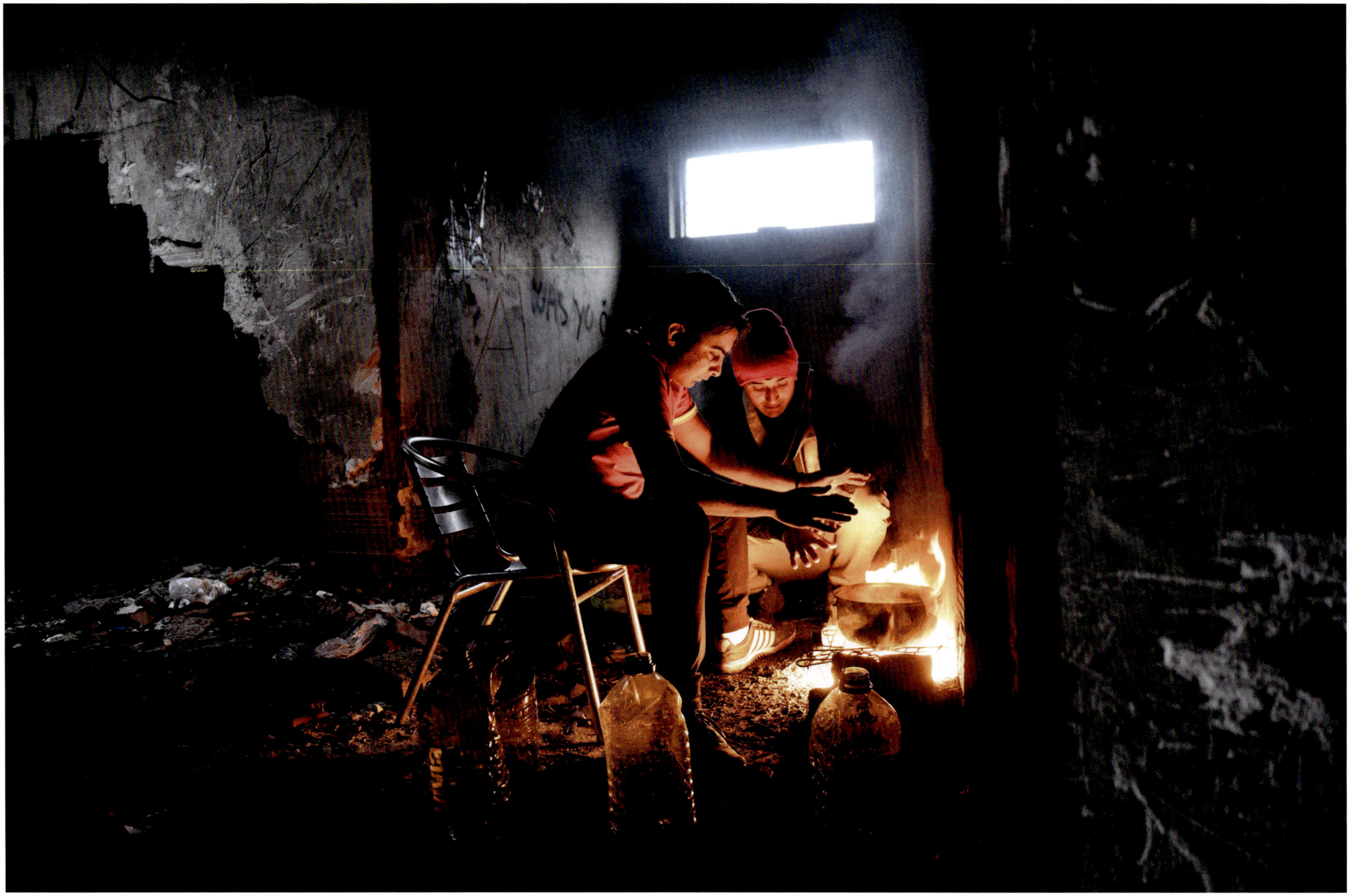

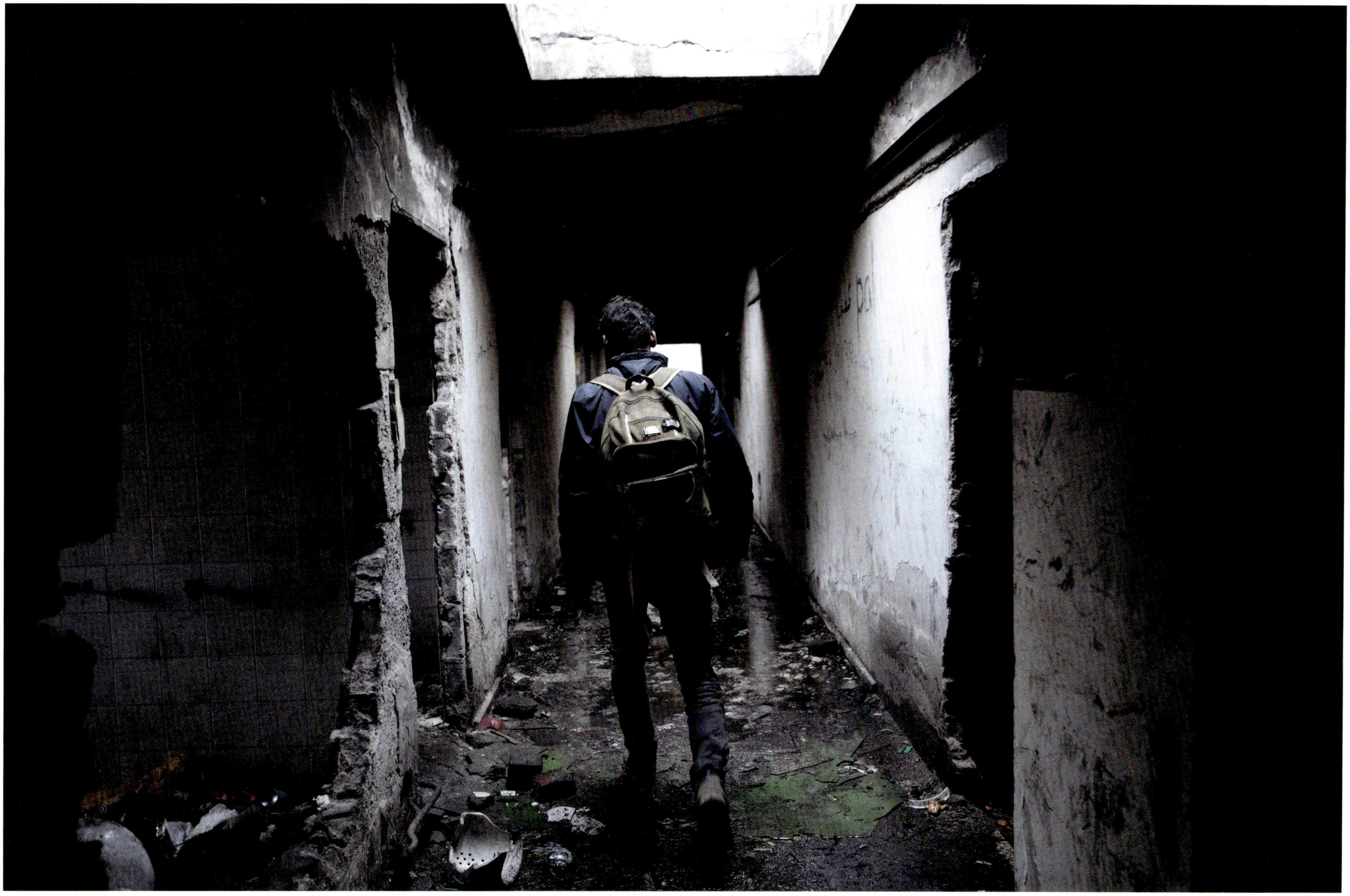

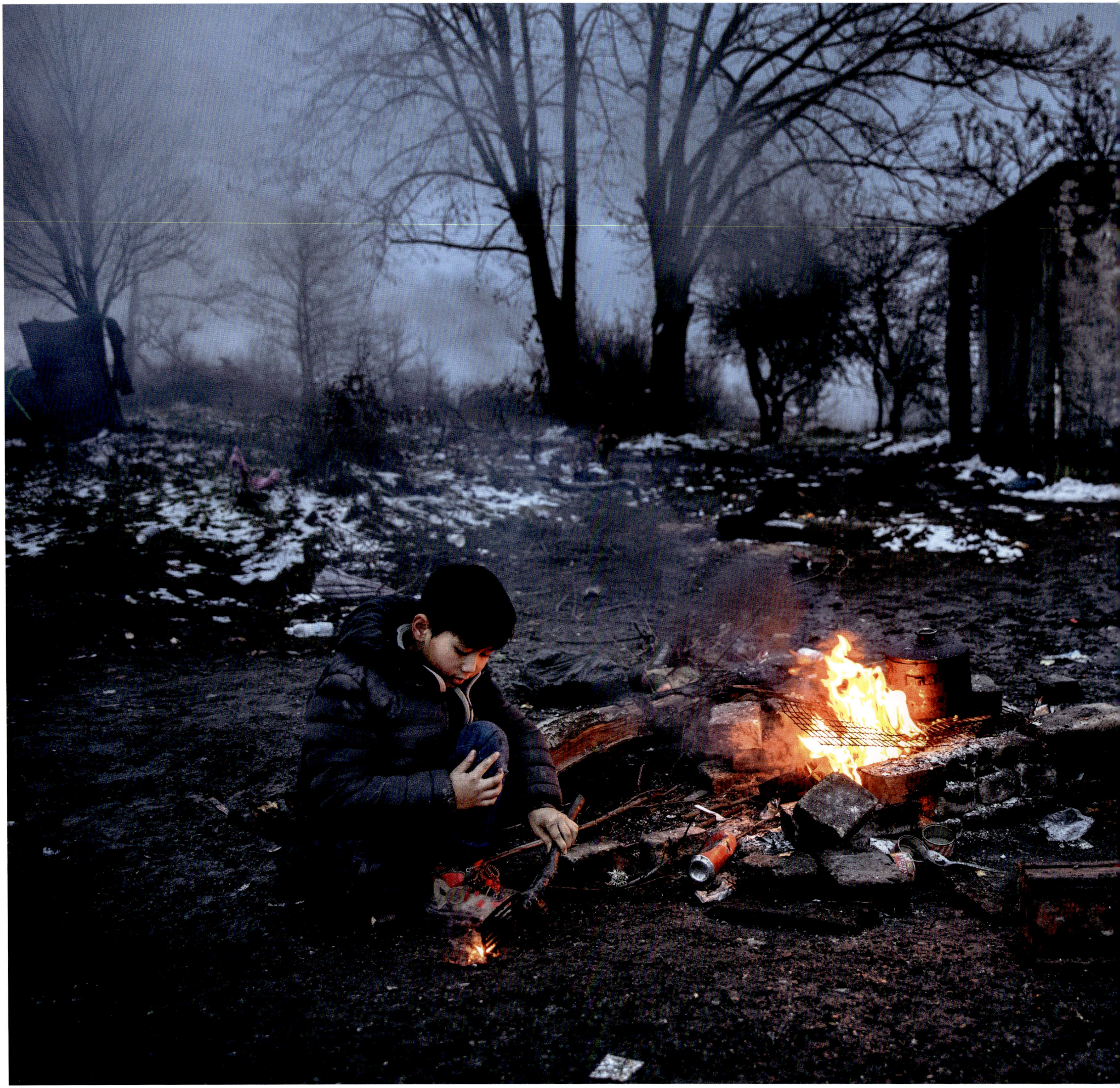

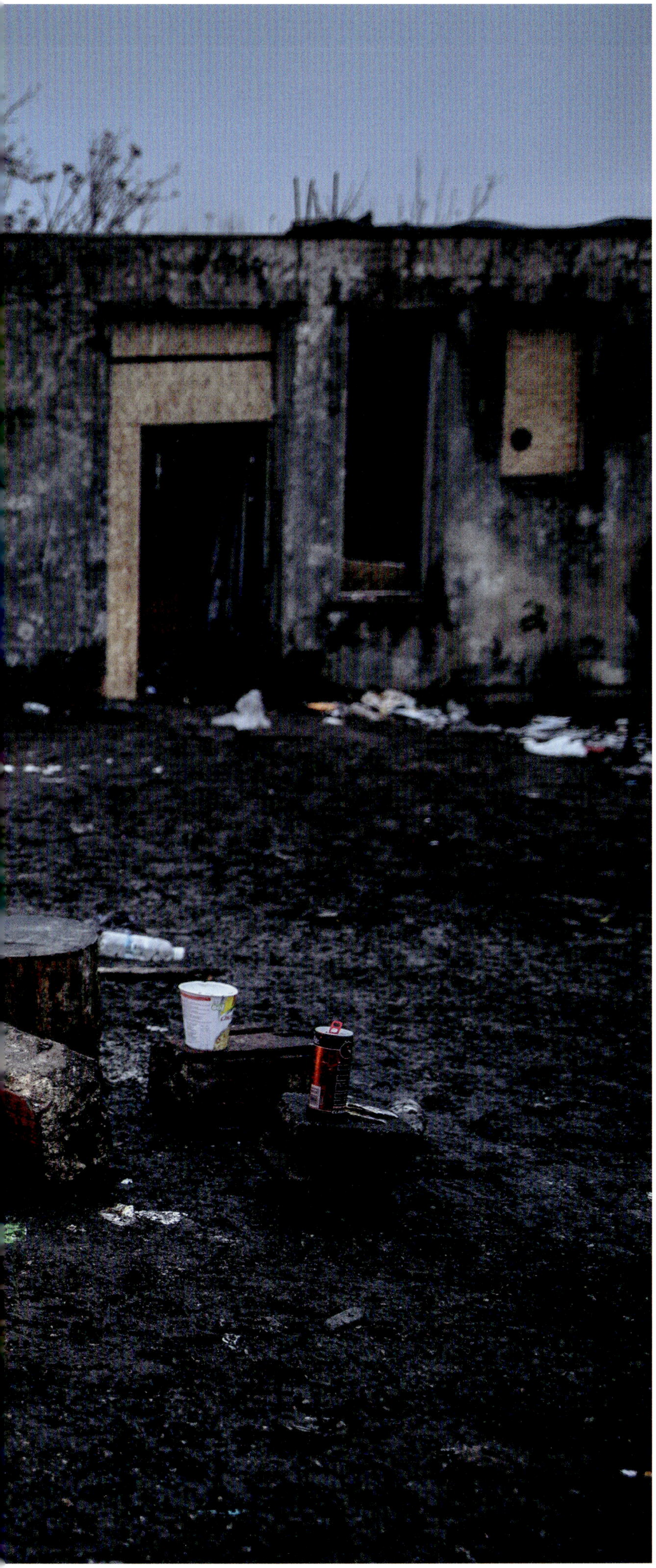

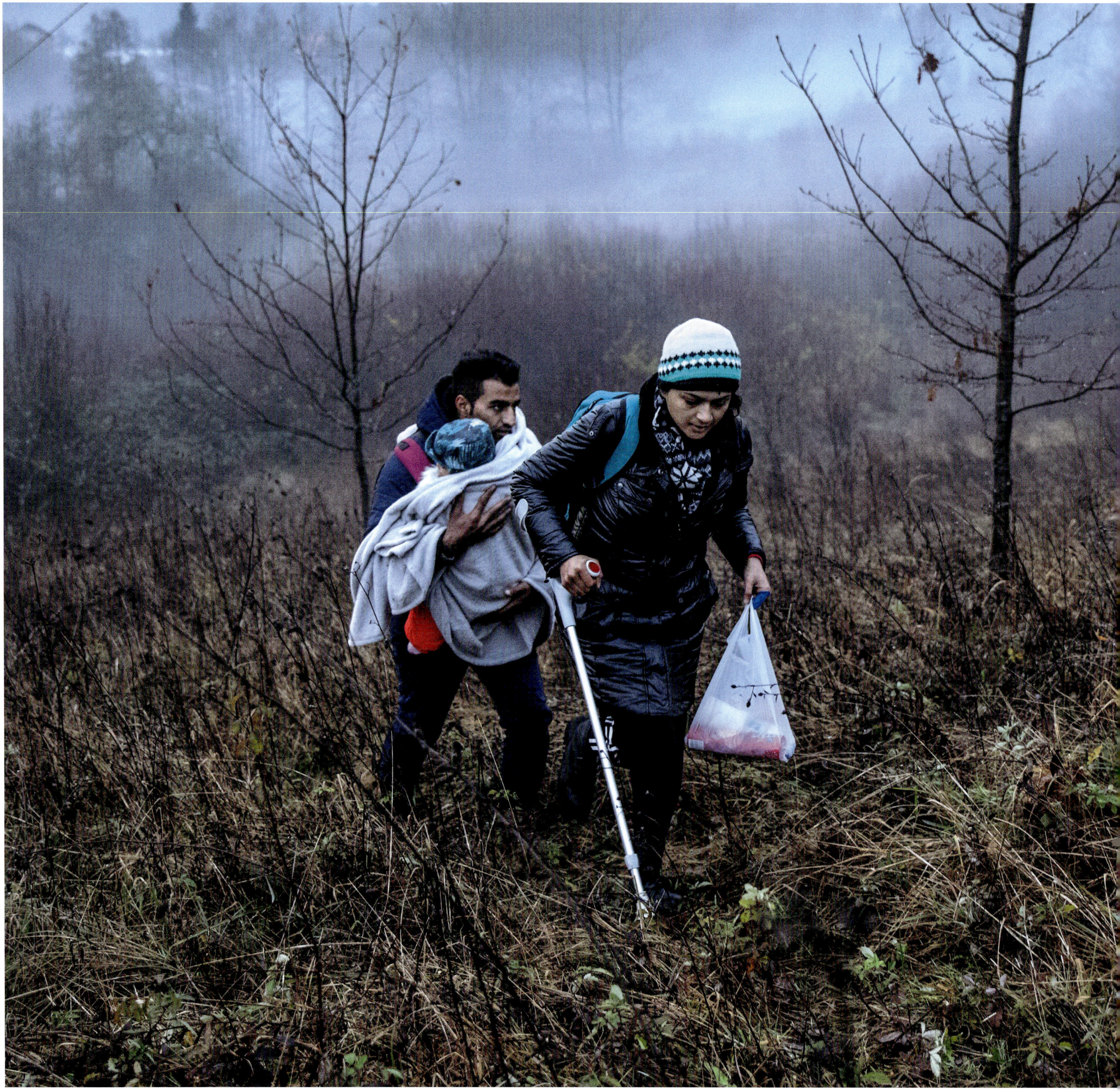

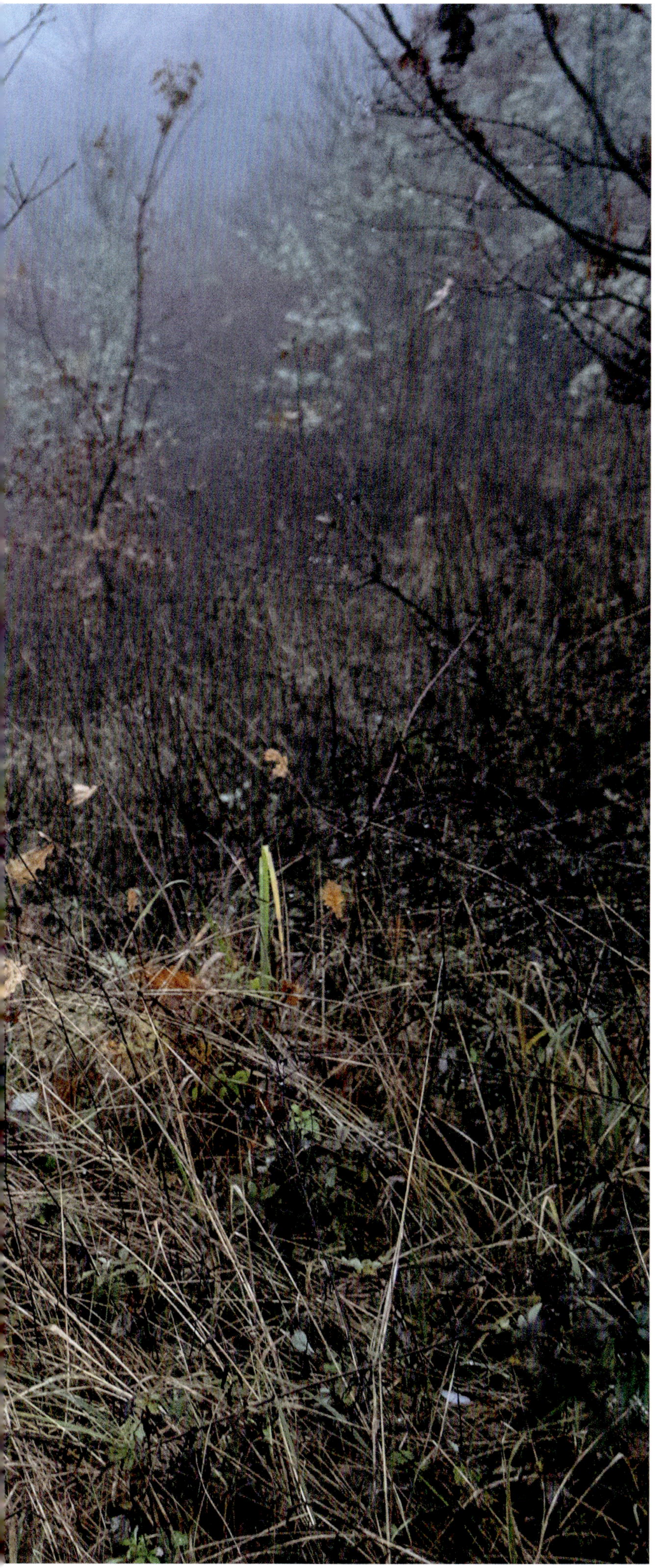

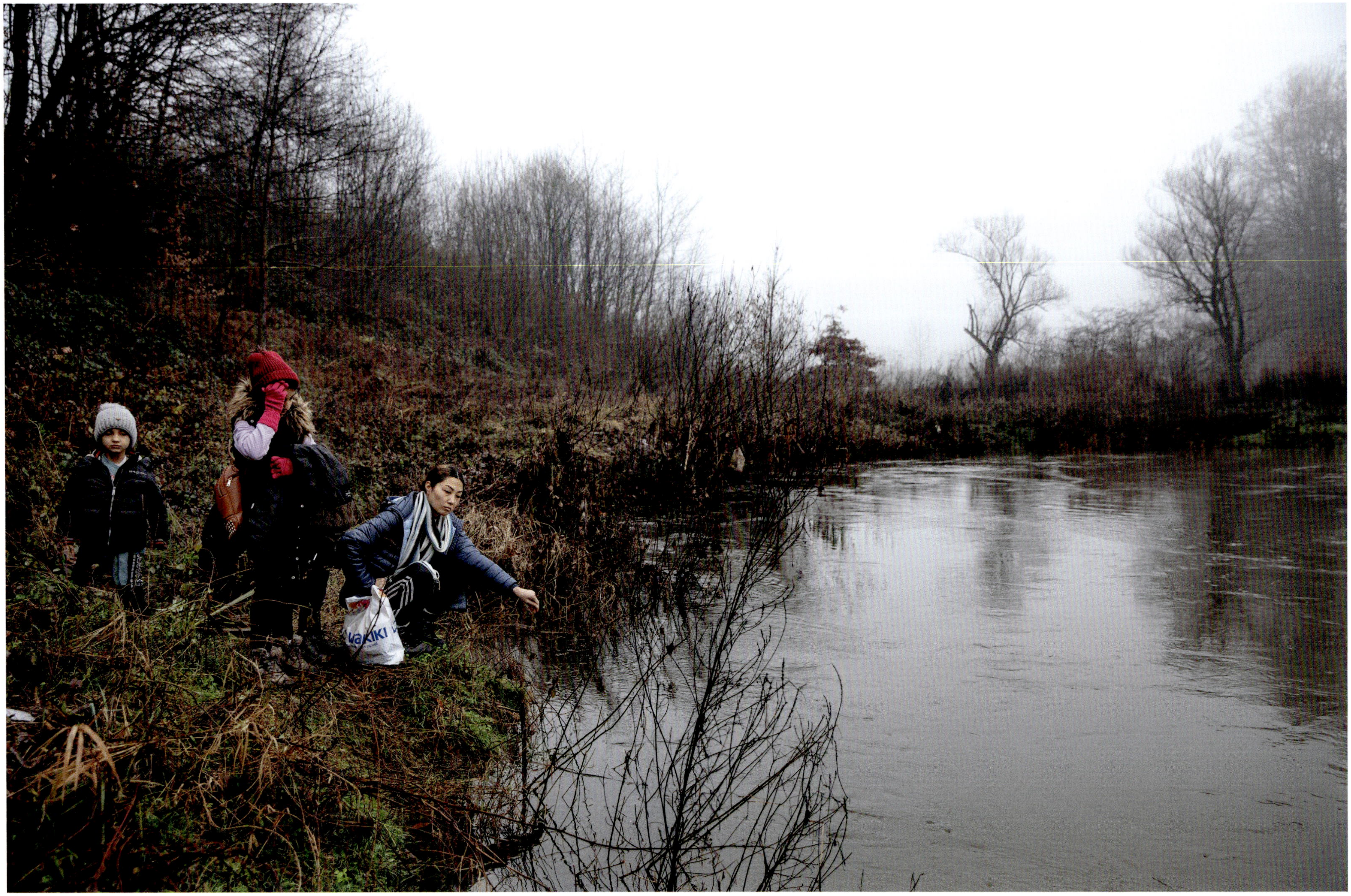

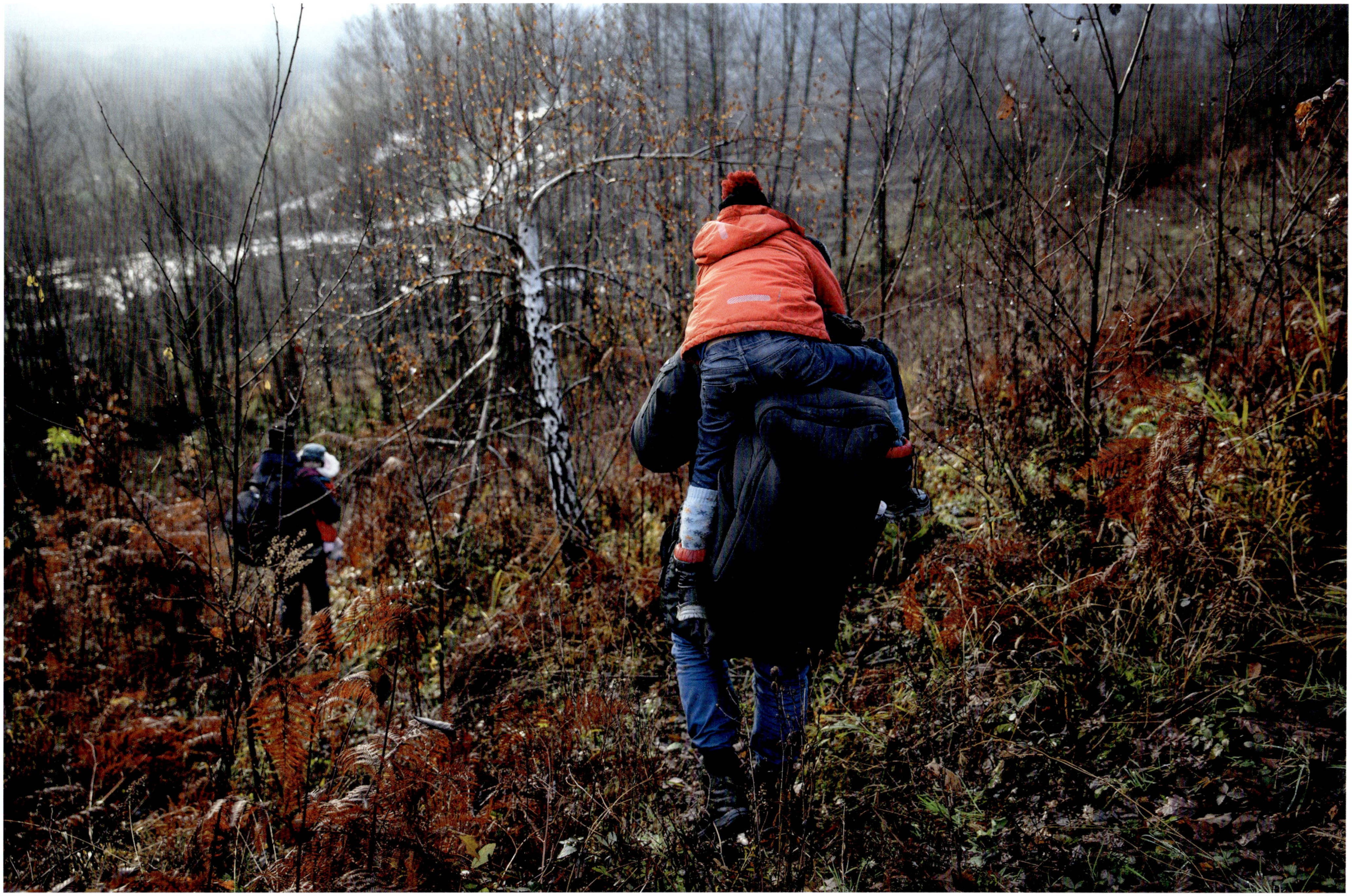

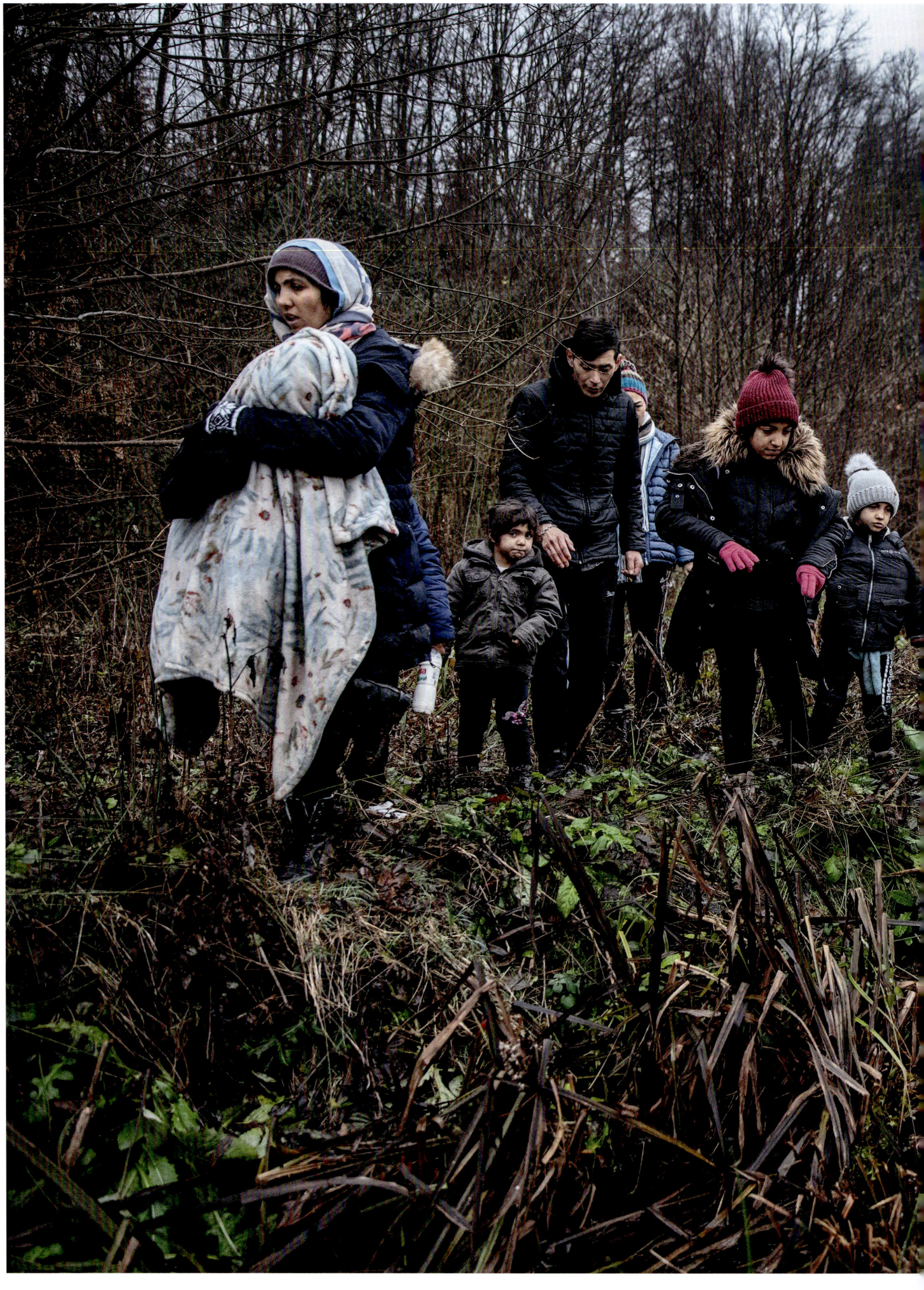

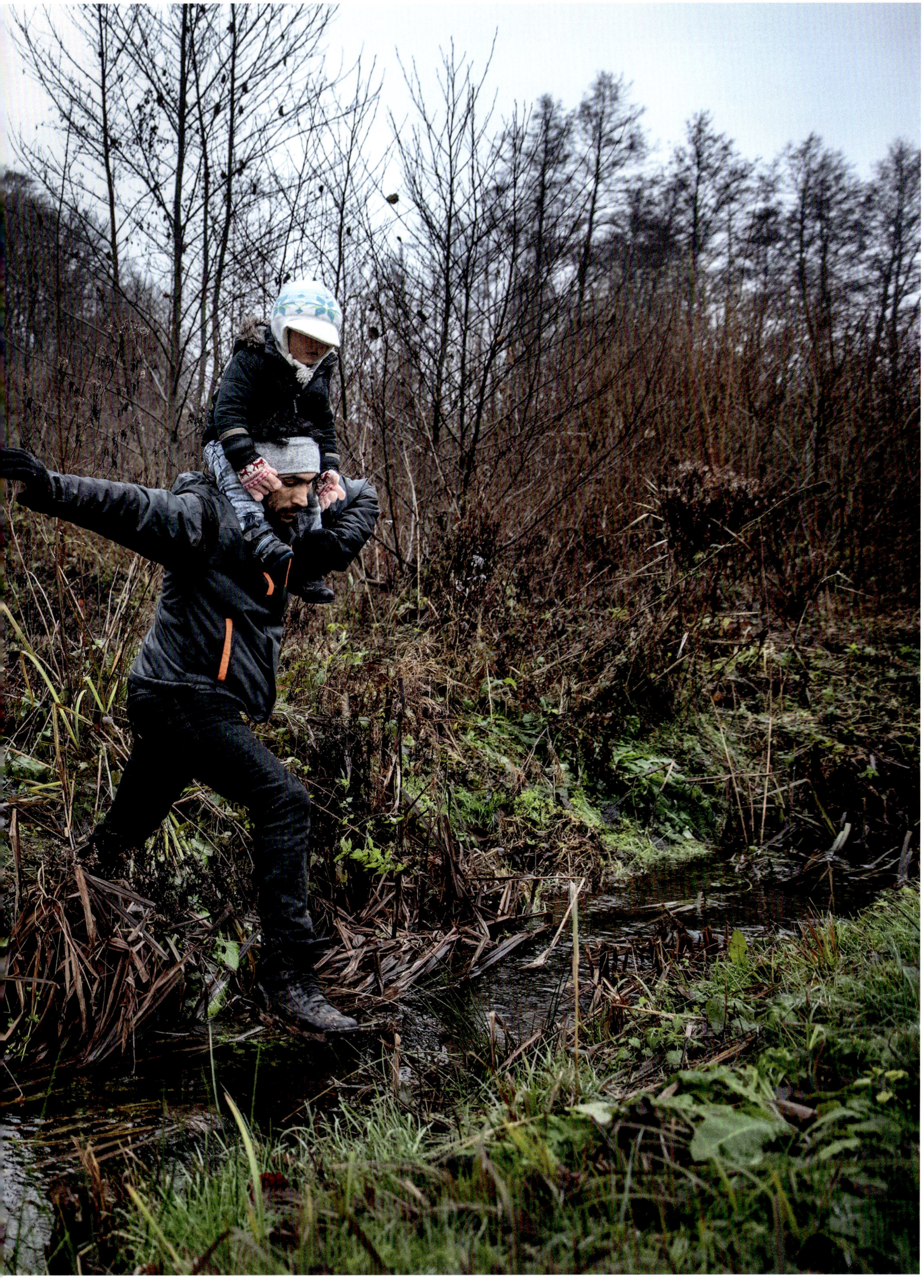

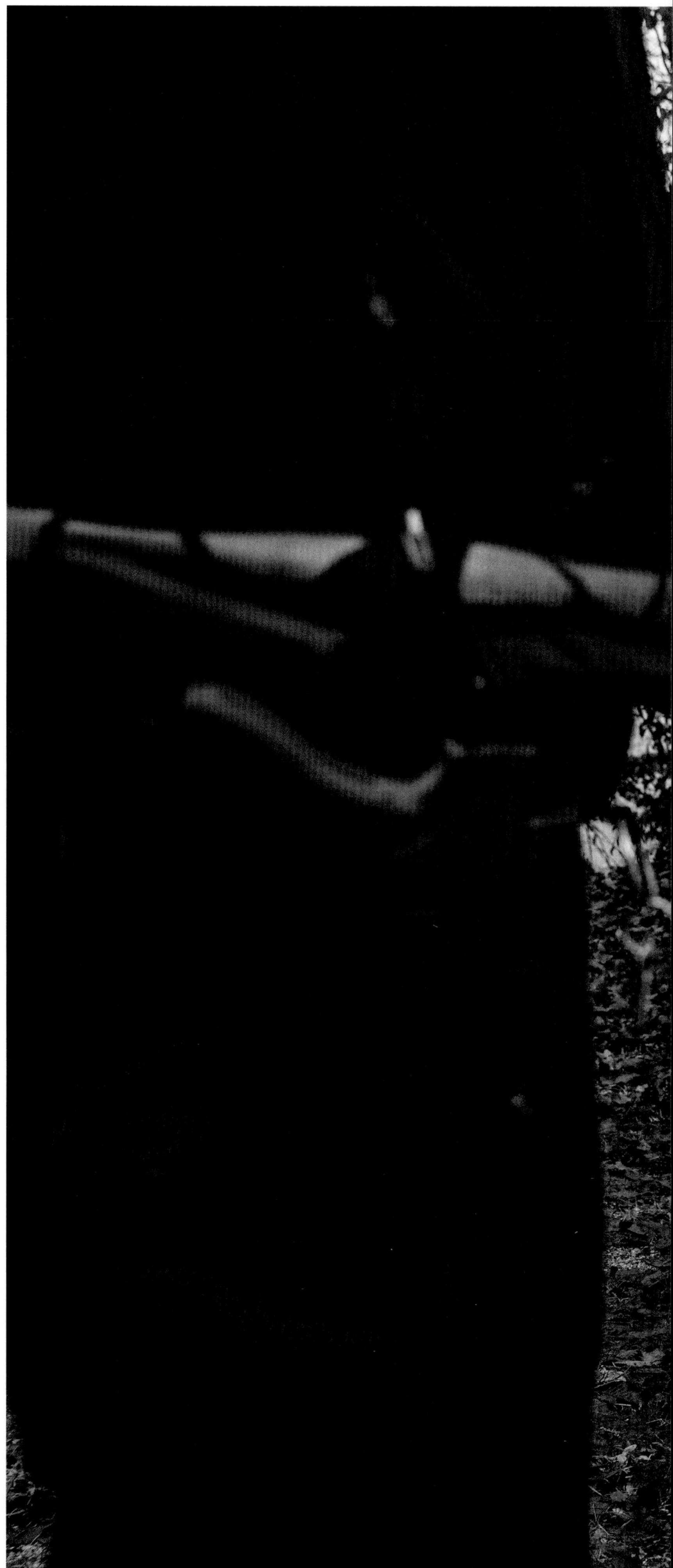

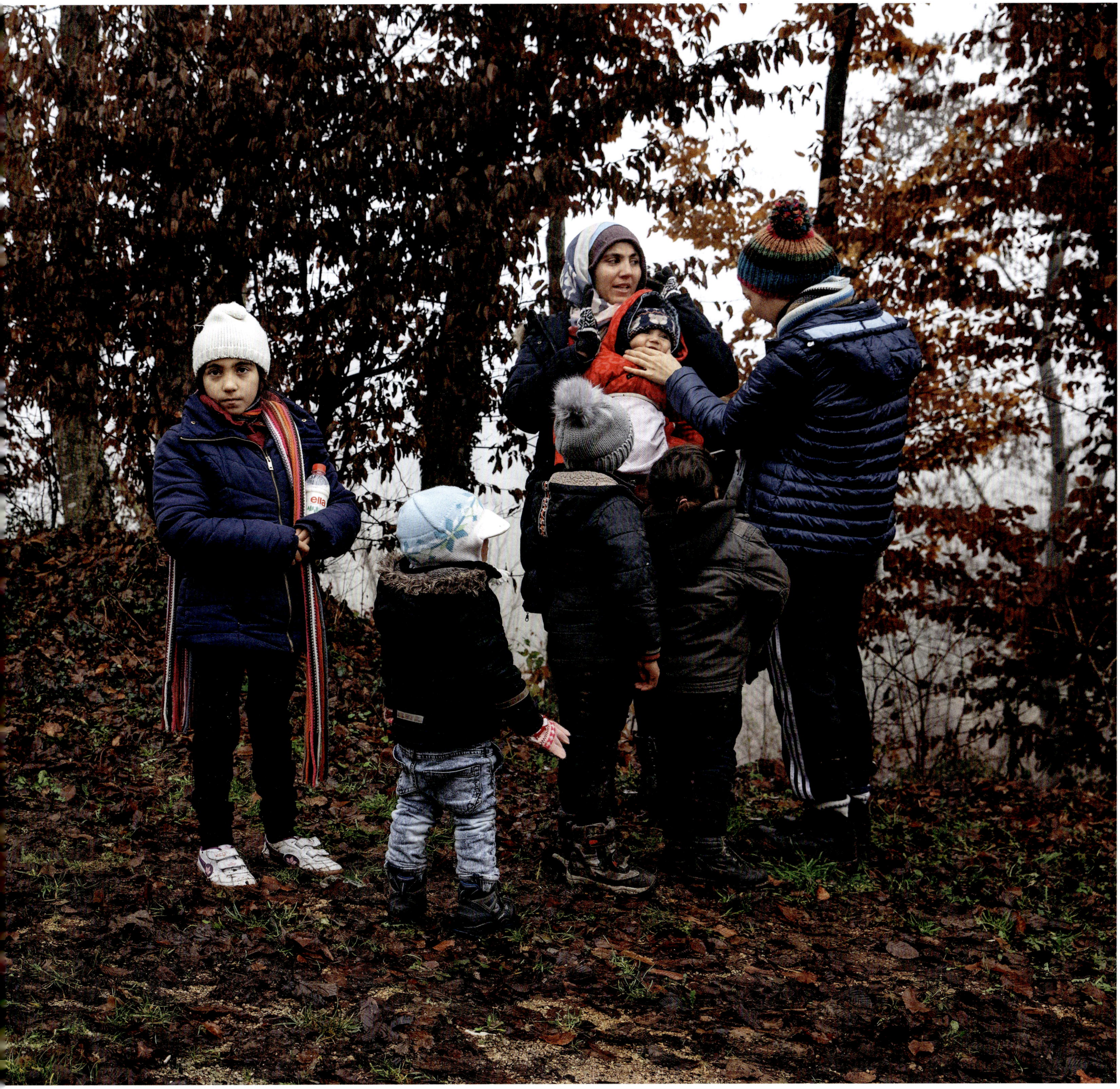
ella

In the summer of 2019 it is four years since the huge stream of people on the run overwhelmed the European asylum systems and the Greeks were confronted with an enormous logistical challenge.

Refugees and migrants continue to come to the Greek islands and they still have to wait a long time before they can move on. It is not unusual that the first interview, which marks the start of an asylum case, is scheduled a year into the future.

Outside the overcrowded reception centres, the improvised 'jungle' camps grow. The asylum seekers live under extremely primitive conditions. There is very limited access to water, electricity and sanitation. It is very hot in the summer and cold in the winter and it is teeming with rats and snakes. Doctors Without Borders (MSF) and local NGOs estimate that up to forty percent of the residents in the camps on Samos and Lesbos are children. They tell of children with self-harming behaviour and suicidal thoughts.

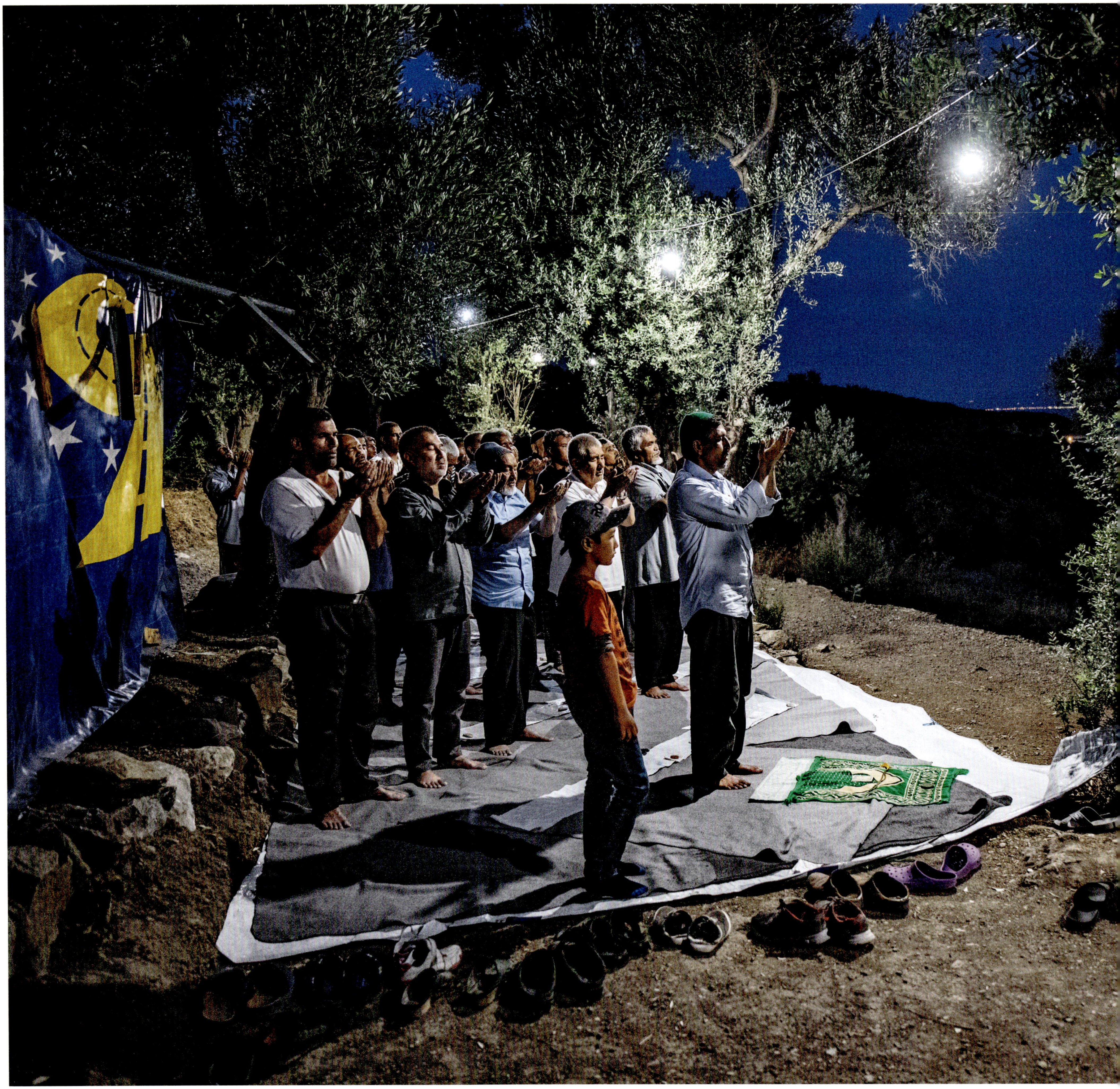

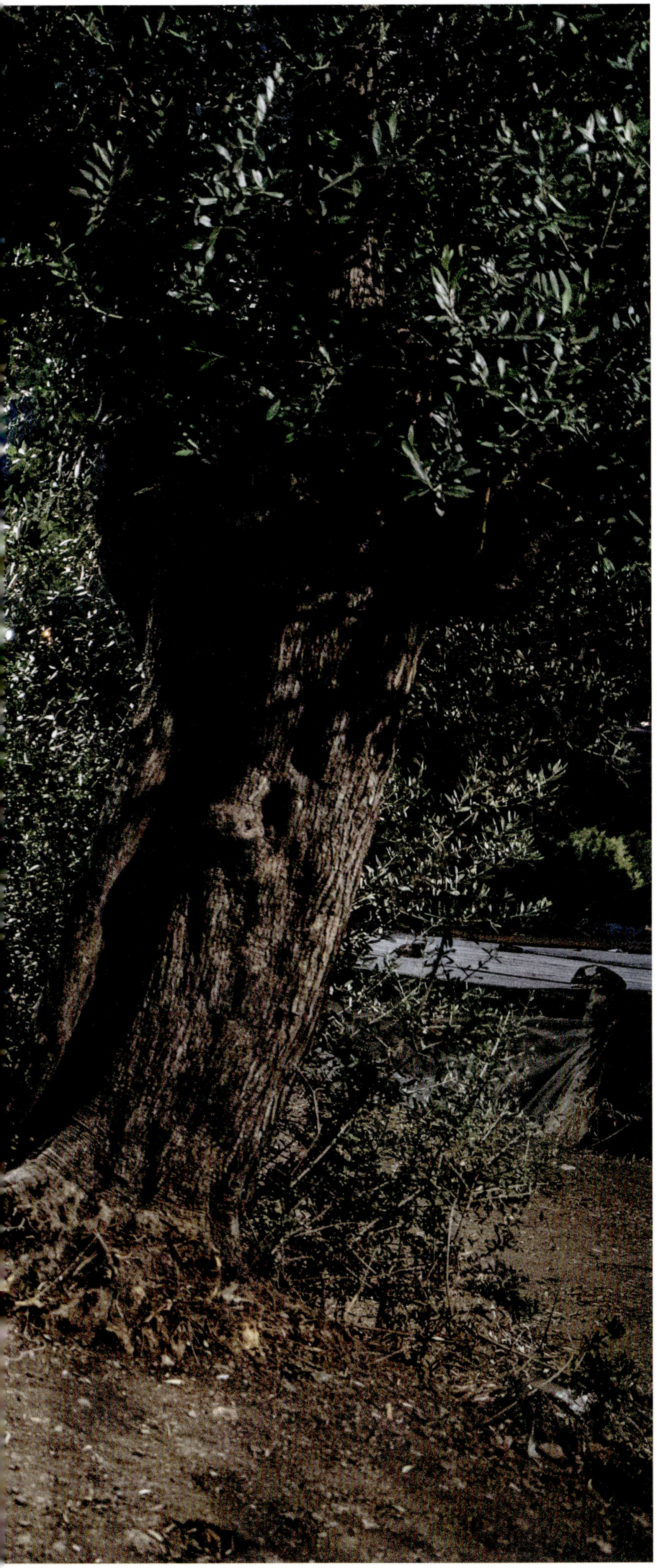

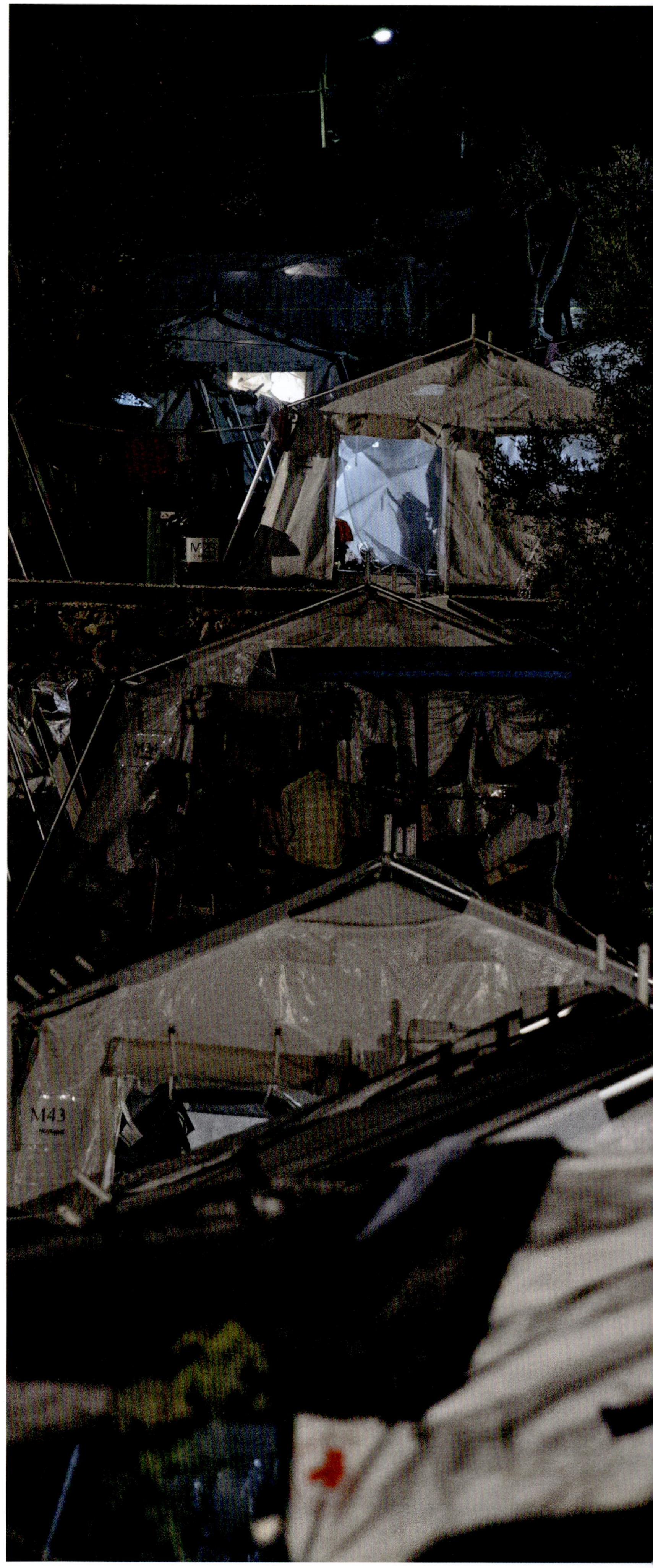
M43

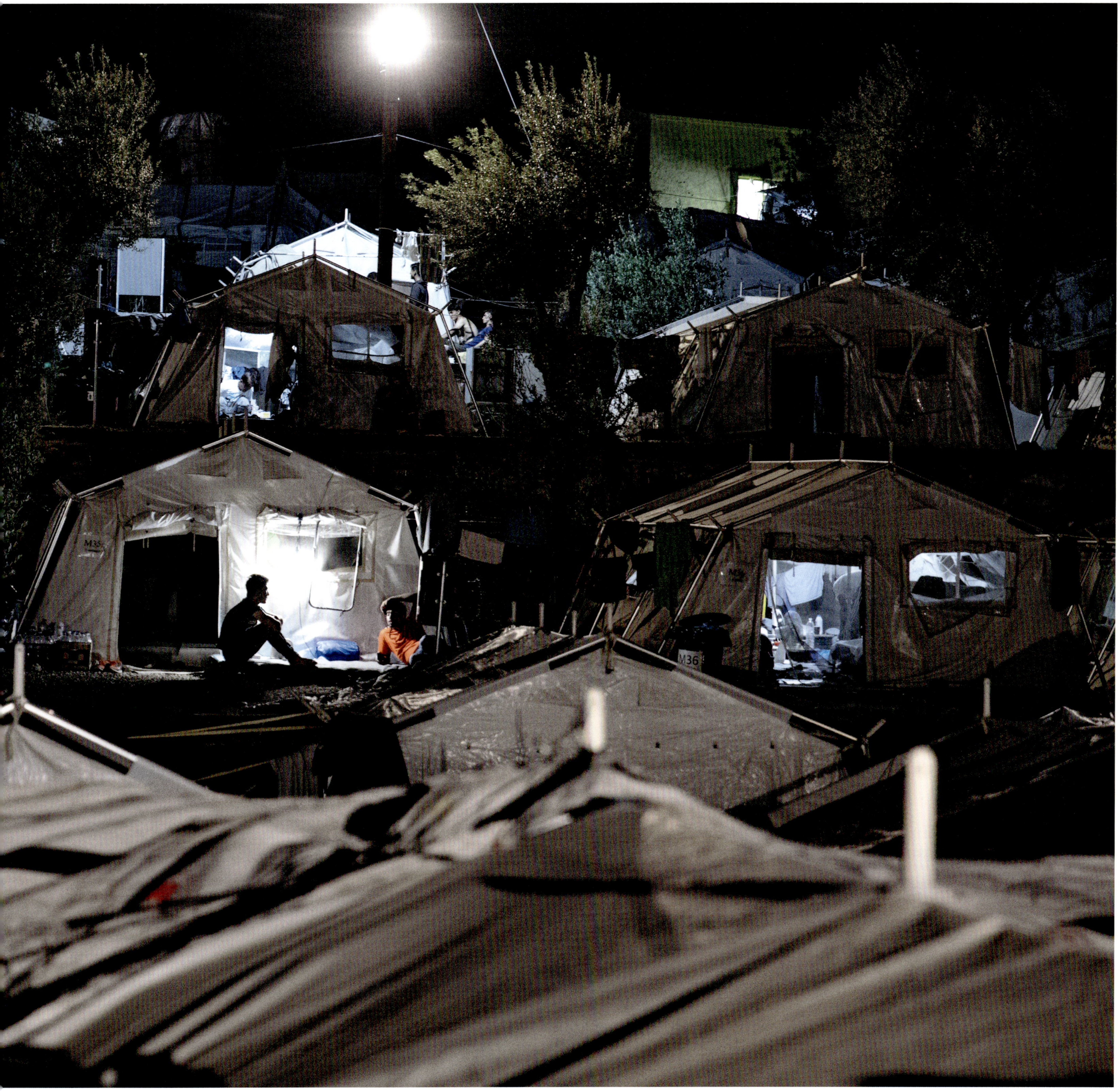
M36

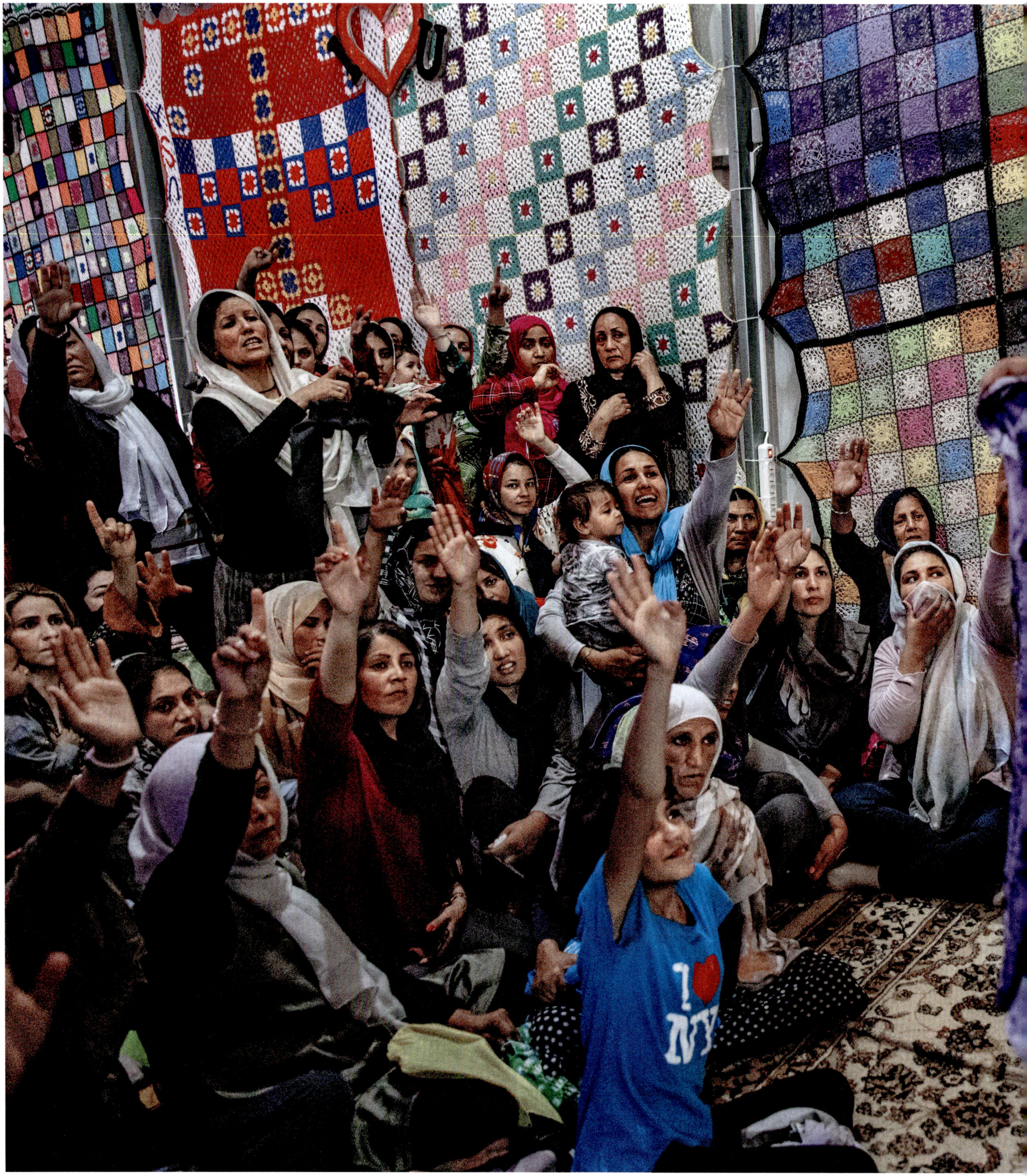
I NY

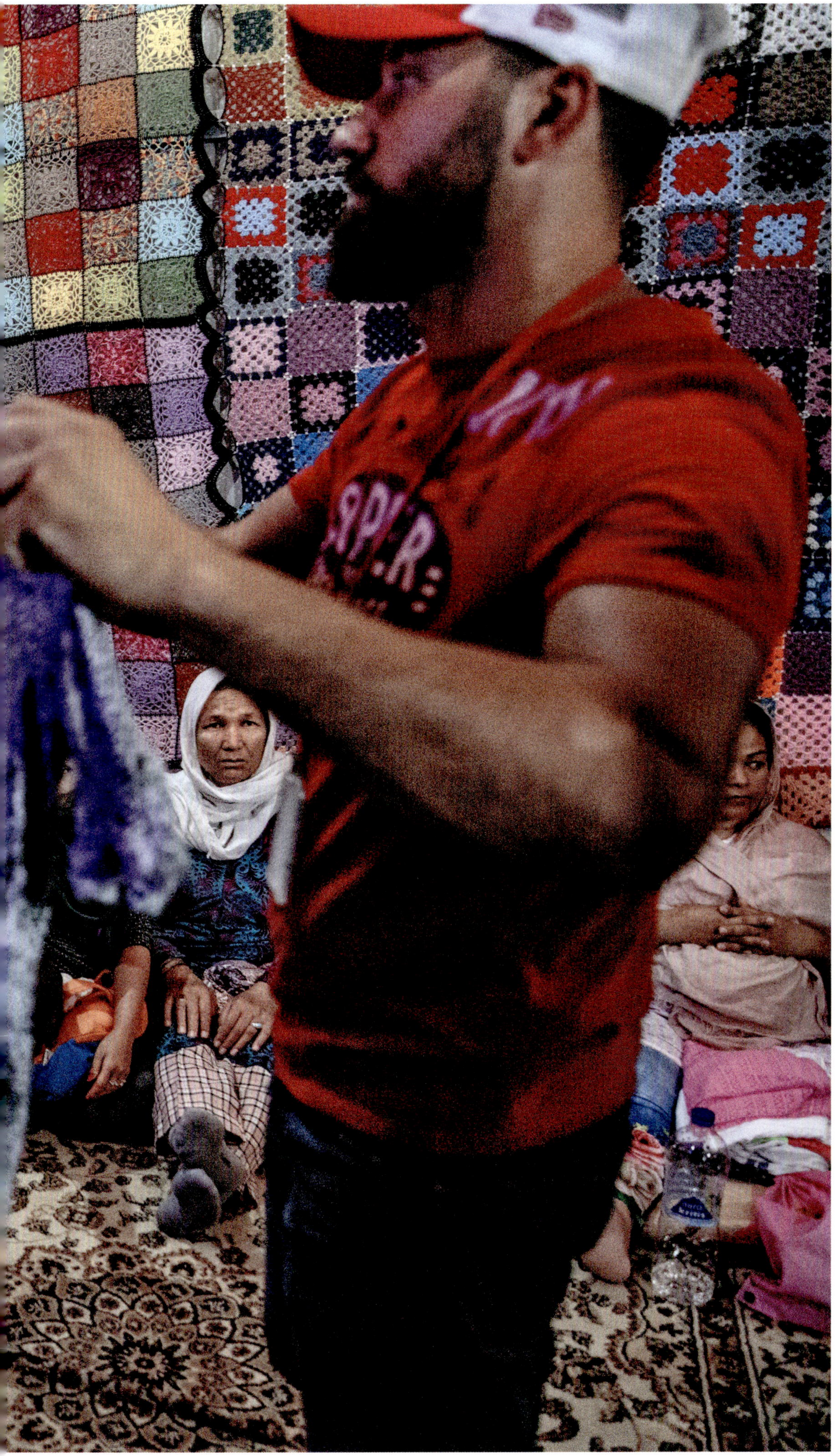

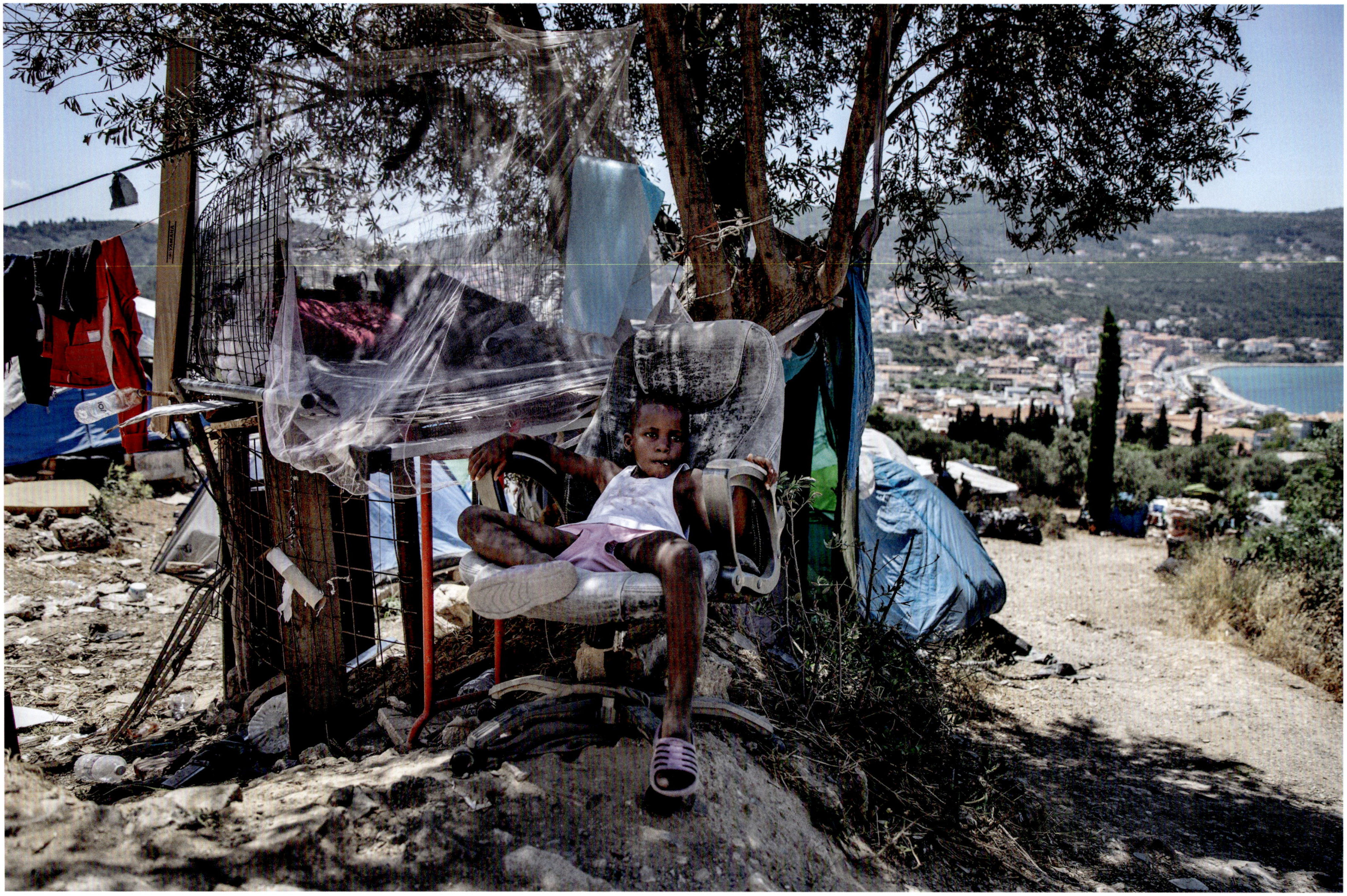

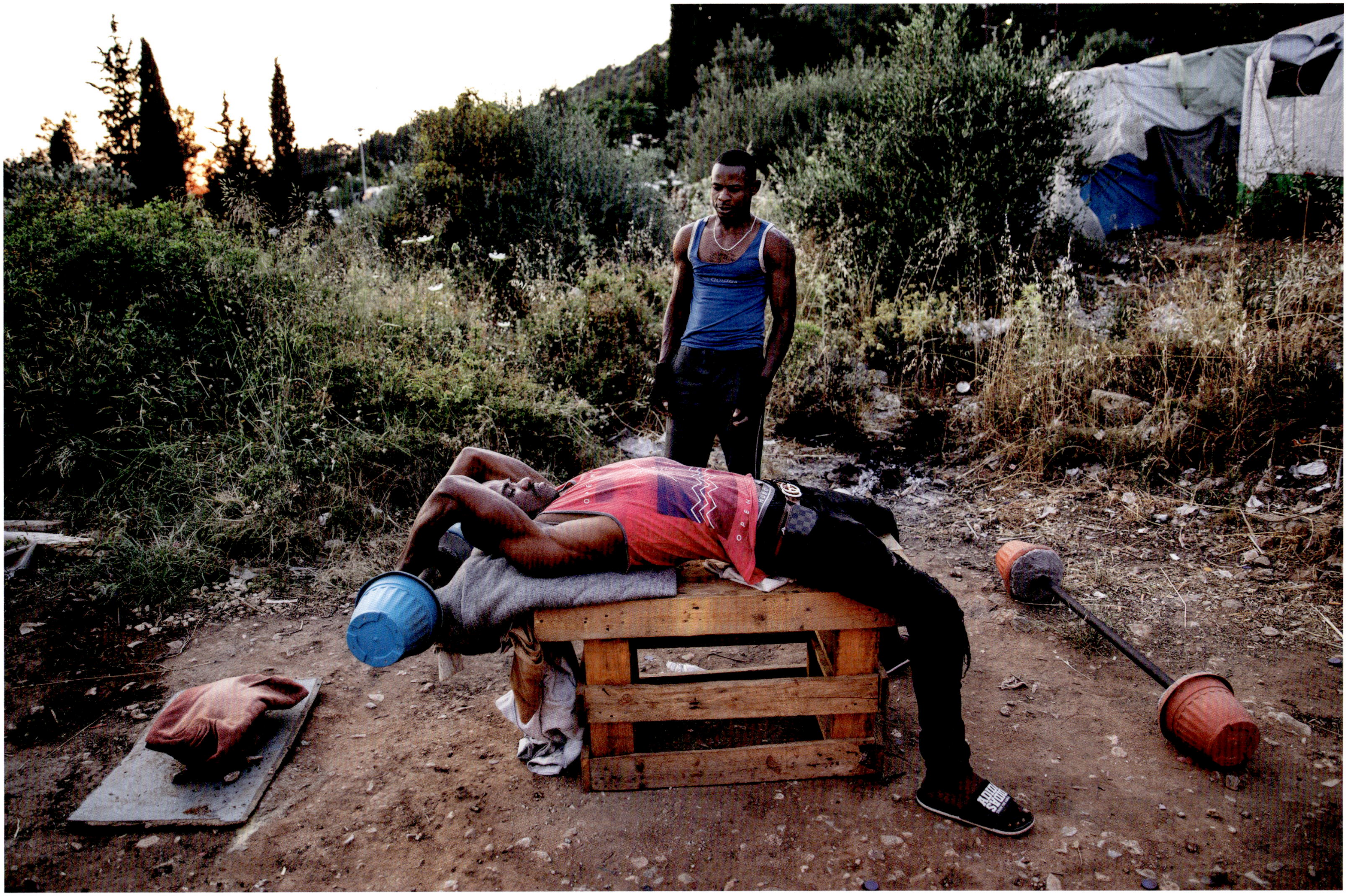

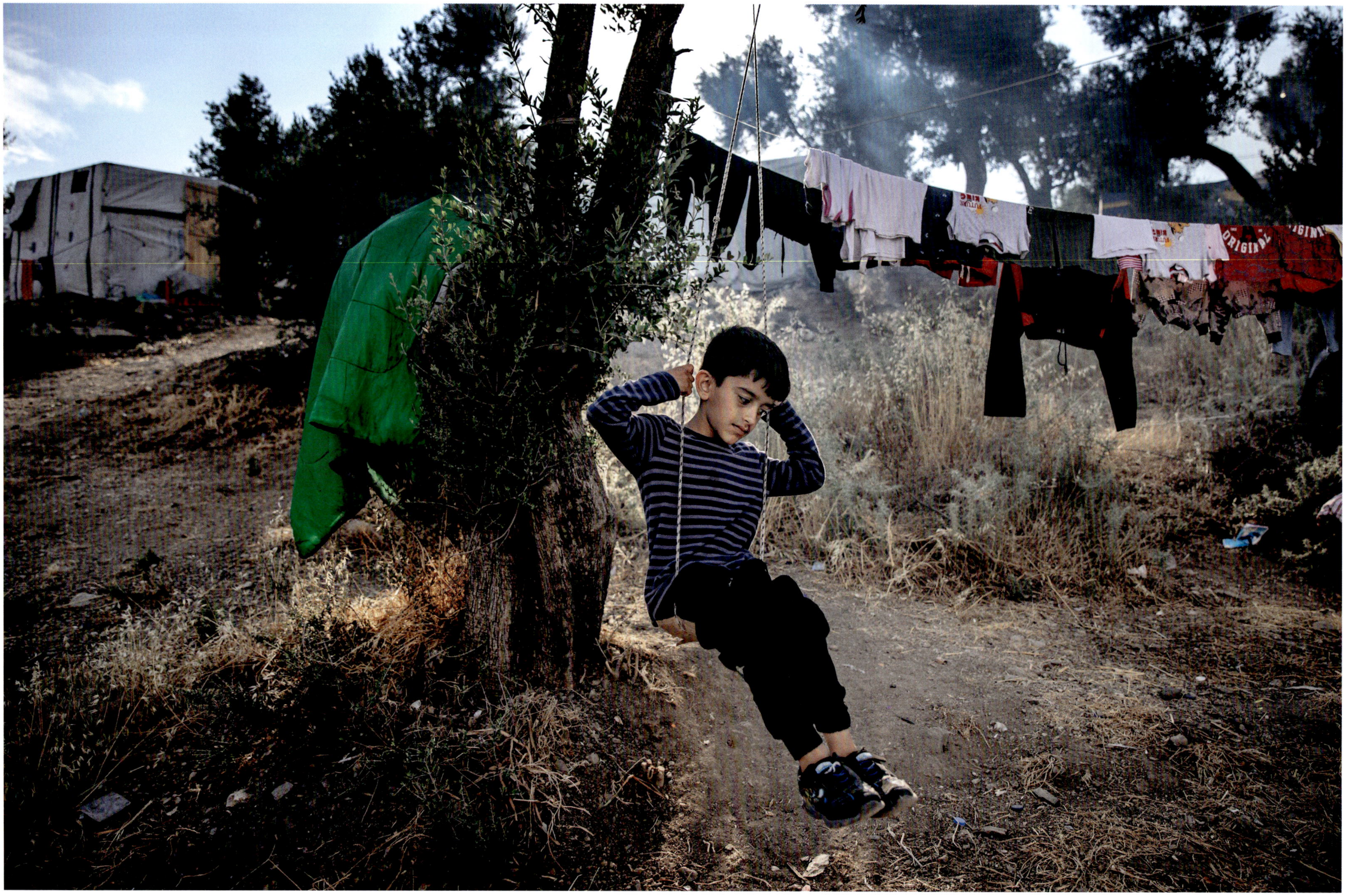
ORIGINAL

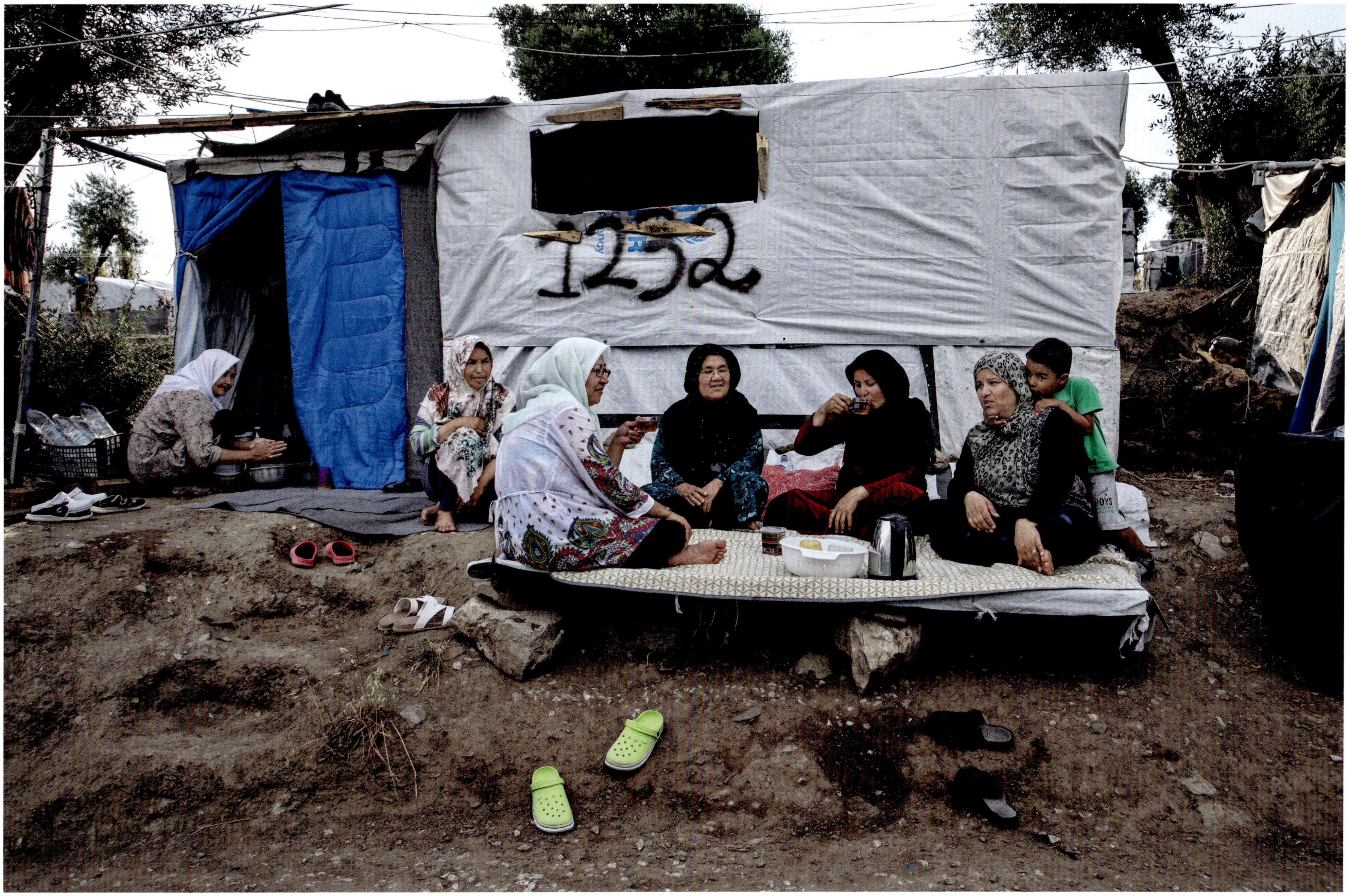
1252

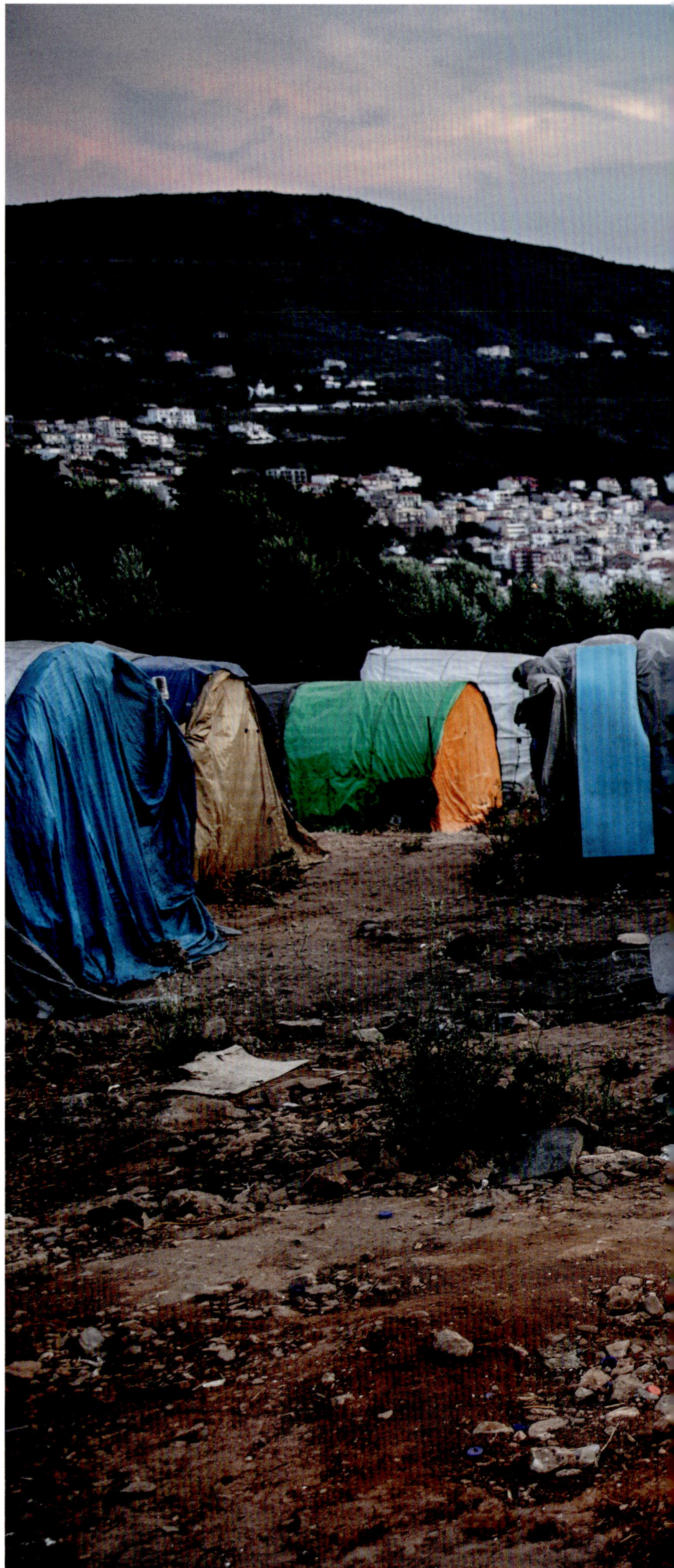

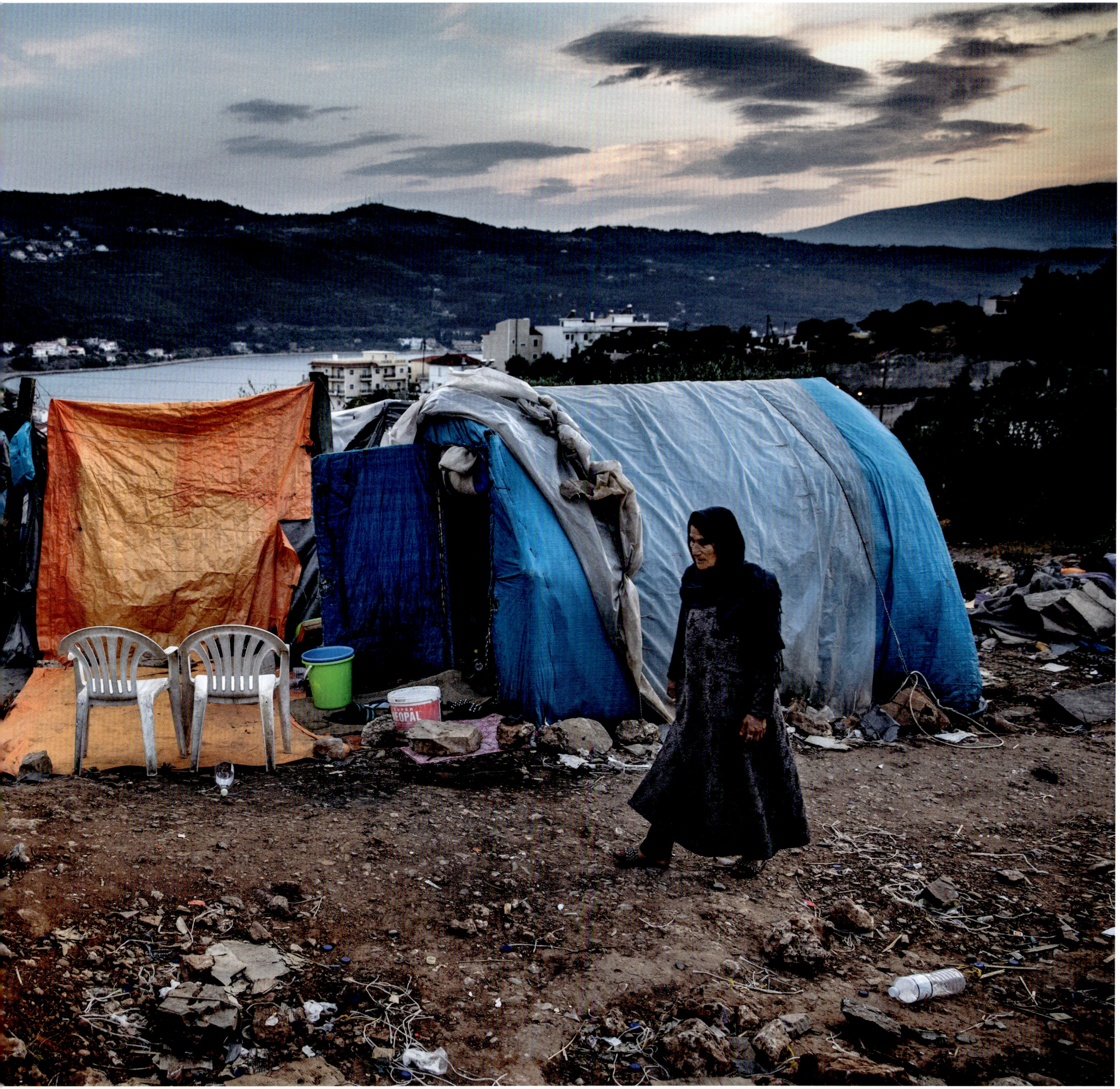

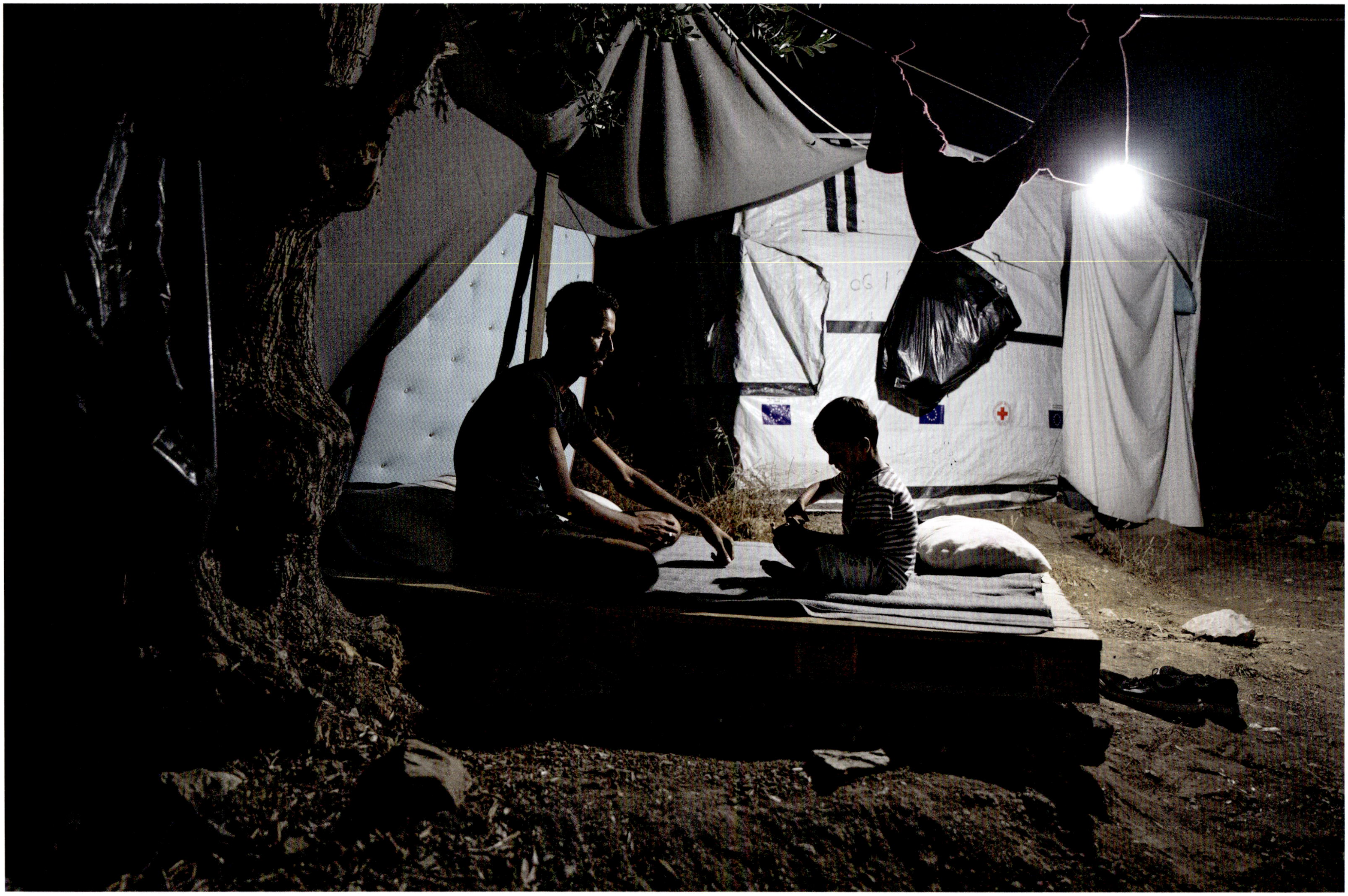

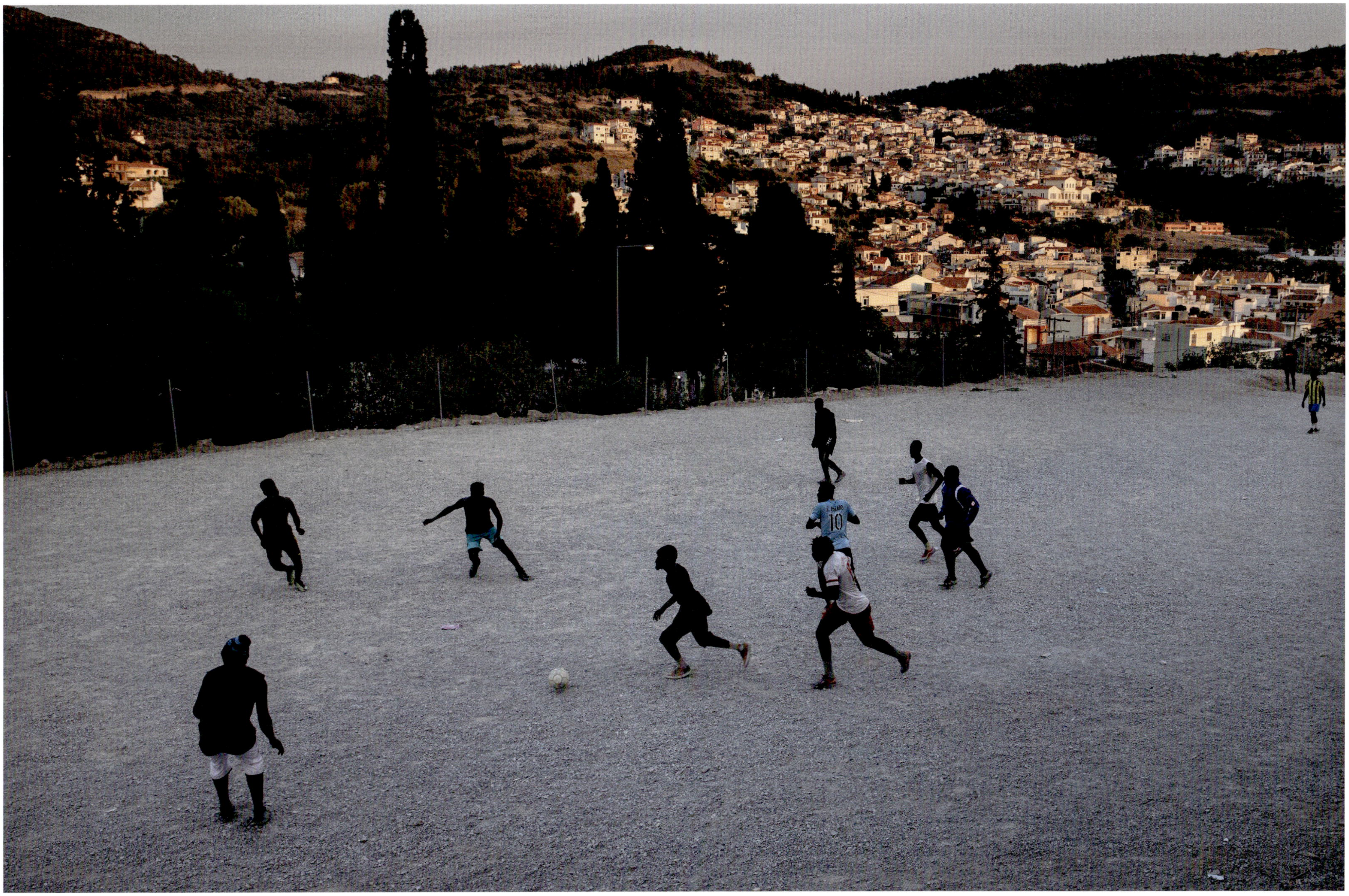

In the spring of 2018 more than 700 refugees and migrants live in a former factory and a former sawmill in the Greek port city of Patras. In the sawmill alone, around 500 people live, mainly young men and boys and mostly from Afghanistan.

All hours of the day and night, they climb over the fence surrounding the port area across the street. It's all about trying to evade the harbour police and reach the fence that surrounds the area where the lorries have passed the security check and are now parked at the quay waiting to drive onto one of the many ferries to Italy. Even if the last fence is successfully crossed, it is not easy to hide on one of the lorries without the police discovering them. But the dream of reaching Italy is powerful and the young men try again and again. They refer to these attempts to get further as 'the game'.

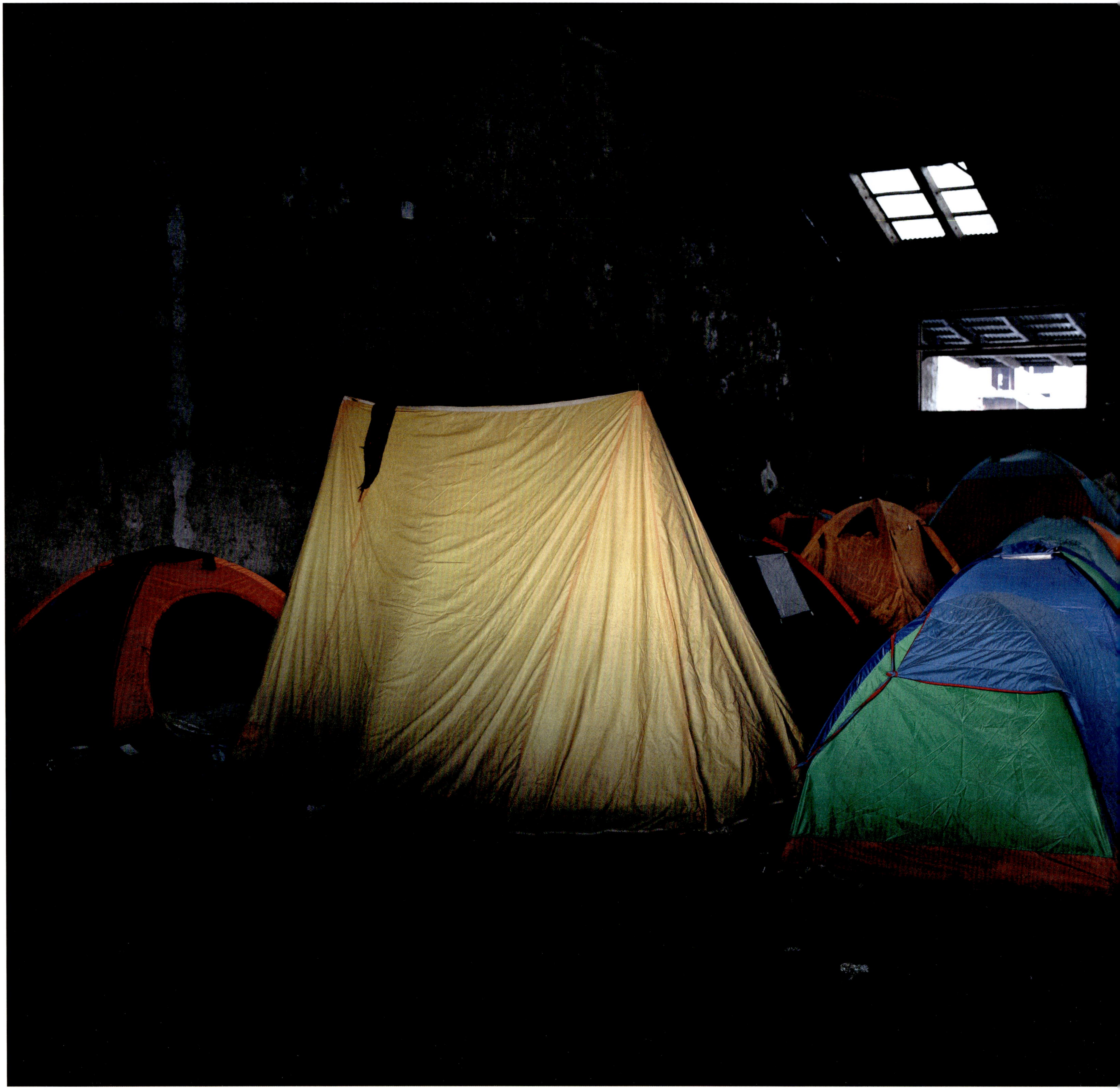

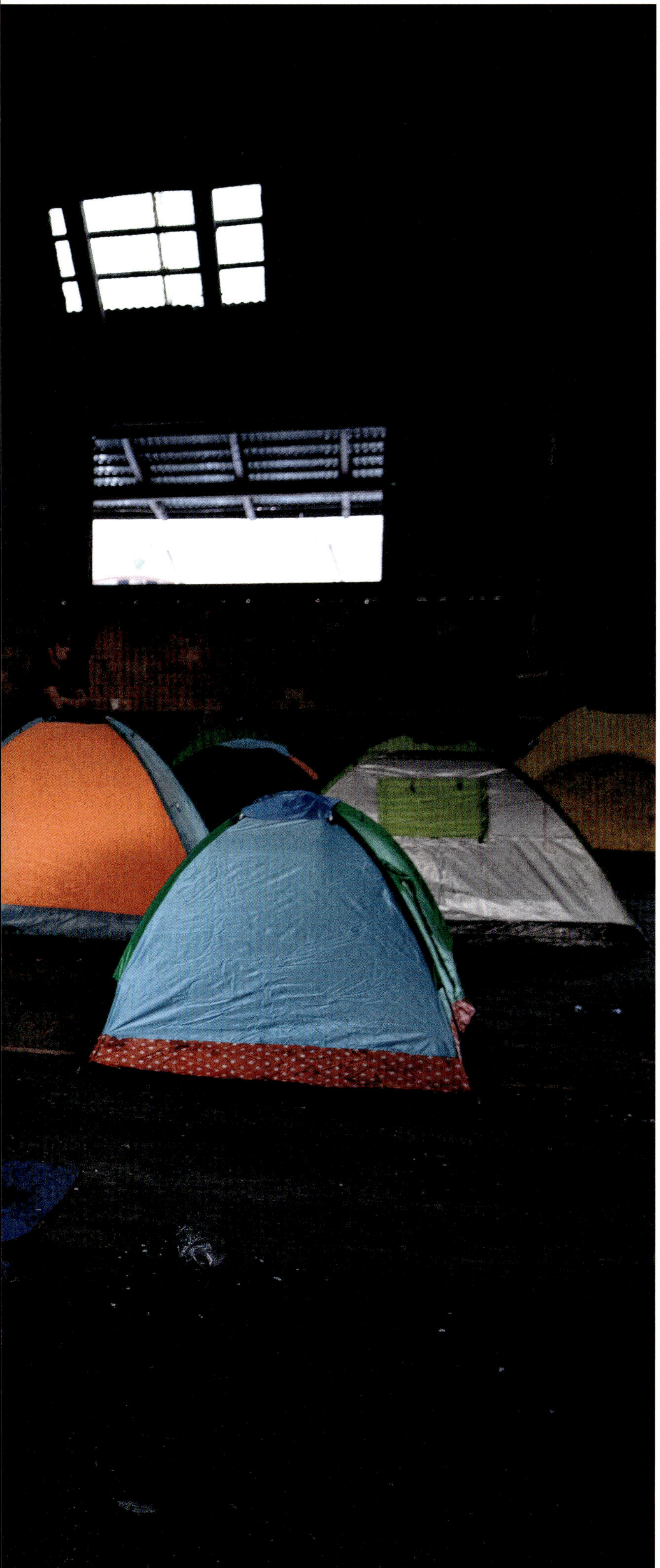

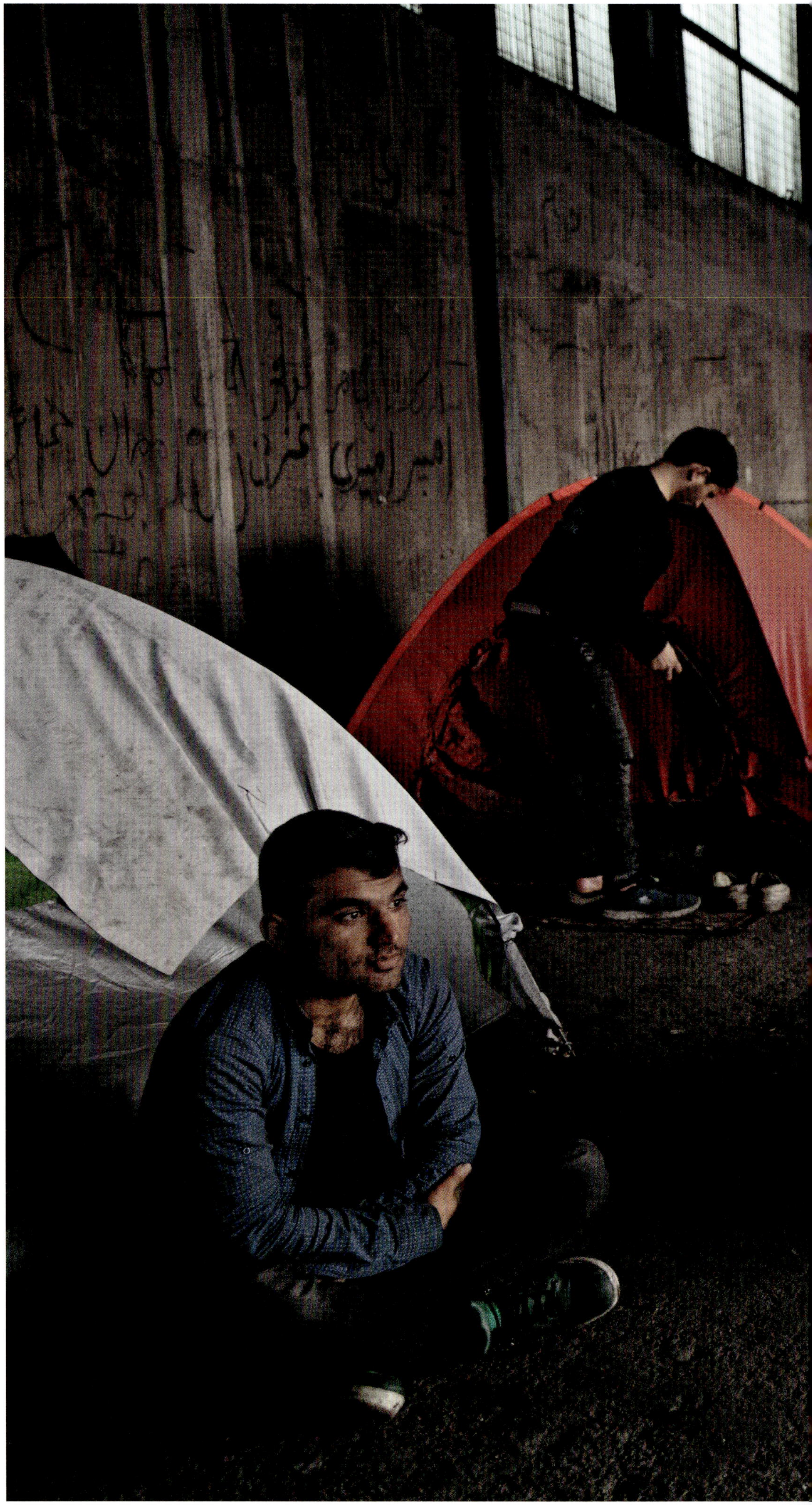

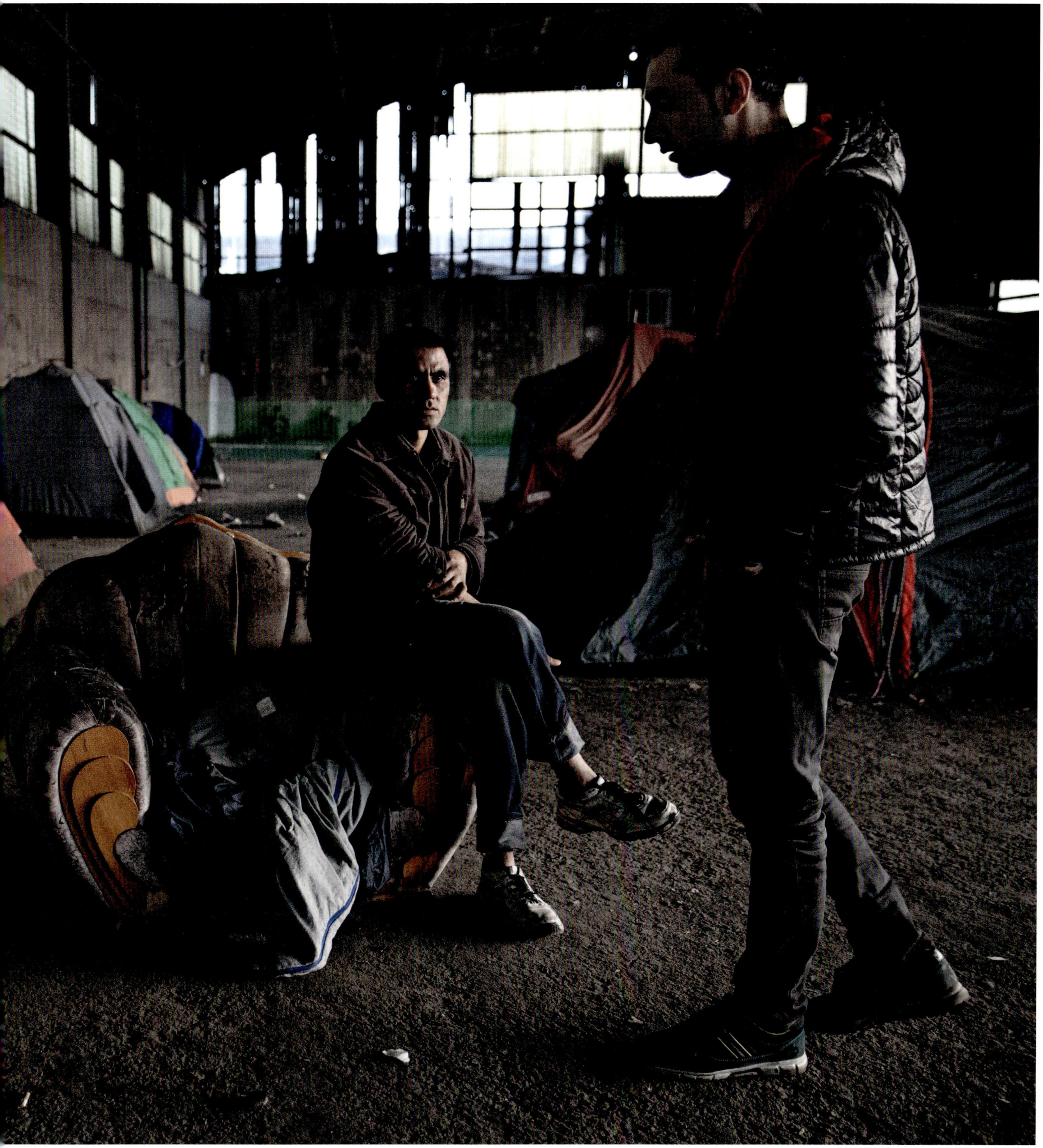

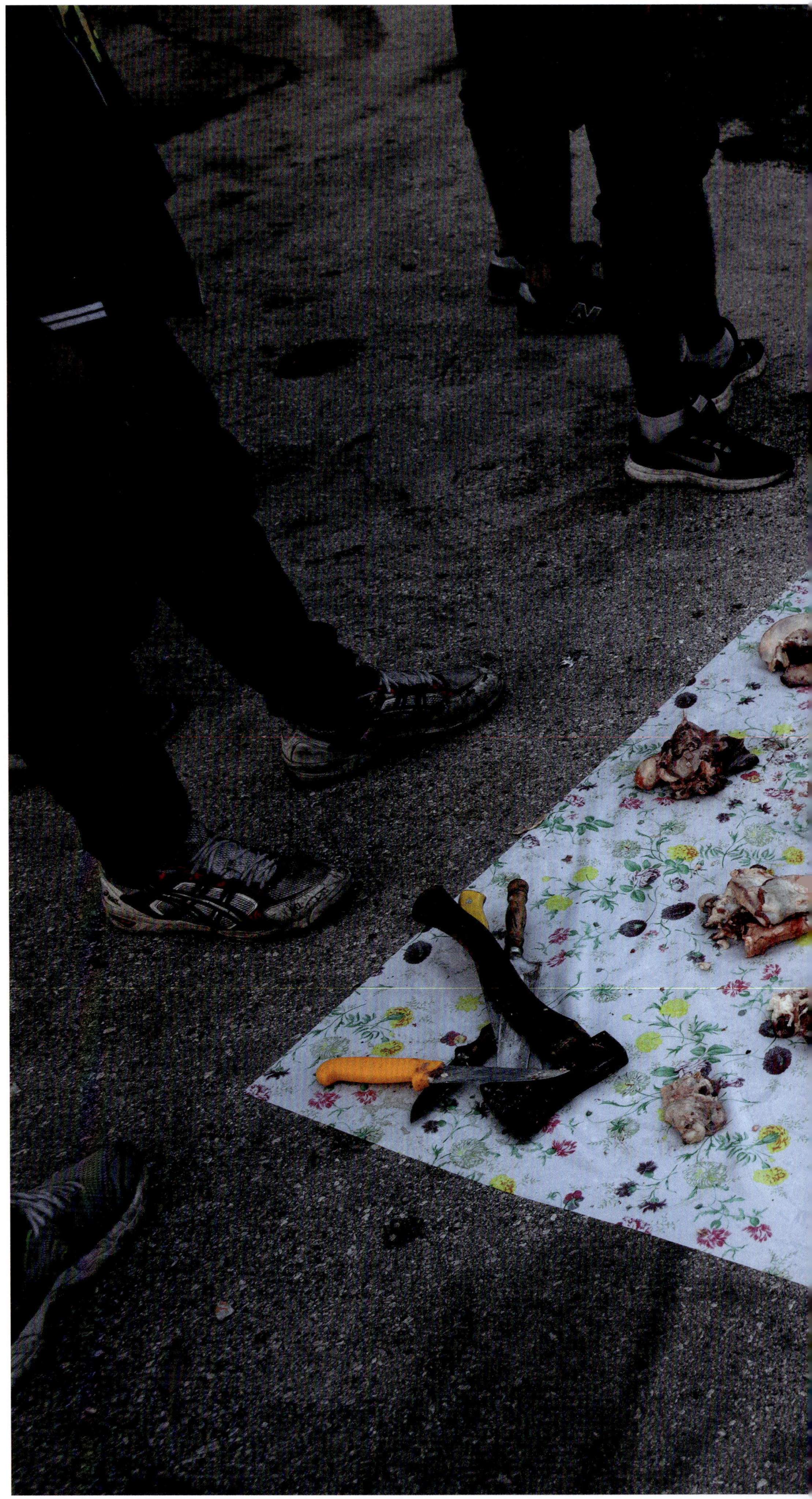

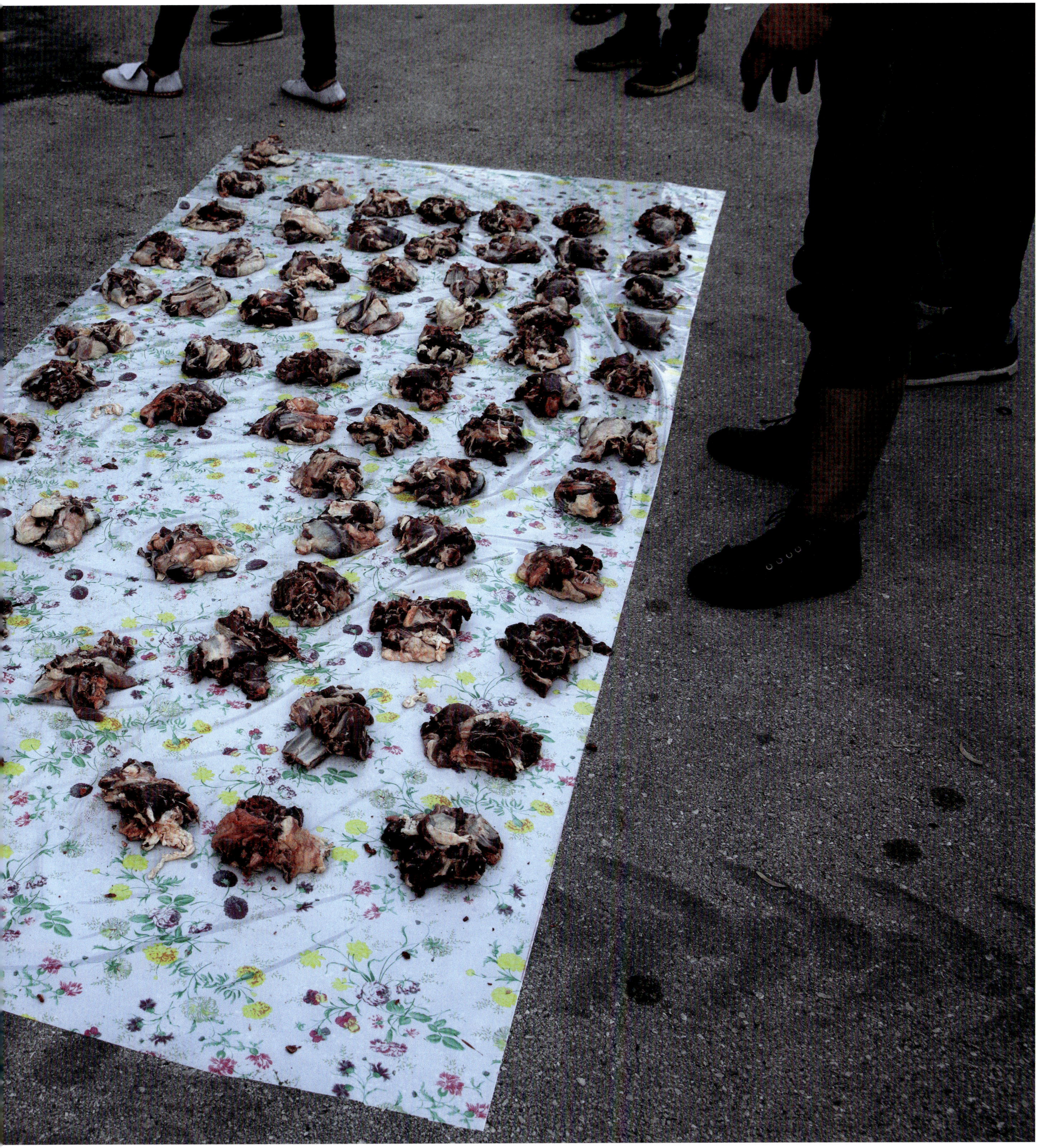

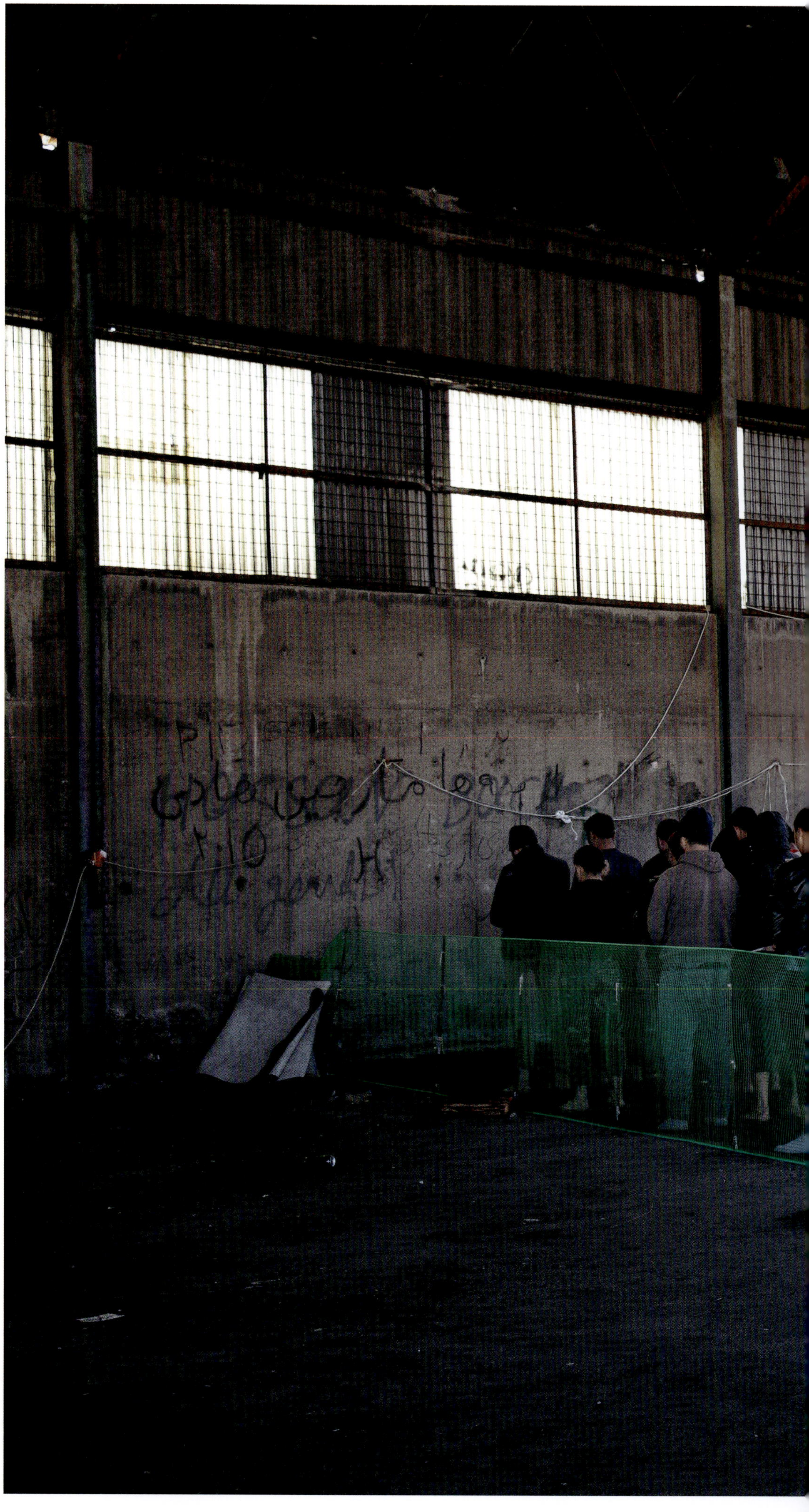

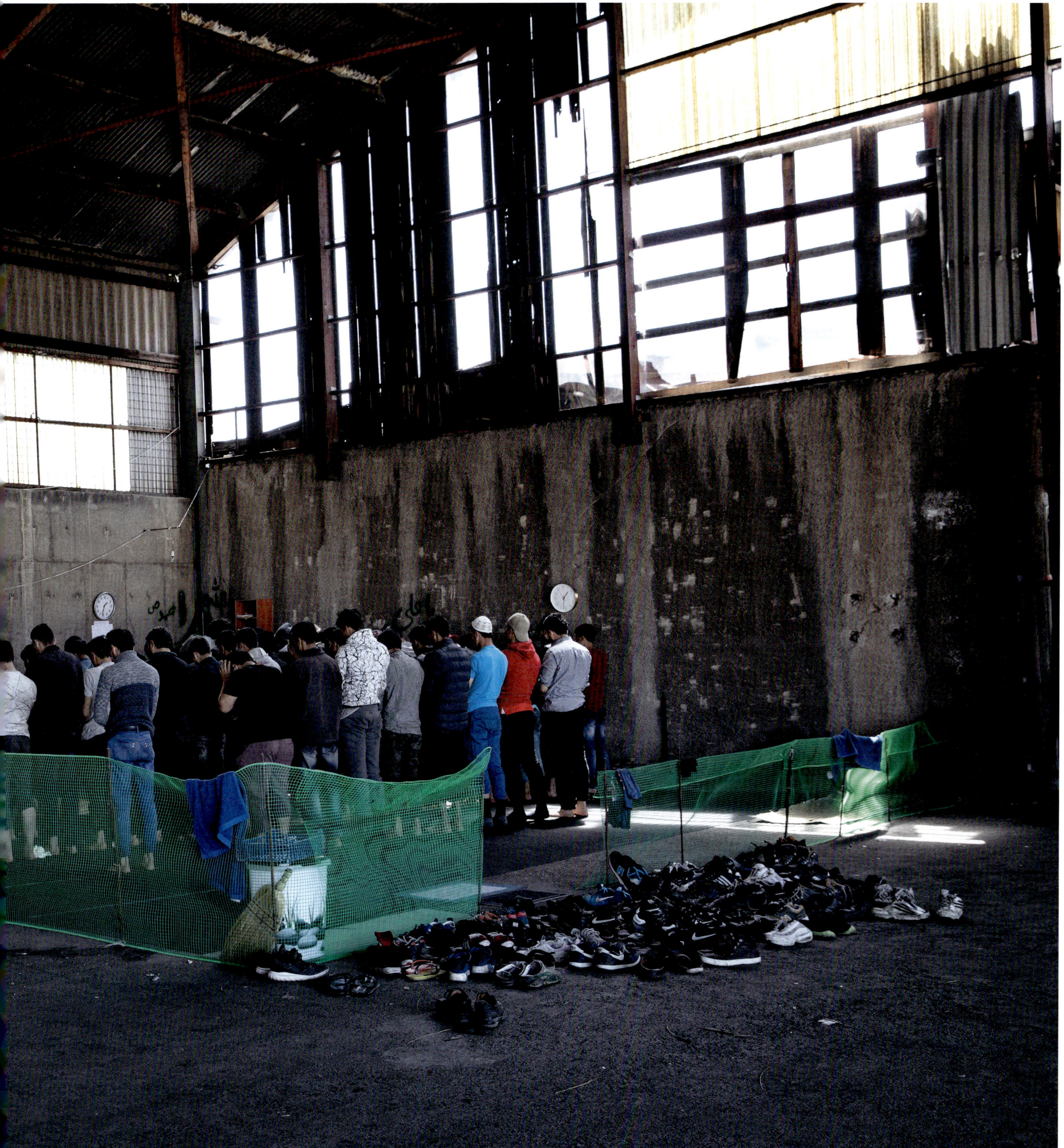

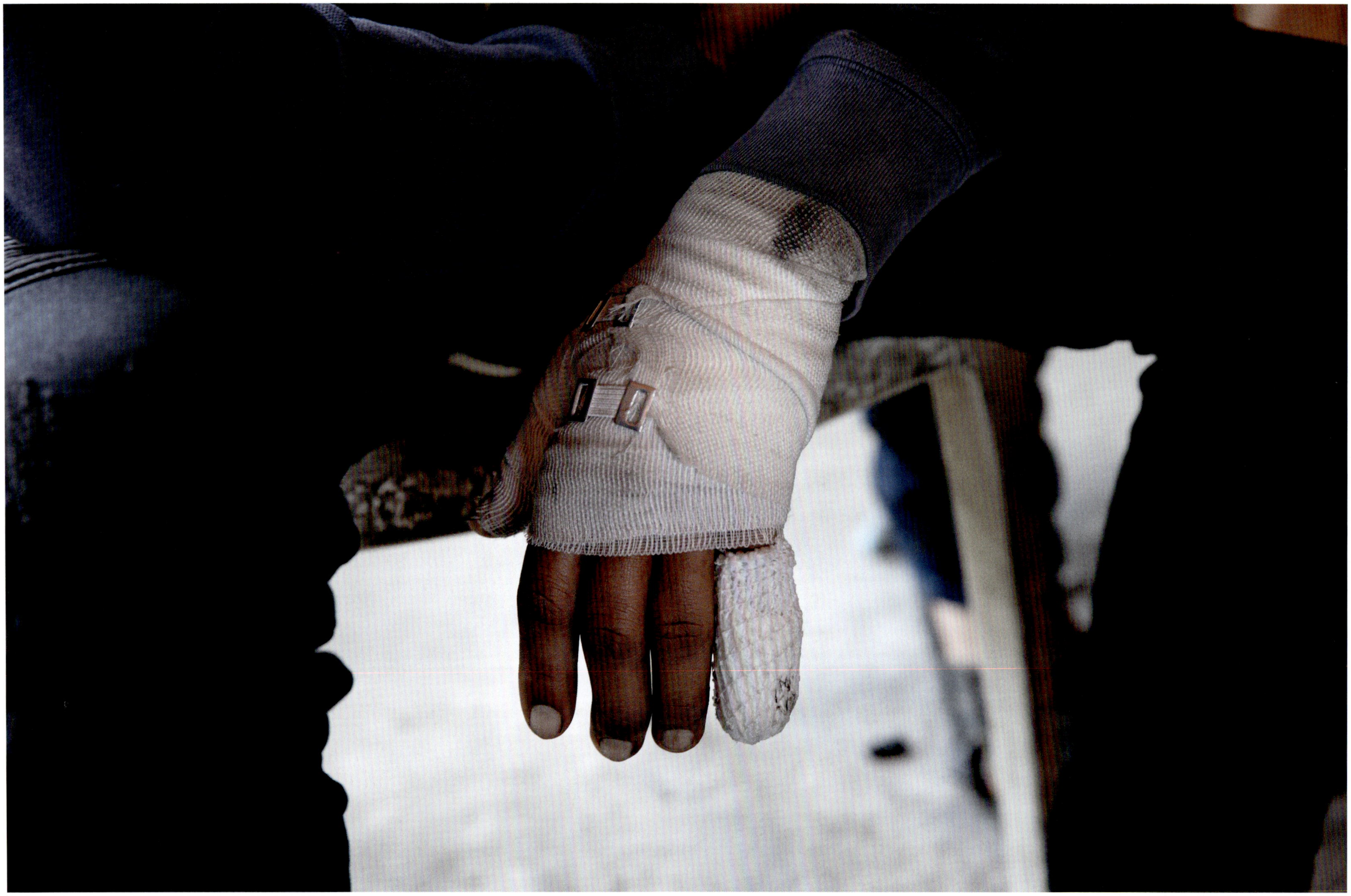

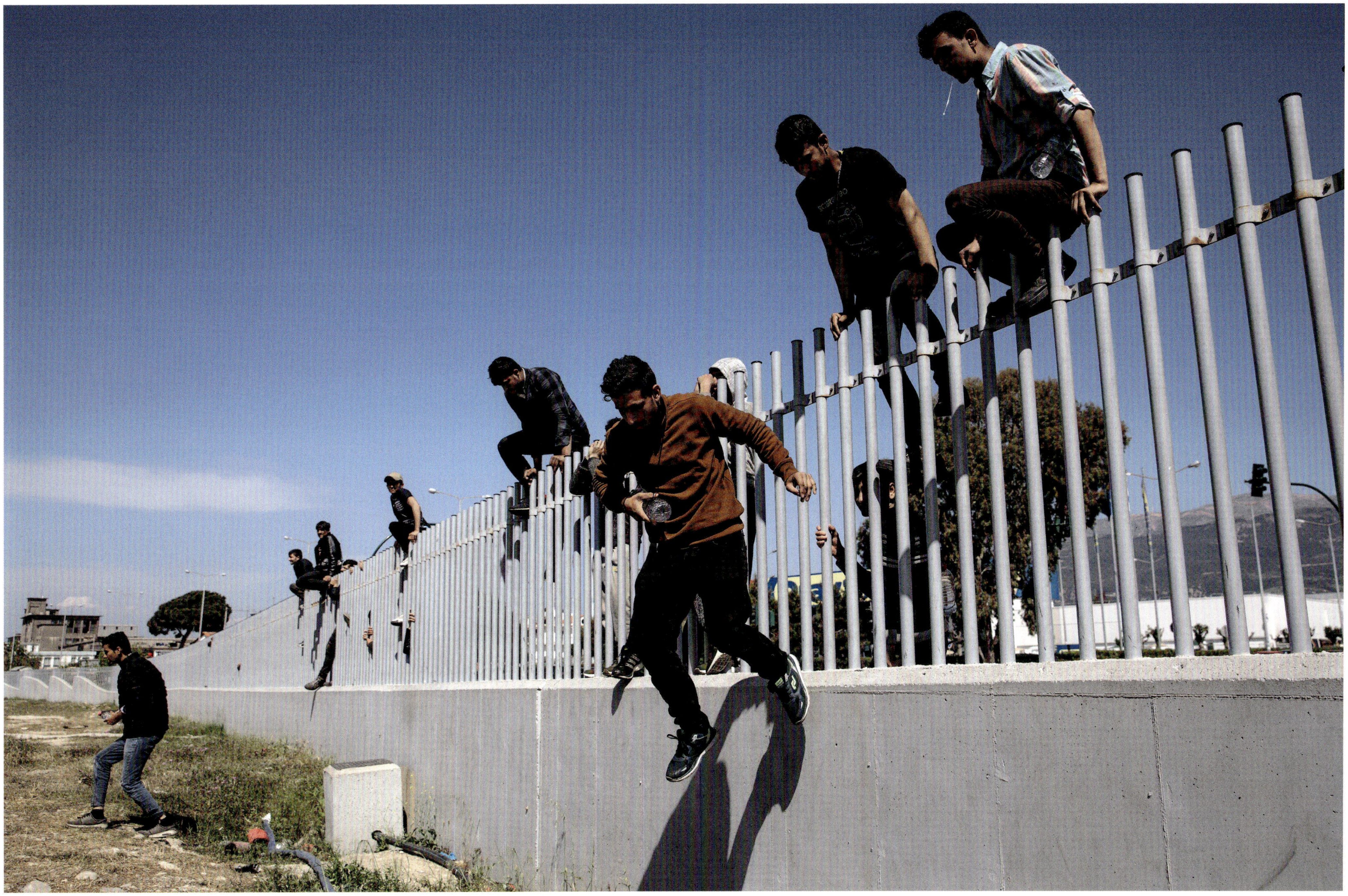

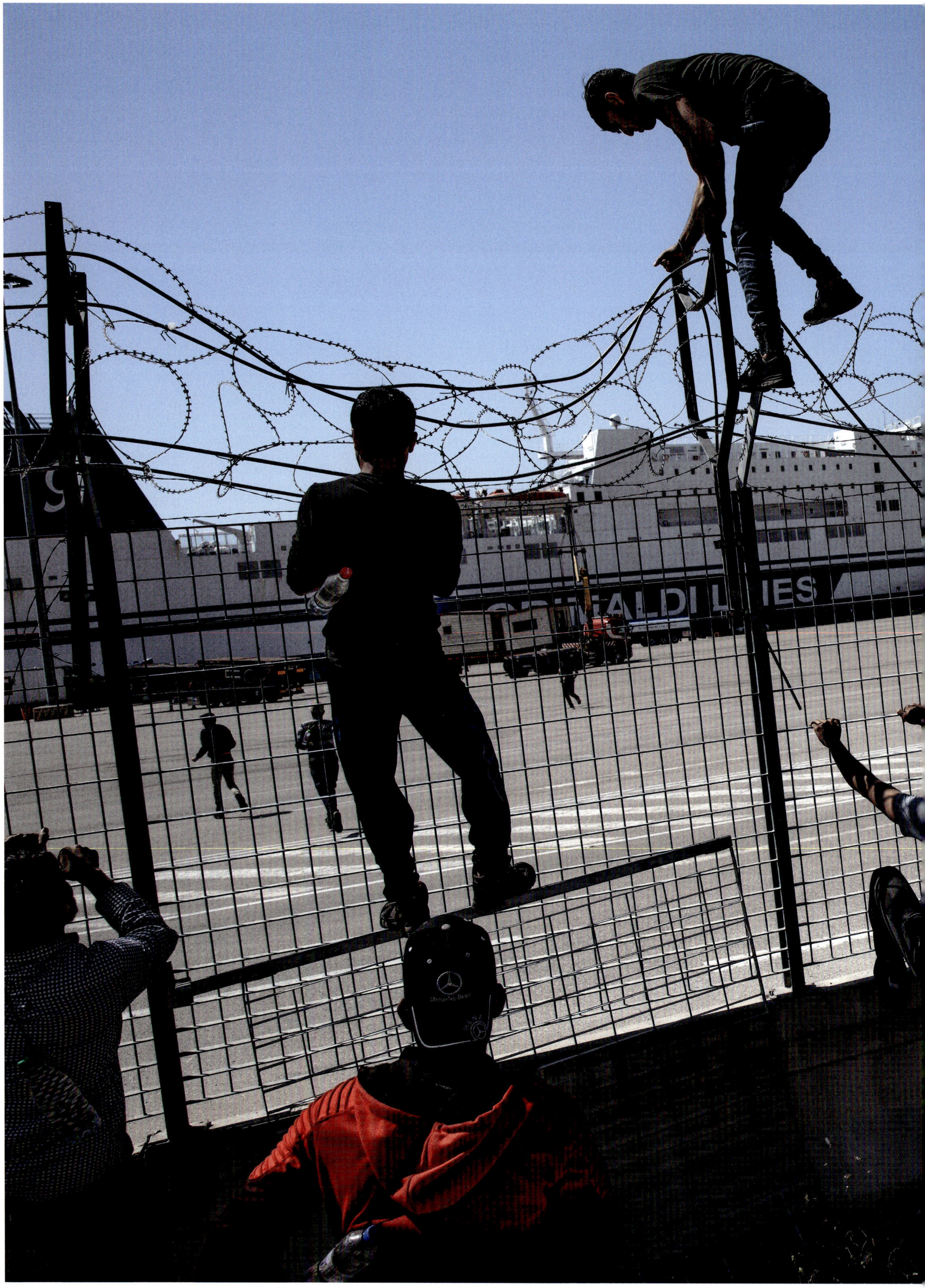
RIMALDI LINES

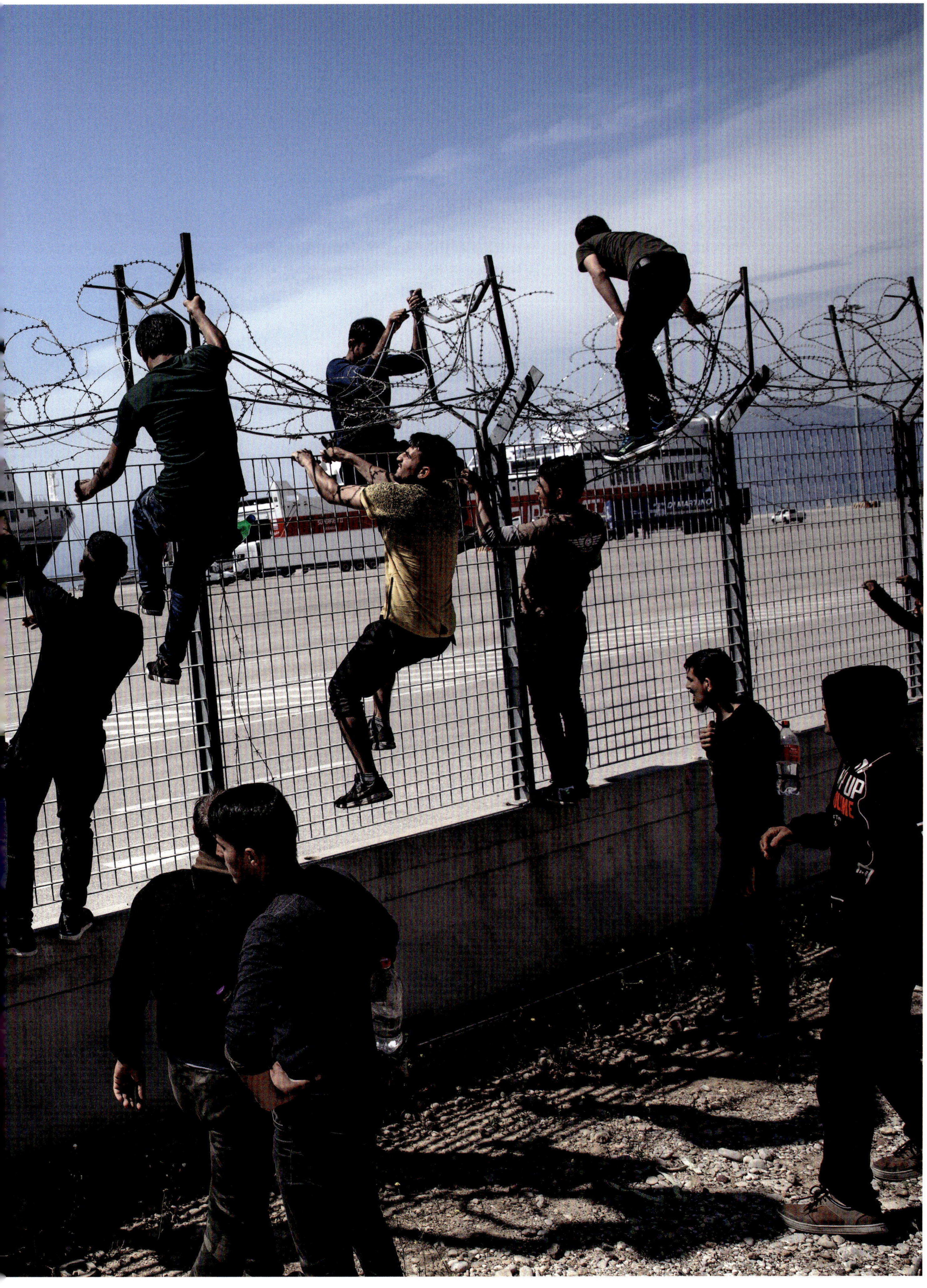

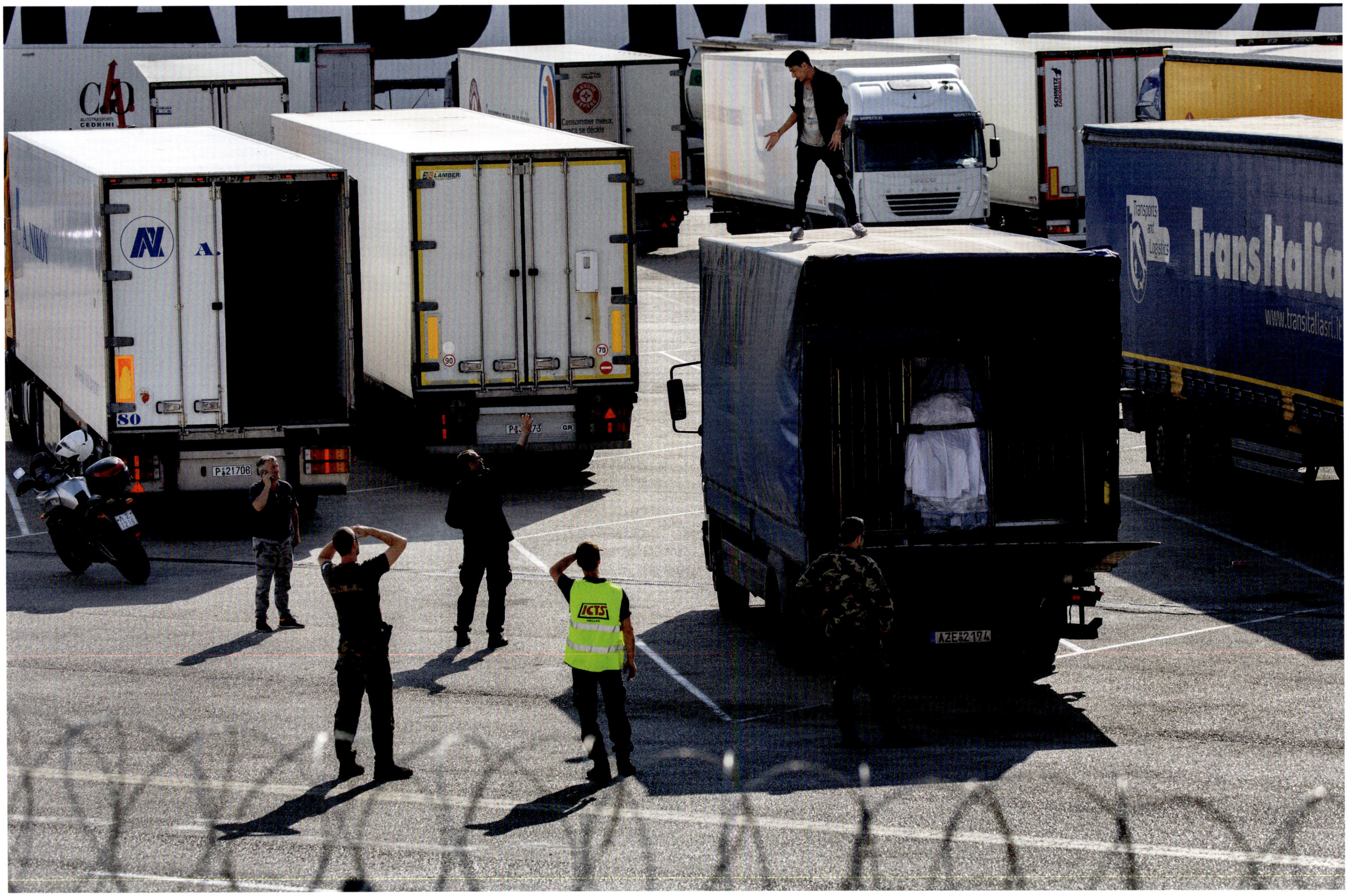
Transports and Logistics
ICTS
LAMBER
CEDRINI

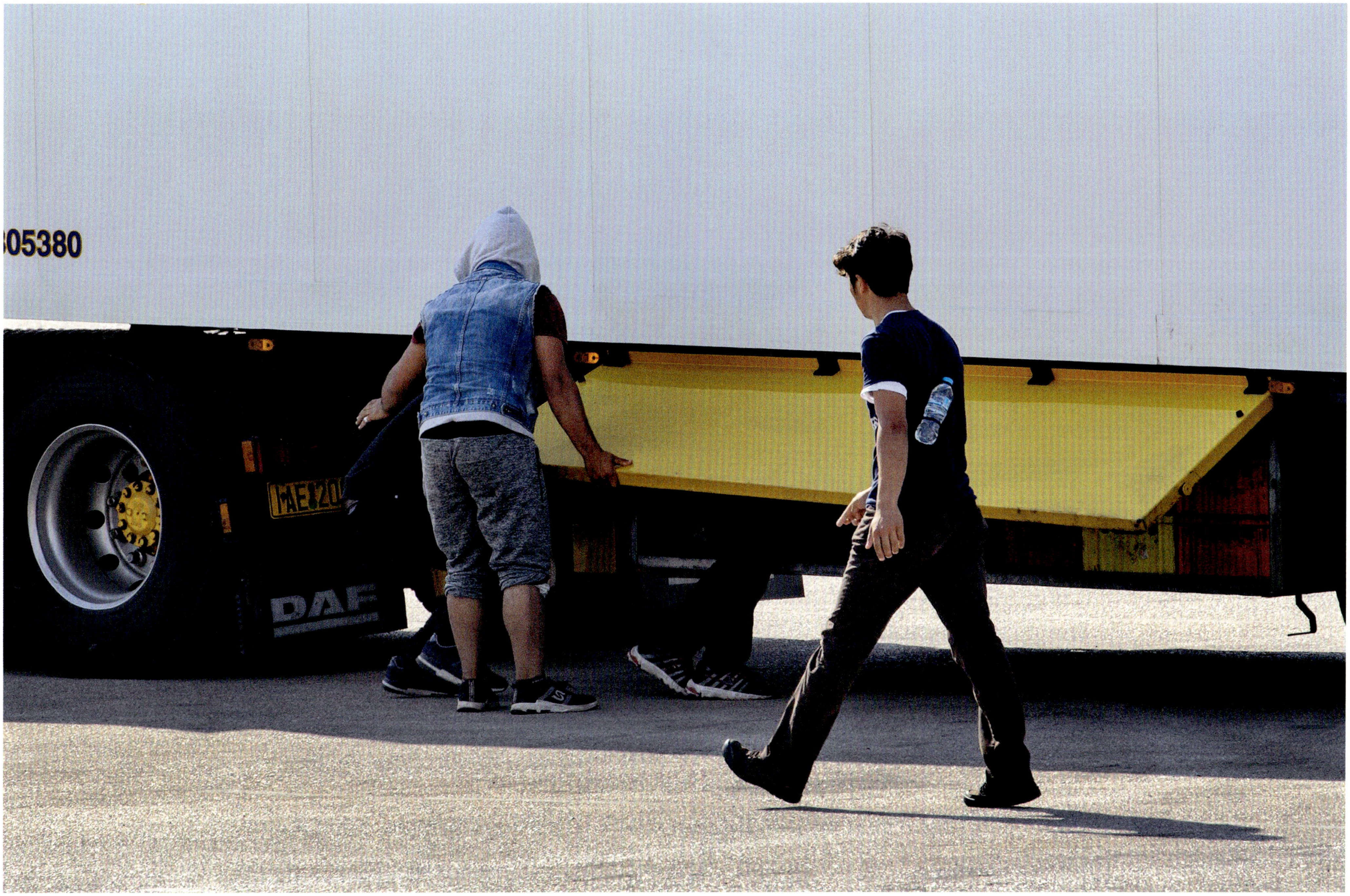
05380
DAF

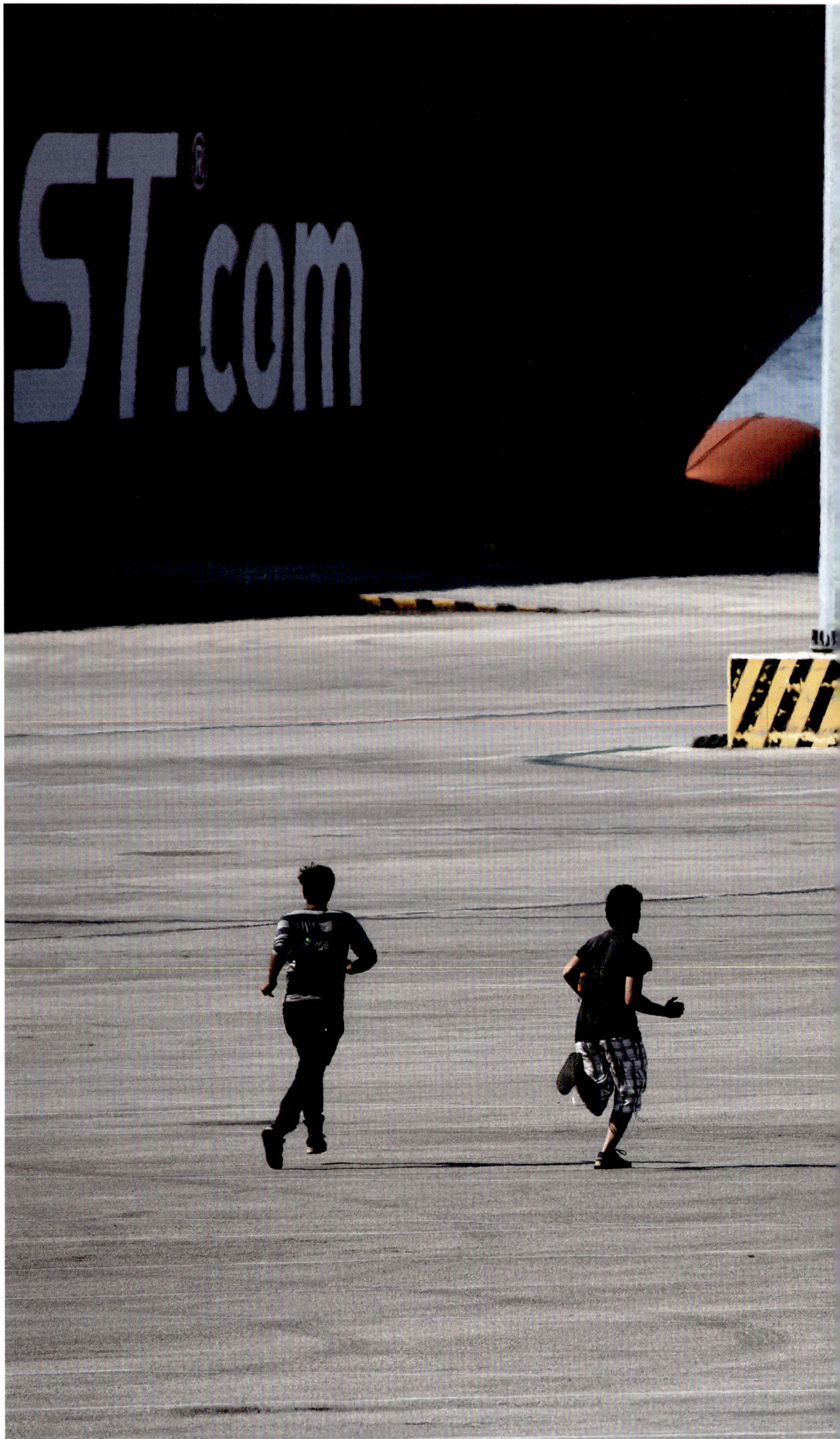
ST.com

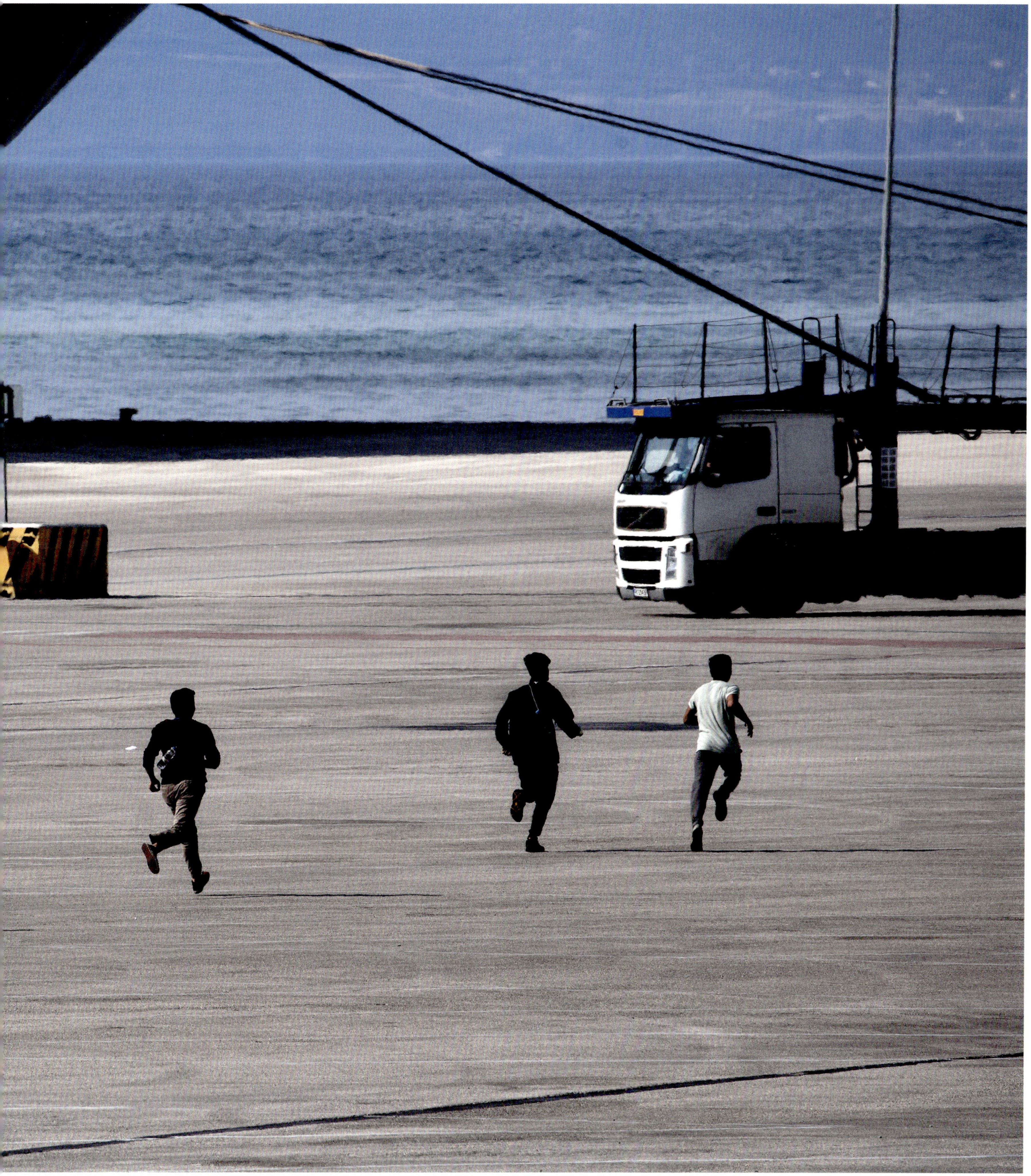

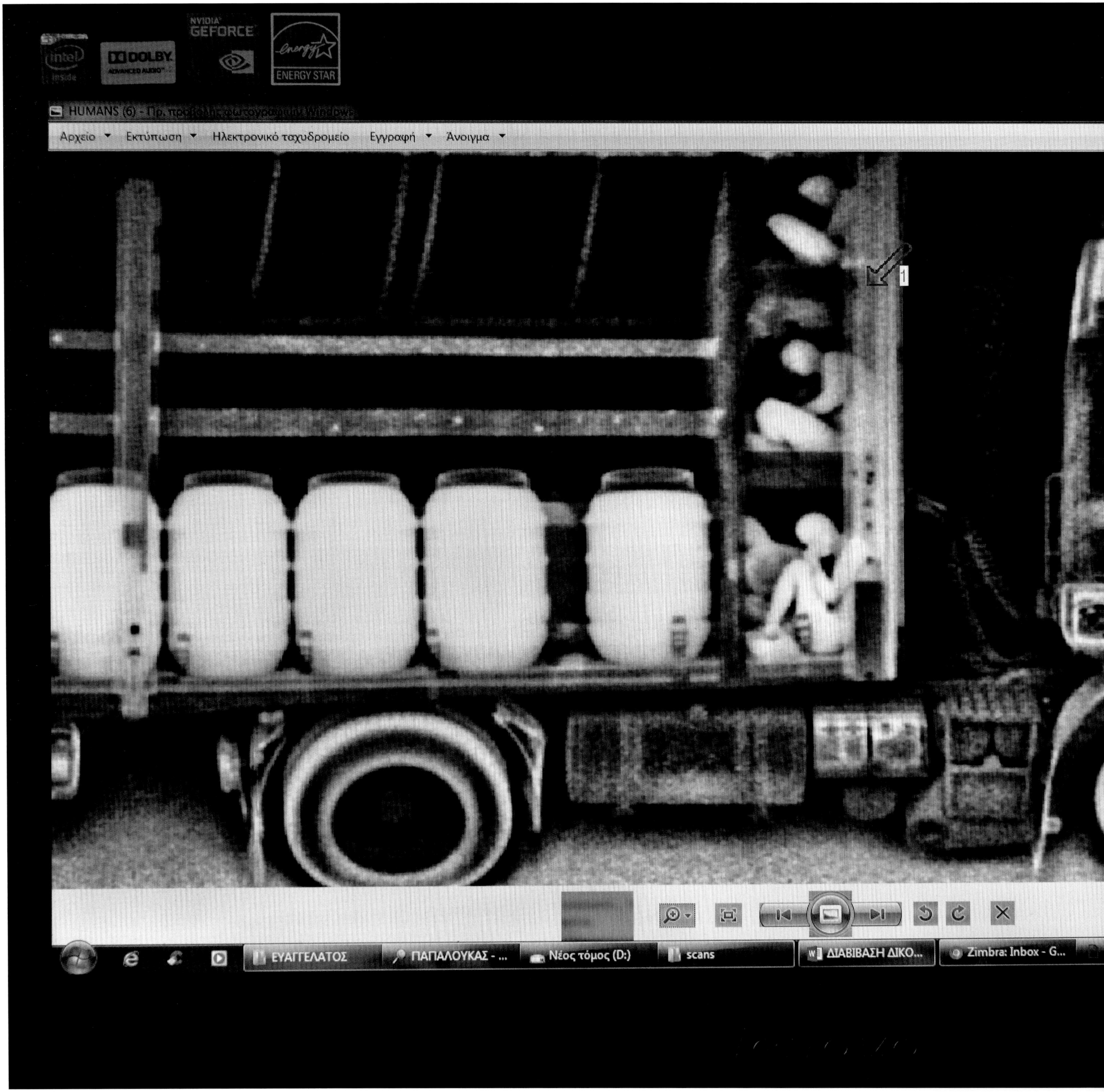
GEFORCE
DOLBY
ENERGY STAR
HUMANS (6) - Πρ. προβολής φωτογραφιών των Windows
Αρχείο
Εκτύπωση
Ηλεκτρονικό ταχυδρομείο
Εγγραφή
Άνοιγμα
1
ΕΥΑΓΓΕΛΑΤΟΣ
ΠΑΠΑΛΟΥΚΑΣ - ...
Νέος τόμος (D:)
scans
ΔΙΑΒΙΒΑΣΗ ΔΙΚΟ...
Zimbra: Inbox - G...

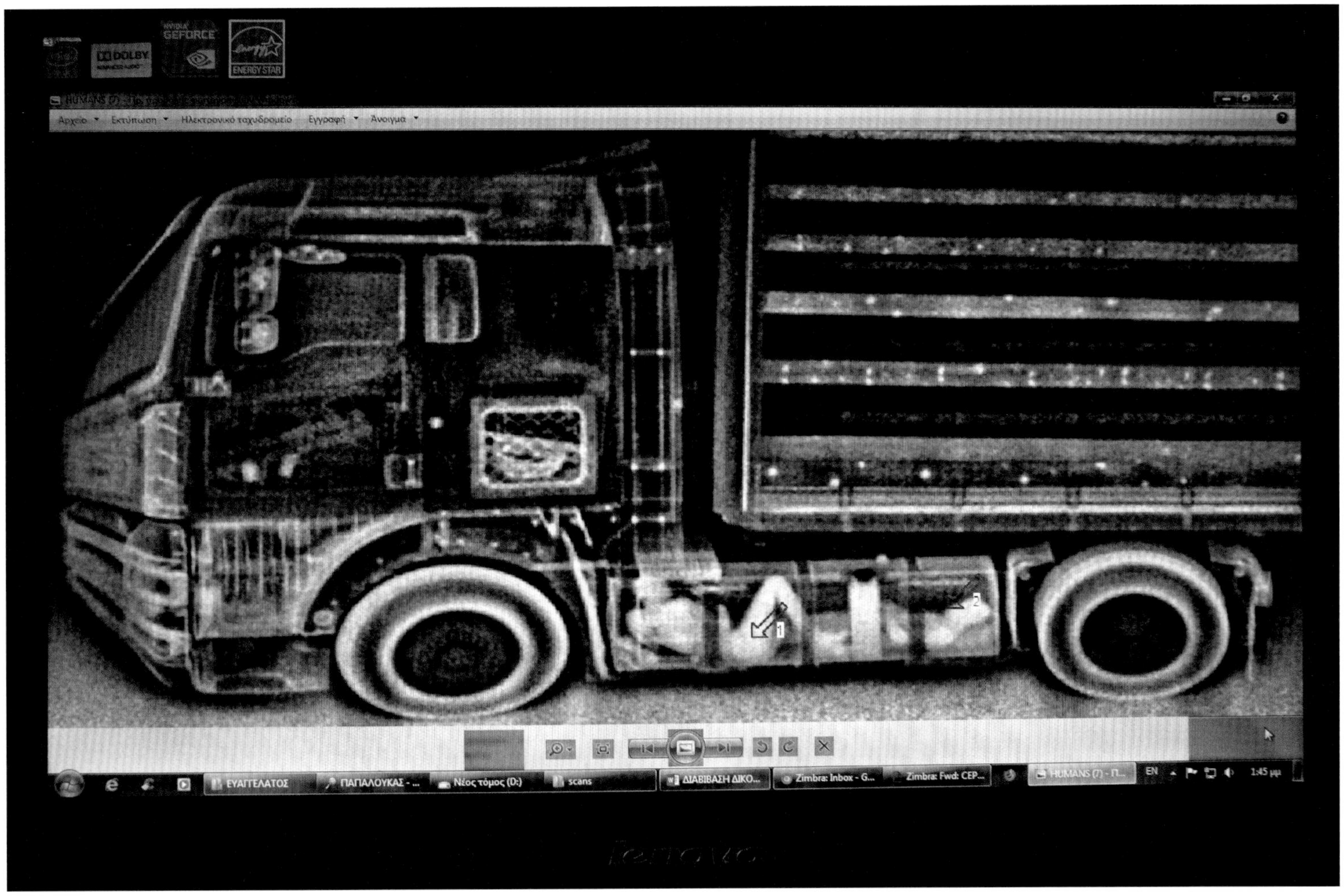
Αρχείο
Εκτύπωση
Ηλεκτρονικό ταχυδρομείο
Εγγραφή
Άνοιγμα
ΕΥΑΓΓΕΛΑΤΟΣ
ΠΑΠΑΛΟΥΚΑΣ - ...
Νέος τόμος (D:)
scans
ΔΙΑΒΙΑΣΗ ΔΙΚΟ...
Zimbra: Inbox - G...
Zimbra: Fwd: CEP...
lenovo

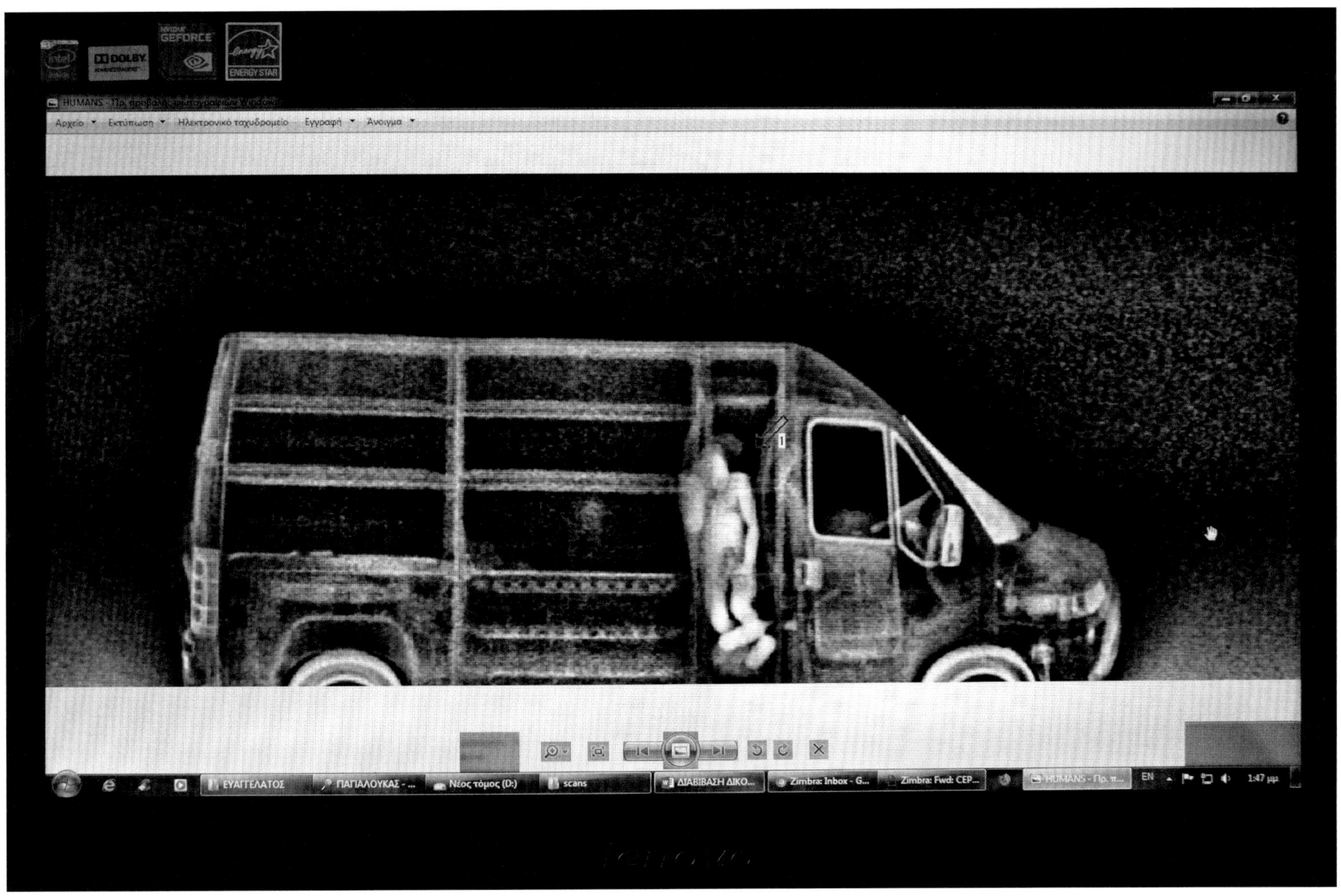
HUMANS
Αρχείο
Εκτύπωση
Ηλεκτρονικό ταχυδρομείο
Εγγραφή
Άνοιγμα
ΕΥΑΓΓΕΛΑΤΟΣ
ΠΑΠΑΛΟΥΚΑΣ - ...
Νέος τόμος (D:)
scans
ΔΙΑΒΙΑΣΗ ΔΙΚΟ...
Zimbra: Inbox - G...
Zimbra: Fwd: CEP...
lenovo

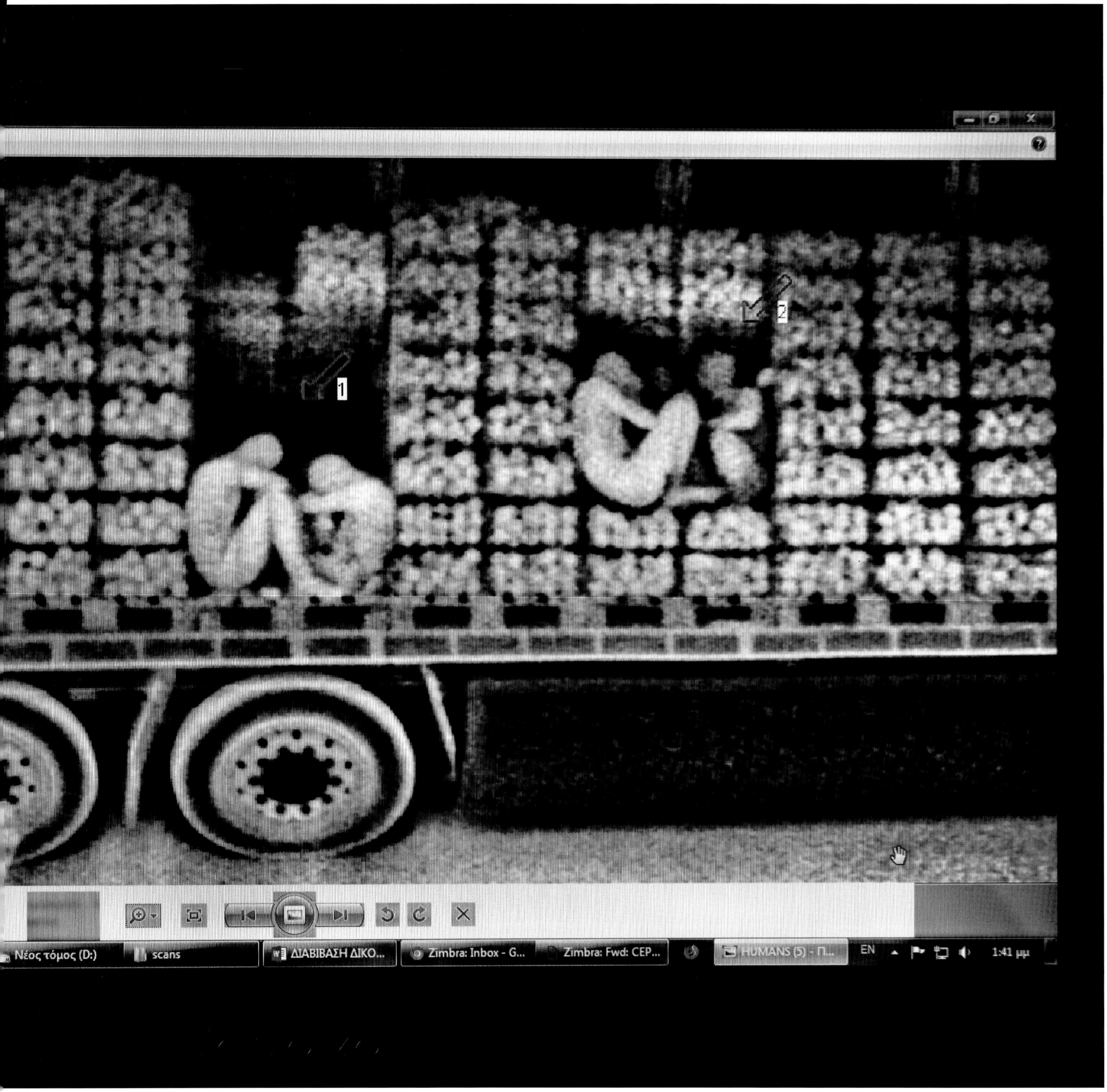
1
2
Νέος τόμος (D:)
scans
ΔΙΑΒΙΒΑΣΗ ΔΙΚΟ...
Zimbra: Inbox - G...
Zimbra: Fwd: CEP...
HUMANS (5) - Π...
EN
1:41 μμ

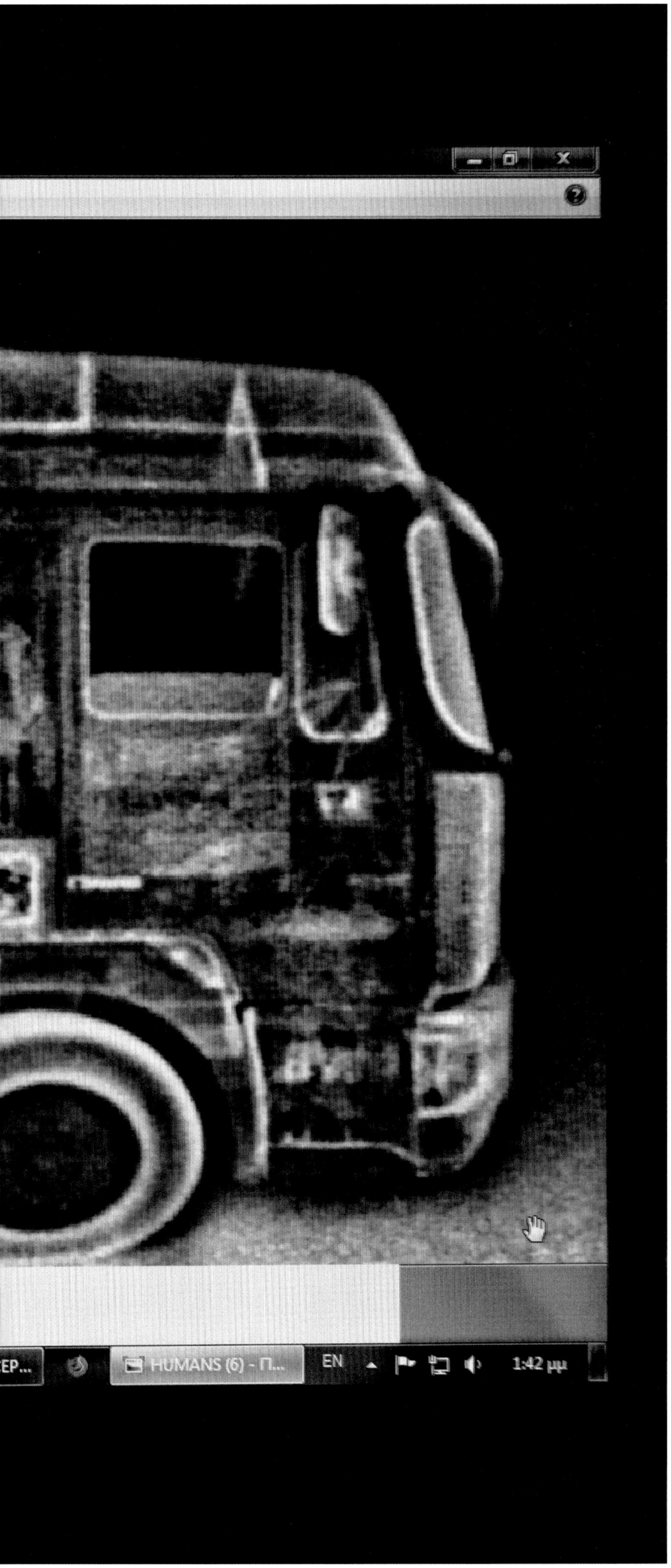
EP...
HUMANS (6) - Π...
EN
1:42 μμ

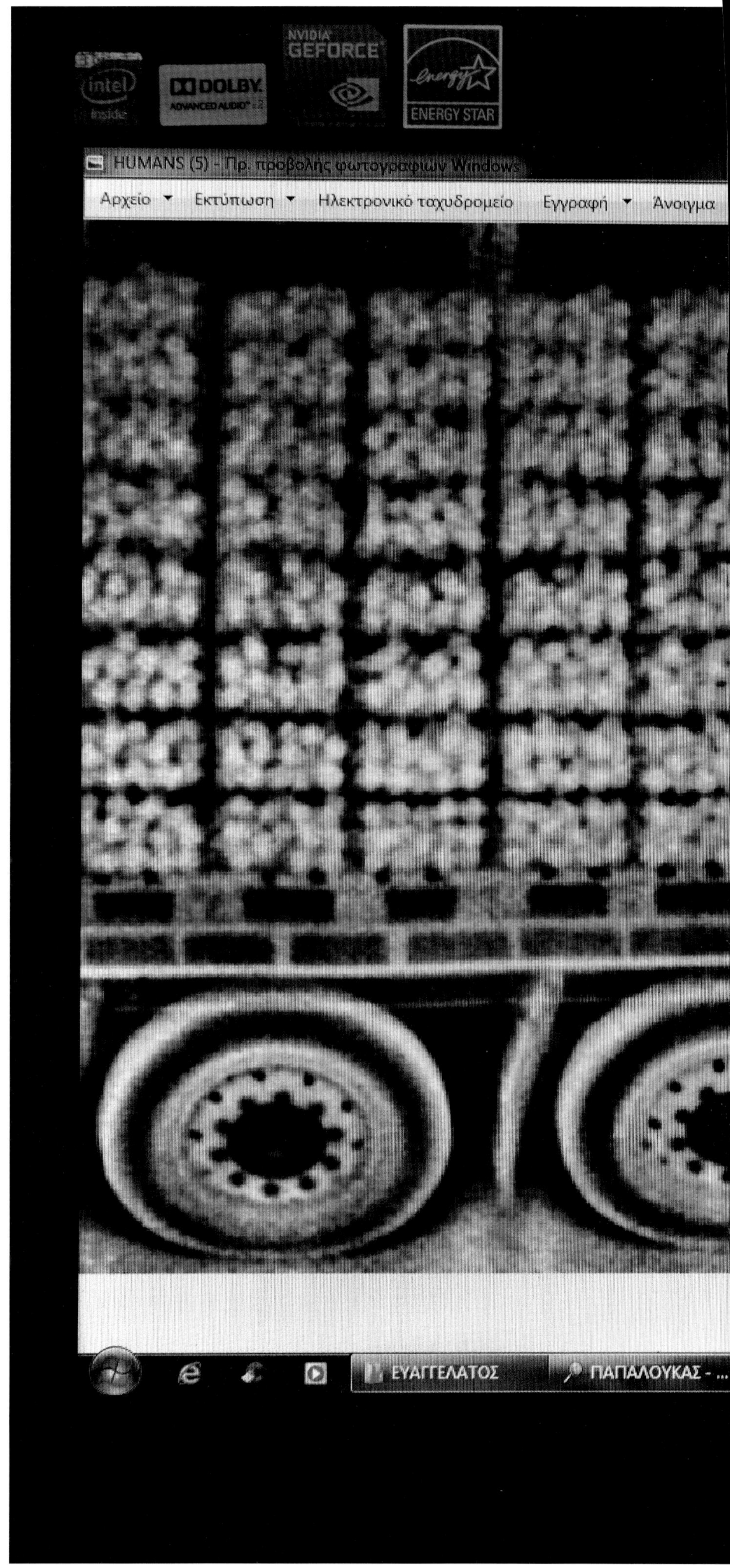
intel inside
DOLBY ADVANCED AUDIO
NVIDIA GEFORCE
ENERGY STAR
HUMANS (5) - Πρ. προβολής φωτογραφιών Windows
Αρχείο
Εκτύπωση
Ηλεκτρονικό ταχυδρομείο
Εγγραφή
Άνοιγμα
ΕΥΑΓΓΕΛΑΤΟΣ
ΠΑΠΑΛΟΥΚΑΣ - ...

In a highly political power game between Turkey and the EU, Turkish president Erdogan announces in February 2020 that Turkey will open its border to Greece. At this point Turkey houses around four million refugees and migrants and it is estimated that 3.6 million of them are refugees from the civil war in Syria.

An agreement reached between Turkey and the EU in 2015 and 2016 has significantly slowed the stream of refugees going from Turkey to Greece, but the agreement is fragile. The EU countries have not achieved a lasting joint model for taking care of the refugees and migrants. Erdogan's repeated threats to withdraw from the agreement if he does not get his way in other foreign policy issues makes it clear that the problems have not been solved.

The announcement of Turkey opening the Turkish border on 29 February prompts tens of thousands of refugees and migrants to take buses, from Istanbul in particular, to northwest Turkey and the Greek border. They hope to enter the EU in a way that is safe and easy, but the Greek border agents have not opened their border barrier and the many refugees and migrants are met with tear gas, rubber bullets and batons.

Most people are stranded in an area near the border crossing at Pazarkule; others settle down in various places on the outskirts of the town of Edirne. After some weeks, all the disappointed refugees and migrants have left the border area and Greece can report that it has kept the outer border of the EU closed.

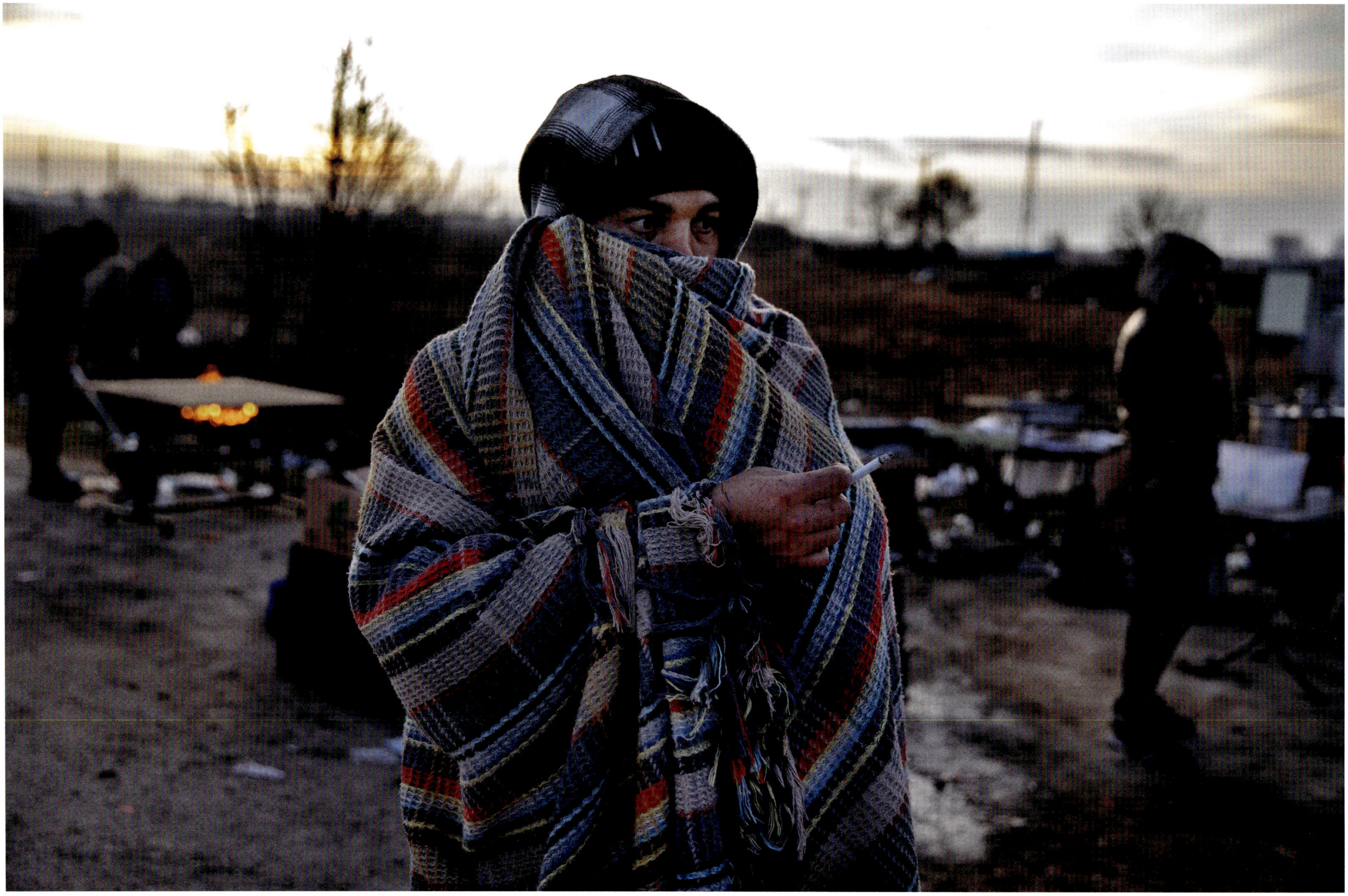

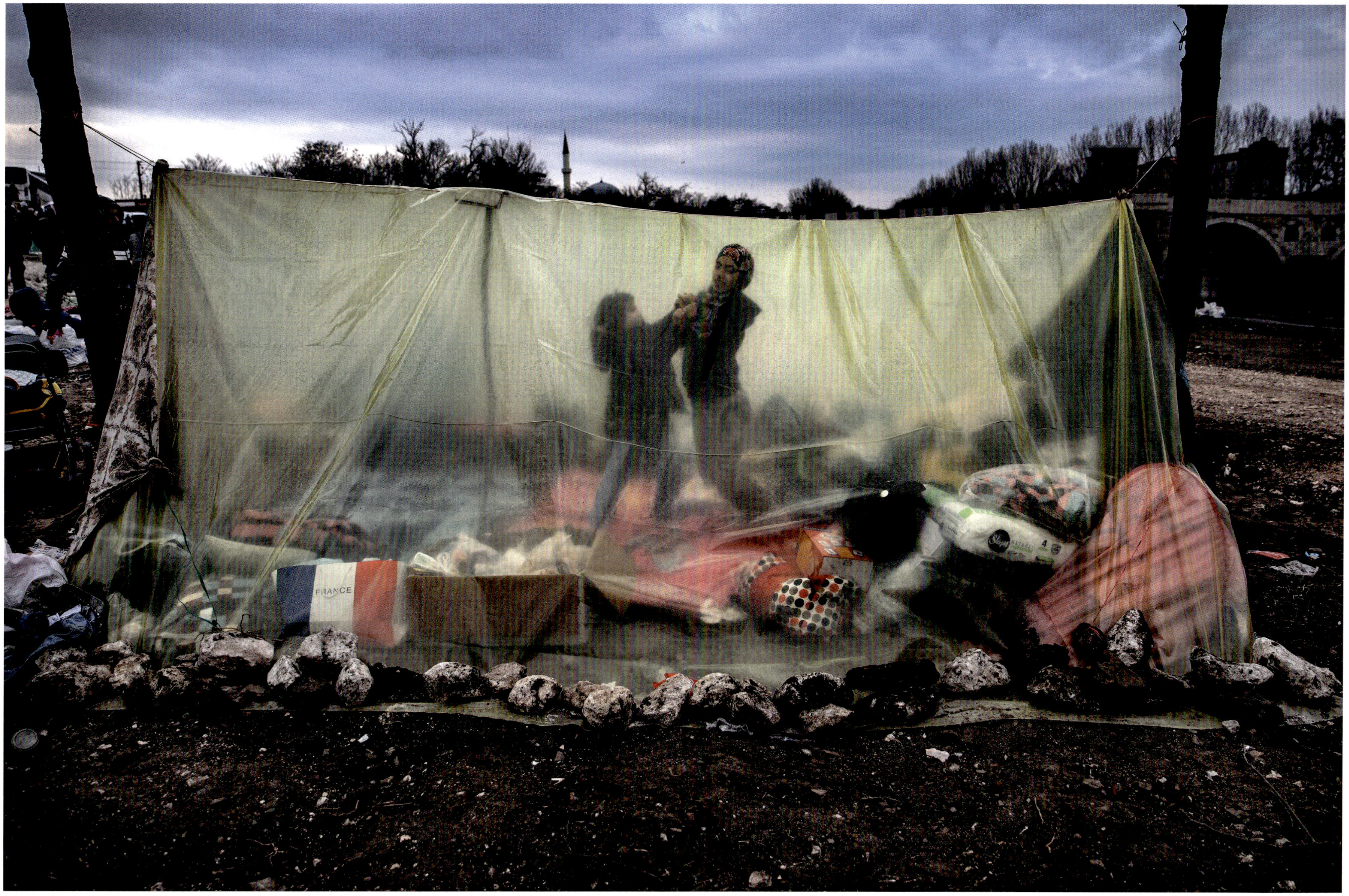
FRANCE

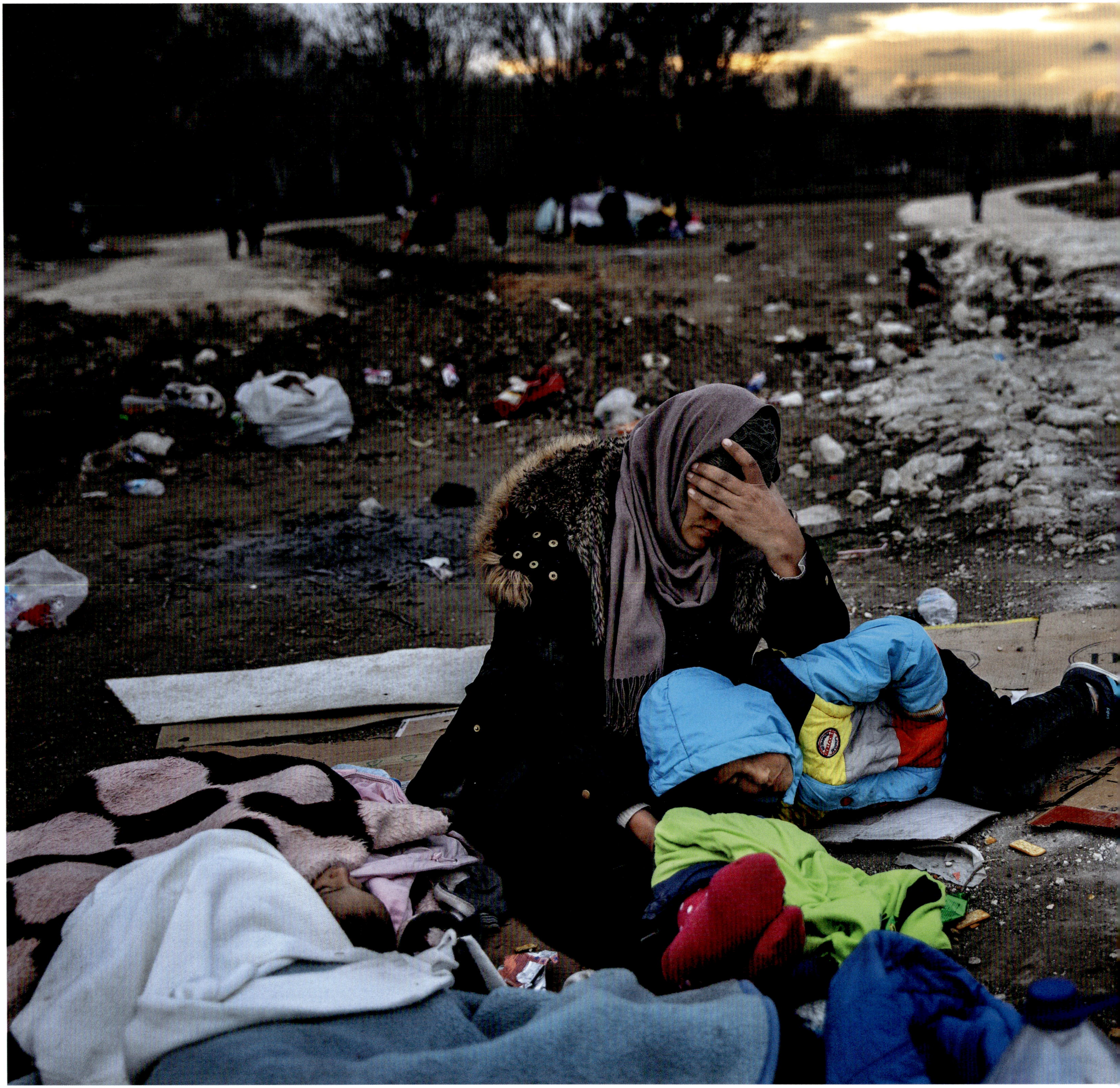

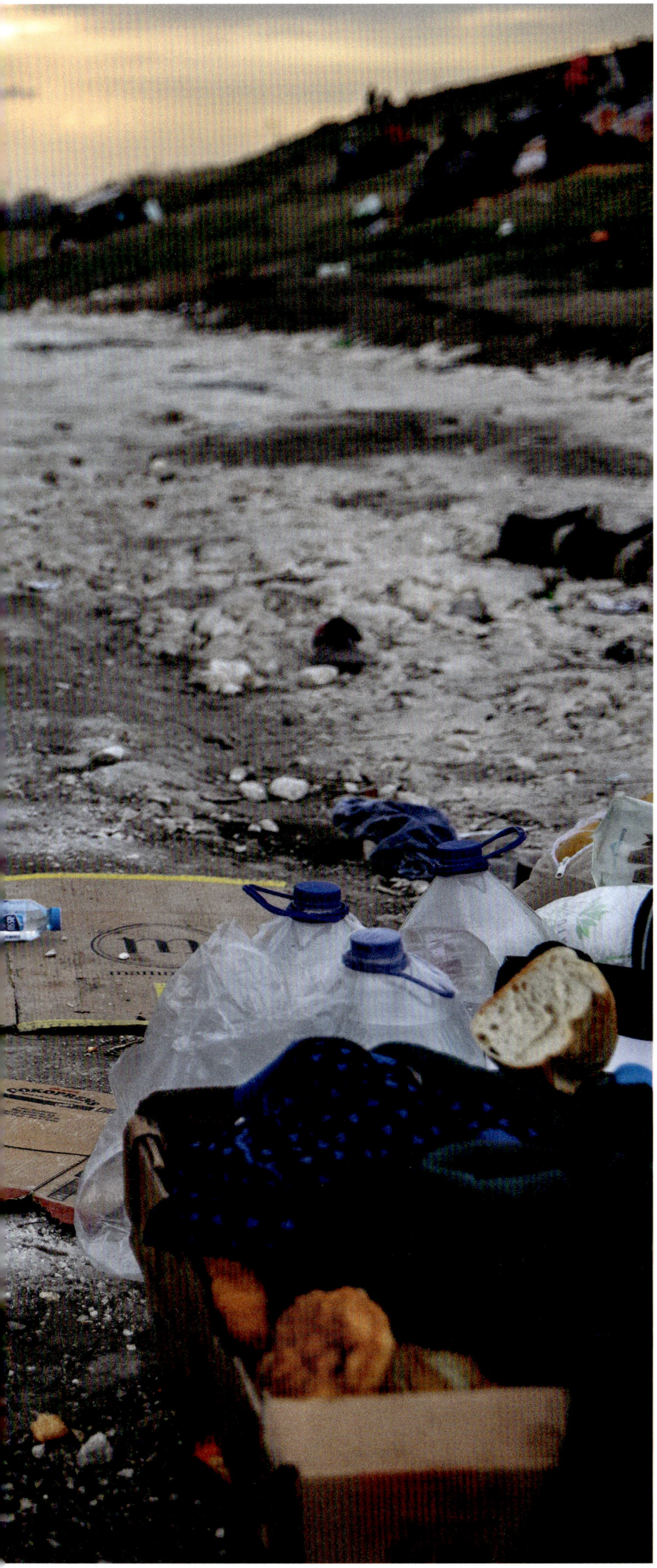

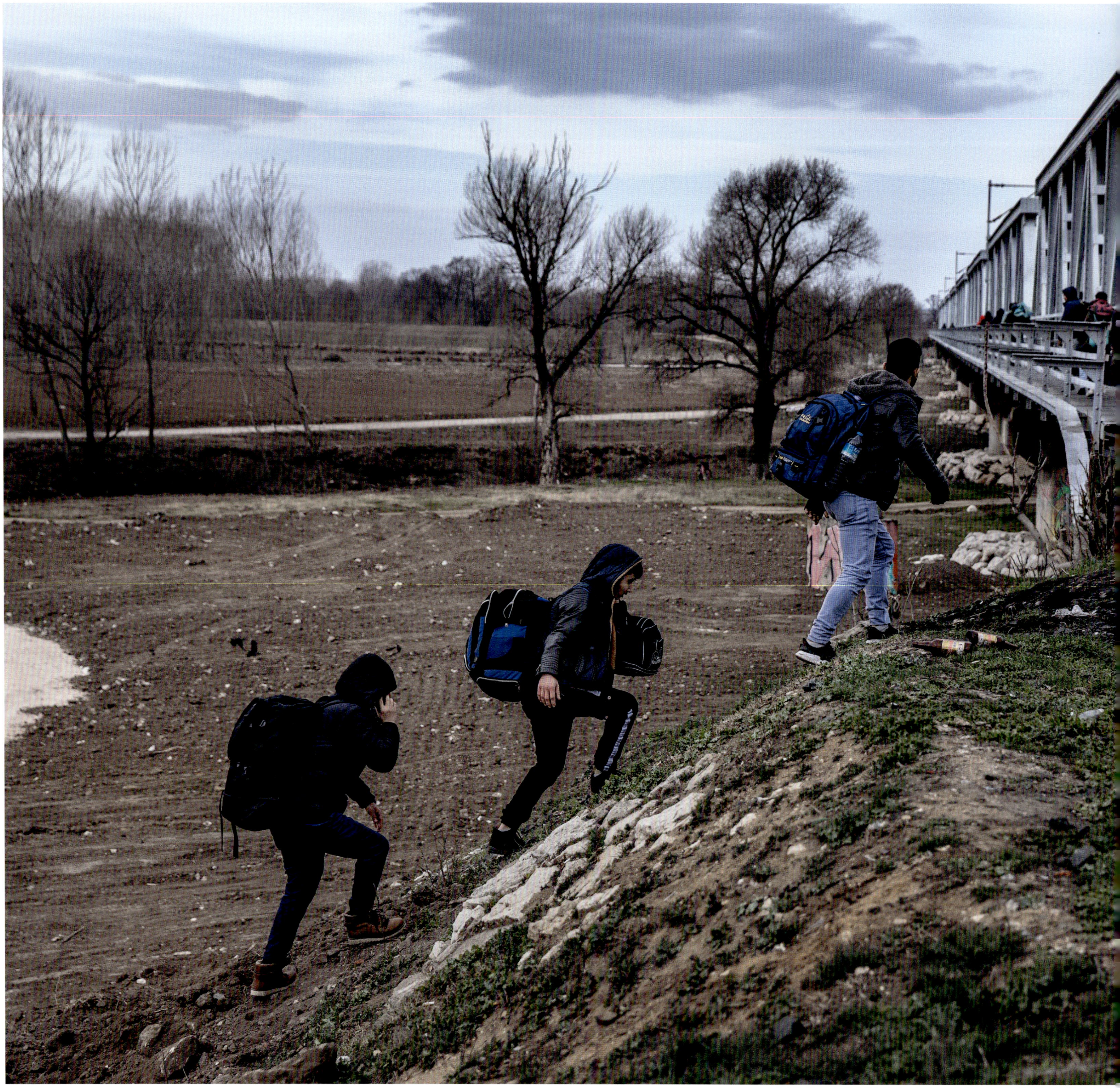

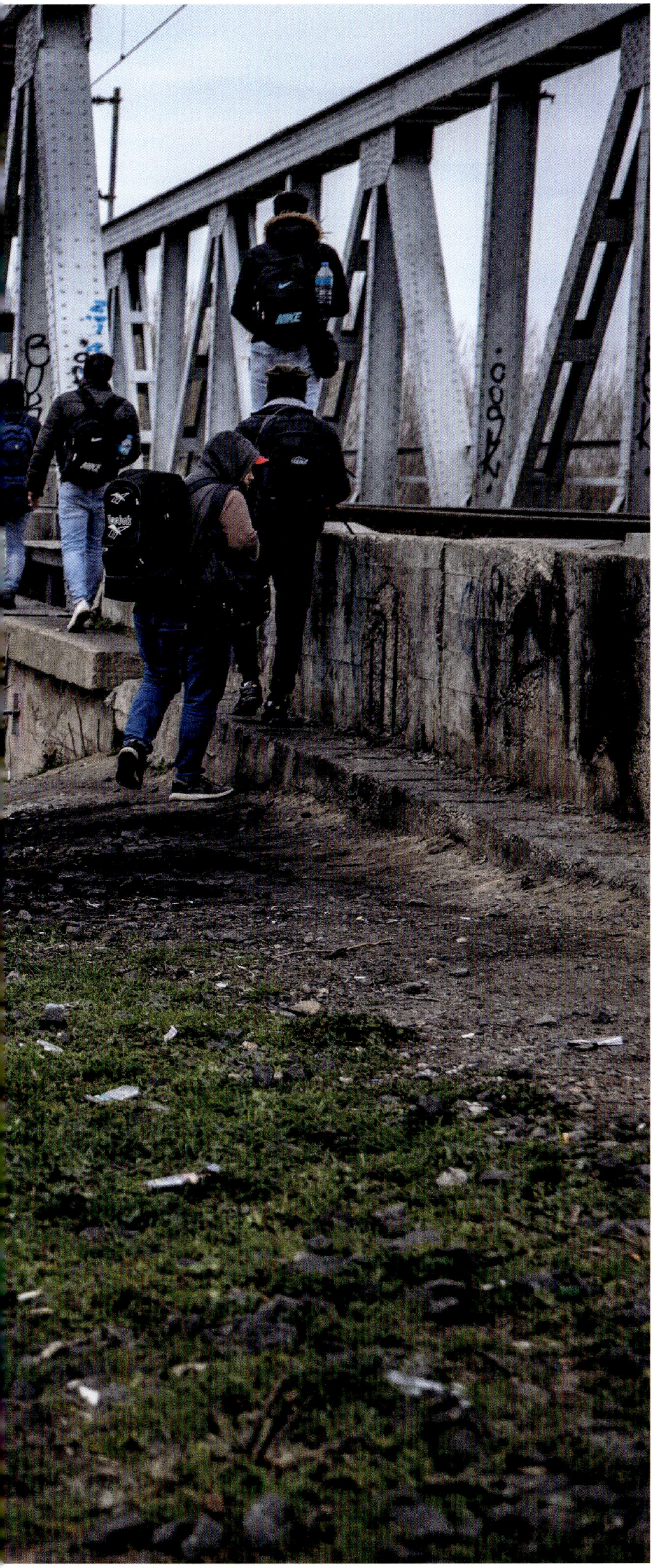

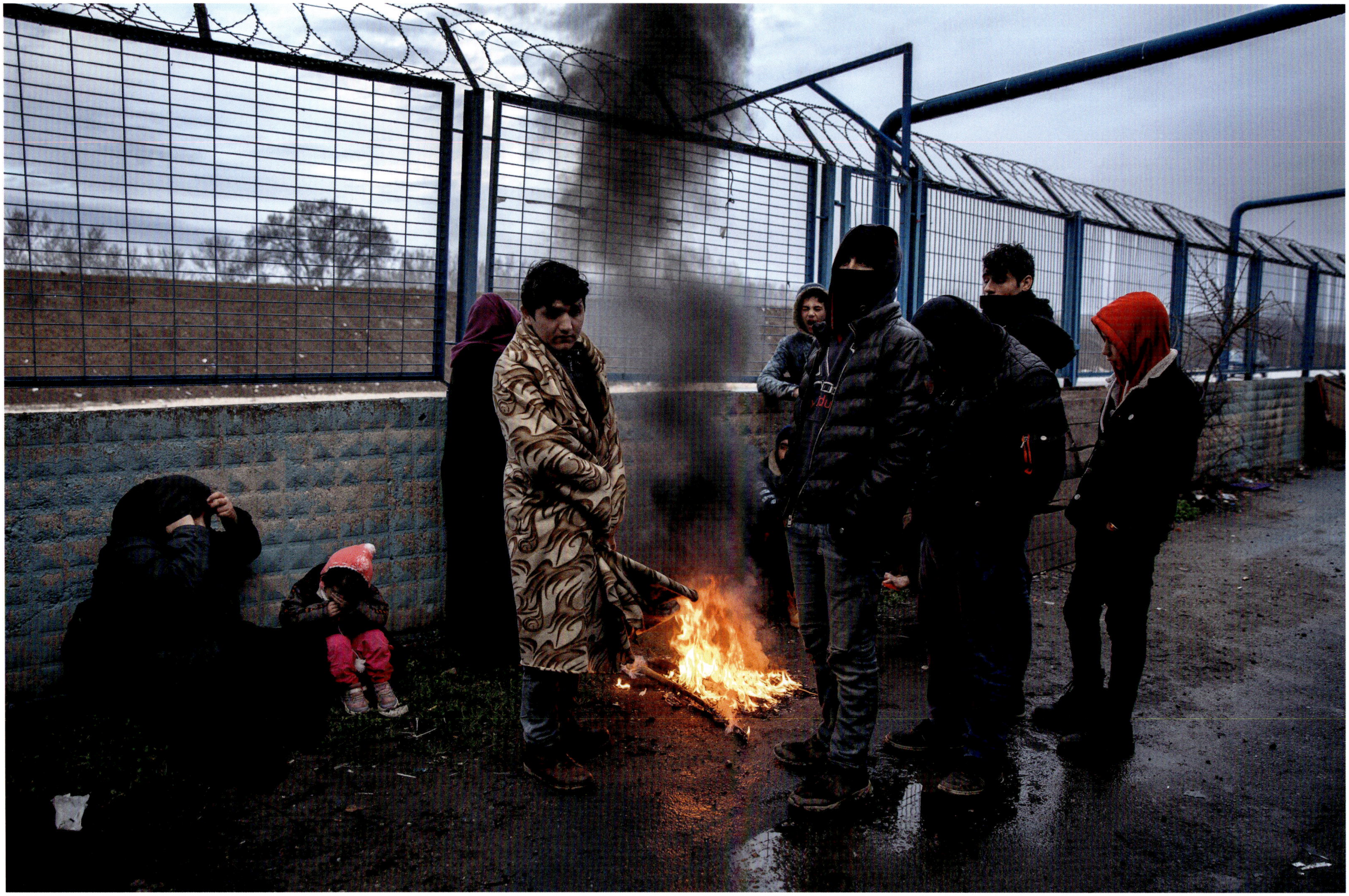

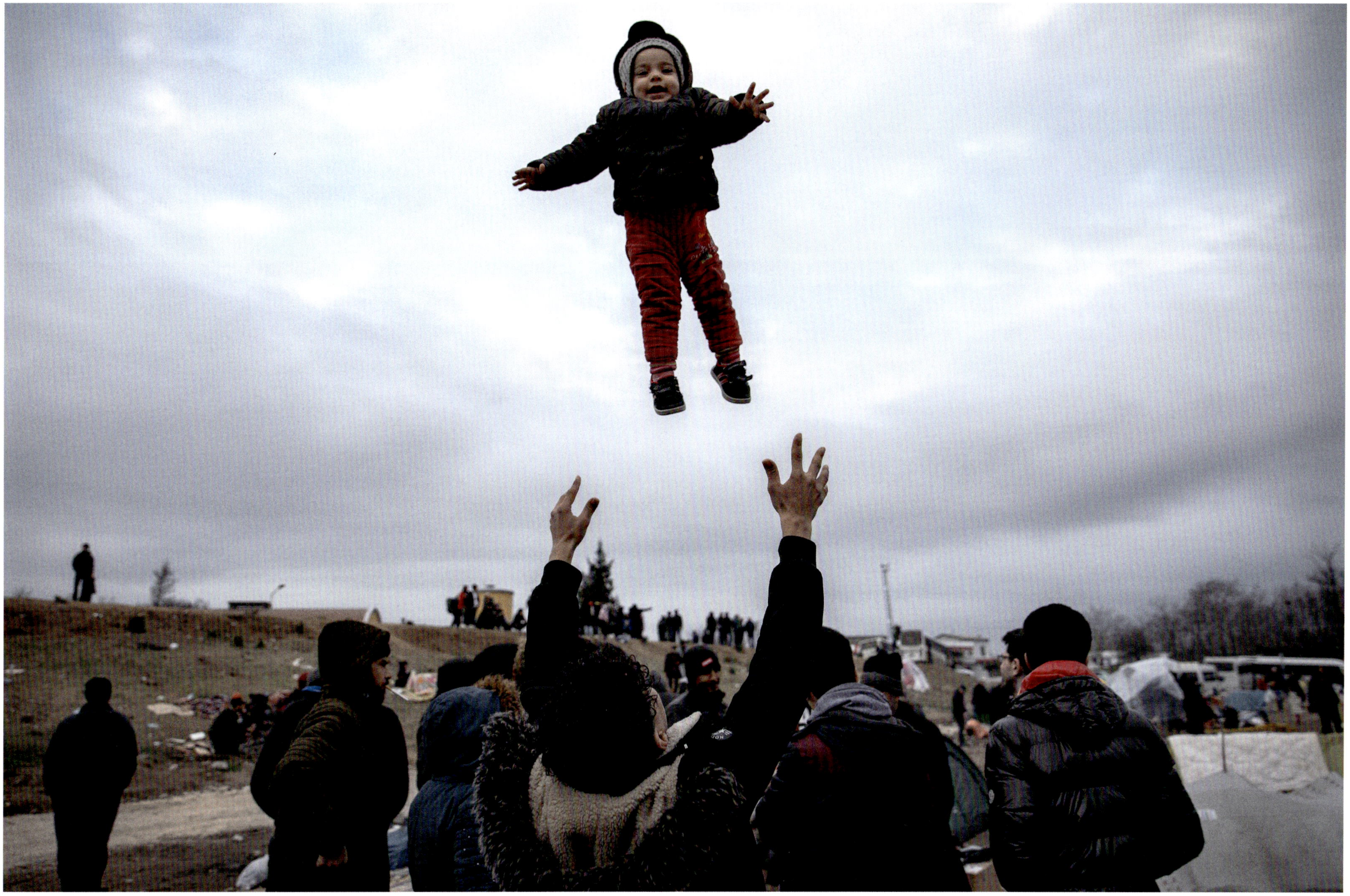

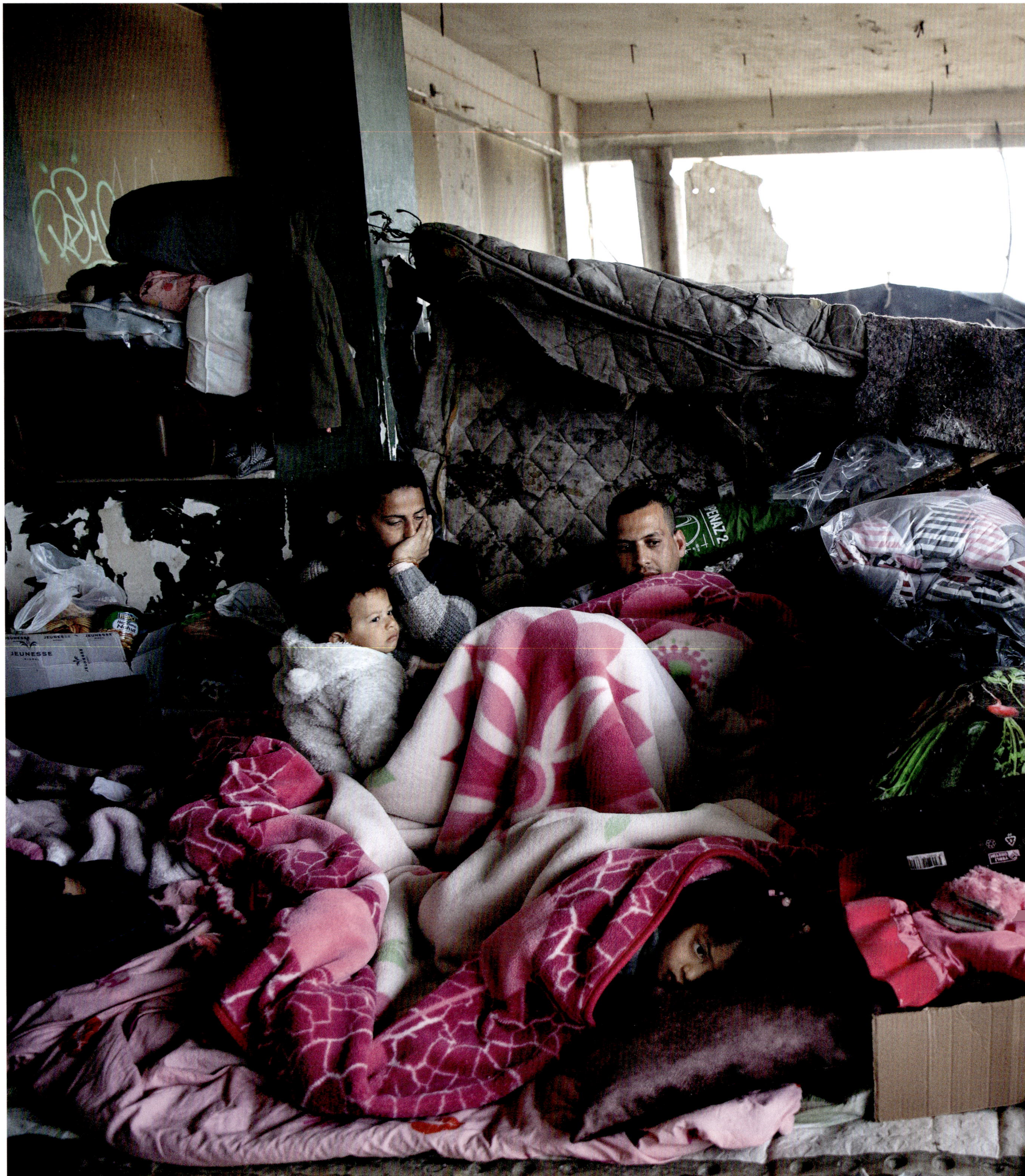
JEUNESSE

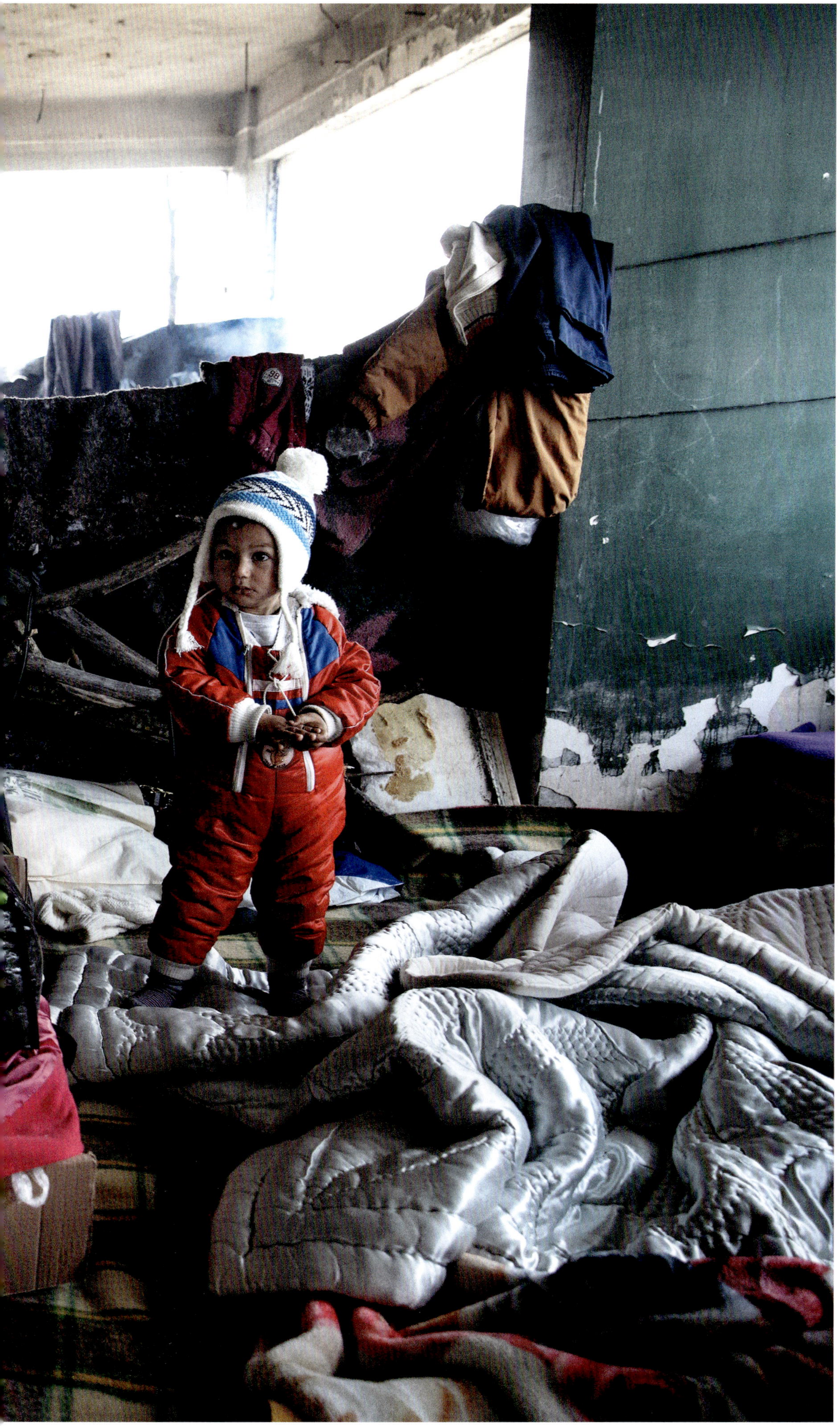

In March 2020 up to 20,000 asylum seekers in the Moria camp live under inhumane conditions. This is more than ever before.

The authorities introduce restrictions on the freedom of movement for asylum seekers due to the Covid-19 outbreak. In practice this means that people are trapped in a place where it is totally impossible for them to follow the most basic guidelines for avoiding infection. The restrictions also mean that they can no longer get away from the camp to catch their breath for a while, and this increases the already high stress levels among the camp residents.

On the night of 9 September 2020, a huge fire breaks out in the Moria camp. The following day smaller fires erupt and eventually the camp burns down completely.

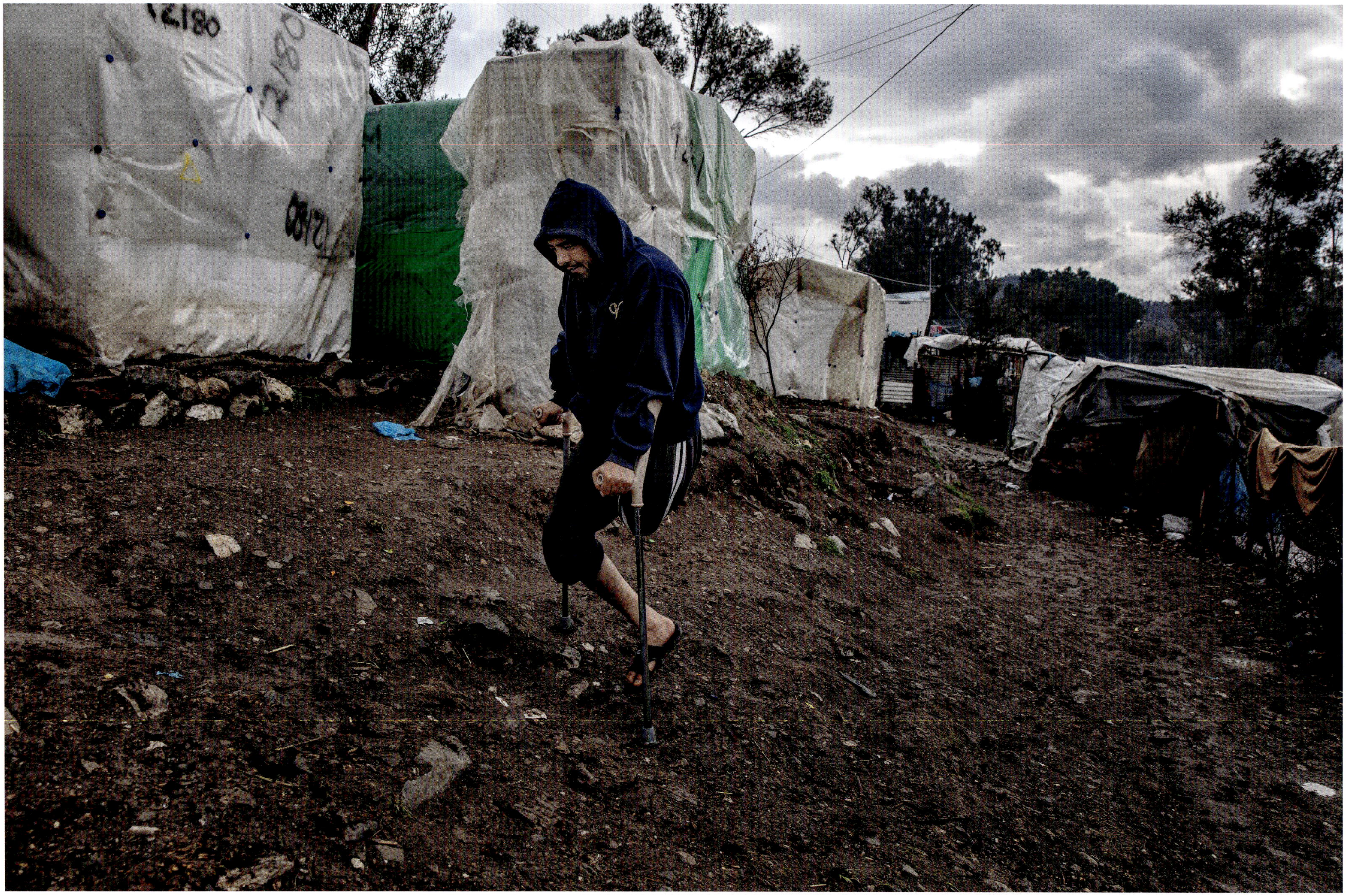

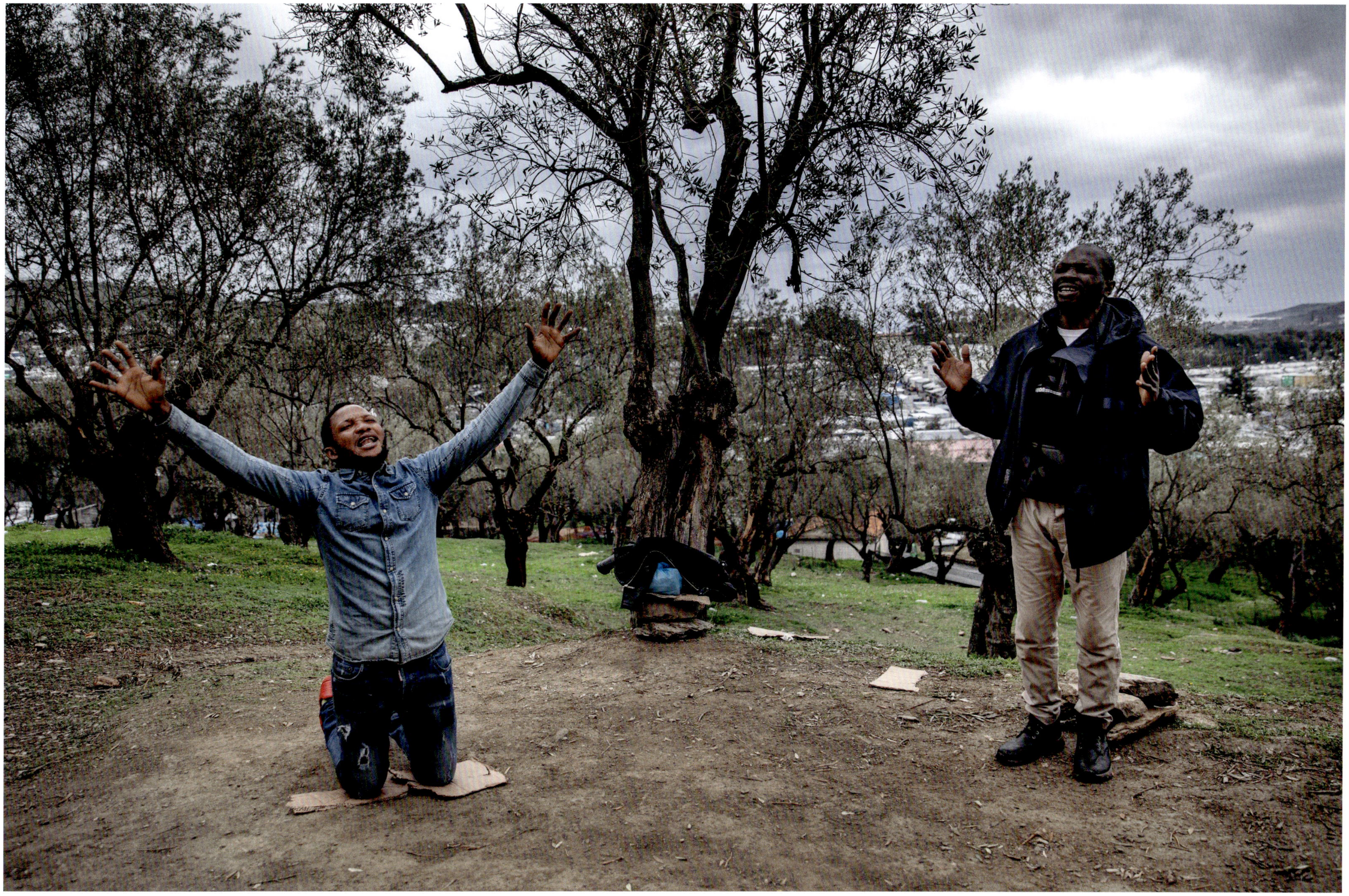

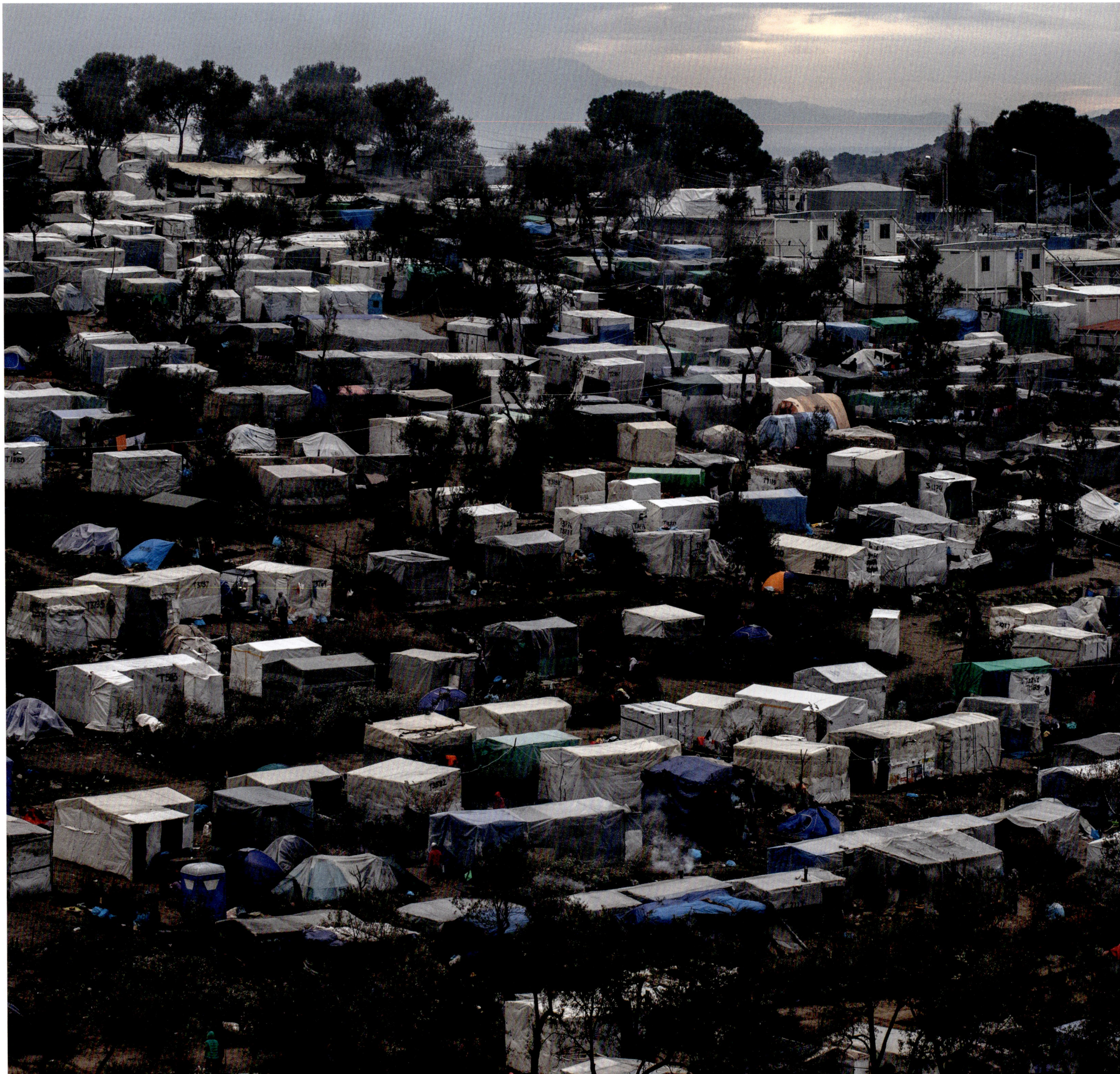

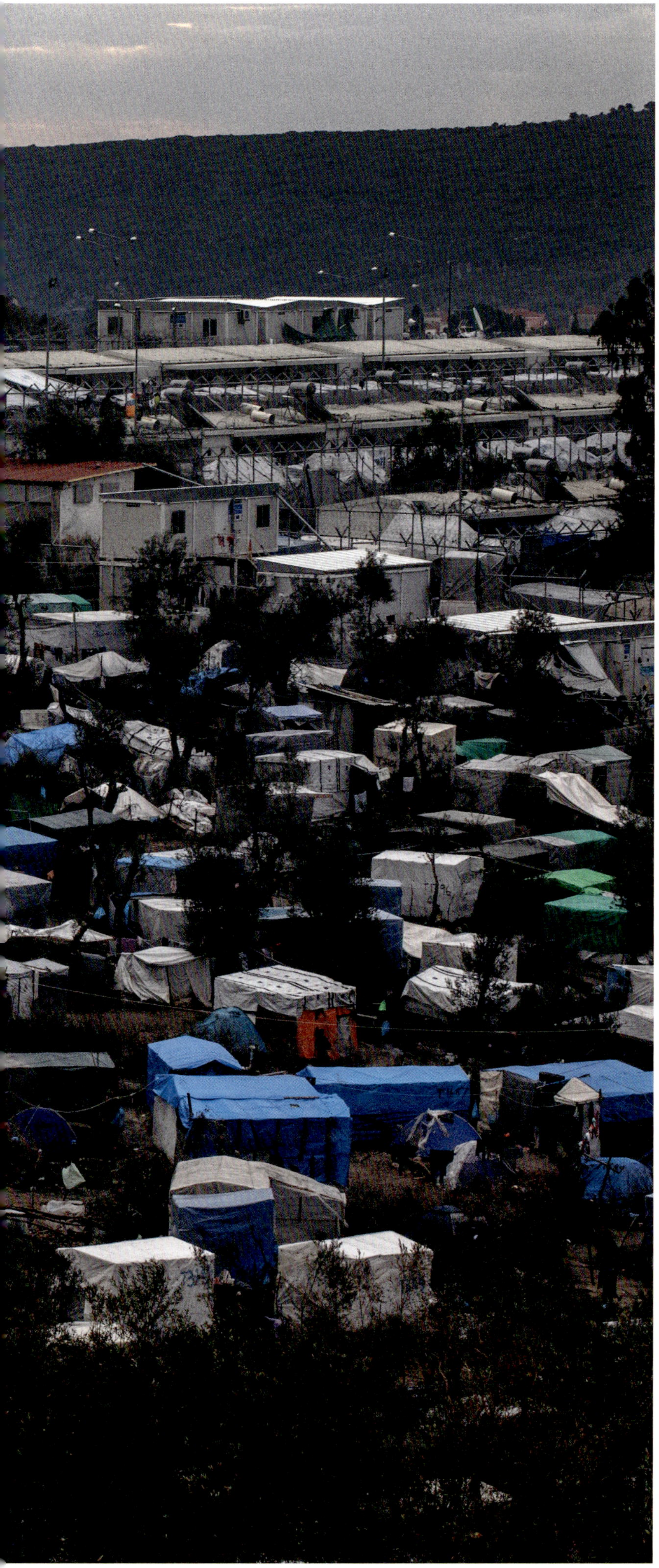

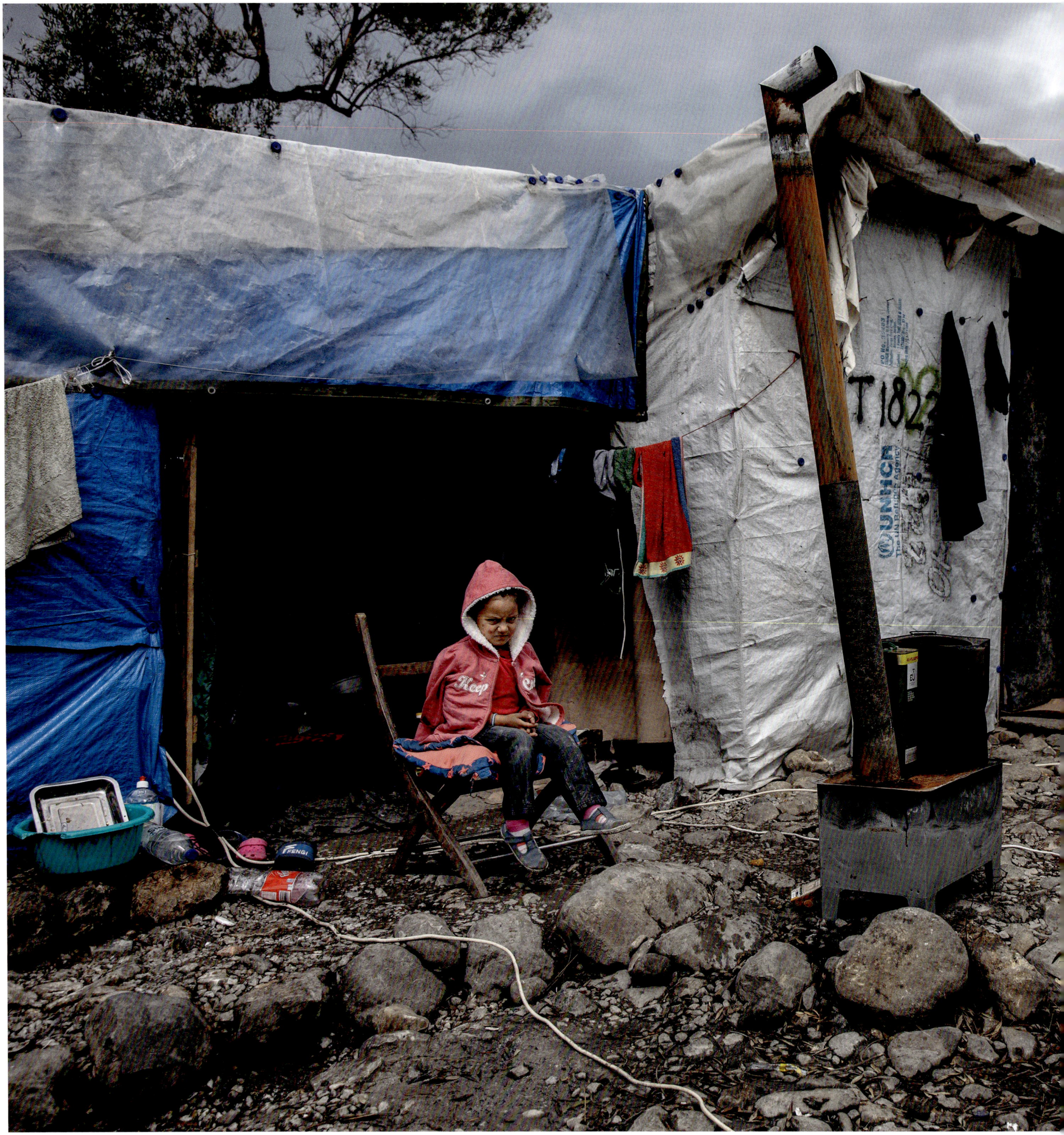
T 1822
UNHCR
The UN Refugee Agency
Keep
FENGI

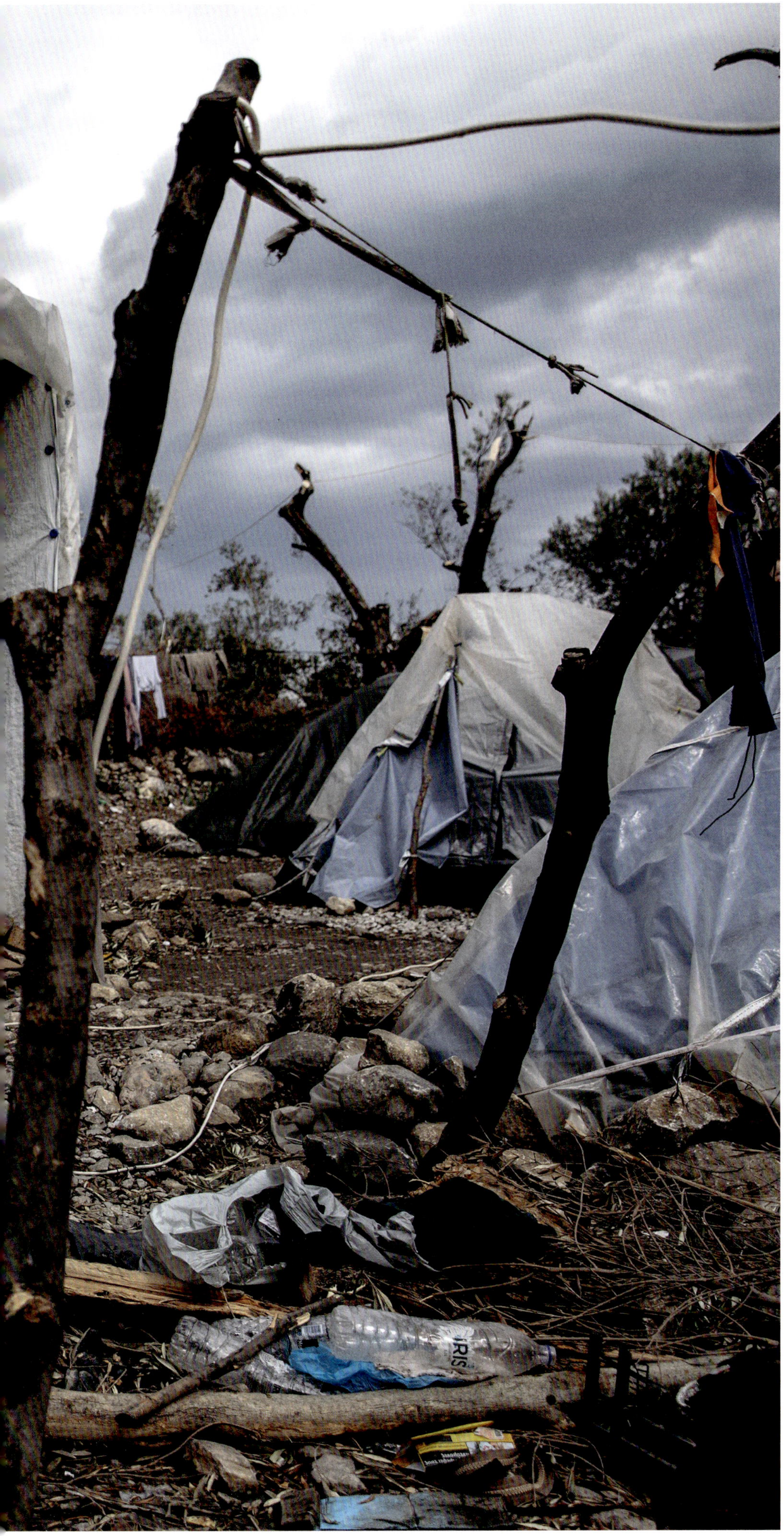

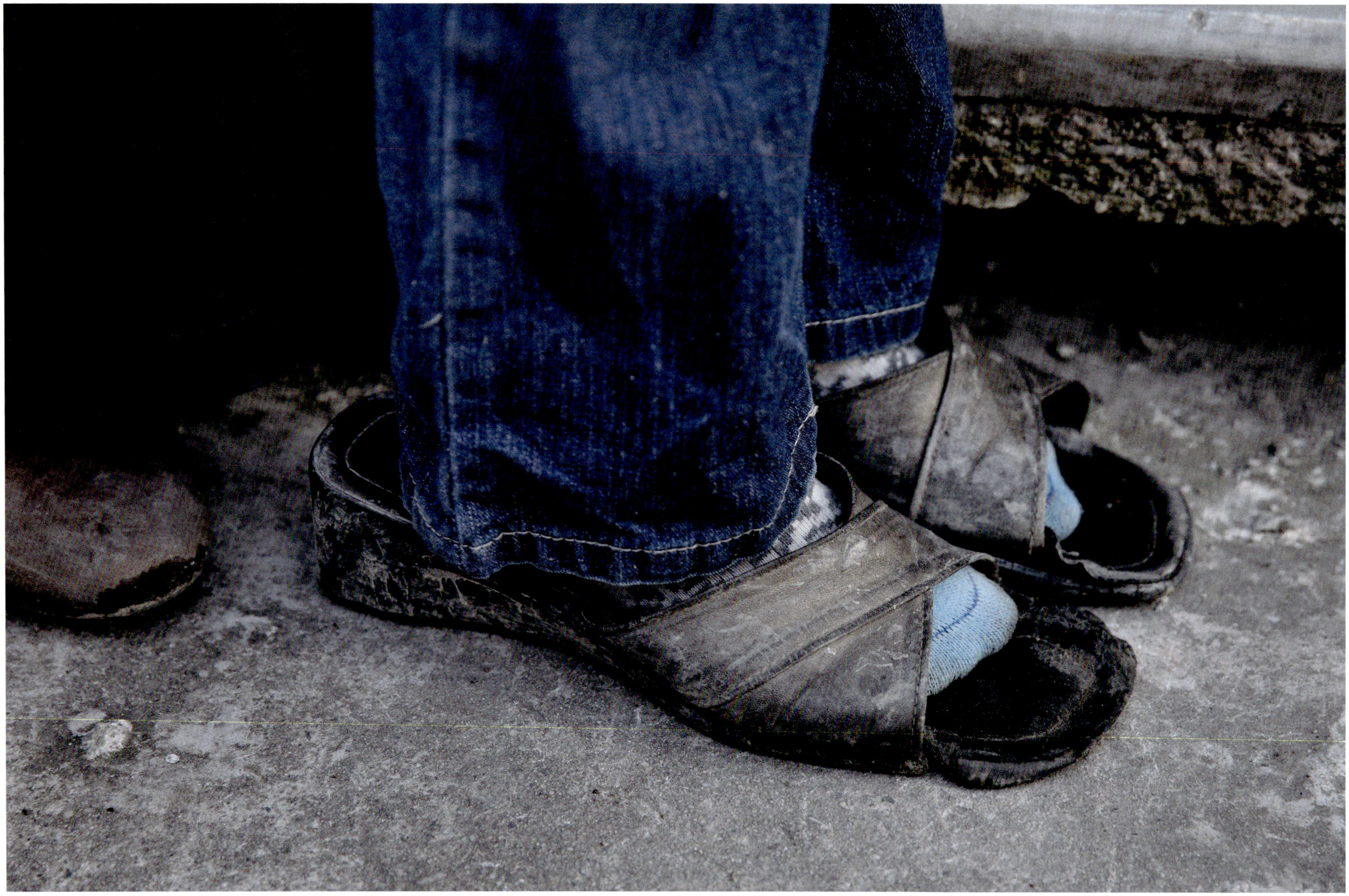

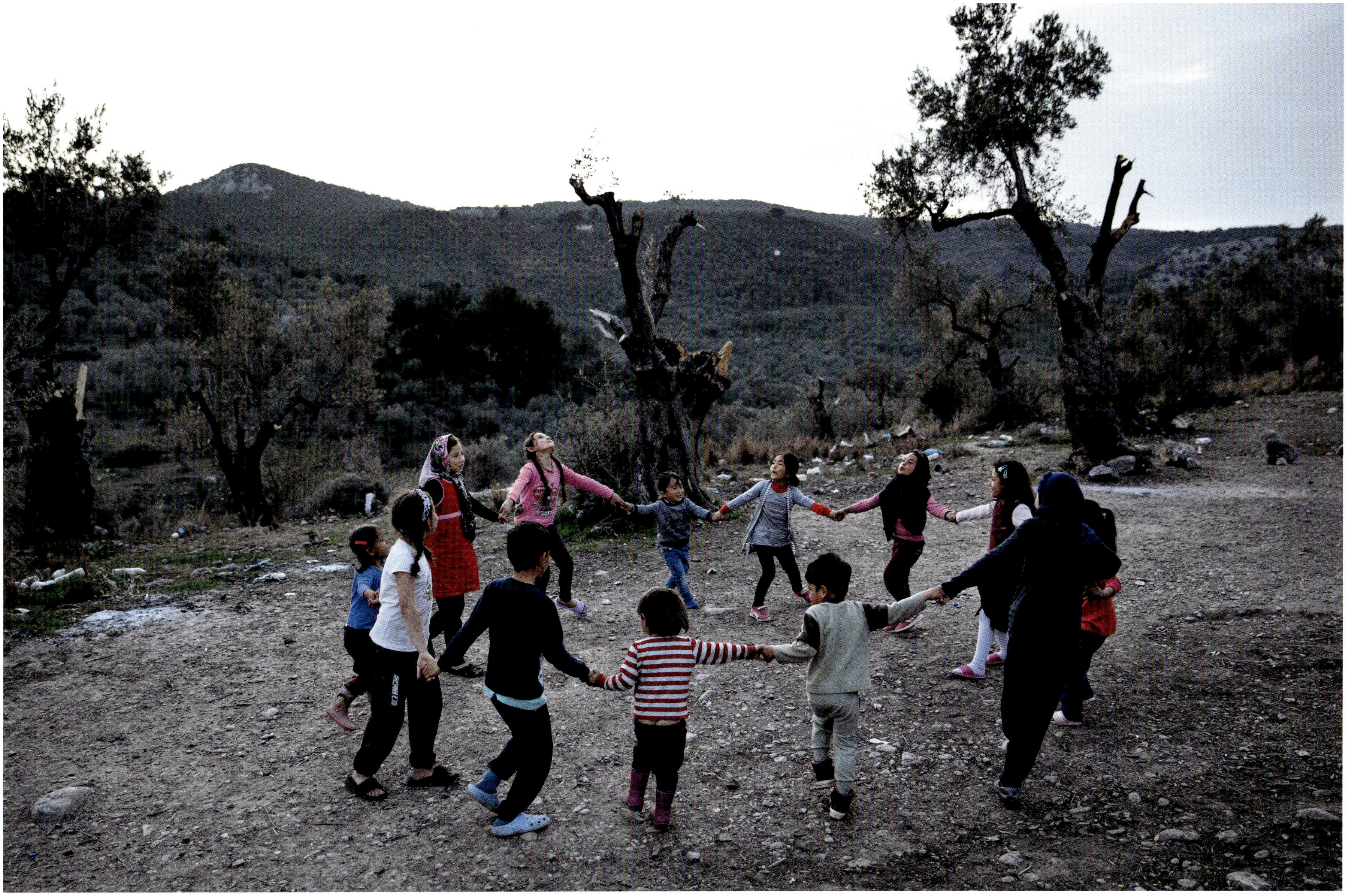

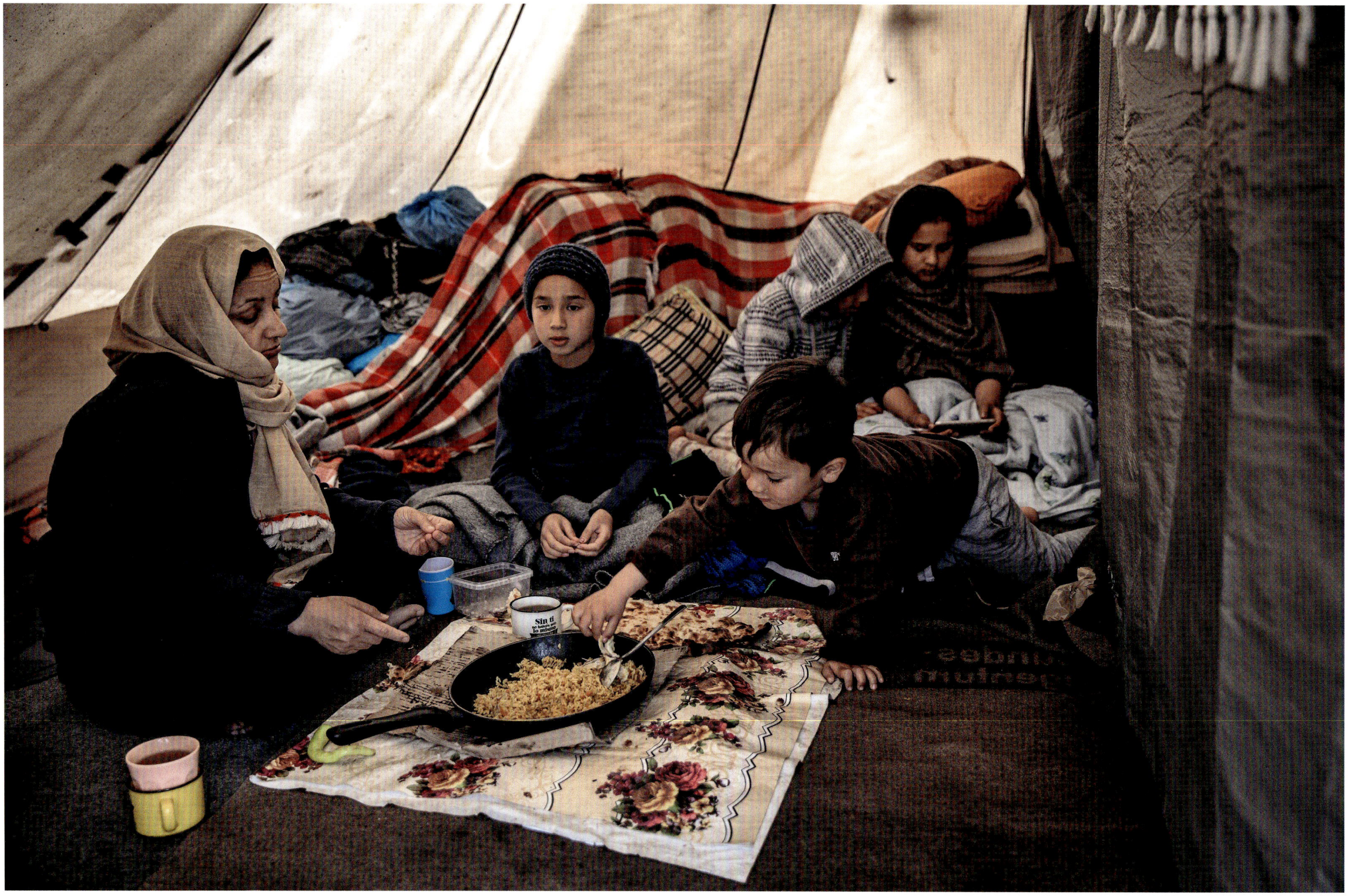

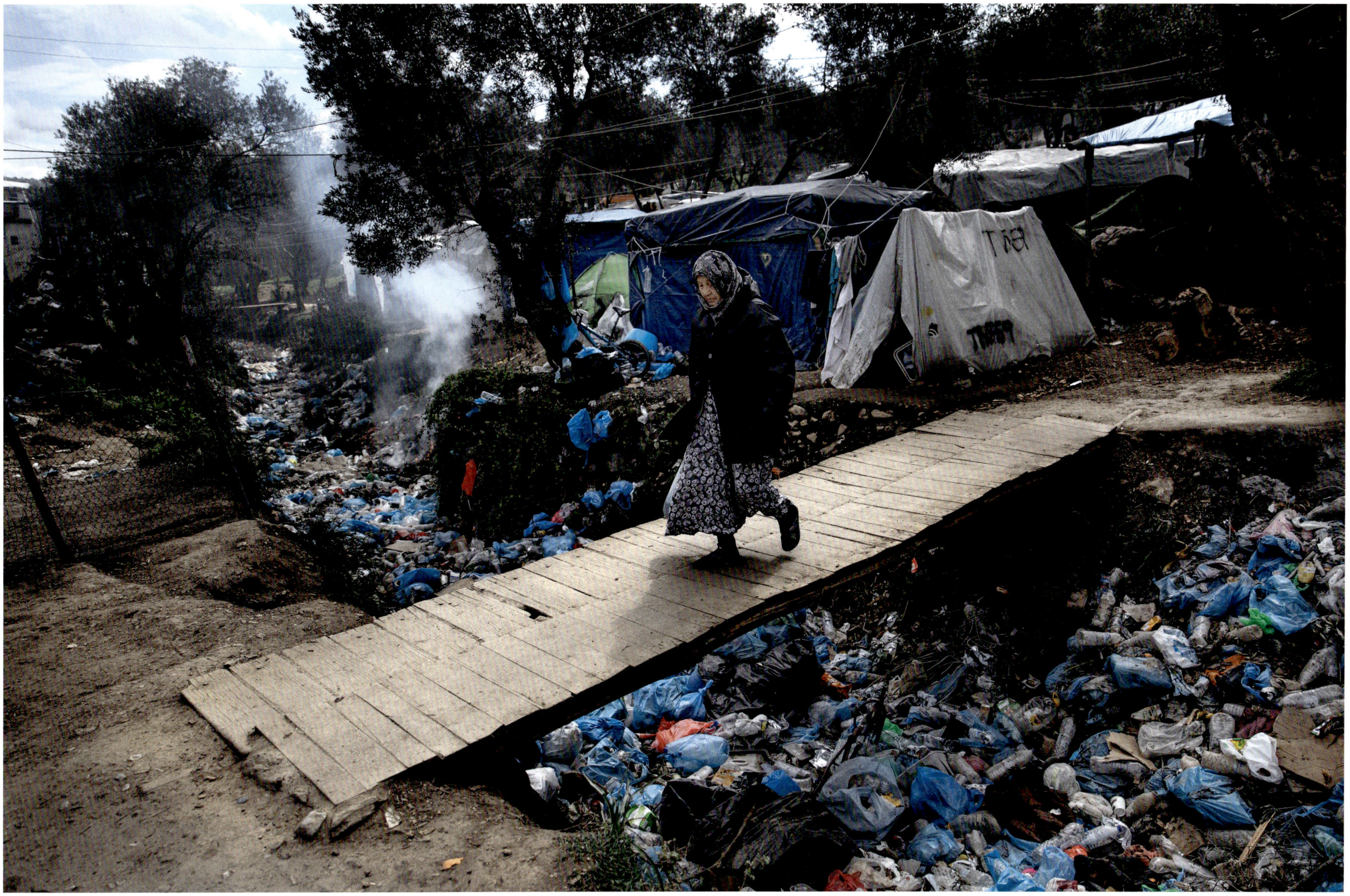

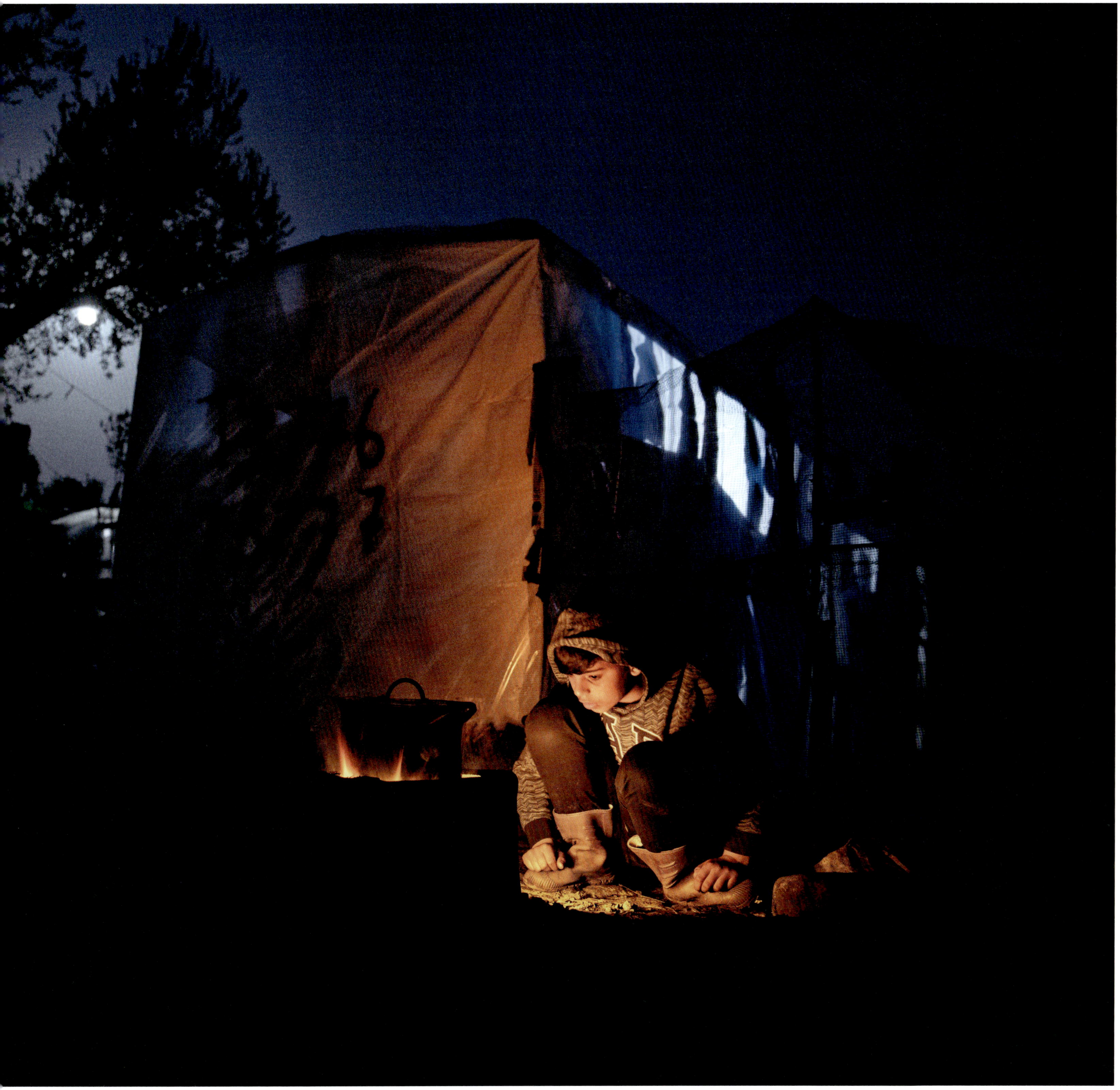

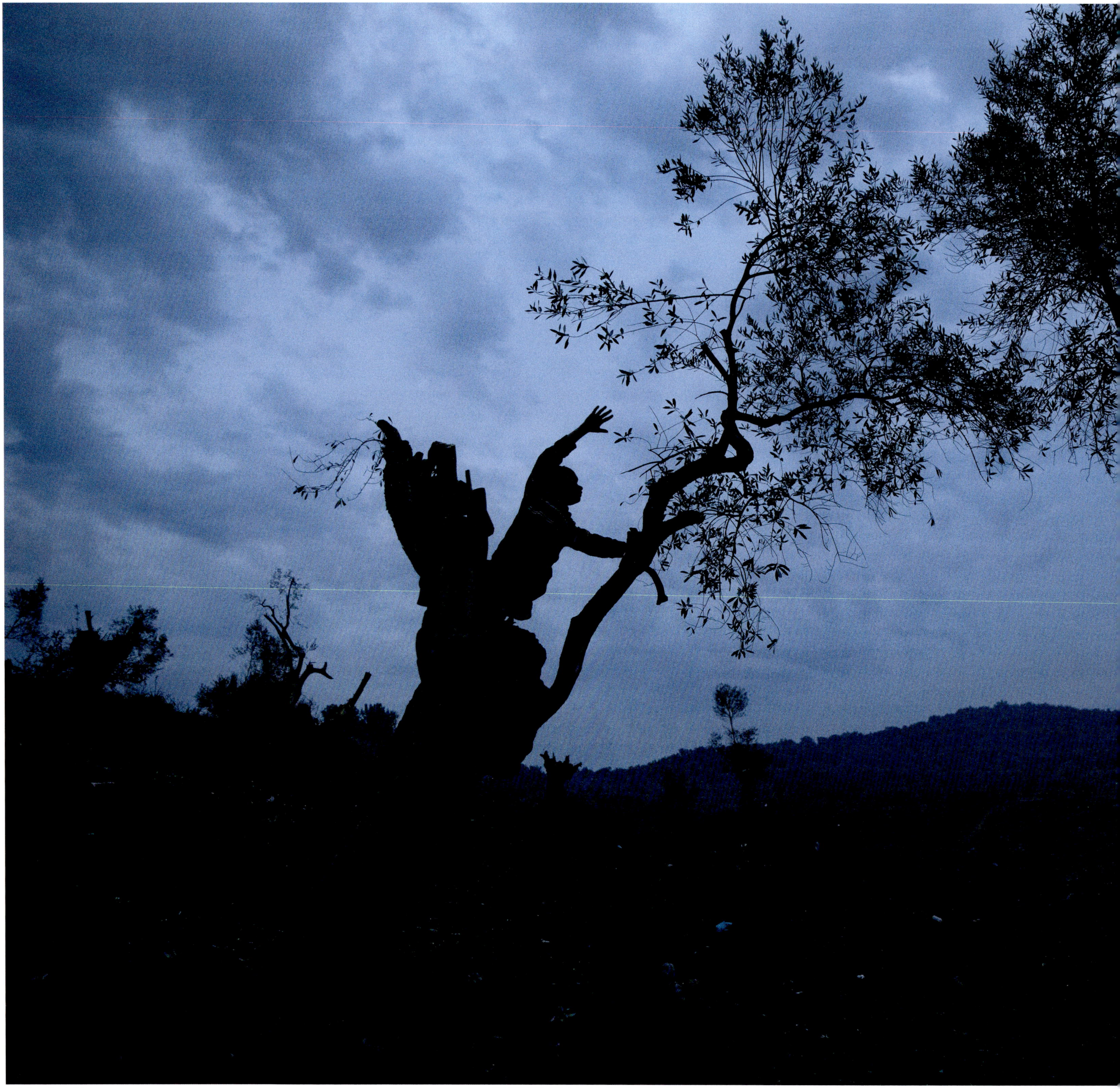

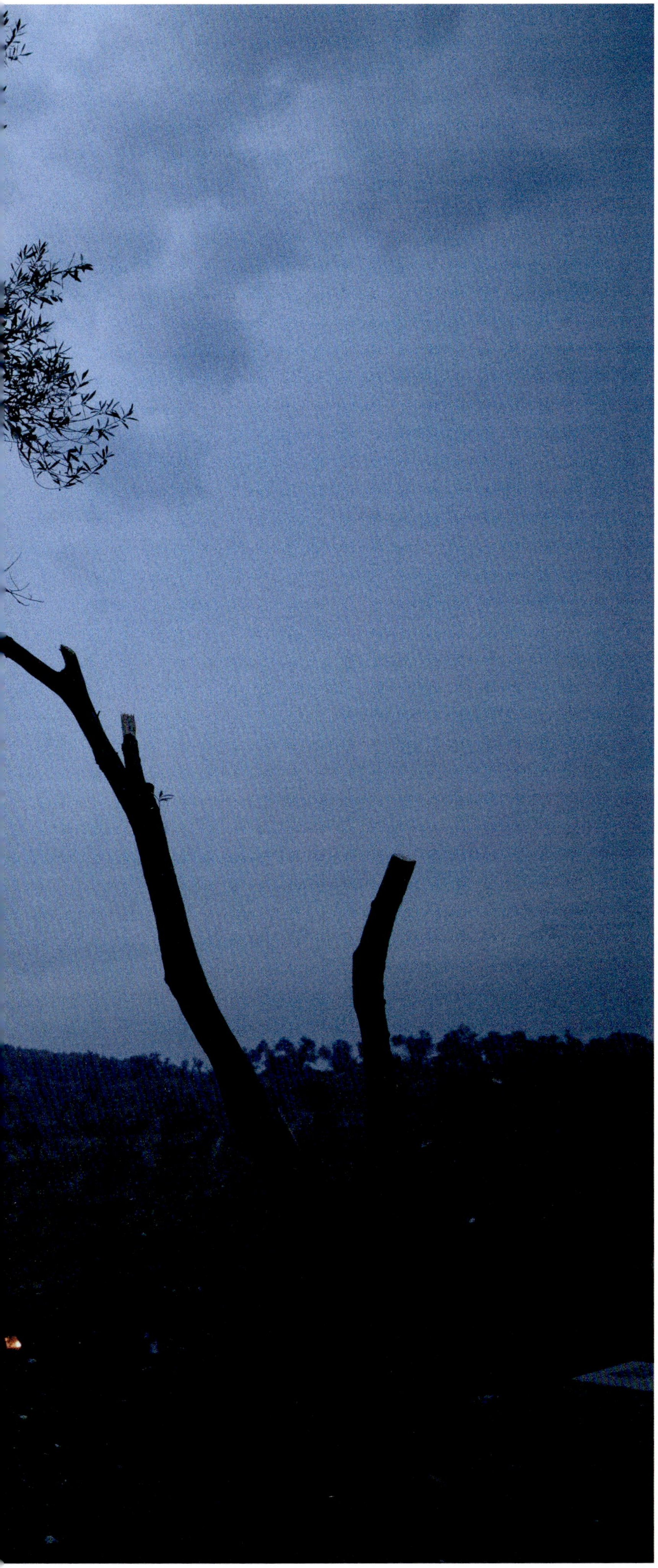

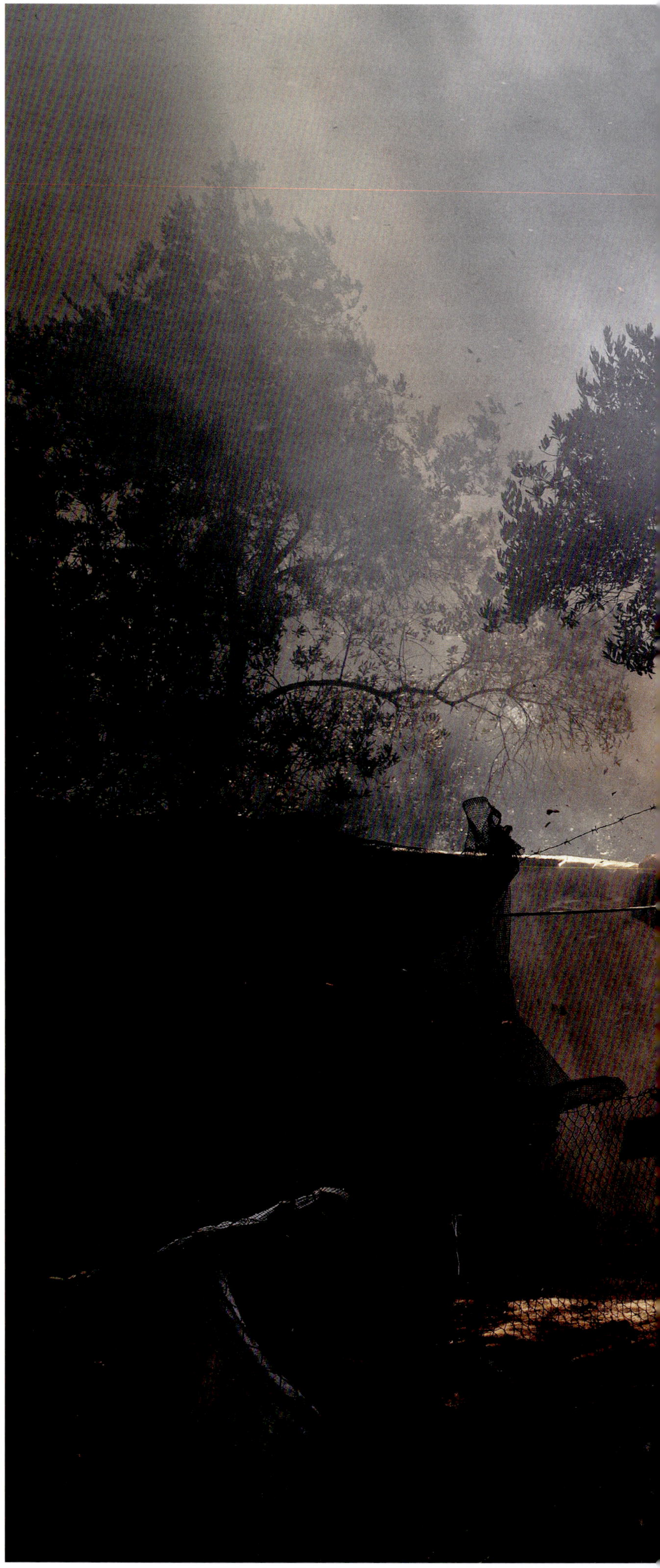

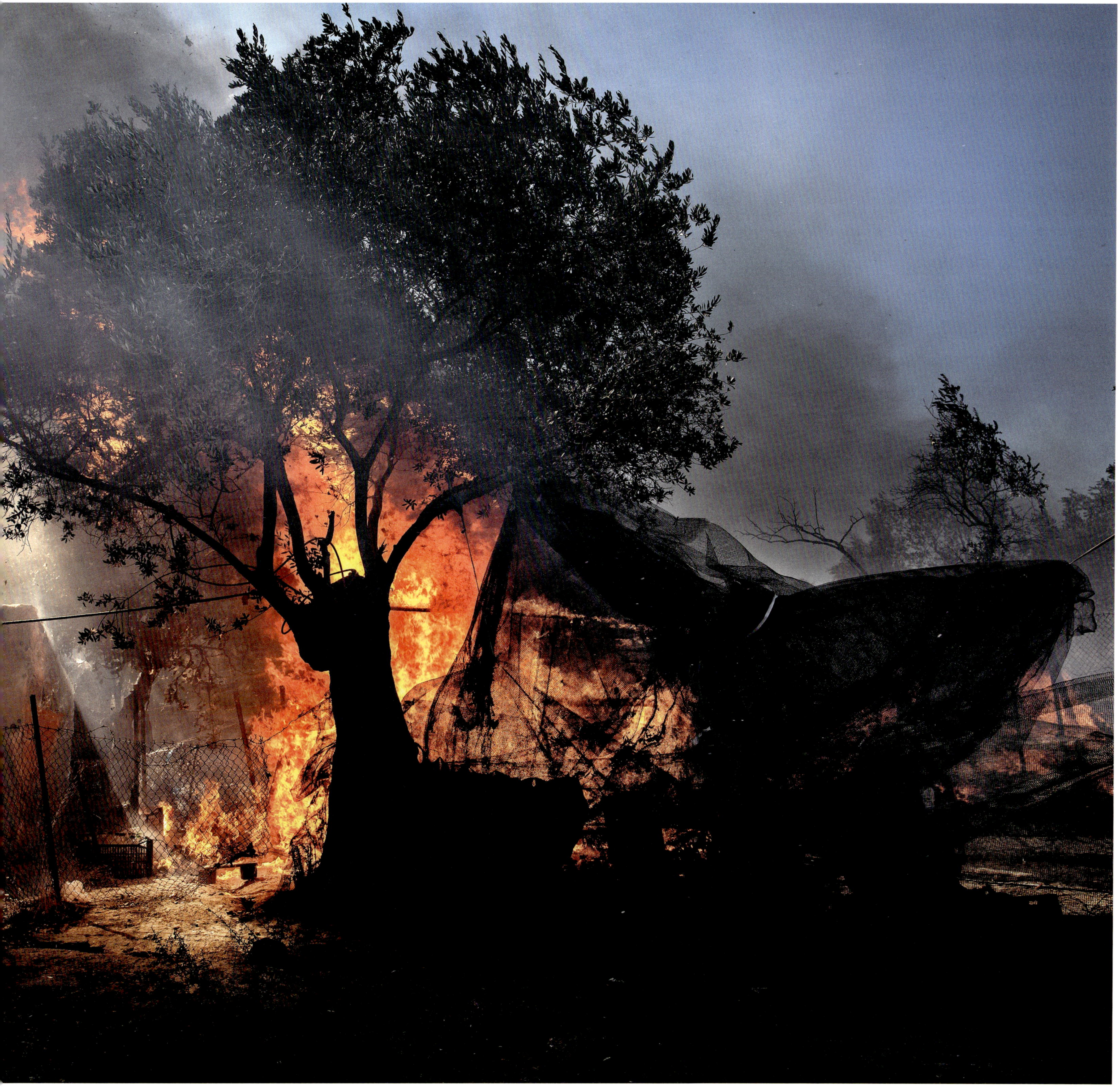

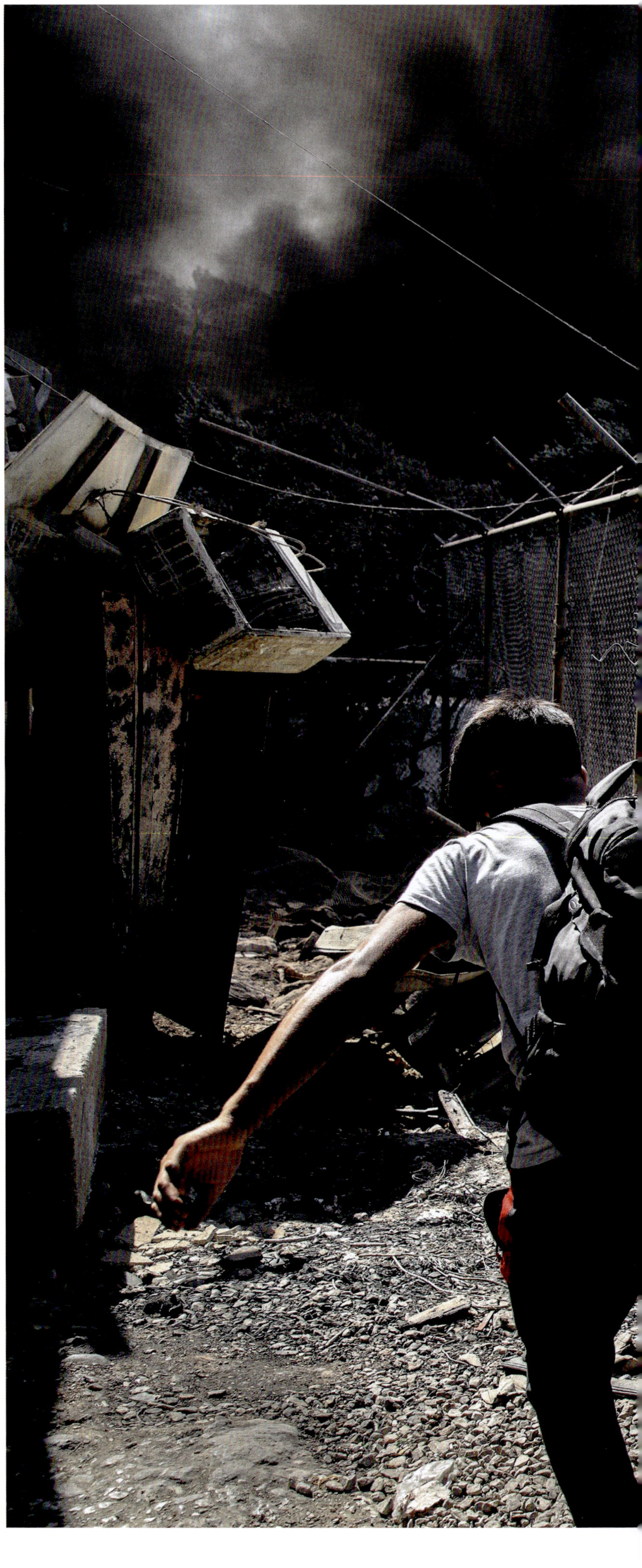

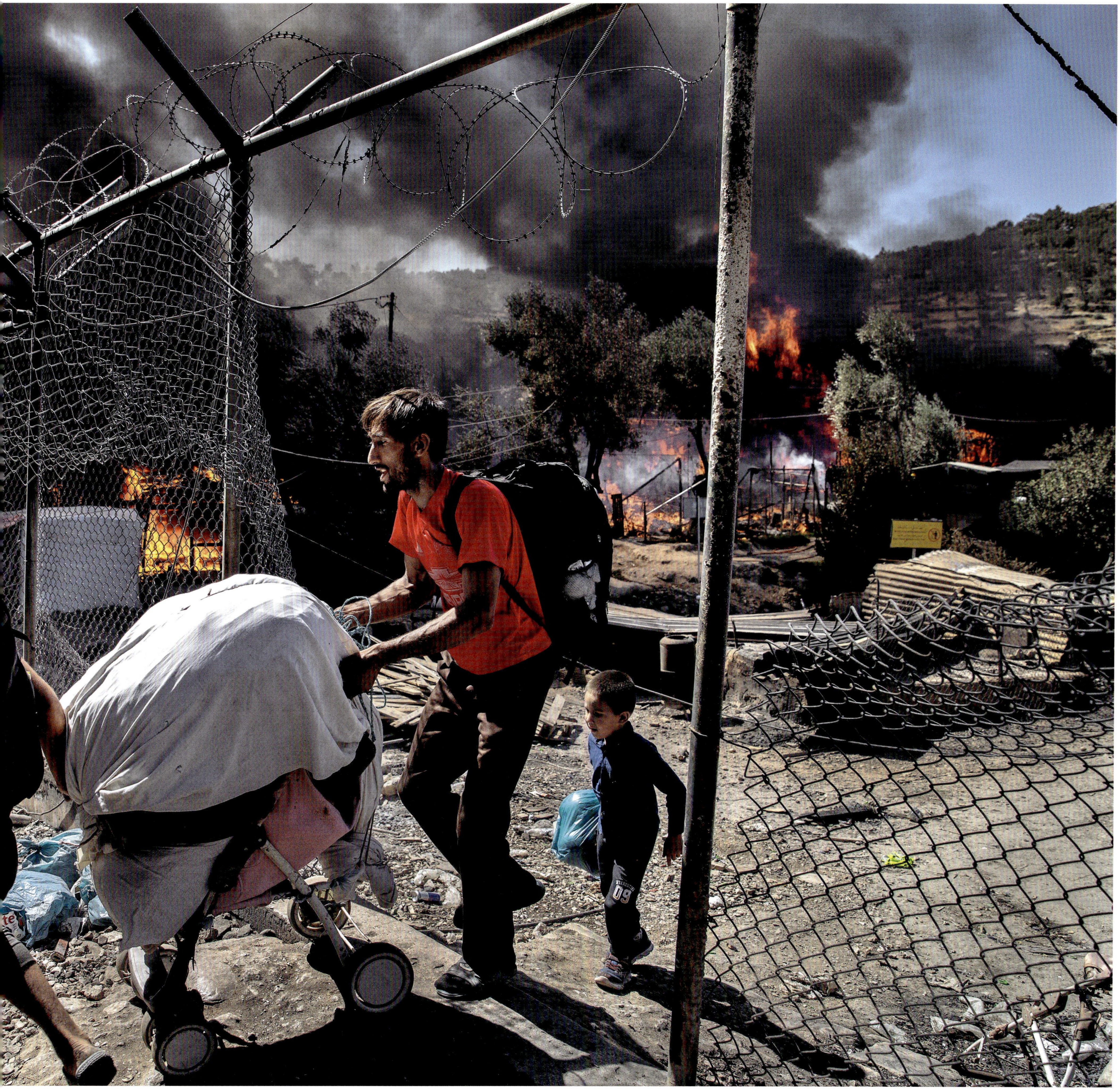

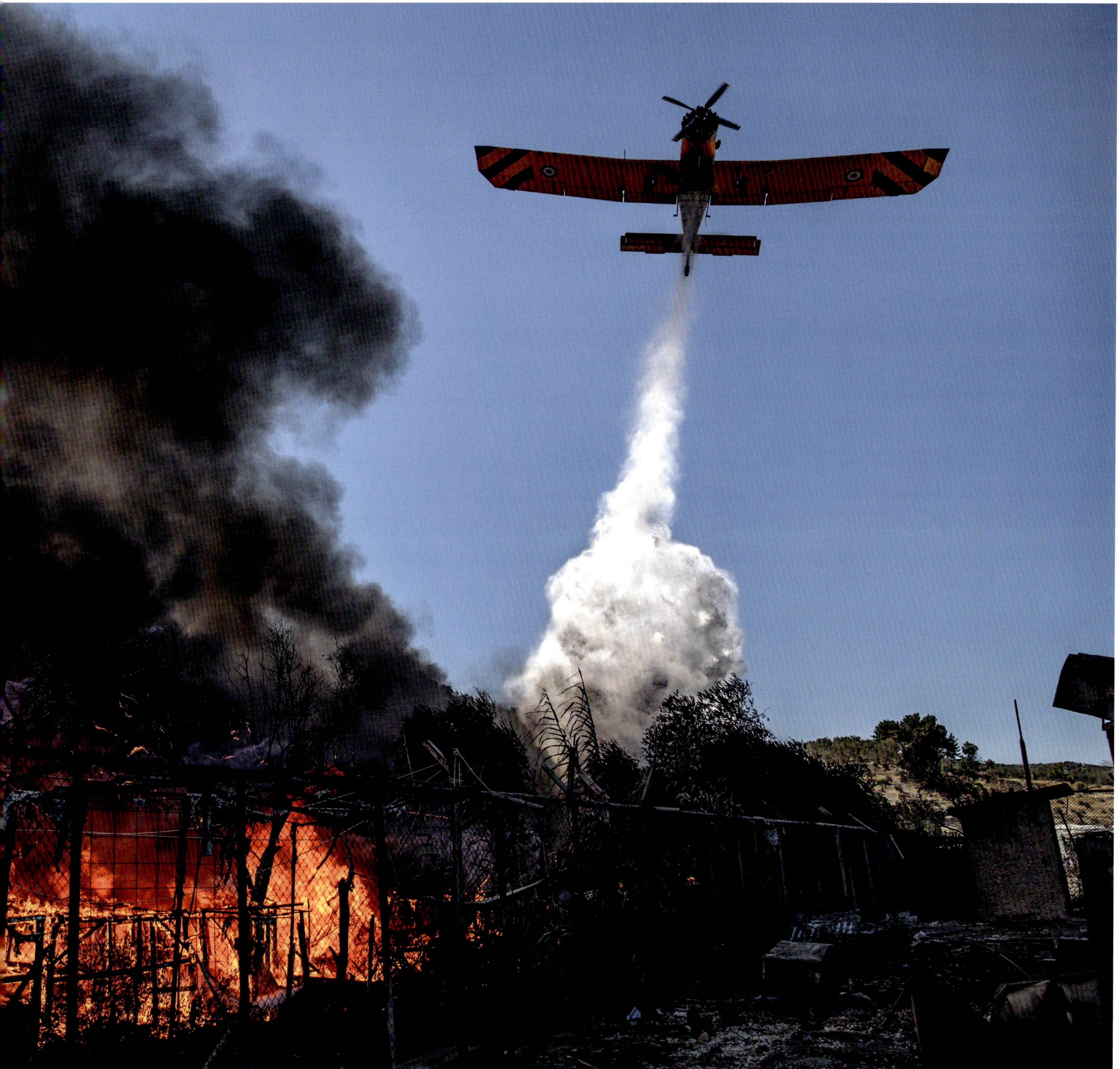

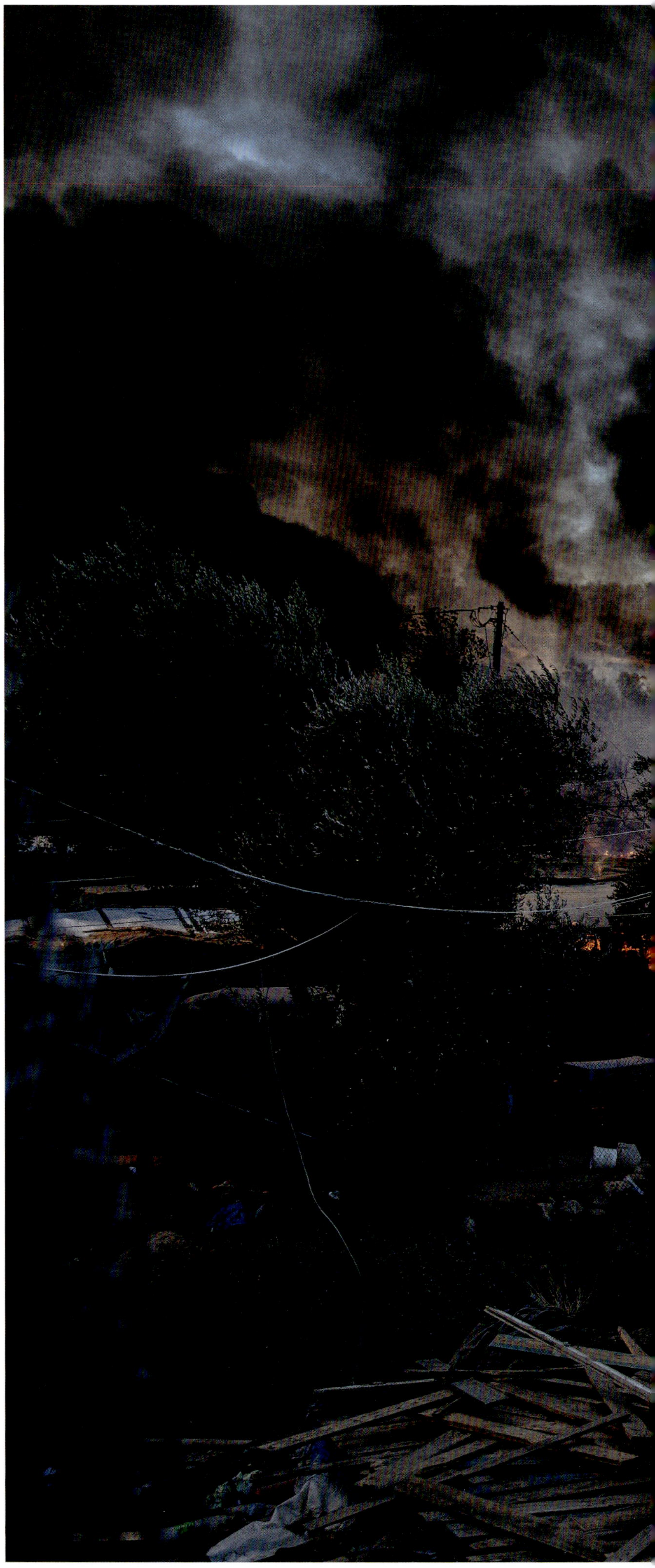

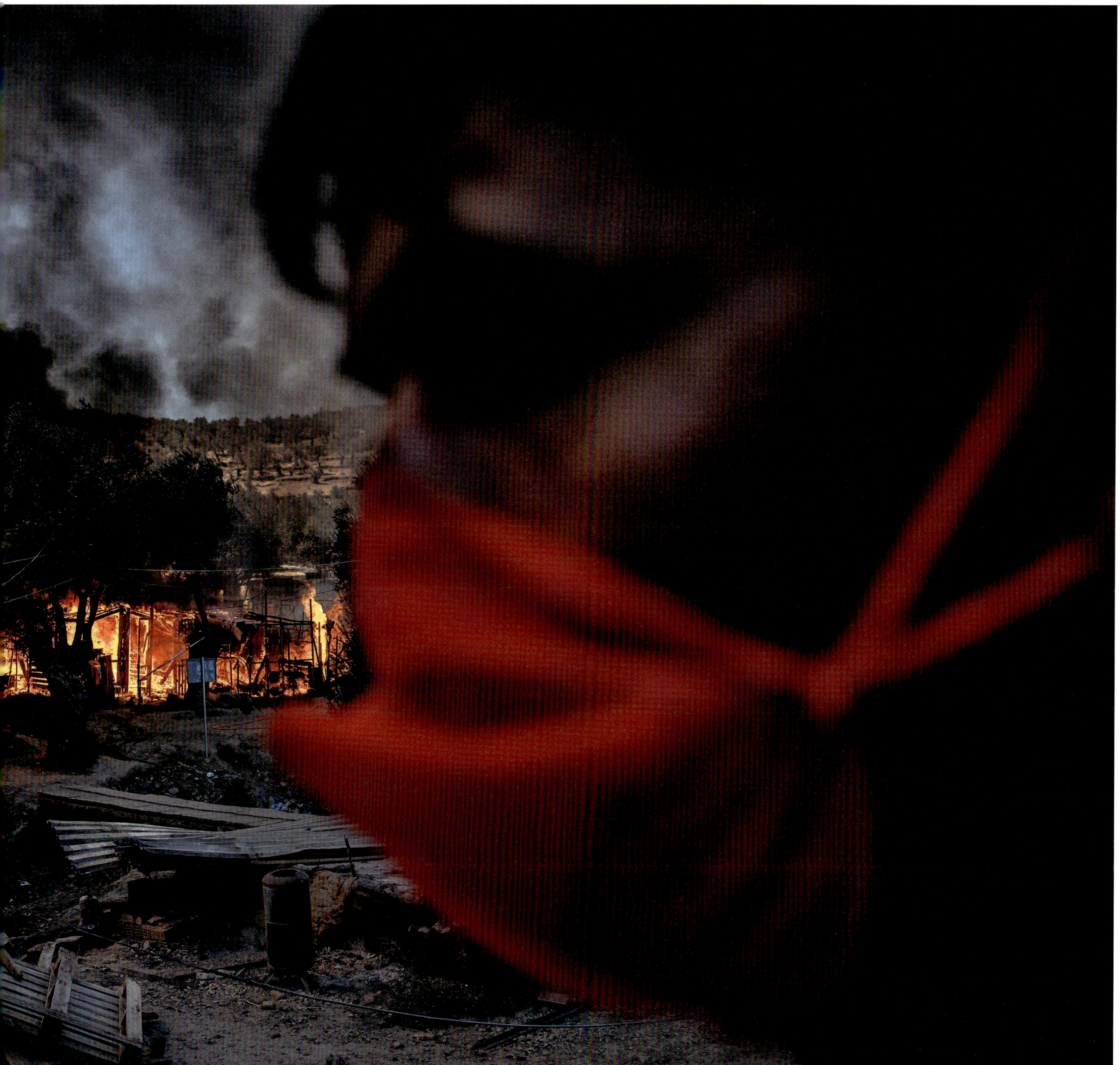

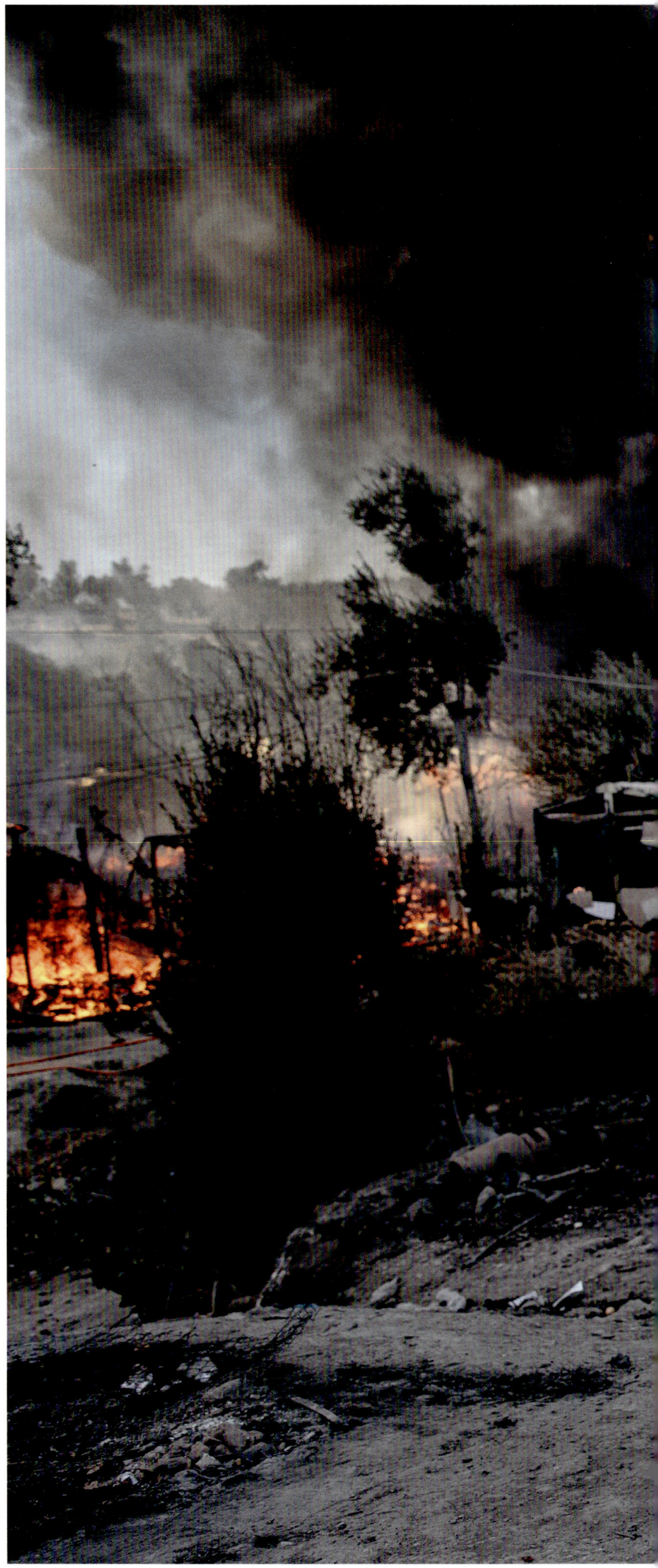

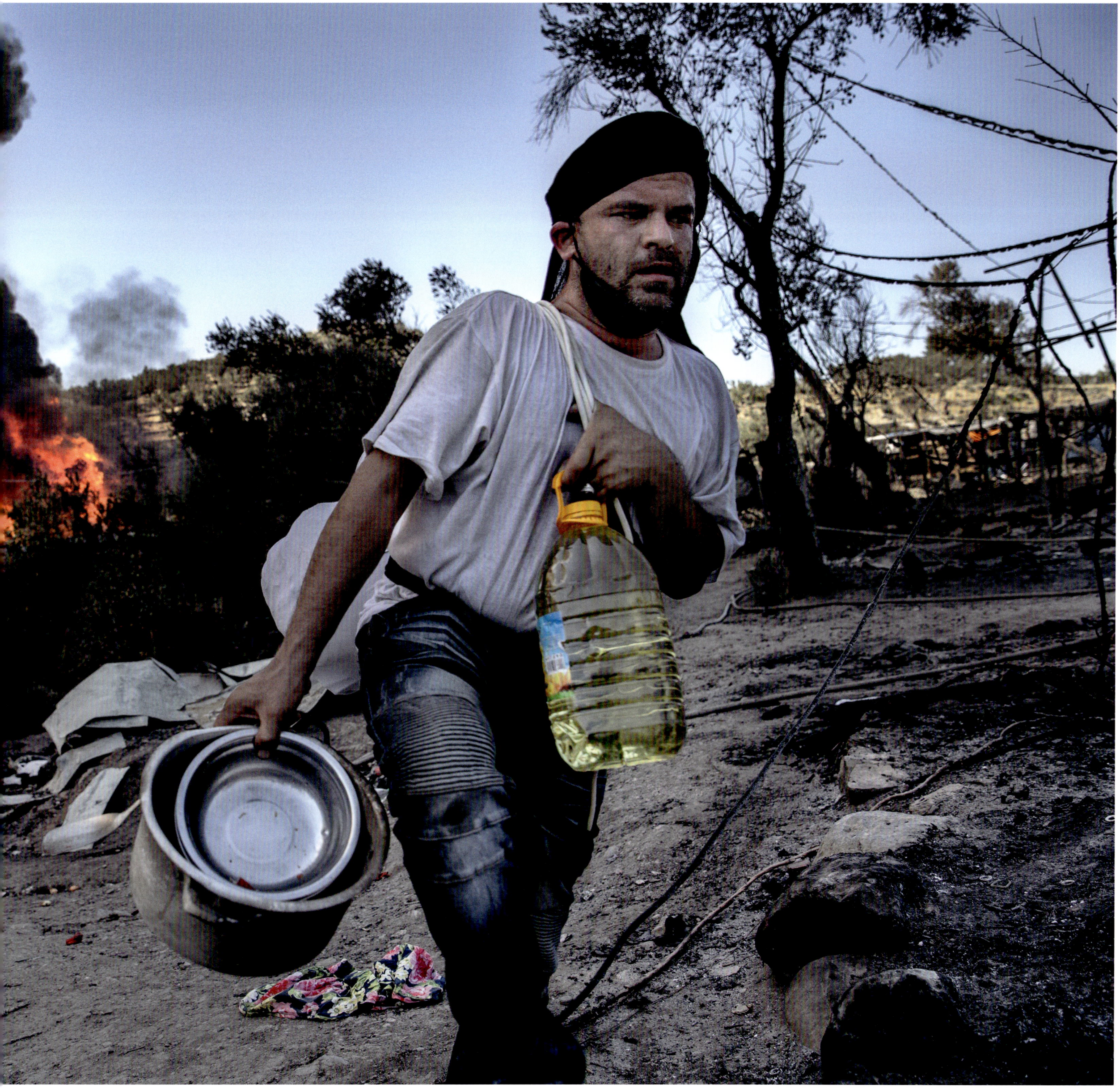

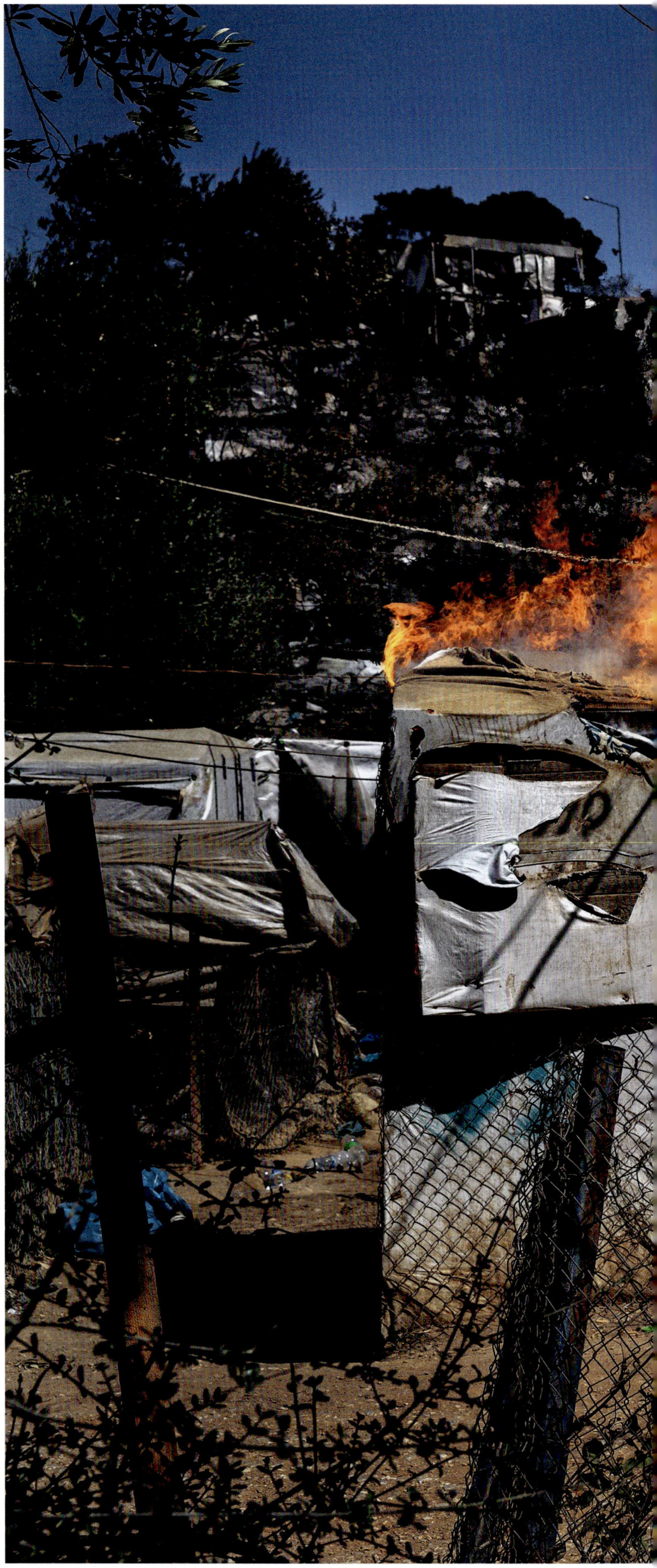

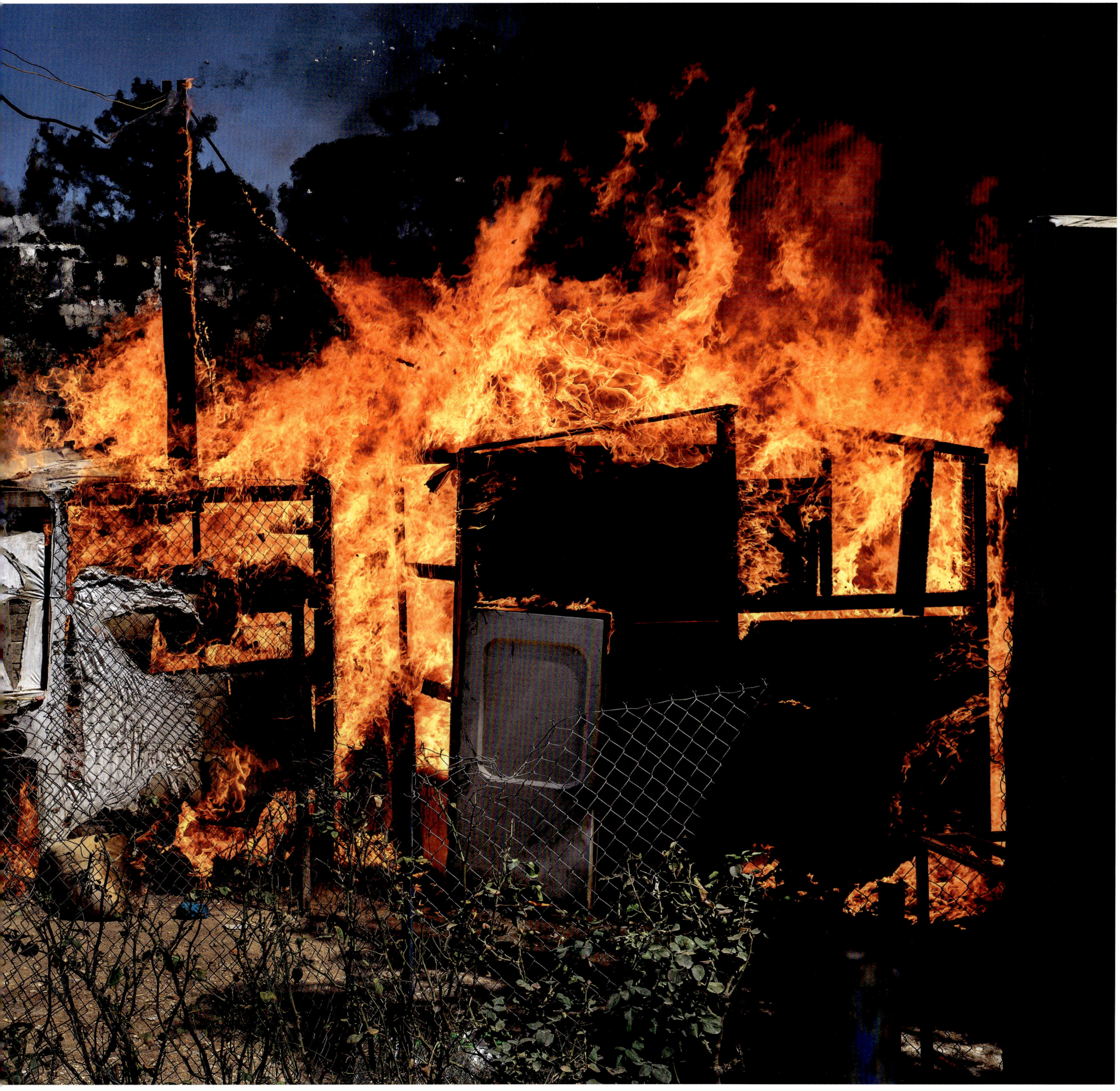

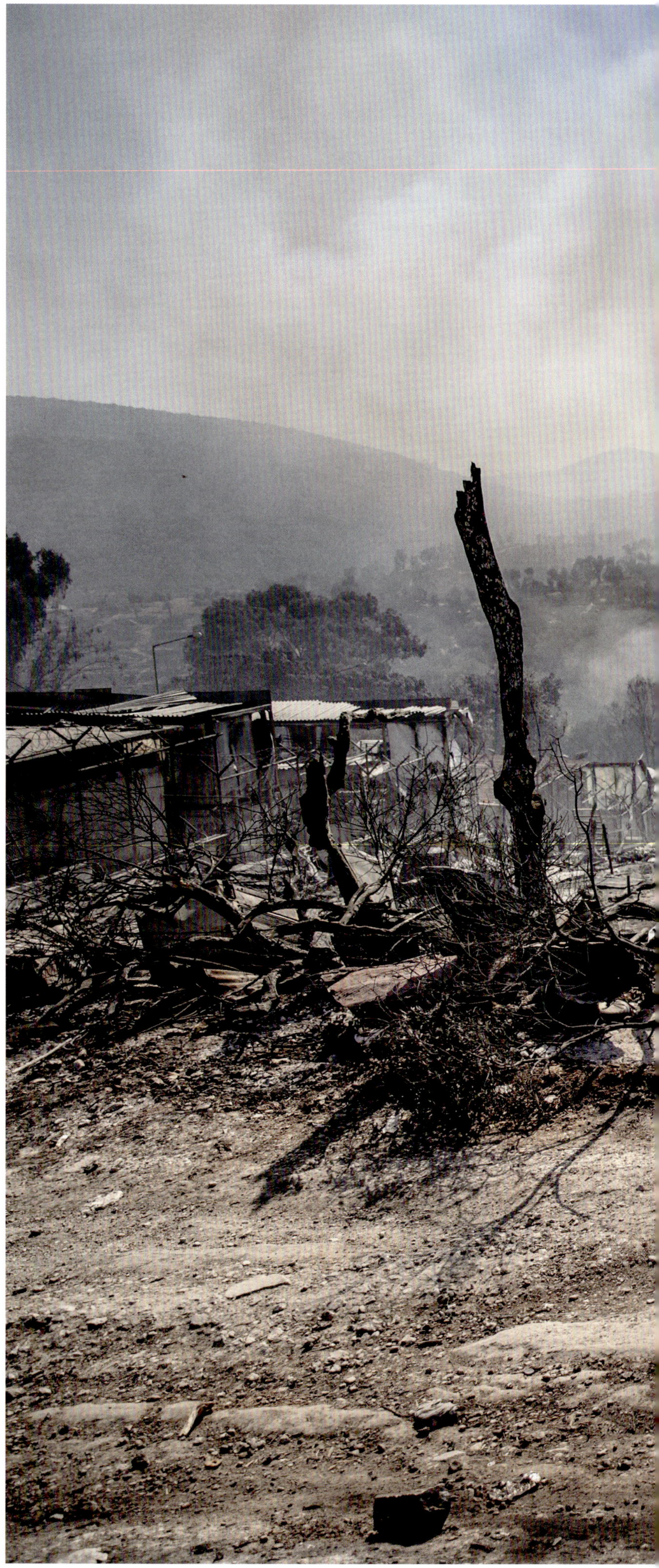

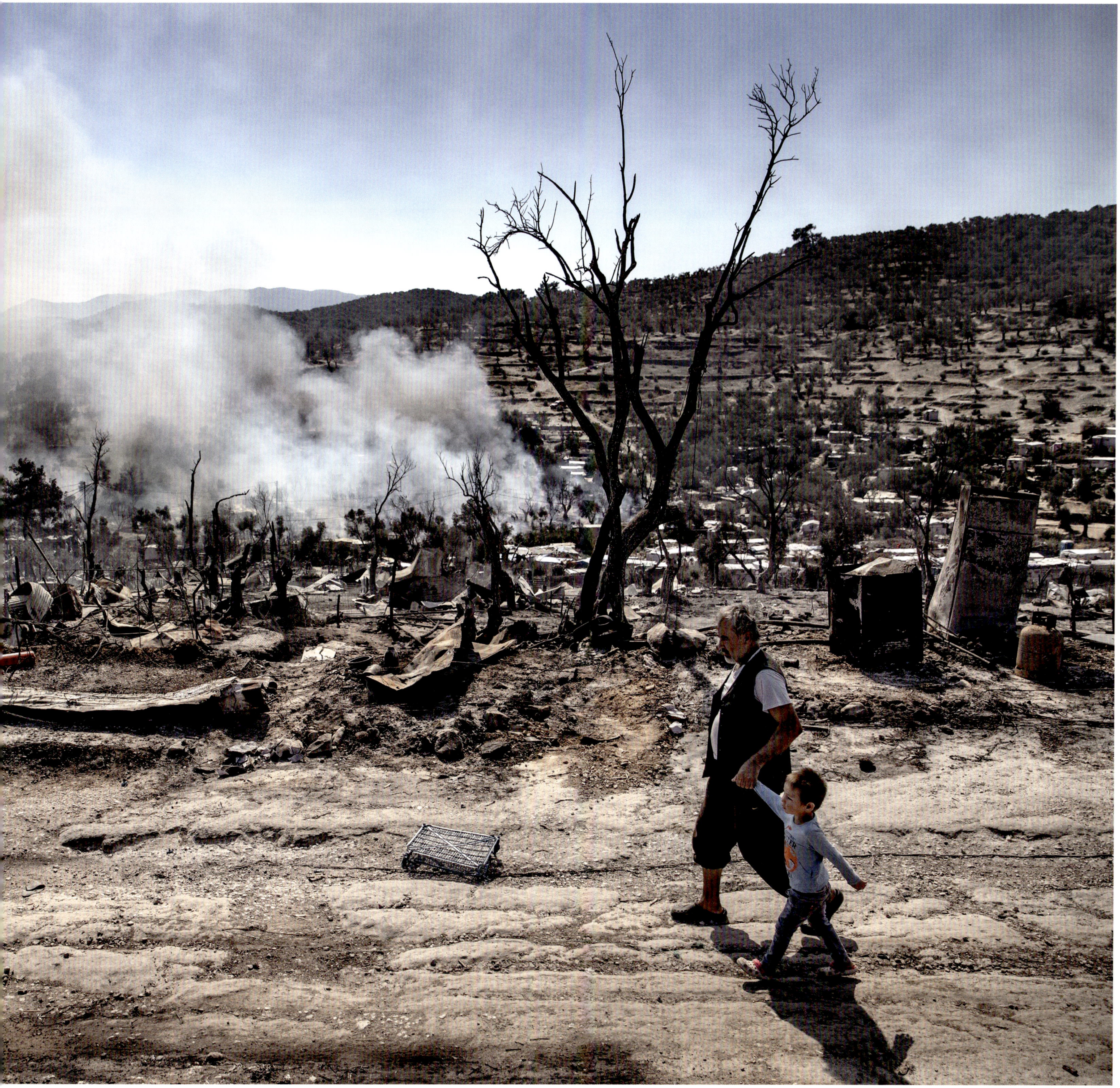

INDEX

9

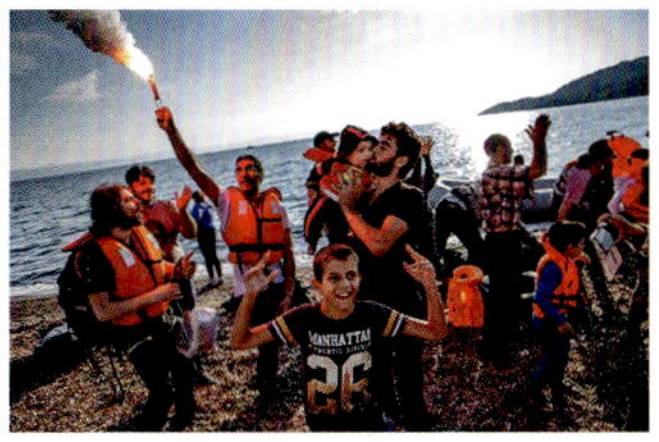

A dinghy with Syrians and Afghans arrives on Lesbos. There is a great sense of relief. Many weep with joy. One man lights a signal flare and people dance, sing, pray and take pictures of each other. The joy is replaced by disappointment when they learn that they will have to walk more than 60 kilometres to a reception centre. 29.06.2015

10

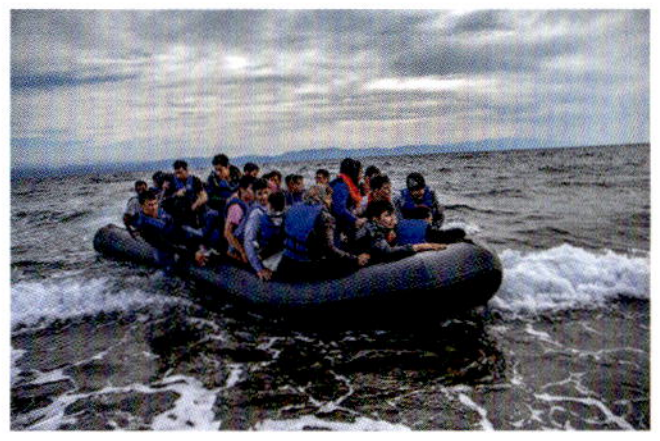

A boat with refugees from Syria and Iraq arrives on a beach near Skala Sikamineas. They have had a difficult passage with two engine failures. 02.07.2015

12

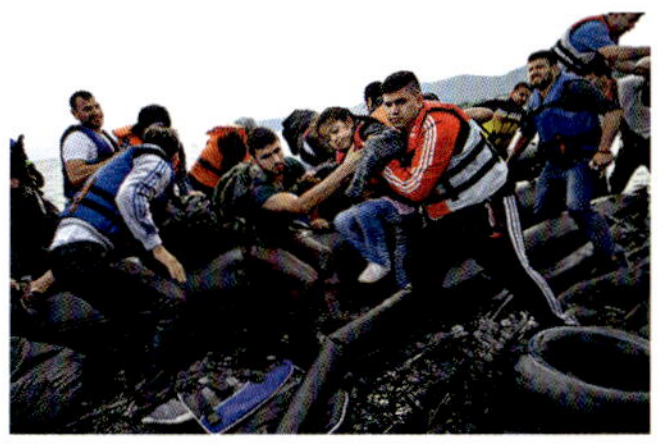

Refugees and migrants from Syria and Iraq go ashore on a beach near Skala Sikamineas. There are typically 40-50 people aboard the overcrowded rubber dinghies that the human traffickers send off from the Turkish coasts. 02.07.2015

13

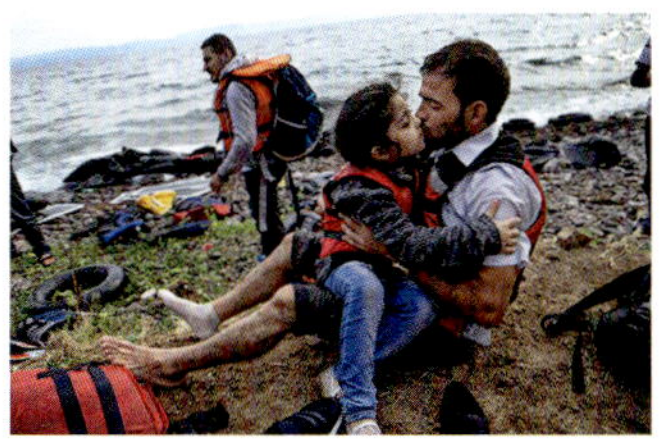

Husam, age 31, from Iraq has just landed on a beach near Skala Sikamineas after a dramatic passage during which the boat almost tipped over. When the boat's engine failed Husam was sitting with two children on top of him. He had to sit perfectly still so that the boat would not take on more water. When they finally reached shore, he was unable to move his legs, so his fellow passengers had to carry him to the beach and massage his legs to get the blood circulating again. His six-year-old daughter, Nawras, is lifted over to him and they can breathe a sigh of relief. His wife and their three-month-old daughter are still in Turkey, as the family could not afford for all of them to take this journey. Husam's plan is to go to Germany and apply for family reunification. 02.07.2015

14

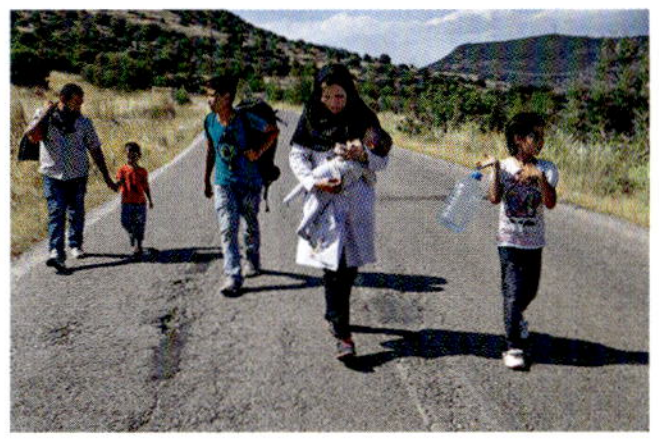

After the journey from Turkey to Lesbos an Afghan family have to walk from Skala Sikaminea to Kara Tepe, a provisional reception camp on the outskirts of Mytilini. The route is about 50 kilometres and runs through hilly terrain. 30.06.2015

15

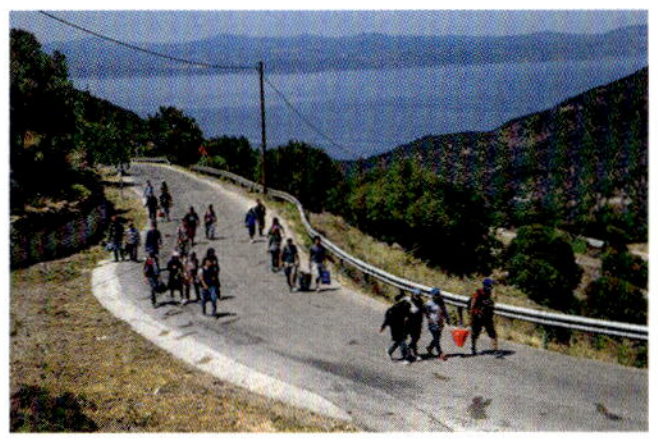

A group of refugees and migrants on the way to Mytilini to present themselves and submit to registration which will allow them to get the documents needed to board a ferry and proceed to Athens. 30.06.2015

16

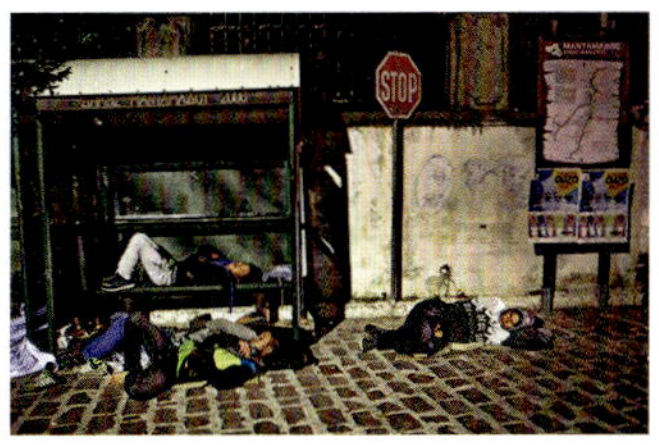

Some Afghan boys have lain down to sleep by a bus stop in the town of Mantamados. Most refugees spend from one to three days to reach the registration point on the outskirts of Mytilini and must sleep in the open along the way. 28.06.2015

20

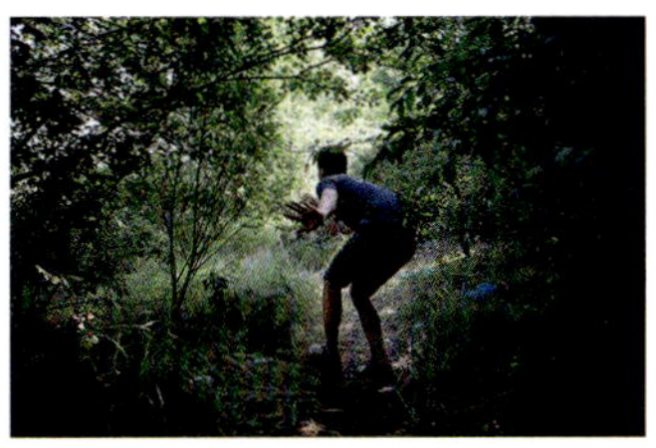

A group of boys who have fled from Aleppo in Syria and just entered Hungary are now moving through fields, forests and thickets to a petrol station on the highway, where they succeed in making contact with some traffickers. For a price of €250 per person, they will be driven to Budapest. They accept the offer without negotiation. 29 .08.2015

23

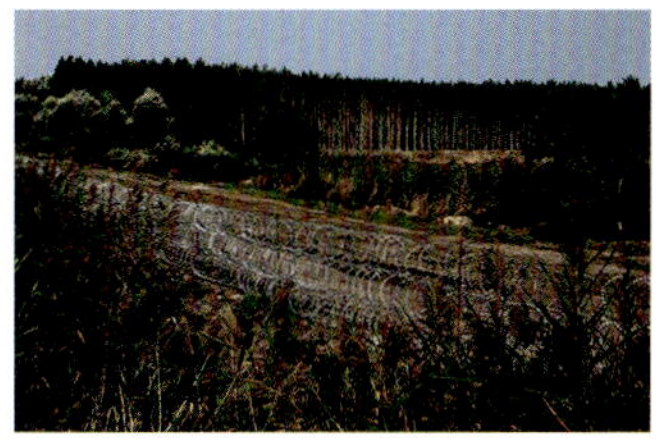

The controversial border fence that Hungary is building, as seen from Serbia. It will be 175 kilometres long, and when it is completed there will also be a four-metre-tall wire fence right behind the barbed-wire fence. Hungary later erects a fence along its border with Croatia as well. 28.08.2015

24

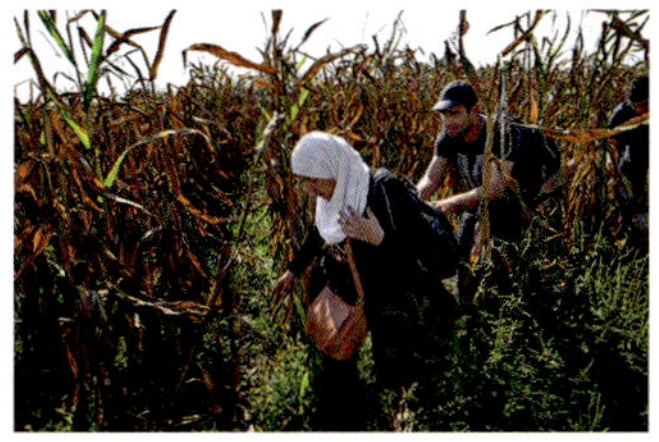

A group of Syrian refugees who have just crossed the border take refuge in a cornfield in order to avoid the police and to avoid being registered. 27.08.2015

25

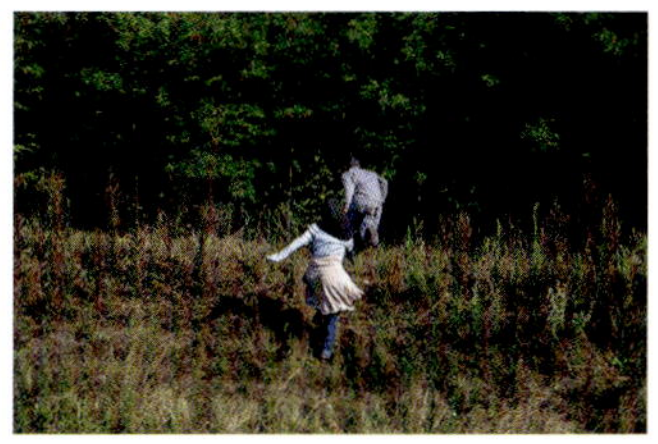

A young couple run into the woods after crawling under the border fence. 27.08.2015

27

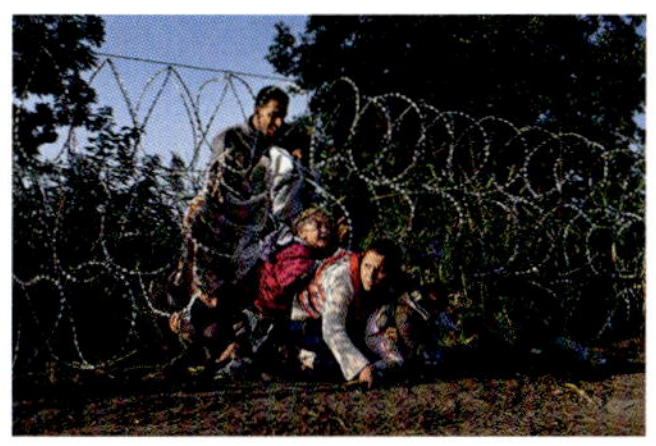

On Thursday 27 August at 08:01, a family of refugees take the chance and crawl under the border fence that Hungary is setting up along the border to Serbia. The barbed wire catches the little girl's hair and it costs some precious seconds to get her free. The man holding the fence doesn't manage to get through before the Hungarian border police arrive at the spot, but an hour and twenty minutes later he takes the chance again and crosses. 27.08.2015

28

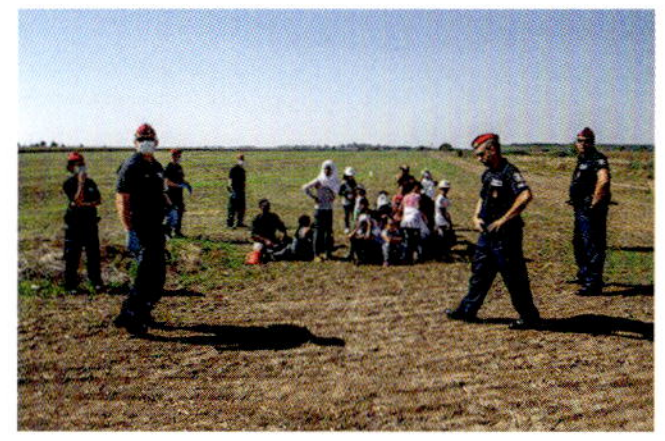

A group of refugees who have entered Hungary by following the railway tracks from Serbia are detained by Hungarian police in a field 500 metres inside the country. They must wait here for buses that will drive them to a registration centre. 29.08.2015

30

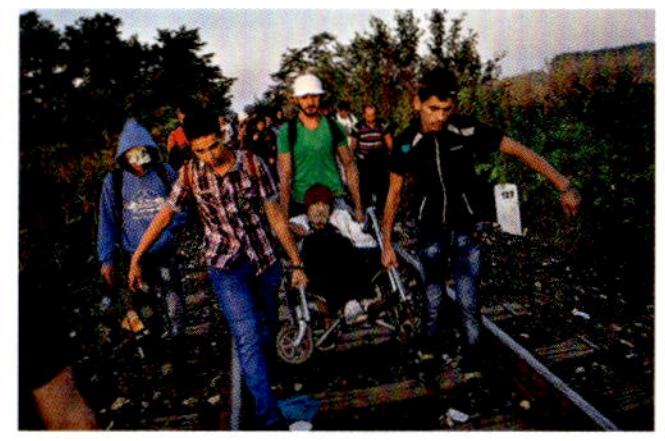

Early one morning 28 refugees cross the border into Hungary via the railway tracks. Most people cross the border in this way. By doing so, they avoid having to force an entrance through the barbed-wire fence. However, the police are waiting for them 500 metres further down the tracks, ready to send them on to a camp that will register them and take their fingerprints. Seeking asylum in Hungary does not fit in with the plans of 20-year-old Majid in the green t-shirt and his 75-year-old father, Talac, in the wheelchair. They would like to go on to Germany. 29.08.2015

31

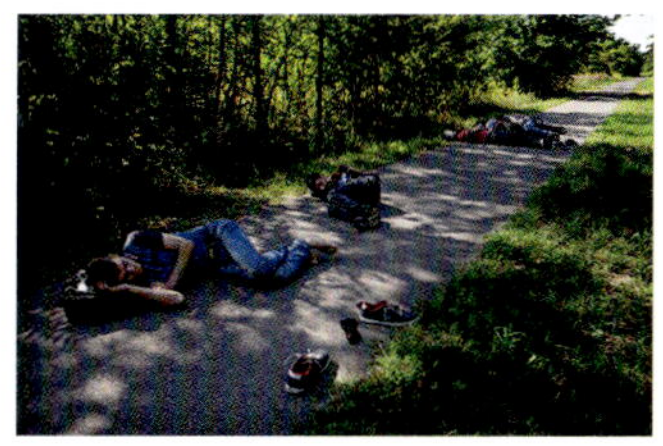

After a 25-day journey from Afghanistan, a group of six boys lie down to sleep on a bicycle path in Hungary. The boys have forced their way through the border fence. They are exhausted and have no money. At this point they do not care if the police discover them. 30.08.2015

32

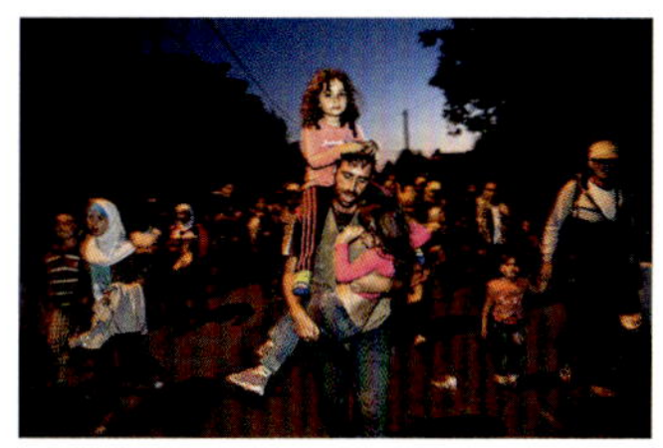

A group of Syrian refugees have entered Hungary from Serbia and are trying to find a railway station so they can reach Germany. Earlier that day they were detained in a field by Hungarian police who wanted to take them to a registration centre, but they became impatient and began to walk. The police, not wanting to start a confrontation, let them walk under surveillance. When they reached a railway crossing after three or four kilometres, most of them gave up and got on the police buses, while others walked along the railway tracks into the darkness. 26.08.2015

34

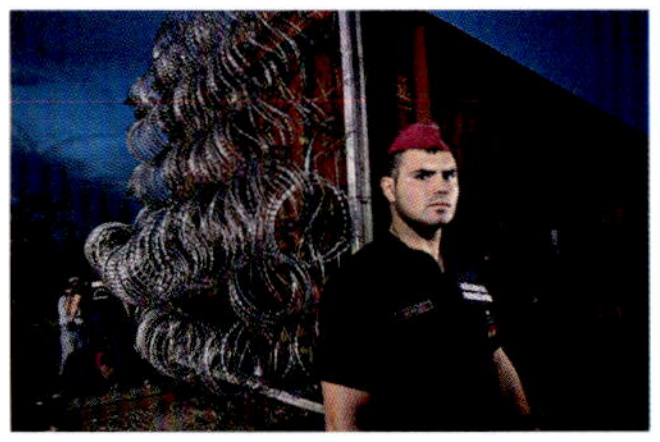

Refugees and migrants are no longer able to follow the railway tracks from Serbia into Hungary. On 14 September, the police and soldiers close the border fence completely. A train wagon with razor wire mounted on a frame arrives to close the hole in the fence where the railway tracks run. 14.09.2015

35

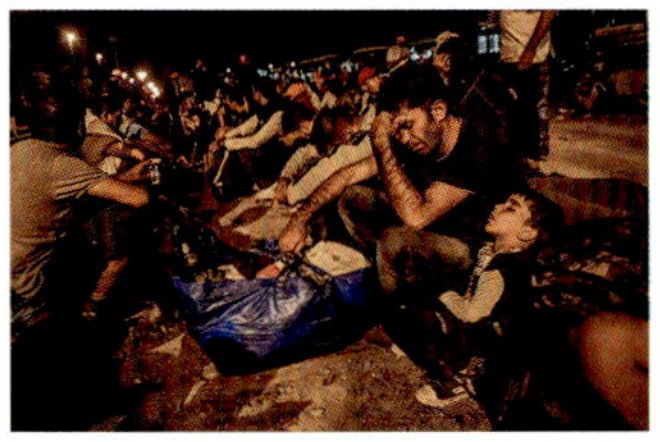

Everyone who manages to enter Hungary before the border fence is completed on 14 September 2015, and who does not want to seek asylum there, is transported to the station in Röszke. Early the next morning they are put on a train that takes them to Austria. 14.09.2015

36

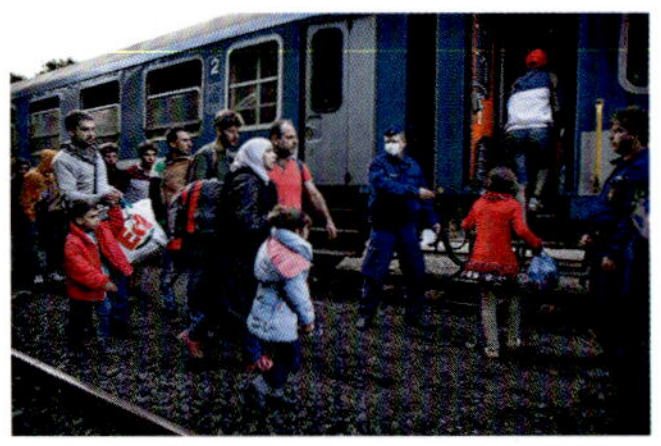

At 7:30 the following morning the train leaves for the border of Austria. 15.09.2015

37

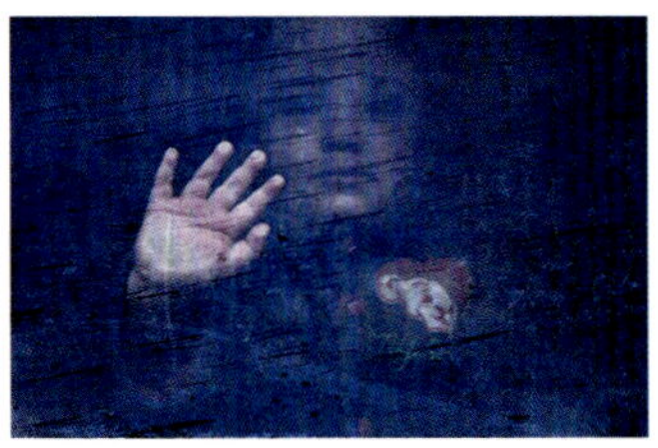

Most of the passengers do not know where the train is heading, but rumour has it that it is going to Austria. 15.09.2015

38

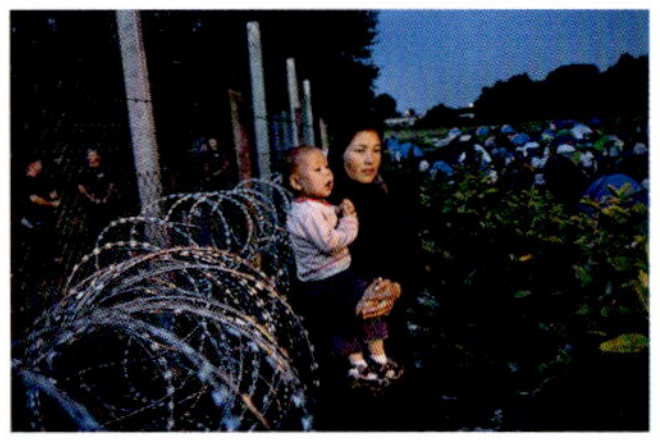

Less than 24 hours after Hungary closes its border to refugees and migrants who are taking the Balkan route through Europe, they began to gather in numbers in an area near the Serbian border crossing of Horgoš. The area is beginning to develop into a regular refugee camp that lacks food, water and sanitation, and no one can tell the refugees what will happen next. 15.09.2015

39

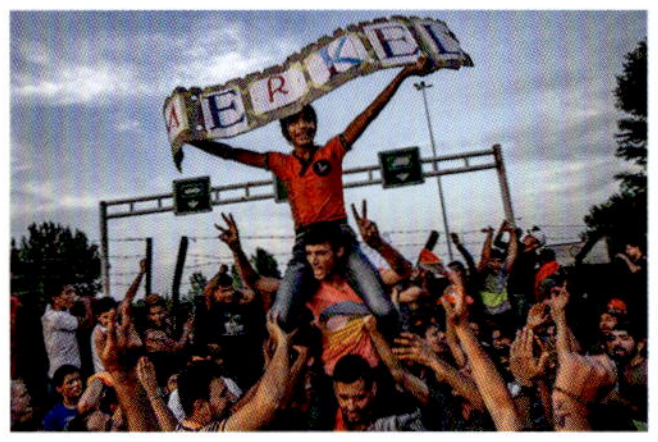

On the Serbian side of the fence near the border crossing Horgoš, refugees and migrants demonstrate against Hungary's closing of the Balkan route. They shout at the Hungarian border guards that they should open the gate and let them enter Hungary. 'No food, no water! Open the border!' and 'Merkel! Merkel! Merkel!' 15.09.2015

40

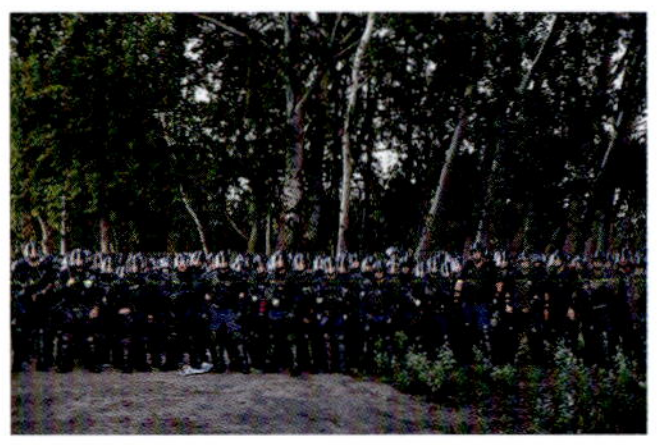

Hungarian police prepare for a confrontation with young refugees and migrants who have begun to throw rocks near the border crossing in the small Serbian village of Horgoš. 16.09.2015

42

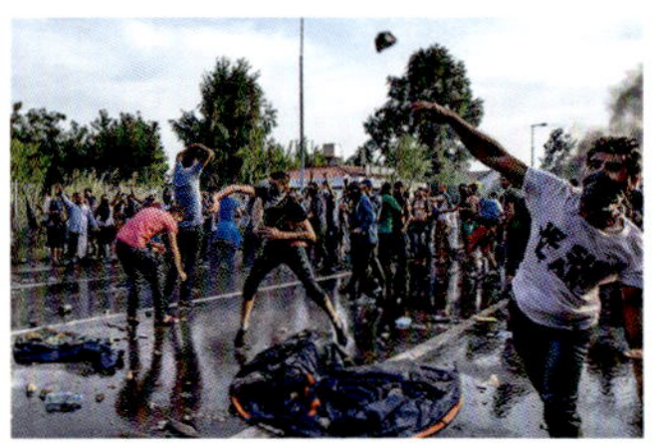

On the afternoon of 16 September, the situation at the border crossing in Horgoš is too much for a group of young men who begin to throw rocks at the Hungarian police. Although they are met with pepper spray, tear gas and water cannons, they succeed in cutting the barbed wire and opening a gate. The police officers dressed in combat gear withdraw 100 metres, they are ready for action and waiting as the situation unfolds. 16.09.2015

44

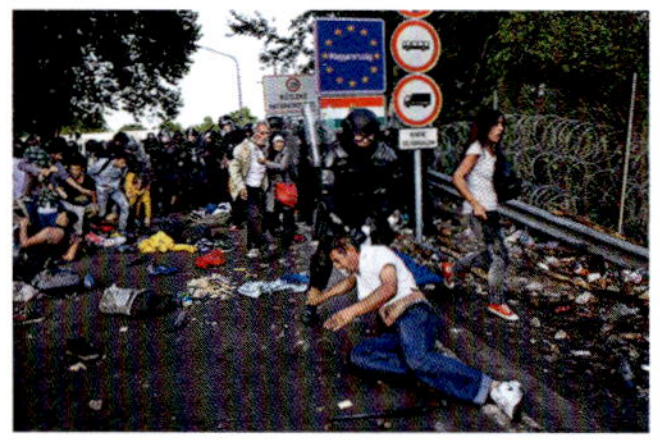

A group of young demonstrators succeed in making an opening in the barrier at the border crossing and the police draw back 100 metres. Rumours circulate that the border has been opened, so now families with children and older people also stream toward the police cordon in the hope of entering Hungary. All at once the area is filled with tear gas. The police cordon quickly advances and starts beating everyone and everything. Chaos breaks out. People bleed, scream and fall on top of each other while trying to escape. 16.09.2015

46

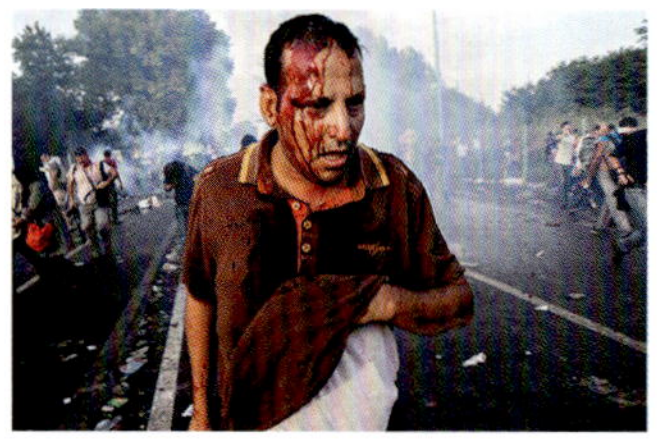

A man in shock leaves the chaos that has erupted at the border crossing. That same evening, the Serbian authorities begin to empty the area and the refugees and migrants are driven to Croatia by bus. 16.09.2015

50

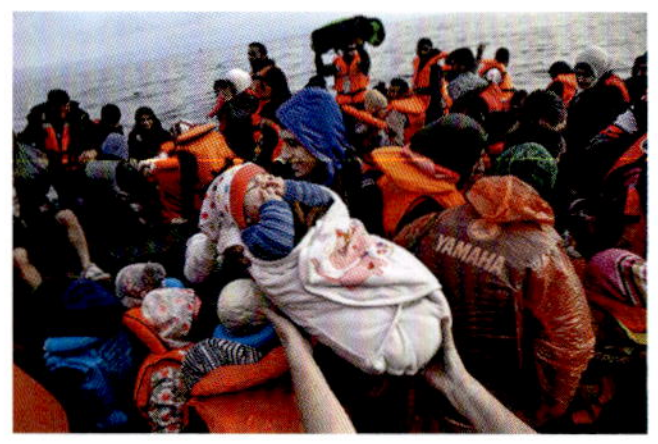

Two large rubber dinghies arrive on a beach near Molivos. The volunteers always make sure to get the children off the boats first. Ziad is three months old and has fled from Syria with his mother and three siblings. His father is still in Turkey. 19.10.2015

51

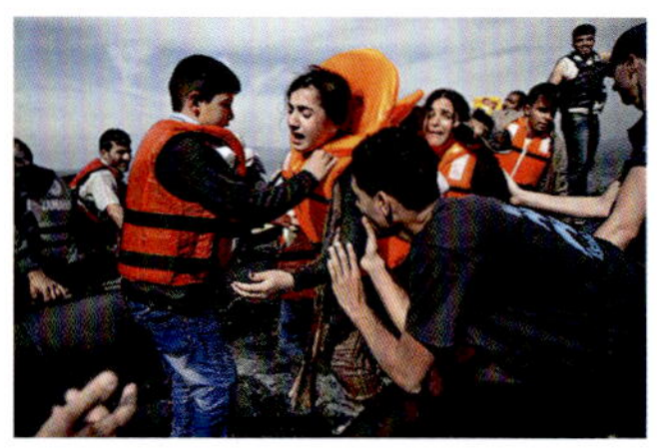

Three children dissolve in tears when an overcrowded rubber dinghy lands on the north coast of the island and volunteers try to help them ashore. It is seven days since they and their parents fled together from Kirkuk, Iraq. 18.10.2015

52

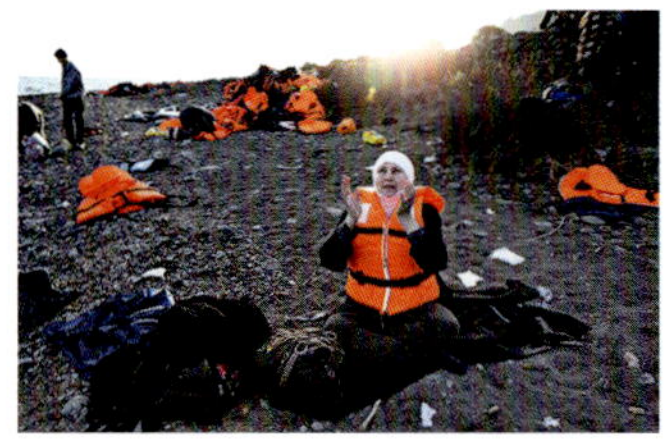

After arriving safely ashore on one of the northern beaches of Lesbos, a woman and a man immediately begin to pray. 18.10.2015

54

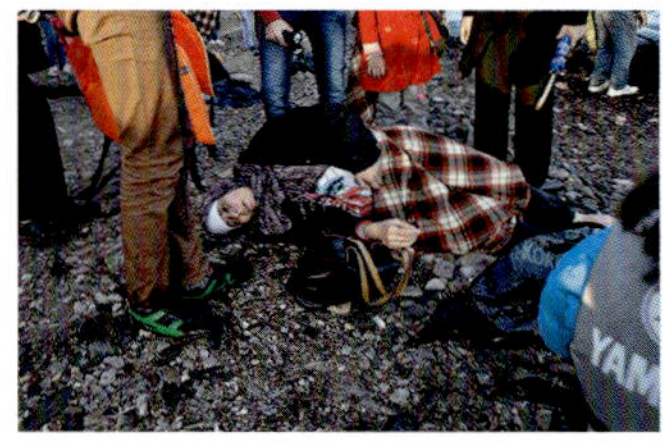

An exhausted woman lies on the beach. After a foot massage that gets her blood back in circulation, she gets on her feet again. 18.10.2015

55

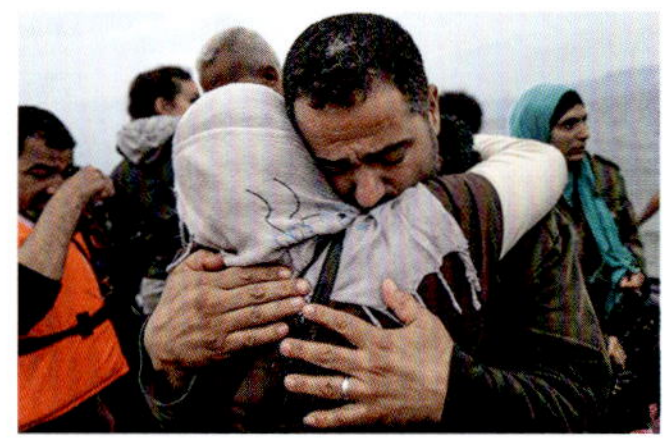

When people arrive safely ashore, emotions flow freely. 21.10.2015

56

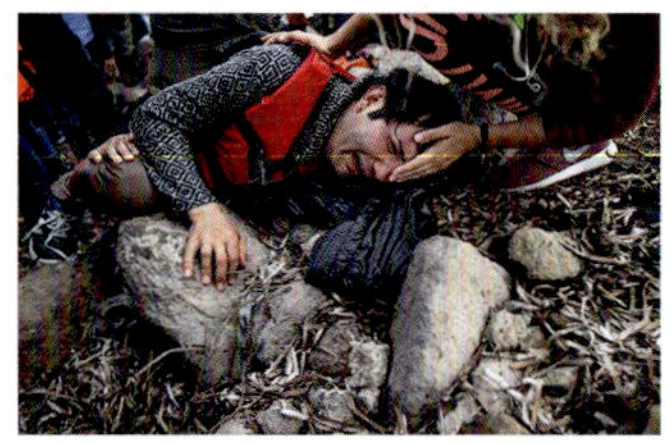

A man falls down weeping and shouts, 'Why no help? Why no help?' Many of the passengers from this journey are beside themselves. They have been at sea for two hours and had to bale water out of the boat for the entire trip. They were very close to capsizing and everything and everyone is soaking wet. 20.10.2015

58

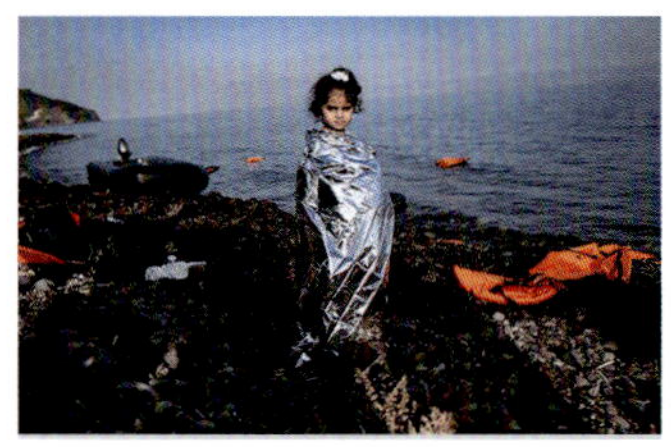

Sima, age four, is on the way to Germany with her two siblings and their mother and father. Unlike earlier this year, now the boats are met by groups of volunteers from around the world who help the refugees and migrants with dry clothes, first aid, food and instructions as to where they should go. 19.10.2015

61

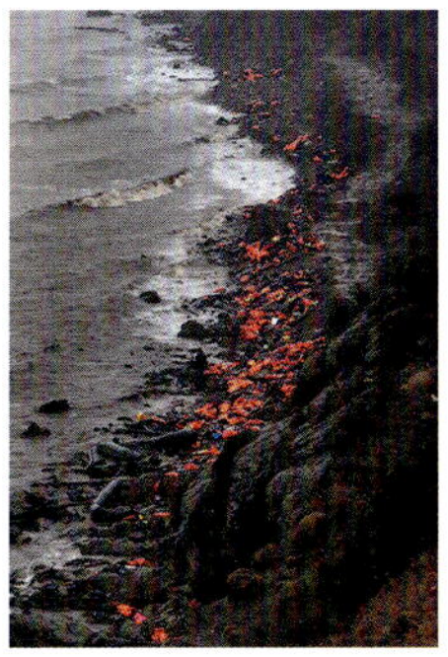

On the rough stretch of coast on the north side of Lesbos, life jackets and worn-out rubber boats pile up. 22.10.2015

62

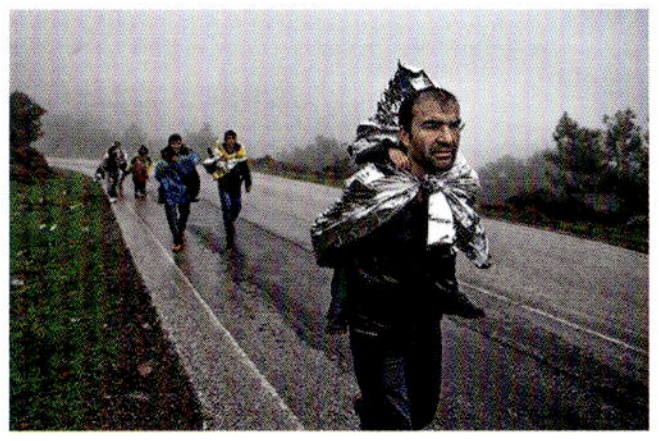

Families with children are sent on a 15 kilometre walk from Skala Sikaminias to a gathering place on the outskirts of Mandamados, where they wait to get picked up and transported to the reception centre in Moria. Since the summer there has been a change in the law so that buses may now carry refugees and migrants from the coasts to Moria, but the buses cannot keep up with the demand, and many people have to walk some of the way. 22.10.2015

64

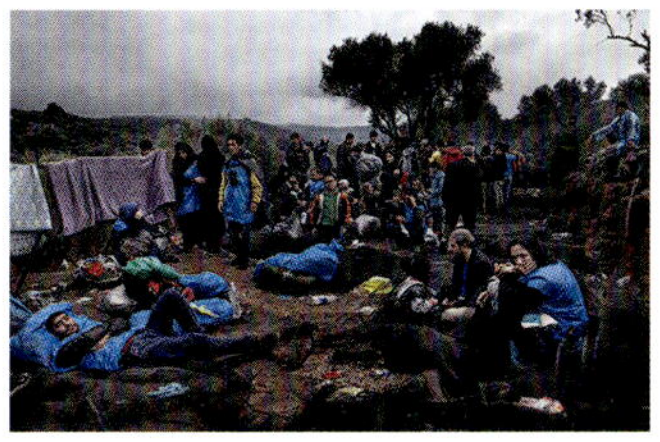

The conditions at the reception centre in Moria are terrible. It has been pouring down for three days in a row. The area is filled with trash and mud, and there is a lack of food, water, medical assistance and sanitary facilities. People wait for up to five days under the open sky to come inside and be registered. On one side of the centre is a queue for Syrians only, and on the other side people of all other nationalities are packed together, as in this queue for families on the non-Syrian side of the reception centre. 22.10.2015

66

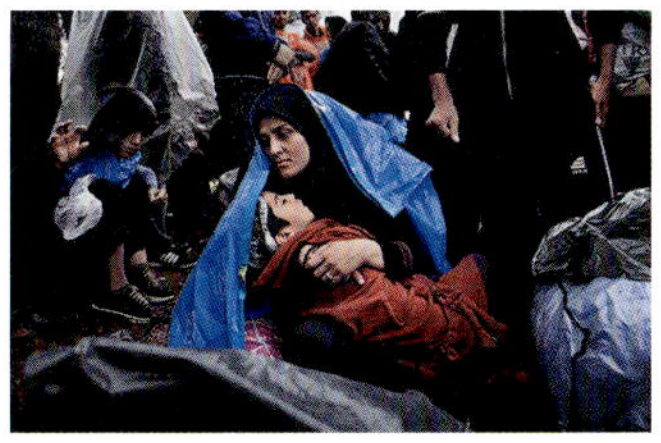

Mahboubeh is 19 years old and from Afghanistan. She has fled from Iran, where she had been living illegally with her husband and their four-year-old son, Matin. Now they are sitting, for the third day, in a queue outside the reception centre in Moria. It has been pouring down, and their son has become ill. They would like to go to Sweden. 22.10.2015

67

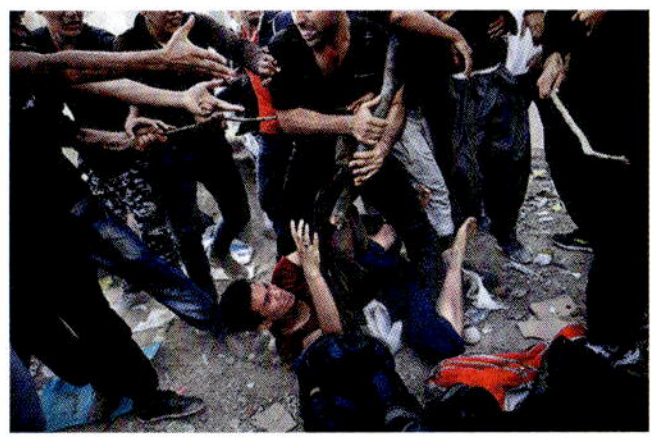

In the queue for non-Syrian men, intense arguments and fights break out over the places in the queue. 20.10.2015

68

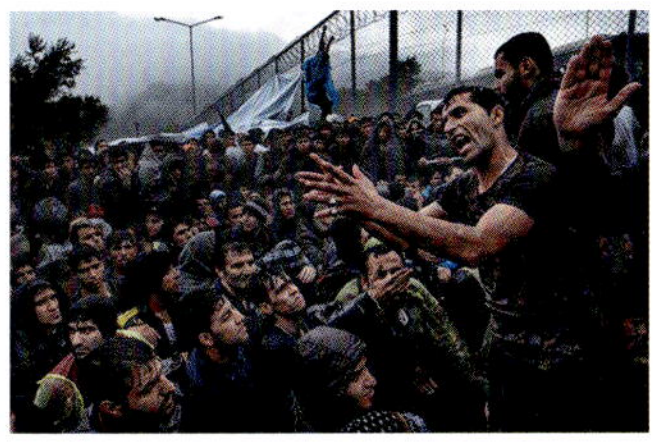

The reception centre in Moria has nowhere near the capacity for the number of people who are arriving in Lesbos now. People wait up to five days under the open sky in order to come inside and be registered. There are no officials keeping a check on the many people outside, so a group of men with sticks function as a kind of self-appointed police force trying to manage the queue and mediate conflicts. 22.10.2015

70

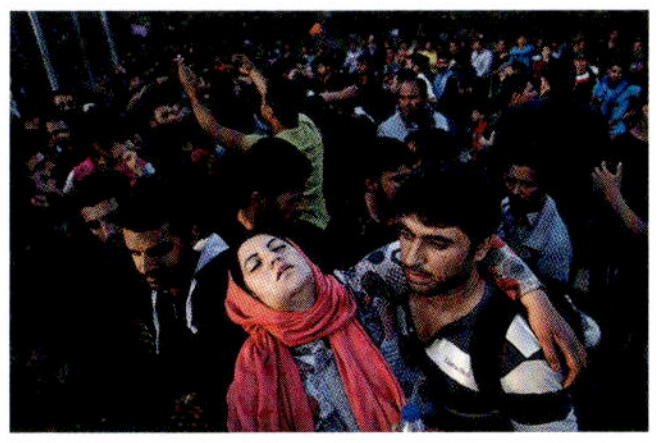

A man brings an exhausted woman to the main entrance of the centre in the hope that they can enter straight away. They are not admitted and must return to the queue. 20.10.2015

73

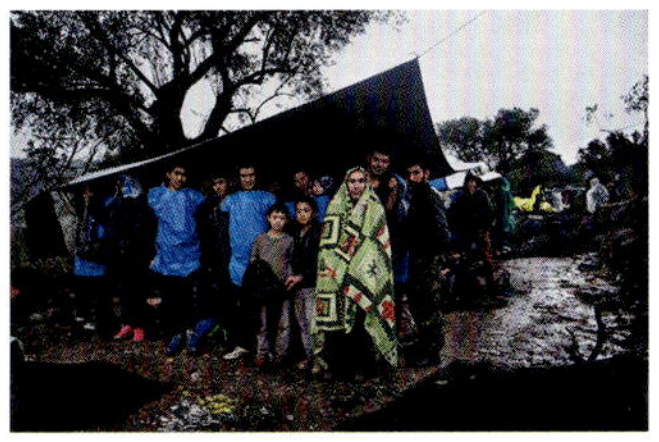

The queue for non-Syrian families outside the Moria camp. 22.10.2015

74

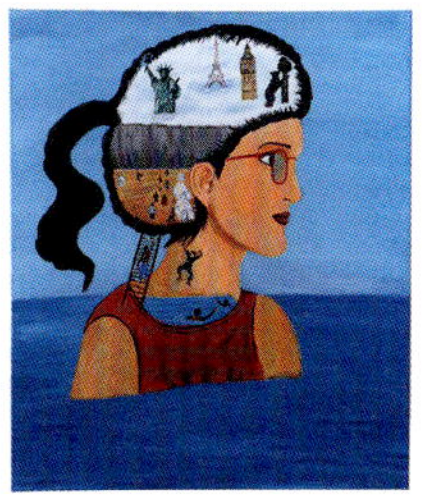

In a warehouse near the Moria camp, married couple Philippa and Eric Kempson have created a free space for refugees and migrants. The space is called The Hope Project and here people can express their creativity through music and painting. The works shown here is painted by Eid Mohammad from Afghanistan. 12.03.2020

74

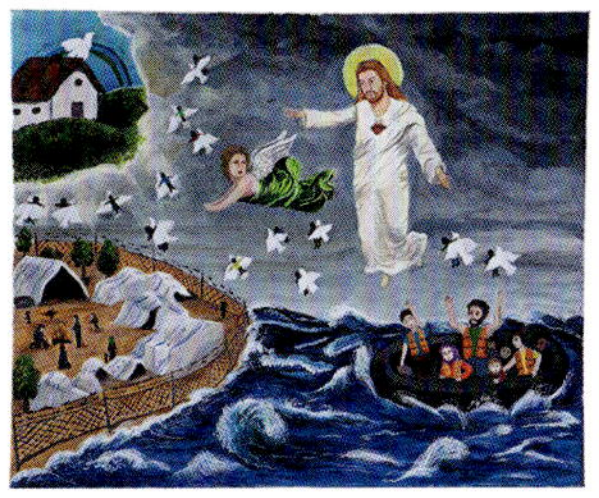

The work shown here is painted by Razieh Gholami from Afghanistan. 12.03.2020

75

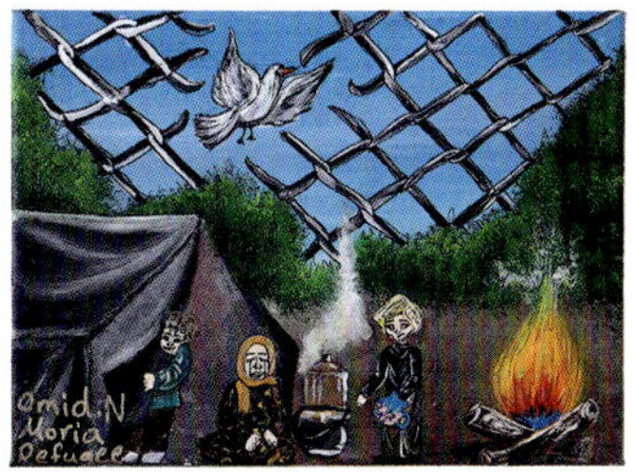

The work shown here is painted by Omid Arvish from Iran. 12.03.2020

75

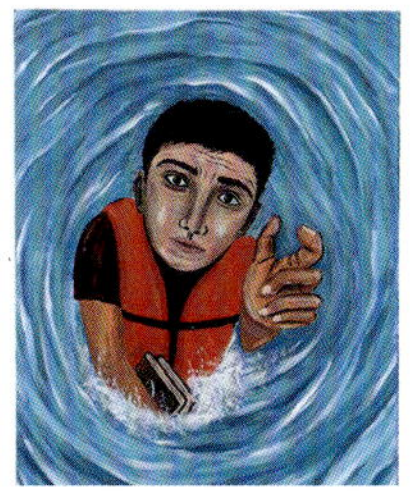

The work shown here is painted by Javad Emami from Afghanistan. 12.03.2020

78

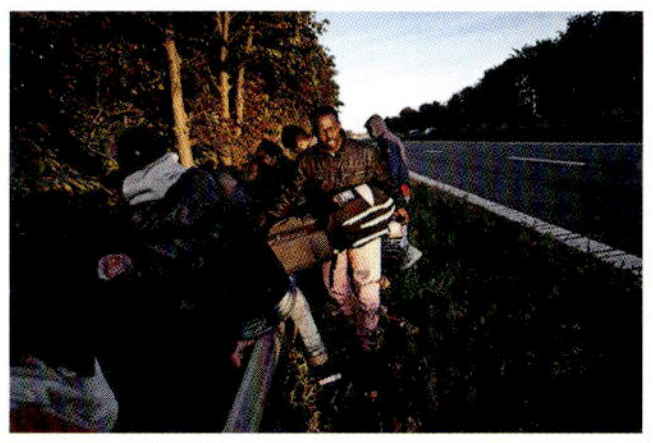

In early September 2015 many refugees and migrants heading for Scandinavian countries reach Denmark. Those who enter the country by train from Germany are stopped by Danish police in Rødby. A large group sneak away from the police. They want to continue to Sweden and begin to walk along the motorway toward Copenhagen. About 25 kilometres north of Rødby, they leave the motorway and begin to walk along a smaller country road instead. Many Danes show up and share food, water, fruit and sweets. Some Danes pick up the refugees in cars and drive them to Copenhagen or Sweden despite police warnings that it is illegal. 07.09.2015

79

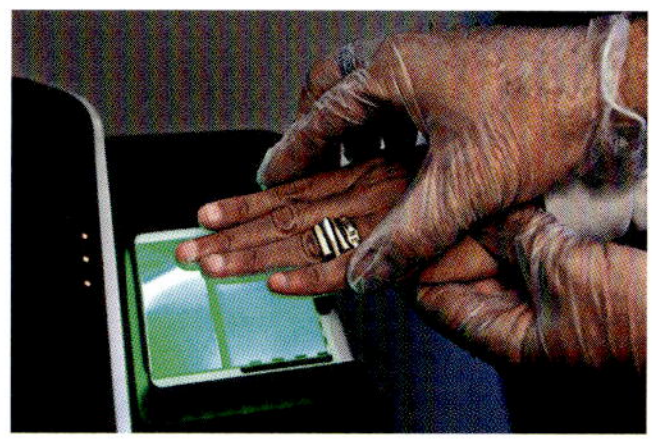

In October 2015 about 1000 refugees and migrants reach Sweden each day. The great majority of them are registered and have fingerprints taken at the Swedish migration agency in Malmö. 02.10.2015

81

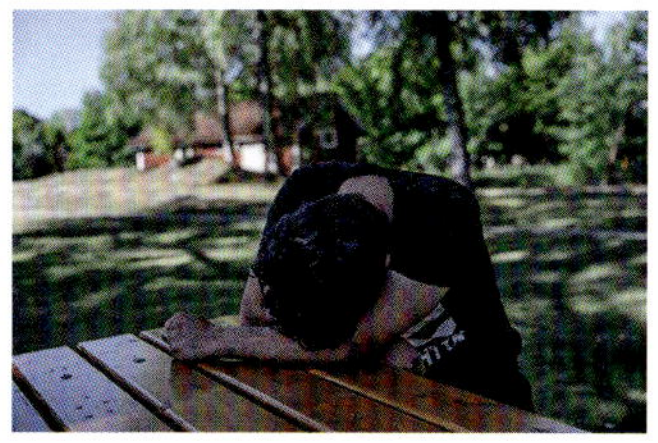

Many of the asylum seekers say that waiting in uncertainty and not being able to plan one's life is highly stressful. Many suffer from headaches and difficulty sleeping. Hussein Mahdavi is 24 years old and has been waiting for two and a half years. When Granbacken closes soon, he must go to Flen, which is a large asylum centre outside Stockholm. 27.06.2018

82

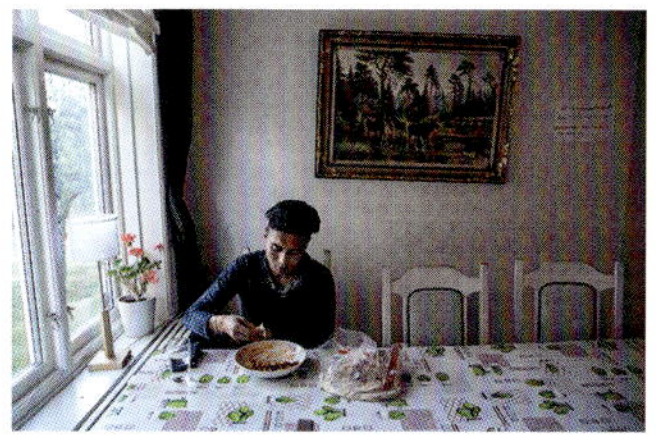

It means a lot for the residents of Granbacken to be able to make their own food, even if the culinary skills of the young men consist of convenience food heated up in a pan. Nineteen-year-old Hussein left Afghanistan three years ago. He eats his meal in the dining room of the old hotel. 27.06.2018

83

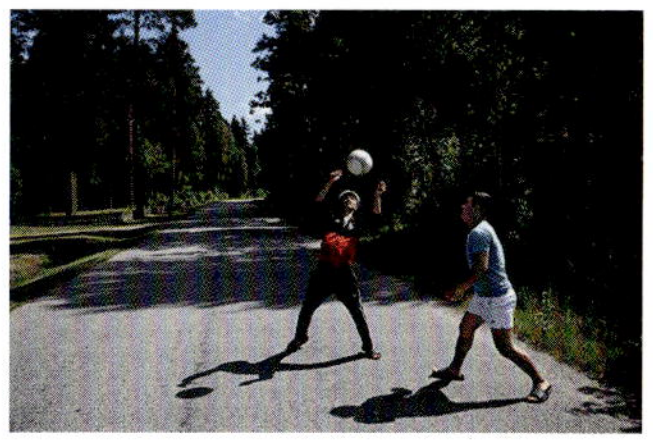

Twenty-year-old Afghan Mustafa Safayee (on the right) has received his first refusal. He came to

Sweden three years ago. At night he paces the main street of Vrigstad restlessly. 'Swedes are friendly, but I don't understand why they say yes to others, but not me. I am confused... When I arrived in Sweden, I didn't imagine that waiting would be like this. I imagined a lot of things I would do, but I am not allowed to study or work. I can't concentrate on anything at all. All I can think of is the refusals from the migration agency. Just waiting, waiting, waiting... This is the opposite of what I dreamt of.' 28.06.2018

84

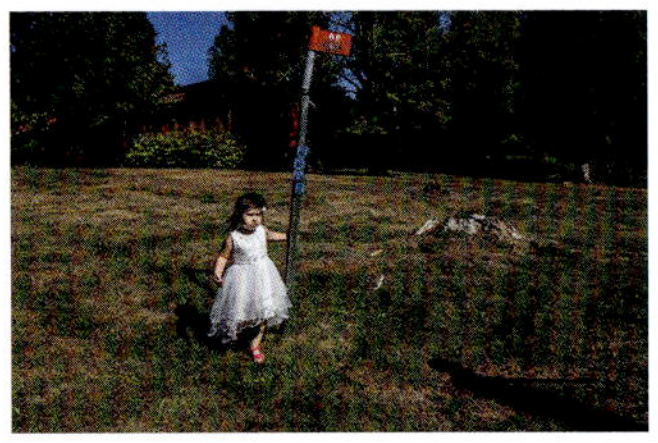

There used to be a lot of children staying at Granbacken, but now only Helen and two other children are left. She lives in a room in the old hotel with her mother and father. 27.06.2018

85

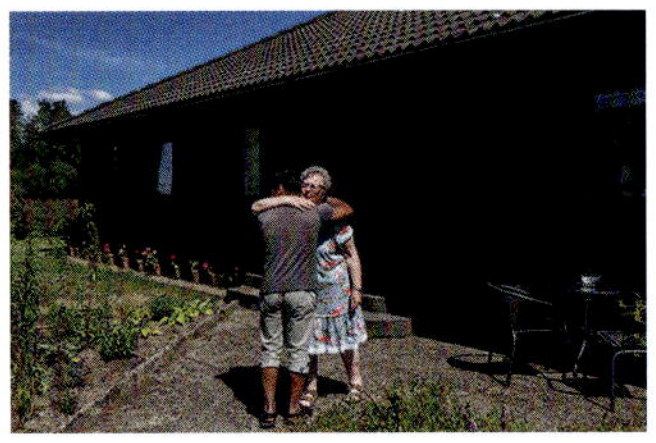

Twenty-two-year-old Afghan Ali Muhammadi has packed his things from his room at Granbacken and is moving in with Berith today. Since her husband moved into a nursing home recently, she has been alone in her big house, and now Ali will move into what used to be a child's bedroom. Ali has been refused asylum, and his first and second appeal have also failed. Three refusals. The last time he pulled out a razor blade in the office of the migration agency and slashed his left wrist. He planned to take his life but was saved by the office staff and an ambulance crew. Now Ali is attempting to use his religion to receive a residence permit, because he converted from Islam to Christianity long ago. But it is not easy to convince the Swedish authorities that it is not just a trick to secure him asylum in Sweden. 27.06.2018

86

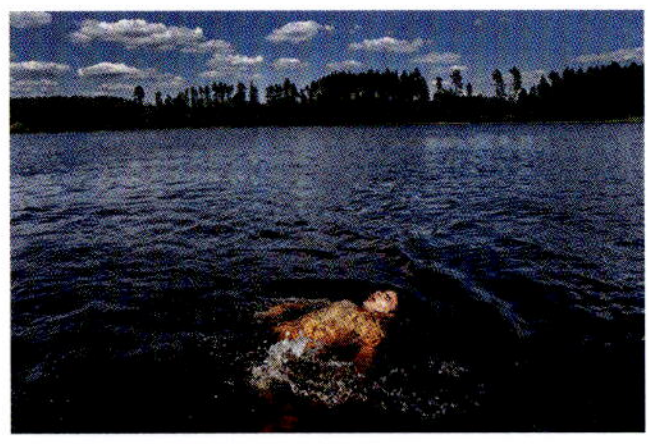

Near the old hotel in Vrigstad is a lake that some of the boys swim in occasionally. Eighteen-year-old Obayd Amin has fled Afghanistan and arrived in Sweden in 2015. He dreams of staying in Sweden, going to school and playing football. He is the substitute goalkeeper on a team in the neighbouring town, and the club has made an agreement with the migration agency that he can remain in the local area when the asylum centre closes. Obayd has not spoken with his family for three years. When he tries to phone home, there is no connection. 28.06.2018

90

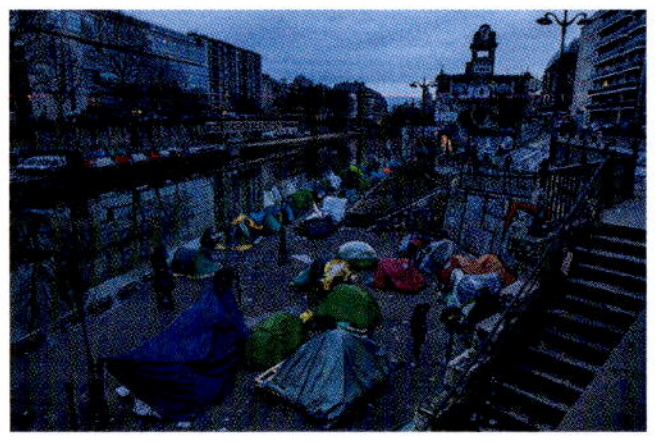

Along the canal by the Jaurès metro station, around 200 Afghans have set up camp. The office where they have to report in order to begin their asylum application is just a stone's throw away. 10.03.2018

92

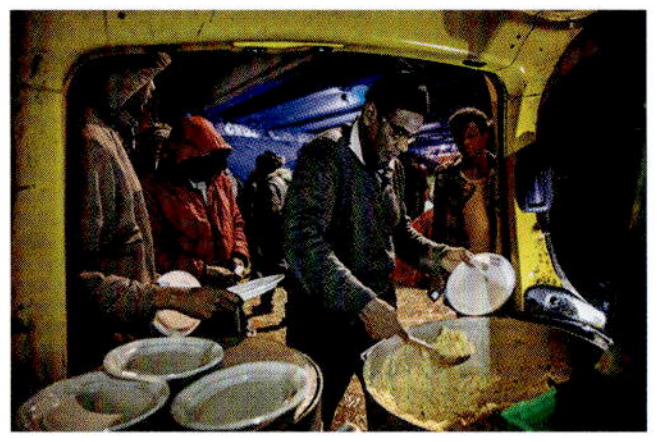

A group of volunteers open the tailboard of their delivery van and serve warm food to the refugees and migrants under a motorway bridge where around 800 Africans have set up camp. People depend on the small NGOs and other volunteers who come by on a daily basis with food, clothes, tents and other basic necessities. 09.03.2018

93

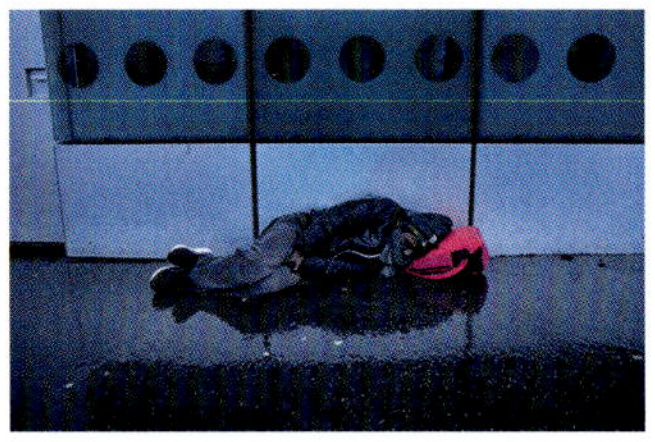

Near a large camp of tents where around 800 Africans have settled, a man lies down to sleep on the street. 10.03.2018

94

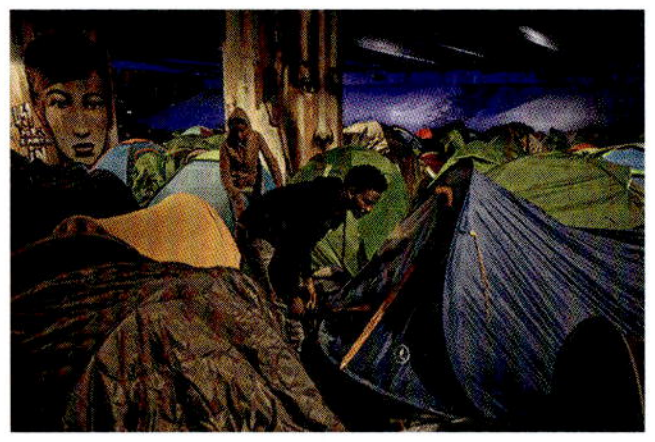

A young man from Eritrea tugs at his tent. Although the motorway bridge provides protection from the rain, water still runs underneath the tents and seeps through the bottom. This means that clothes, sleeping bags and tents have to be dried out constantly. 11.03.2018

95

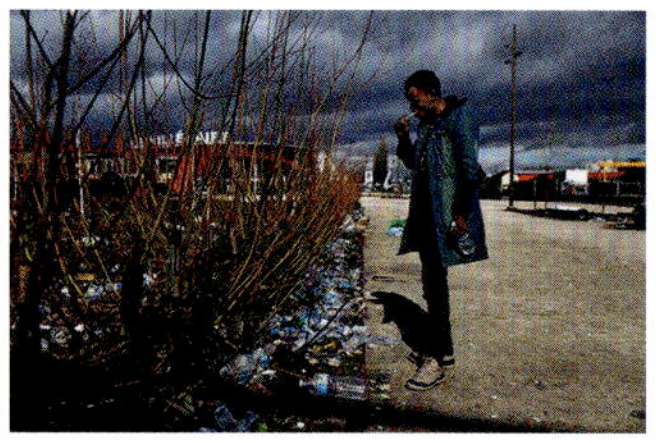

There are no toilet facilities near a makeshift camp of tents under a motorway bridge in the northern part of Paris, so the bushes around the camp quickly start to reek of urine. Bottled water is used for brushing teeth and washing. 12.03.2018

96

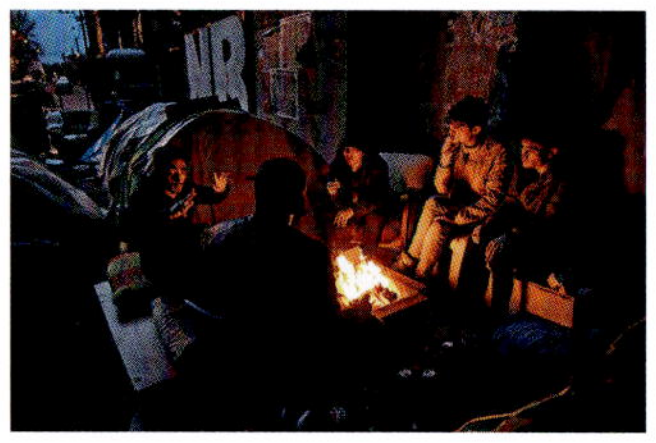

On a street behind the refugee centre in the La Chapelle neighbourhood, a group of refugees and migrants have set up camp. They all hope that there will be room for them inside the centre, where there is food, running water and a roof over their heads. The five young men around the bonfire are from Afghanistan and Sudan. All of them have been in Europe for several years and all have been refused asylum in Sweden, Germany and England. Now they are hoping to be granted asylum in France. 12.03.2018

97

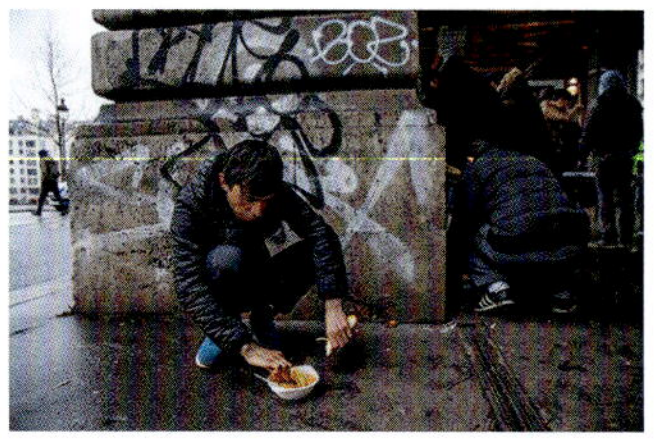

Near the Jaurès metro station a group of volunteers set up large pots and hand out food to refugees and migrants many times a week. The station is close to a makeshift camp of tents with many Afghans. 09.03.2018

98

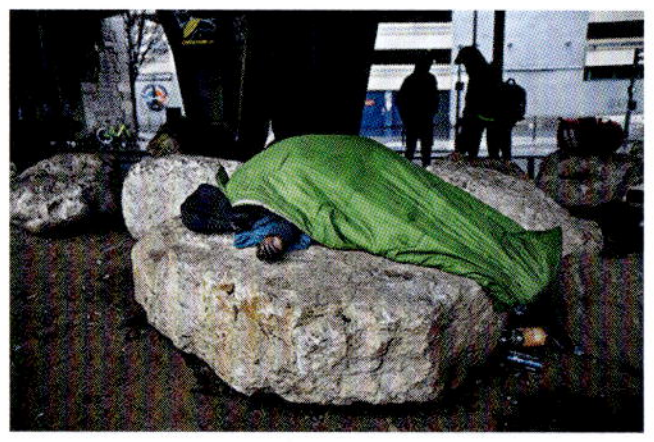

Not far from a refugee centre in the La Chapelle neighbourhood, a young African man sleeps on one of the big stones that the authorities have placed underneath an elevated railway in order to prevent a camp of tents from being set up on the site. 10.03.2018

100

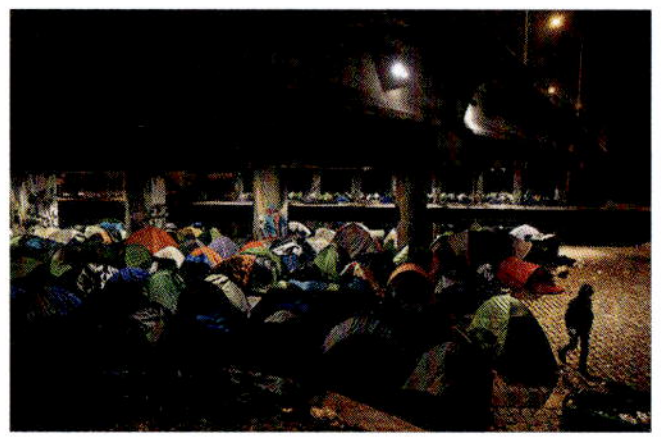

Under a six-lane motorway in the northern part of Paris, around 800 refugees and migrants have set up camp. Most of them are from Sudan and Eritrea, but people come from many other African countries as well. There are very few women in the camp. Once in a while the police clear away the camps that spring up around the city. Tents and other property are destroyed and the refugees are ordered to leave the place. No one knows where they should disappear to, so the camps are quickly reestablished, sometimes in the same places and sometimes in new ones. 09.03.2018

103

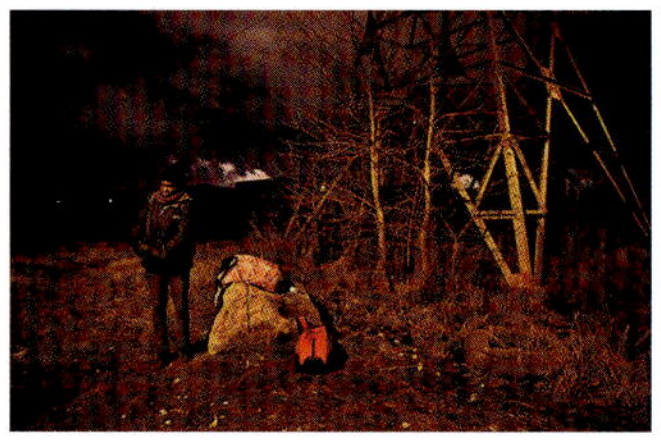

A Sudanese boy has received a hot meal before he has to go off and find a place to sleep on this cold night in Calais. In October 2016 authorities clear the city's notorious makeshift refugee camp 'the Jungle' and many of the residents of the port city of Calais heave a sigh of relief. Nevertheless, many refugees and migrants still come here with the dream of going on to England. Every night many of them meet up in an industrial quarter where the NGO Utopia 56 creates a free space underneath the high-voltage power lines, offering hot food, warm clothes and positive attention for just a couple of hours. Day and night, the police do what they can to make life difficult for the refugees and migrants. Empty buildings, shrubbery and wooded areas are searched thoroughly for tents, sleeping bags, tarpaulins and other things that could be the start of a new 'Jungle' in Calais. 08.02.2017

105

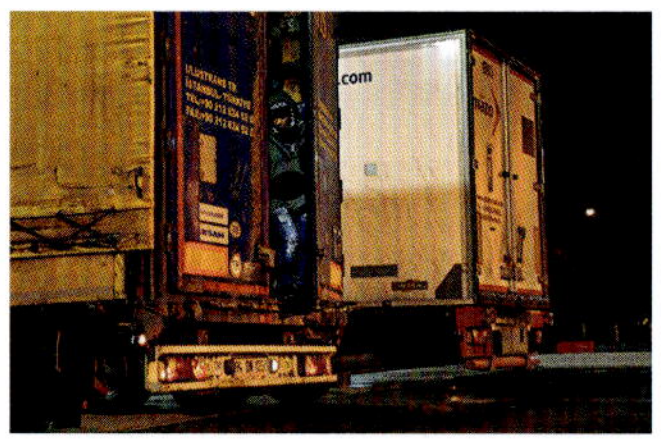

A group of five boys from Eritrea sneak onto a goods lorry at a petrol station on the outskirts of the French port city of Calais. They hope that the goods lorry will drive them to England through the Channel Tunnel, or aboard one of the many ferries that sail day and night. The boys are well aware that they will probably be discovered at a checkpoint before they leave France. That is why they hide one member of the group extra carefully in the lorry. If just one makes it across, it is a success. It is only possible to seek asylum in England if one is found on English soil, so the boys have to try again and again. 05.02.2017

108

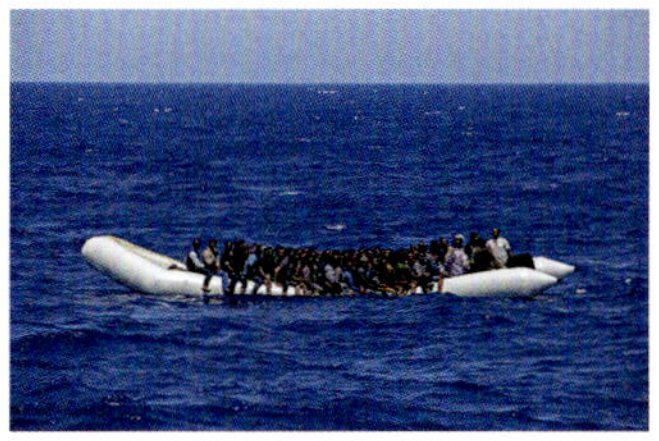

When the NGO rescue ships come across the refugees and migrants this is what they find, people on the open sea, without life jackets, in overcrowded dinghies that are often about to sink and are sometimes patched with duct tape. Shortly after this picture was taken, the wooden bottom of the rubber dinghy collapses and four passengers drown. 03.06.2017

110

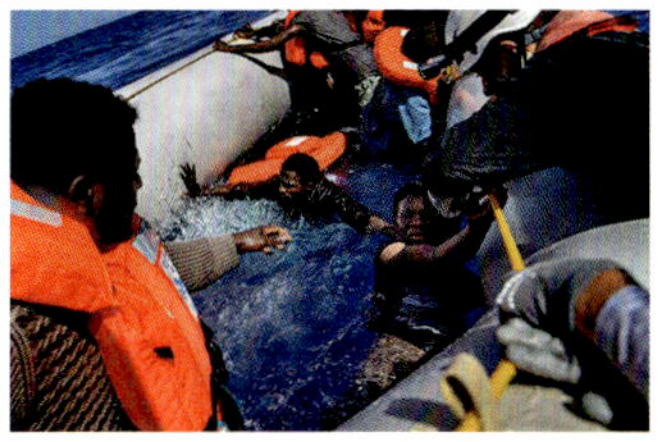

Sea-Watch 2 finds the boat by request from the Maritime Rescue Coordination Centre (MRCC) in Rome and begins a rescue operation 60 kilometres from the Libyan coast. What, at first, looks like a relatively simple task develops into a chaotic situation when large pieces of the wooden base come off the rubber dinghy. It is hard for the rescue workers to reach those who are struggling desperately to stay above the water inside the dinghy. During the operation, the NGO Save the Children joins in the rescue work. One hundred and twenty-five people are saved and subsequently sailed to Italy. Four people drown. 03.06.2017

112

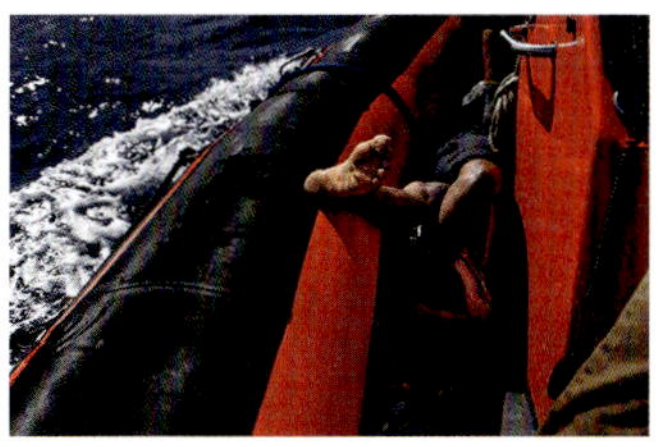

At the last moment, a woman is pulled on board one of Sea-Watch's two rigid inflatable boats and is saved from drowning after the bottom of the dinghy she was on board comes off. She is almost lifeless and is rushed to Sea-Watch 2, where she recovers. 03.06.2017

113

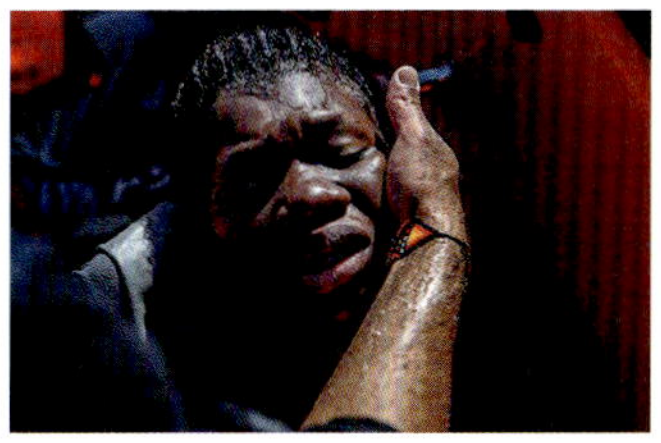

A volunteer from Sea-Watch comforts a woman he has just saved from the water in a dramatic rescue operation in which four people drowned. 03.06.2017

114

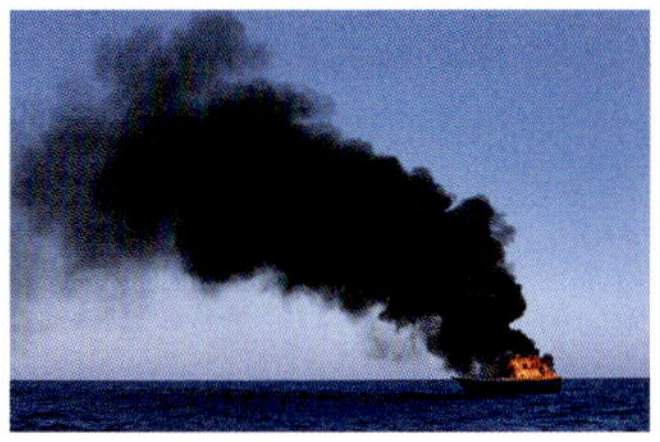

After a major rescue operation in which several NGO ships have collaborated in rescuing people from five different refugee boats, a vessel from the Libyan coast guard sails around setting the empty refugee boats on fire so that human traffickers cannot reuse them. 09.06.2017

117

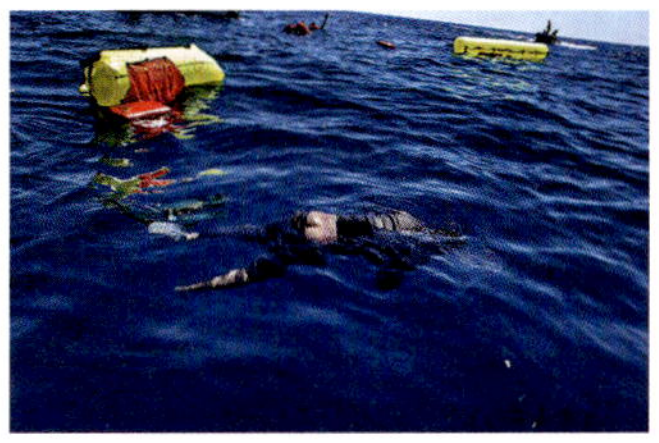

A pregnant woman drowns during a dramatic rescue operation in which an overcrowded refugee boat with about 120 people on board punctures. While the rescue mission is underway, her body drifts between people who are still struggling to survive. A boat with 'motor fishermen' helps to save people and bring them out of the water. "Motor fishermen" are local fishermen who take motors from the empty refugee boats and bring them back to Libya so that they can be used again. 10.06.2017

118

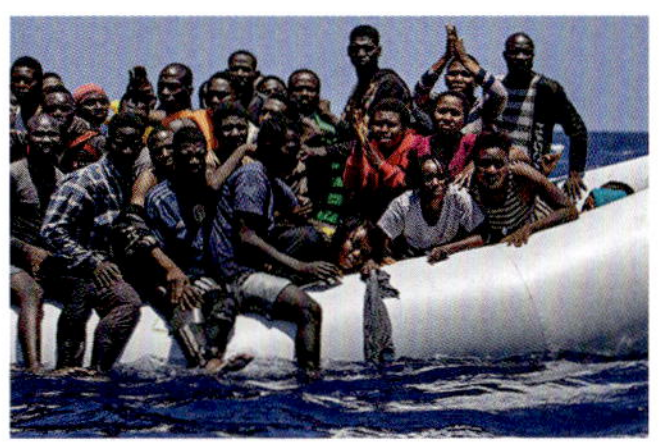

These people have been at sea for three days and have run out of petrol, food and water. They say that three people who had been on the dinghy died the day before and that they are gone now. The almost 130 people on board are in a panic. They beg and pray for the Sea-Watch team in the motorboat to come closer and help them. Some begin to shout and will not sit down. A fight breaks out. The people are so desperate that the rescue team is afraid that chaos will break out and that handing out life vests and lifting people onto the motorboat would be highly dangerous. Instead the rescue team gives fuel for the dinghy and tells them to sail to Sea-Watch 2 where they will be taken aboard. 12.06.2017

120

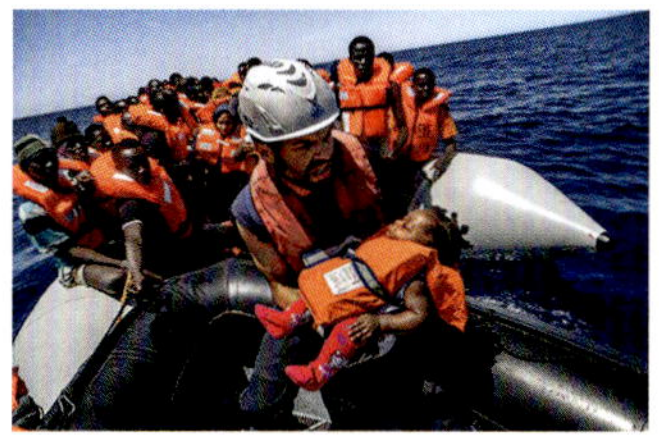

Jakob, one of the ship's two engineers, takes a six-week-old infant from the refugee boat and carries her over to her mother. She has already come over to the motorboat, which will transport them to safety on Sea-Watch 2. When the Sea-Watch crew comes across a refugee boat, they start by asking if there are any sick or dead people and then they distribute life vests. Those on board the rubber boats are asked to keep calm in order to avoid the danger of chaos when some people jump in the water in order to reach the RIB. Groups of 15-20 people are taken to the rescue ship. Many of the people who have been sitting at the bottom of the refugee boats have chemical burns on their legs, bellies and lower bodies from the corrosive mixture of petrol, urine, faeces and salt water. 10.06.2017

121

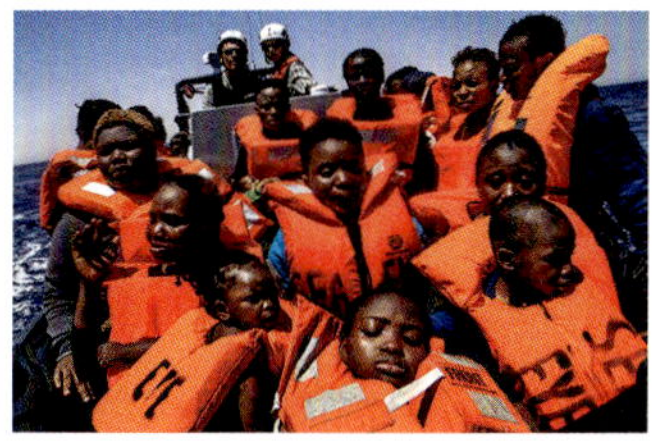

Women, children and sick people are usually the first to be transported to safety. These people are on the way to Sea-Watch 2. Many of the women break out in tears of relief. 10.06.2017

122

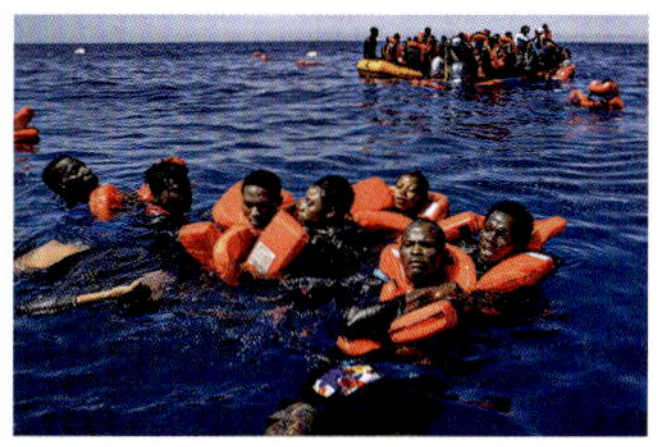

An overcrowded dinghy carrying refugees and migrants suffers a puncture during a rescue operation by German NGO Sea-Watch. Chaos erupts. One of Sea-Watch's two motorboats as well as a lighter vessel carrying life jackets are quickly filled with desperate refugees that threaten to capsize both vessels. A group of people in the water try to remain calm and stay together to help those without life jackets stay above the surface. The body of a drowned pregnant woman drifts between them. The Sea-Watch crew save around 120 people and also recover the corpse. 10.06.2017

124

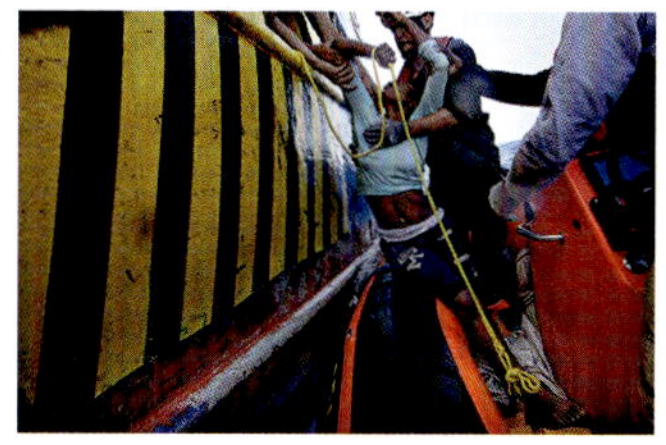

A woman is saved from drowning at the last moment and is rushed to Sea-Watch 2. She is in a state of shock as she is eased aboard the rescue ship, where she is examined by the ship's team of doctors. 03.06.2017

125

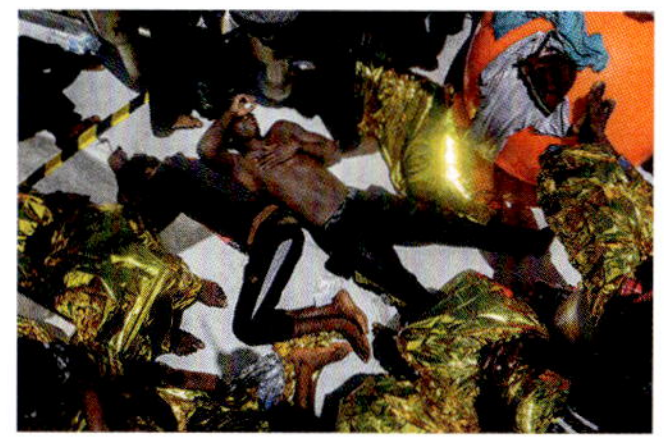

After two rescue operations, there are exhausted people lying about everywhere on the German rescue ship. 10.06.2017

127

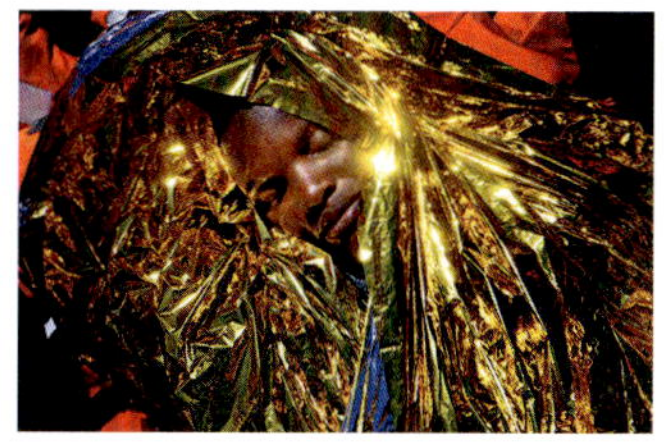

After having survived a dramatic rescue operation an exhausted woman is wrapped in a thermal blanket on the quarterdeck of the Sea-Watch 2. 10.06.2017

128

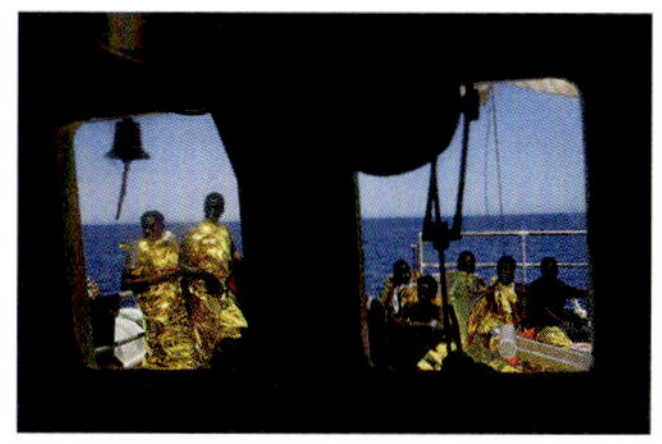

Aboard Sea-Watch 2 the refugees and migrants can relax, have something to eat and drink, and are attended to by a team of doctors. Later they are transferred to another ship with greater capacity that sails them to Italy. 10.06.2017

131

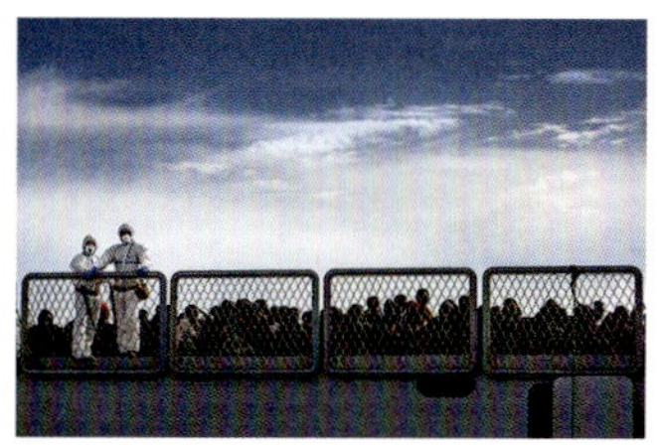

The Italian border police have brought 334 boat refugees to the Sicilian port city of Augusta. The refugees and migrants were rescued the day before off the coast of Libya. 25.04.2015

133

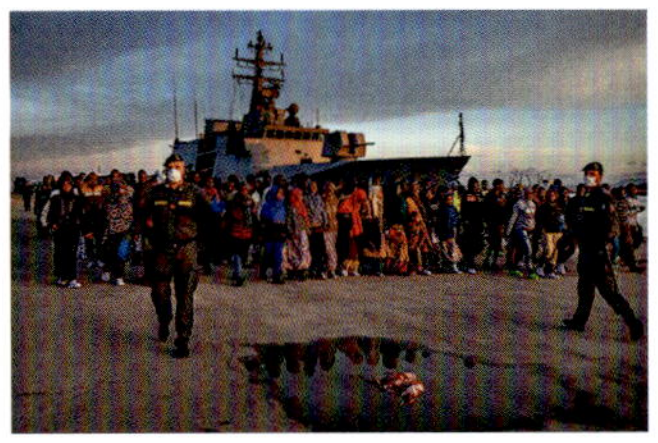

Three hundred and thirty-four boat refugees are led from the border patrol ship to a temporary camp of tents at the harbour in Augusta on the island of Sicily, where they are attended to. Later they are picked up by buses that drive them to a reception centre elsewhere on the island. 25.04.2015

134

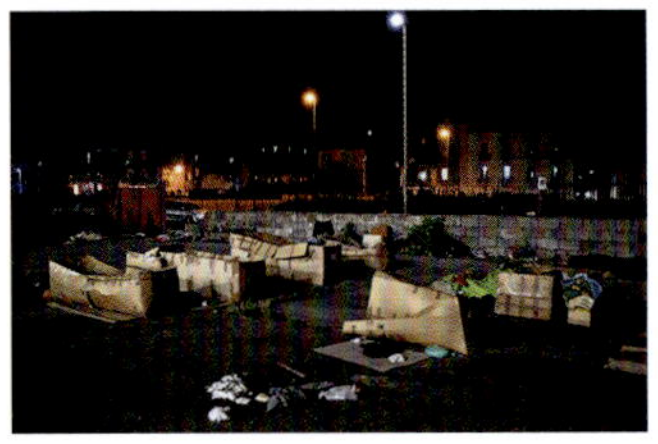

A group of boat refugees from Eritrea have made a temporary camp on a lot adjacent to one of the central squares in Catania. Many of the refugees and migrants arriving in the Sicilian port city stay there for a few days to rest and then move further north through Europe. Others seek residence permits and take accommodation at reception centres. 22.04.2015

139

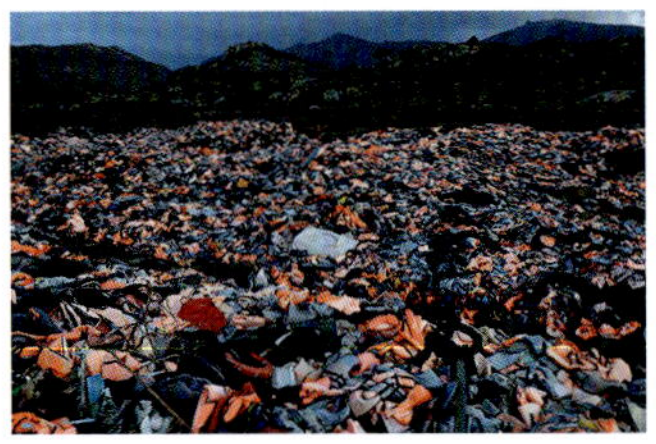

'Lifejacket graveyard' is the name given to the place in the hills not far from Eftalou Beach where the refugees' punctured rubber dinghies and life jackets end their days. 23.01.2018

140

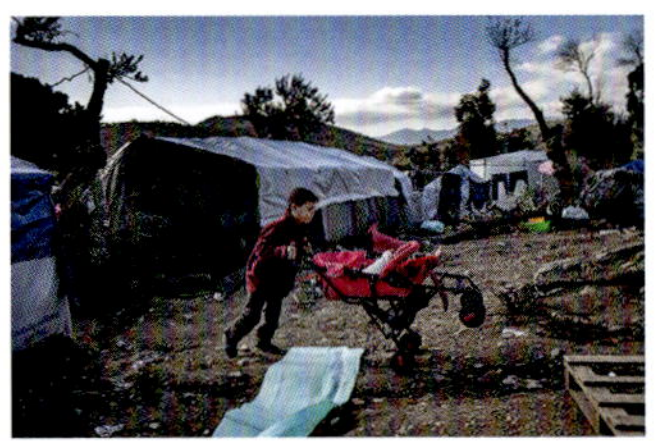

In January the daytime temperature is about ten degrees and when the wind blows it bites, especially on the bare feet of children. 23.01. 2018

142

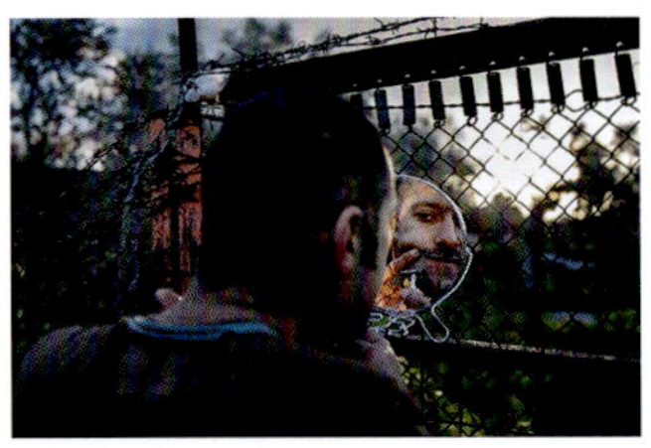

Near the Moria camp a Kurdish man from Iraq puts a mirror on a fence so he can shave. 25.01.2018

143

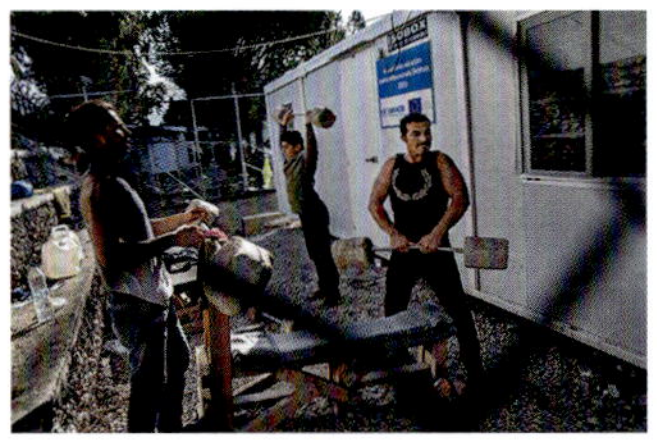

Inside the established part of the Moria camp, a Ghanaian man has created a fitness centre in front of the container where he lives. He charges two euros per month for membership, an offer that three young men from Kabul have bought into. 23.01.2018

144

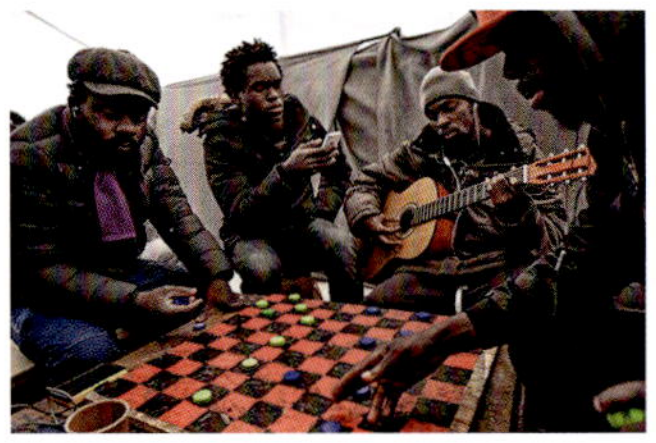

Olive Grove Camp is the name of this part of the Moria camp which has shot up outside of the actual reception centre. Here, around one hundred single men, primarily Africans, are accommodated in a large tent. Between the blanket-covered bunk beds, the young Congolese men play draughts. The playing board is an old piece of chipboard which they have painted, and the pieces are screw caps from water bottles. 27.01.2018

145

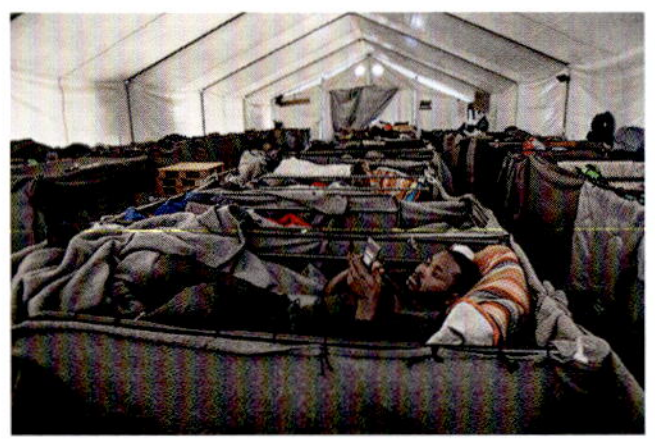

The fan heater that is supposed to heat up the large tent hasn't worked for three days, and so it is freezing cold. Adams is 24 years old and has fled from Cameroon. He has been living in the tent for two months. He has no family in Europe and so does not know where he will go. 27.01.2018

146

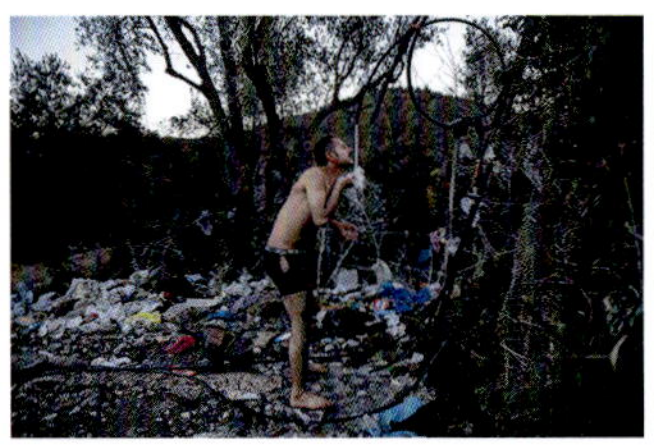

A couple hundred metres down a gravel road near the Moria camp, a farmer has mounted a water hose on a fence and installed a regulator valve to turn the water off and on. A lot of young men come here and wash themselves in the cold water. After a cold bath, and with his teeth chattering, a Kurdish man from Iraq wrings out his torn underpants, puts them back on and walks back to the camp. 25.01.2018

149

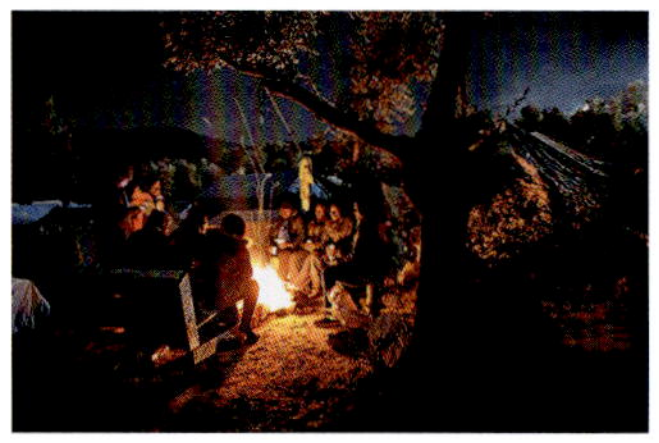

On Saturday night a group of young people from Cameroon try to keep warm by a bonfire in Olive Grove Camp with French rap music blasting through the darkness from a small speaker. 27.01.2018

150

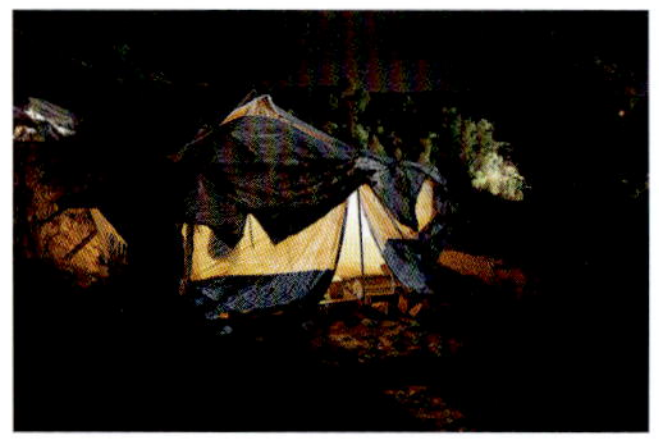

Olive Grove Camp, also known as 'the Jungle' outside the official Moria reception centre, 17.06. 2019

150

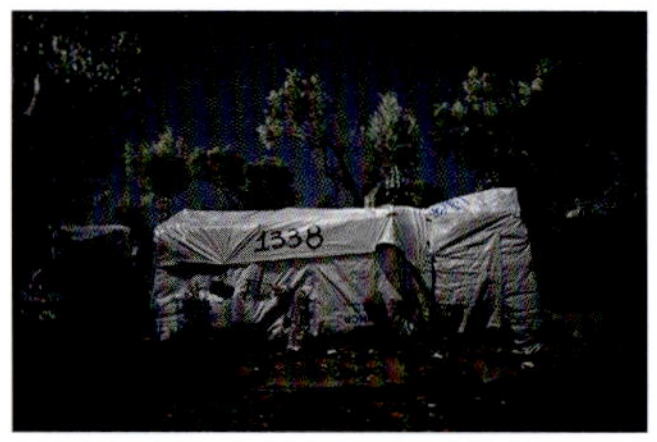

Olive Grove Camp, also known as 'the Jungle' outside the official Moria reception centre, 26.01.2018

151

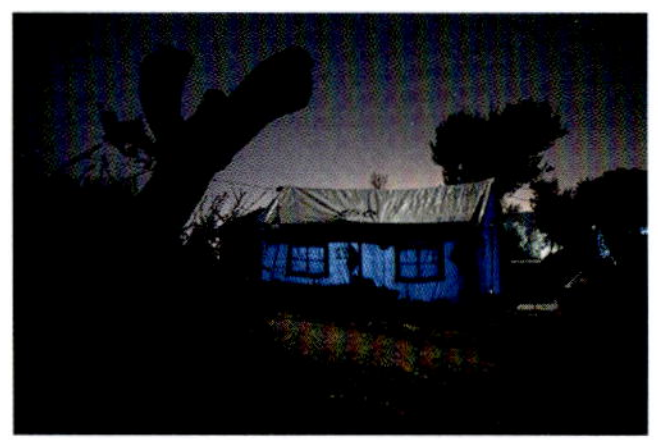

Olive Grove Camp, also known as 'the Jungle' outside the official Moria reception centre, 26.01.2018

151

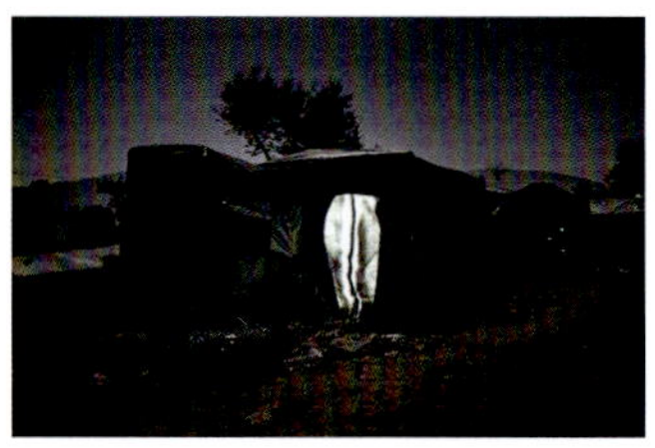

Olive Grove Camp, also known as 'the Jungle' outside the official Moria reception centre, 26.01.2018

155

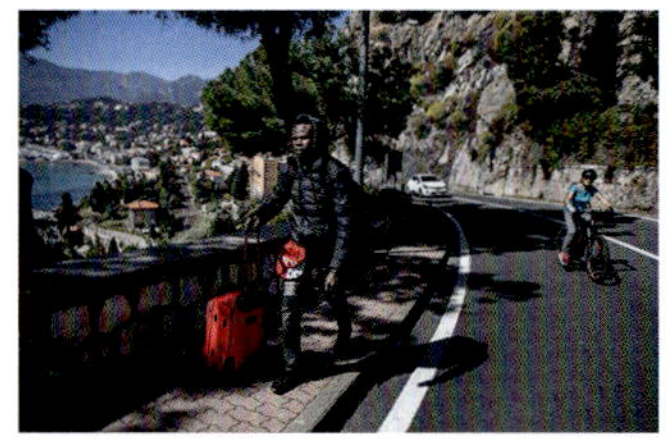

Diallo Demba, a 30-year-old from Senegal, was caught on the train yesterday by the French border police. He has just been released after spending the night in police custody and is on his way back to Ventimiglia, so that he can make another attempt. He lived in Sicily for five years and has worked in a restaurant in Palermo. Now he is attempting to reach Spain, where his father lives. 23.03.2019

157

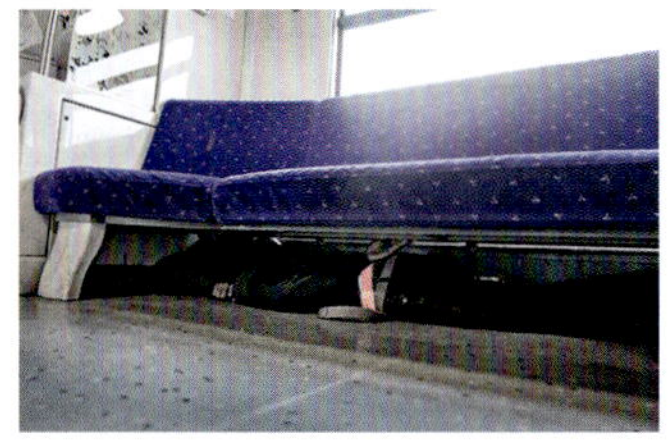

Most of the refugees and migrants who attempt to cross the border from Italy to France hop on the train in the coastal town of Ventimiglia. Some of them purchase a ticket and try to pass themselves off as ordinary passengers. Others hide in the toilet or under a seat in the hope that the French border police will not discover them when they search the train in Menton-Garavan, the first stop on the French side. Although the border police know all the hiding places, this young African man is not found, perhaps because four American tourists in the car drew the attention of the officers. 22.03.2019

158

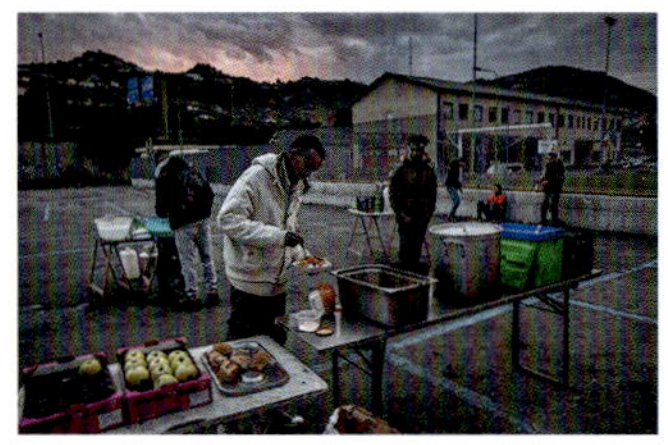

In a parking space on the outskirts of Ventimiglia a group of volunteers who call themselves Kesha Niya meet up every night to serve food mainly to refugees and migrants. Mahamed Dahive Blaiss from Mogadishu in Somalia is 24 years old and shows up this evening. His father died in 1999 and his mother was killed in an explosion in 2009. Mahamed fled through the desert to Libya, where he was kidnapped and imprisoned for three years. His uncle had to sell Mahamed's house in order to pay a ransom. The human traffickers sent him off from Libya in a glass fiber boat along with thirty-seven other refugees, eight containers of petrol and a GPS tracker, the battery of which quickly went dead. After three days at sea, they came across a boat with Tunisian fishermen, who gave them more petrol and contacted the Italian coastal guard, who picked them up and sailed them to Lampedusa. From there, Mahamed journeyed from Sicily to Rome, Milan and Ventimiglia. He has a sweetheart in Toulouse whom he has not seen for five years, but they are in contact by telephone. The next stop is France. 18.03.2019

159 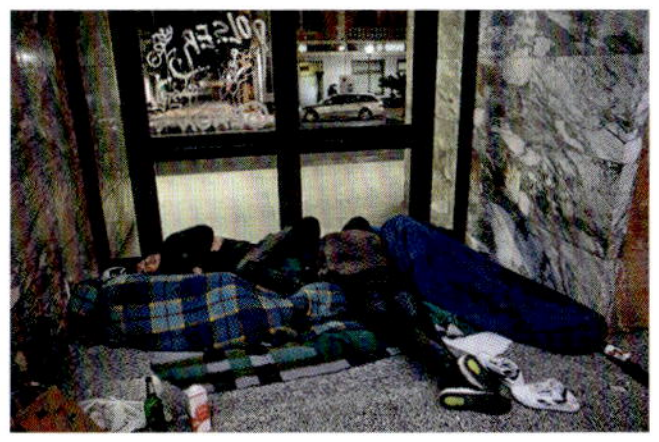

These young men from Tunisia are snoring loudly. They have lain down to sleep at the railway station where it is relatively calm and free from police between 1am and 4am. 21.03.2019

160 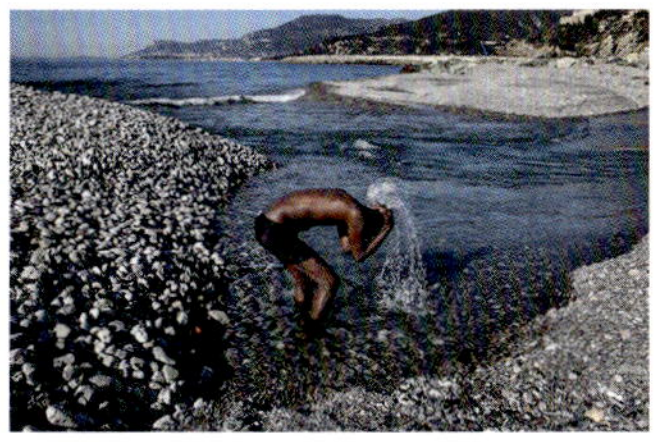

A man from Senegal washes himself on the beach in Ventimiglia where the Roya river discharges into the Mediterranean. He has been in Italy for five years and has been refused asylum here. Now he wants to move on to France or Germany. 22.03.2019

161 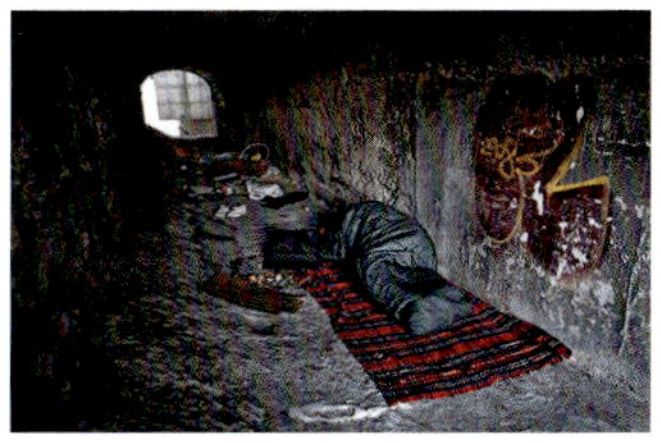

Inside the tunnels that are built into a railway bridge, refugees and migrants sleep, hidden from the outside world. There used to be a makeshift camp of tents under another bridge in Ventimiglia, but the authorities removed it. Now they have to sleep alone or in small groups around town. 21.03.2019

163 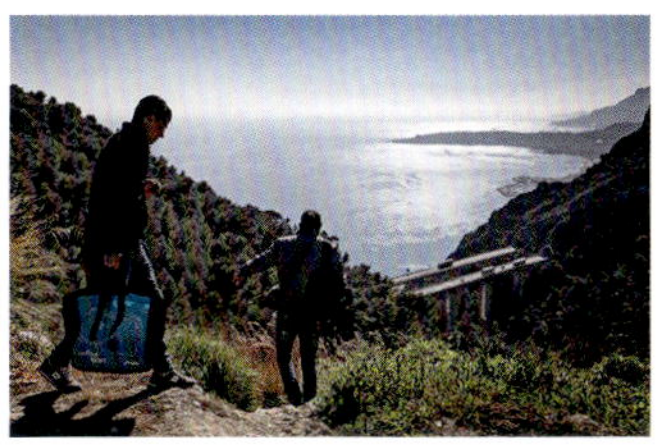

Two men from Algeria are making their way from Italy to France along a narrow mountain path. They hope to avoid both the border police and the army on this route, which was recommended by other refugees. France starts at a point inside the motorway tunnel seen in the background. Further away, on the horizon, is the French town of Menton. 23.03.2019

166 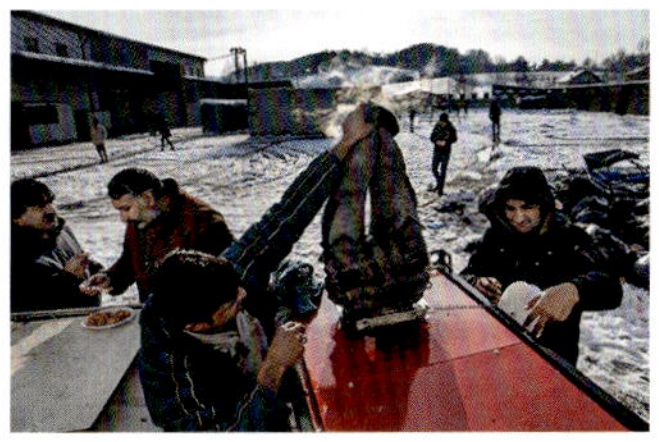

The refugees and migrants who have arrived most recently to the camp in what was formerly a PVC factory in the town of Velika Kladuša are accommodated inside a huge tent in the courtyard of the Miral factory. The tent is heated by two petrol space heaters. Some of the men realize that they can dry their wet clothes by lifting the lid of the exhaust hole of the space heater that is not connected to a pipe. 16.12.2018

168 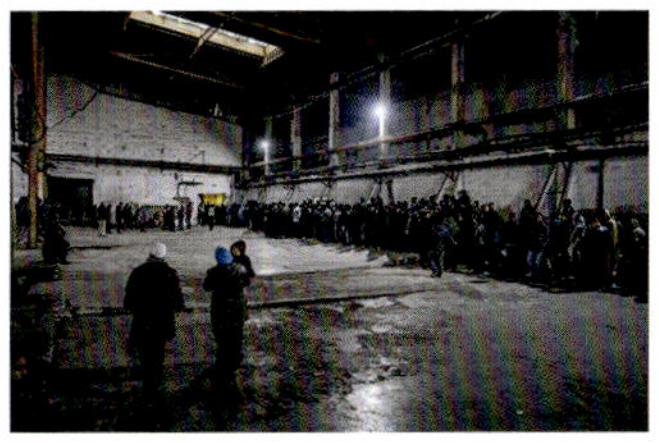

In the town Bihać in northwest Bosnia-Herzegovina, the IOM runs a refugee camp inside a former refrigerator factory. Three times a day people queue up to get a meal. Many residents of Camp Bira complain that the portions are too small. Besides that, there is never enough food for everyone, so many wait in vain in the long queue. 15.12.2018

170 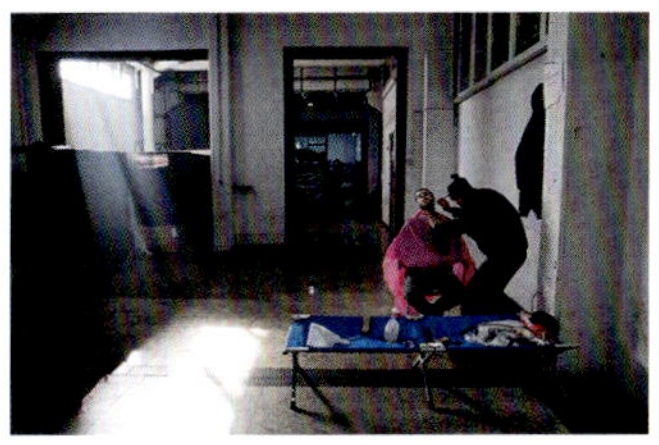

At present the camp in the former PVC factory houses around 600 refugees and migrants. Muhammad is 34 years old and comes from Algeria. He has lived here for five months and earns a bit of money by cutting the hair of the other refugees. He wants to get to Germany where he has a sister. In the chair sits a 25-year-old fellow Algerian, whose name is also Muhammad. 16.12.2018

171 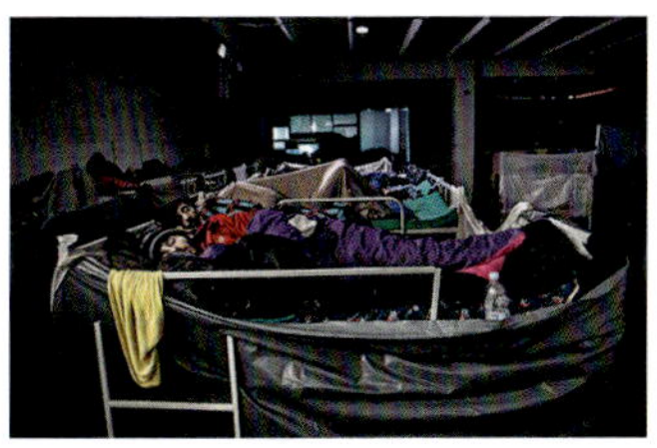

It is not easy to get enough peace and quiet to sleep in the former plastic factory in Velika Kladuša. There is constant noise. If one does fall asleep, there is a risk that any valuables, money, or cell phones may be stolen during the night. 16.12.2018

172 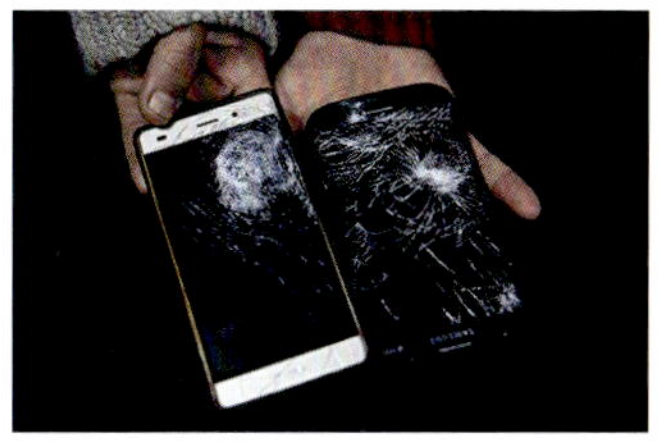

Two young men show their cell phones which have been smashed by the Croatian border guards. 14.12.2018

175 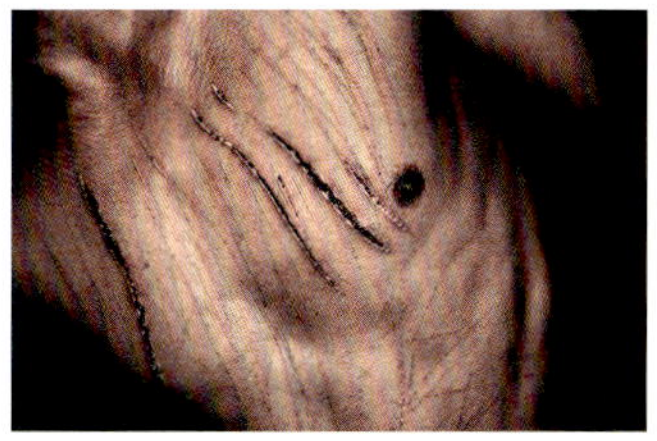

Twenty-nine-year-old Ahmad Hadi from Iraq is trying to get to Italy by following the Balkan route through Bosnia-Herzegovina, Croatia and Slovenia. He says that he has been in Croatia more than 20 times and has been caught every time. He has been beaten many times by the border guards and had many cuts and bruises from moving through the pathless terrain in the Croatian woods. Now he is recovering in the former PVC factory in Velika Kladuša before his next attempt. 16.12.2018

176 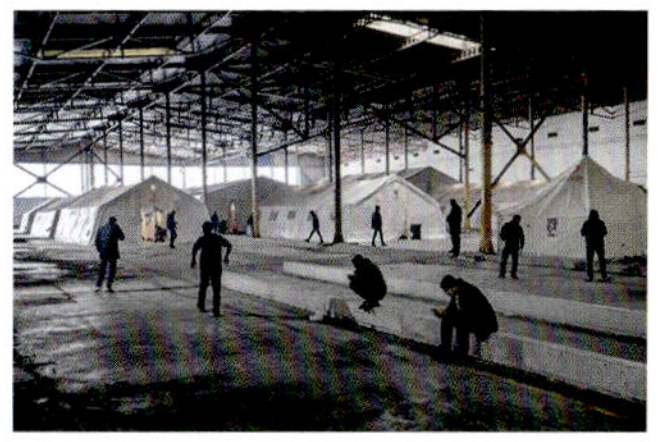

In the town of Bihać, in what was formerly a refrigerator factory, Camp Bira houses around 2,200 refugees and migrants. About 1,700 of them are single young men. They live in large tents set up inside the halls of the factory. Because winter has set in, most of them will wait to cross the Croatian border and continue their walk towards Italy. For now, the journey is too cold and dangerous. 15.12.2018

178 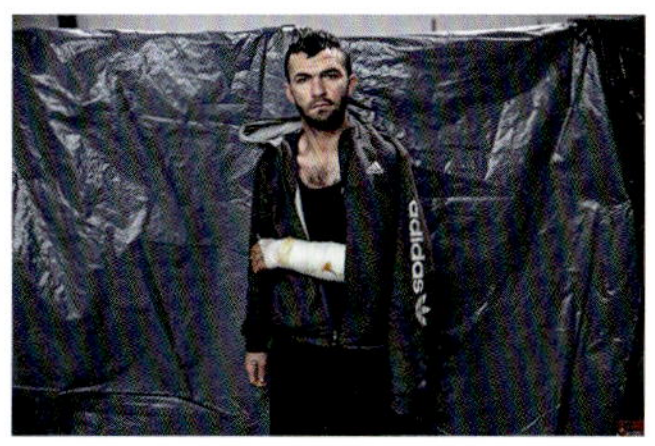

Muhammad Ibrahim, age 24 from Syria, is presently staying at the camp in the former PVC factory. He has attempted to cross the border to Croatia many times but has been caught every time and sent back to Bosnia-Herzegovina. The last time he was beaten so badly by the Croatian border guards that his arm was broken. They also took his personal documents, money, cell phone, two power banks and a bag with his clothes and his shoes. 14.12.2018

179 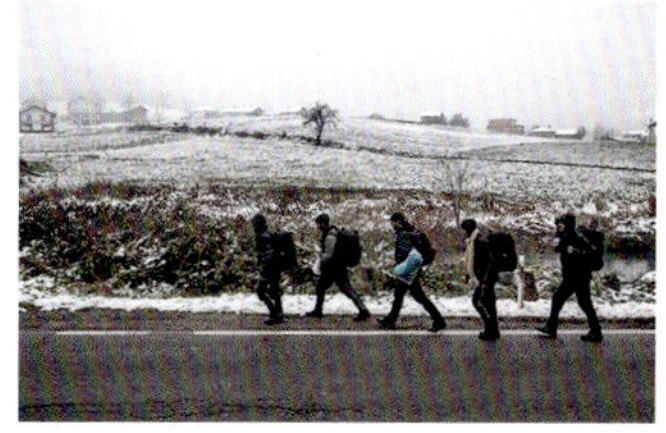

A group of Afghan and Pakistani young men have just been refused admission to the Miral camp in Velika Kladuša. The camp currently houses just over 1,000 men and there is no room for more. So the group sets out on a 60-kilometre walk to Bihać, where they hope to find shelter. 05.12.2020

180 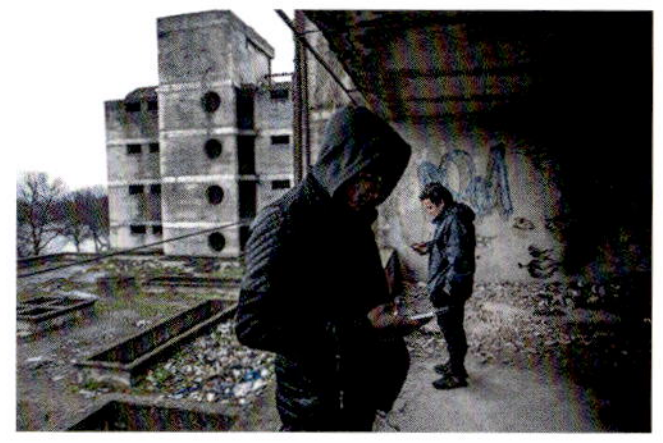

In the centre of Bihać, around 50 young men from Afghanistan and Pakistan are staying in a ruined building next to the river. Originally intended to be a nursing home, construction halted during the wars in former Yugoslavia in the 1990s. The Afghan brothers, Ismail, age 14, and Naeem, age 17, have been staying here for 15 days. They have been pushed back from Croatia twice. Now they are talking to their parents in Jalalabad. Ismail speaks with their father on one phone while Naeem speaks with their mother on another. The boys dream of reaching Belgium and London. 08.12.2020

181 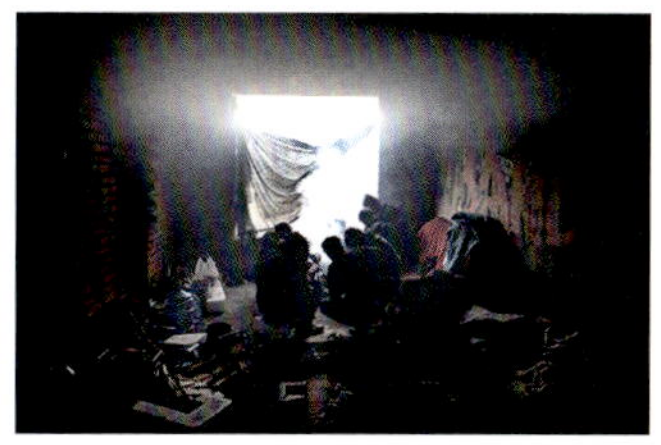

The boys live together in smaller groups inside this decrepit building. Many of them are minors. At night it is extremely cold and many of the boys do not have blankets or warm clothes. The local authorities have forbidden NGOs from distributing clothes, food and other essentials to refugees and migrants in Bihać. 08.12.2020

183 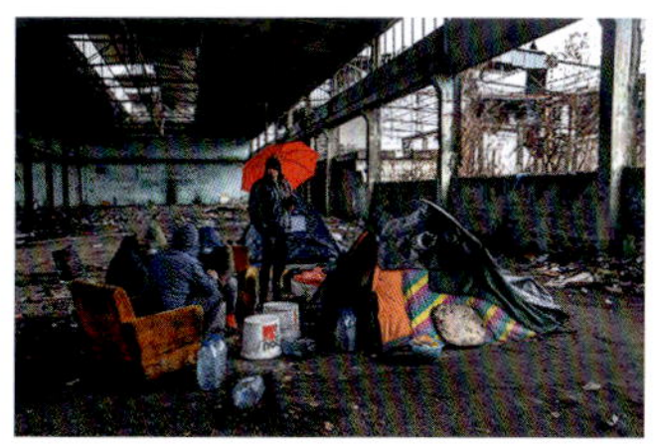

More than 100 young men and boys, primarily from Afghan and Pakistan, have settled in a rundown former metal factory on the outskirts of Bihać. The young man with his back turned is Abas Rahimi. Out of the 13 times he has attempted to cross the border, he has been beaten up ten times. He says, 'They took my shoes, my jacket and my money, and they broke my cell phone with a knife. Then they burnt it all in a fire. The last time it happened was three days ago.' 09.12.2020

184

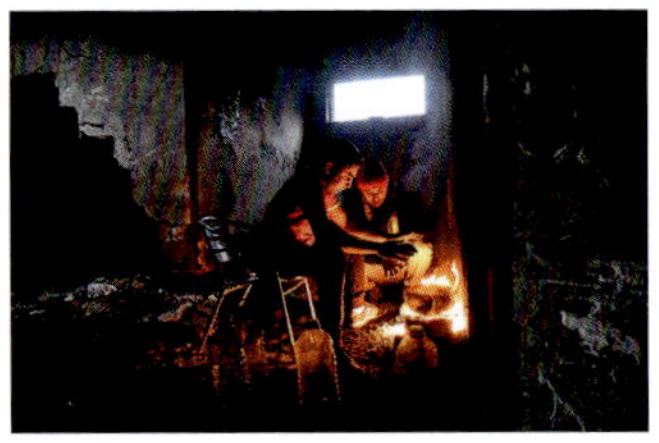

On the top of this ruin of a building, which was built to be a nursing home, two boys sit by the fire warming themselves. Twenty-year-old Sil from Pakistan wants to go to Italy. He has crossed the border to Croatia six times. They call these attempts 'the game'. Sharif, the one with the cap, is 15 years old and comes from Afghanistan. He has crossed the border five times. Three times he made it all the way to Slovenia before the police captured him and drove him back to Bosnia-Hercegovina. Both of them have been living in this building for three months. They have been beaten several times and had their belongings taken from them by the Croatian border police. Sharif would like to go France. 08.12.2020

185

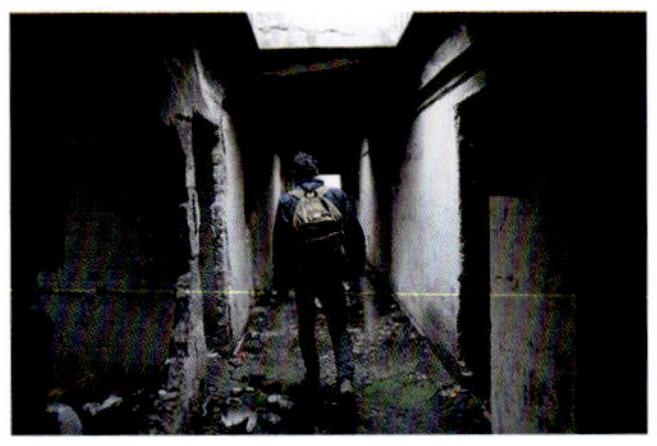

After saying good-bye to the group of boys he has been staying with in the former metal factory, the young man packs his bag and heads for the border on his own. 09.12.2020

187

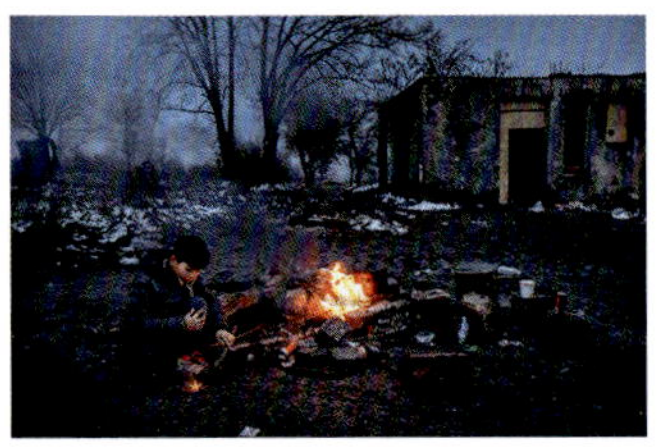

Yesterday the Croatian border police sent eight-year-old Sobhan and his family back over the border to Bosnia-Hercegovina. He has slept in an abandoned house with his parents and three siblings in a village near the border. It is too cold and dangerous to sleep in the ruins, so the Bosnian police who patrol the area have phoned the IOM, which is coming to pick up the family and transport them to a camp in Bihać. 05.12.2020

189

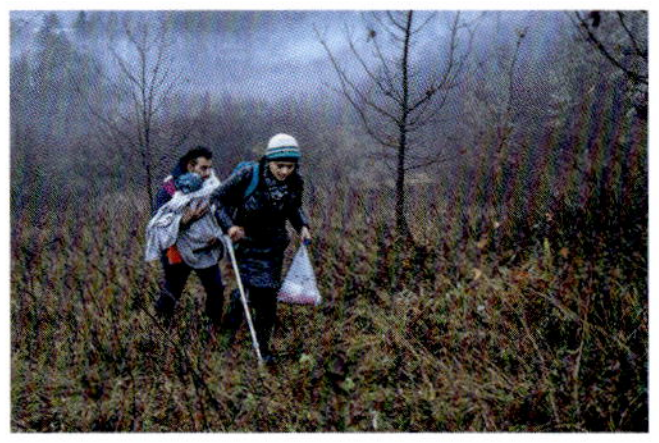

Haseen Afghan, age 29, and his wife Somaya, age 21, are walking toward the Croatian border with their ten-month-old daughter Oswah. Last night they slept in a small hunting lodge in the village of Bosanska Bojna together with another Afghan family. They have tried to cross the border 12 times in the past two weeks. When they enter Croatia, they contact a lawyer, say where they are and that they want to seek asylum. The lawyer then contacts the police, who are supposed to help the family begin the asylum application process. But instead, the family's repeated experience is that the police destroy their cell phones, take their money and send them back across the border. It is almost three years since the couple fled from Herat, where Haseen was an English teacher and Somaya his student. The Taleban murdered Haseen's father and threatened to kill him. Somaya walks with a crutch because she fell and injured her foot earlier in their journey through Europe. 07.12.2020

190

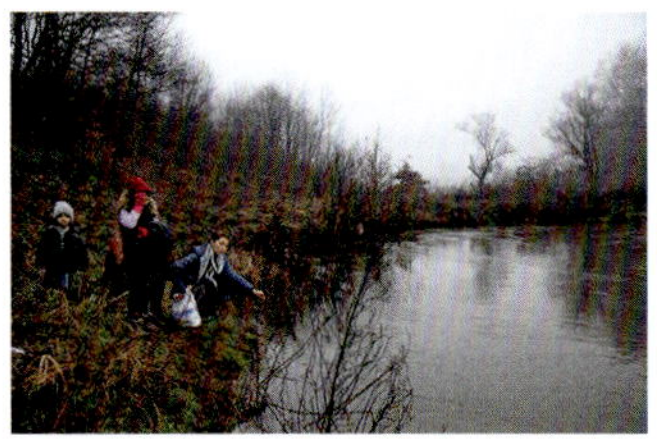

An Afghan family with six children try again and again to cross the border to Croatia along with a young Afghan couple. They had planned to wade across the river that marks the border just outside of Velika Kladuša, as they have done many times before, but the water level has risen and they have to cancel the plan. Next to Somayyeh, age five, and Ayeshe, age ten, sits 26-year-old Mohen Rezaie. 08.12.2020

191

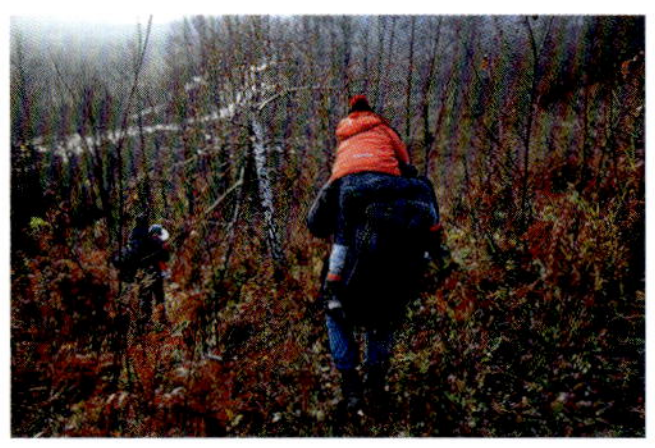

Two Afghan families have just crossed the border and walk into Croatia. The fathers carrying the children lead the way. Many refugees and migrants go to the small village of Bosanska Bojna, 25 kilometres east of Velika Kladuša. They stay in abandoned houses and try to cross the border to Croatia from here. 07.12.2020

192

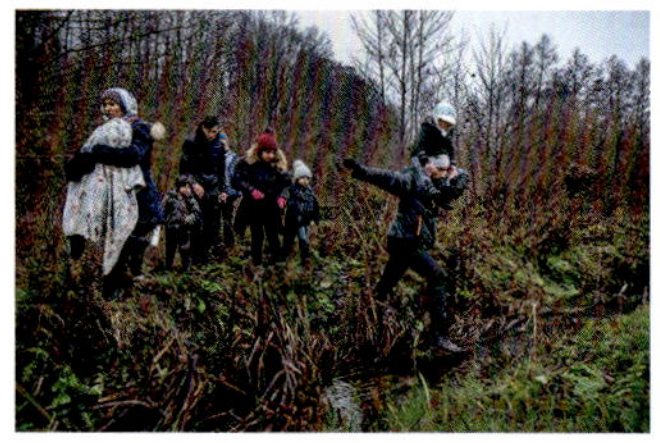

An Afghan family consisting of a mother, a father and their six children aged between five months and ten years old, plan to cross the border to Croatia from the town of Velika Kladuša together with another Afghan couple. They had to give up their original plan to cross a river because the water level was too high. Now they have walked to a place where they have to crawl down a steep muddy slope and jump across a stream to enter Croatia. As soon as the father Hekmatollah Anarkhel lands on the other side of the stream with his two-year-old son Mohammad Taha on his shoulders, a group of Croatian border police come running towards him. He jumps back to his wife Zoleykha who is standing on the other side with their five-month-old son in a baby sling. The couple's four other children are standing on the bank with the young couple the family are travelling with. The families run through the terrain together and up the steep slope back to the main road. This large family have now made 36 unsuccessful border crossings, and the young couple eleven. 08.12.2020

194

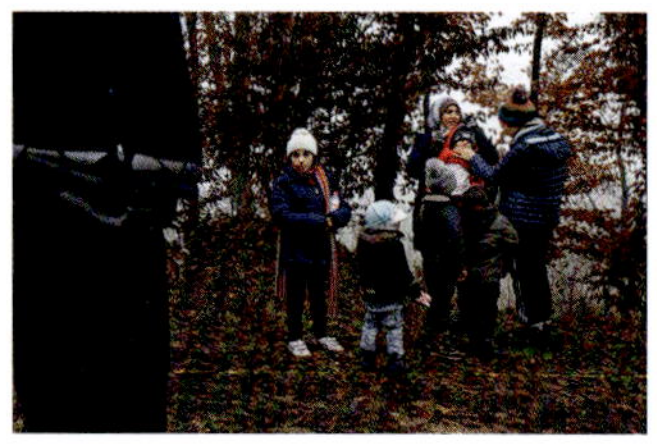

Soon after the two Afghan couples with six children are discovered by the Croatian border police while trying to cross the border on the outskirts of Velika Kladuša, Bosnian police show up and detain them. After speaking with them angrily, the police let them go. Atefeh, age nine, has a bottle of milk for the journey. 08.12.2020

199

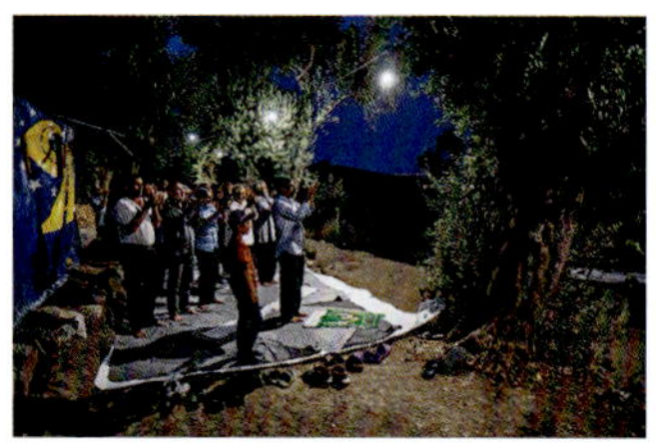

At the Moria camp on Lesbos around 5,000 people are presently living under very primitive conditions in and around the reception centre, originally converted to accommodate 2,800 people. In the makeshift area of the camp, known as 'the Jungle', a group of Afghan men meet every night for prayer. Imam Seead Enajatollh Hossini leads the prayer, accompanied by the singing of a ten-year-old boy named Mahdi Mohammadi. 17.06.2019

200

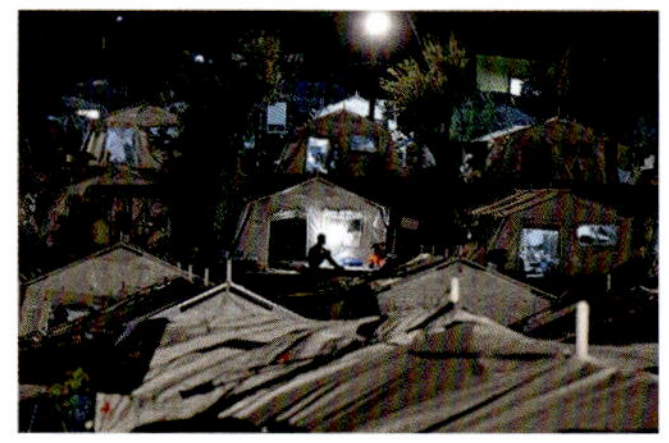

A small area in 'the Jungle' outside Moria's reception centre has been upgraded. Identical tents have been set up on fixed pallets and access to water, toilets and electricity has been established. 16.06.2019

202

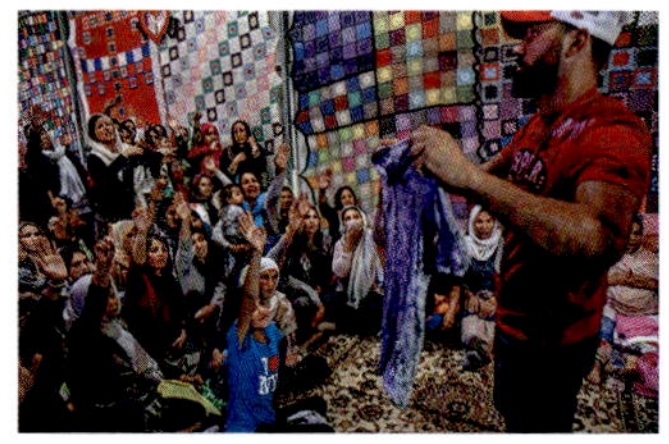

Across from the Moria camp, Salam Aldeen, the co-founder of a small Danish NGO called Team Humanity, rents a large warehouse that he has converted into a club for children and a women's centre. Women and children can come here five days a week to play and enjoy each other's company and forget the hard life in the camp for a while. Today Salam passes out clothes in the women's centre. He shows a piece of clothing, one at a time. If anyone is interested, they raise a hand and hope that he tosses the item of clothing to them. 18.06.2019

204

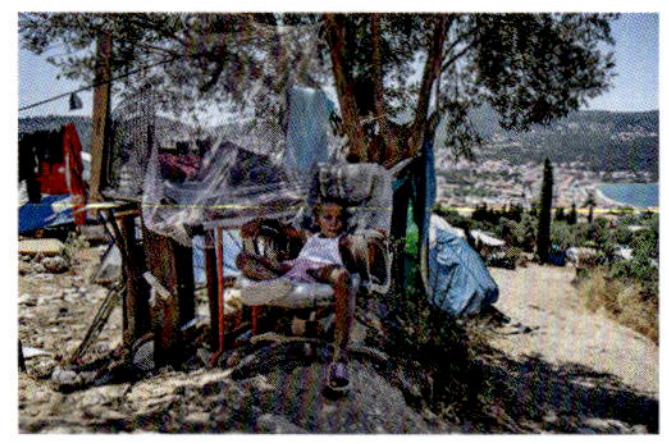

A scene from 'the Jungle' camp that surrounds the official reception centre, located on the outskirts of Samos town. 14.06.2019

205

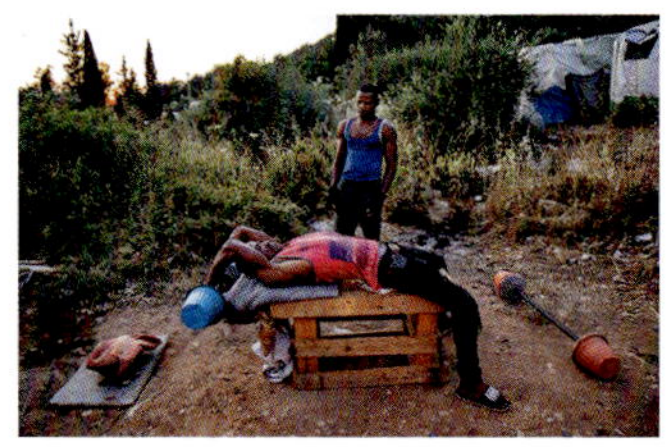

Two men from the Congo work out with weights in an improvised fitness centre in the makeshift camp that has cropped up outside the official reception centre in Samos. 12.06.2019

206

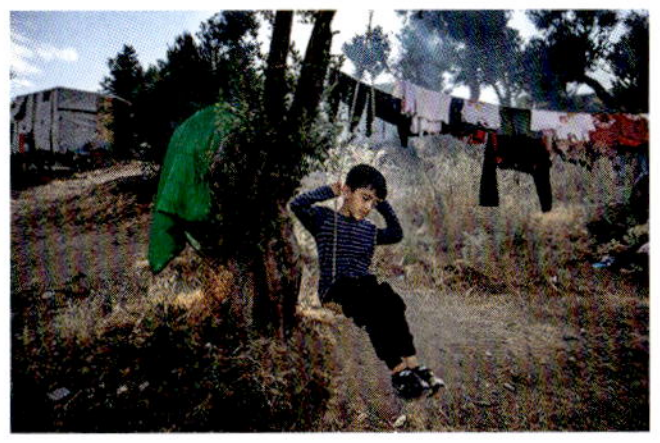

Six-year-old Kamaluddin from Afghanistan lives in 'the Jungle' area of the Moria camp with his parents and four siblings. 17.06.2019

207

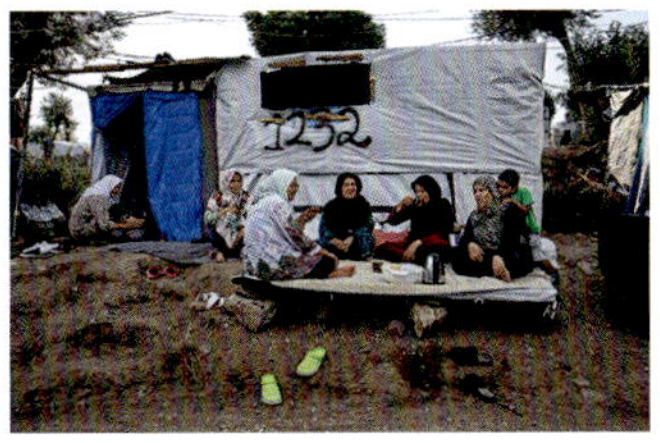

Afghan women drink tea in the Moria camp. 17.06.2019

208

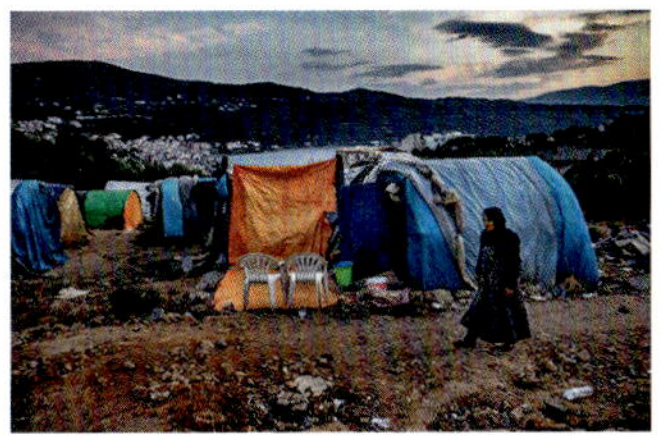

Local NGOs estimate that between 3,000 and 4,000 refugees and migrants live in and around the reception centre on Samos. 12.06.2019

210

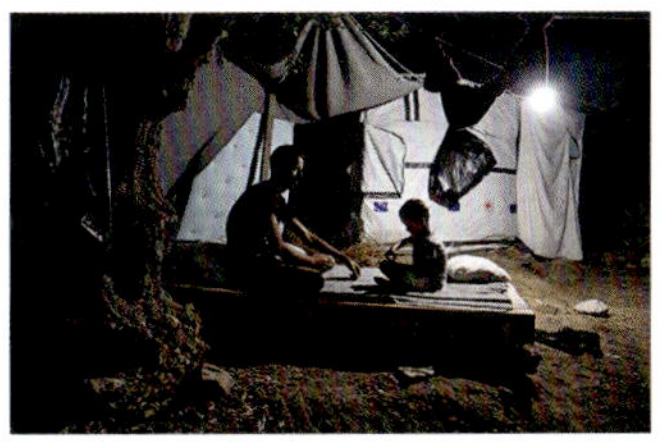

Four-year-old Zoher plays cards with his father, Mojtaba, age 29, in their makeshift house in 'the Jungle' of the Moria camp. They have fled from Afghanistan and have been living here for nine months. 16.06.2019

211

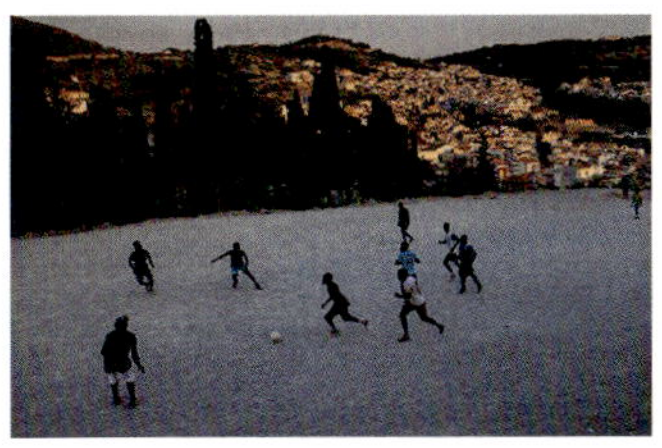

On a mountain slope at the edge of the town of Samos lies the island's reception centre, which is ringed by a makeshift camp. Across from the camp is a gravel court where many of the African men play football every evening. It is one of the few activities that provides the young men with a distraction from the monotonous daily life in the extremely primitive camp. 14.06.2019

215

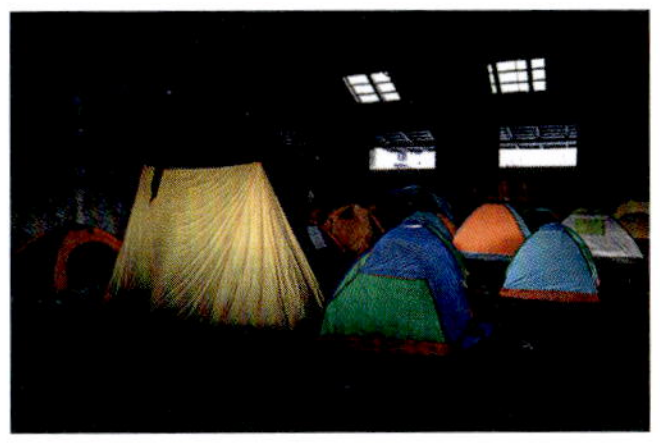

The nearly 500 refugees and migrants at the abandoned sawmill across from the harbour area have set up tents inside. A sign posted on the building says, in many languages, that the building could collapse at any time. 23.04.2018

216

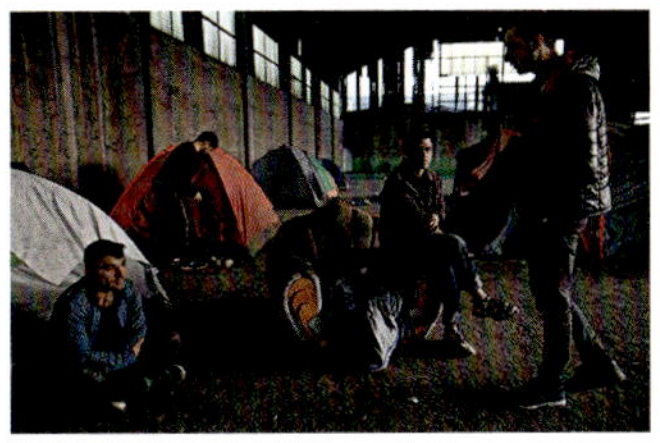

It is not possible to just show up and pitch a tent in the sawmill and start playing 'the game'. First it is necessary to pay a human trafficker. The sawmill is divided into zones that are controlled by different traffickers and their assistants. It costs between 1,000 and 1,500 euros to take part. Once a payment is made one can stay until either successfully boarding a ferry, or until one gives up and tries to find another northbound route through Europe. 23.04.2018

218

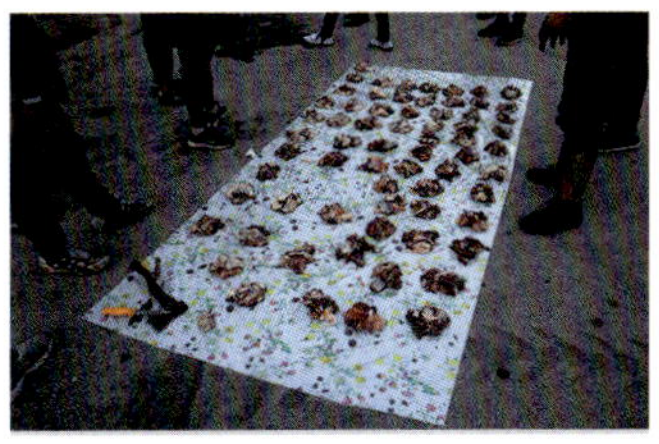

In the courtyard of the sawmill two goats are slaughtered, carved into pieces and divided into portions so that everyone gets some. One of the boys says that one of the sawmill's traffickers has paid for the feast in order to show off in front of the other traffickers, and perhaps to celebrate that he has been successful in getting some of 'his' boys aboard a ship. 24.04.2018

220

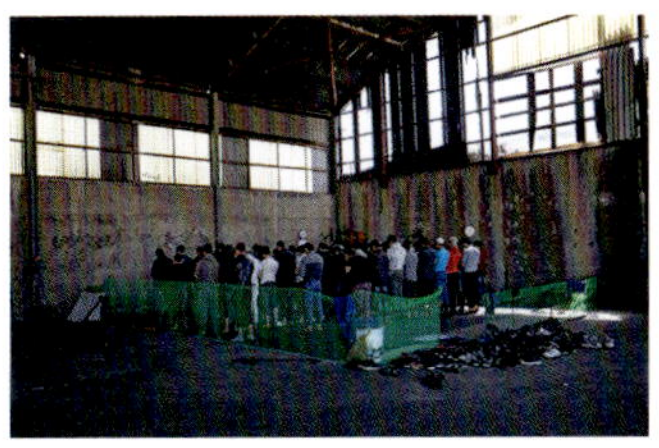

In the corner of one of the large halls inside the sawmill, the residents have made an improvised mosque where people participate in joint prayer several times a day. One of the boys says, 'People here have a lot to pray for.' 24.04.2018

222

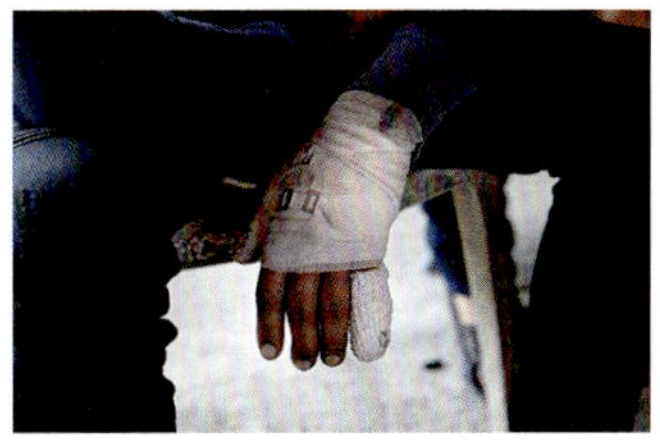

Many people suffer injuries when attempting to enter the port area. When climbing over the fences, they can have a bad fall or cut themselves on the barbed wire. Some also talk of having been beaten with batons by the police. 24.04.2018

223

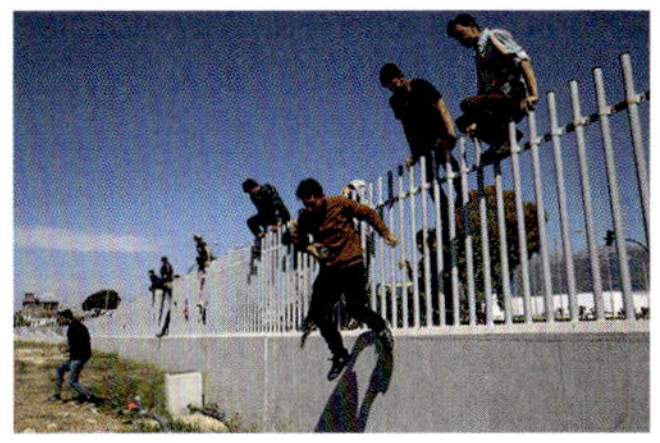

A group of young men and boys jump over the fence surrounding the port area. From here, it's all about evading the port police and reaching the next fence that separates them from the lorries that have passed the security check and are now parked near the quay and ready to be driven aboard one of the many ferries to Italy. The traffickers control when and how the young men scale the fences and hide inside the lorries. 25.04.2018

224

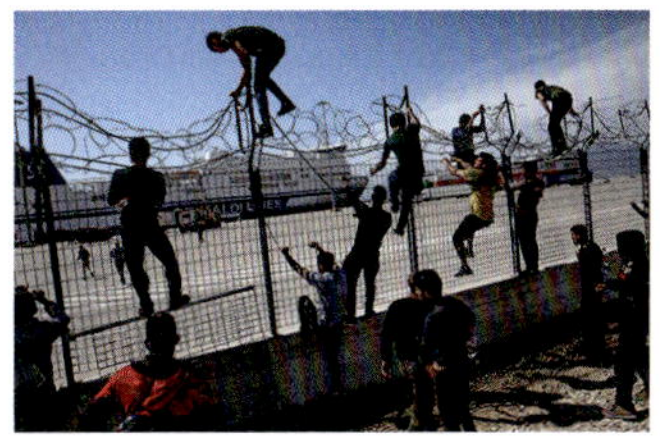

A group of men and boys have evaded the attention of the police and have reached the last fence they have to climb over to reach the lorries. In this case it means that they have to climb over razor wire. Speed is critical. 26.04.2018

226

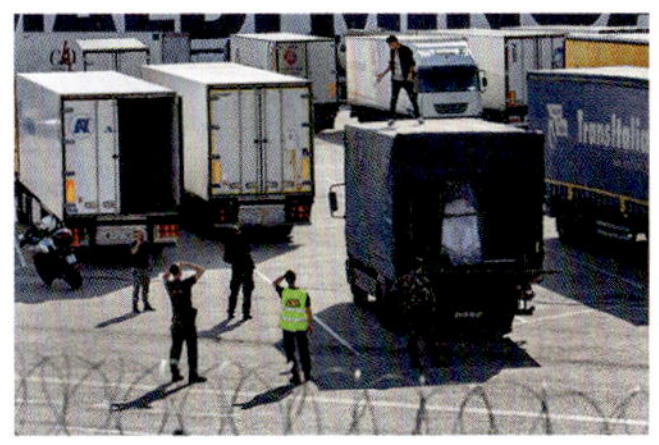

The police discover a boy who was hiding on the roof of a lorry. They try to persuade him to climb down, but the boy is afraid and paces on the roof of the lorry for about fifteen minutes. In the end he jumps down and is allowed to run off. 26.04.2018

227

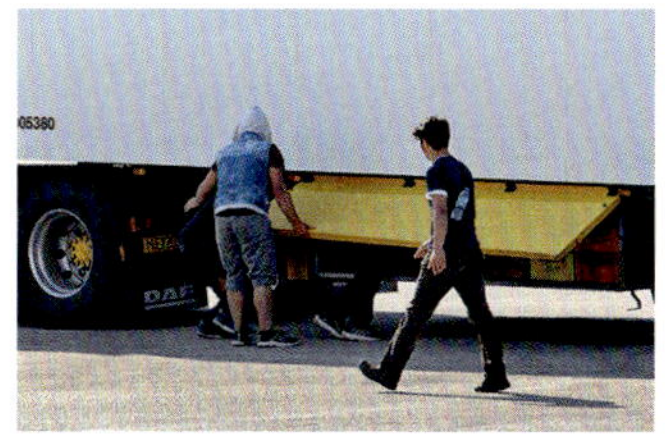

Two boys manage to hide in this storage unit underneath the lorry, which is driven aboard a ferry to Italy shortly thereafter. The voyage takes eighteen hours and it is possible that they could be discovered when the lorry disembarks. If that happens, they are sent back to Greece. 26.04.2018

228

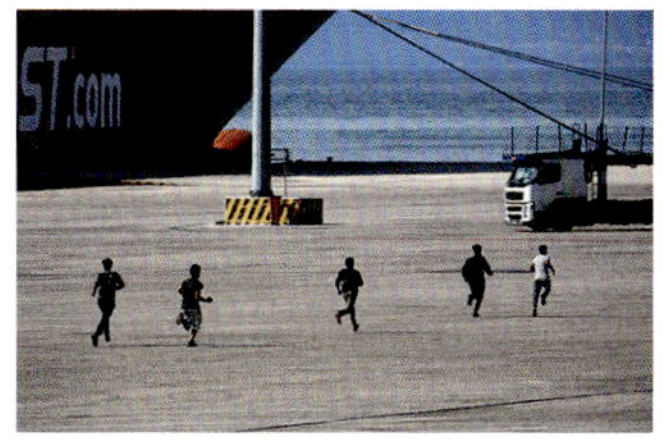

When many refugees and migrants reach the lorries at the same time, it's all about creating confusion. The young men run in all directions and between the lorries, while the police on motorcycles and in cars try to catch them or chase them out of the area. It is in this state of confusion that the chance of getting on a lorry as a stowaway is greatest. 26.04.2018

230-231

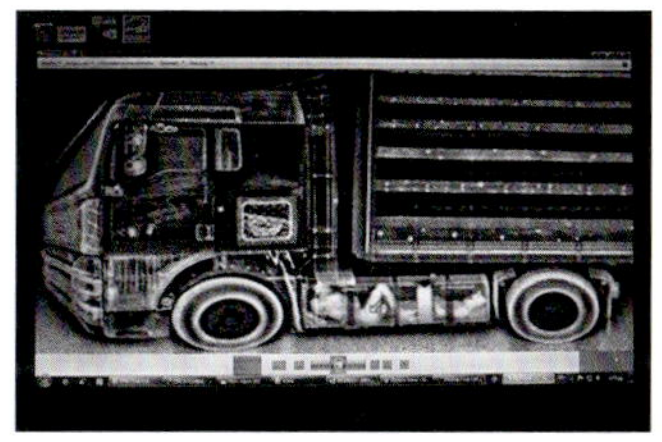

In the Greek port city of Patras, many refugees and migrants attempt to board the ferry to Italy by hiding in lorries. In the port security office, police can show a 'best of' collection of x-ray scans that reveal people hiding in secret compartments built inside the lorries at the behest of the professional human traffickers. The police say that a space costs several thousand euros. Most of the refugees and migrants cannot afford such an organized solution, so they must try to board the lorries in other ways. It is only the most suspect lorries that are scanned. 26.04.2018

234

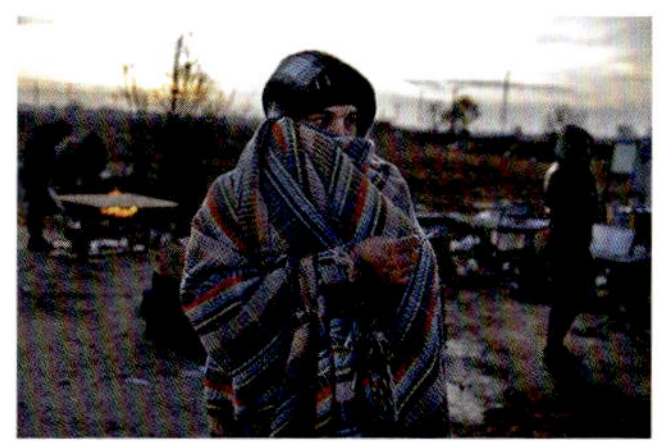

Atef Assir, age 55, from Idlib, Syria, has been staying in the area near the Pazarkule border crossing for five days. The Turkish police have restricted media access. He is here with his wife, his brother, sister-in-law and three children aged three, five and eight. He has left the area to buy a cup of tea and says that there are thousands of people within the police barricade. Seven months ago he and his brother escaped to Turkey. Later they paid traffickers $1,500 to bring their families across the border to Turkey. 04.03.2020

235
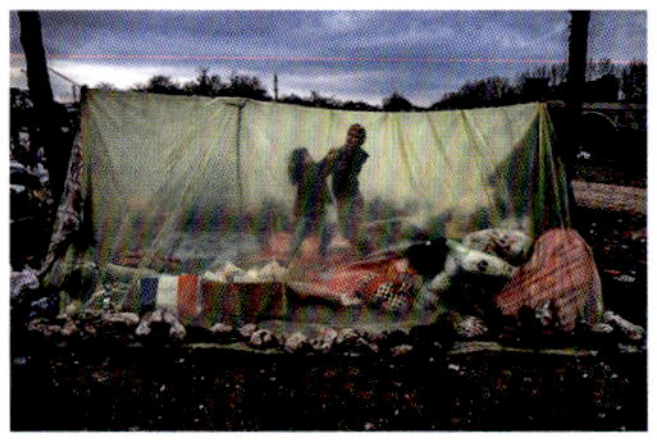

In a park in the Turkish town of Edirne, a Syrian family from Damascus have made a makeshift tent out of a tarpaulin. The two sisters, ages eight and ten, play inside the tent. The father is afraid to say what their names are. The family don't enjoy the tent for long; that night, the police demolish the camp. 05.03.2020

237
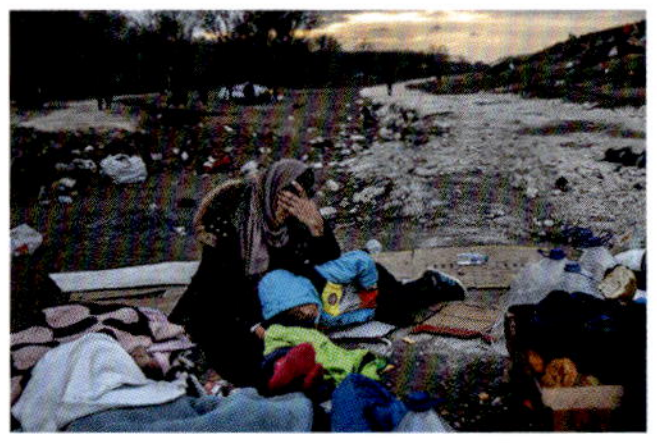

A Syrian woman and her children are among the hundreds of refugees and migrants that have set up a temporary camp in a park near the fork of a river in the Turkish town of Edirne. It is five kilometres to the border of Greece, and they hope that the Greeks will open the barrier at the border soon. 04.03.2020

238
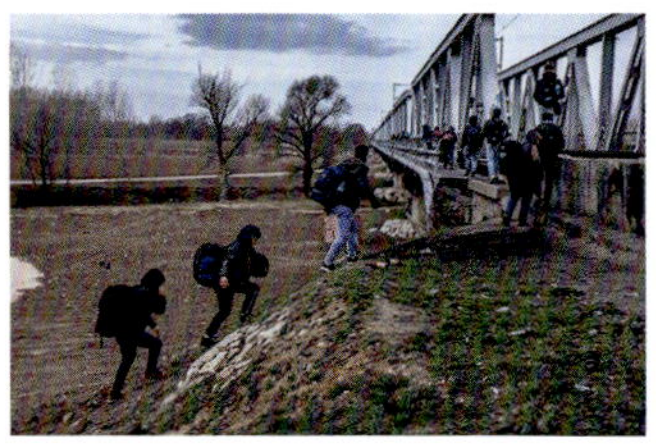

A group of Syrian refugees cross a railway bridge over the junction of two rivers at the edge of the Turkish city of Edirne. They are heading for the Pazarkule border crossing. 04.03.2020

240
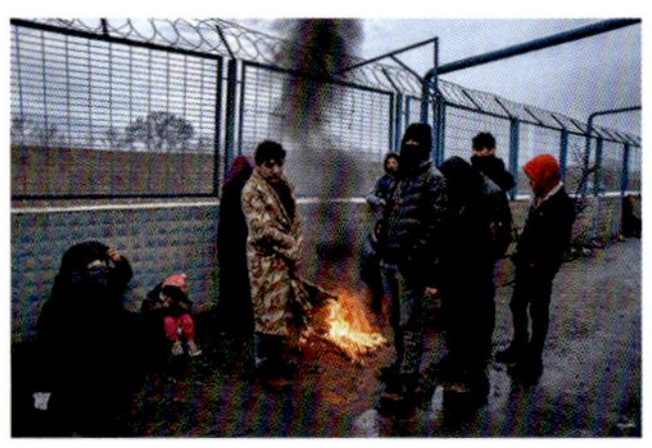

Not far from the Pazarkule border crossing, hundreds of refugees and migrants have settled down in a park. It rained last night, so most of them have sought shelter in an empty market hall next to the park where there is at least a roof over their heads. When day breaks, people begin to light fires inside and outside of the hall to get warm. They hope that the Greeks will open the border soon, even though most of them realize that it will probably not happen. 05.03.2020

241
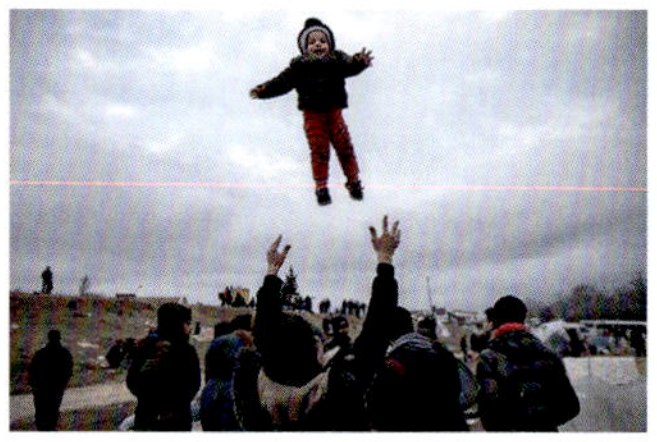

Two-year-old Tasneem is tossed in the air by his older brother. They belong to a Syrian family who moved to Turkey four years ago. They would like to get to Germany, where their older brother lives. Now that the Turkish government has announced that the border to Greece has opened, they have come to Edirne to try to cross the border. They have been here for four days spending the nights in a park at the edge of the town. It is five kilometres to the border, which is not as open as they had anticipated. 05.03.2020

242
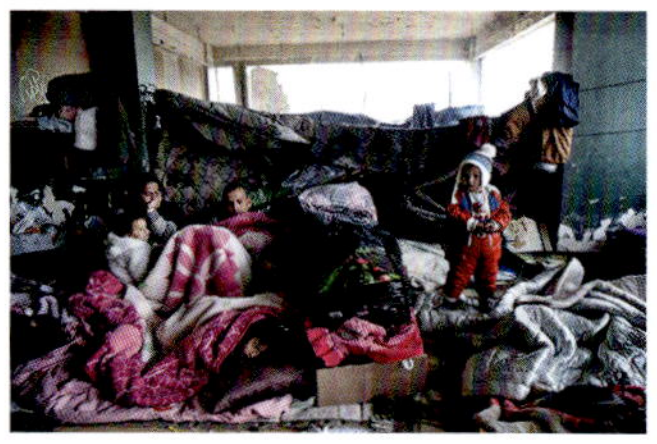

More than 100 refugees from Afghanistan and Syria have settled in an abandoned building near the bus station at the edge of the town of Edirne. Only Afghans live on the ground floor. Among the many is a family that consists of Mohammad Omid, age 33, his wife Rima, age 29, and their four children. Their son Mohammad Akbar, age two, sits on his mother's lap, and their daughter Zohael, age three, is lying down in the foreground. The child on the right belongs to a neighbouring family. This family have been in Turkey for four months and would like to go on to Germany. 06.03.2020

246
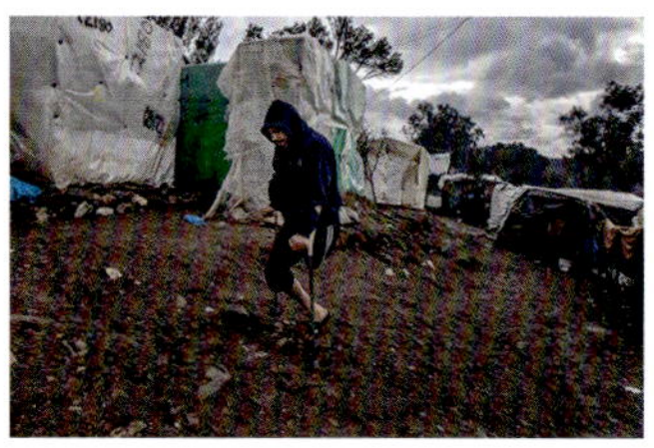

Saiad, age 33, has been living in 'the Jungle' for half a year. He fled from the police and the Taliban in Afghanistan around two years ago. Along the way he has lived in Iran and Turkey. Saiad lost one of his legs when he had to cross a bridge by motorcycle in his hometown, Faryab, and someone let off a roadside bomb. He has a wife and four children in Afghanistan and hopes to be reunited with them in Germany or Canada. He was an imam in his home country and is one here in the Moria camp too. He always tries to create peace between people, but that can be problematic, he says. 11.03.2020

247
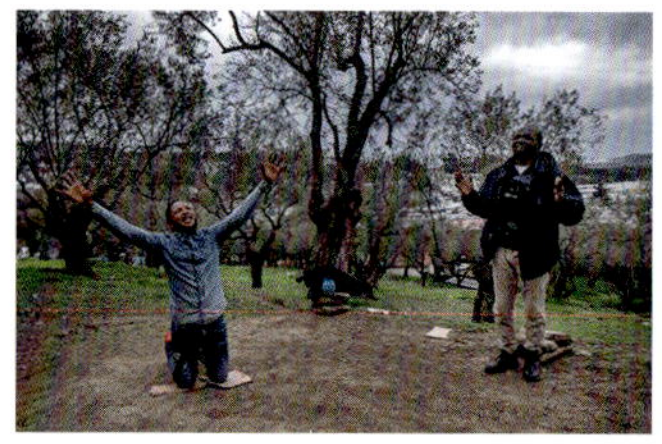

At the edge of Moria's 'jungle' a group of Christians from Congo perform a ritual to ask God for help. Marselo Joni is on his knees. He fled with his wife and their daughter 11 months ago and they have been living in the camp for four months now. They would like to go to a peaceful country in Europe. 10.03.2020

249
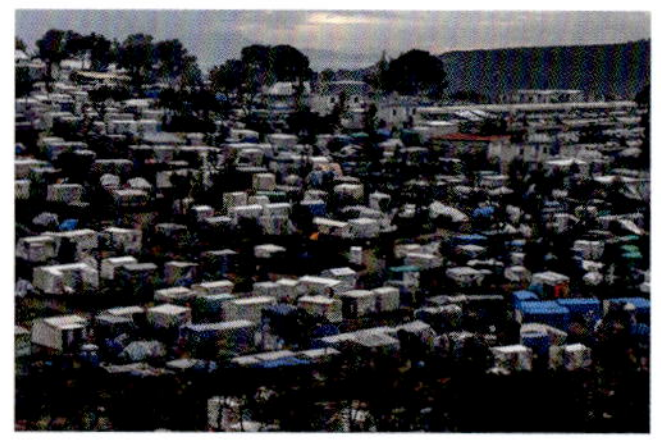

In the summer of 2019 around 5,000 people were living in the Moria camp. Now, in 2020, approximately 20,000 refugees and migrants are bunched together in or around the official part of the camp. Most are Afghans, but there are also many Syrians and people of other nationalities. 11.03.2020

251
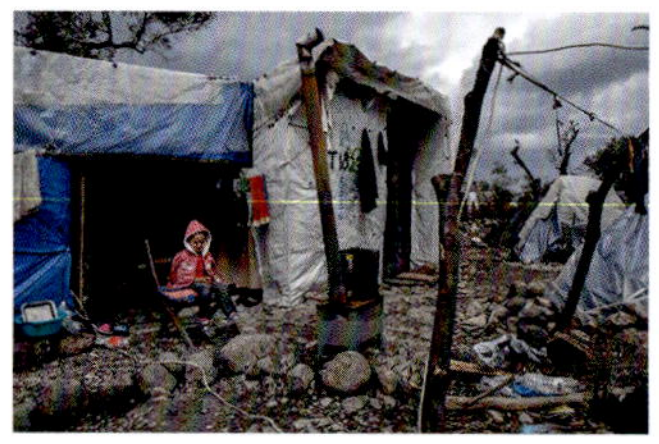

Zaynab Aboud is five years old. She fled with her grandparents from Idlib, a town in Syria that has been devastated by war. Her mother died in a bomb explosion when Zaynab was three months old. Her father has already moved to Germany, so that is where she and her grandparents are going. They have been living in the Moria camp for five months. 11.03.2020

252
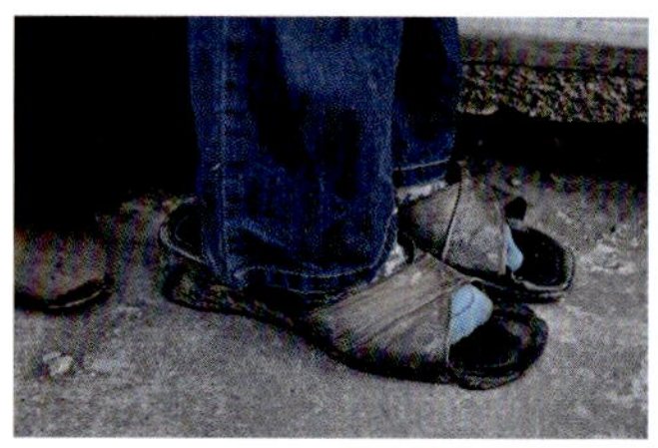

A little girl stands in a queue for food distribution by a small NGO called Team Humanity, based in a warehouse near the Moria camp. 26.01.2018

253
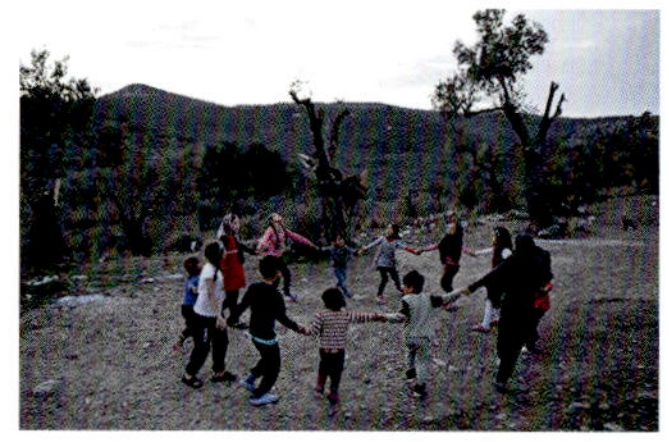

At present around 20,000 refugees and migrants live in the Moria camp. Doctors Without Borders (MSF) and several smaller NGOs estimate that 35 to 40 percent of the residents of the camp are children. Though people live under inhumane conditions, life goes on and sometimes children forget time and place for a while as they laugh and play. 08.03.2020

254
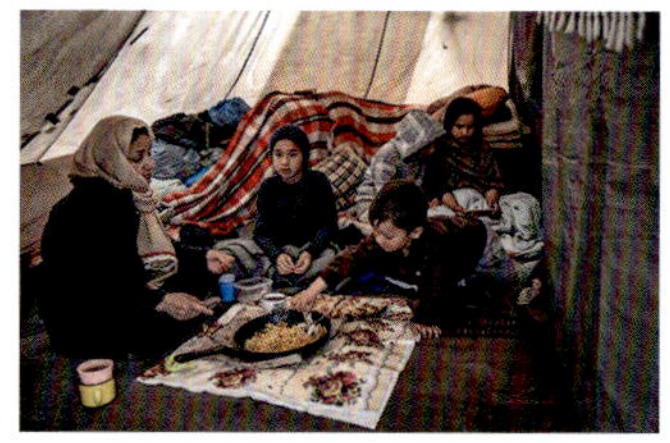

Two Afghan families share a homemade tent at the edge of 'the Jungle'. In one half of the tent live a family with six members. The mother, Fariba, age 33, eats breakfast with her children, Atena, age nine, and younger brother Emran, age five. In the background sits a friend and her daughter Parisa, age twelve, who is playing a game on the cell phone. It is four months since the family arrived at the Moria camp. 10.03.2020

255
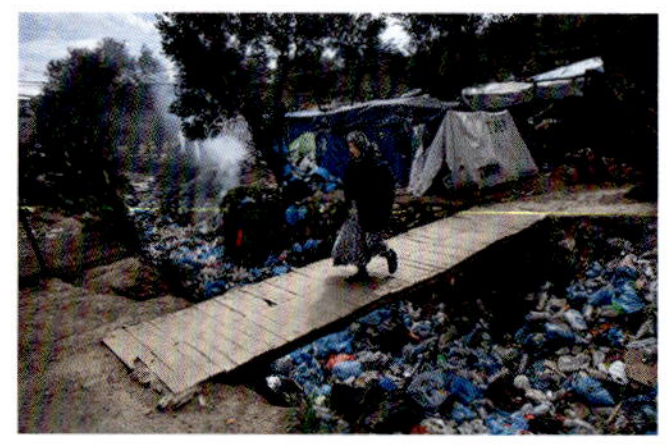

An older woman crosses a river of trash in 'the Jungle' area of the Moria camp. 10.03.2020

256
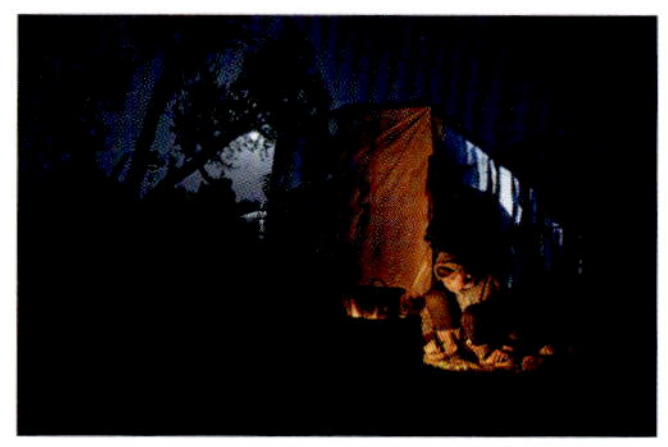

Twelve-year-old Elyas Tahery boils potatoes for the family. He fled Afghanistan with his mother, father, two brothers and a sister a year ago. They have been living in 'the Jungle' for three months. The plan is to continue the journey to Germany, where Elyas' uncle lives. 08.03.2020

259

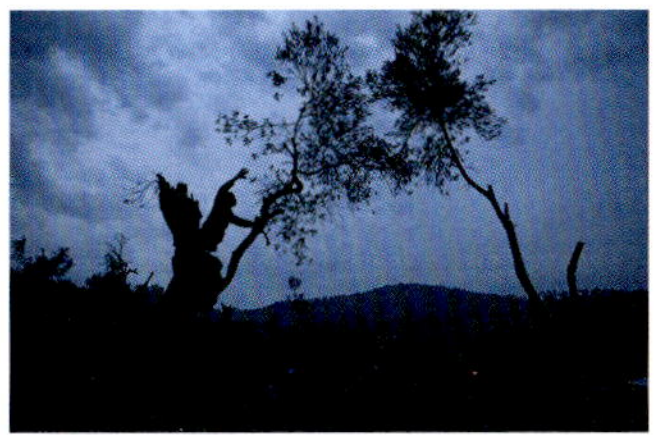

At the edge of 'the Jungle' a boy plays in one of the many olive trees that have been cut back severely because people lack firewood. 09.03.2020

260

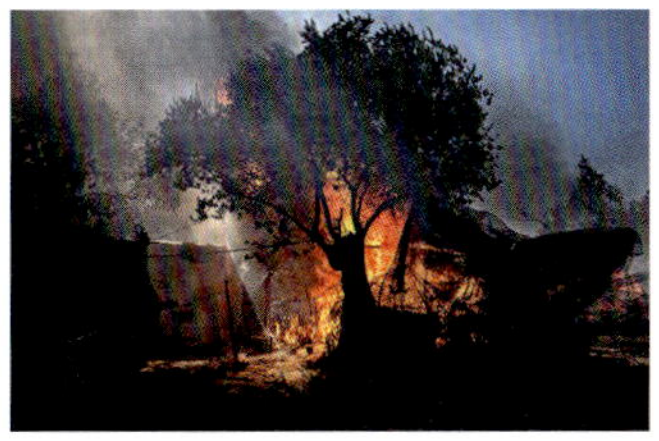

The night before 9 September a huge fire breaks out in the Moria camp, and this makes most of the residents flee. A day and a half later, new fires are still breaking out here and there around the camp. By the end of the day nearly all of the makeshift houses, tents and resident containers have been consumed by flames. 10.09.2020

262

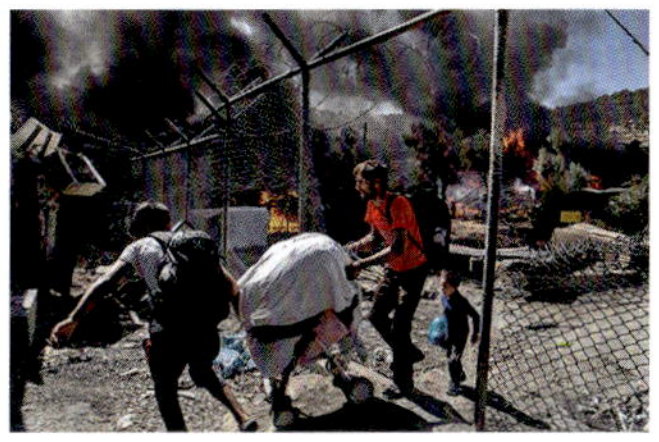

The last residents of the Moria camp salvage what they can and leave the burning ruins. No deaths related to the burning down of the camp have been reported. 10.09.2020

264

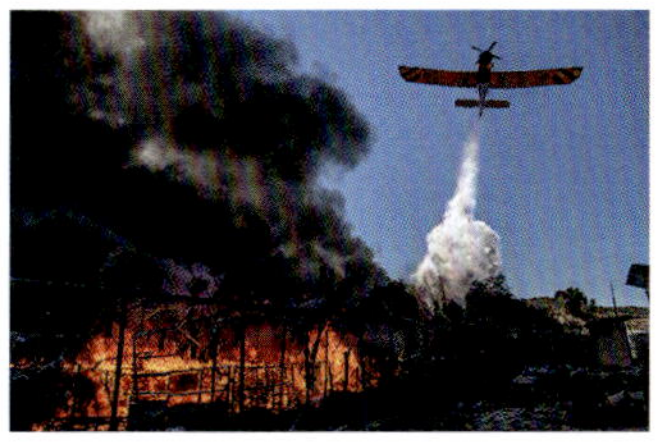

Two aeroplanes and two helicopters fly in shuttle to the camp in order to put out the fires. 10.09.2020

266

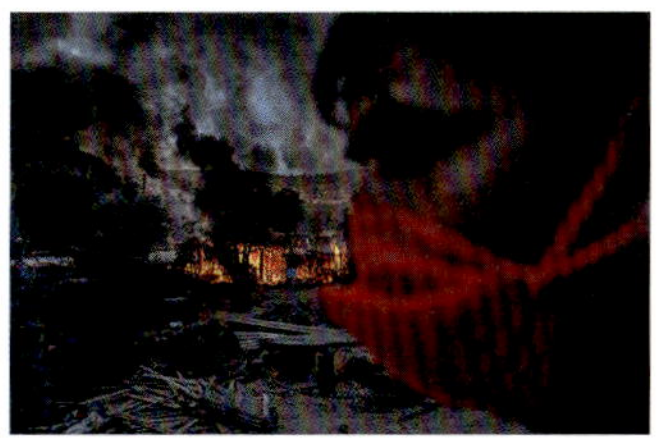

A man recovers his belongings while the flames consume some of the last remaining makeshift houses in 'the Jungle' area of the Moria camp. 10.09.2020

268

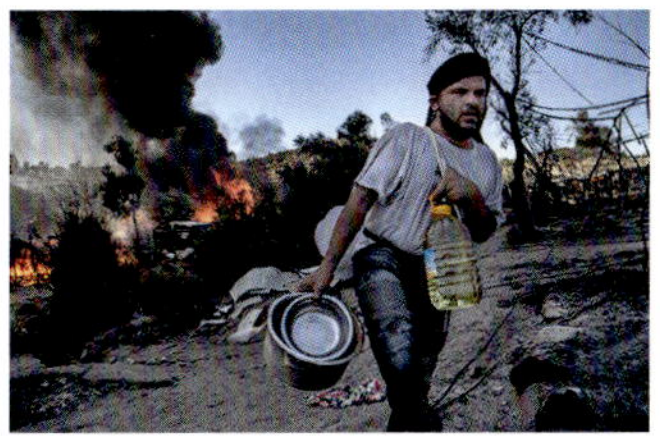

The last residents of the Moria camp salvage what they can and leave the burning ruins. 10.09.2020

270

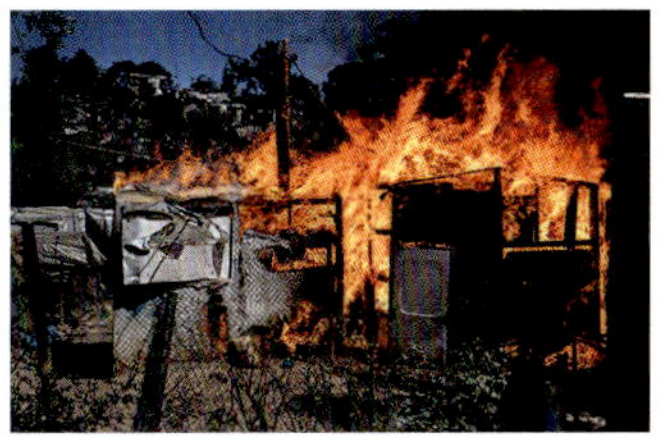

Fanned by the wind, the flames spread quickly from house to house. Soon there is nothing left of the camp. Rumour has it that some Afghan refugees started the fire out of desperation. 10.09.2020

272

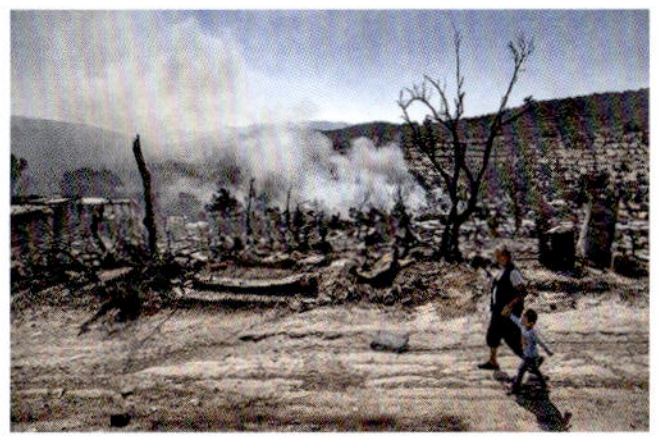

The 12,000 residents living in the Moria camp in September 2020 must now live on the street while the local authorities in collaboration with the UN Refugee Agency set up what is planned to be a temporary, camp of tents in a military area on the outskirts of Mytilini. 10.09.2020

ACKNOWLEDGEMENTS

I would like to express my thanks to:

All of the refugees and migrants I have met and photographed along the way. You have expanded my view of the world.

My wife, Louise, and our children, Anna and Gustav Ehrbahn. For your endless patience and your willingness to put up with me and my absence when I throw myself into my work and engage in projects such as this book. I love you.

Kjeld Hybel. My writing colleague, travel companion, and my firm friend since 2017. We have shared so many intense, tender, tough, and unforgettable experiences. Our friendship and the work that we carry out together means so much to me.

Olav Hergel and Claus Blok Thomsen. My good writing colleagues and travel companions during 2015.

Thomas Borberg. Photo editor-in-chief at Politiken, who gives me space to produce the stories I believe in, and who has supported this book project in every possible way.

Lars Munch. For your sound advice and encouragement over the past six years.

Christian Jensen, Anne Mette Svane, Christian Ilsøe, Michael Jarlner, Henriette Lind. My managers and editors at Politiken, who have enabled us to stay with this major story about the refugees and migrants in Europe and who have continuously published our reports in the best way possible.

Henrik Saxgren. You have confirmed my belief that this publication is important. You prompted me to get started and have given me substantial support and sound advice along the way.

Mads Nissen. My photographer colleague and friend who has been my first mate in the editing of the book. You have spent oceans of time with me and engaged in the project as if it were your own.

All of my colleagues in Politiken's photography department. You are a group of inspiring people. I am glad to be on the same team with every one of you.

Sea-Watch crew from mission six in 2017, Philippa and Eric Kempson/The Hope Project, Salam Aldeen/Team Humanity. You make a huge difference to vulnerable refugees and migrants. You have my greatest respect.

Politiken-Fonden and Sportgoods Fonden. Without your generous financial support, the publication of *Drømmen om Europa* and *A Dream of Europe* would not have been possible.

I would also like to extend my thanks to: *Karsten Orth, Steen Lassen, Peter Christensen, Eva Tandrup Kock, Dewi Lewis, Aske Jonatan Kreilgaard, AQ Afzali, Eid Mohammad, Razieh Gholami, Omid Arvish, Javad Emami, Patras Port Police and Rune Pedersen.*

BIOGRAPHY

Jacob Ehrbahn (1970) is a Danish photojournalist. He graduated from the Danish School of Journalism in 1993. In 2003 he was headhunted by the Danish daily national newspaper *Politiken*, which has long had a strong tradition in photojournalism excellence; he has been working there ever since. Over the years, Ehrbahn has covered prominent international news stories as well as the daily lives of people around the world. He is a persistent photographer who always gets close to the events he covers and portrays people at eye level. Since 2015 his main focus has been on covering stories about refugees and migrants seeking a better life in Europe.

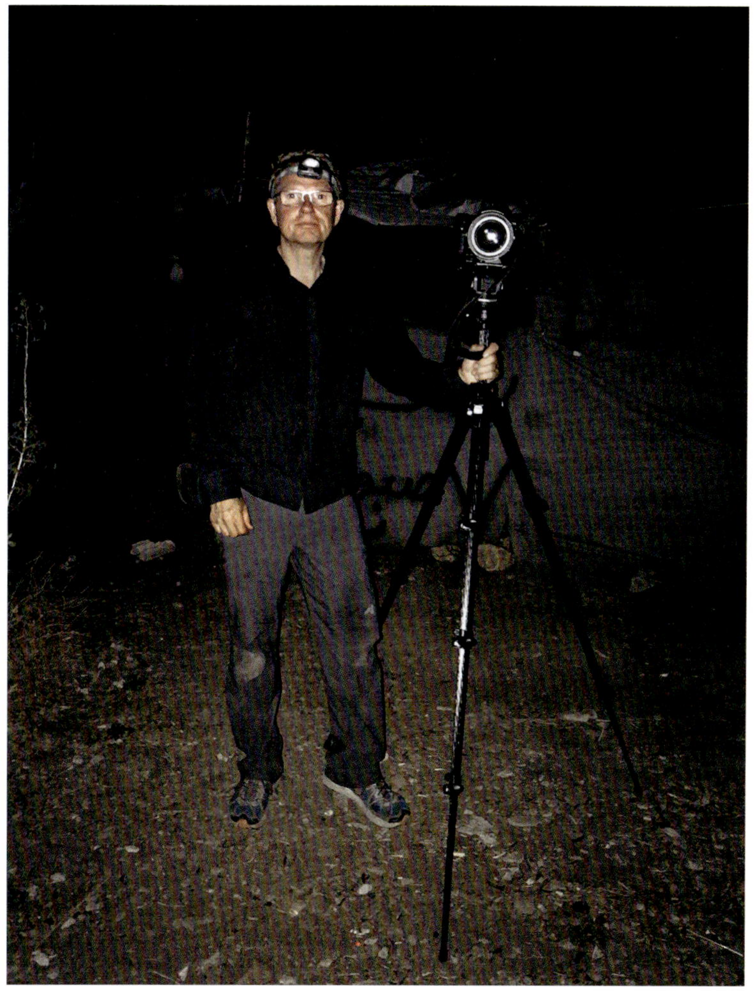

Photo: Kjeld Hybel

Ehrbahn has received numerous awards for his work, including two World Press Photo awards, eleven Pictures of the Year International awards, ten NPPA Best of Photojournalism awards and ten PDN Photo Annual awards. In the Danish Press Photo of the Year contest he has received 24 prizes, including being named Photographer of the Year three times. *A Dream of Europe* is Ehrbahn's third photography monograph.

Previous book releases:

69 – Kampen for et ungdomshus
Published in Denmark, 2008 by Politiken.
For 17 months Ehrbahn followed young activists' struggle to establish a new alternative youth house in Copenhagen, after their former property was demolished by the authorities and riots had broken out.

Headbangers
Published worldwide, 2015 by powerHouse Books.
Taken at European metal festivals, and with a conceptual approach, Jacob Ehrbahn created a collection of intimate portraits of the beauty and chaos of heavy metal rockers in the throes of musical ecstasy. The project resulted in a solo exhibition at Fotografisk Center in Copenhagen.

Published in the UK by
Dewi Lewis Publishing
8 Broomfield Road, Heaton Moor
Stockport SK4 4ND, England
www.dewilewis.com

ISBN: 978-1911306-76-4

Design: Office Hours and Jacob Ehrbahn
Translation from Danish: Pamela Starbird
Print: Narayana Press

MIX
Paper from responsible sources
FSC® C010651

The book has been created with the support of Politiken-Fonden and Sportsgoodfonden.

POLITIKEN-FONDEN

SPORTGOODS FONDEN